Algorithms

THIRD EDITION

in Java

PARTS 1–4

FUNDAMENTALS
DATA STRUCTURES
SORTING
SEARCHING

Robert Sedgewick

Princeton University

✦ Addison-Wesley

Boston • San Francisco • New York • Toronto • Montreal
London • Munich • Paris • Madrid
Capetown • Sydney • Tokyo • Singapore • Mexico City

Many of the designations used by manufacturers and sellers to distinguish their products are claimed as trademarks. Where those designations appear in this book and Addison-Wesley was aware of a trademark claim, the designations have been printed in initial capital letters or all capitals.

The author and publisher have taken care in the preparation of this book, but make no expressed or implied warranty of any kind and assume no responsibility for errors or omissions. No liability is assumed for incidental or consequential damages in connection with or arising out of the use of the information or programs contained herein.

The publisher offers discounts on this book when ordered in quantity for special sales. For more information, please contact:

U. S. Corporate and Government Sales
(800) 382-3410
corpsales@pearsontechgroup.com

For sales outside of the United States, please contact:

International Sales
(317) 581-3793
international@pearsontechgroup.com

Visit Addison-Wesley on the Web: www.awprofessional.com

Library of Congress Cataloging-in-Publication Data

Sedgewick, Robert, 1946 –
    Algorithms in Java / Robert Sedgewick. — 3d ed.
        p.   cm.
    ISBN 0-201-36120-5 (alk. paper)
    Includes bibliographical references and index.
    Contents: v. 1, pts. 1–4. Fundamentals, data structures, sorting, searching.
    1. Java (Computer program language) 2. Computer algorithms.
        I. Title.
    QA76.73.C15S   2003
    005.13'3—dc20   92-901
                                                                        CIP

ISBN 0-201-36120-5

Text printed on recycled paper
1 2 3 4 5 6 7 8 9 10 – CRS – 0605040302
First printing, July 2002

Preface

THIS BOOK IS the first of three volumes that are intended to survey the most important computer algorithms in use today. This first volume (Parts 1–4) covers fundamental concepts (Part 1), data structures (Part 2), sorting algorithms (Part 3), and searching algorithms (Part 4); the second volume (Part 5) covers graphs and graph algorithms; and the (yet to be published) third volume (Parts 6–8) covers strings (Part 6), computational geometry (Part 7), and advanced algorithms and applications (Part 8).

The books are useful as texts early in the computer science curriculum, after students have acquired basic programming skills and familiarity with computer systems, but before they have taken specialized courses in advanced areas of computer science or computer applications. The books also are useful for self-study or as a reference for people engaged in the development of computer systems or applications programs because they contain implementations of useful algorithms and detailed information on these algorithms' performance characteristics. The broad perspective taken makes the series an appropriate introduction to the field.

Together the three volumes comprise the *Third Edition* of a book that has been widely used by students and programmers around the world for many years. I have completely rewritten the text for this edition, and I have added thousands of new exercises, hundreds of new figures, dozens of new programs, and detailed commentary on all the figures and programs. This new material provides both coverage of new topics and fuller explanations of many of the classic algorithms. A new emphasis on abstract data types throughout the books makes the programs more broadly useful and relevant in modern object-oriented programming environments. People who have read previous editions will find a wealth of new information throughout; all readers will find a wealth of pedagogical material that provides effective access to essential concepts.

These books are not just for programmers and computer science students. Everyone who uses a computer wants it to run faster or to solve larger problems. The algorithms that we consider represent a body of knowledge developed during the last 50 years that is the basis for the efficient use of the computer for a broad variety of applications. From N-body simulation problems in physics to genetic-sequencing problems in molecular biology, the basic methods described here have become essential in scientific research; and from database systems to Internet search engines, they have become essential parts of modern software systems. As the scope of computer applications becomes more widespread, so grows the impact of basic algorithms. The goal of this book is to serve as a resource so that students and professionals can know and make intelligent use of these fundamental algorithms as the need arises in whatever computer application they might undertake.

Scope

This book, *Algorithms in Java, Third Edition, Parts 1-4*, contains 16 chapters grouped into four major parts: fundamentals, data structures, sorting, and searching. The descriptions here are intended to give readers an understanding of the basic properties of as broad a range of fundamental algorithms as possible. The algorithms described here have found widespread use for years, and represent an essential body of knowledge for both the practicing programmer and the computer-science student. The second volume is devoted to graph algorithms, and the third consists of four additional parts that cover strings, geometry, and advanced topics. My primary goal in developing these books has been to bring together fundamental methods from these areas, to provide access to the best methods known for solving problems by computer.

You will most appreciate the material here if you have had one or two previous courses in computer science or have had equivalent programming experience: one course in programming in a high-level language such as Java, C, or C++, and perhaps another course that teaches fundamental concepts of programming systems. This book is thus intended for anyone conversant with a modern programming language and with the basic features of modern computer systems.

References that might help to fill in gaps in your background are suggested in the text.

Most of the mathematical material supporting the analytic results is self-contained (or is labeled as beyond the scope of this book), so little specific preparation in mathematics is required for the bulk of the book, although mathematical maturity is definitely helpful.

Use in the Curriculum

There is a great deal of flexibility in how the material here can be taught, depending on the taste of the instructor and the preparation of the students. There is sufficient coverage of basic material for the book to be used to teach data structures to beginners, and there is sufficient detail and coverage of advanced material for the book to be used to teach the design and analysis of algorithms to upper-level students. Some instructors may wish to emphasize implementations and practical concerns; others may wish to emphasize analysis and theoretical concepts.

An elementary course on data structures and algorithms might emphasize the basic data structures in Part 2 and their use in the implementations in Parts 3 and 4. A course on design and analysis of algorithms might emphasize the fundamental material in Part 1 and Chapter 5, then study the ways in which the algorithms in Parts 3 and 4 achieve good asymptotic performance. A course on software engineering might omit the mathematical and advanced algorithmic material, and emphasize how to integrate the implementations given here into large programs or systems. A course on algorithms might take a survey approach and introduce concepts from all these areas.

Earlier editions of this book that are based on other programming languages have been used at scores of colleges and universities as a text for the second or third course in computer science and as supplemental reading for other courses. At Princeton, our experience has been that the breadth of coverage of material in this book provides our majors with an introduction to computer science that can be expanded on in later courses on analysis of algorithms, systems programming, and theoretical computer science, while providing the growing group of students from other disciplines with a large set of techniques that these people can put to good use immediately.

The exercises—nearly all of which are new to this third edition—fall into several types. Some are intended to test understanding of material in the text, and simply ask readers to work through an example or to apply concepts described in the text. Others involve implementing and putting together the algorithms, or running empirical studies to compare variants of the algorithms and to learn their properties. Still others are a repository for important information at a level of detail that is not appropriate for the text. Reading and thinking about the exercises will pay dividends for every reader.

Algorithms of Practical Use

Anyone wanting to use a computer more effectively can use this book for reference or for self-study. People with programming experience can find information on specific topics throughout the book. To a large extent, you can read the individual chapters in the book independently of the others, although, in some cases, algorithms in one chapter make use of methods from a previous chapter.

The orientation of the book is to study algorithms likely to be of practical use. The book provides information about the tools of the trade to the point that readers can confidently implement, debug, and put algorithms to work to solve a problem or to provide functionality in an application. Full implementations of the methods discussed are included, as are descriptions of the operations of these programs on a consistent set of examples.

Because we work with real code, rather than write pseudo-code, you can put the programs to practical use quickly. Program listings are available from the book's home page. You can use these working programs in many ways to help you study algorithms. Read them to check your understanding of the details of an algorithm, or to see one way to handle initializations, boundary conditions, and other awkward situations that often pose programming challenges. Run them to see the algorithms in action, to study performance empirically and check your results against the tables in the book, or to try your own modifications.

Characteristics of the algorithms and of the situations in which they might be useful are discussed in detail. Connections to the analysis of algorithms and theoretical computer science are developed in context. When appropriate, empirical and analytic results are presented to illustrate why certain algorithms are preferred. When interesting, the relationship of the practical algorithms being discussed to purely theoretical results is described. Specific information on performance characteristics of algorithms and implementations is synthesized, encapsulated, and discussed throughout the book.

Programming Language

The programming language used for all of the implementations is Java. The programs use a wide range of standard Java idioms, and the text includes concise descriptions of each construct.

Mike Schidlowsky and I developed a style of Java programming based on abstract data types that we feel is an effective way to present the algorithms and data structures as real programs. We have striven for elegant, compact, efficient, and portable implementations. The style is consistent whenever possible, so programs that are similar look similar.

For many of the algorithms in this book, the similarities hold regardless of the language: Quicksort is quicksort (to pick one prominent example), whether expressed in Ada, Algol-60, Basic, C, C++, Fortran, Java, Mesa, Modula-3, Pascal, PostScript, Smalltalk, or countless other programming languages and environments where it has proved to be an effective sorting method. On the one hand, our code is informed by experience with implementing algorithms in these and numerous other languages (C and C++ versions of this book are also available); on the other hand, some of the properties of some of these languages are informed by their designers' experience with some of the algorithms and data structures that we consider in this book.

Chapter 1 constitutes a detailed example of this approach to developing efficient Java implementations of our algorithms, and Chapter 2 describes our approach to analyzing them. Chapters 3 and 4 are devoted to describing and justifying the basic mechanisms that we use for data type and ADT implementations. These four chapters set the stage for the rest of the book.

Acknowledgments

Many people gave me helpful feedback on earlier versions of this book. In particular, hundreds of students at Princeton and Brown have suffered through preliminary drafts over the years. Special thanks are due to Trina Avery and Tom Freeman for their help in producing the first edition; to Janet Incerpi for her creativity and ingenuity in persuading our early and primitive digital computerized typesetting hardware and software to produce the first edition; to Marc Brown for his part in the algorithm visualization research that was the genesis of so many of the figures in the book; and to Dave Hanson and Andrew Appel for their willingness to answer all of my questions about programming languages. I would also like to thank the many readers who have provided me with comments about various editions, including Guy Almes, Jon Bentley, Marc Brown, Jay Gischer, Allan Heydon, Kennedy Lemke, Udi Manber, Dana Richards, John Reif, M. Rosenfeld, Stephen Seidman, Michael Quinn, and William Ward.

To produce this new edition, I have had the pleasure of working with Peter Gordon and Helen Goldstein at Addison-Wesley, who have patiently shepherded this project as it has evolved. It has also been my pleasure to work with several other members of the professional staff at Addison-Wesley. The nature of this project made the book a somewhat unusual challenge for many of them, and I much appreciate their forbearance. In particular, Marilyn Rash did an outstanding job managing the book's production within a tightly compressed schedule.

I have gained three new mentors in writing this book, and particularly want to express my appreciation to them. First, Steve Summit carefully checked early versions of the manuscript on a technical level and provided me with literally thousands of detailed comments, particularly on the programs. Steve clearly understood my goal of providing elegant, efficient, and effective implementations, and his comments not only helped me to provide a measure of consistency across the implementations, but also helped me to improve many of them substantially. Second, Lyn Dupré also provided me with thousands of detailed comments on the manuscript, which were invaluable in helping me not only to correct and avoid grammatical errors, but also—more important— to find a consistent and coherent writing style that helps bind together the daunting mass of technical material here. Third, Chris Van Wyk, in a long series of spirited electronic mail exchanges, patiently defended the basic precepts of object-oriented programming and helped me develop a style of coding that exhibits the algorithms with clarity and precision while still taking advantage of what object-oriented programming has to offer. The basic approach that we developed for the C++ version of this book has substantially influenced the Java code here and will certainly influence future volumes in both languages (and C as well). I am extremely grateful for the opportunity to learn from Steve, Lyn, and Chris—their input was vital in the development of this book.

Much of what I have written here I have learned from the teaching and writings of Don Knuth, my advisor at Stanford. Although Don had no direct influence on this work, his presence may be felt in the book, for it was he who put the study of algorithms on the scientific footing that makes a work such as this possible. My friend and colleague Philippe Flajolet, who has been a major force in the development of the analysis of algorithms as a mature research area, has had a similar influence on this work.

I am deeply thankful for the support of Princeton University, Brown University, and the Institut National de Recherche en Informatique et Automatique (INRIA), where I did most of the work on the book; and of the Institute for Defense Analyses and the Xerox Palo Alto Research Center, where I did some work on the book while visiting. Many parts of the book are dependent on research that has been generously supported by the National Science Foundation and the Office of Naval Research. Finally, I thank Bill Bowen, Aaron Lemonick, and Neil Rudenstine for their support in building an academic environment at Princeton in which I was able to prepare this book, despite my numerous other responsibilities.

Robert Sedgewick
Marly-le-Roi, France, 1983
Princeton, New Jersey, 1990, 1992
Jamestown, Rhode Island, 1997
Princeton, New Jersey, 1998, 2002

Java Consultant's Preface

In the past decade, Java has become the language of choice for a variety of applications. But Java developers have found themselves repeatedly referring to references such as Sedgewick's *Algorithms in C* for solutions to common programming problems. There has long been an empty space on the bookshelf for a comparable reference work for Java; this book is here to fill that space.

We wrote the sample programs as utility methods to be used in a variety of contexts. To that end, we did not use the Java package mechanism. To focus on the algorithms at hand (and to expose the algorithmic basis of many fundamental library classes), we avoided the standard Java library in favor of more fundamental types. Proper error checking and other defensive practices would both substantially increase the amount of code and distract the reader from the core algorithms. Developers should introduce such code when using the programs in larger applications.

Although the algorithms we present are language independent, we have paid close attention to Java-specific performance issues. The timings throughout the book are provided as one context for comparing algorithms, and will vary depending on the virtual machine. As Java environments evolve, programs will perform as fast as natively compiled code, but such optimizations will not change the performance of algorithms relative to one another. We provide the timings as a useful reference for such comparisons.

I would like to thank Mike Zamansky, for his mentorship and devotion to the teaching of computer science, and Daniel Chaskes, Jason Sanders, and James Percy, for their unwavering support. I would also like to thank my family for their support and for the computer that bore my first programs. Bringing together Java with the classic algorithms of computer science was an exciting endeavor for which I am very grateful. Thank you, Bob, for the opportunity to do so.

Michael Schidlowsky
Oakland Gardens, New York, 2002

To Adam, Andrew, Brett, Robbie,
and especially Linda

Notes on Exercises

Classifying exercises is an activity fraught with peril because readers of a book such as this come to the material with various levels of knowledge and experience. Nonetheless, guidance is appropriate, so many of the exercises carry one of four annotations to help you decide how to approach them.

Exercises that *test your understanding* of the material are marked with an open triangle, as follows:

> ▷ **9.57** Give the binomial queue that results when the keys E A S Y Q U E S T I O N are inserted into an initially empty binomial queue.

Most often, such exercises relate directly to examples in the text. They should present no special difficulty, but working them might teach you a fact or concept that may have eluded you when you read the text.

Exercises that *add new and thought-provoking* information to the material are marked with an open circle, as follows:

> ○ **14.20** Write a program that inserts N random integers into a table of size $N/100$ using separate chaining, then finds the length of the shortest and longest lists, for $N = 10^3$, 10^4, 10^5, and 10^6.

Such exercises encourage you to think about an important concept that is related to the material in the text, or to answer a question that may have occurred to you when you read the text. You may find it worthwhile to read these exercises, even if you do not have the time to work them through.

Exercises that are intended to *challenge you* are marked with a black dot, as follows:

> • **8.46** Suppose that mergesort is implemented to split the file at a *random* position, rather than exactly in the middle. How many comparisons are used by such a method to sort N elements, on the average?

Such exercises may require a substantial amount of time to complete, depending on your experience. Generally, the most productive approach is to work on them in a few different sittings.

A few exercises that are *extremely difficult* (by comparison with most others) are marked with two black dots, as follows:

> •• **15.29** Prove that the height of a trie built from N random bit-strings is about $2 \lg N$.

These exercises are similar to questions that might be addressed in the research literature, but the material in the book may prepare you to enjoy trying to solve them (and perhaps succeeding).

The annotations are intended to be neutral with respect to your programming and mathematical ability. Those exercises that require expertise in programming or in mathematical analysis are self-evident. All readers are encouraged to test their understanding of the algorithms by implementing them. Still, an exercise such as this one is straightforward for a practicing programmer or a student in a programming course, but may require substantial work for someone who has not recently programmed:

> **1.23** Modify Program 1.4 to generate random pairs of integers between 0 and $N-1$ instead of reading them from standard input, and to loop until $N - 1$ *union* operations have been performed. Run your program for $N = 10^3$, 10^4, 10^5, and 10^6 and print out the total number of edges generated for each value of N.

In a similar vein, all readers are encouraged to strive to appreciate the analytic underpinnings of our knowledge about properties of algorithms. Still, an exercise such as this one is straightforward for a scientist or a student in a discrete mathematics course, but may require substantial work for someone who has not recently done mathematical analysis:

> **1.13** Compute the *average* distance from a node to the root in a worst-case tree of 2^n nodes built by the weighted quick-union algorithm.

There are far too many exercises for you to read and assimilate them all; my hope is that there are enough exercises here to stimulate you to strive to come to a broader understanding on the topics that interest you than you can glean by simply reading the text.

Contents

Fundamentals

Data Structures

Sorting

Fundamentals

Introduction

THE OBJECTIVE OF THIS BOOK is to study a broad variety of important and useful *algorithms*—methods for solving problems that are suited for computer implementation. We shall deal with many different areas of application, always concentrating on fundamental algorithms that are important to know and interesting to study. We shall spend enough time on each algorithm to understand its essential characteristics and to respect its subtleties. Our goal is to learn well enough to be able to use and appreciate a large number of the most important algorithms used on computers today.

The strategy that we use for understanding the programs presented in this book is to implement and test them, to experiment with their variants, to discuss their operation on small examples, and to try them out on larger examples similar to what we might encounter in practice. We shall use the Java programming language to describe the algorithms, thus providing useful implementations at the same time. Our programs have a uniform style that is amenable to translation into other modern programming languages as well.

We also pay careful attention to performance characteristics of our algorithms in order to help us develop improved versions, compare different algorithms for the same task, and predict or guarantee performance for large problems. Understanding how the algorithms perform might require experimentation or mathematical analysis or both. We consider detailed information for many of the most important algorithms, developing analytic results directly when feasible, or calling on results from the research literature when necessary.

To illustrate our general approach to developing algorithmic solutions, we consider in this chapter a detailed example comprising a number of algorithms that solve a particular problem. The problem that we consider is not a toy problem; it is a fundamental computational task, and the solution that we develop is of use in a variety of applications. We start with a simple solution, then seek to understand that solution's performance characteristics, which help us to see how to improve the algorithm. After a few iterations of this process, we come to an efficient and useful algorithm for solving the problem. This prototypical example sets the stage for our use of the same general methodology throughout the book.

We conclude the chapter with a short discussion of the contents of the book, including brief descriptions of what the major parts of the book are and how they relate to one another.

1.1 Algorithms

When we write a computer program, we are generally implementing a method that has been devised previously to solve some problem. This method is often independent of the particular computer to be used—it is likely to be equally appropriate for many computers and many computer languages. It is the method, rather than the computer program itself, that we must study to learn how the problem is being attacked. The term *algorithm* is used in computer science to describe a problem-solving method suitable for implementation as a computer program. Algorithms are the stuff of computer science: They are central objects of study in many, if not most, areas of the field.

Most algorithms of interest involve methods of organizing the data involved in the computation. Objects created in this way are called *data structures*, and they also are central objects of study in computer science. Thus, algorithms and data structures go hand in hand. In this book we take the view that data structures exist as the byproducts or end products of algorithms and that we must therefore study them in order to understand the algorithms. Simple algorithms can give rise to complicated data structures and, conversely, complicated algorithms can use simple data structures. We shall study the properties of many data structures in this book; indeed, the book might well have been called *Algorithms and Data Structures in Java*.

When we use a computer to help us solve a problem, we typically are faced with a number of possible different approaches. For small problems, it hardly matters which approach we use, as long as we have one that solves the problem correctly. For huge problems (or applications where we need to solve huge numbers of small problems), however, we quickly become motivated to devise methods that use time or space as efficiently as possible.

The primary reason to learn about algorithm design is that this discipline gives us the potential to reap huge savings, even to the point of making it possible to do tasks that would otherwise be impossible. In an application where we are processing millions of objects, it is not unusual to be able to make a program millions of times faster by using a well-designed algorithm. We shall see such an example in Section 1.2 and on numerous other occasions throughout the book. By contrast, investing additional money or time to buy and install a new computer holds the potential for speeding up a program by perhaps a factor of only 10 or 100. Careful algorithm design is an extremely effective part of the process of solving a huge problem, whatever the applications area.

When a huge or complex computer program is to be developed, a great deal of effort must go into understanding and defining the problem to be solved, managing its complexity, and decomposing it into smaller subtasks that can be implemented easily. Often, many of the algorithms required after the decomposition are trivial to implement. In most cases, however, there are a few algorithms whose choice is critical because most of the system resources will be spent running those algorithms. Those are the types of algorithms on which we concentrate in this book. We shall study a variety of fundamental algorithms that are useful for solving huge problems in a broad variety of applications areas.

The sharing of programs in computer systems is becoming more widespread, so although we might expect to be *using* a large fraction of the algorithms in this book, we also might expect to have to *implement* only a small fraction of them. For example, the Java libraries contain implementations of a host of fundamental algorithms. However, implementing simple versions of basic algorithms helps us to understand them better and thus to more effectively use and tune advanced versions from a library. More important, the opportunity to reimplement basic algorithms arises frequently. The primary reason to do so is that we are faced, all too often, with completely new computing environments (hardware and software) with new features that old implementations may not use to best advantage. In other words, we often implement basic algorithms tailored to our problem, rather than depending on a system routine, to make our solutions more portable and longer lasting. Another common reason to reimplement basic algorithms is that, despite the advances embodied in Java, the mechanisms that we use for sharing software are not always sufficiently powerful to allow us to conveniently tailor library programs to perform effectively on specific tasks.

Computer programs are often overoptimized. It may not be worthwhile to take pains to ensure that an implementation of a particular algorithm is the most efficient possible unless the algorithm is to be used for an enormous task or is to be used many times. Otherwise, a careful, relatively simple implementation will suffice: We can have some confidence that it will work, and it is likely to run perhaps 5 or 10 times slower at worst than the best possible version, which means that it may run for an extra few seconds. By contrast, the proper choice of algorithm in the first place can make a difference of a factor of 100 or 1000 or more, which might translate to minutes, hours, or even more in running time. In this book, we concentrate on the simplest reasonable implementations of the best algorithms. We do pay careful attention to carefully coding the critical parts of the algorithms, and take pains to note where low-level optimization effort could be most beneficial.

The choice of the best algorithm for a particular task can be a complicated process, perhaps involving sophisticated mathematical analysis. The branch of computer science that comprises the study of such questions is called *analysis of algorithms*. Many of the algorithms that we study have been shown through analysis to have excellent performance; others are simply known to work well through experience. Our primary goal is to learn reasonable algorithms for important tasks, yet we shall also pay careful attention to comparative performance of the methods. We should not use an algorithm without having an idea of what resources it might consume, and we strive to be aware of how our algorithms might be expected to perform.

1.2 A Sample Problem: Connectivity

Suppose that we are given a sequence of pairs of integers, where each integer represents an object of some type and we are to interpret the pair p-q as meaning "p is connected to q." We assume the relation "is connected to" to be transitive: If p is connected to q, and q is connected to r, then p is connected to r. Our goal is to write a program to filter out extraneous pairs from the set: When the program inputs a pair p-q, it should output the pair only if the pairs it has seen to that point *do not* imply that p is connected to q. If the previous pairs do imply that p is connected to q, then the program should ignore p-q and should proceed to input the next pair. Figure 1.1 gives an example of this process.

Our problem is to devise a program that can remember sufficient information about the pairs it has seen to be able to decide whether or not a new pair of objects is connected. Informally, we refer to the task of designing such a method as the *connectivity problem*. This problem arises in a number of important applications. We briefly consider three examples here to indicate the fundamental nature of the problem.

For example, the integers might represent computers in a large network, and the pairs might represent connections in the network. Then, our program might be used to determine whether we need to establish a new direct connection for p and q to be able to communicate or whether we could use existing connections to set up a communications path. In this kind of application, we might need to process millions of points and billions of connections, or more. As we shall see, it would be impossible to solve the problem for such an application without an efficient algorithm.

Similarly, the integers might represent contact points in an electrical network, and the pairs might represent wires connecting the points. In this case, we could use our program to find a way to connect all the points without any extraneous connections, if that is possible. There is no guarantee that the edges in the list will suffice to connect all the points—indeed, we shall soon see that determining whether or not they will could be a prime application of our program.

Figure 1.2 illustrates these two types of applications in a larger example. Examination of this figure gives us an appreciation for the

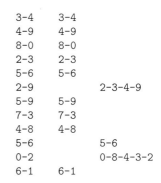

Figure 1.1
Connectivity example

Given a sequence of pairs of integers representing connections between objects (left), the task of a connectivity algorithm is to output those pairs that provide new connections (center). For example, the pair 2-9 is not part of the output because the connection 2-3-4-9 is implied by previous connections (this evidence is shown at right).

Figure 1.2
A large connectivity example

The objects in a connectivity prob-
lem might represent connection
points, and the pairs might be con-
nections between them, as indi-
cated in this idealized example
that might represent wires connect-
ing buildings in a city or compo-
nents on a computer chip. This
graphical representation makes it
possible for a human to spot nodes
that are not connected, but the al-
gorithm has to work with only the
pairs of integers that it is given.
Are the two nodes marked with the
large black dots connected?

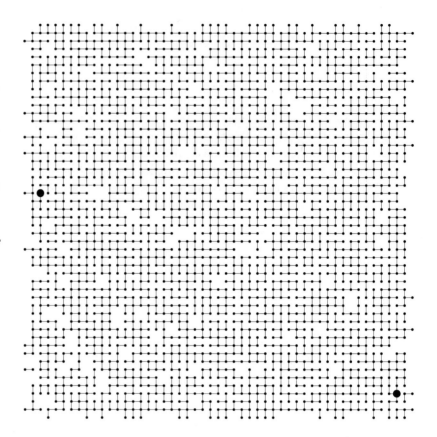

difficulty of the connectivity problem: How can we arrange to tell quickly whether *any* given two points in such a network are connected?

Still another example arises in certain programming environments where it is possible to declare two variable names as equivalent. The problem is to be able to determine whether two given names are equivalent, after a sequence of such declarations. This application is an early one that motivated the development of several of the algorithms that we are about to consider. It directly relates our problem to a simple abstraction that provides us with a way to make our algorithms useful for a wide variety of applications, as we shall see.

Applications such as the variable-name–equivalence problem described in the previous paragraph require that we associate an integer with each distinct variable name. This association is also implicit in the network-connection and circuit-connection applications that we have described. We shall be considering a host of algorithms in Chapters 10 through 16 that can provide this association in an efficient manner. Thus, we can assume in this chapter, without loss of generality, that we have N objects with integer names, from 0 to $N - 1$.

We are asking for a program that does a specific and well-defined task. There are many other related problems that we might want to have solved as well. One of the first tasks that we face in developing an algorithm is to be sure that we have specified the *problem* in a reasonable manner. The more we require of an algorithm, the more time and space we may expect it to need to finish the task. It is impossible to quantify this relationship a priori, and we often modify a problem specification on finding that it is difficult or expensive to solve or, in happy circumstances, on finding that an algorithm can provide information more useful than was called for in the original specification.

For example, our connectivity-problem specification requires only that our program somehow know whether or not any given pair p-q is connected, and not that it be able to demonstrate any or all ways to connect that pair. Adding a requirement for such a specification makes the problem more difficult and would lead us to a different family of algorithms, which we consider briefly in Chapter 5 and in detail in Part 5.

The specifications mentioned in the previous paragraph ask us for *more* information than our original one did; we could also ask for *less* information. For example, we might simply want to be able to answer the question: "Are the M connections sufficient to connect together all N objects?" This problem illustrates that to develop efficient algorithms we often need to do high-level reasoning about the abstract objects that we are processing. In this case, a fundamental result from graph theory implies that all N objects are connected if and only if the number of pairs output by the connectivity algorithm is precisely $N - 1$ (see Section 5.4). In other words, a connectivity algorithm will never output more than $N - 1$ pairs because, once it has output $N - 1$ pairs, any pair that it encounters from that point on will be connected. Accordingly, we can get a program that answers the yes–no question just posed by changing a program that solves the connectivity problem to one that increments a counter, rather than writing out each pair that was not previously connected, answering "yes" when the counter reaches $N - 1$ and "no" if it never does. This question is but one example of a host of questions that we might wish to answer regarding connectivity. The set of pairs in the input is called a *graph*, and the set of pairs output is called a *spanning tree* for that graph, which connects all the objects. We consider properties of graphs, spanning trees, and all manner of related algorithms in Part 5.

It is worthwhile to try to identify the fundamental operations that we will be performing, and so to make any algorithm that we develop for the connectivity task useful for a variety of similar tasks. Specifically, each time that an algorithm gets a new pair, it has first to determine whether it represents a new connection, then to incorporate the information that the connection has been seen into its understanding about the connectivity of the objects such that it can check connections to be seen in the future. We encapsulate these two tasks as *abstract operations* by considering the integer input values to represent elements in abstract sets and then designing algorithms and data structures that can

- *Find* the set containing a given item.
- Replace the sets containing two given items by their *union*.

Organizing our algorithms in terms of these abstract operations does not seem to foreclose any options in solving the connectivity problem, and the operations may be useful for solving other problems. Developing ever more powerful layers of abstraction is an essential process in computer science in general and in algorithm design in particular, and we shall turn to it on numerous occasions throughout this book. In this chapter, we use abstract thinking in an informal way to guide us in designing programs to solve the connectivity problem; in Chapter 4, we shall see how to encapsulate abstractions in Java code.

The connectivity problem is easy to solve with the *find* and *union* abstract operations. We read a new pair from the input and perform a *find* operation for each member of the pair: If the members of the pair are in the same set, we move on to the next pair; if they are not, we do a *union* operation and write out the pair. The sets represent *connected components*—subsets of the objects with the property that any two objects in a given component are connected. This approach reduces the development of an algorithmic solution for connectivity to the tasks of defining a data structure representing the sets and developing *union* and *find* algorithms that efficiently use that data structure.

There are many ways to represent and process abstract sets, some of which we consider in Chapter 4. In this chapter, our focus is on finding a representation that can support efficiently the *union* and *find* operations that we see in solving the connectivity problem.

Exercises

1.1 Give the output that a connectivity algorithm should produce when given the input 0-2, 1-4, 2-5, 3-6, 0-4, 6-0, and 1-3.

1.2 List all the different ways to connect two different objects for the example in Figure 1.1.

1.3 Describe a simple method for counting the number of sets remaining after using the *union* and *find* operations to solve the connectivity problem as described in the text.

1.3 Union–Find Algorithms

The first step in the process of developing an efficient algorithm to solve a given problem is to *implement a simple algorithm that solves the problem.* If we need to solve a few particular problem instances that turn out to be easy, then the simple implementation may finish the job for us. If a more sophisticated algorithm is called for, then the simple implementation provides us with a correctness check for small cases and a baseline for evaluating performance characteristics. We always care about efficiency, but our primary concern in developing the first program that we write to solve a problem is to make sure that the program is a *correct* solution to the problem.

The first idea that might come to mind is somehow to save all the input pairs, then to write a function to pass through them to try to discover whether the next pair of objects is connected. We shall use a different approach. First, the number of pairs might be sufficiently large to preclude our saving them all in memory in practical applications. Second, and more to the point, no simple method immediately suggests itself for determining whether two objects are connected from the set of all the connections, even if we could save them all! We consider a basic method that takes this approach in Chapter 5, but the methods that we shall consider in this chapter are simpler, because they solve a less difficult problem, and more efficient, because they do

<table>
<tr><th colspan="11">Program 1.1 Quick-find solution to connectivity problem</th></tr>
</table>

This program takes an integer N from the command line, reads a sequence of pairs of integers, interprets the pair p q to mean "connect object p to object q," and prints the pairs that represent objects that are not yet connected. The program maintains the array id such that id[p] and id[q] are equal if and only if p and q are connected.

The In and Out methods that we use for input and output are described in the Appendix, and the standard Java mechanism for taking parameter values from the command line is described in Section 3.7.

```java
public class QuickF
  { public static void main(String[] args)
    { int N = Integer.parseInt(args[0]);
      int id[] = new int[N];
      for (int i = 0; i < N ; i++) id[i] = i;
      for( In.init(); !In.empty(); )
        { int p = In.getInt(), q = In.getInt();
          int t = id[p];
          if (t == id[q]) continue;
          for (int i = 0; i < N; i++)
            if (id[i] == t) id[i] = id[q];
          Out.println(" " + p + " " + q);
        }
    }
  }
```

p q	0	1	2	3	4	5	6	7	8	9
3 4	0	1	2	4	4	5	6	7	8	9
4 9	0	1	2	9	9	5	6	7	8	9
8 0	0	1	2	9	9	5	6	7	0	9
2 3	0	1	9	9	9	5	6	7	0	9
5 6	0	1	9	9	9	6	6	7	0	9
2 9	0	1	9	9	9	6	6	7	0	9
5 9	0	1	9	9	9	9	9	7	0	9
7 3	0	1	9	9	9	9	9	9	0	9
4 8	0	1	0	0	0	0	0	0	0	0
5 6	0	1	0	0	0	0	0	0	0	0
0 2	0	1	0	0	0	0	0	0	0	0
6 1	1	1	1	1	1	1	1	1	1	1

Figure 1.3
Example of quick find (slow union)

This sequence depicts the contents of the id array after each of the pairs at left is processed by the quick-find algorithm (Program 1.1). Shaded entries are those that change for the union operation. When we process the pair p q, we change all entries with the value id[p] to have the value id[q].

not require saving all the pairs. They all use an *array* of integers—one corresponding to each object—to hold the requisite information to be able to implement *union* and *find*. Arrays are elementary data structures that we discuss in detail in Section 3.2. Here, we use them in their simplest form: we create an array that can hold N integers by writing int id[] = new int[N]; then we refer to the ith integer in the array by writing id[i], for $0 \leq i < 1000$.

Program 1.1 is an implementation of a simple algorithm called the *quick-find algorithm* that solves the connectivity problem (see Section 3.1 and Program 3.1 for basic information on Java programs). The basis of this algorithm is an array of integers with the property that p and q are connected if and only if the pth and qth array entries are equal. We initialize the ith array entry to i for $0 \leq i < N$. To implement the *union* operation for p and q, we go through the array, changing all the entries with the same name as p to have the same name as q. This choice is arbitrary—we could have decided to change all the entries with the same name as q to have the same name as p.

Figure 1.3 shows the changes to the array for the *union* operations in the example in Figure 1.1. To implement *find*, we just test the indicated array entries for equality—hence the name *quick find*. The *union* operation, on the other hand, involves scanning through the whole array for each input pair.

Property 1.1 *The quick-find algorithm executes at least MN instructions to solve a connectivity problem with N objects that involves M union operations.*

For each of the M *union* operations, we iterate the `for` loop N times. Each iteration requires at least one instruction (if only to check whether the loop is finished). ∎

We can execute tens or hundreds of millions of instructions per second on modern computers, so this cost is not noticeable if M and N are small, but we also might find ourselves with billions of objects and millions of input pairs to process in a modern application. The inescapable conclusion is that we cannot feasibly solve such a problem using the quick-find algorithm (see Exercise 1.10). We consider the process of precisely quantifying such a conclusion precisely in Chapter 2.

Figure 1.4 shows a graphical representation of Figure 1.3. We may think of some of the objects as representing the set to which they belong, and all of the other objects as having a link to the representative in their set. The reason for moving to this graphical representation of the array will become clear soon. Observe that the connections between objects (links) in this representation are *not* necessarily the same as the connections in the input pairs—they are the information that the algorithm chooses to remember to be able to know whether future pairs are connected.

The next algorithm that we consider is a complementary method called the *quick-union algorithm*. It is based on the same data structure—an array indexed by object names—but it uses a different interpretation of the values that leads to more complex abstract structures. Each object has a link to another object in the same set,

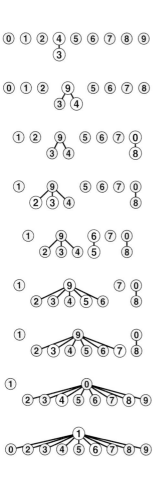

**Figure 1.4
Tree representation of quick find**

This figure depicts graphical representations for the example in Figure 1.3. The connections in these figures do not necessarily represent the connections in the input. For example, the structure at the bottom has the connection 1-7, which is not in the input, but which is made because of the string of connections 7-3-4-9-5-6-1.

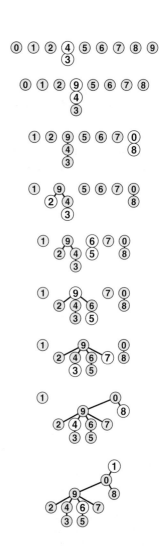

Figure 1.5
Tree representation of quick union

This figure is a graphical representation of the example in Figure 1.3. We draw a line from object i to object id[i].

in a structure with no cycles. To determine whether two objects are in the same set, we follow links for each until we reach an object that has a link to itself. The objects are in the same set if and only if this process leads them to the same object. If they are not in the same set, we wind up at different objects (which have links to themselves). To form the union, then, we just link one to the other to perform the *union* operation; hence the name *quick union*.

Figure 1.5 shows the graphical representation that corresponds to Figure 1.4 for the operation of the quick-union algorithm on the example of Figure 1.1, and Figure 1.6 shows the corresponding changes to the id array. The graphical representation of the data structure makes it relatively easy to understand the operation of the algorithm—input pairs that are known to be connected in the data are also connected to one another in the data structure. As mentioned previously, it is important to note at the outset that the connections in the data structure are not necessarily the same as the connections in the application implied by the input pairs; rather, they are constructed by the algorithm to facilitate efficient implementation of *union* and *find*.

The connected components depicted in Figure 1.5 are called *trees*; they are fundamental combinatorial structures that we shall encounter on numerous occasions throughout the book. We shall consider the properties of trees in detail in Chapter 5. For the *union* and *find* operations, the trees in Figure 1.5 are useful because they are quick to build and have the property that two objects are connected in the tree if and only if the objects are connected in the input. By moving up the tree, we can easily find the root of the tree containing each object, so we have a way to find whether or not they are connected. Each tree has precisely one object that has a link to itself, which is called the *root* of the tree. The self-link is not shown in the diagrams. When we start at any object in the tree, move to the object to which its link refers, then move to the object to which that object's link refers, and so forth, we always eventually end up at the root. We can prove this property to be true by induction: It is true after the array is initialized to have every object link to itself, and if it is true before a given *union* operation, it is certainly true afterward.

The diagrams in Figure 1.4 for the quick-find algorithm have the same properties as those described in the previous paragraph. The difference between the two is that we reach the root from all the nodes

> ### Program 1.2 Quick-union solution to connectivity problem
>
> If we replace the body of the for loop in Program 1.1 by this code, we have a program that meets the same specifications as Program 1.1, but does less computation for the *union* operation at the expense of more computation for the *find* operation. The for loops and subsequent if statement in this code specify the necessary and sufficient conditions on the id array for p and q to be connected. The assignment statement id[i] = j implements the *union* operation.
>
> ```
>         int i, j, p = In.getInt(), q = In.getInt();
>         for (i = p; i != id[i]; i = id[i]);
>         for (j = q; j != id[j]; j = id[j]);
>         if (i == j) continue;
>         id[i] = j;
>         Out.println(" " + p + " " + q);
> ```

in the quick-find trees after following just one link, whereas we might need to follow several links to get to the root in a quick-union tree.

Program 1.2 is an implementation of the *union* and *find* operations that comprise the quick-union algorithm to solve the connectivity problem. The quick-union algorithm would seem to be faster than the quick-find algorithm, because it does not have to go through the entire array for each input pair; but how much faster is it? This question is more difficult to answer here than it was for quick find, because the running time is much more dependent on the nature of the input. By running empirical studies or doing mathematical analysis (see Chapter 2), we can convince ourselves that Program 1.2 is far more efficient than Program 1.1, and that it is feasible to consider using Program 1.2 for huge practical problems. We shall discuss one such empirical study at the end of this section. For the moment, we can regard quick union as an improvement because it removes quick find's main liability (that the program requires at least NM instructions to process M *union* operations among N objects).

This difference between quick union and quick find certainly represents an improvement, but quick union still has the liability that we cannot *guarantee* it to be substantially faster than quick find in every case, because the input data could conspire to make the *find* operation slow.

p q	0 1 2 3 4 5 6 7 8 9
3 4	0 1 2 4 4 5 6 7 8 9
4 9	0 1 2 4 9 5 6 7 8 9
8 0	0 1 2 4 9 5 6 7 0 9
2 3	0 1 9 4 9 5 6 7 0 9
5 6	0 1 9 4 9 6 6 7 0 9
2 9	0 1 9 4 9 6 6 7 0 9
5 9	0 1 9 4 9 6 9 7 0 9
7 3	0 1 9 4 9 6 9 9 0 9
4 8	0 1 9 4 9 6 9 9 0 0
5 6	0 1 9 4 9 6 9 9 0 0
0 2	0 1 9 4 9 6 9 9 0 0
6 1	1 1 9 4 9 6 9 9 0 0
5 8	1 1 9 4 9 6 9 9 0 0

Figure 1.6
Example of quick union (not-too-quick find)

This sequence depicts the contents of the id array after each of the pairs at left are processed by the quick-union algorithm (Program 1.2). Shaded entries are those that change for the union operation (just one per operation). When we process the pair p q, we follow links from p to get an entry i with id[i] == i; then, we follow links from q to get an entry j with id[j] == j; then, if i and j differ, we set id[i] = id[j]. For the find operation for the pair 5–8 (final line), i takes on the values 5 6 9 0 1, and j takes on the values 8 0 1.

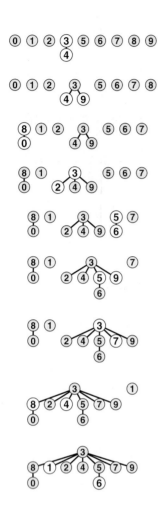

Figure 1.7
Tree representation of weighted quick union

This sequence depicts the result of changing the quick-union algorithm to link the root of the smaller of the two trees to the root of the larger of the two trees. The distance from each node to the root of its tree is small, so the find *operation is efficient.*

Property 1.2 *For $M > N$, the quick-union algorithm could take more than $MN/2$ instructions to solve a connectivity problem with M pairs of N objects.*

Suppose that the input pairs come in the order 1-2, then 2-3, then 3-4, and so forth. After $N - 1$ such pairs, we have N objects all in the same set, and the tree that is formed by the quick-union algorithm is a straight line, with N linking to $N - 1$, which links to $N - 2$, which links to $N - 3$, and so forth. To execute the *find* operation for object N, the program has to follow $N - 1$ links. Thus, the average number of links followed for the first N pairs is

$$(0 + 1 + \ldots + (N - 1))/N = (N - 1)/2.$$

Now suppose that the remainder of the pairs all connect N to some other object. The *find* operation for each of these pairs involves at least $(N - 1)$ links. The grand total for the M *find* operations for this sequence of input pairs is certainly greater than $MN/2$. ∎

Fortunately, there is an easy modification to the algorithm that allows us to guarantee that bad cases such as this one do not occur. Rather than arbitrarily connecting the second tree to the first for *union*, we keep track of the number of nodes in each tree and always connect the smaller tree to the larger. This change requires slightly more code and another array to hold the node counts, as shown in Program 1.3, but it leads to substantial improvements in efficiency. We refer to this algorithm as the *weighted quick-union algorithm*.

Figure 1.7 shows the forest of trees constructed by the weighted union–find algorithm for the example input in Figure 1.1. Even for this small example, the paths in the trees are substantially shorter than for the unweighted version in Figure 1.5. Figure 1.8 illustrates what happens in the worst case, when the sizes of the sets to be merged in the *union* operation are always equal (and a power of 2). These tree structures look complex, but they have the simple property that the maximum number of links that we need to follow to get to the root in a tree of 2^n nodes is n. Furthermore, when we merge two trees of 2^n nodes, we get a tree of 2^{n+1} nodes, and we increase the maximum distance to the root to $n + 1$. This observation generalizes to provide a proof that the weighted algorithm is substantially more efficient than the unweighted algorithm.

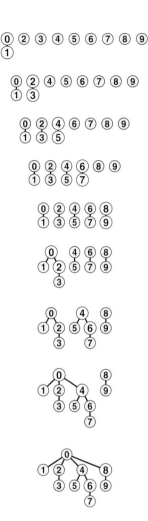

Program 1.3 Weighted version of quick union

This program is a modification to the quick-union algorithm (see Program 1.2) that keeps an additional array sz for the purpose of maintaining, for each object with id[i] == i, the number of nodes in the associated tree so that the *union* operation can link the smaller of the two specified trees to the larger, thus preventing the growth of long paths in the trees.

```
public class QuickUW
  { public static void main(String[] args)
    { int N = Integer.parseInt(args[0]);
      int id[] = new int[N], sz[] = new int[N];
      for (int i = 0; i < N ; i++)
        { id[i] = i; sz[i] = 1; }
      for(In.init(); !In.empty(); )
        { int i, j, p = In.getInt(), q = In.getInt();
          for (i = p; i != id[i]; i = id[i]);
          for (j = q; j != id[j]; j = id[j]);
          if (i == j) continue;
          if (sz[i] < sz[j])
              { id[i] = j; sz[j] += sz[i]; }
          else { id[j] = i; sz[i] += sz[j]; }
          Out.println(" " + p + " " + q);
        }
    }
  }
```

Property 1.3 *The weighted quick-union algorithm follows at most $2 \lg N$ links to determine whether two of N objects are connected.*

We can prove that the *union* operation preserves the property that the number of links followed from any node to the root in a set of k objects is no greater than $\lg k$ (we do not count the self-link at the root). When we combine a set of i nodes with a set of j nodes with $i \leq j$, we increase the number of links that must be followed in the smaller set by 1, but they are now in a set of size $i + j$, so the property is preserved because $1 + \lg i = \lg(i + i) \leq \lg(i + j)$. ∎

The practical implication of Property 1.3 is that the weighted quick-union algorithm uses *at most* a constant times $M \lg N$ instruc-

Figure 1.8
Weighted quick union (worst case)

The worst scenario for the weighted quick-union algorithm is that each union operation links trees of equal size. If the number of objects is less than 2^n, the distance from any node to the root of its tree is less than n.

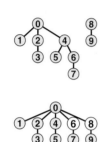

Figure 1.9
Path compression

We can make paths in the trees even shorter by simply making all the objects that we touch point to the root of the new tree for the union operation, as shown in these two examples. The example at the top shows the result corresponding to Figure 1.7. For short paths, path compression has no effect, but when we process the pair 1 6, we make 1, 5, and 6 all point to 3 and get a tree flatter than the one in Figure 1.7. The example at the bottom shows the result corresponding to Figure 1.8. Paths that are longer than one or two links can develop in the trees, but whenever we traverse them, we flatten them. Here, when we process the pair 6 8, we flatten the tree by making 4, 6, and 8 all point to 0.

tions to process M edges on N objects (see Exercise 1.9). This result is in stark contrast to our finding that quick find always (and quick union sometimes) uses *at least* $MN/2$ instructions. The conclusion is that, with weighted quick union, we can guarantee that we can solve huge practical problems in a reasonable amount of time (see Exercise 1.11). For the price of a few extra lines of code, we get a program that is literally millions of times faster than the simpler algorithms for the huge problems that we might encounter in practical applications.

It is evident from the diagrams that relatively few nodes are far from the root; indeed, empirical studies on huge problems tell us that the weighted quick-union algorithm of Program 1.3 typically can solve practical problems in *linear* time. That is, the cost of running the algorithm is within a constant factor of the cost of reading the input. We could hardly expect to find a more efficient algorithm.

We immediately come to the question of whether or not we can find an algorithm that has *guaranteed* linear performance. This question is an extremely difficult one that plagued researchers for many years (see Section 2.7). There are a number of easy ways to improve the weighted quick-union algorithm further. Ideally, we would like every node to link directly to the root of its tree, but we do not want to pay the price of changing a large number of links, as we did in the quick-union algorithm. We can approach the ideal simply by making all the nodes that we do examine link to the root. This step seems drastic at first blush, but it is easy to implement, and there is nothing sacrosanct about the structure of these trees: If we can modify them to make the algorithm more efficient, we should do so. We can easily implement this method, called *path compression*, by adding another pass through each path during the *union* operation, setting the id entry corresponding to each vertex encountered along the way to link to the root. The net result is to flatten the trees almost completely, approximating the ideal achieved by the quick-find algorithm, as illustrated in Figure 1.9. The analysis that establishes this fact is extremely complex, but the method is simple and effective. Figure 1.11 shows the result of path compression for a large example.

There are many other ways to implement path compression. For example, Program 1.4 is an implementation that compresses the paths by making each link skip to the next node in the path on the way up the tree, as depicted in Figure 1.10. This method is slightly easier to

---

Program 1.4 Path compression by halving

If we replace the `for` loops in Program 1.3 by this code, we halve the length of any path that we traverse. The net result of this change is that the trees become almost completely flat after a long sequence of operations.

```
for (i = p; i != id[i]; i = id[i])
    id[i] = id[id[i]];
for (j = q; j != id[j]; j = id[j])
    id[j] = id[id[j]];
```

---

implement than full path compression (see Exercise 1.16), and achieves the same net result. We refer to this variant as *weighted quick-union with path compression by halving*. Which of these methods is the more effective? Is the savings achieved worth the extra time required to implement path compression? Is there some other technique that we should consider? To answer these questions, we need to look more carefully at the algorithms and implementations. We shall return to this topic in Chapter 2, in the context of our discussion of basic approaches to the analysis of algorithms.

The end result of the succession of algorithms that we have considered to solve the connectivity problem is about the best that we could hope for in any practical sense. We have algorithms that are easy to implement whose running time is guaranteed to be within a constant factor of the cost of gathering the data. Moreover, the algorithms are *online* algorithms that consider each edge once, using space proportional to the number of objects, so there is no limitation on the number of edges that they can handle. The empirical studies in Table 1.1 validate our conclusion that Program 1.3 and its path-compression variations are useful even for huge practical applications. Choosing which is the best among these algorithms requires careful and sophisticated analysis (see Chapter 2).

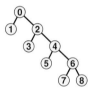

Figure 1.10
Path compression by halving

We can nearly halve the length of paths on the way up the tree by taking two links at a time and setting the bottom one to point to the same node as the top one, as shown in this example. The net result of performing this operation on every path that we traverse is asymptotically the same as full path compression.

Exercises

▷ **1.4** Show the contents of the `id` array after each *union* operation when you use the quick-find algorithm (Program 1.1) to solve the connectivity problem for the sequence 0-2, 1-4, 2-5, 3-6, 0-4, 6-0, and 1-3. Also give the number of times the program accesses the `id` array for each input pair.

▷ **1.5** Do Exercise 1.4, but use the quick-union algorithm (Program 1.2).

Table 1.1 Empirical study of union-find algorithms

These relative timings for solving random connectivity problems using various union–find algorithms demonstrate the effectiveness of the weighted version of the quick-union algorithm. The added incremental benefit due to path compression is less important. In these experiments, M is the number of random connections generated until all N objects are connected. This process involves substantially more *find* operations than *union* operations, so quick union is substantially slower than quick find. Neither quick find nor quick union is feasible for huge N. The running time for the weighted methods is evidently roughly proportional to M.

N	M	F	U	W	P	H
1000	3819	63	53	17	18	15
2500	12263	185	159	22	19	24
5000	21591	698	697	34	33	35
10000	41140	2891	3987	85	101	74
25000	162748			237	267	267
50000	279279			447	533	473
100000	676113			1382	1238	1174

Key:

    F   quick find (Program 1.1)
    U   quick union (Program 1.2)
    W weighted quick union (Program 1.3)
    P   weighted quick union with path compression (Exercise 1.16)
    H   weighted quick union with halving (Program 1.4)

▷ 1.6   Give the contents of the `id` array after each *union* operation for the weighted quick-union algorithm running on the examples corresponding to Figure 1.7 and Figure 1.8.

▷ 1.7   Do Exercise 1.4, but use the weighted quick-union algorithm (Program 1.3).

▷ 1.8   Do Exercise 1.4, but use the weighted quick-union algorithm with path compression by halving (Program 1.4).

1.9   Prove an upper bound on the number of machine instructions required to process M connections on N objects using Program 1.3. You may assume, for example, that any Java assignment statement always requires less than c instructions, for some fixed constant c.

1.10 Estimate the minimum amount of time (in days) that would be required for quick find (Program 1.1) to solve a problem with 10^9 objects and 10^6 input pairs, on a computer capable of executing 10^9 instructions per second. Assume that each iteration of the inner for loop requires at least 10 instructions.

1.11 Estimate the maximum amount of time (in seconds) that would be required for weighted quick union (Program 1.3) to solve a problem with 10^9 objects and 10^6 input pairs, on a computer capable of executing 10^9 instructions per second. Assume that each iteration of the outer for loop requires at most 100 instructions.

1.12 Compute the *average* distance from a node to the root in a worst-case tree of 2^n nodes built by the weighted quick-union algorithm.

▷ 1.13 Draw a diagram like Figure 1.10, starting with eight nodes instead of nine.

○ 1.14 Give a sequence of input pairs that causes the weighted quick-union algorithm (Program 1.3) to produce a path of length 4.

● 1.15 Give a sequence of input pairs that causes the weighted quick-union algorithm with path compression by halving (Program 1.4) to produce a path of length 4.

1.16 Show how to modify Program 1.3 to implement *full* path compression, where we complete each *union* operation by making every node that we touch link to the root of the new tree.

▷ 1.17 Answer Exercise 1.4, but use the weighted quick-union algorithm with full path compression (Exercise 1.16).

●● 1.18 Give a sequence of input pairs that causes the weighted quick-union algorithm with full path compression (Exercise 1.16) to produce a path of length 4.

○ 1.19 Give an example showing that modifying quick union (Program 1.2) to implement full path compression (see Exercise 1.16) is not sufficient to ensure that the trees have no long paths.

● 1.20 Modify Program 1.3 to use the *height* of the trees (longest path from any node to the root), instead of the weight, to decide whether to set id[i] = j or id[j] = i. Run empirical studies to compare this variant with Program 1.3.

●● 1.21 Show that Property 1.3 holds for the algorithm described in Exercise 1.20.

● 1.22 Modify Program 1.4 to generate random pairs of integers between 0 and $N-1$ instead of reading them from standard input, and to loop until $N-1$

Figure 1.11
A large example of the effect of path compression

This sequence depicts the result of processing random pairs from 100 objects with the weighted quick-union algorithm with path compression. All but two of the nodes in the tree are one or two steps from the root.

union operations have been performed. Run your program for $N = 10^3$, 10^4, 10^5, and 10^6, and print out the total number of edges generated for each value of N.

- ● **1.23** Modify your program from Exercise 1.22 to plot the number of edges needed to connect N items, for $100 \leq N \leq 1000$.

- ●● **1.24** Give an approximate formula for the number of random edges that are required to connect N objects, as a function of N.

1.4 Perspective

Each of the algorithms that we considered in Section 1.3 seems to be an improvement over the previous in some intuitive sense, but the process is perhaps artificially smooth because we have the benefit of hindsight in looking over the development of the algorithms as they were studied by researchers over the years (*see reference section*). The implementations are simple and the problem is well specified, so we can evaluate the various algorithms directly by running empirical studies. Furthermore, we can validate these studies and quantify the comparative performance of these algorithms (see Chapter 2). Not all the problem domains in this book are as well developed as this one, and we certainly can run into complex algorithms that are difficult to compare and mathematical problems that are difficult to solve. We strive to make objective scientific judgements about the algorithms that we use, while gaining experience learning the properties of implementations running on actual data from applications or random test data.

The process is prototypical of the way that we consider various algorithms for fundamental problems throughout the book. When possible, we follow the same basic steps that we took for union–find algorithms in Section 1.2, some of which are highlighted in this list:

- Decide on a complete and specific problem statement, including identifying fundamental abstract operations that are intrinsic to the problem.
- Carefully develop a succinct implementation for a straightforward algorithm.
- Develop improved implementations through a process of stepwise refinement, validating the efficacy of ideas for improvement through empirical analysis, mathematical analysis, or both.

- Find high-level abstract representations of data structures or algorithms in operation that enable effective high-level design of improved versions.
- Strive for worst-case performance guarantees when possible, but accept good performance on actual data when available.

The potential for spectacular performance improvements for practical problems such as those that we saw in Section 1.2 makes algorithm design a compelling field of study; few other design activities hold the potential to reap savings factors of millions or billions, or more.

More important, as the scale of our computational power and our applications increases, the gap between a fast algorithm and a slow one grows. A new computer might be 10 times faster and be able to process 10 times as much data as an old one, but if we are using a quadratic algorithm such as quick find, the new computer will take 10 times as long on the new job as the old one took to finish the old job! This statement seems counterintuitive at first, but it is easily verified by the simple identity $(10N)^2/10 = 10N^2$, as we shall see in Chapter 2. As computational power increases to allow us to take on larger and larger problems, the importance of having efficient algorithms increases as well.

Developing an efficient algorithm is an intellectually satisfying activity that can have direct practical payoff. As the connectivity problem indicates, a simply stated problem can lead us to study numerous algorithms that are not only both useful and interesting, but also intricate and challenging to understand. We shall encounter many ingenious algorithms that have been developed over the years for a host of practical problems. As the scope of applicability of computational solutions to scientific and commercial problems widens, so also grows the importance of being able to apply efficient algorithms to solve known problems and of being able to develop efficient solutions to new problems.

Exercises

1.25 Suppose that we use weighted quick union to process 10 times as many connections on a new computer that is 10 times as fast as an old one. How much longer would it take the new computer to finish the new job than it took the old one to finish the old job?

1.26 Answer Exercise 1.25 for the case where we use an algorithm that requires N^3 instructions.

1.5 Summary of Topics

This section comprises brief descriptions of the major parts of the book, giving specific topics covered and an indication of our general orientation toward the material. This set of topics is intended to touch on as many fundamental algorithms as possible. Some of the areas covered are core computer-science areas that we study in depth to learn basic algorithms of wide applicability. Other algorithms that we discuss are from advanced fields of study within computer science and related fields, such as numerical analysis and operations research—in these cases, our treatment serves as an introduction to these fields through examination of basic methods.

The first four parts of the book, which are contained in this volume, cover the most widely used set of algorithms and data structures, a first level of abstraction for collections of objects with keys that can support a broad variety of important fundamental algorithms. The algorithms that we consider are the products of decades of research and development and continue to play an essential role in the ever-expanding applications of computation.

Fundamentals (Part 1) in the context of this book are the basic principles and methodology that we use to implement, analyze, and compare algorithms. The material in Chapter 1 motivates our study of algorithm design and analysis; in Chapter 2, we consider basic methods of obtaining quantitative information about the performance of algorithms.

Data Structures (Part 2) go hand-in-hand with algorithms: We shall develop a thorough understanding of data representation methods for use throughout the rest of the book. We begin with an introduction to basic concrete data structures in Chapter 3, including arrays, linked lists, and strings. In Chapter 4, we consider fundamental abstract data types (ADTs) such as stacks and queues, including implementations using elementary data structures. Then in Chapter 5 we consider recursive programs and data structures, in particular trees and algorithms for manipulating them.

Sorting algorithms (Part 3) for rearranging files into order are of fundamental importance. We consider a variety of algorithms in considerable depth, including shellsort, quicksort, mergesort, heapsort, and radix sorts. We shall encounter algorithms for several related problems, including priority queues, selection, and merging. Many of these algorithms will find application as the basis for other algorithms later in the book.

Searching algorithms (Part 4) for finding specific items among large collections of items are also of fundamental importance. We discuss basic and advanced methods for searching using trees and digital key transformations, including binary search trees, balanced trees, hashing, digital search trees and tries, and methods appropriate for huge files. We note relationships among these methods, comparative performance statistics, and correspondences to sorting methods.

Parts 5 through 8, which are contained in two separate volumes (one for Part 5, another for Parts 6 through 8), cover advanced applications of the algorithms described here for a diverse set of applications— a second level of abstractions specific to a number of important applications areas. We also delve more deeply into techniques of algorithm design and analysis. Many of the problems that we touch on are the subject of ongoing research.

Graph Algorithms (Part 5) are useful for a variety of difficult and important problems. A general strategy for searching in graphs is developed and applied to fundamental connectivity problems, including shortest path, minimum spanning tree, network flow, and matching. A unified treatment of these algorithms shows that they are all based on the same procedure (which depends on the basic priority queue ADT). We also show the broad applicability of graph-processing algorithms by considering general problem-solving models such as the mincost flow problem and the concept of reducing one problem to another.

String Processing algorithms (Part 6) include a range of methods for processing (long) sequences of characters. String searching leads to pattern matching, which leads to parsing. File-compression techniques are also considered. Again, an introduction to advanced topics is given through treatment of some elementary problems that are important in their own right.

Geometric Algorithms (Part 7) are methods for solving problems involving points and lines (and other simple geometric objects) that have found a multitude of applications. We consider algorithms for finding the convex hull of a set of points, for finding intersections among geometric objects, for solving closest-point problems, and for multidimensional searching. Many of these methods nicely complement the more elementary sorting and searching methods.

Advanced Topics (Part 8) are discussed for the purpose of relating the material in the book to several other advanced fields of study. We begin with major approaches to the design and analysis of algorithms, including divide-and-conquer, dynamic programming, randomization, and amortization. We survey linear programming, the fast Fourier transform, NP-completeness, and other advanced topics from an introductory viewpoint to gain appreciation for the interesting advanced fields of study suggested by the elementary problems confronted in this book.

The study of algorithms is interesting because it is a new field (almost all the algorithms that we study are less than 50 years old, and some were just recently discovered) with a rich tradition (a few algorithms have been known for thousands of years). New discoveries are constantly being made, but few algorithms are completely understood. In this book we shall consider intricate, complicated, and difficult algorithms as well as elegant, simple, and easy algorithms. Our challenge is to understand the former and to appreciate the latter in the context of many different potential applications. In doing so, we shall explore a variety of useful tools and develop a style of algorithmic thinking that will serve us well in computational challenges to come.

CHAPTER TWO

Principles of Algorithm Analysis

ANALYSIS IS THE KEY to being able to understand algorithms sufficiently well that we can apply them effectively to practical problems. Although we cannot do extensive experimentation and deep mathematical analysis on each and every program that we run, we can work within a basic framework involving both empirical testing and approximate analysis that can help us to know the important facts about the performance characteristics of our algorithms so that we may compare those algorithms and can apply them to practical problems.

The very idea of describing the performance of a complex algorithm accurately with a mathematical analysis seems a daunting prospect at first, and we do often call on the research literature for results based on detailed mathematical study. Although it is not our purpose in this book to cover methods of analysis or even to summarize these results, it is important for us to be aware at the outset that we are on firm scientific ground when we want to compare different methods. Moreover, a great deal of detailed information is available about many of our most important algorithms through careful application of relatively few elementary techniques. We do highlight basic analytic results and methods of analysis throughout the book, particularly when such activities help us to understand the inner workings of fundamental algorithms. Our primary goal in this chapter is to provide the context and the tools that we need to work intelligently with the algorithms themselves.

The example in Chapter 1 provides a context that illustrates many of the basic concepts of algorithm analysis, so we frequently refer back to the performance of union–find algorithms to make particular points concrete. We also consider a detailed pair of new examples in Section 2.6.

Analysis plays a role at every point in the process of designing and implementing algorithms. At first, as we saw, we can save factors of thousands or millions in the running time with appropriate algorithm design choices. As we consider more efficient algorithms, we find it more of a challenge to choose among them, so we need to study their properties in more detail. In pursuit of the *best* (in some precise technical sense) algorithm, we find both algorithms that are useful in practice and theoretical questions that are challenging to resolve.

Complete coverage of methods for the analysis of algorithms is the subject of a book in itself (*see reference section*), but it is worthwhile for us to consider the basics here so that we can

- Illustrate the process.
- Describe in one place the mathematical conventions that we use.
- Provide a basis for discussion of higher-level issues.
- Develop an appreciation for scientific underpinnings of the conclusions that we draw when comparing algorithms.

Most important, algorithms and their analyses are often intertwined. In this book, we do not delve into deep and difficult mathematical derivations, but we do use sufficient mathematics to be able to understand what our algorithms are and how we can use them effectively.

2.1 Implementation and Empirical Analysis

We design and develop algorithms by layering abstract operations that help us to understand the essential nature of the computational problems that we want to solve. In theoretical studies, this process, although valuable, can take us far afield from the real-world problems that we need to consider. Thus, in this book, we keep our feet on the ground by expressing all the algorithms that we consider in an actual programming language: Java. This approach sometimes leaves us with a blurred distinction between an algorithm and its implementation, but that is small price to pay for the ability to work with and to learn from a concrete implementation.

Indeed, carefully constructed programs in an actual programming language provide an effective means of expressing our algorithms. In this book, we consider a large number of important and efficient algorithms that we describe in implementations that are both concise and precise in Java. English-language descriptions or abstract high-level representations of algorithms are all too often vague or incomplete; actual implementations force us to discover economical representations to avoid being inundated in detail.

We express our algorithms in Java, but this book is about algorithms, rather than about Java programming. Certainly, we consider Java implementations for many important tasks, and when there is a particularly convenient or efficient way to do a task in Java, we will take advantage of it. But the vast majority of the implementation decisions that we make are worth considering in any modern programming environment. Translating the programs in Chapter 1, and most of the other programs in this book, to another modern programming language is a straightforward task. On occasion, we also note when some other language provides a particularly effective mechanism suited to the task at hand. Our goal is to use Java as a vehicle for expressing the algorithms that we consider, rather than to dwell on implementation issues specific to Java.

If an algorithm is to be implemented as part of a large system, we use abstract data types or a similar mechanism to make it possible to change algorithms or implementations after we determine what part of the system deserves the most attention. From the start, however, we need to have an understanding of each algorithm's performance characteristics, because design requirements of the system may have a major influence on algorithm performance. Such initial design decisions must be made with care, because it often does turn out, in the end, that the performance of the whole system depends on the performance of some basic algorithm, such as those discussed in this book.

Implementations of the algorithms in this book have been put to effective use in a wide variety of large programs, operating systems, and applications systems. Our intention is to describe the algorithms and to encourage a focus on their dynamic properties through experimentation with the implementations given. For some applications, the implementations may be quite useful exactly as given; for other applications, however, more work may be required. For example, using a more defensive programming style than the one that we use in this book is justified when we are building real systems. Error conditions must be checked and reported, and programs must be implemented such that they can be changed easily, read and understood quickly by other programmers, interface well with other parts of the system, and be amenable to being moved to other environments.

Notwithstanding all these comments, we take the position when analyzing each algorithm that performance is of critical importance so that we focus our attention on the algorithm's essential performance characteristics. We assume that we are always interested in knowing about algorithms with substantially better performance, particularly if they are simpler.

To use an algorithm effectively, whether our goal is to solve a huge problem that could not otherwise be solved, or whether our goal is to provide an efficient implementation of a critical part of a system, we need to have an understanding of its performance characteristics. Developing such an understanding is the goal of algorithmic analysis.

One of the first steps that we take to understand the performance of algorithms is to do *empirical analysis*. Given two algorithms to solve the same problem, there is no mystery in the method: We run them both to see which one takes longer! This concept might seem too obvious to mention, but it is an all-too-common omission in the comparative study of algorithms. The fact that one algorithm is 10 times faster than another is unlikely to escape the notice of someone who waits 3 seconds for one to finish and 30 seconds for the other to finish, but it is easy to overlook as a small constant overhead factor in a mathematical analysis. When we monitor the performance of careful implementations on typical input, we get performance results that not only give us a direct indicator of efficiency but also provide us with the information that we need to compare algorithms and to validate any mathematical analyses that may apply (see, for example, Table 1.1). When empirical studies start to consume a significant amount of time, mathematical analysis is called for. Waiting an hour or a day for a program to finish is hardly a productive way to find out that it is slow, particularly when a straightforward analysis can give us the same information.

The first challenge that we face in empirical analysis is to develop a correct and complete implementation. For some complex algorithms, this challenge may present a significant obstacle. Accordingly, we typically want to have, through analysis or through experience with similar programs, some indication of how efficient a program might be before we invest too much effort in getting it to work.

The second challenge that we face in empirical analysis is to determine the nature of the input data and other factors that have direct influence on the experiments to be performed. Typically, we have three basic choices: use *actual* data, *random* data, or *perverse* data. Actual data enable us truly to measure the cost of the program in use; random data assure us that our experiments test the algorithm, not the data; and perverse data assure us that our programs can handle any input presented them. For example, when we test sorting algorithms, we run them on data such as the words in *Moby Dick*, on randomly generated integers, and on files of numbers that are all the same value. This problem of determining which input data to use to compare algorithms also arises when we analyze the algorithms.

It is easy to make mistakes when we compare implementations, particularly if differing machines, compilers, or systems are involved, or if huge programs with ill-specified inputs are being compared. The principal danger in comparing programs empirically is that one implementation may be coded more carefully than the other. The inventor of a proposed new algorithm is likely to pay careful attention to every aspect of its implementation and not to expend so much effort on the details of implementing a classical competing algorithm. To be confident of the accuracy of an empirical study comparing algorithms, we must be sure to give the same attention to each implementation.

One approach that we often use in this book, as we saw in Chapter 1, is to derive algorithms by making relatively minor modifications to other algorithms for the same problem so that comparative studies really are valid. More generally, we strive to identify essential abstract operations and start by comparing algorithms on the basis of their use of such operations. For example, the comparative empirical results that we examined in Table 1.1 are likely to be robust across programming languages and environments, as they involve programs that are similar and that make use of the same set of basic operations. For a particular programming environment, we can easily relate these numbers to actual running times. Most often, we simply want to know which of two programs is likely to be faster, or to what extent a certain change will improve the time or space requirements of a certain program.

Perhaps the most common mistake made in selecting an algorithm is to ignore performance characteristics. Faster algorithms are often more complicated than brute-force solutions, and implementors are often willing to accept a slower algorithm to avoid having to deal with added complexity. As we saw with union–find algorithms, however, we can sometimes reap huge savings with just a few lines of code. Users of a surprising number of computer systems lose substantial time waiting for simple quadratic algorithms to finish solving a problem, even though $N \log N$ or linear algorithms are available that are only slightly more complicated and could therefore solve the problem in a fraction of the time. When we are dealing with huge problem sizes, we have no choice but to seek a better algorithm, as we shall see.

Perhaps the second most common mistake made in selecting an algorithm is to pay too much attention to performance characteristics. Improving the running time of a program by a factor of 10 is inconsequential if the program takes only a few microseconds. Even if a program takes a few minutes, it may not be worth the time and effort required to make it run 10 times faster, particularly if we expect to use the program only a few times. The total time required to implement and debug an improved algorithm might be substantially more than the time required simply to run a slightly slower one—we may as well let the computer do the work. Worse, we may spend a considerable amount of time and effort implementing ideas that should improve a program but actually do not do so.

We cannot run empirical tests for a program that is not yet written, but we can analyze properties of the program and estimate the potential effectiveness of a proposed improvement. Not all putative improvements actually result in performance gains, and we need to understand the extent of the savings realized at each step. Moreover, we can include parameters in our implementations and use analysis to help us set the parameters. Most important, by understanding the fundamental properties of our programs and the basic nature of the programs' resource usage, we have the potential to evaluate their effectiveness on computers not yet built and to compare them against new algorithms not yet designed. In Section 2.2, we outline our methodology for developing a basic understanding of algorithm performance.

Exercises

2.1 Translate the programs in Chapter 1 to another programming language, and answer Exercise 1.22 for your implementations.

2.2 How long does it take to count to 1 billion (ignoring overflow)? Determine the amount of time it takes the program

```
int i, j, k, count = 0;
for (i = 0; i < N; i++)
  for (j = 0; j < N; j++)
    for (k = 0; k < N; k++)
      count++;
```

to complete in your programming environment, for $N = 10$, 100, and 1000. If your compiler has optimization features that are supposed to make programs more efficient, check whether or not they do so for this program.

2.2 Analysis of Algorithms

In this section, we outline the framework within which mathematical analysis can play a role in the process of comparing the performance of algorithms and thus lay a foundation for us to be able to consider basic analytic results as they apply to the fundamental algorithms that we consider throughout the book. We shall consider the basic mathematical tools that are used in the analysis of algorithms, both to allow us to study classical analyses of fundamental algorithms and to make use of results from the research literature that help us understand the performance characteristics of our algorithms.

The following are among the reasons that we perform mathematical analysis of algorithms:

- To compare different algorithms for the same task
- To predict performance in a new environment
- To set values of algorithm parameters

We shall see many examples of each of these reasons throughout the book. Empirical analysis might suffice for some of these tasks, but mathematical analysis can be more informative (and less expensive!), as we shall see.

The analysis of algorithms can be challenging indeed. Some of the algorithms in this book are well understood, to the point that accurate mathematical formulas are known that can be used to predict running time in practical situations. People develop such formulas by carefully studying the program to find the running time in terms of fundamental mathematical quantities and then doing a mathematical analysis of the quantities involved. On the other hand, the performance properties of other algorithms in this book are not fully understood—perhaps their analysis leads to unsolved mathematical questions, or perhaps known implementations are too complex for a detailed analysis to be reasonable, or (most likely) perhaps the types of input that they encounter cannot be characterized accurately.

Several important factors in a precise analysis are usually outside a given programmer's domain of influence. First, Java programs are translated into bytecode, and the bytecode is interpreted or translated into runtime code on a virtual machine (VM). The compiler, translator, and VM implementations all have an effect on which instructions on an actual machine are executed, so it can be a challenging task to figure out exactly how long even one Java statement might take to execute. In an environment where resources are being shared, even the same program can have varying performance characteristics at two different times. Second, many programs are extremely sensitive to their input data, and performance might fluctuate wildly depending on the input. Third, many programs of interest are not well understood, and specific mathematical results may not be available. Finally, two programs might not be comparable at all: one may run much more efficiently on one particular kind of input and the second may run efficiently under other circumstances.

All these factors notwithstanding, it is often possible to predict precisely how long a particular program will take, or to know that one program will do better than another in particular situations. Moreover, we can often acquire such knowledge by using one of a relatively small set of mathematical tools. It is the task of the algorithm analyst to discover as much information as possible about the performance of algorithms; it is the task of the programmer to apply such information in selecting algorithms for particular applications. In this and the next several sections, we concentrate on the idealized world of the analyst. To make effective use of our best algorithms, we need to be able to step into this world, on occasion.

The first step in the analysis of an algorithm is to identify the abstract operations on which the algorithm is based in order to separate the analysis from the implementation. Thus, for example, we separate the study of how many times one of our *union–find* implementations executes the code fragment `i = a[i]` from the analysis of how many nanoseconds might be required to execute that particular code fragment on our computer. We need both these elements to determine the actual running time of the program on a particular computer. The former is determined by properties of the algorithm; the latter by properties of the computer. This separation often allows us to compare algorithms in a way that is independent of particular implementations or of particular computers.

Although the number of abstract operations involved can be large, in principle, the performance of an algorithm typically depends on only a few quantities, and typically the most important quantities to analyze are easy to identify. One way to identify them is to use a profiling mechanism (a mechanism available in many Java implementations that gives instruction-frequency counts) to determine the most frequently executed parts of the program for some sample runs. Or, like the union–find algorithms of Section 1.3, our implementation might be built on a few abstract operations. In either case, the analysis amounts to determining the frequency of execution of a few fundamental operations. Our modus operandi will be to look for rough estimates of these quantities, secure in the knowledge that we can undertake a fuller analysis for important programs when necessary. Moreover, as we shall see, we can often use approximate analytic results in conjunction with empirical studies to predict performance accurately.

We also have to study the data and to model the input that might be presented to the algorithm. Most often, we consider one of two approaches to the analysis: we either assume that the input is random and study the *average-case* performance of the program, or we look for perverse input and study the *worst-case* performance of the program. The process of characterizing random inputs is difficult for many algorithms, but for many other algorithms it is straightforward and leads to analytic results that provide useful information. The average case might be a mathematical fiction that is not representative of the data on which the program is being used, and the worst case might be a bizarre construction that would never occur in practice, but these analyses give useful information on performance in most cases. For example, we can test analytic results against empirical results (see Section 2.1). If they match, we have increased confidence in both; if they do not match, we can learn about the algorithm and the model by studying the discrepancies.

In the next three sections, we briefly survey the mathematical tools that we shall be using throughout the book. This material is outside our primary narrative thrust, and readers with a strong background in mathematics or readers who are not planning to check our mathematical statements on the performance of algorithms in detail may wish to skip to Section 2.6 and to refer back to this material when warranted later in the book. The mathematical underpinnings that we consider, however, are generally not difficult to comprehend, and they are too close to core issues of algorithm design to be ignored by anyone wishing to use a computer effectively.

First, in Section 2.3, we consider the mathematical functions that we commonly need to describe the performance characteristics of algorithms. Next, in Section 2.4, we consider the *O-notation*, and the notion of *is proportional to*, which allow us to suppress detail in our mathematical analyses. Then, in Section 2.5, we consider *recurrence relations*, the basic analytic tool that we use to capture the performance characteristics of an algorithm in a mathematical equation. Following this survey, we consider examples where we use the basic tools to analyze specific algorithms, in Section 2.6.

Exercises

- **2.3** Develop an expression of the form $c_0 + c_1 N + c_2 N^2 + c_3 N^3$ that accurately describes the running time of your program from Exercise 2.2. Compare the times predicted by this expression with actual times, for $N = 10$, 100, and 1000.

- **2.4** Develop an expression that accurately describes the running time of Program 1.1 in terms of M and N.

2.3 Growth of Functions

Most algorithms have a *primary parameter* N that affects the running time most significantly. The parameter N might be the degree of a polynomial, the size of a file to be sorted or searched, the number of characters in a text string, or some other abstract measure of the size of the problem being considered: it is most often directly proportional to the size of the data set being processed. When there is more than one such parameter (for example, M and N in the *union–find* algorithms that we discussed in Section 1.3), we often reduce the analysis to just one parameter by expressing one of the parameters as a function of the other or by considering one parameter at a time (holding the other constant) so that we can restrict ourselves to considering a single parameter N without loss of generality. Our goal is to express the resource requirements of our programs (most often running time) in terms of N, using mathematical formulas that are as simple as possible and that are accurate for large values of the parameters. The algorithms in this book typically have running times proportional to one of the following functions.

1   Most instructions of most programs are executed once or at most only a few times. If all the instructions of a program have this property, we say that the program's running time is *constant*.

$\log N$ When the running time of a program is *logarithmic,* the program gets slightly slower as N grows. This running time commonly occurs in programs that solve a big problem by transformation into a series of smaller problems, cutting the problem size by some constant fraction at each step. For our range of interest, we can consider the running time to be less than a large constant. The base of the logarithm changes the constant, but not by much: When N is 1 thousand, $\log N$ is 3 if the base is 10, or is about 10 if the base is 2; when N is 1 million, $\log N$ is only double these values. Whenever N doubles, $\log N$ increases by a constant, but $\log N$ does not double until N increases to N^2.

N When the running time of a program is *linear,* it is generally the case that a small amount of processing is done on each input element. When N is 1 million, then so is the running time. Whenever N doubles, then so does the running time. This situation is optimal for an algorithm that must process N inputs (or produce N outputs).

$N \log N$ The $N \log N$ running time arises when algorithms solve a problem by breaking it up into smaller subproblems, solving them independently, and then combining the solutions.

For lack of a better adjective (*linearithmic*?), we simply say that the running time of such an algorithm is $N \log N$. When N is 1 million, $N \log N$ is perhaps 20 million. When N doubles, the running time more (but not much more) than doubles.

N^2 When the running time of an algorithm is *quadratic,* that algorithm is practical for use on only relatively small problems. Quadratic running times typically arise in algorithms that process all pairs of data items (perhaps in a double nested loop). When N is 1 thousand, the running time is 1 million. Whenever N doubles, the running time increases fourfold.

N^3 Similarly, an algorithm that processes triples of data items (perhaps in a triple-nested loop) has a *cubic* running time and is practical for use on only small problems. When N is 100, the running time is 1 million. Whenever N doubles, the running time increases eightfold.

2^N Few algorithms with *exponential* running time are likely to be appropriate for practical use, even though such algorithms arise naturally as brute-force solutions to problems. When N is 20, the running time is 1 million. Whenever N doubles, the running time squares!

The running time of a particular program is likely to be some constant multiplied by one of these terms (the *leading term*) plus some smaller terms. The values of the constant coefficient and the terms included depend on the results of the analysis and on implementation details. Roughly, the coefficient of the leading term has to do with the number of instructions in the inner loop: At any level of algorithm design, it is prudent to limit the number of such instructions. For large N, the effect of the leading term dominates; for small N or for carefully engineered algorithms, more terms may contribute and comparisons of algorithms are more difficult. In most cases, we will refer to the running time of programs simply as "linear," "$N \log N$," "cubic," and so forth. We consider the justification for doing so in detail in Section 2.4.

Eventually, to reduce the total running time of a program, we focus on minimizing the number of instructions in the inner loop. Each

Table 2.1 Values of commonly encountered functions

This table indicates the relative size of some of the functions that we encounter in the analysis of algorithms. The quadratic function clearly dominates, particularly for large N, and differences among smaller functions may not be as we might expect for small N. For example, $N^{3/2}$ should be greater than $N \lg^2 N$ for huge values of N, but $N \lg^2 N$ is greater for the smaller values of N that might occur in practice. A precise characterization of the running time of an algorithm might involve linear combinations of these functions. We can easily separate fast algorithms from slow ones because of vast differences between, for example, $\lg N$ and N or N and N^2, but distinguishing among fast algorithms involves careful study.

$\lg N$	$\sqrt{N}$	N	$N \lg N$	$N(\lg N)^2$	$N^{3/2}$	N^2
3	3	10	33	110	32	100
7	10	100	664	4414	1000	10000
10	32	1000	9966	99317	31623	1000000
13	100	10000	132877	1765633	1000000	100000000
17	316	100000	1660964	27588016	31622777	10000000000
20	1000	1000000	19931569	397267426	1000000000	1000000000000

instruction comes under scrutiny: Is it really necessary? Is there a more efficient way to accomplish the same task? Some programmers believe that the automatic tools provided by modern Java compilers can produce the best machine code or that modern VMs will optimize program performance; others believe that the best route is to implement critical methods in native C or machine code. We normally stop short of considering optimization at this level, although we do occasionally take note of how many machine instructions are required for certain operations in order to help us understand why one algorithm might be faster than another in practice.

For small problems, it makes scant difference which method we use—a fast modern computer will complete the job in an instant. But as problem size increases, the numbers we deal with can become huge, as indicated in Table 2.1. As the number of instructions to be executed by a slow algorithm becomes truly huge, the time required to execute those instructions becomes infeasible, even for the fastest computers.

seconds

10^2	1.7 minutes
10^4	2.8 hours
10^5	1.1 days
10^6	1.6 weeks
10^7	3.8 months
10^8	3.1 years
10^9	3.1 decades
10^{10}	3.1 centuries
10^{11}	*never*

Figure 2.1
Seconds conversions

The vast difference between numbers such as 10^4 and 10^8 is more obvious when we consider them to measure time in seconds and convert to familiar units of time. We might let a program run for 2.8 hours, but we would be unlikely to contemplate running a program that would take at least 3.1 years to complete. Because 2^{10} is approximately 10^3, this table is useful for powers of 2 as well. For example, 2^{32} seconds is about 124 years.

Table 2.2 Time to solve huge problems

For many applications, our only chance of being able to solve huge
problem instances is to use an efficient algorithm. This table indicates
the minimum amount of time required to solve problems of size 1 million
and 1 billion, using linear, $N \log N$, and quadratic algorithms, when we
can execute 1 million, 1 billion, and 1 trillion instructions per second. A
fast algorithm enables us to solve a problem on a slow machine, but a
fast machine is no help when we are using a slow algorithm.

operations per second	problem size 1 million			problem size 1 billion		
	N	$N \lg N$	N^2	N	$N \lg N$	N^2
10^6	seconds	seconds	weeks	hours	hours	never
10^9	instant	instant	hours	seconds	seconds	decades
10^{12}	instant	instant	seconds	instant	instant	weeks

Figure 2.1 gives conversion factors from large numbers of seconds to
days, months, years, and so forth; Table 2.2 gives examples showing
how fast algorithms are more likely than fast computers to be able to
help us solve problems without facing outrageous running times.

A few other functions do arise. For example, an algorithm with
N^2 inputs that has a running time proportional to N^3 is best thought
of as an $N^{3/2}$ algorithm. Also, some algorithms have two stages of
subproblem decomposition, which lead to running times proportional
to $N \log^2 N$. It is evident from Table 2.1 that both of these functions
are much closer to $N \log N$ than to N^2.

The logarithm function plays a special role in the design and
analysis of algorithms, so it is worthwhile for us to consider it in
detail. Because we often deal with analytic results only to within a
constant factor, we use the notation "$\log N$" without specifying the
base. Changing the base from one constant to another changes the
value of the logarithm by only a constant factor, but specific bases normally suggest themselves in particular contexts. In mathematics, the
natural logarithm (base $e = 2.71828\ldots$) is so important that a special
abbreviation is commonly used: $\log_e N \equiv \ln N$. In computer science,
the *binary logarithm* (base 2) is so important that the abbreviation
$\log_2 N \equiv \lg N$ is commonly used.

The smallest integer larger than $\lg N$ is the number of bits required to represent N in binary, in the same way that the smallest integer larger than $\log_{10} N$ is the number of digits required to represent N in decimal. The Java statement

```
for (lgN = 0; N > 0; lgN++, N /= 2) ;
```

is a simple way to compute the smallest integer larger than $\lg N$. A similar method for computing this function is

```
for (lgN = 0, t = 1; t < N; lgN++, t += t) ;
```

This version emphasizes that $2^n \leq N < 2^{n+1}$ when n is the smallest integer larger than $\lg N$.

Occasionally, we iterate the logarithm: We apply it successively to a huge number. For example, $\lg \lg 2^{256} = \lg 256 = 8$. As illustrated by this example, we generally regard $\log \log N$ as a constant, for practical purposes, because it is so small, even when N is huge.

We also frequently encounter a number of special functions and mathematical notations from classical analysis that are useful in providing concise descriptions of properties of programs. Table 2.3 summarizes the most familiar of these functions; we briefly discuss them and some of their most important properties in the following paragraphs.

Our algorithms and analyses most often deal with discrete units, so we often have need for the following special functions to convert real numbers to integers:

$\lfloor x \rfloor$: largest integer less than or equal to x

$\lceil x \rceil$: smallest integer greater than or equal to x.

For example, $\lfloor \pi \rfloor$ and $\lceil e \rceil$ are both equal to 3, and $\lceil \lg(N+1) \rceil$ is the number of bits in the binary representation of N. Another important use of these functions arises when we want to divide a set of N objects in half. We cannot do so exactly if N is odd, so, to be precise, we divide into one subset with $\lfloor N/2 \rfloor$ objects and another subset with $\lceil N/2 \rceil$ objects. If N is even, the two subsets are equal in size ($\lfloor N/2 \rfloor = \lceil N/2 \rceil$); if N is odd, they differ in size by 1 ($\lfloor N/2 \rfloor + 1 = \lceil N/2 \rceil$). In Java, we can compute these functions directly when we are operating on integers (for example, if $N \geq 0$, then N/2 is $\lfloor N/2 \rfloor$ and N - (N/2) is $\lceil N/2 \rceil$), and we can use floor and ceil from the java.lang.Math package to compute them when we are operating on floating point numbers.

A discretized version of the natural logarithm function called the *harmonic numbers* often arises in the analysis of algorithms. The Nth harmonic number is defined by the equation

$$H_N = 1 + \frac{1}{2} + \frac{1}{3} + \ldots + \frac{1}{N}.$$

The natural logarithm $\ln N$ is the area under the curve $1/x$ between 1 and N; the harmonic number H_N is the area under the step function that we define by evaluating $1/x$ at the integers between 1 and N. This relationship is illustrated in Figure 2.2. The formula

$$H_N \approx \ln N + \gamma + 1/(12N),$$

where $\gamma = 0.57721\ldots$ (this constant is known as *Euler's constant*) gives an excellent approximation to H_N. By contrast with $\lceil \lg N \rceil$ and $\lfloor \lg N \rfloor$, it is better to use the `log` method of `java.lang.Math` to compute H_N than to do so directly from the definition.

The sequence of numbers

$$0\ 1\ 1\ 2\ 3\ 5\ 8\ 13\ 21\ 34\ 55\ 89\ 144\ 233\ 377\ldots$$

that are defined by the formula

$$F_N = F_{N-1} + F_{N-2}, \qquad \text{for } N \geq 2 \text{ with } F_0 = 0 \text{ and } F_1 = 1$$

are known as the *Fibonacci numbers*, and they have many interesting properties. For example, the ratio of two successive terms approaches the *golden ratio* $\phi = (1 + \sqrt{5})/2 \approx 1.61803\ldots$. More detailed analysis shows that F_N is $\phi^N/\sqrt{5}$ rounded to the nearest integer.

We also have occasion to manipulate the familiar *factorial* function $N!$. Like the exponential function, the factorial arises in the brute-force solution to problems and grows much too fast for such solutions to be of practical interest. It also arises in the analysis of algorithms because it represents all the ways to arrange N objects. To approximate $N!$, we use *Stirling's formula*:

$$\lg N! \approx N \lg N - N \lg e + \lg \sqrt{2\pi N}.$$

For example, Stirling's formula tells us that the number of bits in the binary representation of $N!$ is about $N \lg N$.

Figure 2.2
Harmonic numbers

The harmonic numbers are an approximation to the area under the curve $y = 1/x$. The constant γ accounts for the difference between H_N and $\ln N = \int_1^N dx/x$.

Table 2.3 Special functions and constants

This table summarizes the mathematical notation that we use for functions and constants that arise in formulas describing the performance of algorithms. The formulas for the approximate values extend to provide much more accuracy, if desired (*see reference section*).

function	name	typical value	approximation
$\lfloor x \rfloor$	floor function	$\lfloor 3.14 \rfloor = 3$	x
$\lceil x \rceil$	ceiling function	$\lceil 3.14 \rceil = 4$	x
$\lg N$	binary logarithm	$\lg 1024 = 10$	$1.44 \ln N$
F_N	Fibonacci numbers	$F_{10} = 55$	$\phi^N/\sqrt{5}$
H_N	harmonic numbers	$H_{10} \approx 2.9$	$\ln N + \gamma$
$N!$	factorial function	$10! = 3628800$	$(N/e)^N$
$\lg(N!)$		$\lg(100!) \approx 520$	$N \lg N - 1.44N$

$$e = 2.71828\ldots$$
$$\gamma = 0.57721\ldots$$
$$\phi = (1+\sqrt{5})/2 = 1.61803\ldots$$
$$\ln 2 = 0.693147\ldots$$
$$\lg e = 1/\ln 2 = 1.44269\ldots$$

Most of the formulas that we consider in this book are expressed in terms of the few functions that we have described in this section, which are summarized in Table 2.3. Many other special functions can arise in the analysis of algorithms. For example, the classical *binomial distribution* and related *Poisson approximation* play an important role in the design and analysis of some of the fundamental search algorithms that we consider in Chapters 14 and 15. We discuss functions not listed here when we encounter them.

Exercises

▷ **2.5** For what values of N is $10N \lg N > 2N^2$?

▷ **2.6** For what values of N is $N^{3/2}$ between $N(\lg N)^2/2$ and $2N(\lg N)^2$?

2.7 For what values of N is $2NH_N - N < N \lg N + 10N$?

○ **2.8** What is the smallest value of N for which $\log_{10} \log_{10} N > 8$?

○ **2.9** Prove that $\lfloor \lg N \rfloor + 1$ is the number of bits required to represent N in binary.

2.10 Add columns to Table 2.2 for $N(\lg N)^2$ and $N^{3/2}$.

2.11 Add rows to Table 2.2 for 10^7 and 10^8 instructions per second.

2.12 Write a Java method that computes H_N, using the `log` method of `java.lang.Math`.

2.13 Write an efficient Java function that computes $\lceil \lg \lg N \rceil$. Do not use a library function.

2.14 How many digits are there in the decimal representation of 1 million factorial?

2.15 How many bits are there in the binary representation of $\lg(N!)$?

2.16 How many bits are there in the binary representation of H_N?

2.17 Give a simple expression for $\lfloor \lg F_N \rfloor$.

○ **2.18** Give the smallest values of N for which $\lfloor H_N \rfloor = i$ for $1 \le i \le 10$.

2.19 Give the largest value of N for which you can solve a problem that requires at least $f(N)$ instructions on a machine that can execute 10^9 instructions per second, for the following functions $f(N)$: $N^{3/2}$, $N^{5/4}$, $2NH_N$, $N \lg N \lg \lg N$, and $N^2 \lg N$.

2.4 Big-Oh Notation

The mathematical artifact that allows us to suppress detail when we are analyzing algorithms is called the *O-notation*, or "big-Oh notation," which is defined as follows.

Definition 2.1 *A function $g(N)$ is said to be $O(f(N))$ if there exist constants c_0 and N_0 such that $g(N) < c_0 f(N)$ for all $N > N_0$.*

We use the *O*-notation for three distinct purposes:
- To bound the error that we make when we ignore small terms in mathematical formulas
- To bound the error that we make when we ignore parts of a program that contribute a small amount to the total being analyzed
- To allow us to classify algorithms according to upper bounds on their total running times

We consider the third use in Section 2.7 and discuss briefly the other two here.

The constants c_0 and N_0 implicit in the O-notation often hide implementation details that are important in practice. Obviously, saying that an algorithm has running time $O(f(N))$ says nothing about the running time if N happens to be less than N_0, and c_0 might be hiding a large amount of overhead designed to avoid a bad worst case. We would prefer an algorithm using N^2 nanoseconds over one using $\log N$ centuries, but we could not make this choice on the basis of the O-notation.

Often, the results of a mathematical analysis are not exact but rather are approximate in a precise technical sense: The result might be an expression consisting of a sequence of decreasing terms. Just as we are most concerned with the inner loop of a program, we are most concerned with the *leading terms* (the largest terms) of a mathematical expression. The O-notation allows us to keep track of the leading terms while ignoring smaller terms when manipulating approximate mathematical expressions and ultimately allows us to make concise statements that give accurate approximations to the quantities that we analyze.

Some of the basic manipulations that we use when working with expressions containing the O-notation are the subject of Exercises 2.20 through 2.25. Many of these manipulations are intuitive, but mathematically inclined readers may be interested in working Exercise 2.21 to prove the validity of the basic operations from the definition. Essentially, these exercises say that we can expand algebraic expressions using the O-notation as though the O were not there, then drop all but the largest term. For example, if we expand the expression

$$(N + O(1))(N + O(\log N) + O(1)),$$

we get six terms

$$N^2 + O(N) + O(N \log N) + O(\log N) + O(N) + O(1),$$

but can drop all but the largest O-term, leaving the approximation

$$N^2 + O(N \log N).$$

That is, N^2 is a good approximation to this expression when N is large. These manipulations are intuitive, but the O-notation allows us to express them mathematically with rigor and precision. We refer to a formula with one O-term as an *asymptotic expression*.

For a more relevant example, suppose that (after some mathematical analysis) we determine that a particular algorithm has an inner loop that is iterated $2NH_N$ times on the average, an outer section that is iterated N times, and some initialization code that is executed once. Suppose further that we determine (after careful scrutiny of the implementation) that each iteration of the inner loop requires a_0 nanoseconds, the outer section requires a_1 nanoseconds, and the initialization part a_2 nanoseconds. Then we know that the average running time of the program (in nanoseconds) is

$$2a_0NH_N + a_1N + a_2.$$

But it is also true that the running time is

$$2a_0NH_N + O(N).$$

This simpler form is significant because it says that, for large N, we may not need to find the values of a_1 or a_2 to approximate the running time. In general, there could well be many other terms in the mathematical expression for the exact running time, some of which may be difficult to analyze. The O-notation provides us with a way to get an approximate answer for large N without bothering with such terms.

Continuing this example, we also can use the O-notation to express running time in terms of a familiar function, $\ln N$. In terms of the O-notation, the approximation in Table 2.3 is expressed as $H_N = \ln N + O(1)$. Thus, $2a_0N\ln N + O(N)$ is an asymptotic expression for the total running time of our algorithm. We expect the running time to be close to the easily computed value $2a_0N\ln N$ for large N. The constant factor a_0 depends on the time taken by the instructions in the inner loop.

Furthermore, we do not need to know the value of a_0 to predict that the running time for input of size $2N$ will be about twice the running time for input of size N for huge N because

$$\frac{2a_0(2N)\ln(2N) + O(2N)}{2a_0N\ln N + O(N)} = \frac{2\ln(2N) + O(1)}{\ln N + O(1)} = 2 + O\left(\frac{1}{\log N}\right).$$

That is, the asymptotic formula allows us to make accurate predictions without concerning ourselves with details of either the implementation or the analysis. Note that such a prediction would *not* be possible if we were to have only an O-approximation for the leading term.

1	none
$\lg N$	slight increase
N	double
$N\lg N$	slightly more than double
$N^{3/2}$	factor of $2\sqrt{2}$
N^2	factor of 4
N^3	factor of 8
2^N	square

Figure 2.3
Effect of doubling problem size on running time

Predicting the effect of doubling the problem size on the running time is a simple task when the running time is proportional to certain simple functions, as indicated in this table. In theory, we cannot depend on this effect unless N is huge, but this method is surprisingly effective. Conversely, a quick method for determining the functional growth of the running time of a program is to run that program empirically, doubling the input size for N as large as possible, then work backward from this table.

The kind of reasoning just outlined allows us to focus on the leading term when comparing or trying to predict the running times of algorithms. We are so often in the position of counting the number of times that fixed-cost operations are performed and wanting to use the leading term to estimate the result that we normally keep track of *only* the leading term, assuming implicitly that a precise analysis like the one just given could be performed, if necessary.

When a function $f(N)$ is asymptotically large compared to another function $g(N)$ (that is, $g(N)/f(N) \to 0$ as $N \to \infty$), we sometimes use in this book the (decidedly nontechnical) terminology *about* $f(N)$ to mean $f(N)+O(g(N))$. What we seem to lose in mathematical precision we gain in clarity, for we are more interested in the performance of algorithms than in mathematical details. In such cases, we can rest assured that, for large N (if not for all N), the quantity in question will be close to $f(N)$. For example, even if we know that a quantity is $N(N-1)/2$, we may refer to it as being about $N^2/2$. This way of expressing the result is more quickly understood than the more detailed exact result and, for example, deviates from the truth only by 0.1 percent for $N = 1000$. The precision lost in such cases pales by comparison with the precision lost in the more common usage $O(f(N))$. Our goal is to be both precise and concise when describing the performance of algorithms.

In a similar vein, we sometimes say that the running time of an algorithm *is proportional to* $f(N)$ when we can prove that it is equal to $cf(N)+g(N)$ with $g(N)$ asymptotically smaller than $f(N)$. When this kind of bound holds, we can project the running time for, say, $2N$ from our observed running time for N, as in the example just discussed. Figure 2.3 gives the factors that we can use for such projection for functions that commonly arise in the analysis of algorithms. Coupled with empirical studies (see Section 2.1), this approach frees us from the task of determining implementation-dependent constants in detail. Or, working backward, we often can easily develop an hypothesis about the functional growth of the running time of a program by determining the effect of doubling N on running time.

The distinctions among O-bounds, *is proportional to*, and *about* are illustrated in Figures 2.4 and 2.5. We use O-notation primarily to learn the fundamental asymptotic behavior of an algorithm; *is proportional to* when we want to predict performance by extrapolation from

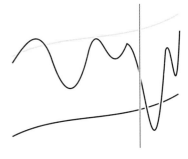

Figure 2.4
Bounding a function with an O-approximation

In this schematic diagram, the oscillating curve represents a function, $g(N)$, which we are trying to approximate; the black smooth curve represents another function, $f(N)$, which we are trying to use for the approximation; and the gray smooth curve represents $cf(N)$ for some unspecified constant c. The vertical line represents a value N_0, indicating that the approximation is to hold for $N > N_0$. When we say that $g(N) = O(f(N))$, we expect only that the value of $g(N)$ falls below some curve the shape of $f(N)$ to the right of some vertical line. The behavior of $f(N)$ could otherwise be erratic (for example, it need not even be continuous).

empirical studies; and *about* when we want to compare performance or to make absolute performance predictions.

Exercises

▷ **2.20** Prove that $O(1)$ is the same as $O(2)$.

2.21 Prove that we can make any of the following transformations in an expression that uses the O-notation:

$$f(N) \rightarrow O(f(N)),$$
$$cO(f(N)) \rightarrow O(f(N)),$$
$$O(cf(N)) \rightarrow O(f(N)),$$
$$f(N) - g(N) = O(h(N)) \rightarrow f(N) = g(N) + O(h(N)),$$
$$O(f(N))O(g(N)) \rightarrow O(f(N)g(N)),$$
$$O(f(N)) + O(g(N)) \rightarrow O(g(N)) \quad \text{if } f(N) = O(g(N)).$$

∘ **2.22** Show that $(N + 1)(H_N + O(1)) = N \ln N + O(N)$.

2.23 Show that $N \ln N = O(N^{3/2})$.

● **2.24** Show that $N^M = O(\alpha^N)$ for any M and any constant $\alpha > 1$.

● **2.25** Prove that

$$\frac{N}{N + O(1)} = 1 + O\left(\frac{1}{N}\right).$$

2.26 Suppose that $H_k = N$. Give an approximate formula that expresses k as a function of N.

● **2.27** Suppose that $\lg(k!) = N$. Give an approximate formula that expresses k as a function of N.

∘ **2.28** You are given the information that the running time of one algorithm is $O(N \log N)$ and that the running time of another algorithm is $O(N^3)$. What does this statement imply about the relative performance of the algorithms?

∘ **2.29** You are given the information that the running time of one algorithm is always about $N \log N$ and that the running time of another algorithm is $O(N^3)$. What does this statement imply about the relative performance of the algorithms?

∘ **2.30** You are given the information that the running time of one algorithm is always about $N \log N$ and that the running time of another algorithm is always about N^3. What does this statement imply about the relative performance of the algorithms?

∘ **2.31** You are given the information that the running time of one algorithm is always proportional to $N \log N$ and that the running time of another algorithm

Figure 2.5
Functional approximations

When we say that $g(N)$ is proportional to $f(N)$ (top), we expect that it eventually grows like $f(N)$ does, but perhaps offset by an unknown constant. Given some value of $g(N)$, this knowledge allows us to estimate it for larger N. When we say that $g(N)$ is about $f(N)$ (bottom), we expect that we can eventually use f to estimate the value of g accurately.

is always proportional to N^3. What does this statement imply about the relative performance of the algorithms?

○ **2.32** Derive the factors given in Figure 2.3: For each function $f(N)$ that appears on the left, find an asymptotic formula for $f(2N)/f(N)$.

2.5 Basic Recurrences

As we shall see throughout the book, a great many algorithms are based on the principle of recursively decomposing a large problem into one or more smaller ones, using solutions to the subproblems to solve the original problem. We discuss this topic in detail in Chapter 5, primarily from a practical point of view, concentrating on implementations and applications. We also consider an example in detail in Section 2.6. In this section, we look at basic methods for analyzing such algorithms and derive solutions to a few standard formulas that arise in the analysis of many of the algorithms that we will be studying. Understanding the mathematical properties of the formulas in this section will give us insight into the performance properties of algorithms throughout the book.

Recursive decomposition in an algorithm is directly reflected in its analysis. For example, the running time of such algorithms is determined by the size and number of the subproblems and the time required for the decomposition. Mathematically, the dependence of the running time of an algorithm for an input of size N on its running time for smaller inputs is captured easily with formulas called *recurrence relations*. Such formulas describe precisely the performance of the corresponding algorithms: To derive the running time, we solve the recurrences. More rigorous arguments related to specific algorithms will come up when we get to the algorithms—here, we concentrate on the formulas themselves.

Formula 2.1 This recurrence arises for a recursive program that loops through the input to eliminate one item:

$$C_N = C_{N-1} + N, \qquad \text{for } N \geq 2 \text{ with } C_1 = 1.$$

Solution: C_N is about $N^2/2$. To solve such a recurrence, we *telescope* it by applying it to itself, as follows:

$$\begin{aligned} C_N &= C_{N-1} + N \\ &= C_{N-2} + (N-1) + N \\ &= C_{N-3} + (N-2) + (N-1) + N \\ &\quad\vdots \end{aligned}$$

Continuing in this way, we eventually find that

$$\begin{aligned} C_N &= C_1 + 2 + \cdots + (N-2) + (N-1) + N \\ &= 1 + 2 + \cdots + (N-2) + (N-1) + N \\ &= \frac{N(N+1)}{2}. \end{aligned}$$

Evaluating the sum $1 + 2 + \cdots + (N-2) + (N-1) + N$ is elementary: The given result follows when we add the sum to itself, but in reverse order, term by term. This result—twice the value sought—consists of N terms, each of which sums to $N+1$.

Formula 2.2 This recurrence arises for a recursive program that halves the input in one step:

$$C_N = C_{N/2} + 1, \qquad \text{for } N \geq 2 \text{ with } C_1 = 1.$$

Solution: C_N is about $\lg N$. As written, this equation is meaningless unless N is even or we assume that $N/2$ is an integer division. For the moment, we assume that $N = 2^n$, so the recurrence is always well-defined. (Note that $n = \lg N$.) But then the recurrence telescopes even more easily than our first recurrence:

$$\begin{aligned} C_{2^n} &= C_{2^{n-1}} + 1 \\ &= C_{2^{n-2}} + 1 + 1 \\ &= C_{2^{n-3}} + 3 \\ &\quad\vdots \\ &= C_{2^0} + n \\ &= n + 1. \end{aligned}$$

The precise solution for general N depends on the interpretation of $N/2$. In the case that $N/2$ represents $\lfloor N/2 \rfloor$, we have a simple solution: C_N is the number of bits in the binary representation of N, and that number is $\lfloor \lg N \rfloor + 1$, by definition. This conclusion follows immediately from the fact that the operation of eliminating the rightmost bit of the binary representation of any integer $N > 0$ converts it into $\lfloor N/2 \rfloor$ (see Figure 2.6).

Formula 2.3 This recurrence arises for a recursive program that halves the input but perhaps must examine every item in the input.

$$C_N = C_{N/2} + N, \qquad \text{for } N \geq 2 \text{ with } C_1 = 0.$$

Solution: C_N is about $2N$. The recurrence telescopes to the sum $N + N/2 + N/4 + N/8 + \dots$. (Like Formula 2.2, the recurrence is precisely defined only when N is a power of 2). If the sequence is infinite, this simple geometric sum evaluates to exactly $2N$. Because we use integer division and stop at 1, this value is an approximation to the exact answer. The precise solution involves properties of the binary representation of N.

Formula 2.4 This recurrence arises for a recursive program that has to make a linear pass through the input, before, during, or after splitting that input into two halves:

$$C_N = 2C_{N/2} + N, \qquad \text{for } N \geq 2 \text{ with } C_1 = 0.$$

Solution: C_N is about $N \lg N$. This solution is the most widely cited of those we are considering here, because the recurrence applies to a family of standard divide-and-conquer algorithms.

$$C_{2^n} = 2C_{2^{n-1}} + 2^n$$
$$\frac{C_{2^n}}{2^n} = \frac{C_{2^{n-1}}}{2^{n-1}} + 1$$
$$= \frac{C_{2^{n-2}}}{2^{n-2}} + 1 + 1$$
$$\vdots$$
$$= n.$$

We develop the solution very much as we did in Formula 2.2, but with the additional trick of dividing both sides of the recurrence by 2^n at the second step to make the recurrence telescope.

Formula 2.5 This recurrence arises for a recursive program that splits the input into two halves and then does a constant amount of

N	$(N)_2$	$\lfloor \lg N \rfloor + 1$
1	1	1
2	10	2
3	11	2
4	100	3
5	101	3
6	110	3
7	111	3
8	1000	4
9	1001	4
10	1010	4
11	1011	4
12	1100	4
13	1101	4
14	1110	4
15	1111	4

**Figure 2.6
Integer functions and binary representations**

Given the binary representation of a number N (center), we obtain $\lfloor N/2 \rfloor$ by removing the rightmost bit. That is, the number of bits in the binary representation of N is 1 greater than the number of bits in the binary representation of $\lfloor N/2 \rfloor$. Therefore, $\lfloor \lg N \rfloor + 1$, the number of bits in the binary representation of N, is the solution to Formula 2.2 for the case that $N/2$ is interpreted as $\lfloor N/2 \rfloor$.

other work (see Chapter 5).

$$C_N = 2C_{N/2} + 1, \qquad \text{for } N \geq 2 \text{ with } C_1 = 1.$$

Solution: C_N is about $2N$. We can derive this solution in the same manner as we did the solution to Formula 2.4.

We can solve minor variants of these formulas, involving different initial conditions or slight differences in the additive term, using the same solution techniques, although we need to be aware that some recurrences that seem similar to these may actually be rather difficult to solve. There is a variety of advanced general techniques for dealing with such equations with mathematical rigor (*see reference section*). We will encounter a few more complicated recurrences in later chapters, but we defer discussion of their solution until they arise.

Exercises

▷ **2.33** Give a table of the values of C_N in Formula 2.2 for $1 \leq N \leq 32$, interpreting $N/2$ to mean $\lfloor N/2 \rfloor$.

▷ **2.34** Answer Exercise 2.33, but interpret $N/2$ to mean $\lceil N/2 \rceil$.

▷ **2.35** Answer Exercise 2.34 for Formula 2.3.

○ **2.36** Suppose that f_N is proportional to a constant and that

$$C_N = C_{N/2} + f_N, \qquad \text{for } N \geq t \text{ with } 0 \leq C_N < c \text{ for } N < t,$$

where c and t are both constants. Show that C_N is proportional to $\lg N$.

● **2.37** State and prove generalized versions of Formulas 2.3 through 2.5 that are analogous to the generalized version of Formula 2.2 in Exercise 2.36.

2.38 Give a table of the values of C_N in Formula 2.4 for $1 \leq N \leq 32$, for the following three cases: (*i*) interpret $N/2$ to mean $\lfloor N/2 \rfloor$; (*ii*) interpret $N/2$ to mean $\lceil N/2 \rceil$; (*iii*) interpret $2C_{N/2}$ to mean $C_{\lfloor N/2 \rfloor} + C_{\lceil N/2 \rceil}$.

2.39 Solve Formula 2.4 for the case when $N/2$ is interpreted as $\lfloor N/2 \rfloor$, by using a correspondence to the binary representation of N, as in the proof of Formula 2.2. *Hint*: Consider all the numbers less than N.

2.40 Solve the recurrence

$$C_N = C_{N/2} + N^2, \qquad \text{for } N \geq 2 \text{ with } C_1 = 0,$$

when N is a power of 2.

2.41 Solve the recurrence

$$C_N = C_{N/\alpha} + 1, \qquad \text{for } N \geq 2 \text{ with } C_1 = 0,$$

when N is a power of α.

○ **2.42** Solve the recurrence
$$C_N = \alpha C_{N/2}, \qquad \text{for } N \geq 2 \text{ with } C_1 = 1,$$
when N is a power of 2.

○ **2.43** Solve the recurrence
$$C_N = (C_{N/2})^2, \qquad \text{for } N \geq 2 \text{ with } C_1 = 1,$$
when N is a power of 2.

● **2.44** Solve the recurrence
$$C_N = (2 + \frac{1}{\lg N})C_{N/2}, \qquad \text{for } N \geq 2 \text{ with } C_1 = 1,$$
when N is a power of 2.

● **2.45** Consider the family of recurrences like Formula 2.1, where we allow $N/2$ to be interpreted as $\lfloor N/2 \rfloor$ or $\lceil N/2 \rceil$, and we require only that the recurrence hold for $N > c_0$ with $C_N = O(1)$ for $N \leq c_0$. Prove that $\lg N + O(1)$ is the solution to all such recurrences.

●● **2.46** Develop generalized recurrences and solutions similar to Exercise 2.45 for Formulas 2.2 through 2.5.

2.6 Examples of Algorithm Analysis

Armed with the tools outlined in the previous three sections, we now consider the analysis of *sequential search* and *binary search*, two basic algorithms for determining whether or not any of a sequence of objects appears among a set of previously stored objects. Our purpose is to illustrate the manner in which we will compare algorithms, rather than to describe these particular algorithms in detail. For simplicity, we assume here that the objects in question are integers. We will consider more general applications in great detail in Chapters 12 through 16. The simple versions of the algorithms that we consider here not only expose many aspects of the algorithm design and analysis problem but also have many direct applications.

For example, we might imagine a credit-card company that has N credit risks or stolen credit cards and wants to check whether any of M given transactions involves any one of the N bad numbers. To be concrete, we might think of N being large (say on the order of 10^3 to 10^6) and M being huge (say on the order of 10^6 to 10^9) for this application. The goal of the analysis is to be able to estimate the

Program 2.1 Sequential search

This function checks whether the number v is among a previously stored
set of numbers in a[l], a[l+1], ..., a[r], by comparing against each
number sequentially, starting at the beginning. If we reach the end without finding the number sought, then we return the value -1. Otherwise,
we return the index of the array position containing the number.

```
static int search(int a[], int v, int l, int r)
  { int i;
    for (i = l; i <= r; i++)
      if (v == a[i]) return i;
    return -1;
  }
```

running times of the algorithms when the values of the parameters fall
within these ranges.

Program 2.1 implements a straightforward solution to the search
problem. It is implemented as a Java method that operates on an
array (see Chapter 3) for better compatibility with other code that
we will examine for the same problem in Part 4. It is not necessary
to understand these details to understand the algorithm: We store all
the objects in an array; then, for each transaction, we look through
the array sequentially, from beginning to end, checking each to see
whether it is the one that we seek.

To analyze the algorithm, we note immediately that the running
time depends on whether or not the object sought is in the array. We
can determine that the search is unsuccessful only by examining each
of the N objects, but a search could end successfully at the first, second,
or any one of the objects.

Therefore, the running time depends on the data. If all the
searches are for the number that happens to be in the first position in
the array, then the algorithm will be fast; if they are for the number
that happens to be in the last position in the array, it will be slow. We
discuss in Section 2.7 the distinction between being able to *guarantee*
performance and being able to *predict* performance. In this case, the
best guarantee that we can provide is that no more than N numbers
will be examined.

To make a prediction, however, we need to make an assumption about the data. In this case, we might choose to assume that all the numbers are randomly chosen. This assumption implies, for example, that each number in the table is equally likely to be the object of a search. On reflection, we realize that it is that property of the search that is critical, because with randomly chosen numbers we would be unlikely to have a successful search at all (see Exercise 2.48). For some applications, the number of transactions that involve a successful search might be high; for other applications, it might be low. To avoid confusing the model with properties of the application, we separate the two cases (successful and unsuccessful) and analyze them independently. This example illustrates that a critical part of an effective analysis is the development of a reasonable model for the application at hand. Our analytic results will depend on the proportion of searches that are successful; indeed, it will give us information that we might need if we are to choose different algorithms for different applications based on this parameter.

Property 2.1 *Sequential search examines N numbers for each unsuccessful search and about $N/2$ numbers for each successful search on the average.*

If each number in the table is equally likely to be the object of a search, then

$$(1 + 2 + \ldots + N)/N = (N + 1)/2$$

is the average cost of a search. ∎

Property 2.1 implies that the running time of Program 2.1 is proportional to N, subject to the implicit assumption that the average cost of comparing two numbers is constant. Thus, for example, we can expect that if we double the number of objects, we double the amount of time required for a search.

We can speed up sequential search for unsuccessful search by putting the numbers in the table in order. Sorting the numbers in the table is the subject of Chapters 6 through 11. A number of the algorithms that we will consider get that task done in time proportional to $N \log N$, which is insignificant by comparison to the search costs when M is huge. In an ordered table, we can terminate the search immediately on reaching a number that is larger than the one that we seek. This change reduces the cost of sequential search to about $N/2$

Program 2.2 Binary search

This program has the same functionality as Program 2.1, but it is much more efficient.

```
static int search(int a[], int v, int l, int r)
  {
    while (r >= l)
      { int m = (l+r)/2;
        if (v == a[m]) return m;
        if (v < a[m]) r = m-1; else l = m+1;
      }
    return -1;
  }
```

---

numbers examined for unsuccessful search, the same as for successful search.

Property 2.2 *Sequential search in an ordered table examines N numbers for each search in the worst case and about N/2 numbers for each search on the average.*

We still need to specify a model for unsuccessful search. This result follows from assuming that the search is equally likely to terminate at any one of the $N + 1$ intervals defined by the N numbers in the table, which leads immediately to the expression

$$(1 + 2 + \ldots + N + N)/N = (N + 3)/2.$$

The cost of an unsuccessful search ending before or after the Nth entry in the table is the same: N. ■

Another way to state the result of Property 2.2 is to say that the running time of sequential search is proportional to MN for M transactions, on the average and in the worst case. If we double either the number of transactions or the number of objects in the table, we can expect the running time to double; if we double both, we can expect the running time to go up by a factor of 4. The result also tells us that the method is not suitable for huge tables. If it takes c microseconds to examine a single number, then, for $M = 10^9$ and $N = 10^6$, the running time for all the transactions would be at least $(c/2)10^9$ seconds or, by Figure 2.1, about $16c$ years, which is prohibitive.

Program 2.2 is a classical solution to the search problem that is much more efficient than sequential search. It is based on the idea that if the numbers in the table are in order, we can eliminate half of them from consideration by comparing the one that we seek with the one at the middle position in the table. If it is equal, we have a successful search. If it is less, we apply the same method to the left half of the table. If it is greater, we apply the same method to the right half of the table. Figure 2.7 is an example of the operation of this method on a sample set of numbers.

Property 2.3 *Binary search never examines more than* $\lfloor \lg N \rfloor + 1$ *numbers.*

The proof of this property illustrates the use of recurrence relations in the analysis of algorithms. If we let T_N represent the number of comparisons required for binary search in the worst case, then the way in which the algorithm reduces search in a table of size N to search in a table half the size immediately implies that

$$T_N \leq T_{\lfloor N/2 \rfloor} + 1, \qquad \text{for } N \geq 2 \text{ with } T_1 = 1.$$

To search in a table of size N, we examine the middle number, then search in a table of size no larger than $\lfloor N/2 \rfloor$. The actual cost could be less than this value either because the comparison might cause us to terminate a successful search or because the table to be searched might be of size $\lfloor N/2 \rfloor - 1$ (if N is even). As we did in the solution of Formula 2.2, we can prove immediately that $T_N \leq n + 1$ if $N = 2^n$ and then verify the general result by induction. ∎

Property 2.3 says that we can solve a huge search problem with up to 1 billion numbers with at most 30 comparisons per transaction, and that is likely to be much less than the time it takes to read the request or write the result on typical computers. The search problem is so important that several techniques have been developed that are even faster than this one, as we shall see in Chapters 12 through 16.

Note that we express Property 2.1 and Property 2.2 in terms of the operations that we perform most often on the data. As noted in the commentary following Property 2.1, we expect that each operation should take a constant amount of time, and we can conclude that the running time of binary search is proportional to $\lg N$ as compared to N for sequential search. As we double N, the running time of

1488	1488			
1578	1578			
1973	1973			
3665	3665			
4426	4426			
4548	4548			
5435	5435	5435	5435	5435
5446	5446	5446	5446	
6333	6333	6333		
6385	6385	6385		
6455	6455	6455		
6504				
6937				
6965				
7104				
7230				
8340				
8958				
9208				
9364				
9550				
9645				
9686				

Figure 2.7
Binary search

To see whether or not 5025 *is in the table of numbers in the left column, we first compare it with* 6504; *that leads us to consider the first half of the array. Then we compare against* 4548 *(the middle of the first half); that leads us to the second half of the first half. We continue, always working on a subarray that would contain the number being sought, if it is in the table. Eventually, we get a subarray with just one element, which is not equal to* 5025, *so* 5025 *is not in the table.*

binary search hardly changes, but the running time of sequential search doubles. As N grows, the gap between the two methods becomes a chasm.

We can verify the analytic evidence of Properties 2.1 and 2.2 by implementing and testing the algorithms. For example, Table 2.4 shows running times for binary search and sequential search for M searches in a table of size N (including, for binary search, the cost of sorting the table) for various values of M and N. We will not consider the implementation of the program to run these experiments in detail here because it is similar to those that we consider in full detail in Chapters 6 and 11, and because we consider the use of library methods and other details of putting together programs from constituent pieces in Chapter 3. For the moment, we simply stress that doing empirical testing is an integral part of evaluating the efficiency of an algorithm.

Table 2.4 validates our observation that the functional growth of the running time allows us to predict performance for huge cases on the basis of empirical studies for small cases. The combination of mathematical analysis and empirical studies provides persuasive evidence that binary search is the preferred algorithm, by far.

This example is a prototype of our general approach to comparing algorithms. We use mathematical analysis of the frequency with which algorithms perform critical abstract operations, then use those results to deduce the functional form of the running time, which allows us to verify and extend empirical studies. As we develop algorithmic solutions to computational problems that are more and more refined, and as we develop mathematical analyses to learn their performance characteristics that are more and more refined, we call on mathematical studies from the literature, so as to keep our attention on the algorithms themselves in this book. We cannot do thorough mathematical and empirical studies of every algorithm that we encounter, but we strive to identify essential performance characteristics, knowing that, in principle, we can develop a scientific basis for making informed choices among algorithms in critical applications.

Exercises

▷ **2.47** Give the average number of comparisons used by Program 2.1 in the case that αN of the searches are successful, for $0 \leq \alpha \leq 1$.

Table 2.4 Empirical study of sequential and binary search

These relative timings validate our analytic results that sequential search takes time proportional to MN and binary search takes time proportional to $M \lg N$ for M searches in a table of N objects. When we increase N by a factor of 2, the time for sequential search increases by a factor of 2 as well, but the time for binary search hardly changes. Sequential search is infeasible for huge M as N increases, but binary search is fast even for huge tables.

N	$M = 1000$		$M = 10000$		$M = 100000$	
	S	B	S	B	S	B
125	3	3	36	12	357	126
250	6	2	63	13	636	130
500	13	1	119	14	1196	137
1250	28	1	286	15	2880	146
2500	57	1	570	16		154
5000	113	1	1172	17		164
12500	308	2	3073	17		173
25000	612	1		19		183
50000	1217	2		20		196
100000	2682	2		21		209

Key:
   S   sequential search (Program 2.1)
   B   binary search (Program 2.2)

•• **2.48** Estimate the probability that at least one of M random 10-digit numbers matches one of a set of N given values, for $M = 10$, 100, and 1000 and $N = 10^3$, 10^4, 10^5, and 10^6.

2.49 Write a driver program that generates M random integers and puts them in an array, then counts the number of N random integers that matches one of the numbers in the array, using sequential search. Run your program for $M = 10$, 100, and 1000 and $N = 10$, 100, and 1000.

• **2.50** State and prove a property analogous to Property 2.3 for binary search.

2.7 Guarantees, Predictions, and Limitations

The running time of most algorithms depends on their input data. Typically, our goal in the analysis of algorithms is somehow to eliminate that dependence: We want to be able to say something about the performance of our programs that depends on the input data to as little an extent as possible, because we generally do not know what the input data will be each time the program is invoked. The examples in Section 2.6 illustrate the two major approaches that we use toward this end: worst-case analysis and average-case analysis.

Studying the *worst-case* performance of algorithms is attractive because it allows us to make *guarantees* about the running time of programs. We say that the number of times certain abstract operations are executed is less than a certain function of the number of inputs, no matter what the input values are. For example, Property 2.3 is an example of such a guarantee for binary search, as is Property 1.3 for weighted quick union. If the guarantees are low, as is the case with binary search, then we are in a favorable situation, because we have eliminated cases for which our program might run slowly. Programs with good worst-case performance characteristics are a basic goal in algorithm design.

There are several difficulties with worst-case analysis, however. For a given algorithm, there might be a significant gap between the time required for it to solve a worst-case instance of the input and the time required for it to solve the data that it might encounter in practice. For example, quick union requires time proportional to N in the worst case, but only $\log N$ for typical data. More important, we cannot always prove that there is an input for which the running time of an algorithm achieves a certain bound; we can prove only that it is guaranteed to be lower than the bound. Moreover, for some problems, algorithms with good worst-case performance are significantly more complicated than are other algorithms. We often find ourselves in the position of having an algorithm with good worst-case performance that is slower than simpler algorithms for the data that occur in practice, or that is not sufficiently faster that the extra effort required to achieve good worst-case performance is justified. For many applications, other considerations—such as portability or reliability—are more important than improved worst-case performance guarantees. For example, as we saw in Chapter 1, weighted quick union with path compression provides provably better performance guarantees than weighted quick union, but the algorithms have about the same running time for typical practical data.

Studying the *average-case* performance of algorithms is attractive because it allows us to make *predictions* about the running time of programs. In the simplest situation, we can characterize precisely the inputs to the algorithm; for example, a sorting algorithm might operate on an array of N random integers, or a geometric algorithm might process a set of N random points in the plane with coordinates between 0 and 1. Then, we calculate the average number of times that each instruction is executed and calculate the average running time of the program by multiplying each instruction frequency by the time required for the instruction and adding them all together.

There are also several difficulties with average-case analysis, however. First, the input model may not accurately characterize the inputs encountered in practice, or there may be no natural input model at all. Few people would argue against the use of input models such as "randomly ordered file" for a sorting algorithm, or "random point set" for a geometric algorithm, and for such models it is possible to derive mathematical results that can predict accurately the performance of programs running on actual applications. But how should one characterize the input to a program that processes English-language text? Even for sorting algorithms, models other than randomly ordered inputs are of interest in certain applications. Second, the analysis might require deep mathematical reasoning. For example, the average-case analysis of union–find algorithms is difficult. Although the derivation of such results is normally beyond the scope of this book, we will illustrate their nature with a number of classical examples, and we will cite relevant results when appropriate (fortunately, many of our best algorithms have been analyzed in the research literature). Third, knowing the average value of the running time might not be sufficient: we may need to know the standard deviation or other facts about the distribution of the running time, which may be even more difficult to derive. In particular, we are often interested in knowing the chance that the algorithm could be dramatically slower than expected.

In many cases, we can answer the first objection listed in the previous paragraph by turning randomness to our advantage. For example, if we randomly scramble an array before attempting to sort it, then the assumption that the elements in the array are in random order is accurate. For such algorithms, which are called *randomized algorithms*, the average-case analysis leads to predictions of the expected running time in a strict probabilistic sense. Moreover, we are often able to prove that the probability that such an algorithm will be slow is negligibly small. Examples of such algorithms include quicksort (see Chapter 9), randomized BSTs (see Chapter 13), and hashing (see Chapter 14).

The field of *computational complexity* is the branch of analysis of algorithms that helps us to understand the fundamental *limitations* that we can expect to encounter when designing algorithms. The overall goal is to determine the worst-case running time of the *best* algorithm to solve a given problem, to within a constant factor. This function is called the *complexity* of the problem.

Worst-case analysis using the O-notation frees the analyst from considering the details of particular machine characteristics. The statement that the running time of an algorithm is $O(f(N))$ is independent of the input and is a useful way to categorize algorithms in a way that is independent of both inputs and implementation details, separating the analysis of an algorithm from any particular implementation. We ignore constant factors in the analysis; in most cases, if we want to know whether the running time of an algorithm is proportional to N or proportional to $\log N$, it does not matter whether the algorithm is to be run on a nanocomputer or on a supercomputer, and it does not matter whether the inner loop has been implemented carefully with only a few instructions or badly implemented with many instructions.

When we can prove that the worst-case running time of an algorithm to solve a certain problem is $O(f(N))$, we say that $f(N)$ is an *upper bound* on the complexity of the problem. In other words, the running time of the best algorithm to solve a problem is no higher than the running time of any particular algorithm to solve the problem.

We constantly strive to improve our algorithms, but we eventually reach a point where no change seems to improve the running time. For every given problem, we are interested in knowing when to stop trying to find improved algorithms, so we seek *lower bounds* on the complexity. For many problems, we can prove that *any* algorithm to solve the problem must use a certain number of fundamental operations. Proving lower bounds is a difficult matter of carefully constructing a machine model and then developing intricate theoretical constructions of inputs that are difficult for any algorithm to solve. We rarely touch on the subject of proving lower bounds, but they represent computational barriers that guide us in the design of algorithms, so we maintain awareness of them when they are relevant.

When complexity studies show that the upper bound of an algorithm matches the lower bound, then we have some confidence that it is fruitless to try to design an algorithm that is fundamentally faster than the best known, and we can start to concentrate on the implementation. For example, binary search is optimal, in the sense that no algorithm that uses comparisons exclusively can use fewer comparisons in the worst case than binary search.

We also have matching upper and lower bounds for pointer-based union–find algorithms. Tarjan showed in 1975 that weighted quick union with path compression requires following less than $O(\lg^* V)$ pointers in the worst case, and that any pointer-based algorithm must follow more than a constant number of pointers in the worst case for some input. In other words, there is no point looking for some new improvement that will guarantee to solve the problem with a linear number of i = a[i] operations. In practical terms, this difference is hardly significant, because $\lg^* V$ is so small; still, finding a simple linear algorithm for this problem was a research goal for many years, and Tarjan's lower bound has allowed researchers to move on to other problems. Moreover, the story shows that there is no avoiding functions like the rather complicated $\log^*$ function, because such functions are intrinsic to this problem.

Many of the algorithms in this book have been subjected to detailed mathematical analyses and performance studies far too complex to be discussed here. Indeed, it is on the basis of such studies that we are able to recommend many of the algorithms that we discuss.

Not all algorithms are worthy of such intense scrutiny; indeed, during the design process, it is preferable to work with approximate performance indicators to guide the design process without extraneous detail. As the design becomes more refined, so must the analysis, and more sophisticated mathematical tools need to be applied. Often, the design process leads to detailed complexity studies that lead to theoretical algorithms that are rather far from any particular application. It is a common mistake to assume that rough analyses from complexity studies will translate immediately into efficient practical algorithms; such assumptions can lead to unpleasant surprises. On the other hand, computational complexity is a powerful tool that tells us when we have reached performance limits in our design work and that can suggest departures in design in pursuit of closing the gap between upper and lower bounds.

In this book, we take the view that algorithm design, careful implementation, mathematical analysis, theoretical studies, and empirical analysis all contribute in important ways to the development of elegant and efficient programs. We want to gain information about the properties of our programs using any tools at our disposal, then modify or develop new programs on the basis of that information. We will not be able to do exhaustive testing and analysis of every algorithm that we run in every programming environment on every machine, but we can use careful implementations of algorithms that we know to be efficient, then refine and compare them when peak performance is necessary. Throughout the book, when appropriate, we shall consider the most important methods in sufficient detail to appreciate why they perform well.

Exercise

○ **2.51** You are given the information that the time complexity of one problem is $N \log N$ and that the time complexity of another problem is N^3. What does this statement imply about the relative performance of specific algorithms that solve the problems?

References for Part One

The number of introductory textbooks on programming is too numerous for us to recommend a specific one here. The standard reference for Java is the book by Arnold and Gosling, and the books by Gosling, Yellin, and "The Java Team" are indispensible references for Java programmers.

The many variants on algorithms for the union–find problem of Chapter 1 are ably categorized and compared by van Leeuwen and Tarjan.

Bentley's books describe, again in the same spirit as much of the material here, a number of detailed case studies on evaluating various approaches to developing algorithms and implementations for solving numerous interesting problems.

The classic reference on the analysis of algorithms based on asymptotic worst-case performance measures is Aho, Hopcroft, and Ullman's book. Knuth's books cover average-case analysis more fully and are the authoritative source on specific properties of numerous algorithms. The books by Gonnet and Baeza-Yates and by Cormen, Leiserson, and Rivest are more recent works; both include extensive references to the research literature.

The book by Graham, Knuth, and Patashnik covers the type of mathematics that commonly arises in the analysis of algorithms, and such material is also sprinkled liberally throughout Knuth's books. The book by Sedgewick and Flajolet is a thorough introduction to the subject.

A. V. Aho, J. E. Hopcroft, and J. D. Ullman, *The Design and Analysis of Algorithms*, Addison-Wesley, Reading, MA, 1975.

K. Arnold and J. Gosling, *The Java Programming Language*, Addison-Wesley, Reading, MA, 1996.

R. Baeza-Yates and G. H. Gonnet, *Handbook of Algorithms and Data Structures*, second edition, Addison-Wesley, Reading, MA, 1984.

J. L. Bentley, *Programming Pearls*, second edition, Addison-Wesley, Boston, MA, 2000; *More Programming Pearls*, Addison-Wesley, Reading, MA, 1988.

T. H. Cormen, C. E. Leiserson, and R. L. Rivest, *Introduction to Algorithms*, second edition, MIT Press/McGraw-Hill, Cambridge, MA, 2002.

J. Gosling, F. Yellin, and The Java Team, *The Java Application Programming Interface. Volume 1: Core Packages*, Addison-Wesley, Reading, MA, 1996; *Volume 2: Window Toolkit and Applets*, Addison-Wesley, Reading, MA, 1996.

R. L. Graham, D. E. Knuth, and O. Patashnik, *Concrete Mathematics: A Foundation for Computer Science*, second edition, Addison-Wesley, Reading, MA, 1994.

D. E. Knuth, *The Art of Computer Programming. Volume 1: Fundamental Algorithms*, third edition, Addison-Wesley, Reading, MA, 1997; *Volume 2: Seminumerical Algorithms*, third edition, Addison-Wesley, Reading, MA, 1998; *Volume 3: Sorting and Searching*, second edition, Addison-Wesley, Reading, MA, 1998.

R. Sedgewick and P. Flajolet, *An Introduction to the Analysis of Algorithms*, Addison-Wesley, Reading, MA, 1996.

J. van Leeuwen and R. E. Tarjan, "Worst-case analysis of set-union algorithms," *Journal of the ACM*, 1984.

Data Structures

CHAPTER THREE

Elementary Data Structures

O RGANIZING THE DATA for processing is an essential step in the development of a computer program. For many applications, the choice of the proper data structure is the only major decision involved in the implementation: once the choice has been made, the necessary algorithms are simple. For the same data, some data structures require more or less space than others; for the same operations on the data, some data structures lead to more or less efficient algorithms than others. The choices of algorithm and of data structure are closely intertwined, and we continually seek ways to save time or space by making the choice properly.

A data structure is not a passive entity: We also must consider the operations to be performed on it (and the algorithms used for these operations). This concept is formalized in the notion of a *data type*. In this chapter, our primary interest is in concrete implementations of the fundamental approaches that we use to structure data. We consider basic methods of organization and methods for manipulating data, work through a number of specific examples that illustrate the benefits of each, and discuss related issues such as storage management. In Chapter 4, we discuss *abstract data types*, where we separate the definitions of data types from implementations.

We discuss properties of arrays, linked lists, and strings. These classical data structures have widespread applicability: with trees (see Chapter 5), they form a basis for virtually all the algorithms considered in this book. We consider primitive operations for manipulating these data structures in order to develop a basic set of tools that we can use to develop sophisticated algorithms for difficult problems.

The study of storing data as variable-sized objects and in linked data structures requires an understanding of how the system manages the storage that it allocates to programs for their data. We do not cover this subject exhaustively because many of the important considerations are system and machine dependent and because one of Java's prime features is to free programmers from some of the basic problems that can arise. However, we do discuss some approaches to storage management and some basic underlying mechanisms.

At the end of the chapter, we consider several examples of *compound structures*, such as arrays of linked lists and arrays of arrays. The notion of building abstract mechanisms of increasing complexity from lower-level ones is a recurring theme throughout this book. We consider a number of examples that serve as the basis for more advanced algorithms later in the book.

The data structures that we consider in this chapter are important building blocks that we can use in a natural manner in Java and many other programming languages. In Chapter 5, we consider another important data structure, the *tree*. Arrays, strings, linked lists, and trees are the basic elements underlying most of the algorithms that we consider in this book. In Chapter 4, we discuss the use of the concrete representations developed here in building basic abstract data types that can meet the needs of a variety of applications. In the rest of the book, we develop numerous variations of the basic tools discussed here, trees, and abstract data types in order to create algorithms that can solve more difficult problems and that can serve us well as the basis for higher-level abstract data types in diverse applications.

3.1 Building Blocks

In this section, we review the primary low-level constructs that we use to store and process information in Java. All the data that we process on a computer ultimately decompose into individual bits, but writing programs that exclusively process bits would be tiresome indeed. *Types* allow us to specify how we will use particular sets of bits, and *methods* allow us to specify the operations that we will perform on the data. We use Java *classes* to describe the information that we process, to define the methods for processing them, and to make *objects* that actually hold the information. All of our data structures are comprised of objects and *references* to objects. In this section, we consider these basic Java mechanisms, in the context of presenting a general approach to organizing our programs. Our primary goal is to lay the groundwork for the development, in the rest of the chapter and in Chapters 4 and 5, of the higher-level constructs that will serve as the basis for most of the algorithms that we consider in this book.

We write programs that process information derived from mathematical or natural-language descriptions of the world in which we live; accordingly, computing environments need to provide built-in support for the basic building blocks of such descriptions—numbers and characters. In Java, our programs are all built from just a few basic types of data:

- Boolean values (`booleans`).
- Characters (`chars`).
- 8-bit integers (`bytes`).
- 16-bit integers (`shorts`).
- 32-bit integers (`ints`).
- 64-bit integers (`longs`).
- 32-bit floating-point numbers (`floats`).
- 64-bit floating-point numbers (`doubles`).

It is customary to refer to these basic types by their Java names—`int`, `float`, `char`, and so forth—although we often use the generic terminology *integer*, *floating-point number*, and *character*, as well. We use data of type `boolean` to store the logical values `true` or `false`, usually to record facts about other data that will affect decision-making later in a computation. Characters are most often used in higher-level abstractions—for example, to make words and sentences—so we defer consideration of character data to Section 3.6. All of the other primitive types are used to represent numbers.

We use a fixed number of bits to represent numbers, so when we represent integers we are working with a specific range of values that depends on the number of bits that we use to represent them. Floating-point numbers approximate real numbers, and the number of bits that we use to represent them affects the precision with which we can approximate a real number. In Java, we trade space for accuracy by choosing from among the types `int`, `long`, `short`, or `byte` for integers and from among `float` or `double` for floating-point numbers. On most systems, these types correspond to underlying hardware representations, but the number of bits used for the representation, and therefore the range of values (in the case of integers or precision (in the case of floating-point numbers), is guaranteed for each type by Java. In this book, we normally use `int` and `double`.

In modern programming, we think of the type of the data more in terms of the needs of the program than the capabilities of the machine, primarily in order to make programs portable. Thus, for example, we think of a `short` as an object that can take on values between $-32{,}768$ and $32{,}767$, instead of as a 16-bit object. Moreover, our concept of an integer includes the operations that we perform on them: addition, multiplication, and so forth.

Definition 3.1 *A* **data type** *is a set of values and a collection of operations on those values.*

Operations are associated with types, not the other way around. When we perform an operation, we need to ensure that its operands and result are of the correct type. Neglecting this responsibility is a common programming error. In some situations, Java performs implicit type conversions; in other situations, we use *casts*, or explicit type conversions. For example, if x and N are integers, the expression

```
((float) x) / N
```

includes both types of conversion: the (`float`) is a cast that converts the value of x to floating point; then an implicit conversion is performed for N to make both arguments of the divide operator floating point, according to Java's rules for implicit type conversion.

Many of the operations associated with standard data types (for example, the arithmetic operations) are built into the Java language. Other operations are found in the form of methods that are defined in standard Java libraries; still others take form in the Java methods that we define in our programs. That is, the concept of a data type is relevant not just to integer, floating point, and character primitive types. We often define our own data types, as an effective way of organizing our software. When we define a simple method in Java, we are effectively creating a new data type, with the operation implemented by that method added to the operations defined for the types of data represented by its parameters. Indeed, in a sense, *each* Java program is a data type—a list of sets of values (primitive or other types) and associated operations (methods). This point of view is perhaps too broad

Program 3.1 Method definition

To implement new operations on data in Java, we *define* methods in Java *class*, as illustrated here. Each Java program is a class that includes a definition of the method `main`, and this code also defines `lg`.

Each Java class is kept in a file with the same name as the class and a `.java` extension (`LogTable.java` in this case). Environments differ on the way that we compile or interpret and actually run programs: some have interactive interfaces and others respond to typed commands such as `java LogTable`.

The method `lg` implements a single-argument mathematical function: the integer binary logarithm function (see Section 2.3). In Java, we refer to the arguments as *parameters* and the value as the *return value*. A method may have any number of parameters but at most one return value. The method `main` takes a parameter (not used here) that contains information from the command line that was used to start the application and has no return value (see Appendix).

A method's definition begins with its *signature*, which defines the type of its return value, its name, and the types of its parameters. This information identifies the method and is needed by other methods in order to *invoke* the method, using objects of the proper type in place of each parameter. The invoking method can use the method in an expression, in the same way as it uses variables of the return-value type. Following the signature, enclosed in braces, is the Java code that implements the method. In a method definition, we name the parameters and express the computation in terms of those names, as if they were local variables. When the method is invoked, these variables are initialized with values supplied for each parameter by the invoking method and the method code is executed. The `return` statement ends execution of the method and provides the return value to the calling method.

```
class LogTable
  {
    static int lg(int N)
      { int i = 0;
        while (N > 0) { i++; N/= 2; }
        return i;
      }
    public static void main(String[] args)
      {
        for (int N = 1000; N <= 1000000000; N *= 10)
          Out.println(lg(N) + " " + N);
      }
  }
```

to be useful, but we shall see that narrowing our focus to understand our programs in terms of data types is valuable.

All Java programs are based upon its class mechanism. The simplest Java program is a class consisting of a single method named main, as in the programs in Chapter 1. The first step in organizing a large program is to break it into smaller pieces by defining other methods, as illustrated in Program 3.1. The second simplest Java program is a class consisting of several methods (one of which is named main) that invoke one another. This programming model is a powerful one of great utility, but it breaks down in large programs with complex relationships among the methods and the data they operate upon. In this section and in Chapter 4, we describe the process of building more complicated programs by defining data types and implementing them as classes.

One goal that we have when writing programs is to organize them such that they apply to as broad a variety of situations as possible. The reason for adopting such a goal is that it might put us in the position of being able to reuse an old program to solve a new problem, perhaps completely unrelated to the problem that the program was originally intended to solve. First, by taking care to understand and to specify precisely which operations a program uses, we can easily extend it to any type of data for which we can support those operations. Second, by taking care to understand and to specify precisely what a program does, we can add the abstract operation that it performs to the operations at our disposal in solving new problems.

We often want to build data structures that allow us to handle collections of data. The data structures may be huge, or they may be used extensively, so we are interested in identifying the important operations that we will perform on the data and in knowing how to implement those operations efficiently. Doing these tasks is taking the first steps in the process of incrementally building lower-level abstractions into higher-level ones; that process allows us to conveniently develop ever more powerful programs. The Java class mechanism provides us with direct support for doing so.

One property of classes is that they are aggregate types that we can use to define collections of data such that we can manipulate an entire collection as a unit, but can still refer to individual components of a given datum by name. Classes are not at the same level as primitive types such as int or float in Java, because the only operations that are defined for them (beyond referring to their components) are to create objects and to manipulate references to them. Creating an object of a given class is known as *instantiation*. Thus, we can use a class to define a new type of data, name variables, and pass those variables as parameters to methods, but we have to define specifically as methods any operations that we want to perform.

For example, when processing geometric data we might want to work with the abstract notion of points in the plane. Accordingly, we can write

```
class Point { double x; double y; }
```

to indicate that we will use Point to create objects that consist of pairs of floating-point numbers. To instantiate objects, we use the Java new operator. For example, the code

```
Point a = new Point(), b = new Point();
```

creates two Point objects and puts references to them in the variables a and b. We can then use the references to refer to individual members of an object by name. For example, the statements

```
a.x = 1.0; a.y = 1.0; b.x = 4.0; b.y =5.0;
```

set a to represent the point $(1, 1)$ and b to represent the point $(4, 5)$.

When we create a variable of type int or double or any of the primitive types, the name that we use is a synonym for the address of the memory location that contains the information. For all other objects, the name is a synonym for what is known in Java as a *reference*: it specifies the address of a memory location that contains the address of the memory location that contains the information. Figure 3.1 illustrates this extra level of indirection for our Point example. Referring to an object indirectly via a reference is often more convenient than referring directly to the object, and it can also be more efficient, particularly for large objects. We will see many examples of this advantage in Sections 3.3 through 3.7. Even more important, as we shall see, we can use references to structure our data in ways that support efficient algorithms for processing the data. References are the basis for many data structures and algorithms.

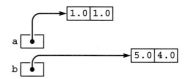

Figure 3.1
Object representation

This diagram depicts how Java represents simple objects that aggregate data, for the two objects of the Point class described in the text. Each object's data is stored in a contiguous block of memory, and programs access the data and manipulate it with references to the data. The reference to point a is the memory address of the chunk of memory where the values 1.0 and 1.0 are stored; the reference to point b is the memory address of the chunk of memory where the values 4.0 and 5.0 are stored. To access the data, the Java system must follow the reference, but in programs we use the object reference to mean both the reference and the object itself.

For example, references make it easy for us to pass objects as parameters to methods. The code

```
double distance(Point a, Point b)
  { double dx = a.x - b.x; dy = a.y - b.y;
    return Math.sqrt(dx*dx + dy*dy); }
```

defines a method that computes the distance between two given points. It is easily coded because the references that are passed as parameters provide it with easy access to each point's data.

In C and many other languages, references are known as *pointers*, and they are commonly used. In Java programs, there is no distinction between the reference and the object, so we have no choice but to refer to objects through references. This feature of Java simplifies many aspects of our programs, but it comes at a cost. When objects are large, it is much more efficient to use pointers to manipulate them than to actually move data around, but when objects are small, there is a performance penalty to pay for following the pointer every time that we need to get at the data. Full treatment of the reasons that the designers of Java chose this approach is beyond the scope of this book, but we will again touch upon this issue when it is relevant (for example, when doing performance studies).

Thus, classes allow us to aggregate our data in typical applications. We can define a class that specifies all the types of the data that we want to collect, create objects of that type (with those types of data), and write code that refers to those objects via references to them. The Point class example just given is a simple one that aggregates two data items of the same type. In general, we can mix different types of data in classes. We shall be working extensively with such classes throughout the rest of this chapter.

Normally, we go one step further and use the Java class mechanism to define data types, not just aggregate data. That is, we also specify methods that define the operations that we will perform on the data. For example, Program 3.2 is a class that embodies our definition of a data type for points in the plane. It specifies that points are an aggregate type comprised of pairs of floating-point numbers and includes definitions of several operations that we might perform on the points.

Every class consists of a collection of *data fields* that define the set of values for its data type and a collection of *methods* that operate

---

Program 3.2 Point class implementation

This code, kept in a file named `Point.java`, is a class implemention of a data type for points in the plane. It specifies that all points will have `double` values representing their x- and y-coordinates, and it defines six methods that programs can use to manipulate points. The first two are constructors: a client can create a new `Point` object via `new`, either with random coordinates (no parameters) or specified coordinates (two parameters).

The operations that programs can perform on `Point` objects (besides creating them) are to compute its polar coordinates, compute the distance to another point, and compute a string representation of the point (for use in printing its value).

```
class Point
  { double x, y;
    Point()
      { x = Math.random(); y = Math.random(); }
    Point(double x, double y)
      { this.x = x; this.y = y; }
    double r()
      { return Math.sqrt(x*x + y*y); }
    double theta()
      { return Math.atan2(y, x); }
    double distance(Point p)
      { double dx = x - p.x, dy = y - p.y;
        return Math.sqrt(dx*dx + dy*dy);
      }
    public String toString()
      { return "(" + x + ", " + y + ")"; }
  }
```

---

upon the data. We also refer to the data fields and the methods as the class *members*. Program 3.2 has two data fields (x and y) and six methods (two POINTs, r, theta, distance, and toString).

Methods that have the same name as the class and no return type are known as *constructors*. When a constructor is invoked via `new`, Java creates an object, then passes control to the constructor method, which generally initializes the data fields. For example, we use the code `Point a = new Point(1.0, 1.0);` to use the class in

Program 3.2 to create an object a that represents the point $(1, 1)$, `Point b = new Point(4.0, 5.0);` to create an object b that represents the point $(4, 5)$, and `Point c = new Point();` to create a new point with random coordinates. All other methods are invoked through point objects: for example, we can use the expression `c.r()` to compute the distance to the origin from c, or the expression `a.distance(b)` (or `b.distance(a)`) to compute the distance between a and b.

Using identical names for two different methods is known as *overloading*, and it is perfectly acceptable as long as the system can distinguish them by differences in their signatures. In Program 3.2, the constructor is overloaded—the two `Point` methods differ because one has no parameters and the other has two. The types of parameters and the presence or absence of a return value also can serve to distinguish methods with identical names.

This style of programming, which is sometimes called *object-oriented programming*, is directly supported by the Java `class` construct. We may think of classes as mechanisms that not only allow us to aggregate data but also define operations on that data. There may be many different objects that belong to a class, but all of them are similar in that the set of values that their data members can take on is the same, and the collection of operations that can be performed on their data members is the same; in short, they are instances of the same data type. In object-oriented programming, we direct objects to process their member data (as opposed to having free methods processing the data stored in objects).

We could also, if desired, prepend the keyword `static` to the distance method implementation given above that takes two points as parameters and include it as a method in our `Point` class. The `static` designation is for methods that are associated with the class (as opposed to methods that are associated with class objects). They are invoked by using the class name instead of an object name. If we make this change, the expressions `Point.distance(a, b)`, `a.distance(b)`, and `b.distance(a)` all represent the same value, and each might be preferable to the others in specific programming contexts.

Each Java class definition is kept in a separate file with the same name as the class and a `.java` suffix. Any Java program can then use the class. For example, Programs 3.7 and 3.18 build upon the abstraction implemented by Program 3.2.

Program 3.3 Statistics of a sequence of random numbers

This program computes the average μ and standard deviation σ of a sequence $x_1, x_2, \ldots, x_N$ of random nonnegative four-digit integers, following the mathematical definitions

$$\mu = \frac{1}{N} \sum_{1 \le i \le N} x_i \quad \text{and} \quad \sigma^2 = \frac{1}{N} \sum_{1 \le i \le N} (x_i - \mu)^2 = \frac{1}{N} \sum_{1 \le i \le N} x_i^2 - \mu^2.$$

Note that a direct implementation from the definition of σ^2 requires one pass to compute the average and another to compute the sums of the squares of the differences between the members of the sequence and the average, but rearranging the formula makes it possible for us to compute σ^2 in one pass through the data (without having to store any of it!).

```
class PrintStats
  {
    public static void main(String[] args)
      { int N = Integer.parseInt(args[0]);
        double m = 0.0, s = 0.0;
        for (int i = 0; i < N; i++)
          { int x = (int) (Math.random()*10000);
            double d = (double) x;
            m += d/N; s += (d*d)/ N;
          }
        s = Math.sqrt(s - m*m);
        Out.println("    Avg.: " + m);
        Out.println("Std. dev.: " + s);
      }
  }
```

We use classes like Point to define data types whenever possible because they encapsulate the definition of the data type in a clear and direct manner. We normally take further steps to make sure that other programs can use points without having to make any assumption about how they are represented. Such mechanisms are the topic of Chapter 4, but we briefly introduce them next.

Program 3.3 implements a simple computation on four-digit numbers: computing the average and standard deviation of a long sequence of random values. It is interesting from an algorithmic point of view because it computes both statistics in one pass through the numbers. Computing the average in one pass is easy, but a naive implementation for the standard deviation that follows the mathematical definition would require storing all the numbers in order to be able to sum the squares of the deviation of each from the average. This difference means that Program 3.3 can compute the average and standard deviation of a huge sequence of numbers (limited only by the time it might take), while the naive implementation is limited by the amount of space available.

What changes do we need to make Program 3.3 work with other types of numbers (say, floating-point numbers in the unit interval) rather than with four-digit integers? There are a number of different options. For such a small program, the simplest is to make a copy of the file, then to change the two lines involving x to

```
double d = Math.random();
```

Even for such a small program, this approach is inconvenient because it leaves us with two copies of the main program, and we will have to make sure that any later changes in that program are reflected in both copies.

In Java, an alternative approach is to define a separate data type for sequences of numbers, as follows:

```
class NumberSeq
  { public double next() { return Math.random(); } }
```

To use this class in Program 3.3, we insert the following code before the for loop:

```
NumberSeq NS = new NumberSeq();
```

(to create an object that can give us sequences of number); and we replace the two lines involving x in Program 3.3 by

```
double d = NS.next();
```

(to use that object to give us the numbers). These changes allow us to use Program 3.3 to test different kinds of numbers (by substituting different implementations of NumberSeq) without modifying *it* at all.

By recasting Program 3.3 in terms of the NumberSeq class, we significantly extend its potential utility. We can do the computation for 3-digit numbers, or 20-digit numbers, or floats, or any other type of number. We could even arrange for Program 3.3 to process items of type Point by defining how we want to extract values of type double for a sequence of points:

```
class NumberSeq
   { double next() { return (new Point()).r(); } }
```

If we use this implementation of NumberSeq with Program 3.3, then it generates random points and computes the average and standard deviation of their distance from the origin (see Exercise 3.11). Generally speaking, this approach is likely to extend the useful lifetime of a program. When some new circumstance (a new application, or perhaps a new compiler or computer) presents us with a new type of number with which we need to work, we can update our program just by changing the data type.

Conceptually, these changes amount to splitting the computation into three distinct parts:

- An *interface*, which declares the methods to be used
- An *implementation* of the methods in the interface
- A *client* program that uses the methods in the interface to work at a higher level of abstraction

We may think of the interface as a definition of the data type. It is a contract between the client and the implementation. The client agrees to access the data only through the methods defined in the interface, and the implementation agrees to deliver the promised methods.

For the example just given, the *interface* is the classname NumberSeq and the methods NumberSeq() and next(). Changing the two lines in Program 3.3 involving x to use NumberSeq, as just described, makes it a *client* of this interface.

An *implementation* of this interface includes the Java code that defines the body of the methods. If we put another version of NumberSeq with different code for each of the methods in the file NumberSeq.java and compile it with a client, then we can get different behavior, without changing the client code at all.

If we were to try to do operations other than arithmetic operations, we would soon find the need to add more operations to the data type. For example, if we want to print the numbers, we need to implement a toString method. Whenever we strive to develop a data type based on identifying the operations of importance in a program, we need to strike a balance between the level of generality that we choose and the ease of implementation and use that results.

Often, we want to build a new data type by adding features to an existing one. To facilitate this process, Java provides the ability to define a class that *extends* another one. The data type defined by the extended class is defined by the members of the base class plus all the members in the extended class. The extended class can either define new members or redefine members from the base class. We say that the extended class *inherits* the members of the base class. For example, we could extend the Point class to give us a class where we can associate a string with each point, as follows:

```
class LabeledPoint extends Point
  {
    String id;
    void label(String name) { id = name; }
    public String toString()
      { return name + "(" + x + ", " + y + ")"; }
  }
```

The extends keyword means that LabeledPoint inherits all the data fields and methods from Point. We add the new data field String and redefine the toString method without having to make another copy of (or even know the details of) the code for Point.

This ability to use previously defined high-level abstract operations, even for newly defined types, is one of the essential and distinctive features of Java programming. Extended classes provide a convenient way for programmers to build upon the work of others and are an integral feature of object-oriented programming systems. However, we use inheritance sparingly in this book because it makes parts of interfaces implicit, where we normally strive to make the interfaces that correspond to fundamental data types fully explicit.

There are other ways to support data types besides the client–interface–implementation scenario just described, but we will not dwell on distinctions among various alternatives because such distinctions are best drawn in a systems-programming context rather than in an algorithm-design context (*see reference section*). However, we do often make use of this basic design paradigm because it provides us with a natural way to substitute improved implementations for old ones and therefore to compare different algorithms for the same problem. Chapter 4 is devoted to this topic.

Object-oriented programming is based on our ability to directly define our own data types by associating data and precisely defining the operations on the data (and the data structures and algorithms that support them) with classes. Classes form the basis for our code throughout the book, but before considering our methodology in further detail (in Chapter 4), we need to consider a number of lower-level mechanisms for manipulating and associating data.

So far, we have primarily talked about defining individual pieces of information for our programs to process. In many instances, we are need to work with potentially huge *collections* of data, and we now turn to basic methods for doing so. In general, we use the term *data structure* to refer to a mechanism for organizing our information to provide convenient and efficient mechanisms for accessing and manipulating it. Many important data structures are based on one or both of the two elementary approaches that we shall consider in this chapter. We may use an *array*, where we organize objects in a fixed sequential fashion that is more suitable for access than for manipulation; or a *list*, where we organize objects in a logical sequential fashion that is more suitable for manipulation than for access.

Exercises

▷ **3.1** Define a class suitable for representing playing cards, including methods for testing whether two cards are in the same suit and whether one has a higher value than the other. Also include a toString() method.

▷ **3.2** Write a class that uses the Point class to implement a data type for *triangles* in the unit square. Include both a method for testing whether the triangle is a right triangle and a toString method for printing the coordinates of the vertices.

3.3 Write a client program that uses the data type in Program 3.2 for the following task: Read a sequence of points (pairs of floating-point numbers) from standard input, and find the one that is closest to the first.

● **3.4** Add a method to the point data type (Program 3.2) that determines whether or not three points are collinear, to within a numerical tolerance of 10^{-4}. Assume that the points are all in the unit square.

▷ **3.5** Give a NumberSeq implementation that allows you to use Program 3.3 (modified to be a NumberSeq client, as described in the text) to print the average and standard deviation of a sequence of random 4-digit integers.

● **3.6** Add to your class from Exercise 3.2 a method for computing the area of the triangle. Then write a myNUMBER implementation that allows you to use

Program 3.3 (modified as described in the text) to generate random triangles and compute their average area.

3.7 Test the random-number generator on your system by generating N random integers between 0 and $r-1$ with `((int) (1000*Math.random()))` `% r` and computing the average and standard deviation for $r = 10$, 100, and 1000 and $N = 10^3$, 10^4, 10^5, and 10^6.

3.8 Test the random-number generator on your system by generating N random integers between 0 and $r-1$ with `((int) (r*Math.random()))` and computing the average and standard deviation for $r = 10$, 100, and 1000 and $N = 10^3$, 10^4, 10^5, and 10^6.

○ **3.9** Do Exercises 3.7 and 3.8 for $r = 2$, 4, and 16.

3.10 Adapt Program 3.3 to be used for random *bits* (numbers that can take only the values 0 or 1).

● **3.11** Give an analytic expression for the expected distance to the origin of a random point in the unit square and compare with the result of using Program 3.3 (in the manner described in the text) to find the average and standard deviation of this quantity for N random points, for $N = 10^3$, 10^4, 10^5, and 10^6.

3.2 Arrays

Perhaps the most fundamental data structure is the *array*, which is defined as a primitive in Java and in most other programming languages. We have already seen, in the examples in Chapter 1, the use of an array as the basis for the development of an efficient algorithm; we shall see many more examples in this section.

An array is a fixed collection of same-type data that are stored contiguously and are accessible by an index. We refer to the `i`th element of an array a as `a[i]`. It is the responsibility of the programmer to store something meaningful in an array position `a[i]` before referring to `a[i]`. In Java, it is also the responsibility of the programmer to use indices that are nonnegative and smaller than the array size. Neglecting these responsibilities are two of the more common programming mistakes.

Arrays are fundamental data structures in that they have a direct correspondence with memory systems on virtually all computers. To retrieve the contents of a word from memory in machine language, we provide an address. Thus, we could think of the entire computer memory as an array, with the memory addresses corresponding to

Program 3.4 Sieve of Eratosthenes

The goal of this program is to print all the primes less than the integer given as a command-line argument. To do so, it computes an array of boolean values with a[i] set to true if i is prime, and to false if i is not prime. First, it sets to true all array elements in order to indicate that no numbers are known to be nonprime. Then it sets to false array elements corresponding to indices that are known to be nonprime (multiples of known primes). If a[i] is still true after all multiples of smaller primes have been set to false, then we know it to be prime.

```
class Primes
  {
    public static void main(String[] args)
      { int N = Integer.parseInt(args[0]);
        boolean[] a = new boolean[N];
        for (int i = 2; i < N; i++) a[i] = true;
        for (int i = 2; i < N; i++)
          if (a[i] != false)
            for (int j = i; j*i < N; j++)
              a[i*j] = false;
        for (int i = 2; i < N; i++)
          if (i > N - 100)
            if (a[i]) Out.print(" " + i);
        Out.println();
      }
  }
```

i	2	3	5	a[i]
2	1			1
3	1			1
4	1	0		
5	1			1
6	1	0		
7	1			1
8	1	0		
9	1		0	
10	1	0		
11	1			1
12	1	0	0	
13	1			1
14	1	0		
15	1		0	
16	1	0		
17	1			1
18	1	0	0	
19	1			1
20	1	0		
21	1		0	
22	1	0		
23	1			1
24	1	0	0	
25	1			0
26	1	0		
27	1		0	
28	1	0		
29	1			1
30	1	0	0	0
31	1			1

Figure 3.2
Sieve of Eratosthenes

To compute the prime numbers less than 32, we initialize all the array entries to 1 (second column) in order to indicate that no numbers are known to be nonprime (a[0] and a[1] are not used and are not shown). Then, we set array entries whose indices are multiples of 2, 3, and 5 to 0, since we know these multiples to be nonprime. Indices corresponding to array entries that remain 1 are prime (rightmost column).

array indices. Most computer-language processors translate programs that involve arrays into efficient code that directly accesses memory, and we are safe in assuming that an array access such as a[i] translates to just a few machine instructions.

A simple example of the use of an array is given by Program 3.4, which prints out all prime numbers less than a specified value. The method used, which dates back to the third century B.C., is called the *sieve of Eratosthenes*. It is typical of algorithms that exploit the fact that we can access efficiently any item of an array, given that item's index. Figure 3.2 traces the operation of the program when computing the primes less than 32. For economy, we use the numbers 1 and 0 in the figure to denote the values true and false, respectively.

Program 3.5 Robust array allocation

If a user of Program 3.4 types a huge number as command-line argument, it will throw an `OutOfMemoryError` exception. It is good programming practice to check for all errors that might occur, so we should replace the line that creates the boolean array a in Program 3.4 with this code. We frequently allocate arrays in code in this book, but, for brevity, we will omit these insufficient-memory tests.

```
boolean[] a;
try
  { a = new boolean[N]; }
catch (OutOfMemoryError e)
  { Out.println("Out of memory"); return; }
```

The implementation has four loops, three of which access the items of the array sequentially, from beginning to end; the fourth skips through the array, i items at a time. In some cases, sequential processing is essential; in other cases, sequential ordering is used because it is as good as any other. For example, we could change the first loop in Program 3.4 to

```
for (i = N-1; i > 1; i--) a[i] = true;
```

without any effect on the computation. We could also reverse the order of the inner loop in a similar manner, or we could change the final loop to print out the primes in decreasing order, but we could not change the order of the outer loop in the main computation, because it depends on all the integers less than i being processed before `a[i]` is tested for being prime.

We will not analyze the running time of Program 3.4 in detail because that would take us astray into number theory, but it is clear that the running time is proportional to

$$N + N/2 + N/3 + N/5 + N/7 + N/11 + \ldots$$

which is less than $N + N/2 + N/3 + N/4 + \ldots = NH_N \sim N \ln N$.

As with other objects, references to arrays are significant because they allow us to manipulate the arrays efficiently as higher-level objects. In particular, we can pass a reference to an array as an parameter to a method, thus enabling that method to access objects in the array without having to make a copy of the whole array. This capability is indispensable when we write programs to manipulate huge arrays. For example, the search methods that we examined in Section 2.6 use this feature. We shall see other examples in Section 3.7.

The second basic mechanism that we use in Program 3.4 is the new operator that *allocates* the amount of memory that we need for our array at execution time and returns, for our exclusive use, a reference to the array. Dynamic allocation is an essential tool in programs that manipulate multiple arrays, some of which might have to be huge. In this case, without memory allocation, we would have to predeclare an array as large as any value that the user is allowed to type. In a large program where we might use many arrays, it is not feasible to do so for each array. For Java, the underlying mechanism new is the same as for any other object, but its use is particularly important for arrays, which could be huge. A robust version of Program 3.4 would also check that there is sufficient memory available for the array, as illustrated in Program 3.5.

Not only do arrays closely reflect the low-level mechanisms for accessing data in memory on most computers, but also they find widespread use because they correspond directly to natural methods of organizing data for applications. For example, arrays also correspond directly to *vectors*, the mathematical term for indexed lists of objects.

The Java standard library provides the class Vector, an abstract object that we can index like an array but that can also grow and shrink. We get some of the benefit of arrays but can work with abstract operations for making an array larger or smaller without having to worry about the details of coding them. Programs that use Vector objects are more cumbersome than programs that use arrays, because to access the ith element of a Vector we have to call its get method instead of using square braces. The implementation of Vector most likely uses an internal array, so using a Vector instead of an array just leads to an extra level of indirection for most references. Therefore, for simplicity and efficiency, we use arrays in all of our code while recognizing that it could be adapted to use Vectors if desired (see Exercise 3.15).

Program 3.6 is an example of a simulation program that uses an array. It simulates a sequence of *Bernoulli trials*, a familiar abstract concept from probability theory. If we flip a coin N times, the

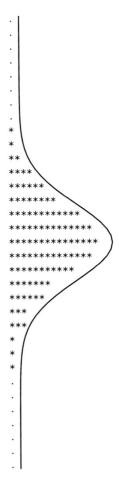

**Figure 3.3
Coin-flipping simulation**

This table shows the result of running Program 3.6 with $N = 32$ and $M = 1000$, simulating 1000 experiments of flipping a coin 32 times. The number of heads that we should see is approximated by the normal distribution function, which is drawn over the data.

Program 3.6 Coin-flipping simulation

If we flip a coin N times, we expect to get $N/2$ heads, but could get anywhere from 0 to N heads. This program runs the experiment M times, taking both N and M from the command line. It uses an array f to keep track of the frequency of occurrence of the outcome "i heads" for $0 \leq i \leq N$, then prints out a histogram of the result of the experiments, with one asterisk for each 10 occurrences. The operation on which this program is based—indexing an array with a computed value—is critical to the efficiency of many computational procedures.

```
class CoinFlip
  {
    static boolean heads()
      { return Math.random() < 0.5; }
    public static void main(String[] args)
      { int i, j, cnt;
        int N = Integer.parseInt(args[0]);
        int M = Integer.parseInt(args[1]);
        int[] f = new int[N+1];
        for (j = 0; j <= N; j++) f[j] = 0;
        for (i = 0; i < M; i++, f[cnt]++)
          for (cnt = 0, j = 0; j <= N; j++)
            if (heads()) cnt++;
        for (j = 0; j <= N; j++)
          {
            if (f[j] == 0) Out.print(".");
            for (i = 0; i < f[j]; i+=10)
              Out.print("*");
            Out.println();
          }
      }
  }
```

probability that we see k heads is

$$\binom{N}{k}\frac{1}{2^N} \approx \frac{e^{-(k-N/2)^2/N}}{\sqrt{\pi N/2}}.$$

The approximation is known as the *normal approximation*—the familiar bell-shaped curve. Figure 3.3 illustrates the output of Program 3.6

for 1000 trials of the experiment of flipping a coin 32 times. Many more details on the Bernoulli distribution and the normal approximation can be found in any text on probability. In the present context, our interest in the computation is that we use the numbers as indices into an array to count their frequency of occurrence. The ability of arrays to support this kind of operation is one of their prime virtues.

Programs 3.4 and 3.6 both compute array indices from the data at hand. In a sense, when we use a computed value to access an array of size N, we are taking N possibilities into account with just a single operation. This gain in efficiency is compelling when we can realize it, and we shall be encountering algorithms throughout the book that make use of arrays in this way.

We use arrays to organize all different manner of types of objects, not just integers. In Java, we can declare arrays of any primitive or class type. An array of integers contains the values of the integers themselves, and the same is true of any other primitive type. But an array of objects is an array of *references* to the objects, as depicted in Figure 3.4.

Program 3.7 illustrates the use of an array of points in the plane using the class definition for points that we considered in Section 3.1. This program also illustrates a common use of arrays: to save data away so that they can be quickly accessed in an organized manner in some computation.

Incidentally, Program 3.7 is also interesting as a prototypical quadratic algorithm, which checks all pairs of a set of N data items, and therefore takes time proportional to N^2. In this book, we look for improvements whenever we see such an algorithm, because its use becomes infeasible as N grows. In this case, we shall see how to use a compound data structure to perform this computation in linear time, in Section 3.7.

We can create compound types of arbitrary complexity in a similar manner: We can have not just arrays of objects, but also arrays of arrays, or objects containing arrays. We will consider these different options in detail in Section 3.7. Before doing so, however, we will examine *linked lists*, which serve as the primary alternative to arrays for organizing collections of objects.

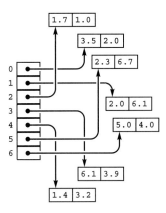

Figure 3.4
Array of points

An array of objects in Java is actually an array of references to the objects, as depicted in this diagram of an array of Point *objects.*

Program 3.7 Closest-point computation

This program illustrates the use of an array of objects and is representative of the typical situation where we save items in an array to process them later, during some computation. It counts the number of pairs of N randomly generated points in the unit square that can be connected by a straight line of length less than d, using the data type for points described in Section 3.1. The running time is $O(N^2)$, so this program cannot be used for huge N. Program 3.18 provides a faster solution.

```
class ClosePoints
  { public static void main(String[] args)
      { int cnt = 0, N = Integer.parseInt(args[0]);
        double d = Double.parseDouble(args[1]);
        Point[] a = new Point[N];
        for (int i = 0; i < N; i++)
          a[i] = new Point();
        for (int i = 0; i < N; i++)
          for (int j = i+1; j < N; j++)
            if (a[i].distance(a[j]) < d) cnt++;
        Out.print(cnt + " pairs ");
        Out.println("closer than " + d);
      }
  }
```

Exercises

3.12 Modify our implementation of the sieve of Eratosthenes (Program 3.4) to use an array of ints; instead of booleans. Determine the effects of these changes on the amount of space and time used by the program.

▷ **3.13** Use the sieve of Eratosthenes to determine the number of primes less than N, for $N = 10^3$, 10^4, 10^5, and 10^6.

○ **3.14** Use the sieve of Eratosthenes to draw a plot of N versus the number of primes less than N for N between 1 and 1000.

○ **3.15** The Java package java.util includes the Vector data type as an alternative to arrays. Find out how to use this data type and determine the effect on the runtime when you replace the array in Program 3.4 by a Vector.

● **3.16** Empirically determine the effect of removing the test of a[i] from the inner loop of Program 3.4, for $N = 10^3$, 10^4, 10^5, and 10^6, and explain the effect that you observe.

▷ **3.17** Suppose that `a` is declared as `int[] a = new int[99]`. Give the contents of the array after the following two statements are executed:

```
for (i = 0; i < 99; i++) a[i] = 98-i;
for (i = 0; i < 99; i++) a[i] = a[a[i]];
```

▷ **3.18** Write a program that counts the number of different integers less than 1000 that appear in an input stream.

○ **3.19** Write a program that determines empirically the number of random positive integers less than 1000 that you can expect to generate before getting a repeated value.

○ **3.20** Write a program that determines empirically the number of random positive integers less than 1000 that you can expect to generate before getting each value at least once.

3.21 Modify Program 3.6 to simulate a situation where the coin turns up heads with probability p. Run 1000 trials for an experiment with 32 flips with $p = 1/6$ to get output that you can compare with Figure 3.3.

3.22 Modify Program 3.6 to simulate a situation where the coin turns up heads with probability λ/N. Run 1000 trials for an experiment with 32 flips to get output that you can compare with Figure 3.3. This distribution is the classical *Poisson* distribution.

○ **3.23** Modify Program 3.7 to print out the coordinates of the closest pair of points.

● **3.24** Modify Program 3.7 to perform the same computation in d dimensions.

3.3 Linked Lists

When our primary interest is to go through a collection of items sequentially, one by one, we can organize the items as a *linked list*—a basic data structure where each item contains the information that we need to get to the next item. The primary advantage of linked lists over arrays is that the links provide us with the capability to rearrange the items efficiently. This flexibility is gained at the expense of quick access to any arbitrary item in the list, because the only way to get to an item in the list is to follow links from the beginning.

Definition 3.2 *A* **linked list** *is a set of items where each item is part of a* **node** *that also contains a* **link** *to a node.*

We define nodes by referring to nodes, so linked lists are sometimes called *self-referent* structures. Moreover, although a node's link usually refers to a different node, it could refer to the node itself, so linked lists can also be *cyclic* structures. The implications of these two facts will become apparent as we begin to consider concrete representations and applications of linked lists.

Normally, we think of linked lists as implementing a sequential arrangement of a set of items: Starting at a given node, we consider its item to be first in the sequence. Then, we follow its link to another node, which gives us an item that we consider to be second in the sequence, and so forth. Since the list could be cyclic, the sequence could seem infinite. We most often work with lists that correspond to a simple sequential arrangement of the items, adopting one of the following conventions for the link in the final node:

- It is a *null link* that points to no node.
- It refers to a *dummy node* that contains no item.
- It refers back to the first node, making the list a *circular list*.

In each case, following links from the first node to the final one defines a sequential arrangement of items. Arrays define a sequential ordering of items as well; in an array, however, the sequential organization is provided implicitly by the position in the array. (Arrays also support arbitrary access by index, which lists do not.)

We first consider nodes with precisely one link, and, in most applications, we work with one-dimensional lists where all nodes except possibly the first and the final each have precisely one link referring *to* them. This corresponds to the simplest situation, which is also the one that interests us most, where linked lists correspond to sequences of items. We will consider more complicated situations in due course.

Linked lists are primitive constructs in some programming environments, but not in Java. However, the basic building blocks that we discussed in Section 3.1 are well suited to implementing linked lists. Specifically, we use objects for nodes and references to objects for links, as follows:

```
class Node
  { Object item; Node next; }
```

This code is nothing more than Java code for Definition 3.2. We implement linked-list nodes as objects of type Node: each node consists of an item (whose type is unspecified here) and a reference to a node. That is, we use references to nodes to implement links. We shall see more complicated representations in Chapter 4 that provide more flexibility and allow more efficient implementations of certain operations, but this simple representation will suffice for us to consider the fundamentals of list processing. We use similar conventions for other linked structures throughout the book.

Memory allocation is a central consideration in the effective use of linked lists. We have defined a class Node, but we will have many objects that instantiate this class, one for each node that we want to use. Whenever we want to use a new node, we need to create an object of type Node. For example, as for any other class, the line of code

```
Node x = new Node();
```

creates an object of type Node and returns a reference to it in x. In Section 3.5, we shall briefly consider how the system goes about reserving memory, because addressing that task is a good application of linked lists (!).

When working with linked structures, it is wise to initialize all the members of each object when we create it. Since invoking a constructor is part of the process of instantiating an object, we can adhere to this policy by assigning values to each data field in every constructor. For example, we might define list nodes with the code

```
Class Node
  { Object item; Node next;
    Node(Object v)
      { item = v; next = null; }
  }
```

so that the statement t = new Node(x); not only reserves memory for a node and assigns a reference to it to t, but also sets the item field of the node to the value v and the next field to the value null. Proper use of constructors helps us to avoid programming bugs associated with uninitialized data.

Now, once a list node is created, how do we refer to the information it comprises—its item and its link? We have already seen the basic operations that we need for this task: We simply use the class data field names—the item in the node referenced by x (which is an Object) is x.item, and the link (which is a reference to a Node) is x.next. As with all other Java references, we so often need to use the phrase "the node referenced by link x" that we simply say "node x"—the link *does* name the node.

The correspondence between links and Java references is essential, but we must bear in mind that the former is an abstraction and

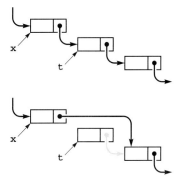

Figure 3.5
Linked-list deletion

To delete, or remove, the node following a given node x from a linked list, we set t to refer to the node to be removed, then change x's link to t.next. The reference t can be used to refer to the removed node (to add it to some other list, for example). Although its link still refers to a node in the list, we generally do not use such a link after removing the node from the list.

the latter a concrete representation. We can design algorithms that use nodes and links, and we can choose one of many possible implementations of that idea. For example, we could also represent links with array indices, as we shall see at the end of this section.

Figures 3.5 and 3.6 show the two fundamental operations that we perform on linked lists. We can *remove* any item from a linked list, to make it shrink by 1 in length; and we can *insert* an item into a linked list at any point, to make it grow by 1 in length. For simplicity, we assume in these figures that the lists are circular and never become empty. We will consider null links, dummy nodes, and empty lists in Section 3.4. As shown in the figures, insertion and deletion each require just two statements in Java. To remove the node following node x, we use the statements

```
t = x.next; x.next = t.next;
```

or simply

```
x.next = x.next.next;
```

To insert node t into a list at a position following node x, we use the statements

```
t.next = x.next; x.next = t;
```

The simplicity of insertion and deletion is the *raison d'être* of linked lists. The corresponding operations are unnatural and inconvenient in arrays because they require moving all of the array's contents following the affected item.

By contrast, linked lists are *not* well suited for the *find the kth item* (find an item given its index) operation that characterizes efficient access in arrays. In an array, we find the kth item simply by accessing a[k]; in a list, we have to traverse k links. Another operation that is unnatural on singly linked lists is "find the item *before* a given item."

When we remove a node from a linked list using x.next = x.next.next, we may never be able to access it again. In Java, this is no special concern because Java *automatically* reclaims memory to which there is no reference. In many other systems, it is necessary to inform the system when memory may be used for some other purpose and to pay particular attention to doing so when processing large list objects or large numbers of them. We will revisit this issue in Section 3.5.

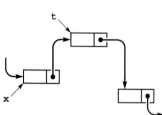

Figure 3.6
Linked-list insertion

To insert a given node t *into a linked list at a position following another given node* x *(top), we set* t.next *to* x.next *(center), then set* x.next *to* t *(bottom).*

We will see many examples of applications of these and other basic operations on linked lists in later chapters. Since the operations involve only a few statements, we often manipulate the lists directly rather than defining methods for inserting, deleting, and so forth. As an example, we consider next a program for solving the *Josephus problem* which provides an interesting contrast with the sieve of Eratosthenes.

We imagine that N people have decided to elect a leader by arranging themselves in a circle and eliminating every Mth person around the circle, closing ranks as each person drops out. The problem is to find out which person will be the last one remaining (a mathematically inclined potential leader will figure out ahead of time which position in the circle to take).

The identity of the elected leader is a function of N and M that we refer to as the *Josephus function*. More generally, we may wish to know the order in which the people are eliminated. For example, as shown in Figure 3.7, if $N = 9$ and $M = 5$, the people are eliminated in the order 5 1 7 4 3 6 9 2, and 8 is the leader chosen. Program 3.8 reads in N and M and prints out this ordering.

Program 3.8 uses a *circular* linked list to simulate the election process directly. First, we build the list for 1 to N: We build a circular list consisting of a single node for person 1, then insert the nodes for people 2 through N, in that order, following that node in the list, using the insertion code illustrated in Figure 3.6. Then, we proceed through the list, counting through $M - 1$ items, deleting the next one using the code illustrated in Figure 3.5, and continuing until only one node is left (which then points to itself).

The sieve of Eratosthenes and the Josephus problem clearly illustrate the distinction between using arrays and using linked lists to represent a sequentially organized collection of objects. Using a linked list instead of an array for the sieve of Eratosthenes would be costly because the algorithm's efficiency depends on being able to access any array position quickly, and using an array instead of a linked list for the Josephus problem would be costly because the algorithm's efficiency depends on the ability to remove items quickly.

When we choose a data structure, we *must* be aware of the effects of that choice upon the efficiency of the algorithms that will process the data. This interplay between data structures and algorithms is at

Figure 3.7
Example of Josephus election

This diagram shows the result of a Josephus-style election, where the group stands in a circle, then counts around the circle, eliminating every fifth person and closing the circle.

Program 3.8 Circular list example (Josephus problem)

To represent people arranged in a circle, we build a circular linked list, with a link from each person to the person on the left in the circle.

```
class Josephus
  {
    static class Node
      { int val; Node next;
        Node(int v) { val = v; }
      }
    public static void main(String[] args)
      { int N = Integer.parseInt(args[0]);
        int M = Integer.parseInt(args[1]);
        Node t = new Node(1);
        Node x = t;
        for (int i = 2; i <= N; i++)
          x = (x.next = new Node(i));
        x.next = t;
        while (x != x.next)
          {
            for (int i = 1; i < M; i++) x = x.next;
            x.next = x.next.next;
          }
        Out.println("Survivor is " + x.val);
      }
  }
```

---

the heart of the design process and is a recurring theme throughout this book.

In Java, objects and references to objects provide a direct and convenient concrete realization of the abstract concept of a linked list, but the essential value of the abstraction does not depend on any particular implementation. For example, Figure 3.8 shows how we could use arrays of integers to implement the linked list for the Josephus problem. That is, we could implement links using array indices, instead of references to objects. Linked lists were useful well before constructs such as objects and references to them were available in high-level languages such as Java. Even in modern systems, array-based implementations are sometimes convenient.

Exercises

▷ 3.25 Write a method that returns the number of nodes on a circular list, given a reference to one of the nodes on the list.

3.26 Write a code fragment that determines the number of nodes that are between the nodes referenced by two given references x and t to nodes on a circular list.

3.27 Write a code fragment that, given references x and t to nodes on two disjoint circular lists, inserts all the nodes on the list containing node t into the list containing node x, at the point following x.

• 3.28 Given references x and t to nodes on a circular list, write a code fragment that moves the node following t to the position following the node following x on the list.

3.29 Modify Program 3.8 so that it maintains a circular list after each node is inserted.

3.30 Give the running time of Program 3.8, within a constant factor, as a function of M and N.

3.31 Use Program 3.8 to determine the value of the Josephus function for $M = 2, 3, 5, 10$, and $N = 10^3, 10^4, 10^5$, and 10^6.

3.32 Use Program 3.8 to plot the Josephus function versus N for $M = 10$ and N from 2 to 1000.

○ 3.33 Redo the table in Figure 3.8, beginning with item i initially at position N-i in the array.

3.34 Develop a version of Program 3.8 that uses an array of indices to implement the linked list (see Figure 3.8).

3.4 Elementary List Processing

Linked lists bring us into a world of computing that is markedly different from that of arrays and simple classes. With arrays and classes, we save an item in memory and later refer to it by name (or by index) in much the same manner as we might put a piece of information in a file drawer or an address book; with linked lists, the manner in which we save information makes it more difficult to access but easier to rearrange. Working with data that are organized in linked lists is called *list processing*.

	0	1	2	3	4	5	6	7	8
val	1	2	3	4	5	6	7	8	9
next	1	2	3	4	5	6	7	8	0
5	1	2	3	4	5	6	7	8	9
	1	2	3	5	5	6	7	8	0
1	1	2	3	4	5	6	7	8	9
	1	2	3	5	5	6	7	8	1
7	1	2	3	4	5	6	7	8	9
	1	2	3	5	5	7	7	8	1
4	1	2	3	4	5	6	7	8	9
	1	2	5	5	5	7	7	8	1
3	1	2	3	4	5	6	7	8	9
	1	5	5	5	5	7	7	8	1
6	1	2	3	4	5	6	7	8	9
	1	7	5	5	5	7	7	8	1
9	1	2	3	4	5	6	7	8	9
	1	7	5	5	5	7	7	1	1
2	1	2	3	4	5	6	7	8	9
	1	7	5	5	5	7	7	7	1

**Figure 3.8
Array representation of a
 linked list**

This sequence shows a linked list for the Josephus problem (see Figure 3.7), built from two arrays using indices instead of references for links. The index of the item following the item with index 0 in the list is next[0]*, and so forth. Initially* (top three rows), *the item for person* i *has index* i-1*, and we form a circular list by setting* next[i] *to* i+1 *for* i *from 0 to 8 and* next[8] *to 0. To simulate the Josephus-election process, we change the links (*next *array entries) but do not move the items. Each pair of lines shows the result of moving through the list four times with* x = next[x]*, then deleting the fifth item (displayed at the left) by setting* next[x] *to* next[next[x]]*.*

When we use arrays, we are susceptible to program bugs involving out-of-bounds array accesses. The most common bug that we encounter when using linked lists is a similar bug where we reference an undefined object. Another common mistake is to use a reference that we have changed unknowingly. One reason that this problem arises is that we may have multiple references to the same node without necessarily realizing that that is the case. Program 3.8 avoids several such problems by using a circular list that is never empty, so that each link always refers to a well-defined node, and each link can also be interpreted as referring to the list.

Developing correct and efficient code for list-processing applications is an acquired programming skill that requires practice and patience to develop. In this section, we consider examples and exercises that will increase our comfort with working with list-processing code. We shall see numerous other examples throughout the book, because linked structures are at the heart of some of our most successful algorithms.

As mentioned in Section 3.3, we use a number of different conventions for the first and final links in a list. We consider some of them in this section, even though we adopt the policy of reserving the term *linked list* to describe the simplest situation.

Definition 3.3   *A linked list is either a null link or a link to a node that contains an item and a link to a linked list.*

This definition is more restrictive than Definition 3.2, but it corresponds more closely to the mental model that we have when we write list-processing code. Rather than exclude all the other various conventions by using only this definition, and rather than provide specific definitions corresponding to each convention, we let both stand, with the understanding that it will be clear from the context which type of linked list we are using.

Program 3.9 is an implementation of a simple list-processing task, reversing the order of the nodes on a list. It takes a linked list as an parameter, and returns a linked list comprising the same nodes, but with the order reversed. Figure 3.9 shows the change that the method makes for each node in its main loop. Such a diagram makes it easier for us to check each statement of the program to be sure that the code changes the links as intended, and programmers typically use these diagrams to understand the operation of list-processing implementations.

Program 3.9 List reversal

This method reverses the links in a list, returning a pointer to the final node, which then points to the next-to-final node, and so forth, with the link in the first node of the original list set to null. To accomplish this task, we need to maintain links to three consecutive nodes in the list.

```
static Node reverse(Node x)
  { Node t, y = x, r = null;
    while (y != null)
      { t = y.next; y.next = r; r = y; y = t; }
    return r;
  }
```

One of the most common operations that we perform on lists is to *traverse* them: We scan through the items on the list sequentially, performing some operation on each. For example, if x refers to the first node of a list, the final node has a null link, and visit is a method that takes an item as a parameter, then we might write

```
for (Node t = x; t != null; t = t.next) visit(t.item);
```

to traverse the list. This loop (or its equivalent while form) is as ubiquitous in list-processing programs as is the corresponding loop of the form for (int i = 0; i < N; i++) in array-processing programs.

Program 3.10 illustrates the implementation of three other basic list-processing tasks: it builds a list from a sequence of numbers on standard input, rearranges the nodes of the list to put the items in sorted order, and prints out the sorted sequence. As we discuss in Chapter 6, the expected running time of this program is proportional to N^2, so the program is not useful for large N. Beyond this observation, we defer discussing the sort aspect of this program to Chapter 6, because we shall see a great many methods for sorting in Chapters 6 through 10. Our purpose now is to present the implementation as an example of a list-processing application.

The lists in Program 3.10 illustrate another commonly used convention: We maintain a dummy node called a *head node* at the beginning of each list. We ignore the item field in a list's head node but maintain its link as a reference to the node containing the first item in the list. The program uses two lists: one to collect the random

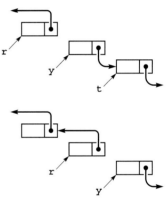

Figure 3.9
List reversal

To reverse the order of a list, we maintain a pointer r to the portion of the list already processed, and a pointer y to the portion of the list not yet seen. This diagram shows how the pointers change for each node in the list. We save a pointer to the node following y in t, change y's link to point to r, and then move r to y and y to t.

Program 3.10 List insertion sort

This code builds a linked list with one number from standard input per node (create method), then rearranges the nodes so that the numbers appear in order on the list (sort method), then prints the numbers out in sorted order (print method). To accomplish the sort, it maintains two lists, an input (unsorted) list and an output (sorted) list. On each iteration of the loop, it removes a node from the input and inserts it into position in the output. The code is simplified by the use of head nodes for each list that contain the links to the first nodes on the lists.

```
class ListSortExample
  {
    static class Node
      { int val; Node next;
        Node(int v, Node t) { val = v; next = t; }
      }
    static Node create()
      { Node a = new Node(0, null);
        for (In.init(); !In.empty(); )
          a.next = new Node(In.getInt(), a.next);
        return a;
      }
    static Node sort(Node a)
      { Node t, u, x, b = new Node(0, null);
        while (a.next != null)
          {
            t = a.next; u = t.next; a.next = u;
            for (x = b; x.next != null; x = x.next)
              if (x.next.val > t.val) break;
            t.next = x.next; x.next = t;
          }
        return b;
      }
    static void print(Node h)
      { for (Node t = h.next; t != null; t = t.next)
          Out.println(t.val + ""); }
    public static void main(String[] args)
      { print(sort(create())); }
  }
```

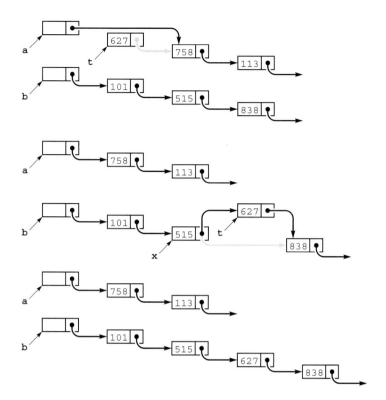

Figure 3.10
Linked-list sort

This diagram depicts one step in transforming an unordered linked list (referred to by a*) into an ordered one (referred to by* b*), using insertion sort. We take the first node of the unordered list, keeping a pointer to it in* t *(top). Then, we search through* b *to find the first node* x *with* x.next.item > t.item *(or* x.next = null*), and insert* t *into the list following* x *(center). These operations reduce the length of* a *by one node, and increase the length of* b *by one node, keeping* b *in order (bottom). Iterating, we eventually exhaust* a *and have the nodes in order in* b*.*

input in the first loop, and the other to collect the sorted output in the second loop. Figure 3.10 diagrams the changes that Program 3.10 makes during one iteration of its main loop. We take the next node off the input list, find where it belongs in the output list, and link it into position.

The primary reason to use the head node at the beginning becomes clear when we consider the process of adding the *first* node to the sorted list. This node is the one in the input list with the smallest item, and it could be anywhere on the list. We have three options:

- Duplicate the for loop that finds the smallest item and start with a one-node list in the same manner as in Program 3.8.
- Test whether the output list is empty every time that we wish to insert a node.
- Use a dummy head node whose link points to the first node on the list, as in the given implementation.

The first option is inelegant and requires extra code; the second is also inelegant and requires extra time. Incidentally, the concise body of the main method in Program 3.10 provides an example of what is known as *functional programming*: it consists entirely of method invocations (function calls).

The use of a head node does incur some cost (the extra node), and we can avoid the head node in many common applications. For example, we can also view Program 3.9 as having an input list (the original list) and an output list (the reversed list), but we do not need to use a head node in that program because all insertions into the output list are at the beginning. We shall see still other applications that are more simply coded when we use a dummy node, rather than a null link, at the *tail* of the list. There are no hard-and-fast rules about whether or not to use dummy nodes—the choice is a matter of style combined with an understanding of effects on performance. Good programmers enjoy the challenge of picking the convention that most simplifies the task at hand. We shall see several such tradeoffs throughout this book.

For reference, a number of options for linked-list conventions are laid out in Table 3.1; others are discussed in the exercises. In all the cases in Table 3.1, we use a reference head to refer to the list, and we maintain a consistent stance that our program manages references to nodes, using the given code for various operations. Instantiating nodes and filling them with information is the same for all the conventions. Robust methods implementing the same operations would have extra code to check for error conditions (for example, every use of new should be enclosed in a try-catch block, as in Program 3.5). The purpose of the table is to expose similarities and differences among the various options.

To this point, our programs have implemented the linked-list abstraction with code that directly manipulates data fields (items and links) in nodes, relying on programming conventions to ensure that the lists themselves have the desired structure. An alternative is to define a data type for the lists themselves, making the conventions an explicit part of the implementation. This approach frees client programs from tedious low-level operations. For example, Program 3.11 is a class that implements the circular-list abstraction, and Program 3.12 is our Josephus-election program (Program 3.8) recast as a client program that uses this class. The CircularList class has the responsiblity of

---

Table 3.1 Head and tail conventions in linked lists

This table gives implementations of basic list-processing operations with four commonly used conventions. This type of code is used in simple applications where the list-processing code is inline.

Circular, never empty

```
        first insert: head.next = head;
  insert t after x: t.next = x.next; x.next = t;
   remove after x: x.next = x.next.next;
    traversal loop: t = head;
                    do { ...  t = t.next; } while (t != head);
 test if one item: if (head.next == head)
```

Head reference, null tail

```
          initialize: head = null;
  insert t after x: if (x == null) { head = t; head.next = null; }
                    else { t.next = x.next; x.next = t; }
   remove after x: t = x.next; x.next = t.next;
    traversal loop: for (t = head; t != null; t = t.next)
     test if empty: if (head == null)
```

Dummy head node, null tail

```
          initialize: head = new Node();
                    head.next = null;
  insert t after x: t.next = x.next; x.next = t;
   remove after x: t = x.next; x.next = t.next;
    traversal loop: for (t = head.next; t != null; t = t.next)
     test if empty: if (head.next == null)
```

Dummy head and tail nodes

```
          initialize: head = new Node();
                    z = new Node();
                    head.next = z; z.next = z;
  insert t after x: t.next = x.next; x.next = t;
   remove after x: x.next = x.next.next;
    traversal loop: for (t = head.next; t != z; t = t.next)
     test if empty: if (head.next == z)
```

Program 3.11 Circular-list class

This class implements basic operations on circular linked lists. Its purpose is to allow clients to manipulate such lists and to ensure that they do so without dependence upon implementation details. Clients can insert a new node with a given value after a given node in a list (and, by convention, create a one-node list if the first parameter is null) and remove the node following a given node (remove has no effect if the list has only one node). The accessor methods next and val provide the values of fields to the clients; their use gives us the freedom to change the implementation (see Chapter 4).

```
class CircularList
  {
    static class Node
      { int val; Node next;
        Node(int v) { val = v; }
      }
    Node next(Node x)
      { return x.next; }
    int val(Node x)
      { return x.val; }
    Node insert(Node x, int v)
      { Node t = new Node(v);
        if (x == null) t.next = t;
        else { t.next = x.next;   x.next = t; }
        return t;
      }
    void remove(Node x)
      { x.next = x.next.next; }
  }
```

making sure that the list is always a proper circular list, and the client program works with high-level operations such as "insert a new node into the list" rather than low-level operations such as assigning specific values to links.

We consider a completely different class implementation with the same interface in Section 3.5. This example is yet another illustration of the client-interface-implementation scenario that we use throughout the book. We can use any class implementation that has the same

---

Program 3.12 Solving the Josephus problem with circular lists

This program for the Josephus problem is an example of a client program that utilizes the circular-list class of Program 3.13. The low-level details of maintaining the list structure are left to the class implementation.

```
class JosephusY
  {
    public static void main(String[] args)
      { int N = Integer.parseInt(args[0]);
        int M = Integer.parseInt(args[1]);
        CircularList L = new CircularList();
        CircularList.Node x = null;
        for (int i = 1; i <= N; i++)
          x = L.insert(x, i);
        while (x != L.next(x))
          {
            for (int i = 1; i < M; i++)
              x = L.next(x);
            L.remove(x);
          }
        Out.println("Survivor is " + L.val(x));
      }
  }
```

---

methods without changing Program 3.12 at all. Identifying the important operations that we use in a computation and encapsulating them all in a single class has two advantages:

- We can work at a higher level of abstraction in the client.
- We consider different concrete implementations of critical operations and test their effectiveness.

In this case, our purpose is to expose underlying mechanisms, not find more efficient implementations.

Some programmers prefer to encapsulate all operations on data structures such as linked lists by defining methods for every operation that a client might need in classes like Program 3.11. Indeed, as just illustrated and as we shall see in Chapter 4, the Java class mechanism makes it easy to do so. However, that extra layer of abstraction sometimes masks the fact that just a few low-level operations are involved.

In this book, when we are implementing higher-level interfaces, we usually write low-level operations on linked structures directly in order to clearly expose the essential details of our algorithms and data structures. We shall see many examples in Chapter 4.

By adding more links, we can add the capability to move backward through a linked list. For example, we can support the operation "find the item *before* a given item" by using a *doubly linked list* in which we maintain two links for each node: one (prev) to the item before, and another (next) to the item after. With dummy nodes or a circular list, we can ensure that x, x.next.prev, and x.prev.next are the same for every node in a doubly linked list. Figures 3.11 and 3.12 show the basic link manipulations required to implement *remove, insert after*, and *insert before*, in a doubly linked list. Note that, for *remove*, we do not need extra information about the node before it (or the node after it) in the list, as we did for singly linked lists—that information is contained in the node itself.

Indeed, the primary significance of doubly linked lists is that they allow us to remove a node when the *only* information that we have about that node is a link to it. Typical situations are when the link is passed as an parameter in a method invocation, and when the node has other links and is also part of some other data structure. Providing this extra capability doubles the space needed for links in each node and doubles the number of link manipulations per basic operation, so doubly linked lists are not normally used unless specifically called for. We defer considering detailed implementations to a few specific situations where we have such a need—for example, in Section 9.5.

We use linked lists throughout this book, first for basic ADT implementations (see Chapter 4), then as components in more complex data structures. For many programmers, linked lists provide the first exposure to an abstract data structure that is under their direct control. They represent an essential tool for our use in developing the high-level abstract data structures that we need for a host of important problems, as we shall see.

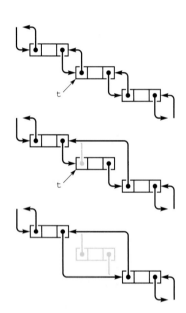

Figure 3.11
Deletion in a doubly linked list

In a doubly linked list, a reference to a node is sufficient information for us to be able to remove it, as diagrammed here. Given t, we set t.next.prev *to* t.prev *(center)and* t.prev.next *to* t.next *(bottom).*

Exercises

▷ **3.35** Write a method that moves the largest item on a given list to be the final node on the list.

3.36 Write a method that moves the smallest item on a given list to be the first node on the list.

3.37 Write a method that rearranges a linked list to put the nodes in even positions after the nodes in odd positions in the list, preserving the relative order of both the evens and the odds.

3.38 Implement a code fragment for a linked list that exchanges the positions of the nodes after the nodes referenced by two given links t and u.

○ **3.39** Write a method that takes a link to a list as an parameter and returns a link to a copy of the list (a new list that contains the same items, in the same order).

3.40 Write a method that takes two parameters—a link to a list and an object with a method that takes a link as an parameter—and removes all items on the given list for which the method returns a nonzero value.

3.41 Solve Exercise 3.40, but make copies of the nodes that pass the test and return a link to a list containing those nodes, in the order that they appear in the original list.

3.42 Implement a version of Program 3.9 that uses a head node.

3.43 The create() method in Program 3.10 builds a list with the numbers in the nodes in the list appearing in the reverse of the order in which they appear in standard input. Give an implementation of that method that preserves the order.

3.44 Implement a version of Program 3.10 that does not use head nodes.

3.45 Implement a method that exchanges two given nodes on a doubly linked list.

○ **3.46** Give an entry for Table 3.1 for a list that is never empty, is referred to with a link to the first node, and for which the final node has a link to itself.

3.47 Give an entry for Table 3.1 for a circular list that has a dummy node, which serves as both head and tail.

3.5 Memory Allocation for Lists

An advantage of linked lists over arrays is that linked lists gracefully grow and shrink during their lifetime. In particular, their maximum size does not need to be known in advance. One important practical ramification of this observation is that we can have several data structures share the same space, without paying particular attention to their relative size at any time.

The crux of the matter is to consider what happens when we use new to instantiate an object that is to be used as a node on a list. How does the system decide which piece of memory to reserve for

Figure 3.12
Insertion in a doubly linked list

To insert a node into a doubly linked list, we need to set four references, whether we want to insert the new node after a given node (diagrammed here) or before a given node. We insert a given node t after another given node x by setting t.next to x.next and x.next.prev to t(center), and then setting x.next to t and t.prev to x (bottom).

that object? For example, when we remove a node from a list, it is one thing for us to rearrange the links so that the node is no longer hooked into the list, but what does the system do with the space that the node occupied? And how does the system recycle space such that it can always find space for a node when new is invoked and more space is needed? The mechanisms behind these questions provide another example of the utility of elementary list processing.

Some programming languages, such as C++, have an operator delete that is the counterpart to new. When we are done using a chunk of allocated memory in a C++ program, we invoke delete to inform the system that the chunk is available for later use. *Dynamic memory allocation* is the process of managing memory and responding to invocations of new and delete from client programs. In Java, we do not explicitly invoke a method to free memory, but the system still must do dynamic memory allocation.

When we are invoking new directly in applications such as Program 3.8 or Program 3.10, all the calls request memory blocks of the same size. This case is typical, and an alternate method of keeping track of memory available for allocation immediately suggests itself: Simply use a linked list! All nodes that are not on any list that is in use can be kept together on a single linked list. We refer to this list as the *free list*. When we need to allocate space for a node, we get it by *removing* it from the free list; when we remove a node from any of our lists, we dispose of it by *inserting* it onto the free list.

Program 3.13 is a class that implements the same interface as Program 3.11, but which does its own memory allocation for list nodes. Client programs do not refer to list nodes except by declaring variables of type Node and using them as parameters to methods defined in the interface. This program implements the same interface as Program 3.11 so that it can be used with a client such Program 3.12 (to compute the same result!) without changing the client code at all.

This implementation is not intended to be of practical use but rather to serve as a precise description of how a memory allocator might be built in a lower-level language where we could view the memory available as an array and provide clients with array indices (integers) as references to nodes, as in the example in Figure 3.8. Continuing this example, Figure 3.13 illustrates how the free list grows as nodes are freed, for Program 3.12. Program 3.13 is not a direct

Program 3.13 Circular-list class with memory allocation

This program gives an alternate implementation of the circular-list class
of Program 3.11 that illustrates a standard approach to allocating memory for fixed-size nodes. We create an array to hold all of the nodes,
then build a free list that is initialized to the maximum number of nodes
that our program will use, all linked together. When a client program
creates a node, we remove that node from the free list; when a client
program is finished with a node, we link that node in to the free list.

```
class CircularList
  {
    static class Node
      { int val; int next; }
    static Node M[];
    static int free, max = 10000;
    CircularList()
      {
        M = new Node[max+1];
        for (int i = 0; i < max; i++)
          { M[i] = new Node(); M[i].next = i+1; }
        M[max] = new Node(); M[max].next = 0;
        free = 0;
      }
    Node next(Node x)
      { return M[x.next]; }
    int val(Node x)
      { return x.val; }
    Node insert(Node x, int v)
      {
        int i = free; free = M[free].next;
        M[i].val = v;
        if (x == null) M[i].next = i;
        else { M[i].next = x.next;  x.next = i; }
        return M[i];
      }
    void remove(Node x)
      { int i = x.next; x.next = M[i].next;
        M[i].next = free; free = i;
      }
  }
```

Figure 3.13
Array representation of a linked list, with free list

This version of Figure 3.8 shows the result of maintaining a free list with the nodes deleted from the circular list, with the index of the first node on the free list given at the left. At the end of the process, the free list is a linked list containing all the items that were deleted. Following the links, starting at 1, we see the items in the order 2 9 6 3 4 7 1 5, which is the reverse of the order in which they were deleted.

implementation of this scenario because it works with an array of references to nodes, not an array of nodes. Regardless, all of this is hidden from the client program: the task of memory management is completely separate from the task of solving a problem like the Josephus problem.

In this case, maintaining the free list for fixed-size nodes is a trivial task, given the basic operations for inserting nodes onto and deleting nodes from a list. The general-purpose memory allocator in the Java environment is much more complex than is suggested by this simple example. The implementation of new is not as simple as is indicated by Program 3.13, and finding unreferenced nodes to put on the free list (a process known as *garbage collection*) is a significant part of the computational burden. One reason that new is more complicated is that it has to handle storage-allocation requests for nodes of varying sizes, ranging from tiny to huge. Several clever storage management algorithms have been developed to do memory management and garbage collection; in Java, the system implements these.

Programs that can take advantage of specialized knowledge about an application often are more efficient than general-purpose programs for the same task. Memory allocation is no exception to this maxim. An algorithm that has to handle storage requests of varying sizes cannot know that we are always going to be making requests for blocks of one fixed size, and it therefore cannot take advantage of that fact. Paradoxically, another reason to avoid general-purpose library methods is that doing so makes programs more portable—we can protect ourselves against unexpected performance changes when the library changes or when we move to a different system. Many programmers have found that using a simple memory allocator like the one illustrated in Program 3.13 is an effective way to develop efficient and portable programs that use linked lists. This approach applies to a number of the algorithms that we will consider throughout this book, which make similar kinds of demands on the memory-management system. That said, we shall use the standard Java new operator to create objects and leave memory management and garbage collection to the Java system throughout the rest of the book.

Exercises

○ **3.48** Write a method that removes all the nodes on a circular list, given a reference to one of its nodes.

▷ **3.49** Write a program that removes the nodes in positions that are divisible by 5 in a circular list (the fifth, tenth, fifteenth, and so forth), starting at a given node.

○ **3.50** Write a program that removes the nodes in even positions in a circular list (the second, fourth, sixth, and so forth), starting at a given node.

3.51 Run empirical studies comparing the running times of the circular-list implementations in Program 3.11 and in Program 3.13 for Program 3.12 with $M = 2$ and $N = 10^3, 10^4, 10^5,$ and 10^6.

3.52 Instrument Program 3.13 to provide a trace such as Figure 3.13.

○ **3.53** Suppose that you have a set of nodes with no null links (each node refers to itself or to some other node in the set). Prove that you ultimately get into a cycle if you start at any given node and follow links.

● **3.54** Under the conditions of Exercise 3.53, write a code fragment that, given a link to a node, finds the number of different nodes that it ultimately reaches by following links from that node, *without* modifying any nodes. Do not use more than a constant amount of extra memory space.

●● **3.55** Under the conditions of Exercise 3.54, write a method that determines whether or not two given links, if followed, eventually end up on the same cycle.

3.6 Strings

In C and some other languages, the term *string* refers to a variable-length array of characters, defined by a starting point and by a string-termination character marking the end. Programmers use library functions to process strings and also work directly with the low-level representation. In Java, strings are a higher-level abstraction with built-in language support whose representation is hidden. To work at a lower level of abstraction, programmers convert strings to concrete representations such as arrays of characters and back. In this section, we consider some examples that illustrate these points.

Strings are valuable data structures, for two basic reasons. First, many computing applications involve processing textual data, which can be represented directly with strings. Second, many computer systems provide direct and efficient access to *bytes* of memory, which correspond directly to characters in strings. That is, in a great many situations, the string abstraction matches needs of the application to the capabilities of the machine.

The abstract notion of a sequence of characters could be implemented in many ways. For example, we could use a linked list. That choice would exact a cost of one reference per character, but could make more efficient operations such as concatenating together two long strings to make a third. Many algorithms are based upon the concrete array-based implementation of C-style strings, but many others are also amenable to the other representations. Generally, we assume that we can perform the following two operations in constant time:

- Index a string (access its kth character for a given k)
- Determine the number of characters in a string

We make these assumptions despite the fact that the first does not hold for strings represented as linked lists; the second does not hold for C-style strings; and we can have no guarantee that either will hold for Java strings, because their representation is hidden. In cases where performance is critical or an algorithm is best expressed using a particular representation, we can usually convert to a given representation without much difficulty. We return to the topic of representing strings (in considerable detail) at the beginning of Part 6, which is entirely devoted to string processing.

One of the most important operations that we perform on strings is the *compare* operation, which tells us which of two strings would appear first in the dictionary. This operation is provided in the compareTo method in the String class; but for purposes of discussion, we assume an idealized dictionary (since the actual rules for strings that contain punctuation, uppercase and lowercase letters, numbers, and so forth are rather complex) and compare strings character-by-character, from beginning to end. This ordering is called *lexicographic order*. We also use the compare method to tell whether strings are equal—by convention, the compare method returns a negative number if the first parameter string appears before the second in the dictionary, returns 0 if they are equal, and returns a positive number if the first appears after the second in lexicographic order. It is critical to take note that doing equality testing is *not* the same as determining whether two string *references* are equal—if two string referencess are equal, then so are the referenced strings (they are the *same* string), but we also could have different string references that point to equal strings (identical sequences of characters). Numerous applications involve storing

---

Program 3.14 String search

This method discovers all occurrences of the pattern string given as its
first parameter in the (presumably much larger) text string given as its
second parameter.

For each starting position i in the text, we try matching the substring starting at that position with the pattern, testing for equality
character by character. Whenever we reach the end of p successfully, we
increment the count of the number of occurrences of the pattern in the
text.

```
static int countMatches(String p, String s)
  {
    int cnt = 0, M = p.length(), N = s.length();
    if (M > N) return 0;
    for (int i = 0; i < N; i++)
      { int j;
        for (j = 0; j < M; j++)
          if (s.charAt(i+j) != p.charAt(j)) break;
        if (j == p.length()) cnt++;
      }
    return cnt;
  }
```

---

information as strings, then processing or accessing that information
by comparing the strings, so the compare operation is a particularly
critical one.

Program 3.14 is an implementation of a simple string-processing
task, which counts the number of occurences of a short pattern string
within a long text string. Several sophisticated algorithms have been
developed for this task (see Chapter 23), but this simple one illustrates
several of the basic facilities available for processing strings in Java. In
practice, as we shall see, we are normally more interested in variations
of this program that tell us where in the text the matches occur (see
Exercises 3.56 and 3.57).

String processing provides a convincing example of the need to
be knowledgeable about the performance of library methods. Consider an implementation where determining the length of a string takes
time proportional to the length of the string, as it does in C-style
strings. Ignoring this fact can lead to severe performance problems.

For example, if we have such a length method and we code a for loop with

```
for (i = 0; i < s.length(); i++)
```

then the time required is proportional to at least the *square* of the length of s, no matter what code is in the body of the loop! This cost can be considerable, even prohibitive: Running such code to check whether this book (which has more than 1 million characters) contains a certain word would require trillions of instructions. Problems such as this one are difficult to detect because a program might work fine when we are debugging it for small strings, but then slow down or even never finish when it goes into production. Moreover, we can avoid such problems only if we know about them—we have no way of knowing if some remote or future Java user will encounter a slow length method, because the Java string representation is hidden from us.

This kind of error is called a *performance bug*, because the code can be verified to be correct, but it does not perform as efficiently as we (implicitly) expect. Before we can even begin the study of efficient algorithms, we must be certain to have eliminated performance bugs of this type. Although built-in language support and standard libraries have many virtues, we must be wary of the dangers of using them for simple methods of this kind. In this particular case, there is not much to worry about, because typical Java implementations have source code which we can examine to check assumptions about performance, and they also typically have constant-time string indexing and length methods.

Java strings are *immutable*—they cannot be changed. When we use the + operator to concatenate two strings, we create a new string with the result. Accordingly, when implementing algorithms that involve substantial changes to a String, we convert the string to an array of characters, perform the computation, and convert the resulting array of characters back to a String. This approach provides concise code with performance guarantees.

Program 3.15 is an example of such a computation which replaces sequences of blanks in a string by a single blank. Conceptually, we might think of implementing this by, every time we encounter a sequence of blanks, moving the tail of the string to the left to cover all but one of them. Indeed, the System library provides an arraycopy operation that we could use as the basis for such an implementation. We do

---

Program 3.15 Manipulating strings

This method returns a string that is the same as the string given as its parameter except that each sequence of blank characters is replaced with a single blank character. Since Java `String` objects cannot be changed, this program illustrates a typical approach that we use to manipulate strings: copy into a character array (using the `toCharArray` method from the `String` class), then change the character array, then create a new `String` with the result (using a `String` constructor).

The index N refers to the next character in the result: the main loop copies the next string character into `a[N]` if it is not a blank or if `a[N-1]` is not a blank.

```
static String squeeze(String s)
  {
    char[] a = s.toCharArray();
    int N = 1;
    for (int i = 1; i < a.length; i++)
      {
        a[N] = a[i];
        if (a[N] != ' ') N++;
        else if (a[N-1] != ' ') N++;
      }
    return new String(a, 0, N);
  }
```

---

not use this approach because it could be very slow: for example, if we have a huge string with plenty of blanks, the running time approaches the *product* of the length of the string and the number of sequences of blanks, which is excessive and perhaps prohibitive. By contrast, the implementation in Program 3.15 runs in time proportional to the length of the string.

Memory allocation for strings is typically more difficult than for linked lists because strings vary in size; but again, the Java system takes care of all the details. Indeed, a fully general mechanism to reserve space for strings is neither more nor less than the general memory allocation mechanism required for all Java objects. As mentioned in Section 3.6, various algorithms, whose performance characteristics are system and machine dependent, have been developed for this problem. Often, memory allocation is a less severe problem when we are working with strings than it might first appear, because we often work with *references* to the strings, rather than with the characters themselves.

Exercises

▷ **3.56** Modify Program 3.14 to print out all character positions in the text where a substring is found that matches the pattern.

▷ **3.57** Modify Program 3.14 to return a linked list with all the character positions in the text where a substring is found that matches the pattern.

▷ **3.58** Write a method that takes a string as an parameter and prints out a table giving, for each character that occurs in the string, the character and its frequency of occurrence.

▷ **3.59** Write a method that checks whether a given string is a palindrome (reads the same backward or forward), ignoring blanks. For example, your program should report success for the string if i had a hifi.

3.60 Write a method that takes a string as a parameter and reads a sequence of words (sequences of characters separated by blank space) from standard input, printing out those that appear as substrings somewhere in the parameter string.

3.61 Write a method that takes a string and a character as parameters and returns a string that is the result of removing all occurrences of the character from the string. Your implementation should run in time proportional to the length of the string.

○ **3.62** Write an efficient method that finds the length of the longest sequence of blanks in a given string, examining as few characters in the string as possible. *Hint*: Your program should become faster as the length of the sequence of blanks increases.

3.63 Write a version of Program 3.15 that, instead of a character array, uses an interface that supports just two methods: one that returns the next character in a string, and another that appends a character to a string.

3.64 Implement your interface from Exercise 3.63 using a character array representation, and test it with your client program from Exercise 3.63.

3.65 Implement your interface from Exercise 3.63 using a linked-list representation, and test it with your client program from Exercise 3.63.

3.7 Compound Data Structures

Arrays, linked lists, and strings all provide simple ways to structure data sequentially. They provide a first level of abstraction that we can use to group objects in ways amenable to processing the objects efficiently. Having settled on these abstractions, we can use them in a hierarchical fashion to build up more complex structures. We can contemplate arrays of arrays, arrays of lists, arrays of strings, and so forth. In this section, we consider examples of such structures.

In the same way that one-dimensional arrays correspond to vectors, *two-dimensional* arrays, with two indices, correspond to *matrices*, and are widely used in mathematical computations. For example, we would use the Java code double[][] c = new double[N][N]; to declare that we are going to use a two-dimensional array c to represent an N-by-N matrix. Then we might use the following code to set all of c's entries to 0.0:

```
for (i = 0; i < N; i++)
  for (j = 0; j < N; j++)
    c[i][j] = 0.0;
```

With similar representations for two other matrices, we then might use the following code to multiply a and b, leaving the result in c.

```
for (i = 0; i < N; i++)
  for (j = 0; j < N; j++)
    for (k = 0; k < N; k++)
      c[i][j] += a[i][k]*b[k][j];
```

We frequently encounter mathematical computations like this one that are naturally expressed in terms of multidimensional arrays.

Beyond mathematical applications, a familiar way to structure information is to use a table of numbers organized into rows and columns. A table of students' grades in a course might have one row for each student and one column for each assignment. Such a table would be represented as a two-dimensional array with one index for the row and one for the column. If we were to have 100 students and 10 assignments, we would write grades[100][10] to declare the array, and then refer to the ith student's grade on the jth assignment as grade[i][j]. To compute the average grade on an assignment, we sum together the elements in a column and divide by the number of rows; to compute a particular student's average grade in the course, we sum together the elements in a row and divide by the number of columns, and so forth. Two-dimensional arrays are widely used in applications of this type. On a computer, it is often convenient and straightforward to use more than two dimensions. For example, an instructor might use a third index to keep student-grade tables for a sequence of years.

Figure 3.14
String sort

When processing strings, we work with references into a system buffer that contains the string objects (top). The string representation is hidden in Java, so here we show a stylized representation that consists of the length followed by a character array that contains the strings' characters. To manipulate the strings, programs move their references but do not change the string characters. For example, a sort method would rearrange the references such that accessing them in order would give the strings in alphabetical (lexicographic) order.

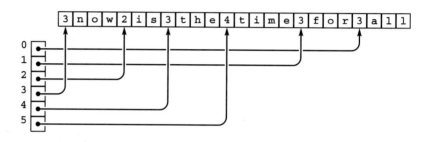

Two-dimensional arrays are a notational convenience, as the numbers are ultimately stored in the computer memory, which is essentially a one-dimensional array. In many programming environments, two-dimensional arrays are stored in *row-major order* in a one-dimensional array: In an array a[M][N], the first N positions would be occupied by the first row (elements a[0][0] through a[0][N-1]), the second N positions by the second row (elements a[1][0] through a[1][N-1]), and so forth. With row-major order, the final line in the matrix-multiplication code in the previous paragraph is precisely equivalent to

```
c[N*i+j] = a[N*i+k]*b[N*k+j]
```

The same scheme generalizes to provide a facility for arrays with more dimensions. In Java, multidimensional arrays may be implemented in a more general manner: we can define them to be compound data structures (arrays of arrays). This provides the flexibility, for example, to have an array of arrays that differ in size.

The basic facilities of Java make it easy to create and manipulate compound structures. For example, an array of strings in Java is an array of references to strings. When the strings are represented as

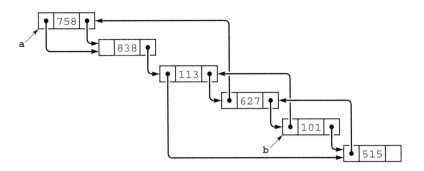

Figure 3.15
A multilist

We can link together nodes with two link fields in two independent lists, one using one link field, the other using the other link field. Here, the right link field links together nodes in one order (for example, this order could be the order in which the nodes were created) and the left link field links together nodes in a different order (for example, in this case, sorted order, perhaps the result of insertion sort using the left link field only). Following right links from a, we visit the nodes in the order created; following left links from b, we visit the nodes in sorted order.

arrays of characters, this representation is essentially an array of arrays that differ in size. By manipulating the references, we get the effect of manipulating the strings. For example, as illustrated in Figure 3.14, we then can get the effect of rearranging strings simply by rearranging the references in the array. To accomplish this sort in Java, we can use the Arrays.sort method in the Java utilities package or, as described in Chapter 6, any one of numerous algorithms from Part 2 of this book.

We have already encountered another use of arrays of strings: the args array that is used to pass parameter strings to main in Java programs. The system creates a string for each string in the command line typed by the user and passes to main an array of references to those strings. We use conversion methods to calculate numbers corresponding to some parameters; we use other parameters as strings, directly.

We can also build compound data structures exclusively with links. Figure 3.15 shows an example of a *multilist*, where nodes have multiple link fields and belong to independently maintained linked lists. In algorithm design, we often use more than one link to build up complex data structures, but in such a way that they are used to allow us to process them efficiently. For example, a doubly linked list is a multilist that satisfies the constraint that x.l.r and x.r.l are both equal to x. We shall examine a much more important data structure with two links per node in Chapter 5.

If a multidimensional matrix is *sparse* (relatively few of the entries are nonzero), then we might use a multilist rather than a multidimensional array to represent it. We could use one node for each value in the matrix and one link for each dimension, with the link pointing to the next item in that dimension. This arrangement reduces the storage required from the product of the maximum indices in the dimensions to be proportional to the number of nonzero entries, but increases the time required for many algorithms, because they have to traverse links to access individual elements.

To see more examples of compound data structures and to highlight the distinction between indexed and linked data structures, we next consider data structures for representing graphs. A *graph* is a fundamental combinatorial object that is defined simply as a set of objects (called *vertices*) and a set of connections among the vertices (called *edges*). We have already encountered graphs, in the connectivity problem of Chapter 1.

We assume that a graph with V vertices and E edges is defined by a set of E pairs of integers between 0 and V-1. That is, we assume that the vertices are labeled with the integers 0, 1, ..., V-1, and that the edges are specified as pairs of vertices. As in Chapter 1 we take the pair i-j as defining a connection between i and j and thus having the same meaning as the pair j-i. Graphs that comprise such edges are called *undirected* graphs. We shall consider other types of graphs in Part 7.

One straightforward method for representing a graph is to use a two-dimensional array, called an *adjacency matrix*. With an adjacency matrix, we can determine immediately whether or not there is an edge from vertex i to vertex j, just by checking whether the entry at row i and column j of the matrix is true. For the undirected graphs that we are considering, if the entry in row i and column j is true, then so must be the entry in row j and column i—the matrix is symmetric. Figure 3.16 shows an example of an adjacency matrix for an undirected graph; Program 3.16 shows how we can create an adjacency matrix, given a sequence of edges as input.

Another straightforward method for representing a graph is to use an array of linked lists, called *adjacency lists*. We keep a linked list for each vertex, with a node for each vertex connected to that vertex. For the undirected graphs that we are considering, if there is a node for j in i's list, then there must be a node for i in j's list. Figure 3.17 shows an example of the adjacency-lists representation of an undirected graph; Program 3.17 shows how we can create an

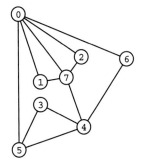

Program 3.16 Adjacency-matrix graph representation

This program reads a set of edges that define an undirected graph and builds an adjacency-matrix representation for the graph, setting a[i][j] and a[j][i] to true if there is an edge from i to j or j to i in the graph, or to false if there is no such edge.

```
class AdjacencyMatrix
  {
    public static void main(String[] args)
      { int V = Integer.parseInt(args[0]);
        int E = Integer.parseInt(args[1]);
        boolean adj[][] = new boolean[V][V];
        for (int i = 0; i < V; i++)
          for (int j = 0; j < V; j++)
            adj[i][j] = false;
        for (int i = 0; i < V; i++)
          adj[i][i] = true;
        for (In.init(); !In.empty() ;)
          {
            int i = In.getInt(), j = In.getInt();
            adj[i][j] = true; adj[j][i] = true;
          }

      }
  }
```

	0	1	2	3	4	5	6	7
0	1	1	1	0	0	1	1	1
1	1	1	0	0	0	0	0	1
2	1	0	1	0	0	0	0	1
3	0	0	1	1	1	0	0	0
4	0	0	0	1	1	1	1	0
5	1	0	0	1	1	1	1	0
6	1	0	0	0	1	0	1	0
7	1	1	1	0	1	0	0	1

Figure 3.16
Graph with adjacency-matrix representation

A graph is a set of vertices and a set of edges connecting the vertices. For simplicity, we assign indices (nonnegative integers, consecutively, starting at 0) to the vertices. An adjacency matrix is a two-dimensional array of boolean values where we represent a graph by putting in row i and column j true *if there is an edge from vertex i to vertex j and* false *otherwise (in the diagram, we represent* true *with 1 and* false *with 0). The array is symmetric about the diagonal. By convention, we assign* true *values on the diagonal (each vertex is connected to itself). For example, the sixth row (and the sixth column) says that vertex 6 is connected to vertices 0, 4, and 6.*

adjacency-lists representation of a graph, given a sequence of edges as input.

Both graph representations are arrays of simpler data structures—one for each vertex describing the edges incident on that vertex. For an adjacency matrix, the simpler data structure is implemented as an indexed array; for an adjacency list, it is implemented as a linked list.

Thus, we face straightforward space tradeoffs when we represent a graph. The adjacency matrix uses space proportional to V^2; the adjacency lists use space proportional to $V + E$. If there are few edges (such a graph is said to be *sparse*), then the adjacency-lists representation uses far less space; if most pairs of vertices are connected by edges (such a graph is said to be *dense*), the adjacency-matrix representation

Figure 3.17
Adjacency-lists representation of a graph

This representation of the graph in Figure 3.16 uses an array of lists. The space required is proportional to the number of nodes plus the number of edges. To find the indices of the vertices connected to a given vertex i, we look at the ith position in an array, which contains a reference to a linked list containing one node for each vertex connected to i.

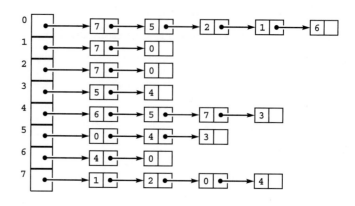

might be preferable, because it involves no links. Some algorithms will be more efficient with the adjacency-matrix representation, because it allows the question "is there an edge between vertex i and vertex j?" to be answered in constant time; other algorithms will be more efficient with the adjacency-lists representation, because it allows us to process all the edges in a graph in time proportional to $V + E$, rather than to V^2. We see a specific example of this tradeoff in Section 5.8.

Both the adjacency-matrix and the adjacency-lists graph representations can be extended straightforwardly to handle other types of graphs (see, for example, Exercise 3.74). They serve as the basis for most of the graph-processing algorithms that we shall consider in Part 7.

To conclude this chapter, we consider an example that shows the use of compound data structures to provide an efficient solution to the simple geometric problem that we considered in Section 3.2. Given d, we want to know how many pairs from a set of N points in the unit square can be connected by a straight line of length less than d. Program 3.18 uses a two-dimensional array of linked lists to improve the running time of Program 3.7 by a factor of about $1/d^2$ when N is sufficiently large. It divides the unit square up into a grid of equal-sized smaller squares. Then, for each square, it builds a linked list of all the points that fall into that square. The two-dimensional array provides the capability to access immediately the set of points close to a given point; the linked lists provide the flexibility to store the points where

---

Program 3.17 Adjacency-lists graph representation

This program reads a set of edges that define a graph and builds an adjacency-matrix representation for the graph. An adjacency list for a graph is an array of lists, one for each vertex, where the *j*th list contains a linked list of the nodes connected to the *j*th vertex.

```
class AdjacencyLists
  {
    static class Node
      { int v; Node next;
        Node (int v, Node t)
          { this.v = v; next = t; }
      }
    public static void main(String[] args)
      { int V = Integer.parseInt(args[0]);
        int E = Integer.parseInt(args[1]);
        Node adj[] = new Node[V];
        for (int i = 0; i < V; i++) adj[i] = null;
        for (In.init(); !In.empty() ;)
          {
            int i = In.getInt(), j = In.getInt();
            adj[j] = new Node(i, adj[j]);
            adj[i] = new Node(j, adj[i]);
          }
      }
  }
```

---

they may fall without our having to know ahead of time how many points fall into each grid square.

The space used by Program 3.18 is proportional to $1/d^2 + N$, but the running time is $O(d^2 N^2)$, which is a substantial improvement over the brute-force algorithm of Program 3.7 for small d. For example, with $N = 10^6$ and $d = 0.001$, we can solve the problem in time and space that is effectively linear, whereas the brute-force algorithm would require a prohibitive amount of time. We can use this data structure as the basis for solving many other geometric problems, as well. For example, combined with a union-find algorithm from Chapter 1, it gives a near-linear algorithm for determining whether a set of

Program 3.18 A two-dimensional array of lists

This program illustrates the effectiveness of proper data-structure choice, for the geometric computation of Program 3.7. It divides the unit square into a grid and maintains a two-dimensional array of linked lists, with one list corresponding to each grid square. The grid is chosen to be sufficiently fine that all points within distance d of any given point are either in the same grid square or an adjacent one.

```
class ClosePoints
  {
    static class Node
      { Point p; Node next;
        Node(Point x, Node t) { p = x; next = t; }
      }
    static int G, cnt = 0;
    static double d;
    static Node[][] g;
    static void gridInsert(Point p)
      { int X = (int)(p.x*G)+1, Y = (int)(p.y*G)+1;
        Node s, t = new Node(p, g[X][Y]);
        for (int i = X-1; i <= X+1; i++)
          for (int j = Y-1; j <= Y+1; j++)
            for (s = g[i][j]; s != null; s = s.next)
              if (s.p.distance(t.p) < d) cnt++;
        g[X][Y] = t;
      }
    public static void main(String[] args)
      { int i, N = Integer.parseInt(args[0]);
        d = Double.parseDouble(args[1]);
        G = (int) (1.0/d);
        g = new Node[G+2][G+2];
        for (i = 0; i < G+2; i++)
          for (int j = 0; j < G+2; j++)
            g[i][j] = null;
        for (i = 0; i < N; i++)
          gridInsert(new Point());
        Out.print(cnt + " pairs ");
        Out.println("closer than " + d);
      }
  }
```

N random points in the plane can be connected together with lines of length d—a fundamental problem of interest in networking and circuit design.

As suggested by the examples that we have seen in this section, there is no end to the level of complexity that we can build up from the basic abstract constructs that we can use to structure data of differing types into objects and sequence the objects into compound objects, either implicitly or with explicit links. These examples still leave us one step away from full generality in structuring data, as we shall see in Chapter 5. Before taking that step, however, we shall consider the important abstract data structures that we can build with linked lists and arrays—basic tools that will help us in developing the next level of generality.

Exercises

3.66 Extend Program 3.18 (and Program 3.2) to *three* dimensions so that it finds the number of pairs of N randomly generated points in the unit cube that can be connected by a straight line of length less than d.

3.67 Write a program that reads strings from standard input and prints them out in sorted order, taking the number of strings to be sorted from the command line.

3.68 Write a program to fill in a two-dimensional array of boolean values by setting a[i][j] to true if the greatest common divisor of i and j is 1, and to false otherwise.

3.69 Use Program 3.18 in conjunction with Program 1.4 to develop an efficient program that can determine whether a set of N points can be connected with edges of length less than d.

3.70 Write a program to convert a sparse matrix from a two-dimensional array to a multilist with nodes for only nonzero values.

• **3.71** Implement matrix multiplication for matrices represented with multilists.

▷ **3.72** Show the adjacency matrix that is built by Program 3.16 given the input pairs 0-2, 1-4, 2-5, 3-6, 0-4, 6-0, and 1-3.

▷ **3.73** Show the adjacency lists that are built by Program 3.17 given the input pairs 0-2, 1-4, 2-5, 3-6, 0-4, 6-0, and 1-3.

○ **3.74** A *directed* graph is one where vertex connections have orientations: edges go *from* one vertex *to* another. Do Exercises 3.72 and 3.73 under the assumption that the input pairs represent a directed graph, with i-j signifying that there is an edge from i to j. Also, draw the graph, using arrows to indicate edge orientations.

○ **3.75** Write a method that uses the adjacency matrix of a graph to calculate, given vertices a and b, the number of vertices c with the property that there is an edge from a to c and from c to b.

○ **3.76** Answer Exercise 3.75, but use adjacency lists.

Abstract Data Types

D EVELOPING ABSTRACT MODELS for our data and for the
ways in which our programs process those data is an essential
ingredient in the process of solving problems with a computer. We see
examples of this principle at a low level in everyday programming (for
example, when we use arrays and linked lists, as discussed in Chapter 3) and at a high level in problem-solving (as we saw in Chapter 1,
when we used union–find forests to solve the connectivity problem).
In this chapter, we consider *abstract data types (ADTs)*, which allow
us to build programs that use high-level abstractions. With abstract
data types, we can separate the conceptual transformations that our
programs perform on our data from any particular data-structure representation and algorithm implementation.

All computer systems are based on *layers of abstraction*: We
adopt the abstract model of a bit that can take on a binary 0–1 value
from certain physical properties of silicon and other materials; then
we adopt the abstract model of a machine from dynamic properties of
the values of a certain set of bits; then we adopt the abstract model
of a programming language that we realize by controlling the machine
with a machine-language program; then we adopt the abstract notion
of an algorithm implemented as a Java language program. Abstract
data types allow us to take this process further to develop abstract
mechanisms for certain computational tasks at a higher level than
provided by the Java system, to develop application-specific abstract
mechanisms that are suitable for solving problems in numerous applications areas, and to build higher-level abstract mechanisms that use

these basic mechanisms. Abstract data types give us an ever-expanding set of tools that we can use to attack new problems.

On the one hand, our use of abstract mechanisms frees us from detailed concern about how they are implemented; on the other hand, when performance matters in a program, we need to be cognizant of the costs of basic operations. We use many basic abstractions that are built into the computer hardware and provide the basis for machine instructions; we implement others in software; and we use still others that are provided in previously written systems software. Often we build higher-level abstract mechanisms in terms of more primitive ones. The same basic principle holds at all levels: We want to identify the critical operations in our programs and the critical characteristics of our data, to define both precisely at an abstract level, and to develop efficient concrete mechanisms to support them. We consider many examples of this principle in this chapter.

To develop a new layer of abstraction, we need to *define* the abstract objects that we want to manipulate and the operations that we perform on them; we need to *represent* the data in some data structure and to *implement* the operations; and (the point of the exercise) we want to ensure that the objects are convenient to *use* to solve an applications problem. Moreover, we want to *separate* the client from the implementation so that a single client can use multiple implementations and so that a single implementation can be used by many clients, without having to change any code. In Java systems, this concept is familiar: the Java virtual machine is a layer of abstraction that separates Java programs from virtual machine implementations so that we know that we can run a Java program on a variety of different computers without having to change any code. In this chapter, we consider how to adapt the basic Java class mechanism to achieve this same kind of separation in layers of abstraction built with Java code.

Definition 4.1 *An* **abstract data type** (ADT) *is a data type (a set of values and a collection of operations on those values) that is accessed only through an* **interface**. *We refer to a program that uses an ADT as a* **client**, *and a program that specifies the data type as an* **implementation**.

The key distinction that makes a data type abstract is drawn by the word *only*: with an ADT, client programs do not access any data values except through the operations provided in the interface. The representation of the data and the methods that implement the operations are in the implementation and are completely separated from the client, by the interface. We say that the interface is *opaque*: the client cannot see the implementation through the interface. In Java programs, we normally draw a slightly finer distinction, because the simplest way to set up an interface involves including the data representation in the interface but specifying that client programs are not allowed to access data directly. That is, client programmers may know the data representation, but they have no way to *use* it.

As an example, we start with the data type for points (Program 3.2) that we considered in Section 3.1, which explicitly declares that points are represented as classes with pairs of floating-point numbers, with data fields named x and y. Indeed, this use of data types is common in large software systems: we develop a set of conventions for how data is to be represented (and define a number of associated operations) and make those conventions available in an interface for use by client programs that comprise a large system. The data type ensures that all parts of the system are in agreement on the representation of core system-wide data structures. While valuable, this strategy has a flaw: if we need to *change* the data representation, we then need to change all the client programs. Program 3.2 again provides a simple example: one reason for developing the data type is to make it convenient for client programs to manipulate points, and we expect that clients will access the individual coordinates when needed. But we cannot change to a different representation (polar coordinates, say, or three dimensions, or even different data types for the individual coordinates) without changing all the client programs.

Program 4.1 is a more elaborate version of Program 3.2 (which we can still use with Program 3.7) that includes two additional methods and some modifications to make it an ADT implementation. The key distinction that makes its data type abstract has to do with access to information, as specified by the keyword `private`. A *private* class member can be referred to only *within* the class; a member that is not *private* can be referred to by other classes. Private members can be either fields or methods: in Program 4.1 only the fields are private, but we shall see numerous examples of classes that use private methods as well.

Program 4.1 Point class implementation

This class defines a data type consisting of the set of values "pairs of floating-point numbers" (which are presumably interpreted as points in the Cartesian plane). The class includes eight methods: two constructors, two *accessor methods* that return the values of the data fields, two methods for converting to polar coordinates, a method for computing the distance to another `Point`, and a `toString` method. The data representation is `private` and can be accessed or modified only by the class methods, but the methods can be used by any client.

```
class Point
  {
    private double x, y;
    Point()
      { x = Math.random(); y = Math.random(); }
    Point(double x, double y)
      { this.x = x; this.y = y; }
    double x() { return x; }
    double y() { return y; }
    double r() { return Math.sqrt(x*x + y*y); }
    double theta() { return Math.atan2(y, x); }
    double distance(Point p)
      { double dx = this.x() - p.x();
        double dy = this.y() - p.y();
        return Math.sqrt(dx*dx + dy*dy);
      }
    public String toString()
      { return "(" + x + ", " + y + ")"; }
  }
```

For example, no client program that uses the `Point` class of Program 4.1 can refer directly to the fields p.x, q.y, and so forth (as can any client of the `Point` class of Program 3.2) because the x and y fields are private. All that a client *can* do is use the public methods to process points. Those methods do have direct access to the members of any object in the class. For example, when a client invokes the distance method in Program 4.1 with the call p.distance(q), the name x within the distance method refers to the x field in the point p (because distance was invoked as a member of the instance p), but the name p.x refers to the x field in the point q (because q is the actual parameter corresponding to the formal parameter p). We can also say this.x instead of x to eliminate possible ambiguity or confusion—the keyword this refers to the object for which a method is invoked.

Each member in a Java class has one of four possible access control states: private, protected, and public and no modifier (default). Informally, throughout this book we use the term *private* to mean private or protected and the term *public* to mean default or public. We do so solely for economy in presenting our programs: most of our class members have no access control modifier (default); those that need to be hidden are private; and some (like main and toString) are public so as to adhere to Java system conventions.

The two added methods x() and y() in Program 4.1 provide client programs with the capability to read the values of data fields (since they cannot access them directly). These methods do not modify the fields of the object on which they are called; they just provide their values. Such methods are known as *accessor methods*. We often include methods of this kind in Java classes. Note that we do not provide a way to change the values of the data fields once the object is constructed: objects that cannot be changed are said to be *immutable* and are common in Java. To define a different kind of Point that *can move* we could add a method move with the same code as the two-parameter constructor, which allows clients to change the values of the x and y fields.

Program 4.2 illustrates the fundamental reason that we go to the trouble of carefully defining ADTs: By not allowing clients to access directly the data representation, we are free to change it! In this case, we switch to polar coordinates to represent points, but any client program should perform the same computation with one implementation as with the other.

Why would we want to make such a change? The most common reason to do so is to improve the implementation. Suppose that we have a large system with numerous client programs using an ADT and we discover a bug in the implementation of one of the methods, which causes it to give an incorrect answer in some circumstances. We have no way of knowing how the existence of that bug affects clients, but we can go ahead and fix it without having to change the clients at all. Or, in the case of the Point class, perhaps we notice that clients use the r()

> **Program 4.2 Point class (alternate implementation)**
>
> This implementation of the data type for points uses polar coordinates for its internal representation. In principle, clients such as Programs 3.7 and 3.18 should be able to substitute this implementation for Program 4.1 without noticing the difference, except possibly for performance characteristics.
>
> ```
> class Point
>   {
>     private double r, theta;
>     Point()
>       { double x = Math.random(), y = Math.random();
>         this = new Point(x, y); }
>     Point(double x, double y)
>       { r = Math.sqrt(x*x + y*y);
>         theta = Math.atan2(y, x); }
>     double r() { return r; }
>     double theta() { return theta; }
>     double x() { return r*Math.cos(theta); }
>     double y() { return r*Math.sin(theta); }
>     double distance(Point p)
>       { double dx = x() - p.x();
>         double dy = y() - p.y();
>         return Math.sqrt(dx*dx + dy*dy);
>       }
>     public String toString()
>       { return "(" + x() + ", " + y() + ")"; }
>   }
> ```

method frequently and the other methods infrequently. Then we can improve performance for these clients by switching to Program 4.2. In this case, the performance gain is relatively modest, but we shall see many examples in this book where we can reap huge savings. Indeed, we will investigate many situations where the potential exists for performance gains that can vastly expand the scope of applicability of client programs, without having to change them at all.

For many applications, the ability to change implementations is a requirement. For example, suppose that we are developing software for a company that needs to process mailing lists of potential customers. With a Java class, we can define methods that allow client programs to manipulate the data without directly accessing it. With an ADT, we instead provide methods that return the data of interest. For example, we might provide client programs with an interface defining operations such as *extract customer name* or *add customer record*. The most important implication of this arrangement is that we can use the same client programs even if we need to change the format used for the mailing lists. That is, we can change the data representation and the implementation of the methods that access the data without having to change the client programs.

We also can take advantage of the flexibility afforded by ADTs in implementing methods themselves—for example, since we use method invocations like `p.x()` instead of field references like `p.x` in the implementation of `distance` in Program 4.1 we do not have to change that code when we change the data representation. By making these methods private, we can give ourselves this flexibility even in classes where we do not want the client to have access to the data

How does the Java class concept relate to the client-interface-implementation paradigm and ADTs? It provides direct language support but is sufficiently general that there are a number of different approaches that we could take. We shall usually adopt a simple convention: *the signatures of the methods that are not private in a class comprise its interface*. In other words, *class members that are not part of its interface are private*. That is, we keep the data representation hidden, where it cannot be accessed by programs that use the class (client programs). All the client programs "know" about the class is the non-private information about its methods (name, type of return value, and types of parameters).

In this book, to emphasize the nature of the interface defined by a class, we will often consider interfaces *before* examining implementations. The essential point is that this arrangement makes it easy for us to consider other implementations, with different data representations and different implementations of the methods, and to test and compare implementations without changing the client programs at all. The convention that we use to define interfaces is illustrated in Program 4.3: we derive an interface definition from a class implementation by deleting the private members, the implementations of the

---

Program 4.3 Point ADT interface

By convention, we derive the interface associated with a class ADT implementation by removing the private members and by replacing methods with their signatures. This interface is derived in this way from Programs 4.1 and 4.2 (which implement the same interface). We can use different implementations that have the same interface without changing any code in the client programs that use the ADT.

```
class Point // ADT interface
  { // implementations and private members hidden
    Point()
    Point(double, double)
    double x()
    double y()
    double r()
    double theta()
    double distance(Point)
    public String toString()
  }
```

---

public methods, and the parameter names, leaving only the signatures of the public methods. Doing so for any two classes that implement the interface should result in the same interface. The order in which the method signatures appear might differ, but that order is immaterial. These interface definitions are not Java code, but each serves as a concise and complete description of the contract between clients and implementations that is the basis for an effective ADT design.

Our use of Java classes to implement ADTs with the convention that the public method signatures comprise the interface is not a perfect arrangement because interface and implementation are not completely separate, and we use a convention, not Java code, to define interfaces. In Section 4.6, we briefly discuss Java's interface facility, which does not fully support ADTs as we have defined them. For example, we cannot put constructors in a Java interface, so clients access constructors without going through the interface, which violates Definition 4.1.

Class data-type implementations of this sort are sometimes called *concrete data types*. This terminology is ironic because a data type that adheres to these conventions actually meets our definition of an *abstract* data type (Definition 4.1)—the distinction is a matter of precisely defining words like "access," "refer," and "specify," which is tricky business that we shall leave to programming-language theorists. Indeed, Definition 4.1 does not specify what an interface is or how the data type and the operations are to be described. This imprecision is necessary because specifying such information in full generality requires a formal mathematical language and eventually leads to difficult mathematical questions. This question is central in programming language design. We shall discuss the specification issue further after we consider examples of ADTs.

ADTs have emerged as an effective mechanism supporting *modular programming* as an organizing principle for large modern software systems. They provide a way to limit the size and complexity of the connections between (potentially complicated) algorithms and associated data structures and (a potentially large number of) programs that use the algorithms and data structures. This arrangement makes it easier to understand a large applications program as a whole. Moreover, unlike simple data types, ADTs provide the flexibility necessary to make it convenient to change or improve the fundamental data structures and algorithms in the system. Most important, the ADT interface defines a contract between users and implementors that provides a precise means of communicating what each can expect of the other.

With a carefully designed ADT, we can make use of the separation between client and implementations in many interesting ways. For example, we commonly use driver programs when developing or debugging ADT implementations. Similarly, we often use incomplete implementations of ADTs, called *stubs*, as placeholders while building systems in order to learn properties of clients.

We examine ADTs in detail in this chapter because they also play an important role in the study of data structures and algorithms. Indeed, the essential motivation behind the development of nearly all the algorithms that we consider in this book is to provide efficient implementations of the basic operations for certain fundamental ADTs that play a critical role in many computational tasks. Designing an ADT is only the first step in meeting the needs of applications programs—we also need to develop viable implementations of the associated operations and underlying data structures that enable them. Those tasks are the topic of this book. Moreover, we use abstract models directly to develop and to compare the performance characteristics of algorithms and data structures, as in the example in Chapter 1: Typically, we develop an applications program that uses an ADT to solve a problem, then develop multiple implementations of the ADT and compare their effectiveness. In this chapter, we consider this general process in detail, with numerous examples.

Java programmers use data types and ADTs regularly. At a low level, when we process integers using only the operations provided by Java for integers, we are essentially using a system-defined abstraction for integers. The integers could be represented and the operations implemented some other way on some new machine, but a program that uses only the operations specified for integers will work properly on the new machine. In this case, the various Java operations for integers constitute the interface, our programs are the clients, and the Java virtual machine provides the implementation. We can run our program on a different computer with, say, different representations for integers or floating-point numbers, without having to change our programs at all.

Most Java classes are examples of data-type implementations, though they exist in a more complex context than we have sketched and do not always conform completely to the standards outlined here. They allow us to not only use different implementations of the methods, but also base them upon different underlying data structures. Again, the key distinction that characterizes ADTs is that we can make such changes without modifying any client programs at all, because of the requirement that the data type be accessed *only* through the interface. In Java, we enforce this restriction by making `private` everything but the public methods that constitute the interface.

We shall see numerous examples throughout this chapter of using Java classes to build ADT implementations. After we have developed a feel for the concept, we shall return at the end of the chapter to a discussion of philosophical and practical implications.

Exercises

▷ **4.1** Suppose that we wish to modify Programs 3.7 and 4.1 to count the number of pairs of points that fall within a *square* of size d. First, show how to solve this problem by modifying the `distance` method in the implementation (so that the client does not have to be changed). Second, show how to solve this problem by changing the client to use the accessor methods in the implementation (so that the implementation does not have to be changed).

▷ **4.2** Give an implementation of the point interface (Program 4.3) for points with *three* coordinates.

4.3 Define two points to *coincide* if the distance between them is less than 10^{-6}. Add a method to the `Point` interface for testing whether two points coincide, then write a client program that takes an integer N from the command line and fills an array with N points, no two of which coincide.

○ **4.4** Change both implementations of `Point` (Programs 4.1 and 4.2) such that the no-parameter constructor creates a random point in the unit circle.

4.1 Collections of Items

The data structures that we use in applications often contain a great deal of information of various types, and certain pieces of information may belong to multiple independent data structures. For example, a file of personnel data may contain records with names, addresses, and various other pieces of information about employees; and each record may need to belong to one data structure for searching for particular employees, to another data structure for answering statistical queries, and so forth.

Despite this diversity and complexity, a large class of computing applications involve generic manipulation of data items and need access to the information associated with them for a limited number of specific reasons. ADTs provide a way for us to make explicit any assumptions about the operations that we perform on data items.

Many of the manipulations that are required are concerned with *collections* of items. We shall see that these manipulations are a natural outgrowth of basic computational procedures and are therefore needed in a broad variety of applications. Several of the fundamental algorithms that we consider in this book can be applied effectively to the task of building a layer of abstraction that can provide client programs with the ability to perform such manipulations efficiently. Thus, we shall consider in detail numerous ADTs that are associated with such manipulations. They define various operations on collections of items that are valid for many different types of items.

In particular, several of the data structures and algorithms that we consider in this book are used to implement fundamental ADTs comprising collections of abstract objects that are built up from just two operations:

- *insert* a new item into the collection.
- *remove* an item from the collection.

We refer to such ADTs as *generalized queues*. For convenience, we also typically include explicit operations to *construct* the data structure (constructors) and to *count* the number of items in the data structure (or just to test whether it is empty). We also might need an operation to *copy* the data structure (clone it); we shall discuss that in Section 4.9.

When we *insert* an item, our intent is clear, but which item do we get when we *remove* an item from the collection? Different ADTs for collections of items are characterized by different criteria for deciding which item to remove for the *remove* operation and by different conventions associated with the various criteria. Moreover, we shall encounter a number of other natural operations beyond *insert* and *remove*. Several of the algorithms and data structures that we consider in this book were designed to support efficient implementation of various subsets of these operations for various different *remove* criteria and other conventions. These ADTs are conceptually simple, used widely, and lie at the core of a great many computational tasks, so they deserve the careful attention that we pay them.

In this chapter, we consider several of these fundamental data structures, their properties, and examples of their application, while at the same time using them as examples to illustrate the basic mechanisms that we use to develop ADTs. In Section 4.2, we consider the *pushdown stack*, where the rule for removing an item is to remove the one that was most recently inserted. We consider applications of stacks in Section 4.3 and implementations in Section 4.4, including a specific approach to keeping the applications and implementations separate. After stepping back to consider the process of creating a new ADT, in the context of the union–find abstraction for the connectivity problem that we considered in Chapter 1, we return to collections of items, to consider FIFO and generalized queues (which differ from stacks on the abstract level only in that they involve using a different rule to remove items) and generalized queues where we disallow duplicate items.

As we saw in Chapter 3, arrays and linked lists provide basic mechanisms that allow us to *insert* and *remove* specified items. Indeed, linked lists and arrays are the underlying data structures for several of the implementations of generalized queues that we consider. As we know, the cost of insertion and deletion is dependent on the specific structure that we use and the specific item being inserted or removed. For a given ADT, our challenge is to choose a data structure that allows us to perform the required operations efficiently. In this chapter, we examine in detail several examples of ADTs for which linked lists and arrays provide appropriate solutions. ADTs that support more powerful operations require more sophisticated implementations, which are the prime impetus for many of the algorithms that we consider in this book.

Data types comprising collections of items (generalized queues) are a central object of study in computer science because they directly support a fundamental paradigm of computation. For a great many computations, we find ourselves in the position of having many objects with which to work, but being able to process only one object at a time. Therefore, we need to save the others while processing that one. This processing might involve examining some of the items already saved away or adding more to the collection, but operations of saving the items away and retrieving them according to some criterion are the basis of the computation. Many classical data structures and algorithms fit this mold, as we shall see.

4.2 Pushdown Stack ADT

Of the data types that support *insert* and *remove* for collections of items, the most important is called the *pushdown stack*.

A stack operates somewhat like a busy professor's "in" box: work piles up in a stack, and whenever the professor has a chance to get some work done, it comes off the top. A student's paper might well get stuck at the bottom of the stack for a day or two, but a conscientious professor might manage to get the stack emptied at the end of the week. As we shall see, computer programs are naturally organized in this way. They frequently postpone some tasks while doing others; moreover, they frequently need to return to the most

```
L           L
A           L A
*       A   L
S           L S
T           L S T
I           L S T I
*       I   L S T
N           L S T N
*       N   L S T
F           L S T F
I           L S T F I
R           L S T F I R
*       R   L S T F I
S           L S T F I S
T           L S T F I S T
*       T   L S T F I S
*       S   L S T F I
O           L S T F I O
U           L S T F I O U
*       U   L S T F I O
T           L S T F I O T
*       T   L S T F I O
*       O   L S T F I
*       I   L S T F
*       F   L S T
*       T   L S
*       S   L
*       L
```

Figure 4.1
Pushdown stack (LIFO queue) example

This list shows the result of the sequence of operations in the left column (top to bottom), where a letter denotes push *and an asterisk denotes* pop. *Each line displays the operation, the letter popped for* pop *operations, and the contents of the stack after the operation, in order from least recently inserted to most recently inserted, left to right.*

Program 4.4 Pushdown-stack ADT interface

Using the same convention that we used in Program 4.3, we define an ADT for a pushdown stack that contains integers with method signatures, so that the stack representation and any other implementation-dependent code can be kept private in implementations, thereby allowing us to change implementations without changing client code. The parameter to the Stack constructor specifies the maximum number of integers expected on the stack.

```
class intStack // ADT interface
  { // implementations and private members hidden
    intStack(int)
    int empty()
    void push(int)
    int pop()
  }
```

---

recently postponed task first. Thus, pushdown stacks appear as the fundamental data structure in many computational applications.

Definition 4.2 *A* **pushdown stack** *is an ADT that comprises two basic operations: insert (**push**) a new item, and remove (**pop**) the item that was most recently inserted.*

That is, when we speak of a *pushdown stack ADT*, we are referring to both a description of the *push* and *pop* operations that is sufficiently well specified that a client program can make use of them as well as to some implementation of the operations enforcing the rule that characterizes a pushdown stack: items are removed according to a *last-in, first-out (LIFO)* discipline.

Figure 4.1 shows how a sample stack evolves through a series of *push* and *pop* operations. Each *push* increases the size of the stack by 1, and each *pop* decreases the size of the stack by 1. In the figure, the items in the stack are listed in the order that they are put on the stack so that it is clear that the rightmost item in the list is the one at the top of the stack—the item that is to be returned if the next operation is *pop*. In an implementation, we are free to organize the items any way that we want, as long as we allow clients to maintain the illusion that the items are organized in this way.

As we have discussed, in order to write programs that use the pushdown stack abstraction, we need first to define the interface. To this end, our convention is to declare a collection of public methods to be used in class implementations, as illustrated in Program 4.4. We keep all other class members `private`, so that Java will ensure that these methods are the only connection between client programs and implementations. This mechanism allows us to write programs that use these abstract operations. To enforce the abstraction, we use the class mechanism to hide the data structure and the implementation from the client. In Section 4.3, we consider examples of client programs that use the stack abstraction; in Section 4.4, we consider implementations.

The stack ADT interface of Program 4.4 defines stacks of integers, when we would like to be able to work with stacks of items of any type. Indeed, our example in Figure 4.1 uses stacks of characters, which would require that we define an interface like Program 4.4 for `charStack` classes where the parameter to push and the return value from pop are of type `char`. In order to separate our discussion of implementing and using stacks from our discussion of doing so in a generic way, we will defer discussion of the latter to Section 4.5.

In an ADT, the purpose of the interface is to serve as a contract between client and implementation. If both client and implementation use methods with the signatures in the interface, then we know that the calls in the client program and the method definitions in the implementation match. The interface otherwise contains no information about how the methods are to be implemented, or even how they are to behave. How can we explain what a stack is to a client program? For simple structures like stacks, one possibility is to exhibit the code, but this solution is clearly not effective in general. Most often, programmers resort to English-language descriptions in documentation that accompanies the code.

A rigorous treatment of this situation requires a full description, in some formal mathematical notation, of how the methods are supposed to behave. Such a description is sometimes called a *specification*. Developing a specification is generally a challenging task. It has to describe *any* program that implements the methods in a mathematical metalanguage, whereas we are used to specifying the behavior of methods with code written in a programming language. In practice, we describe behavior in English-language descriptions. Before getting drawn further into epistemological issues, we move on. In this book, we give detailed examples, English-language descriptions, and multiple implementations for most of the ADTs that we consider.

To emphasize that our specification of the pushdown stack ADT is sufficient information for us to write meaningful client programs, in Section 4.3 we consider (before thinking about any implementation) two client programs that use pushdown stacks.

Exercises

▷ **4.5**   A letter means *push* and an asterisk means *pop* in the sequence

$$E A S * Y * Q U E * * * S T * * * I O * N * * *.$$

Give the sequence of values returned by the *pop* operations.

4.6   Using the conventions of Exercise 4.5, give a way to insert asterisks in the sequence E A S Y so that the sequence of values returned by the *pop* operations is (*i*) E A S Y ; (*ii*) Y S A E ; (*iii*) A S Y E ; (*iv*) A Y E S ; or, in each instance, prove that no such sequence exists.

•• **4.7**   Given two sequences, give an algorithm for determining whether or not asterisks can be added to make the first produce the second, when interpreted as a sequence of stack operations in the sense of Exercise 4.6.

4.3 Examples of Stack ADT Clients

We shall see a great many applications of stacks in the chapters that follow. As an introductory example, we now consider the use of stacks for evaluating arithmetic expressions. For example, suppose that we need to find the value of a simple arithmetic expression involving multiplication and addition of integers, such as

```
5 * ( ( ( 9 + 8 ) * ( 4 * 6 ) ) + 7 )
```

The calculation involves saving intermediate results: For example, if we calculate 9 + 8 first, then we have to save the result 17 while, say, we compute 4 * 6. A pushdown stack is the ideal mechanism for saving intermediate results in such a calculation.

We begin by considering a simpler problem, where the expression that we need to evaluate is in a form where each operator appears *after* its two arguments, rather than between them. As we shall see, any arithmetic expression can be arranged in this form, which is called *postfix*, by contrast with *infix*, the customary way of writing arithmetic expressions. The postfix representation of the expression in the previous paragraph is

```
5 9 8 + 4 6 * * 7 + *
```

The reverse of postfix is called *prefix*, or *Polish notation* (because it was invented by the Polish logician Lukasiewicz).

In infix, we need parentheses to distinguish, for example,

```
5 * ( ( ( 9 + 8 ) * ( 4 * 6 ) ) + 7 )
```

from

```
( ( 5 * 9 ) + 8 ) * ( ( 4 * 6 ) + 7 )
```

but parentheses are unnecessary in postfix (or prefix). To see why, we can consider the following process for converting a postfix expression to an infix expression: We replace all occurrences of two operands followed by an operator by their infix equivalent (with parentheses) to indicate that the result can be considered to be an operand. That is, we replace any occurrence of a b * and a b + by (a * b) and (a + b), respectively. Then, we perform the same transformation on the resulting expression, continuing until all the operators have been processed. For our example, the transformation happens as follows:

```
5 9 8 + 4 6 * * 7 + *
5 ( 9 + 8 ) ( 4 * 6 ) * 7 + *
5 ( ( 9 + 8 ) * ( 4 * 6 ) ) 7 + *
5 ( ( ( 9 + 8 ) * ( 4 * 6 ) ) + 7 ) *
( 5 * ( ( ( 9 + 8 ) * ( 4 * 6 ) ) + 7 ) )
```

We can determine the operands associated with any operator in the postfix expression in this way, so no parentheses are necessary.

Alternatively, with the aid of a stack, we can actually perform the operations and evaluate any postfix expression, as illustrated in Figure 4.2. Moving from left to right, we interpret each operand as the command to "push the operand onto the stack," and each operator as the commands to "pop the two operands from the stack, perform the operation, and push the result." Program 4.5 is a Java implementation of this process.

Postfix notation and an associated pushdown stack give us a natural way to organize a series of computational procedures. Some calculators and some computing languages explicitly base their method

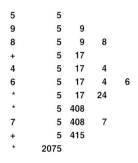

5	5		
9	5	9	
8	5	9	8
+	5	17	
4	5	17	4
6	5	17	4	6
*	5	17	24
*	5	408	
7	5	408	7
+	5	415	
*	2075		

**Figure 4.2
Evaluation of a postfix expression**

*This sequence shows the use of a stack to evaluate the postfix expression 5 9 8 + 4 6 * * 7 + * . Proceeding from left to right through the expression, if we encounter a number, we push it on the stack; and if we encounter an operator, we push the result of applying the operator to the top two numbers on the stack.*

Program 4.5 Postfix-expression evaluation

This pushdown-stack client reads any postfix expression involving multiplication and addition of integers, then evaluates the expression (saving intermediate results on a stack) and prints the computed result.
Operands are pushed onto the stack; operators are applied to the top
two entries popped from the stack, with the result pushed back onto the
stack.

   The program assumes that the integers and operators are delimited
by other characters of some kind (blanks, say), but does not check the
legality of the input at all. The final if statement and the while loop
perform a calculation similar to the Java Integer.parseInt method,
which converts from string to integer representation.

```
class Postfix
  {
    public static void main(String[] args)
      { char[] a = args[0].toCharArray();
        int N = a.length;
        intStack s = new intStack(N);
        for (int i = 0; i < N; i++)
          {
            if (a[i] == '+')
              s.push(s.pop() + s.pop());
            if (a[i] == '*')
              s.push(s.pop() * s.pop());
            if ((a[i] >= '0') && (a[i] <= '9'))
              s.push(0);
            while((a[i] >= '0') && (a[i] <= '9'))
              s.push(10*s.pop() + (a[i++]-'0'));
          }
        Out.println(s.pop() + "");
      }
  }
```

of calculation on postfix and stack operations—every operation pops
its arguments from the stack and returns its results to the stack.

   One example of such a language is the PostScript language, which
is used to print this book. It is a complete programming language
where programs are written in postfix and are interpreted with the

aid of an internal stack, precisely as in Program 4.5. Although we cannot cover all the aspects of the language here (*see reference section*), it is sufficiently simple that we can study some actual programs to appreciate the utility of the postfix notation and the pushdown-stack abstraction. For example, the string

```
5 9 8 add 4 6 mul mul 7 add mul
```

is a PostScript program! Programs in PostScript consist of operators (such as add and mul) and operands (such as integers). As we did in Program 4.5 we interpret a program by reading it from left to right: If we encounter an operand, we push it onto the stack; if we encounter an operator, we pop its operands (if any) from the stack and push the result (if any). Thus, the execution of this program is fully described by Figure 4.2: The program leaves the value 2075 on the stack.

PostScript has a number of primitive operators that serve as instructions to an abstract plotting device; we can also define our own operators, or functions, which are like methods in Java. These functions are invoked with arguments on the stack in the same way as any other function. For example, the PostScript code

```
0 0 moveto 144 hill 0 72 moveto 72 hill stroke
```

corresponds to the sequence of actions "call moveto with arguments 0 and 0, then call hill with argument 144," and so forth. Some operators refer directly to the stack itself. For example the operator dup duplicates the entry at the top of the stack so, for example, the PostScript code

```
144 dup 0 rlineto 60 rotate dup 0 rlineto
```

corresponds to the sequence of actions "call rlineto with arguments 144 and 0, then call rotate with argument 60, then call rlineto with arguments 144 and 0," and so forth. The PostScript program in Figure 4.3 defines and uses the function hill. Functions in PostScript are like macros: The sequence /hill { A } def makes the name hill equivalent to the operator sequence inside the braces. Figure 4.3 is an example of a PostScript program that defines a function and draws a simple diagram.

In the present context, our interest in PostScript is that this widely used programming language is based on the pushdown-stack abstraction. Indeed, many computers implement basic stack operations in hardware because they naturally implement a function-call

```
/hill {
    dup 0 rlineto
    60 rotate
    dup 0 rlineto
    -120 rotate
    dup 0 rlineto
    60 rotate
    dup 0 rlineto
    pop
  } def
0 0 moveto
144 hill
0 72 moveto
72 hill
stroke
```

Figure 4.3
Sample PostScript program

The diagram at the top was drawn by the PostScript program below it. The program is a postfix expression that uses the built-in functions moveto, rlineto, rotate, stroke and dup as well as the user-defined function hill (see text). The graphics commands are instructions to a plotting device: moveto instructs that device to go to the specified position on the page (coordinates are in points, which are $\frac{1}{72}$ inch); rlineto instructs it to move to the specified position in coordinates relative to its current position, adding the line it makes to its current path; rotate instructs it to turn left the specified number of degrees; and stroke instructs it to draw the path that it has traced.

(			
5	5		
*		*	
(		*	
(		*	
(		*	
9	9	*	
+		*	+
8	8	*	+
)	+	*	
*		*	*
(		*	*
4	4	*	*
*		*	*	*
6	6	*	*	*
)	*	*	*
)	*	*	
+		*	+
7	7	*	+
)	+	*	
)	*		

Figure 4.4
Conversion of an infix expression to postfix

This sequence shows the use of a stack to convert the infix expression (5*(((9+8)*(4*6))+7)) *to its postfix form* 5 9 8 + 4 6 * * 7 + * *. We proceed from left to right through the expression: If we encounter a number, we write it to the output; if we encounter a left parenthesis, we ignore it; if we encounter an operator, we push it on the stack; and if we encounter a right parenthesis, we write the operator at the top of the stack to the output.*

Program 4.6 Infix-to-postfix conversion

This program is another example of a pushdown-stack client. In this case, the stack contains characters. To convert (A+B) to the postfix form A B +, we ignore the left parenthesis, convert A to postfix, save the + on the stack, convert B to postfix, then, on encountering the right parenthesis, pop the stack and output the +.

```
class InfixToPostfix
  {
    public static void main(String[] args)
      { char[] a = args[0].toCharArray();
        int N = a.length;
        charStack s = new charStack(N);
        for (int i = 0; i < N; i++)
          {
            if (a[i] == ')')
              Out.print(s.pop() + " ");
            if ((a[i] == '+') || (a[i] == '*'))
              s.push(a[i]);
            if ((a[i] >= '0') && (a[i] <= '9'))
              Out.print(a[i] + " ");
          }
        Out.println("");
      }
  }
```

mechanism: Save the current environment on entry to a procedure by pushing information onto a stack; restore the environment on exit by using information popped from the stack. As we see in Chapter 5, this connection between pushdown stacks and programs organized as functions that call functions is an essential paradigm of computation.

Returning to our original problem, we can also use a pushdown stack to convert fully parenthesized arithmetic expressions from infix to postfix, as illustrated in Figure 4.4. For this computation, we push the *operators* onto a stack and simply pass the operands through to the output. Then, each right parenthesis indicates that both arguments for the last operator have been output, so the operator itself can be popped and output. Note that arguments appear in the postfix expression in the same order as in the infix expression. It is also amusing to note that the left parentheses are not needed in the infix expression. The left parentheses would be required, however, if we could have operators that take differing numbers of operands (see Exercise 4.11). Program 4.6 is an implementation of this process that uses a stack of characters.

In addition to providing two different examples of the use of the pushdown-stack abstraction, the entire algorithm that we have developed in this section for evaluating infix expressions is itself an exercise in abstraction. First, we convert the input to an intermediate representation (postfix). Second, we simulate the operation of an abstract stack-based machine to interpret and evaluate the expression. This same schema is followed by many modern programming-language translators, for efficiency and portability: The problem of compiling a Java program for a particular computer is broken into two tasks centered around an intermediate representation so that the problem of translating the program is separated from the problem of executing that program, just as we have done in this section. We shall see a related, but different, intermediate representation in Section 5.7.

This application also illustrates the value of ADTs and the need for generic implementations. Not only do we use two different stacks, but also one of the stacks holds items of type char (operators), whereas the other holds items of type int (operands). We might even combine both of the clients just considered into one program that would need both stacks (see Exercise 4.15). In Section 4.5, we consider the idea of using a single implementation for both stacks. While this approach is attractive, we should be aware that it might not always be desirable, because different implementations may have different performance characteristics; consequently, we might not wish to decide a priori that one implementation will serve both purposes. Indeed, our main focus is on the implementations and their performance, and we turn now to those topics for pushdown stacks.

Exercises

▷ **4.8** Extend Programs 4.5 and 4.6 to include the − (subtract) and / (divide) operations.

▷**4.9** Convert to postfix the expression

(5 * ((9 * 8) + (7 * (4 + 6)))) .

▷**4.10** Give, in the same manner as Figure 4.2, the contents of the stack as the following expression is evaluated by Program 4.5:

5 9 * 8 7 4 6 + * 2 1 3 * + * + * .

4.11 Extend your solution to Exercise 4.8 to include the unary operators – (negation) and $ (square root). Also, modify the abstract stack machine in Program 4.5 to use floating point. For example, given the expression

(-(-1) + $((-1) * (-1)-(4 * (-1))))/2

your program should print the value 1.618034.

4.12 Write a PostScript program that draws this figure:

● **4.13** Prove by induction that Program 4.5 correctly evaluates any postfix expression.

○ **4.14** Write a program that converts a postfix expression to infix, using a pushdown stack.

○ **4.15** Combine Program 4.5 and Program 4.6 into a single class that uses two stacks (an `intStack` and a `charStack`).

●● **4.16** Implement a compiler and interpreter for a programming language where each program consists of a single arithmetic expression preceded by a sequence of assignment statements with arithmetic expressions involving integers and variables named with single lower case characters. For example, given the input

```
(x = 1)
(y = (x + 1))
(((x + y) * 3) + (4 * x))
```

your program should print the value 13.

4.4 Stack ADT Implementations

In this section, we consider two implementations of the stack ADT: one using arrays and one using linked lists. The implementations are both straightforward applications of the basic tools that we covered in Chapter 3. They differ only, we expect, in their performance characteristics.

If we use an array to represent the stack, each of the methods declared in Program 4.4 is trivial to implement, as shown in Program 4.7. We put the items in the array precisely as diagrammed in Figure 4.1,

---

Program 4.7 Array implementation of a pushdown stack

When there are N items in the stack, this implementation keeps them in s[0], ... , s[N-1], in order from least recently inserted to most recently inserted. The top of the stack (the place for the next item to be pushed) is s[N]. The client program passes the maximum number of items expected on the stack as the parameter to the constructor for intStack, which allocates an array of that size, but this code does not check for errors such as pushing onto a full stack (or popping an empty one).

```
class intStack
  {
    private int[] s;
    private int N;
    intStack(int maxN)
      { s = new int[maxN]; N = 0; }
    boolean isEmpty()
      { return (N == 0); }
    void push(int item)
      { s[N++] = item; }
    int pop()
      { return s[--N]; }
  }
```

---

keeping track of the index of the top of the stack. Doing the *push* operation amounts to storing the item in the array position indicated by the top-of-stack index, then incrementing the index; doing the *pop* operation amounts to decrementing the index, then returning the item that it designates. The *construct* operation (constructor) involves allocating an array of the indicated size, and the *test if empty* operation involves checking whether the index is 0. This code provides an efficient and effective pushdown stack of integers for a client program such as Program 4.5.

To implement the class charStack for stacks of characters that is needed by Program 4.6, we can use the same code as in Program 4.7, changing to char the types of s, push's parameter, and pop's return value. Doing so amounts to defining and implementing a different ADT interface. We can use the same method to implement stacks for any type of item. This approach has the potential advantage of allow-

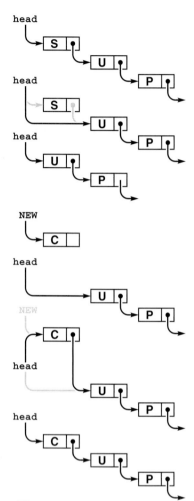

Figure 4.5
Linked-list pushdown stack

The stack is represented by a pointer head, *which points to the first (most recently inserted) item. To* pop *the stack (top), we remove the item at the front of the list by setting* head *from its link. To push a new item onto the stack (bottom), we link it in at the beginning by setting its link field to* head, *then setting* head *to point to it.*

ing us to specify different implementations tailored to the item type and the potential disadvantage of leaving us with multiple class implementations comprised of essentially the same code. We will return to this issue, but, for the moment, our focus is on different ways to implement stacks of integers.

We know one potential drawback to using an array representation: As is usual with data structures based on arrays, we need to know the maximum size of the array before using it so that we can allocate memory for it. In this implementation, we make that information an parameter to the constructor. This constraint is an artifact of our choice to use an array implementation; it is not an essential part of the stack ADT. We may have no easy way to estimate the maximum number of elements that our program will be putting on the stack: If we choose an arbitrarily high value, this implementation will make inefficient use of space, and that may be undesirable in an application where space is a precious resource. If we choose too small a value, our program might not work at all. By using an ADT, we make it possible to consider other alternatives, in other implementations, without changing any client program.

For example, to allow the stack to grow and shrink gracefully, we may wish to consider using a linked list, as in the implementation in Program 4.8. We keep the stack in reverse order from the array implementation, from most recently inserted element to least recently inserted element, to make the basic stack operations easier to implement, as illustrated in Figure 4.5. To *pop*, we remove the node from the front of the list and return its item; to *push*, we create a new node and add it to the front of the list. Because all linked-list operations are at the beginning of the list, we do not need to use a head node. Note that the constructor ignores its first parameter in this implementation.

We could also change the types in Program 4.8 to get implementations of the charStack class for stacks of characters or classes for stacks of any other types of items. As mentioned for Program 4.7, this approach has the disadvantage of leaving us with different classes comprised of essentially the same code. In the next section, we consider alternate approaches that allow us to use existing code instead of having to write a new class each time we want to use a stack for a new type of item.

Program 4.8 Linked-list implementation of a pushdown stack

This code implements the pushdown stack ADT using a linked list. The data representation for linked-list nodes is organized in the usual way (see Section 3.3), including a constructor for nodes that fills in each new node with the given item and link.

```
class intStack
  {
    private Node head;
    private class Node
      {
        int item; Node next;
        Node(int item, Node next)
          { this.item = item; this.next = next; }
      }
    intStack(int maxN)
      { head = null; }
    boolean isEmpty()
      { return (head == null); }
    void push(int item)
      { head = new Node(item, head); }
    int pop()
      { int v = head.item; Node t = head.next;
        head = t; return v; }
  }
```

Programs 4.7 and 4.8 are two different implementations for the same ADT. We can substitute one for the other without making *any* changes in client programs such as the ones that we examined in Section 4.3. They differ in only their performance characteristics. The array implementation uses the amount of space necessary to hold the maximum number of items expected throughout the computation. The list implementation uses space proportional to the number of items, but it always uses both extra space for one link per item and extra time to allocate memory for each *push* and (eventually) deallocate memory for each *pop*. If we need a huge stack that is usually nearly full, we might prefer the array implementation; if we have a stack whose size varies dramatically and other data structures that could make use of the space not being used when the stack has only a few items in it, we might prefer the linked-list implementation.

These same considerations about space usage hold for many ADT implementations, as we shall see throughout the book. We often are in the position of choosing between the ability to access any item quickly but having to predict the maximum number of items needed ahead of time (in an array implementation) and the flexibility of always using space proportional to the number of items in use while giving up the ability to access every item quickly (in a linked-list implementation).

Beyond basic space-usage considerations, we normally are most interested in performance differences among ADT implementations that relate to running time. In this case, there is little difference between the two implementations that we have considered.

Property 4.1 *We can implement the* **push** *and* **pop** *operations for the pushdown stack ADT in constant time, using either arrays or linked lists.*

This fact follows immediately from Programs 4.7 and 4.8. ∎

That the stack items are kept in different orders in the array and the linked-list implementations is of no concern to the client program. The implementations are free to use any data structure whatever, as long as they maintain the illusion of an abstract pushdown stack. In both cases, the implementations are able to create the illusion of an efficient abstract entity that can perform the requisite operations with just a few machine instructions. Throughout this book, our goal is to find data structures and efficient implementations for other important ADTs.

The linked-list implementation supports the illusion of a stack that can grow without bound. Such a stack is impossible in practical terms: at some point, new will raise an exception when the request for more memory cannot be satisfied. It is also possible to arrange for an array-based stack to grow and shrink dynamically, by doubling the size of the array when the stack becomes half full, and halving the size of the array when the stack becomes half empty. We leave the details of implementing such a strategy as an exercise in Chapter 14, where we consider the process in detail for a more advanced application. On the other hand, it is sometimes useful to have the client pass the maximum stack size to the constructor (for example, suppose that an application needs a huge number of small stacks).

The code in Programs 4.7 and 4.8 does not check for errors such as popping an empty stack, pushing onto a full stack, or running out of memory. To make our code robust for practical applications, we can modify it to check for such conditions and throw exceptions as appropriate (see Exercises 4.19 and 4.20). To keep our code compact and focus on algorithms, we generally do not show such error checks, but it is good programming practice to include them at every opportunity. Note that exceptions constitute a change in the interface, since clients should know which exceptions might be thrown; but fully capturing exception-handling in our client-interface-implementation scenario is a complicated matter.

Exercises

▷ **4.17** Give the contents of s[0], ..., s[4] after the execution of the operations illustrated in Figure 4.1, using Program 4.7.

○ **4.18** Suppose that you change the pushdown-stack interface to replace *test if empty* by *count*, which should return the number of items currently in the data structure. Provide implementations for *count* for the array representation (Program 4.7) and the linked-list representation (Program 4.8).

4.19 Modify the array-based pushdown-stack implementation in the text (Program 4.7) to throw exceptions if there is not enough memory available from new to allocate the stack in the constructor, if the client attempts to *pop* when the stack is empty, or if the client attempts to *push* when the stack is full.

4.20 Modify the linked-list–based pushdown-stack implementation in the text (Program 4.8) to throw exceptions if the client attempts to *pop* when the stack is empty, if the client attempts to *push* when the stack is full, or if there is no memory available from new for a *push*. *Hint*: You need to keep a counter that keeps track of the number of items in the stack.

4.21 Modify the linked-list–based pushdown-stack implementation in the text (Program 4.8) to use an array of integers and an array of indices to implement the list (see Figure 3.7).

4.22 Write a linked-list–based pushdown-stack implementation that keeps items on the list in order from least recently inserted to most recently inserted. You will need to use a doubly linked list.

● **4.23** Develop an ADT that provides clients with two different pushdown stacks. Use an array implementation. Keep one stack at the beginning of the array and the other at the end. (If the client program is such that one stack grows while the other one shrinks, this implementation will use less space than other alternatives.)

● **4.24** Implement an infix-expression–evaluation program for integers based upon Programs 4.5 and 4.6 (see Exercise 4.15) that uses your ADT from

Exercise 4.23. *Note*: You have to cope with the fact that both stacks have to contain items of the same type.

4.5 Generic Implementations

How can we develop one stack implementation that allows us to build both a stack of integers and a stack of characters as required, for example, by the clients in Section 4.3? The most straightforward way to do so in Java is to use inheritance: we define an interface and implementation for stacks of items of type Object, then cast each item to the desired type when we pop it from the stack. Since all objects in Java are derived from type Object, the cast is always valid.

Program 4.9 is a generic stack implementation that uses an array representation. It is the same code as Program 4.7, except with the types of s, push's parameter, and pop's return value all changed to Object. We can push any Java object onto the stack, then cast it to the required type when we pop it. For example, if a and b are objects of type Item, the following code would exchange them:

```
Stack S = new Stack(2);
s.push(a); s.push(b);
a = ((Item) s.pop());
b = ((Item) s.pop());
```

This approach is widely used to develop generic implementations in Java, but it has two limitations, which we now consider.

First, to use stacks of items of type Object for primitive types such as int or char, we have to make use of wrapper classes such as Integer or Character. For example, rather than writing s.push(x) to push a variable x of type int onto the stack, we have to write

```
s.push(new Integer(x))
```

and rather than using s.pop() as an integer value in an expression, we would have to use

```
((Integer) s.pop()).intValue() .
```

This approach adds an extra level of indirection, as illustrated in Figure 4.6: a stack of objects is a stack of references. In an application where we are using huge numbers of items of a primitive type, this extra cost may be unacceptable.

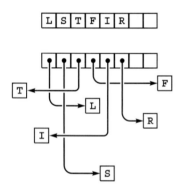

Figure 4.6
Array representations

When we use an array to represent a stack of primitive types such as characters (top), we reserve space for one character per stack entry. For any other type of object, we have to reserve space for one reference per object, in addition to the objects themselves (bottom).

The second problem with using inheritance from `Object` to develop generic implementations is that doing so can expose us to subtle bugs in our programs that cannot be detected until runtime. For example, there is nothing to stop a programmer from putting different types of objects on the same stack, then encountering a runtime type-checking error, as in the following example:

```
Apple a = new Apple();
Orange b = new Orange();
s.push(a);
s.push(b);
a = ((Apple) s.pop()); // throws a ClassCastException
b = ((Orange) s.pop());
```

This toy example illustrates a basic problem, which could arise even in a stack whose items are all of the same type. The code cannot be type-checked at compile time: there might be an incorrect cast that occurs in a complex piece of code that could escape detection until some particular runtime circumstance arises. Such an error is to be avoided at all costs because it could happen long after an implementation is delivered to a client, who would have no way to fix it.

In other words, when we use type casting with an implementation such as Program 4.9 to reuse code for different types of items, we are assuming that clients will cast objects popped from the stack to the proper type. This implicit assumption contradicts our requirement for ADTs that operations are to be accessed only through an explicit interface. One reason that programmers use precisely defined ADTs such as Program 4.4 is to protect future clients against errors that arise from such implicit assumptions.

One way to address this problem is to use the generic `Stack` class to implement the `intStack` interface, as shown in Program 4.10. We still have to have a class for every type of object, but their implementations are trivial and we do not have to duplicate the (potentially complicated) algorithm and data-structure implementations. It is actually quite common in Java programming to define a class whose sole purpose is to match the needs of a client with the capability of an existing class. Such a class is called an *adapter* class.

Another approach that we could use to enable compile-time type checking is to define an ADT for the items that we are going to put on stacks so that we can get stacks of different types of items by using

Program 4.9 Generic pushdown stack

This code implements a pushdown stack ADT for the Object type. It does *not* implement the interface of Program 4.4 because push's parameter and pop's return value do not match the specification.

      The code for pop is more complicated than in Program 4.7 because the reference to the popped item in the array has to be replaced by null—otherwise, the Java garbage collection system has no way to know that this reference will never be used and will not reclaim the memory associated with the popped object.

```
class Stack
  {
    private Object[] s;
    private int N;
    Stack(int maxN)
      { s = new Object[maxN]; N = 0; }
    boolean isEmpty()
      { return (N == 0); }
    void push(Object item)
      { s[N++] = item; }
    Object pop()
      { Object t = s[--N]; s[N] = null; return t; }
  }
```

different implementations of that ADT. We will use this approach in the more complicated algorithms and data structures that we consider in Parts 3 and 4 because they make certain assumptions about the item type that we need to build into the ADT. This approach still leaves us with an extra level of indirection for primitive types and requires that we use adapter classes to have, for example, stacks of two different types of items in a single program.

      In client programs, we use specified classes like intStack. This approach will accommodate either a direct implementation for primitive types or a a generic implementation with an adapter class while still using code that can be fully type-checked at compile time.

Exercises

▷ **4.25** Give a class that implements that same interface as Program 4.9 but uses a linked-list representation.

> **Program 4.10 Adapter class for stack of integers**
>
> This code does implement the interface of Program 4.4. With this technique, we can reuse the code of Program 4.9 for different types of data, while still being sure that clients and implementations agree on an explicit interface.
>
> ```
> class intStack
>   {
>     private Stack S;
>     intStack(int maxN)
>       { S = new Stack(maxN); }
>     boolean isEmpty()
>       { return S.isEmpty(); }
>     void push(int item)
>       { S.push(new Integer(item)); }
>     int pop()
>       { return ((Integer) S.pop()).intValue(); }
>   }
> ```

4.26 Write a generic static method that exchanges two items in an array. Test your code in a driver program that creates one array of items of type `Integer` and another array of type `Character` and then uses your method to exchange objects in each array.

• **4.27** Implement an infix-expression–evaluation program for integers based upon Programs 4.5 and 4.6, that uses the generic stack class in Program 4.9. *Note*: You have to cope with the fact that the stack has to contain items of different types (see Exercise 4.23).

•• **4.28** Write an adapter class for stacks of type `String`, then use it in a client that takes simple PostScript programs as input and draws the intended output using the Java `Graphics` library. Your program should handle at least `moveto`, `lineto`, and `stroke`, but tackle as rich a subset of PostScript as you can.

4.6 Creation of a New ADT

Sections 4.2 through 4.4 present a complete example of Java code that captures one of our most important abstractions: the pushdown stack. The *interface* in Section 4.2 defines the basic operations; *client programs* such as those in Section 4.3 can use those operations without dependence on how the operations are implemented; and *implemen-*

tations such as those in Section 4.4 provide the necessary concrete representation and program code to realize the abstraction.

To design a new ADT, we often enter into the following process: Starting with the task of developing a client program to solve an applications problem, we identify operations that seem crucial—that is, what would we *like* to be able to do with our data? Then, we define an interface and write client code to test the hypothesis that the existence of the ADT would make it easier for us to implement the client program. Next, we consider the idea of whether or not we *can* implement the operations in the ADT with reasonable efficiency. If we cannot, we perhaps can seek to understand the source of the inefficiency and to modify the interface to include operations that are better suited to efficient implementation. These modifications affect the client program, and we modify it accordingly. After a few iterations, we have a working client program and a working implementation, so we freeze the interface by adopting a policy of not changing it. At this moment, the development of client programs and the development of implementations are separable: We can write other client programs that use the same ADT (perhaps we write some driver programs that allow us to test the ADT), we can write other implementations, and we can compare the performance of multiple implementations.

In other situations, we might define the ADT first. This approach might involve asking questions such as these: What basic operations would client programs want to perform on the data at hand? Which operations do we know how to implement efficiently? After we develop an implementation, we might test its efficacy on client programs. We might modify the interface and do more tests before eventually freezing the interface.

In Chapter 1, we considered a detailed example where thinking on an abstract level helped us to find an efficient algorithm for solving a complex problem. We consider next the use of the general approach that we are discussing in this chapter to encapsulate the specific abstract operations that we exploited in Chapter 1.

Program 4.11 defines the interface, in terms of two operations (in addition to *construct*) that seem to characterize the algorithms that we considered in Chapter 1 for connectivity, at a high abstract level. Whatever the underlying algorithms and data structures, we want to

Program 4.11 Equivalence-relations ADT interface

Our ADT interface mechanism makes it convenient for us to encode precisely our decision to consider the connectivity algorithm in terms of a class that suppports three abstract operations: *initialize* an abstract data structure to keep track of connections among the given number of nodes, *find* whether two given nodes are connected, and *unite* two given nodes to consider them connected henceforth.

```
class UF // ADT interface
  { // implementations and private members hidden
    UF(int)
    boolean find(int, int)
    void unite(int, int)
  }
```

be able both to check whether or not two nodes are known to be connected and to declare that two nodes are connected.

Program 4.12 is a client program that uses the ADT defined in the interface of Program 4.11 to solve the connectivity problem. One benefit of using the ADT is that this program is easy to understand, because it is written in terms of abstractions that allow the computation to be expressed in a natural way.

Program 4.13 is an implementation of the union–find interface defined in Program 4.11 that uses a forest of trees represented by two arrays as the underlying representation of the known connectivity information, as described in Section 1.3. The different algorithms that we considered in Chapter 1 represent different implementations of this ADT, and we can test them as such without changing the client program at all.

This ADT leads to programs that are slightly less efficient than those in Chapter 1 for the connectivity application, because it does not take advantage of the property of that client that every *union* operation is immediately preceded by a *find* operation. We sometimes incur extra costs of this kind as the price of moving to a more abstract representation. In this case, there are numerous ways to remove the inefficiency, perhaps at the cost of making the interface or the implementation more complicated (see Exercise 4.30). In practice, the paths

---

Program 4.12 Equivalence-relations ADT client

The ADT of Program 4.11 allows us to separate the connectivity algorithm of Program 1.1 from the union–find implementation, thereby making both more accessible. For example, using the ADT allows us to try various union–find implementations such as Programs 1.2 through 1.4 without changing the connectivity code at all.

```
class Equivalence
  {
    public static void main(String[] args)
      { int p, q, N = Integer.parseInt(args[0]);
        UF info = new UF(N);
        for (In.init(); !In.empty(); )
          { p = In.getInt(); q = In.getInt();
            if (!info.find(p, q))
              {
                info.unite(p, q);
                Out.println(p + "-" + q);
              }
          }
      }
  }
```

---

are extremely short (particularly if we use path compression), so the extra cost is likely to be negligible in this case.

Programs 4.12 and 4.13 are equivalent to Program 1.3, but splitting the program into two parts is a better approach because it

- Separates the task of solving the high-level (connectivity) problem from the task of solving the low-level (union–find) problem, allowing us to work on the two problems independently
- Gives us a natural way to compare different algorithms and data structures for solving the problem
- Defines, through the interface, a way to check that the software is operating as expected
- Provides a mechanism that allows us to upgrade to new representations (new data structures or new algorithms) without changing the client program at all
- Gives us an abstraction that we can use to build other algorithms

Program 4.13 Equivalence-relations ADT implementation

This code for the weighted-quick-union code from Chapter 1 implements the interface of Program 4.11, packaging the code in a form that
makes it convenient for use in other applications.

```
class UF
  {
    private int[] id, sz;
    private int find(int x)
      { while (x != id[x]) x = id[x]; return x; }
    UF(int N)
      { id = new int[N]; sz = new int[N];
        for (int i = 0; i < N; i++)
          { id[i] = i; sz[i] = 1; }
      }
    boolean find(int p, int q)
      { return (find(p) == find(q)); }
    void unite(int p, int q)
      { int i = find(p), j = find(q);
        if (i == j) return;
        if (sz[i] < sz[j])
              { id[i] = j; sz[j] += sz[i]; }
        else { id[j] = i; sz[i] += sz[j]; }
      }
  }
```

These benefits are widely applicable to many tasks that we face when
developing computer programs, so the basic tenets underlying ADTs
are widely used.

How do we switch from one implementation to another? The
simplest method is to rename files. Java always expects the implementation of, say, the UF class to be in a file named UF.java, so we can
substitute a different implementation by renaming it to be UF.java
(after, presumably, giving the old one some different name or saving
it somewhere). However, moving around multiple files with the same
name can be confusing and cumbersome, and this task is so common
that many Java environments provide a specific mechanism to support
it: a programmer can specify a *class path* sequence that tells the Java

> **Program 4.14 Abstract class for equivalence-relations ADT**
>
> This Java code constitutes an interface for the equivalence-relations ADT that provides complete separation between client and implementation (*see text*).
>
> ```
> interface uf
>   {
>     int find(int x);
>     boolean find(int p, int q);
>     void unite(int p, int q);
>   }
> ```

interpreter which directories it should check to look for the code that implements the classes. Thus, we can keep one implementation in one directory and another in another directory, then choose between them by specifying an appropriate class path.

Our code in Program 4.13 mixes the interface with the implementation and therefore does not provide the full separation of client, interface, and implementation that we would prefer to have for ADTs. With `private`, we can keep client programs from any dependence on the data representation, but if we make any changes in the data representation, we have to recompile all the clients. In many software engineering scenarios, we may have no information about the clients, so this would be an onerous requirement. In other scenarios, this arrangement does make sense. For a huge and complex ADT, we might settle on a data representation and an interface, then have multiple programmers working on different parts of the implementation. In this case, the public part of the interface serves as a contract between the programmers and the clients, and the private part of the interface serves as a contract among programmers. This strategy also often provides precisely what we need in this book, when we want to consider different algorithms that use a particular data structure. In this way, we might be able to realize performance gains by changing a small part of a huge system.

The Java language does provide a mechanism that is specifically designed to allow us to write programs with a well-defined interface that completely separates clients from implementations. It is based on the Java inheritance mechanism. Through inheritance, we *can* add members to an existing class or redefine any of its methods; including abstract in a method declaration means that the method *must* be redefined in some extended class. A class that has any abstract methods is known as an *abstract class*. No implementation is provided for an abstract method in an abstract class (only its signature is needed): some extended class will provide the implementation. An abstract class whose public methods are all abstract is similar to what we refer to as an ADT interface.

Java also has an *interface* mechanism that is similar to an abstract class whose methods are all abstract. Any class that extends an interface must define all of the methods in an interface; so, in our terminology, it is an implementation. Clients can use the interface and the Java system can enforce the contract between clients and implementations, even when clients and implementations are compiled separately. For example, Program 4.14 shows an interface uf for equivalence relations; changing the first line of Program 4.13 to

```
class UF implements uf
```

would indicate that UF defines (at least) all of the methods in uf—that is, it is an implementation of interface uf.

Unfortunately, using an abstract class or a Java interface incurs significant runtime costs, because every call to an abstract method requires (at least) following a reference through a table of references to methods. Since the algorithms and data structures that we consider in this book are often in performance-critical parts of systems, we may not wish to pay these penalties to gain the flexibility that abstract classes and interfaces provide. Moreover, there is not an exact match between the Java interface mechanism and the ADT interface that we have been discussing: for example, constructors cannot be part of a Java interface, but a proper ADT interface needs to specify just which constructors clients can use and implementations must include. Also, a Java interface cannot have static methods, but we might need them in an ADT interface.

Another reason that we use an informal mechanism to define interfaces rather than a language construct is that when we use inheritance to extend a class, we are defining an implicit interface whose scope we may not even wish to explicitly articulate. For example, the methods equals, hashCode, clone, getClass, and finalize are defined for all Java objects through inheritance, but we do not list them in every interface that we design. The convention that we use is very similar to the standard used to document Java class libraries: to describe what a client can expect from a class, we list the signatures of its public methods.

The kind of flexibility that we can achieve with interfaces and inheritance still leaves open the possibility that the implied contract between clients and implementations about what an ADT is to be may be broken, perhaps unwittingly, at some future time. All of these mechanisms ensure that client programs and implementations connect up properly, but they also depend on one another to *do* things, in ways that we generally cannot specify formally. For example, suppose that some uninformed programmer finds our weighted quick-union algorithm too difficult to understand and decides to replace it with a quick-find algorithm (or worse, an implementation that does not even give the right answer). We have insisted on allowing such a change to be made easily, but in this case it might cripple a client in a critical application that depends upon the implementation's having good performance for huge problems. Programming lore is filled with tales of such problems, and it is quite difficult to protect against them.

Such considerations are drawing us into considering properties of languages, compilers, interpreters, and virtual machines, and are rather far afield from algorithms. Accordingly, we will most often stick to our simple two-file convention where we implement ADTs with Java classes, the public methods constituting the interface. Our primary reason for doing so is to provide is a convenient and compact expression of our data structures and algorithms. If, for a particular application, we need the extra flexibility afforded by the other approaches just mentioned, we can restructure our classes along these lines.

Exercises

4.29 Give a class that implements the same interface as Program 4.13, but uses path compression by halving.

4.30 Remove the inefficiency mentioned in the text by adding an operation to Program 4.11 that combines *union* and *find*, providing an implementation in Program 4.13 and modifying Program 4.12 accordingly.

○ **4.31** Modify our equivalence-relations interface (Program 4.11) and implementation (Program 4.13) to provide a method that will return the number of nodes known to be connected to a given node.

4.32 Modify Program 4.13 to use an array of objects instead of parallel arrays for the underlying data structure.

○ **4.33** Build a solution to the postfix-expression evaluation problem that uses a Java `interface` for the stack-of-integers ADT interface. Make sure that your client program (your version of Program 4.5) can be compiled separately from your stack implementation (your version of Program 4.7).

● **4.34** Create a full implementation of the equivalence-relations ADT based on a Java `interface`, and compare its performance against Program 4.13 on huge connectivity problems, in the style of Table 1.1.

4.7 FIFO Queues and Generalized Queues

The *first-in, first-out (FIFO) queue* is another fundamental ADT that is similar to the pushdown stack but uses the opposite rule to decide which element to remove for *remove*. Rather than removing the most recently inserted element, we remove the element that has been in the queue the longest.

Perhaps our busy professor's "in" box *should* operate like a FIFO queue, since the first-in, first-out order seems to be an intuitively fair way to decide what to do next. However, that professor might not ever answer the phone or get to class on time. In a stack, a memorandum can get buried at the bottom, but emergencies are handled when they arise; in a FIFO queue, we work methodically through the tasks, but each has to wait its turn.

FIFO queues are abundant in everyday life. When we wait in line to see a movie or to buy groceries, we are being processed according to a FIFO discipline. Similarly, FIFO queues are frequently used within computer systems to hold tasks that are yet to be accomplished when we want to provide services on a first-come, first-served basis. Another example, which illustrates the distinction between stacks and FIFO queues, is a grocery store's inventory of a perishable product. If the grocer puts new items on the front of the shelf and customers take items from the front, then we have a stack discipline, which is a problem for the grocer because items at the back of the shelf may stay there for a very long time and therefore spoil. By putting new items at the back of the shelf, the grocer ensures that the length of time any item has to stay on the shelf is limited by the length of time it takes customers to purchase the maximum number of items that fit on the shelf. This same basic principle applies to numerous similar situations.

```
F       F
I       F I
R       F I R
S       F I R S
*    F  I R S
T       I R S T
*  I    R S T
I       R S T I
N       R S T I N
*   R   S T I N
*   S   T I N
*   T   I N
F       I N F
I       I N F I
*  I    N F I
R       N F I R
S       N F I R S
*  N    F I R S
*  F    I R S
*  I    R S
T       R S T
*  R    S T
O       S T O
U       S T O U
T       S T O U T
*  S    T O U T
*  T    O U T
*  O    U T
*  U    T
*  T
```

Figure 4.7
FIFO queue example

This list shows the result of the sequence of operations in the left column (top to bottom), where a letter denotes put *and an asterisk denotes* get. *Each line displays the operation, the letter returned for* get *operations, and the contents of the queue in order from least recently inserted to most recently inserted, left to right.*

Program 4.15 FIFO queue ADT interface

This interface is identical to the pushdown stack interface of Program 4.4, except for the names of the methods. The two ADTs differ only in the specification, which is not reflected in the interface code.

```
class intQueue // ADT interface
  { // implementations and private members hidden
    intQueue(int)
    int empty()
    void put(int)
    int get()
  }
```

Definition 4.3 *A* **FIFO queue** *is an ADT that comprises two basic operations: insert (**put**) a new item, and remove (**get**) the item that was least recently inserted.*

Program 4.15 is the interface for a FIFO queue ADT. This interface differs only in the nomenclature from the stack interface that we considered in Section 4.2: to a compiler, say, the two interfaces are identical! This observation underscores the fact that the abstraction itself, which programmers normally do not define formally, is the essential component of an ADT. For large applications, which may involve scores of ADTs, the problem of defining them precisely is critical. In this book, we work with ADTs that capture essential concepts that we define in the text, but not in any formal language other than via specific implementations. To discern the nature of ADTs, we need to consider examples of their use and to examine specific implementations.

Figure 4.7 shows how a sample FIFO queue evolves through a series of *get* and *put* operations. Each *get* decreases the size of the queue by 1, and each *put* increases the size of the queue by 1. In the figure, the items in the queue are listed in the order that they are put on the queue so that it is clear that the first item in the list is the one that is to be returned by the *get* operation. Again, in an implementation we are free to organize the items any way that we want, as long as we maintain the illusion that the items are organized in this way.

To implement the FIFO queue ADT using a linked list, we keep the items in the list in order from least recently inserted to most recently

---

Program 4.16 FIFO queue linked-list implementation

The difference between a FIFO queue and a pushdown stack (Program 4.8) is that new items are inserted at the end, rather than the beginning. This class keeps a pointer `tail` to the last node of the list so that the method `put` can add a new node by linking that node to the node referenced by `tail` and updating `tail` to point to the new node. The constructor, `get`, and `empty` are identical to their counterparts for the linked-list–pushdown-stack implementation of Program 4.8. The node constructor has only one parameter because new nodes are always inserted at the end of the list and thus have a null `next` field.

```
class intQueue
  {
    private class Node
      { int item; Node next;
        Node(int item)
          { this.item = item; next = null; }
      }
    private Node head, tail;
    intQueue(int max)
      { head = null; tail = null; }
    boolean empty()
      { return (head == null); }
    void put(int item)
      { Node t = tail; tail = new Node(item);
        if (empty()) head = tail; else t.next = tail;
      }
    int get()
      { int v = head.item; Node t = head.next;
        head = t; return v; }
  }
```

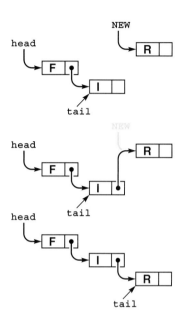

Figure 4.8
Linked-list queue

In this linked-list representation of a queue, we insert new items at the end, so the items in the linked list are in order from least recently inserted to most recently inserted, from beginning to end. The queue is represented by two pointers `head` and `tail`, which point to the first and final item, respectively. To get an item from the queue, we remove the item at the front of the list, in the same way as we did for stacks (see Figure 4.5). To put a new item onto the queue, we set the link field of the node referenced by `tail` to point to it (center), then update `tail` (bottom).

inserted, as diagrammed in Figure 4.7. This order is the reverse of the order that we used for the stack implementation, but allows us to develop efficient implementations of the queue operations. We maintain two pointers into the list: one to the beginning (so that we can *get* the first element), and one to the end (so that we can *put* a new element onto the queue), as shown in Figure 4.8 and in the implementation in Program 4.16.

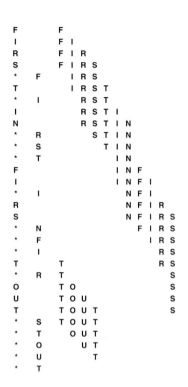

Figure 4.9
FIFO queue example, array implementation

This sequence shows the data manipulation underlying the abstract representation in Figure 4.7 when we implement the queue by storing the items in an array, keeping indices to the beginning and end of the queue, and wrapping the indices back to the beginning of the array when they reach the end of the array. In this example, the tail index wraps back to the beginning when the second T is inserted, and the head index wraps when the second S is removed.

We can also use an array to implement a FIFO queue, although we have to exercise care to keep the running time constant for both the *put* and *get* operations. That performance goal dictates that we can not move the elements of the queue within the array, unlike what might be suggested by a literal interpretation of Figure 4.7. Accordingly, as we did with the linked-list implementation, we maintain two indices into the array: one to the beginning of the queue and one to the end of the queue. We consider the contents of the queue to be the elements between the indices. To *get* an element, we remove it from the beginning (head) of the queue and increment the head index; to *put* an element, we add it to the end (tail) of the queue and increment the tail index. A sequence of *put* and *get* operations causes the queue to appear to move through the array, as illustrated in Figure 4.9. When it hits the end of the array, we arrange for it to wrap around to the beginning. The details of this computation are in the code in Program 4.17.

Property 4.2 *We can implement the* **get** *and* **put** *operations for the FIFO queue ADT in constant time, using either arrays or linked lists.*

This fact is immediately clear when we inspect the code in Programs 4.16 and 4.17. ∎

The same considerations that we discussed in Section 4.4 apply to space resources used by FIFO queues. The array representation requires that we reserve enough space for the maximum number of items expected throughout the computation, whereas the linked-list representation uses space proportional to the number of elements in the data structure, at the cost of extra space for the links and extra time to allocate and deallocate memory for each operation.

Although we encounter stacks more often than we encounter FIFO queues, because of the fundamental relationship between stacks and recursive programs (see Chapter 5) we shall also encounter algorithms for which the queue is the natural underlying data structure. As we have already noted, one of the most frequent uses of queues and stacks in computational applications is to postpone computation. Although many applications that involve a queue of pending work operate correctly no matter what rule is used for *remove*, the overall running time or other resource usage may be dependent on the rule. When such applications involve a large number of *insert* and *remove*

Program 4.17 FIFO queue array implementation

The contents of the queue are all the elements in the array between `head` and `tail`, taking into account the wraparound back to 0 when the end of the array is encountered. If `head` and `tail` are equal, then we consider the queue to be empty; but if put would make them equal, then we consider it to be full. As usual, we do not check such error conditions, but we make the size of the array 1 greater than the maximum number of elements that the client expects to see in the queue, so that we could augment this program to make such checks.

```
class intQueue
  {
    private int[] q; private int N, head, tail;
    intQueue(int maxN)
      { q = new int[maxN + 1];
        N = maxN + 1; head = N; tail = 0; }
    boolean empty()
      { return (head % N == tail); }
    void put(int item)
      { q[tail++] = item; tail = tail % N; }
    int get()
      { head = head % N; return q[head++]; }
  }
```

operations on data structures with a large number of items on them, performance differences are paramount. Accordingly, we devote a great deal of attention in this book to such ADTs. If we ignored performance, we could formulate a single ADT that encompassed *insert* and *remove*; since we do not ignore performance, each rule, in essence, constitutes a different ADT. To evaluate the effectiveness of a particular ADT, we need to consider two costs: the implementation cost, which depends on our choice of algorithm and data structure for the implementation, and the cost of the particular decision-making rule in terms of effect on the performance of the client. To conclude this section, we will describe a number of such ADTs, which we will be considering in detail throughout the book.

Specifically, pushdown stacks and FIFO queues are special instances of a more general ADT: the *generalized queue*. Instances of generalized queues differ in only the rule used when items are removed. For stacks, the rule is "remove the item that was most recently inserted"; for FIFO queues, the rule is "remove the item that was least recently inserted"; and there are many other possibilities.

A simple but powerful alternative is the *random queue*, where the rule is to "remove a random item," and the client can expect to get any of the items on the queue with equal probability. We can implement the operations of a random queue in constant time using an array representation (see Exercise 4.47). As do stacks and FIFO queues, the array representation requires that we reserve space ahead of time. The linked-list alternative is less attractive than for stacks and FIFO queues because implementing both insertion and deletion efficiently is a challenging task (see Exercise 4.48). We can use random queues as the basis for randomized algorithms in order to avoid, with high probability, worst-case performance scenarios (see Section 2.7).

We have described stacks and FIFO queues by identifying items according to the time that they were inserted into the queue. Alternatively, we can describe these abstract concepts in terms of a sequential listing of the items in order and refer to the basic operations of inserting and deleting items from the beginning and the end of the list. If we insert at the end and remove at the end, we get a stack (precisely as in our array implementation); if we insert at the beginning and remove at the beginning, we also get a stack (precisely as in our linked-list implementation); if we insert at the end and remove at the beginning, we get a FIFO queue (precisely as in our linked-list implementation); and if we insert at the beginning and remove at the end, we also get a FIFO queue (this option does not correspond to any of our implementations—we could switch our array implementation to implement it precisely, but the linked-list implementation is not suitable because of the need to back up the pointer to the end when we remove the item at the end of the list). Building on this point of view, we are led to the *deque* ADT, where we allow either insertion or deletion at either end. We leave the implementations for exercises (see Exercises 4.42 through 4.46), noting that the array-based implementation is a straightforward extension of Program 4.17, and that the linked-list implementation requires a doubly linked list unless we restrict the deque to allow deletion at only one end.

In Chapter 9, we consider *priority queues*, where the items have keys and the rule for deletion is "remove the item with the smallest key." The priority-queue ADT is useful in a variety of applications, and the problem of finding efficient implementations for this ADT has been a research goal in computer science for many years. Identifying and using the ADT in applications has been an important factor in this research: we can get an immediate indication whether or not a new algorithm is correct by substituting its implementation for an old implementation in a huge, complex application and checking that we get the same result. Moreover, we get an immediate indication whether a new algorithm is more efficient than an old one by noting the extent to which substituting the new implementation improves the overall running time. The data structures and algorithms that we consider in Chapter 9 for solving this problem are interesting, ingenious, and effective.

In Chapters 12 through 16, we consider *symbol tables*, which are generalized queues where the items have keys and the rule for deletion is "remove an item whose key is equal to a given key, if there is one." This ADT is perhaps the most important one that we consider, and we shall examine dozens of implementations.

Each of these ADTs also give rise to a number of related, but different, ADTs that suggest themselves as an outgrowth of careful examination of client programs and the performance of implementations. In Sections 4.7 and 4.8, we consider numerous examples of changes in the specification of generalized queues that lead to yet more different ADTs, which we shall consider later in this book.

Exercises

▷ **4.35** Give the contents of q[0], . . . , q[4] after the execution of the operations illustrated in Figure 4.7, using Program 4.17. Assume that maxN is 10, as in Figure 4.8.

▷ **4.36** A letter means *put* and an asterisk means *get* in the sequence

EAS*Y*QUE***ST***IO*N***.

Give the sequence of values returned by the *get* operations when this sequence of operations is performed on an initially empty FIFO queue.

4.37 Modify the array-based FIFO queue implementation in the text (Program 4.17) to throw exceptions if there is not enough memory available from new to allocate the queue in the constructor, if the client attempts to *get* when the queue is empty, or if the client attempts to *put* when the queue is full.

4.38 Modify the linked-list–based FIFO queue implementation in the text (Program 4.16) to throw exceptions if the client attempts to *get* when the queue is empty, if the client attempts to *put* when the queue is full, or if there is no memory available from new for a *put*.

▷**4.39**   An uppercase letter means *put* at the beginning, a lowercase letter means *put* at the end, a plus sign means *get* from the beginning, and an asterisk means *get* from the end in the sequence

$$\text{E A s} + \text{Y} + \text{Q U E} * * + \text{s t} + * + \text{l O} * \text{n} + + *.$$

Give the sequence of values returned by the *get* operations when this sequence of operations is performed on an initially empty deque.

▷**4.40**   Using the conventions of Exercise 4.39, give a way to insert plus signs and asterisks in the sequence E a s Y so that the sequence of values returned by the *get* operations is (*i*) E s a Y ; (*ii*) Y a s E ; (*iii*) a Y s E ; (*iv*) a s Y E ; or, in each instance, prove that no such sequence exists.

•**4.41**   Given two sequences, give an algorithm for determining whether or not it is possible to add plus signs and asterisks to make the first produce the second when interpreted as a sequence of deque operations in the sense of Exercise 4.40.

▷**4.42**   Give an ADT interface for the deque ADT.

4.43   Provide an implementation for your deque interface (Exercise 4.42) that uses an array for the underlying data structure.

4.44   Provide an implementation for your deque interface (Exercise 4.42) that uses a doubly linked list for the underlying data structure.

4.45   Provide an implementation for the FIFO queue interface in the text (Program 4.15) that uses a circular list for the underlying data structure.

4.46   Write a client that tests your deque ADTs (Exercise 4.42) by reading, as the first argument on the command line, a string of commands like those given in Exercise 4.39, then performing the indicated operations. Add a method dump to the interface and implementations, and print out the contents of the deque after each operation, in the style of Figure 4.7.

○**4.47**   Build a random-queue ADT by writing an ADT interface and an implementation that uses an array as the underlying data structure. Make sure that each operation takes constant time.

••**4.48**   Build a random-queue ADT by writing an interface and an implementation that uses a linked list as the underlying data structure. Provide implementations for *insert* and *remove* that are as efficient as you can make them, and analyze their worst-case cost.

▷**4.49**   Write a client that picks numbers for a lottery by putting the numbers 1 through 99 on a random queue, then prints the result of removing five of them.

4.50   Write a client that takes an integer $N < 11$ from the command line, then prints out N poker hands, by putting 52 items on a random queue (see

Exercise 3.1), then printing out the result of picking five cards from the queue, N times.

● 4.51 Write a program that solves the connectivity problem by inserting all the pairs on a random queue and then taking them from the queue, using the weighted-quick-union algorithm (Program 1.3).

4.8 Duplicate and Index Items

For many applications, the abstract items that we process are *unique*, a quality that leads us to consider modifying our idea of how stacks, FIFO queues, and other generalized ADTs should operate. Specifically, in this section, we consider the effect of changing the specifications of stacks, FIFO queues, and generalized queues to disallow duplicate items in the data structure.

For example, our company that maintains a mailing list of customers might want to try to grow the list by performing *insert* operations from other lists gathered from many sources, but it would not want the list to grow for an *insert* operation that refers to a customer already on the list. We shall see that the same principle applies in a variety of applications. For another example, consider the problem of routing a message through a complex communications network. We might try going through several paths simultaneously in the network, but there is only one message, so any particular node in the network would want to have only one copy in its internal data structures.

One approach to handling this situation is to leave up to the clients the task of ensuring that duplicate items are not presented to the ADT, a task that clients presumably might carry out using some different ADT. But since the purpose of an ADT is to provide clients with clean solutions to applications problems, we might decide that detecting and resolving duplicates is a part of the problem that the ADT should help to solve.

The policy of disallowing duplicate items is a change in the *abstraction*: the interface, names of the operations, and so forth for such an ADT are the same as those for the corresponding ADT without the policy, but the behavior of the implementation changes in a fundamental way. In general, whenever we modify the specification of an ADT, we get a completely new ADT—one that has completely different properties. This situation also demonstrates the precarious nature of

```
L            L
A            L A
*    A       L
S            L S
T            L S T
I            L S T I
*    I       L S T
N            L S T N
*    N       L S T
F            L S T F
I            L S T F I
R            L S T F I R
*    R       L S T F I
S            L S T F I
T            L S T F I
*    I       L S T F
*    F       L S T
*    T       L S
O            L S O
U            L S O U
*    U       L S O
T            L S O T
*    T       L S O
*    O       L S
*    S       L
```

Figure 4.10
Pushdown stack with no duplicates

This sequence shows the result of the same operations as those in Figure 4.1, but for a stack with no duplicate objects allowed. The gray squares mark situations where the stack is left unchanged because the item to be pushed is already on the stack. The number of items on the stack is limited by the number of possible distinct items.

```
F        F
I        F I
R        F I R
S        F I R S
*   F      I R S
T        I R S T
*   I      R S T
I        R S T I
N        R S T I N
*   R      S T I N
*   S      T I N
*   T      I N
F        I N F
I        I N F ▨
*   I      N F
R        N F R
S        N F R S
*   N      F R S
*   F      R S
*   R      S
T        S T
*   S      T
O        T O
U        T O U
T        T O U ▨
*   T      O U
*   O      U
*   U
```

Figure 4.11
FIFO queue with no dupli-
cates, ignore-the-new-item
policy

*This sequence shows the result of
the same operations as those in
Figure 4.7, but for a queue with
no duplicate objects allowed. The
gray squares mark situations where
the queue is left unchanged because the item to be put onto the
queue is already there.*

ADT specification: Being sure that clients and implementations adhere to the specifications in an interface is difficult enough, but enforcing a high-level policy such as this one is another matter entirely. Still, we are interested in algorithms that do so because clients can exploit such properties to solve problems in new ways, and implementations can take advantage of such restrictions to provide more efficient solutions.

Figure 4.10 shows how a modified no-duplicates stack ADT would operate for the example corresponding to Figure 4.1; Figure 4.11 shows the effect of the change for FIFO queues.

In general, we have a policy decision to make when a client makes an *insert* request for an item that is already in the data structure. Should we proceed as though the request never happened, or should we proceed as though the client had performed a *remove* followed by an *insert*? This decision affects the order in which items are ultimately processed for ADTs such as stacks and FIFO queues (see Figure 4.12), and the distinction is significant for client programs. For example, the company using such an ADT for a mailing list might prefer to use the new item (perhaps assuming that it has more up-to-date information about the customer), and the switching mechanism using such an ADT might prefer to ignore the new item (perhaps it has already taken steps to send along the message). Furthermore, this policy choice affects the implementations: the forget-the-old-item policy is generally more difficult to implement than the ignore-the-new-item policy, because it requires that we modify the data structure.

To implement generalized queues with no duplicate items, we need a method for testing item equality. The equals method is defined for all objects, but the default implementation takes an object to be equal only to itself, whereas in this context, we want to make a decision about equality based on the contents of its fields. Even given such an operation, we still need to be able to determine whether a new item to be inserted is already in the data structure. This general case amounts to implementing the symbol table ADT, so we shall consider it in the context of the implementations given in Chapters 12 through 15.

There is an important special case for which we have a straight-forward solution, which is illustrated for the pushdown stack ADT in Program 4.18. This implementation assumes that the items are integers in the range 0 to $M - 1$. Then, it uses a second array, indexed by the item itself, to determine whether that item is in the stack. When we insert item i, we set the ith entry in the second array to true; when we remove item i, we set the ith entry in the array to false. Otherwise, we use the same code as before to insert and remove items, with one additional test: Before inserting an item, we can test to see whether it is already in the stack. If it is, we ignore the *push*. This solution does not depend on whether we use an array or linked-list (or some other) representation for the stack. Implementing an ignore-the-old-item policy involves more work (see Exercise 4.56).

In summary, one way to implement a stack with no duplicates using an ignore-the-new-item policy is to maintain *two* data structures: the first contains the items in the stack, as before, to keep track of the order in which the items in the stack were inserted; the second is an array that allows us to keep track of which items are in the stack, by using the item as an index. Using an array in this way is a special case of a symbol-table implementation that is discussed in Section 12.2. We can apply the same technique to any generalized queue ADT, when we know the items to be integers in the range 0 to $M - 1$.

This special case arises frequently. The most important example is when the items in the data structure are themselves array indices, so we refer to such items as *index items*. Typically, we have a set of M objects, kept in yet another array, that we need to pass through a generalized queue structure as a part of a more complex algorithm. Objects are put on the queue by index and processed when they are removed, and each object is to be processed precisely once. Using array indices in a queue with no duplicates accomplishes this goal directly.

Each of these choices (disallow duplicates, or do not; and use the new item, or do not) leads to a new ADT. The differences may seem minor, but they obviously affect the dynamic behavior of the ADT as seen by client programs, and affect our choice of algorithm and data structure to implement the various operations, so we have no alternative but to treat all the ADTs as different. Furthermore, we have other options to consider: For example, we might either wish to modify the interface to inform the client program when it attempts to insert a duplicate item or to give the client the option whether to ignore the new item or to forget the old one.

When we informally use a term such as *pushdown stack*, *FIFO queue*, *deque*, *priority queue*, or *symbol table*, we are potentially referring to a *family* of ADTs, each with different sets of defined operations

```
F           F
I           F I
R           F I R
S           F I R S
*  F        I R S
T           I R S T
*  I        R S T
I           R S T I
N           R S T I N
*  R        S T I N
*  S        T I N
*  T        I N
F           I N F
I           N F I
*  N        F I
R           F I R
S           F I R S
*  F        I R S
*  I        R S
*  R        S
T           S T
*  S        T
O           T O
U           T O U
T           O U T
*  O        U T
*  U        T
*  T
```

Figure 4.12
FIFO queue with no duplicates, forget-the-old-item policy

This sequence shows the result of the same operations as in Figure 4.11, but using the (more difficult to implement) policy by which we always add a new item at the end of the queue. If there is a duplicate, we remove it.

Program 4.18 Stack with index items and no duplicates

This pushdown-stack implementation assumes that the integers on the
stack are in the range 0 and maxN-1, so that it can maintain an array
t that has a boolean value corresponding to each item in the stack.
The array enables an efficient implementation of an ignore-the-new-
item policy, where push takes no action its parameter is already on the
stack.

```
class intStack
  {
    private int[] s;
    private boolean[] t;
    private int N;
    intStack(int maxN)
      { s = new int[maxN]; N = 0;
        t = new boolean[maxN];
        for (int i = 0; i < maxN; i++) t[i] = false;
      }
    boolean empty()
      { return N == 0; }
    public void push(int item)
      { if (t[item]) return;
        s[N++] = item;
        t[item] = true;
      }
    public int pop()
      { t[s[--N]] = false; return s[N]; }
  }
```

and different sets of conventions about the meanings of the operations, each requiring different and, in some cases, more sophisticated
implementations to be able to support those operations efficiently.

Exercises

▷**4.52** Draw a figure corresponding to Figure 4.10 for the stack ADT that
disallows duplicates using a forget-the-old-item policy.

4.53 Modify the standard array-based stack implementation in Section 4.4
(Program 4.7) to disallow duplicates with an ignore-the-new-item policy. Use
a brute-force approach that involves scanning through the whole stack.

4.54 Modify the standard array-based stack implementation in Section 4.4 (Program 4.7) to disallow duplicates with a forget-the-old-item policy. Use a brute-force approach that involves scanning through, and possibly rearranging, the whole stack.

• **4.55** Do Exercises 4.53 and 4.54 for the linked-list–based stack implementation in Section 4.4 (Program 4.8).

○ **4.56** Develop a pushdown-stack implementation for integer items between 0 and $M - 1$ that disallows duplicates (using a forget-the-old-item policy) and that uses constant time for both *push* and *pop*. *Hint*: Use a doubly linked list representation for the stack and keep pointers to nodes, rather than true–false values, in an item-indexed array.

4.57 Do Exercises 4.53 and 4.54 for the FIFO queue ADT.

4.58 Do Exercise 4.55 for the FIFO queue ADT.

4.59 Do Exercise 4.56 for the FIFO queue ADT.

4.60 Do Exercises 4.53 and 4.54 for the randomized-queue ADT.

4.61 Write a client program for your ADT from Exercise 4.60, which exercises a randomized queue with no duplicates.

4.9 First-Class ADTs

ADTs help us manage the complexity of creating client programs that address the needs of increasingly more complicated applications by building increasingly powerful layers of abstraction. Throughout this process, it is often natural to want to use the data types in our programs in the same way that we use primitive types such as int or float. In this section, we consider the pitfalls that arise when we try to do so.

Definition 4.4 *A* **first-class data type** *is one which we can use in our programs in the same way as we use primitive data types.*

If a first-class data type is accessed only through an interface, it is a first-class ADT.

In general, Java does not support first-class data types because its primitive (built-in) data types are fundamentally different from its class (user-defined) data types. Java also provides direct language support for the String type, making it different from both primitive types and other class types. First, arithmetic operators such as + and * are defined for primitive data types (and + is defined for the String type), but we cannot arrange to write a+b when a and b are objects of a user-defined type. Second, we can define methods for class types and extend them, but we cannot do either for primitive types. Third, the meaning of a = b depends on whether or not a and b are primitive types: if they are primitive, a gets a copy of the value of b; if not, a gets a copy of a *reference* to b. The same holds true of method parameters and return values.

As with our other definitions related to data types, we cannot be precise in defining the concept of first-class types without straying into deep issues relating to semantics of operations. It is one thing to expect that we be able to write a = b when a and b are objects from a user-defined class, but it is quite another thing to precisely specify what we mean by that statement.

In a perfect world, we might envision all data types having some universal set of well-defined methods. An example is the convention that all Java objects have a toString method. In practice, each data type is characterized by its own set of methods. This difference between data types in itself militates against a precise definition of the concept of first-class data types, because it implies that we should provide definitions for *every* operation that is defined for built-in types, which we rarely do. Most often, only a few crucial operations are of importance to us, and we try to use those operations for our own data types in the same way as we do for built-in types.

As an illustration, we consider an ADT for the *complex-number* abstraction. Our goal is to be able to write programs that perform algebraic operations on complex numbers using operations defined in the ADT. We would like to declare and initialize complex numbers and use arithmetic operations on complex numbers to perform various computations involving them. As just mentioned, we will not be able to write clients that use the arithmetic operators * and + on complex numbers; we will have to define and use appropriate methods for these operations. Still, it is natural to want to compute with complex numbers in much the same way as we compute with real numbers or integers.

We now digress to consider briefly a few mathematical properties of complex numbers. In one sense, we are not digressing at all, because it is interesting to contemplate the relationship between complex numbers themselves as a mathematical abstraction and how to represent them in a computer program.

The number $i = \sqrt{-1}$ is an *imaginary* number. Although $\sqrt{-1}$ is meaningless as a real number, we name it i and perform algebraic manipulations with i, replacing i^2 with -1 whenever it appears. A *complex number* consists of two parts, real and imaginary—complex numbers can be written in the form $a + bi$, where a and b are reals. To multiply complex numbers, we apply the usual algebraic rules, replacing i^2 with -1 whenever it appears. For example,

$$(a + bi)(c + di) = ac + bci + adi + bdi^2 = (ac - bd) + (ad + bc)i.$$

The real or imaginary parts might cancel out (have the value 0) when we perform a complex multiplication. For example,

$$(1 - i)(1 - i) = 1 - i - i + i^2 = -2i,$$

$$(1 + i)^4 = 4i^2 = -4,$$

$$(1 + i)^8 = 16.$$

Scaling the preceding equation by dividing through by $16 = (\sqrt{2})^8$, we find that

$$\left(\frac{1}{\sqrt{2}} + \frac{i}{\sqrt{2}}\right)^8 = 1.$$

In general, there are many complex numbers that evaluate to 1 when raised to a power. These are the *complex roots of unity*. Indeed, for each N, there are exactly N complex numbers z with $z^N = 1$. The numbers

$$\cos\left(\frac{2\pi k}{N}\right) + i\sin\left(\frac{2\pi k}{N}\right),$$

for $k = 0, 1, \ldots, N - 1$ are easily shown to have this property (see Exercise 4.68). For example, taking $k = 1$ and $N = 8$ in this formula gives the particular eighth root of unity that we just discovered.

As an example of a client, consider the task of writing a program that computes each of the Nth roots of unity for any given N and checks the computation by raising each of them to the Nth power. This process should produce the output shown in Figure 4.13: We expect that each number raised to the Nth power gives the same result: 1, or $1 + 0i$. (The real and imaginary parts that we compute may not be exactly one and zero, respectively, because of limitations on the precision of our calculations.)

```
0  1.000  0.000 1.000 0.000
1  0.707  0.707 1.000 0.000
2  0.000  1.000 1.000 0.000
3 -0.707  0.707 1.000 0.000
4 -1.000  0.000 1.000 0.000
5 -0.707 -0.707 1.000 0.000
6  0.000 -1.000 1.000 0.000
7  0.707 -0.707 1.000 0.000
```

Figure 4.13
Complex roots of unity

This table gives the output that would be produced by Program 4.19 when invoked with a.out 8, *with an implementation of the overloaded* toString *method that does appropriate output formatting (see Exercise 4.70). The eight complex roots of unity are* ± 1, $\pm i$, *and*

$$\pm\frac{\sqrt{2}}{2} \pm \frac{\sqrt{2}}{2}i$$

(left two columns). *Each of these eight numbers gives the result* $1 + 0i$ *when raised to the eighth power (right two columns).*

Program 4.19 Complex numbers driver (roots of unity)

This client program performs a computation on complex numbers using an ADT that allows it to compute directly with the abstraction of interest by using objects of type `Complex`. This program checks the ADT implementation by computing the powers of the roots of unity. With an appropriate `toString` method(see Exercise 4.70), it prints the table in Figure 4.13.

```java
public class RootsOfUnity
  {
    public static void main(String[] args)
      { int N = Integer.parseInt(args[0]);
        Out.println(N + " roots of unity");
        for (int k = 0; k < N; k++)
          { double x = Math.cos(2.0*Math.PI*k/N),
                   y = Math.sin(2.0*Math.PI*k/N);
            Complex t = new Complex(x, y);
            Out.print(k + ": "+ t);
            Complex z = (Complex) t.clone();
            for (int j = 0; j < N-1; j++) z.mult(t);
            Out.println(" " + z);
          }
      }
  }
```

How should we arrange to multiply two complex numbers? Ideally, we would want to write expressions like

```java
a = b * c;
```

where a, b, and c are all of type `Complex`, but, again, Java does not support this style of programming. One idea is to try to mimic this style by writing a static method that takes two `Complex` objects as parameters and returns a `Complex`, so that we can write

```java
a = Complex.mult(b, c);
```

Another approach is to use a single-parameter class method `mult` that we use to multiply a `Complex` object by the given parameter. This approach mimics the use of expressions like a `*=` b with primitive types. We faced a similar tradeoff in Section 3.1 when discussing the

---

Program 4.20 ADT interface for complex numbers

This interface for complex numbers allows implementations to create objects of type `Complex` (initialized with two `double` values), to access the real and imaginary parts, and to use the `mult` method. While not explicitly specified, system default mechanisms that work for all classes allow us to use `Complex` objects as parameters or return values in methods. The `clone()` method provides a way for clients to mimic an assignment statement (copy the value of one `Complex` into another) (*see text*).

```
class Complex implements Cloneable // ADT interface
  { // implementations and private members hidden
    Complex(double re, double im)
    double re()
    double im()
    Complex mult(Complex rhs)
    public Object clone()
    public String toString()
  }
```

---

implementation of a method for computing the distance between two points. Here there is an additional important performance difference: when we use the static two-parameter method, we have to create a new `Complex` (for the result) every time we perform an arithmetic operation and, in an extended computation, are likely to leave numerous objects to be gathered by the garbage collector. When we use the class method, we do not pay this price (see Exercise 4.63).

Suppose that we have a `float` named `t` and an `int` named `N`, and we wish to compute the value of `t` raised to the Nth power. If `N` is not large, a natural way to perform this computation is to use the following code:

```
float z = t;
for (int j = 0; j < N-1; j++) z *= t;
```

Accordingly, if `t` is `Complex`, we would expect to be able to write

```
Complex z = t;
for (int j = 0; j < N-1; j++) z.mult(t);
```

But we would be mistaken in this expectation, because `z` and `t` are references to the same complex object, not different ones. This code

---

Program 4.21 ADT implementation for complex numbers

This code implements the ADT defined in Program 4.20 using doubles
to represent the real and imaginary parts of each complex number. Like
toString, a default implementation of the clone() method (which
copies the data fields of this object into a new object) exists in Object
and may be redefined by any implementation but must have the given
signature.

```java
class Complex implements Cloneable
  {
    private double re, im;
    Complex(double re, double im)
      { this.re = re; this.im = im; }
    double re()
      { return re; }
    double im()
      { return im; }
    void add(Complex rhs)
      {
        re = re() + rhs.re();
        im = im() + rhs.im();
      }
    void mult(Complex rhs)
      { double t = re();
        re = re() * rhs.re() - im() * rhs.im();
        im = t * rhs.im() + im() * rhs.re();
      }
    public String toString()
      { return re() + " " + im(); }
  }
```

---

actually computes the value of t^{2^N}, not t^N. The problem is that we
expect the assignment statement to make a copy of the object, but it
actually makes a copy of a reference to the object.

Java has a mechanism that specifically addresses this problem:
any class can implement the Cloneable interface. In such a class,
clients can invoke an object's clone method that returns a copy of the
object (a different object with the same data fields). Program 4.19 is a

client that uses this capability to print and check the roots of unity, as desired.

Program 4.20 is an ADT for complex numbers based on the discussion above, and Program 4.21 is an implementation that uses a standard data representation (one `double` for the real part and one `double` for the imaginary part). Even for this simple example, it is important that the data type be abstract because there is another standard representation that we might wish to consider using: polar coordinates (see Exercise 4.67).

Another place to use cloning is when we use objects as method parameters. For primitive types, we expect to have an object of our own for use within the method; for object types, we are passing a reference to the object and need to clone it if we want the method to have a copy. The same holds true for return values.

This issue of *copy semantics* is an important one to address in any ADT design. When an object's data fields are just primitive types, as in Program 4.21, the default implementation of `clone` in `Object` suffices (since it copies the values of the object's data fields to the corresponding fields in the clone); but if the data fields contain references to other objects, we need to clone those objects; if those objects contain references to other objects, we need to clone them, and so forth. Next, we consider an example that will help us examine this issue in more detail.

Program 4.22 exemplifies a client program that manipulates FIFO queues. It simulates a certain situation involving customers arriving and being served in a set of M queues. Figure 4.14 is an example of the output produced by this program. Our interest in this program is as an example of working with queues as objects—we can imagine writing similar programs to test various methods of organizing queues to serve customers, and so forth. This program prints out the contents of the queues on the last five times through the simulation loop.

For the present discussion, our interest is in the `for` loop at the end, which is intended to print out the contents of each queue. Suppose that we use the linked-list queue implementation that we considered in Program 4.16. We know that when we say `t = Q[k]` (where `t` and `Q[k]` are both `intQueue` objects) we would just be making them refer to the same queue, but what behavior do we want when we make `intQueue` clonable and say `t = (intQueue) Q[k].clone()`?

Program 4.22 Queue client program (queue simulation)

This client program simulates a situation where we assign customers waiting for service at random to one of M service queues, then choose a queue at random (possibly the same one) and, if it is nonempty, perform the service (remove a customer from the queue). To see the effect on the queues, we print out the customer added, the customer served, and the contents of the queues for the last five iterations.

This implementation uses the clonable queue ADT interface of Program 4.23 and requires a clone implementation such as the one given in Program 4.24 to make a copy of the appropriate queue for t each time through the inner for loop.

```
public class SimulateQueues
  { private static int M = 4;
    public static void main(String[] args)
      { int N = Integer.parseInt(args[0]);
        intQueue[] Q = new intQueue[M];
        for (int i = 0; i < M; i++)
          Q[i] = new intQueue(N);
        for (int i = 0; i < N; i++)
          { int in = (int) (Math.random() * M);
            int out = (int) (Math.random() * M);
            Q[in].put(i);
            if (!Q[out].empty()) Q[out].get();
            if (i < N - 5) continue;
            Out.print(in + " in ");
            Out.println(out + " out");
            for (int k = 0; k < M; k++)
              { intQueue t;
                t = (intQueue) Q[k].clone();
                Out.print(k + ": ");
                while(!t.empty())
                  Out.print(t.get() + " ");
                Out.println("");
              }
          }
      }
  }
```

Program 4.23 Clonable queue ADT interface

To make a user-defined class whose data members may contain pointers behave more like a built-in type, we need to include a `clone()` implementation in its interface, as in this version of the basic FIFO queue interface that we considered in Program 4.15.

```
class intQueue implements Cloneable // ADT interface
  { // private members and implementations hidden
    intQueue(int)
    public Object clone()
    boolean empty()
    void put(int)
    int get()
  }
```

The default implementation of `clone` will simply make a new object `t` with a copy of `Q[k]`'s data fields. In this case, the `head` and `tail` fields of `t` would be references to the first and last objects (respectively) on `Q[k]`. But this would result in unintended behavior (see Exercise 4.71) because we were clearly expecting to have a copy of the whole list. The system cannot know how to do that—we have to provide the code. To do so, we override the implementation of `clone`, as illustrated in Program 4.24.

Such methods are generally based on straightforward traversals of our data structures. However, we do not always take these extra steps, because

- We often use only a single instance of an object from a class.
- If we do have multiple instances, we want to avoid inadvertently copying huge data structures.

In short, while cognizant of our ability to clone objects we remain aware of the tradeoff between convenience and cost when doing so, particularly when huge amounts of data are involved.

As another example, we might envision modifying Program 4.22 to periodically print just the first few items on each queue, so that we can track progress even when the queues become huge. But we might eventually be surprised by poor performance when the queues do become huge, because initialization of the local variable in the `for` loop invokes the copy constructor, which makes a copy of the entire queue,

```
75 in 74 out
0: 58 59 60 67 68 73
1:
2: 64 66 72
3: 75

76 in
0: 58 59 60 67 68 73
1:
2: 64 66 72
3: 75 76

77 in 58 out
0: 59 60 67 68 73
1: 77
2: 64 66 72
3: 75 76

78 in 77 out
0: 59 60 67 68 73
1: 78
2: 64 66 72
3: 75 76

79 in 78 out
0: 59 60 67 68 73
1: 79
2: 64 66 72
3: 75 76
```

**Figure 4.14
Random-queue simulation**

This listing gives the tail end of the output produced when Program 4.22 is invoked with 80 as the command-line argument. It shows the contents of the queues after the indicated operations, where we choose a queue at random and put *the next item in, then choose another queue at random and, if it is nonempty,* get *an item out.*

Program 4.24 Linked-list implementation of a clonable queue

Adding this method upgrades the FIFO queue class implementation in
Program 4.16 to implement the interface in Program 4.23. It makes a
copy of the list by traversing it and building a new list from the same
items.

```
public Object clone()
  {
    intQueue Q = new intQueue(0);
    for (Node t = head; t != null; t = t.next)
      Q.put(t.item);
    return Q;
  }
```

---

even if we only want to access a few elements. Eventually that entire
queue is collected as garbage, because it is the value of a local variable.
For Program 4.22 as it stands, where we access every item on the copy,
the extra cost of allocating and garbage collection affects the running
time by only a constant factor, but it would be an unreasonable price
to pay if we merely wanted to access a few items. In such a situation,
we would prefer to use the default pointer-assignment implementation
for *copy*, and modify the ADT to add operations allowing us to access
items on the queue without modifying it.

The list of questions that can arise when we consider ADT implementations is long, even for simple ADTs like the ones that we have
been considering in this chapter. Do we want to be able to have different types of objects on the same queue? Do we want to use different
implementations for queues of the same type in a single client because
we know of performance differences? Should information about the
efficiency of implementations be included in the interface? What form
should that information take? Such questions underscore the importance of understanding the basic characteristics of our algorithms and
data structures and how client programs may use them effectively,
which is, in a sense, the topic of this book. Though full implementations are often exercises in software engineering instead of algorithms
design, we strive to remain cognizant of the relevant issues so that our
algorithms and data structures can serve as the basis for software tools
in a broad variety of applications (*see reference section*).

Exercises

▷ **4.62** Develop a version of the Complex class in this section (Program 4.21) that uses static methods instead of class methods for add and mult, and write a version of the roots-of-unity client (Program 4.19) that uses your class.

4.63 Compare the performance of your solution to Exercise 4.62 with the programs in the text, by removing the println statements and comparing running times for $N = 100$, 1000, and 10000.

4.64 Write a clone method for the equivalence-relations ADT in Section 4.5.

4.65 Create an ADT with a clone method for use in programs that process playing cards.

●● **4.66** Write a program to determine empirically the probability that various poker hands are dealt, using your ADT from Exercise 4.65.

○ **4.67** Develop an implementation for the complex-number ADT (a program with the same public methods as Program 4.21 that is based on representing complex numbers in polar coordinates (that is, in the form $re^{i\theta}$).

● **4.68** Use the identity $e^{i\theta} = \cos\theta + i\sin\theta$ to prove that $e^{2\pi i} = 1$ and that the N complex Nth roots of unity are

$$\cos\left(\frac{2\pi k}{N}\right) + i\sin\left(\frac{2\pi k}{N}\right),$$

for $k = 0, 1, \ldots, N - 1$.

4.69 List the Nth roots of unity for N from 2 through 8.

● **4.70** Provide an implementation of toString for Program 4.21 that produces the output in Figure 4.13 for Program 4.19.

▷ **4.71** Describe precisely what happens when you run the queue simulation program Program 4.22 using a clonable version of Program 4.16 or Program 4.17, but with the default clone method.

4.72 Develop an implementation of the clonable FIFO queue ADT given in the text (Program 4.23) that uses an array as the underlying data structure.

▷ **4.73** Write an interface for a pushdown-stack ADT that includes a clone method.

4.74 Develop an implementation of your interface from Exercise 4.73 that uses an array as the underlying data structure.

4.75 Develop an implementation of your interface from Exercise 4.73 that uses a linked list as the underlying data structure.

○ **4.76** Modify the postfix-evaluation program in Section 4.3 to evaluate postfix expressions consisting of complex numbers with integer coefficients, using the complex-numbers ADT in the text (Program 4.21). For simplicity, assume that the complex numbers all have nonnull integer coefficients for both real and imaginary parts and are written with no spaces. For example, your program should print the output 8+4i when given the input

```
1+1i 0+1i + 1-2i * 3+4i + .
```

●● **4.77** Do a mathematical analysis of the queue-simulation process in Program 4.22 to determine, as a function of N and M, the probability that the queue selected for the Nth get is empty and the expected number of items in the queues after N iterations of the for loop.

4.10 Application-Based ADT Example

As a final example, we consider in this section an application-specific ADT that is representative of the relationship between application domains and the algorithms and data structures of the type that we consider in this book. The example that we shall consider is the *polynomial* ADT. It is drawn from *symbolic mathematics*, where we use the computer to help us manipulate abstract mathematical objects.

Our goal is to be able to write programs that can manipulate polynomials and perform computations such as

$$\left(1 - x + \frac{x^2}{2} - \frac{x^3}{6}\right)\left(1 + x + x^2 + x^3\right) = 1 + \frac{x^2}{2} + \frac{x^3}{3} - \frac{2x^4}{3} + \frac{x^5}{3} - \frac{x^6}{6}.$$

We also want to be able to evaluate the polynomial for a given value of x. For $x = 0.5$, both sides of this equation have the value 1.1328125. The operations of multiplying, adding, and evaluating polynomials are at the heart of a great many mathematical calculations.

The first step is to define the polynomial ADT, as illustrated in the interface Program 4.26. For a well-understood mathematical abstraction such as a polynomial, the specification is so clear as to be unspoken: We want instances of the ADT to behave precisely in the same manner as the well-understood mathematical abstraction. As for the ADT for complex numbers that we discussed in Section 4.8, our first preference might be to have a first-class ADT where we could use arithmetic operators such as * and + (which are well defined for polynomials), but Java does not support operator overloading, so we have to define standard methods. Just as we found for complex numbers, it is natural instead in Java to use an object-oriented approach where we define methods add and mult for any polynomial object to multiply itself by another polynomial.

Program 4.25 ADT interface for polynomials

This interface defines a polynomial ADT with integer coefficients. The constructor, when invoked with parameters c and N, is to create a polynomial corresponding to cx^N.

```
class Poly // ADT interface
  { // implementations and private members hidden
    Poly(int, int)
    double eval(double)
    void add(Poly)
    void mult(Poly)
    public String toString()
  }
```

Program 4.25 is a simple example of a client that performs the symbolic operations corresponding to the polynomial equations

$$(x + 1)^2 = x^2 + 2x + 1,$$
$$(x + 1)^3 = x^3 + 3x^2 + 3x + 1,$$
$$(x + 1)^4 = x^4 + 4x^3 + 6x^2 + 4x + 1,$$
$$(x + 1)^5 = x^5 + 5x^4 + 10x^3 + 10x^2 + 5x + 1,$$

. . .

and then evaluates the polynomial that results for a given value of x.

To implement the methods defined in the interface, we need to choose a particular data structure to represent polynomials and then to implement algorithms that manipulate the data structure to produce the behavior that client programs expect from the ADT. As usual, the choice of data structure affects the potential efficiency of the algorithms, and we are free to consider several. As with stacks and queues, we have the choice of using a linked representation or an array representation. Program 4.27 is an implementation using an array representation; the linked-list representation is left as an exercise (see Exercise 4.80).

To *add* two polynomials, we add their coefficients. If the polynomials are represented as arrays, the *add* method amounts to a single loop through the arrays, as shown in Program 4.27. To *multiply* two polynomials, we use the elementary algorithm based on the distribu-

Program 4.26 Polynomial client (binomial coefficients)

This client program uses the polynomial ADT that is defined in the interface Program 4.26 to perform algebraic manipulations on polynomials with integer coefficients. It takes an integer N and a floating-point number p from the command line, computes $(x+1)^N$, and checks the result by evaluating the resulting polynomial at $x = p$.

```
public class Binomial
  {
    public static void main(String[] args)
      { int N = Integer.parseInt(args[0]);
        double p = Double.parseDouble(args[1]);
        Poly y = new Poly(1, 0);
        Poly t = new Poly(1, 0);
        t.add(new Poly(1, 1));
        for (int i = 0; i < N; i++)
          { y.mult(t); Out.println(y + ""); }
        Out.println("value: " + y.eval(p));
      }
  }
```

tive law. We multiply one polynomial by each term in the other, line up the results so that powers of x match, then add the terms to get the final result. The following table summarizes the computation for $\left(1 - x + x^2/2 - x^3/6\right)\left(1 + x + x^2 + x^3\right)$:

$$
\begin{array}{cccccccc}
1 & -x & +\dfrac{x^2}{2} & -\dfrac{x^3}{6} & & & & \\[2mm]
 & +x & -x^2 & +\dfrac{x^3}{2} & -\dfrac{x^4}{6} & & & \\[2mm]
 & & +x^2 & -x^3 & +\dfrac{x^4}{2} & -\dfrac{x^5}{6} & & \\[2mm]
 & & & +x^3 & -x^4 & +\dfrac{x^5}{2} & -\dfrac{x^6}{6} & \\[2mm]
\hline
1 & & +\dfrac{x^2}{2} & +\dfrac{x^3}{3} & -\dfrac{2x^4}{3} & +\dfrac{x^5}{3} & -\dfrac{x^6}{6} &
\end{array}
$$

The computation seems to require time proportional to N^2 to multiply two polynomials. Finding a faster algorithm for this task is a significant challenge. We shall consider this topic in detail in Part 8, where we shall see that it is possible to accomplish the task in time proportional to $N^{3/2}$ using a divide-and-conquer algorithm, and in time proportional to $N \lg N$ using the fast Fourier transform.

The implementation of the *evaluate* method in Program 4.27 uses a classic efficient algorithm known as *Horner's algorithm*. A naive implementation of the method involves a direct computation using a method that computes x^N. This approach takes quadratic time. A less naive implementation involves saving the values of x^i in a table, then using them in a direct computation. This approach takes linear extra space. Horner's algorithm is a direct optimal linear algorithm based on parenthesizations such as

$$a_4 x^4 + a_3 x^3 + a_2 x^2 + a_1 x + a_0 = (((a_4 x + a_3)x + a_2)x + a_1)x + a_0.$$

Horner's method is often presented as a time-saving trick, but it is actually an early and outstanding example of an elegant and efficient algorithm, which reduces the time required for this essential computational task from quadratic to linear. The calculation that we performed in Program 4.5 for converting ASCII strings to integers is a version of Horner's algorithm. We shall encounter Horner's algorithm again, in Chapter 14 and Part 5, as the basis for an important computation related to certain symbol-table and string-search implementations.

The add and mult operators construct new arrays to hold their results. We overwrite references to the old ones leaving a (potentially huge) number of objects with no references to them. We depend upon the Java garbage-collection mechanism to reclaim the memory associated with these objects (see Exercise 4.79). Because we have to create new objects anyway, the use of static methods instead of class methods is a reasonable alternative for this application (see Exercise 4.78).

As usual, the array representation for implementing the polynomial ADT is but one possibility. If exponents are huge and there are not many terms, a linked-list representation might be more appropriate (see Exercise 4.80). For example, we might not want to use Program 4.27 to perform a multiplication such as

$$(1 + x^{1000000})(1 + x^{2000000}) = 1 + x^{1000000} + x^{2000000} + x^{3000000},$$

because it would use an array with space for millions of unused coefficients while a linked-list implementation would only use a few nodes.

Program 4.27 Array implementation of polynomial ADT

In this implementation of an ADT for polynomials, the data representation consists of the degree and a pointer to an array of coefficients.

```
class Poly
  { private int n; private int[] a;
    Poly(int c, int N)
      { a = new int[N+1]; n = N+1; a[N] = c;
        for (int i = 0; i < N; i++) a[i] = 0;
      }
    double eval(double d)
      { double t = 0.0;
        for (int i = n-1; i >= 0; i--)
          t = t*d + (double) a[i];
        return t;
      }
    void add(Poly p)
      { int[] t = new int[(p.n > n) ? p.n : n];
        for (int i = 0; i < p.n; i++)
          t[i] = p.a[i];
        for (int j = 0; j < n; j++)
          t[j] += a[j];
        a = t; n = t.length;
      }
    void mult(Poly p)
      { int[] t = new int[p.n + n -1];
        for (int i = 0; i < p.n; i++)
          for (int j = 0; j < n; j++)
            t[i+j] += p.a[i] * a[j];
        a = t; n = t.length;
      }
    public String toString()
      { String s = "";
        for (int i = 0; i < n; i++)
          s += a[i] + " ";
        return s;
      }
  }
```

Exercises

▷ **4.78** Develop a version of the `Poly` class in this section (Program 4.27) that uses static methods instead of class methods for `add` and `mult`, and write a version of the binomial-coefficients client (Program 4.25) that uses your class.

4.79 Compare the performance of your solution to Exercise 4.62 with the programs in the text, by removing the `println` statements and comparing running times for $N = 100$, 1000, and 10000.

○ **4.80** Provide an implementation for the polynomial ADT given in the text (Program 4.26) that uses linked lists as the underlying data structure. Your lists should not contain any nodes corresponding to terms with coefficient value 0.

▷ **4.81** Write a `clone` method for the `Poly` class of Program 4.27 so that it can implement `Cloneable`.

○ **4.82** Extend the polynomial ADT given in the text to include integration and differentiation of polynomials.

4.83 Modify your polynomial ADT from Exercise 4.82 to ignore all terms with exponents greater than or equal to an integer M, which is provided by the client at initialization.

●● **4.84** Extend your polynomial ADT from Exercise 4.82 to include polynomial division and composition.

● **4.85** Develop an ADT that allows clients to perform addition and multiplication of arbitrarily long integers.

● **4.86** Modify the postfix-evaluation program in Section 4.3 to evaluate postfix expressions consisting of arbitrarily long integers, using the ADT that you developed for Exercise 4.85.

●● **4.87** Write a client program that uses your polynomial ADT from Exercise 4.84 to evaluate integrals by using Taylor series approximations of functions, manipulating them symbolically.

4.88 Develop an ADT that provides clients with the ability to perform algebraic operations on vectors of floating-point numbers.

4.89 Develop an ADT that provides clients with the ability to perform algebraic operations on matrices of abstract objects for which addition, subtraction, multiplication, and division are defined.

4.90 Write an interface for a character-string ADT, which includes operations for creating a string, comparing two strings, concatenating two strings, copying one string to another, and returning the string length. *Note*: Your interface will be quite similar to the interface provided for the standard Java `String` type.

4.91 Provide an adapter class that implements your string ADT interface from Exercise 4.90, using the standard Java `String` type where appropriate.

4.92 Provide an implementation for your string interface from Exercise 4.90, using a linked list for the underlying representation. Analyze the worst-case running time of each operation.

4.93 Write an interface and an implementation for an index set ADT, which processes sets of integers in the range 0 to $M - 1$ (where M is a defined constant) and includes operations for creating a set, computing the union of two sets, computing the intersection of two sets, computing the complement of a set, computing the difference of two sets, and printing out the contents of a set. In your implementation, use an array of $M - 1$ boolean values to represent each set.

4.94 Write a client program that exercises your ADT from Exercise 4.93.

4.11 Perspective

There are three primary reasons for us to be aware of the fundamental concepts underlying ADTs as we embark on the study of algorithms and data structures:

- ADTs are an important software-engineering tool in widespread use, and many of the algorithms that we study serve as implementations for fundamental ADTs that are widely applicable.
- ADTs help us to encapsulate the algorithms that we develop, so that we can use the same code for many different purposes.
- ADTs provide a convenient mechanism for our use in the process of developing and comparing the performance of algorithms.

Ideally, ADTs embody the common-sense principle that we are obligated to describe precisely the ways in which we manipulate our data. The client-interface-implementation mechanism that we have considered in detail in this chapter is convenient for this task in Java, and provides us with Java code that has a number of desirable properties. Many modern languages have specific support that allows the development of programs with similar properties, but the general approach transcends particular languages—when we do not have specific language support, we adopt programming conventions to maintain the separation that we would like to have among clients, interfaces, and implementations.

As we consider an ever-expanding set of choices in specifying the behavior of our ADTs, we are faced with an ever-expanding set of challenges in providing efficient implementations. The numerous

ABSTRACT DATA TYPES §4.11 195

examples that we have considered illustrate ways of meeting such challenges. We continually strive to achieve the goal of implementing all the operations efficiently, but we are unlikely to have a general-purpose implementation that can do so for all sets of operations. This situation works against the principles that lead us to ADTs in the first place, because in many cases implementors of ADTs need to know properties of client programs to know which implementations of associated ADTs will perform most efficiently, and implementors of client programs need to know performance properties of various implementations to know which to choose for a particular application. As ever, we must strike a balance. In this book, we consider numerous approaches to implementations for variants of fundamental ADTs, all of which have important applications.

We can use one ADT to build another. We have used the pointer and structure abstractions provided by Java to build linked lists, then we have used linked lists or the array abstraction provided by Java to build pushdown stacks, then we have used pushdown stacks to get the capability to evaluate arithmetic expressions. The ADT concept allows us to construct large systems on different layers of abstraction, from the machine-language instructions provided by the computer, to the various capabilities provided by the programming language, to sorting, searching and other higher-level capabilities provided by algorithms as discussed in Parts 3 and 4 of this book, to the even higher levels of abstraction that the various applications require, as discussed in Parts 5 through 8. ADTs are one point on the continuum of developing ever more powerful abstract mechanisms, which is the essence of using computers effectively in problem solving.

CHAPTER FIVE

Recursion and Trees

THE CONCEPT OF recursion is fundamental in mathematics and computer science. The simple definition is that a recursive program in a programming language is one that invokes itself (just as a recursive function in mathematics is one that is defined in terms of itself). A recursive program cannot invoke itself always, or it would never stop (just as a recursive function cannot be defined in terms of itself always, or the definition would be circular); so a second essential ingredient is that there must be a *termination condition* when the program can cease to invoke itself (and when the mathematical function is not defined in terms of itself). All practical computations can be couched in a recursive framework.

The study of recursion is intertwined with the study of recursively defined structures known as *trees*. We use trees both to help us understand and analyze recursive programs and as explicit data structures. We have already encountered an application of trees (although not a recursive one) in Chapter 1. The connection between recursive programs and trees underlies a great deal of the material in this book. We use trees to understand recursive programs; we use recursive programs to build trees; and we draw on the fundamental relationship between both (and recurrence relations) to analyze algorithms. Recursion helps us to develop elegant and efficient data structures and algorithms for all manner of applications.

Our primary purpose in this chapter is to examine recursive programs and data structures as practical tools. First, we discuss the relationship between mathematical recurrences and simple recursive

197

programs, and we consider a number of examples of practical recursive programs. Next, we examine the fundamental recursive scheme known as *divide and conquer*, which we use to solve fundamental problems in several later sections of this book. Then, we consider a general approach to implementing recursive programs known as *dynamic programming*, which provides effective and elegant solutions to a wide class of problems. Next, we consider trees, their mathematical properties, and associated algorithms in detail, including basic methods for *tree traversal* that underlie recursive tree-processing programs. Finally, we consider closely related algorithms for processing graphs— we look specifically at a fundamental recursive program, *depth-first search*, that serves as the basis for many graph-processing algorithms.

As we shall see, many interesting algorithms are simply expressed in Java with recursive methods, and many algorithm designers prefer to express computations recursively. We also investigate nonrecursive alternatives in detail. Not only can we often devise simple stack-based algorithms that are essentially equivalent to recursive algorithms, but also we can often find nonrecursive alternatives that achieve the same final result through a different sequence of computations. The recursive formulation provides a structure within which we can seek more efficient alternatives.

A full discussion of recursion and trees could fill an entire book, for they arise in many applications throughout computer science and are pervasive outside of computer science as well. Indeed, it might be said that *this* book is filled with a discussion of recursion and trees, for they are present, in a fundamental way, in every one of the book's chapters.

5.1 Recursive Algorithms

A *recursive algorithm* is one that solves a problem by solving one or more smaller instances of the same problem. To implement recursive algorithms in Java, we use *recursive methods*—a recursive method is one that calls itself. Recursive methods in Java correspond to recursive definitions of mathematical functions. We begin our study of recursion by examining programs that directly evaluate mathematical functions. The basic mechanisms extend to provide a general-purpose programming paradigm, as we shall see.

Program 5.1 Factorial function (recursive implementation)

This recursive method computes the function $N!$, using the standard recursive definition. It returns the correct value when called with N nonnegative and sufficiently small that $N!$ can be represented as an int.

```
static int factorial(int N)
  {
    if (N == 0) return 1;
    return N*factorial(N-1);
  }
```

Recurrence relations (see Section 2.5) are recursively defined functions. A recurrence relation defines a function whose domain is the nonnegative integers either by some initial values or (recursively) in terms of its own values on smaller integers. Perhaps the most familiar such function is the *factorial* function, which is defined by the recurrence relation

$$N! = N \cdot (N-1)!, \qquad \text{for } N \geq 1 \text{ with } 0! = 1.$$

This definition corresponds directly to the recursive Java method in Program 5.1.

Program 5.1 is equivalent to a simple loop. For example, the following for loop performs the same computation:

```
for ( t = 1, i = 1; i <= N; i++) t *= i;
```

As we shall see, it is always possible to transform a recursive program into a nonrecursive one that performs the same computation. Conversely, we can also use recursion to express without loops any computation that involves loops.

We use recursion because it often allows us to express complex algorithms in a compact form, without sacrificing efficiency. For example, the recursive implementation of the factorial function obviates the need for local variables. The cost of the recursive implementation is borne by the mechanisms in the programming systems that support method invocations, which use the equivalent of a built-in pushdown stack. Most modern programming systems have carefully engineered mechanisms for this task. Despite this advantage, as we shall see, it is all too easy to write a simple recursive method that is extremely

---

Program 5.2 A questionable recursive program

If the argument N is odd, this method calls itself with $3N + 1$ as an argument; if N is even, it calls itself with $N/2$ as an argument. We cannot use induction to prove that this program terminates, because not every recursive call uses an argument smaller than the one given.

```
static int puzzle(int N)
  {
    if (N == 1) return 1;
    if (N % 2 == 0)
        return puzzle(N/2);
    else return puzzle(3*N+1);
  }
```

---

inefficient, and we need to exercise care to avoid being burdened with intractable implementations.

Program 5.1 illustrates the basic features of a recursive program: it calls itself (with a smaller value of its argument), and it has a termination condition in which it directly computes its result. We can use mathematical induction to convince ourselves that the program works as intended:

- It computes 0! (basis).
- Under the assumption that it computes $k!$ for $k < N$ (inductive hypothesis), it computes $N!$.

Reasoning like this can provide us with a quick path to developing algorithms that solve complex problems, as we shall see.

In a programming language such as Java, there are few restrictions on the kinds of programs that we write, but we strive to limit ourselves in our use of recursive methods to those that embody inductive proofs of correctness like the one outlined in the previous paragraph. Although we do not consider formal correctness proofs in this book, we are interested in putting together complicated programs for difficult tasks, and we need to have some assurance that the tasks will be completed properly. Mechanisms such as recursive methods can provide such assurances while giving us compact implementations. Practically speaking, the connection to mathematical induction tells us that we should ensure that all of our recursive methods satisfy two basic properties:

```
puzzle(3)
  puzzle(10)
    puzzle(5)
      puzzle(16)
        puzzle(8)
          puzzle(4)
            puzzle(2)
              puzzle(1)
```

Figure 5.1
Example of a recursive method invocation chain

This nested sequence of method invocations eventually terminates, but we cannot prove that the recursive method in Program 5.2 does not have arbitrarily deep nesting for some argument. We prefer recursive programs that always invoke themselves with smaller arguments.

Program 5.3 Euclid's algorithm

One of the oldest known algorithms, dating back over 2000 years, is this recursive method for finding the greatest common divisors of two integers.

```
static int gcd(int M, int N)
  {
    if (N == 0) return M;
    return gcd(N, M % N);
  }
```

• They must explicitly solve a basis case.

• Each recursive call must involve smaller values of the arguments. These points are vague—they amount to saying that we should have a valid inductive proof for each recursive method that we write. Still, they provide useful guidance as we develop implementations.

Program 5.2 is an example that illustrates the need for an inductive argument. It is a recursive method that violates the rule that each recursive call must involve smaller values of the arguments, so we cannot use mathematical induction to understand it. Indeed, it is not known whether or not this computation terminates for every N if there are no bounds on the size of N. For small integers that can be represented as ints, we can check that the program terminates (see Figure 5.1 and Exercise 5.4), but for large integers (64-bit words, say), we do not know whether or not this program goes into an infinite loop.

Program 5.3 is a compact implementation of *Euclid's algorithm* for finding the greatest common divisor of two integers. It is based on the observation that the greatest common divisor of two integers x and y with $x > y$ is the same as the greatest common divisor of y and $x \bmod y$ (the remainder when x is divided by y). A number t divides both x and y if and only if t divides both y and $x \bmod y$, because x is equal to $x \bmod y$ plus a multiple of y. The recursive calls made for an example invocation of this program are shown in Figure 5.2. For Euclid's algorithm, the depth of the recursion depends on arithmetic properties of the arguments (it is known to be logarithmic).

Program 5.4 is an example with multiple recursive calls. It is another expression evaluator that performs essentially the same compu-

```
gcd(314159, 271828)
  gcd(271828, 42331)
    gcd(42331, 17842)
      gcd(17842, 6647)
        gcd(6647, 4458)
          gcd(4458, 2099)
            gcd(2099, 350)
              gcd(350, 349)
                gcd(349, 1)
                  gcd(1, 0)
```

Figure 5.2
Example of Euclid's algorithm

This nested sequence of method invocations illustrates the operation of Euclid's algorithm in discovering that 314159 and 271828 are relatively prime.

Program 5.4 Recursive program to evaluate prefix expressions

To evaluate a prefix expression, we either convert a number from ASCII to binary (in the `while` loop at the end) or perform the operation indicated by the first character in the expression on the two operands, evaluated recursively. This method is recursive, but it uses a global array containing the expression and an index to the current character in the expression. The index is advanced past each subexpression evaluated.

```
static char[] a;
static int i;
static int eval()
  { int x = 0;
    while (a[i] == ' ') i++;
    if (a[i] == '+')
      { i++; return eval() + eval(); }
    if (a[i] == '*')
      { i++; return eval() * eval(); }
    while ((a[i] >= '0') && (a[i] <= '9'))
      x = 10*x + (a[i++]-'0');
    return x;
  }
```

```
eval() * + 7 * * 4 6 + 8 9 5
  eval() + 7 * * 4 6 + 8 9
    eval() 7
    eval() * * 4 6 + 8 9
      eval() * 4 6
        eval() 4
        eval() 6
        return 24 = 4*6
      eval() + 8 9
        eval() 8
        eval() 9
        return 17 = 8 + 9
      return 408 = 24*17
    return 415 = 7+408
  eval() 5
  return 2075 = 415*5
```

Figure 5.3
Prefix expression evaluation example

This nested sequence of method invocations illustrates the operation of the recursive prefix-expression–evaluation algorithm on a sample expression. For simplicity, the expression arguments are shown here. The algorithm itself never explicitly decides the extent of its argument string: rather, it takes what it needs from the front of the string.

tations as Program 4.5 but on prefix (rather than postfix) expressions and lets recursion take the place of the explicit pushdown stack. In this chapter, we shall see many other examples of recursive programs and equivalent programs that use pushdown stacks. We shall examine the specific relationship between several pairs of such programs in detail.

Figure 5.3 shows the operation of Program 5.4 on a sample prefix expression. The multiple recursive calls mask a complex series of computations. Like most recursive programs, this program is best understood inductively: Assuming that it works properly for simple expressions, we can convince ourselves that it works properly for complex ones. This program is a simple example of a *recursive descent parser*—we can use the same process to convert Java programs into machine code.

A precise inductive proof that Program 5.4 evaluates the expression properly is certainly much more challenging to write than are the proofs for methods with integer arguments that we have been discussing, and we shall encounter recursive programs and data structures that are even more complicated than this one throughout this book. Accordingly, we do not pursue the idealistic goal of providing complete inductive proofs of correctness for every recursive program that we write. In this case, the ability of the program to "know" how to separate the operands corresponding to a given operator seems mysterious at first (perhaps because we cannot immediately see how to do this separation at the top level), but it is actually a straightforward calculation (because the path to pursue at each method invocation is unambiguously determined by the first character in the expression).

In principle, we can replace any `for` loop by an equivalent recursive program. Often, the recursive program is a more natural way to express the computation than the `for` loop, so we may as well take advantage of the mechanism provided by the programming system that supports recursion. There is one hidden cost, however, that we need to bear in mind. As is plain from the examples that we examined in Figures 5.1 through 5.3, when we execute a recursive program, we are nesting method invocations until we reach a point where we do not do a recursive invocation, and we return instead. In most programming environments, such nested method invocations are implemented using the equivalent of built-in pushdown stacks. We shall examine the nature of such implementations throughout this chapter. The *depth of the recursion* is the maximum degree of nesting of the method invocations over the course of the computation. Generally, the depth will depend on the input. For example, the depths of the recursions for the examples depicted in Figures 5.2 and 5.3 are 9 and 4, respectively. When using a recursive program, we need to take into account that the programming environment has to maintain a pushdown stack of size proportional to the depth of the recursion. For huge problems, the space needed for this stack might prevent us from using a recursive solution.

Data structures built from objects with fields that are references to objects of the same type are inherently recursive. For example, our definition of linked lists in Chapter 3 (Definition 3.3) is recursive. Therefore, recursive programs provide natural implementations of many commonly used functions for manipulating such data structures. Program 5.5 comprises four examples. We use such implementations frequently throughout the book, primarily because they are so much easier to understand than are their nonrecursive counterparts. However, we must exercise caution in using programs such as those in Program 5.5 when processing huge lists: the depth of the recursion for those methods can be proportional to the length of the lists, so the space required for the recursive stack might become prohibitive.

Some programming environments automatically detect and eliminate *tail recursion* (when the last action of a method is a recursive invocation) because it is not strictly necessary to add to the depth of the recursion in such a case. This improvement would effectively transform the count, traversal, and deletion methods in Program 5.5 into loops, but it does not apply to the reverse-order traversal method.

In Sections 5.2 and 5.3, we consider two families of recursive algorithms that represent essential computational paradigms. Then, in Sections 5.4 through 5.7, we consider recursive data structures that serve as the basis for a very large fraction of the algorithms that we consider.

Exercises

▷ **5.1** Write a recursive program to compute $\lg(N!)$.

5.2 Modify Program 5.1 to compute $N! \bmod M$, so that overflow is no longer an issue. Try running your program for $M = 997$ and $N = 10^3$, 10^4, 10^5, and 10^6 in order to get an indication of how your programming system handles deeply nested recursive calls.

▷ **5.3** Give the sequences of argument values that result when Program 5.2 is invoked for each of the integers 1 through 9.

● **5.4** Find the value of $N < 10^6$ for which Program 5.2 makes the maximum number of recursive calls.

▷ **5.5** Provide a nonrecursive implementation of Euclid's algorithm.

▷ **5.6** Give the figure corresponding to Figure 5.2 for the result of running Euclid's algorithm for the inputs 89 and 55.

○ **5.7** Give the recursive depth of Euclid's algorithm when the input values are two consecutive Fibonacci numbers (F_N and F_{N+1}).

▷ **5.8** Give the figure corresponding to Figure 5.3 for the result of recursive prefix-expression evaluation for the input + * * 12 12 12 144.

5.9 Write a recursive program to evaluate postfix expressions.

5.10 Write a recursive program to evaluate infix expressions. You may assume that operands are always enclosed in parentheses.

○ **5.11** Write a recursive program that converts infix expressions to postfix.

Program 5.5 Examples of recursive functions for linked lists

These recursive methods for simple list-processing tasks are easy to express but may not be useful for huge lists because the depth of the recursion may be proportional to the length of the list.

The first method, count, counts the number of nodes on the list. The second, traverse, calls visit for each node on the list, from beginning to end. These two methods are both also easy to implement with a for or while loop. The third method, traverseR, does not have a simple iterative counterpart. It calls visit for every node on the list, but in reverse order.

The fourth method, remove, removes all the nodes having a given item value from a list. The structural changes for each invocation are the same as diagrammed in Figure 3.5.

```
int count(Node h)
  {
    if (h == null) return 0;
    return 1 + count(h.next);
  }
void traverse(Node h)
  {
    if (h == null) return;
    h.item.visit();
    traverse(h.next);
  }
void traverseR(Node h)
  {
    if (h == null) return;
    traverseR(h.next);
    h.item.visit();
  }
Node remove(Node h, Item v)
  {
    if (h == null) return null;
    if (eq(h.item, v)) return remove(h.next, v);
    h.next = remove(h.next, v);
    return h;
  }
```

○ 5.12 Write a recursive program that converts postfix expressions to infix.

5.13 Write a recursive program for solving the Josephus problem (see Section 3.3).

5.14 Write a recursive program that deletes the final element of a linked list.

○ 5.15 Write a recursive program for reversing the order of the nodes in a linked list (see Program 3.9). *Hint*: Use a global variable.

5.2 Divide and Conquer

Many of the recursive programs that we consider in this book use two recursive calls, each operating on about one-half of the input. This recursive scheme is perhaps the most important instance of the well-known *divide-and-conquer* paradigm for algorithm design, which serves as the basis for many of our most important algorithms.

As an example, let us consider the task of finding the maximum among N items stored in an array a[0], ..., a[N-1]. We can easily accomplish this task with a single pass through the array, as follows:

```
for (t = a[0], i = 1; i < N; i++)
  if (a[i] > t) t = a[i];
```

The recursive divide-and-conquer solution given in Program 5.6 is also a simple (and entirely different) algorithm for the same problem; we use it to illustrate the divide-and-conquer concept.

Most often, we use the divide-and-conquer approach because it provides solutions faster than those available with simple iterative algorithms (we shall discuss several examples at the end of this section); this approach is also worthy of close examination as a way of understanding the nature of certain fundamental computations.

As usual, the code itself suggests the proof by induction that it performs the desired computation:

- It finds the maximum for arrays of size 1 explicitly and immediately.
- For $N > 1$, it partitions the array into two arrays of size less than N, finds the maximum of the two parts by the inductive hypothesis, and returns the larger of these two values, which must be the maximum value in the whole array.

Moreover, we can use the recursive structure of the program to understand its performance characteristics.

```
  0 1 2 3 4 5 6 7 8 9 10
  T I N Y E X A M P L E

  Y max(0, 10)
    Y max(0, 5)
      T max(0, 2)
        T max(0, 1)
          T max(0, 0)
          I max(1, 1)
        N max(2, 2)
      Y max(3, 5)
        Y max(3, 4)
          Y max(3, 3)
          E max(4, 4)
        X max(5, 5)
    P max(6, 10)
      P max(6, 8)
        M max(6, 7)
          A max(6, 6)
          M max(7, 7)
        P max(8, 8)
      L max(9, 10)
        L max(9, 9)
        E max(10, 10)
```

Figure 5.4
A recursive approach to finding the maximum

This sequence of method invocations illustrates the dynamics of finding the maximum with a recursive algorithm.

Program 5.6 Divide-and-conquer to find the maximum

This method divides an array of doubles a[1], ..., a[r] into a[1], ... , a[m] and a[m+1], ..., a[r], finds the maximum elements in the two parts (recursively), and returns the larger of the two as the maximum element in the whole array. If the array size is even, the two parts are equal in size; if the array size is odd, the sizes of the two parts differ by 1.

```
static double max(double a[], int l, int r)
  {
    if (l == r) return a[l];
    int m = (l+r)/2;
    double u = max(a, l, m);
    double v = max(a, m+1, r);
    if (u > v) return u; else return v;
  }
```

Figure 5.4 shows the recursive invocations that are made when Program 5.6 is invoked for a sample array. The underlying structure seems complicated, but we normally do not need to worry about it— we depend on a proof by induction that the program works, and we use a recurrence relation to analyze the program's performance.

Property 5.1 *A recursive method that divides a problem of size N into two independent (nonempty) parts that it solves recursively calls itself less than N times.*

If the parts are one of size k and one of size $N - k$, then the total number of recursive method invocations that we use is

$$T_N = T_k + T_{N-k} + 1, \qquad \text{for } N \geq 1 \text{ with } T_1 = 0.$$

The solution $T_N = N - 1$ is immediate by induction. If the sizes sum to a value less than N, the proof that the number of calls is less than $N - 1$ follows the same inductive argument. We can prove analogous results under general conditions (see Exercise 5.20). ■

Program 5.6 is representative of many divide-and-conquer algorithms with precisely the same recursive structure, but other examples may differ in two primary respects. First, Program 5.6 does a constant amount of work on each method invocation, so its total running time is

```
 0  10
 0   5   6  10
 0   2   3   5   6  10
 0   1   2   2   3   5   6  10
 0   0   1   1   2   2   3   5   6  10
 1   1   2   2   3   5   6  10
 2   2   3   5   6  10
 3   5   6  10
 3   4   5   5   6  10
 3   3   4   4   5   5   6  10
 4   4   5   5   6  10
 5   5   6  10
 6  10
 6   8   9  10
 6   7   8   8   9  10
 6   6   7   7   8   8   9  10
 7   7   8   8   9  10
 8   8   9  10
 9  10
 9   9  10  10
10  10
```

Figure 5.5
Example of internal stack dynamics

This sequence is an idealistic representation of the contents of the internal stack during the sample computation of Figure 5.4. We start with the left and right indices of the whole subarray on the stack. Each line depicts the result of popping two indices and, if they are not equal, pushing four indices, which delimit the left subarray and the right subarray after the popped subarray is divided into two parts. In practice, the system keeps return addresses and local variables on the stack, instead of this specific representation of the work to be done, but this model suffices to describe the computation.

linear. Other divide-and-conquer algorithms may perform more work on each method invocation, as we shall see, so determining the total running time requires more intricate analysis. The running time of such algorithms depends on the precise manner of division into parts. Second, Program 5.6 is representative of divide-and-conquer algorithms for which the parts sum to make the whole. Other divide-and-conquer algorithms may divide either into smaller parts that constitute less than the whole problem or into overlapping parts that total up to more than the whole problem. These algorithms are still proper recursive algorithms because *each* part is smaller than the whole, but analyzing them is more difficult than analyzing Program 5.6. We shall consider the analysis of these different types of algorithms in detail as we encounter them.

For example, the binary-search algorithm that we studied in Section 2.6 is a divide-and-conquer algorithm that divides a problem in half, then works on just one of the halves. We examine a recursive implementation of binary search in Chapter 12.

Figure 5.5 indicates the contents of the internal stack maintained by the programming environment to support the computation in Figure 5.4. The model depicted in the figure is idealistic, but it gives useful insights into the structure of the divide-and-conquer computation. If a program has two recursive calls, the actual internal stack contains one entry corresponding to the first method invocation while that method is being executed (which contains values of arguments, local variables, and a return address), then a similar entry corresponding to the second method invocation while that method is being executed. The alternative that is depicted in Figure 5.5 is to put the two entries on the stack at once, keeping all the subtasks remaining to be done explicitly on the stack. This arrangement plainly delineates the computation and sets the stage for more general computational schemes, such as those that we examine in Sections 5.6 and 5.8.

Figure 5.6 depicts the structure of the divide-and-conquer find-the-maximum computation. It is a recursive structure: the node at the top contains the size of the input array, the structure for the left subarray is drawn at the left, and the structure for the right subarray is drawn at the right. We will formally define and discuss tree structures of this type in in Sections 5.4 and 5.5. They are useful for understanding the structure of any program involving nested method

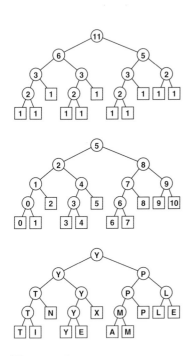

Figure 5.6
Recursive structure of find-the-maximum algorithm.

The divide-and-conquer algorithm splits a problem of size 11 into one of size 6 and one of size 5, a problem of size 6 into two problems of size 3, and so forth, until reaching problems of size 1 (top). Each circle in these diagrams represents a call on the recursive method, to the nodes just below connected to it by lines (squares are those calls for which the recursion terminates). The diagram in the middle shows the value of the index into the middle of the file that we use to effect the split; the diagram at the bottom shows the return value.

Program 5.7 Solution to the towers of Hanoi

We shift the tower of disks to the right by (recursively) shifting all but the bottom disk to the left, then shifting the bottom disk to the right, then (recursively) shifting the tower back onto the bottom disk.

```
static void hanoi(int N, int d)
  {
    if (N == 0) return;
    hanoi(N-1, -d);
    shift(N, d);
    hanoi(N-1, -d);
  }
```

---

invocations—recursive programs in particular. Also shown in Figure 5.6 is the same tree, but with each node labeled with the return value for the corresponding method invocation. In Section 5.7, we shall consider the process of building explicit linked structures that represent trees like this one.

No discussion of recursion would be complete without the ancient *towers of Hanoi* problem. We have three pegs and N disks that fit onto the pegs. The disks differ in size and are initially arranged on one of the pegs, in order from largest (disk N) at the bottom to smallest (disk 1) at the top. The task is to move the stack of disks to the right one position (peg), while obeying the following rules: (*i*) only one disk may be shifted at a time; and (*ii*) no disk may be placed on top of a smaller one. One legend says that the world will end when a certain group of monks accomplishes this task in a temple with 40 golden disks on three diamond pegs.

Program 5.7 gives a recursive solution to the problem. It specifies which disk should be shifted at each step, and in which direction (+ means move one peg to the right, cycling to the leftmost peg when on the rightmost peg; and - means move one peg to the left, cycling to the rightmost peg when on the leftmost peg). The recursion is based on the following idea: To move N disks one peg to the right, we first move the top $N-1$ disks one peg to the left, then shift disk N one peg to the right, then move the $N-1$ disks one more peg to the left (onto disk N). We can verify that this solution works by induction. Figure 5.7

Figure 5.7
Towers of Hanoi

This diagram depicts the solution to the towers of Hanoi problem for five disks. We shift the top four disks left one position (left column)*, then move disk 5 to the right, then shift the top four disks left one position* (right column)*. The sequence of method invocations that follows constitutes the computation for three disks. The computed sequence of moves is* +1 −2 +1 +3 +1 −2 +1*, which appears four times in the solution (for example, the first seven moves).*

```
hanoi(3, +1)
  hanoi(2, -1)
    hanoi(1, +1)
      hanoi(0, -1)
      shift(1, +1)
      hanoi(0, -1)
    shift(2, -1)
    hanoi(1, +1)
      hanoi(0, -1)
      shift(1, +1)
      hanoi(0, -1)
  shift(3, +1)
  hanoi(2, -1)
    hanoi(1, +1)
      hanoi(0, -1)
      shift(1, +1)
      hanoi(0, -1)
    shift(2, -1)
    hanoi(1, +1)
      hanoi(0, -1)
      shift(1, +1)
      hanoi(0, -1)
```

shows the moves for $N = 5$ and the recursive calls for $N = 3$. An underlying pattern is evident, which we now consider in detail.

First, the recursive structure of this solution immediately tells us the number of moves that the solution requires.

Property 5.2 *The recursive divide-and-conquer algorithm for the towers of Hanoi problem produces a solution that has $2^N - 1$ moves.*

As usual, it is immediate from the code that the number of moves satisfies a recurrence. In this case, the recurrence satisfied by the number of disk moves is similar to Formula 2.5:

$$T_N = 2T_{N-1} + 1, \qquad \text{for } N \geq 2 \text{ with } T_1 = 1.$$

We can verify the stated result directly by induction: we have $T(1) = 2^1 - 1 = 1$; and, if $T(k) = 2^k - 1$ for $k < N$, then $T(N) = 2(2^{N-1} - 1) + 1 = 2^N - 1$. ∎

If the monks are moving disks at the rate of one per second, it will take at least 348 centuries for them to finish (see Figure 2.1), assuming that they do not make a mistake. The end of the world is likely to be even further off than that because those monks presumably never have had the benefit of being able to use Program 5.7, and might not be able to figure out so quickly which disk to move next. We now consider an analysis of the method that leads to a simple (nonrecursive) method that makes the decision easy. While we may not wish to let the monks in on the secret, it is relevant to numerous important practical algorithms.

To understand the towers of Hanoi solution, let us consider the simple task of drawing the markings on a ruler. Each inch on the ruler has a mark at the $\frac{1}{2}$ inch point, slightly shorter marks at $\frac{1}{4}$ inch intervals, still shorter marks at $\frac{1}{8}$ inch intervals, and so forth. Our task is to write a program to draw these marks at any given resolution, assuming that we have at our disposal a procedure mark(x, h) to make a mark h units high at position x.

If the desired resolution is $\frac{1}{2^n}$ inches, we rescale so that our task is to put a mark at every point between 0 and 2^n, endpoints not included. Thus, the middle mark should be n units high, the marks in the middle of the left and right halves should be $n - 1$ units high, and so forth. Program 5.8 is a straightforward divide-and-conquer algorithm to accomplish this objective; Figure 5.8 illustrates it in operation on a

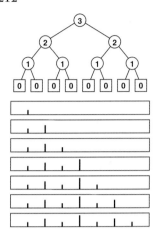

```
rule(0, 8, 3)
  rule(0, 4, 2)
    rule(0, 2, 1)
      rule(0, 1, 0)
      mark(1, 1)
      rule(1, 2, 0)
    mark(2, 2)
    rule(2, 4, 1)
      rule(2, 3, 0)
      mark(3, 1)
      rule(3, 4, 0)
  mark(4, 3)
  rule(4, 8, 2)
    rule(4, 6, 1)
      rule(4, 5, 0)
      mark(5, 1)
      rule(5, 6, 0)
    mark(6, 2)
    rule(6, 8, 1)
      rule(6, 7, 0)
      mark(7, 1)
      rule(7, 8, 0)
```

Figure 5.8
Ruler-drawing method invocations

This sequence of method invocations constitutes the computation for drawing a ruler of length 8, resulting in marks of lengths 1, 2, 1, 3, 1, 2, and 1.

Program 5.8 Divide and conquer to draw a ruler

To draw the marks on a ruler, we draw the marks on the left half, then draw the longest mark in the middle, then draw the marks on the right half. This program is intended to be used with $r - l$ equal to a power of 2—a property that it preserves in its recursive calls (see Exercise 5.27).

```
static void rule(int l, int r, int h)
  { int m = (l+r)/2;
    if (h > 0)
      {
        rule(l, m, h-1);
        mark(m, h);
        rule(m, r, h-1);
      }
  }
```

small example. Recursively speaking, the idea behind the method is the following: To make the marks in an interval, we first divide the interval into two equal halves. Then, we make the (shorter) marks in the left half (recursively), the long mark in the middle, and the (shorter) marks in the right half (recursively). Iteratively speaking, Figure 5.8 illustrates that the method makes the marks in order, from left to right—the trick lies in computing the lengths. The recursion tree in the figure helps us to understand the computation: Reading down, we see that the length of the mark decreases by 1 for each recursive method invocation. Reading across, we get the marks in the order that they are drawn, because, for any given node, we first draw the marks associated with the method invocation on the left, then the mark associated with the node, then the marks associated with the method invocation on the right.

We see immediately that the sequence of lengths is precisely the same as the sequence of disks moved for the towers of Hanoi problem. Indeed, a simple proof that they are identical is that the recursive programs are the same. Put another way, our monks could use the marks on a ruler to decide which disk to move.

Moreover, both the towers of Hanoi solution in Program 5.7 and the ruler-drawing program in Program 5.8 are variants of the basic divide-and-conquer scheme exemplified by Program 5.6. All three solve a problem of size 2^n by dividing it into two problems of size 2^{n-1}. For finding the maximum, we have a linear-time solution in the size of the input; for drawing a ruler and for solving the towers of Hanoi, we have a linear-time solution in the size of the output. For the towers of Hanoi, we normally think of the solution as being *exponential* time, because we measure the size of the problem in terms of the number of disks, n.

It is easy to draw the marks on a ruler with a recursive program, but is there some simpler way to compute the length of the ith mark, for any given i? Figure 5.9 shows yet another simple computational process that provides the answer to this question. The ith number printed out by both the towers of Hanoi program and the ruler program is nothing other than the number of trailing 0 bits in the binary representation of i. We can prove this property by induction by correspondence with a divide-and-conquer formulation for the process of printing the table of n-bit numbers: Print the table of $(n-1)$-bit numbers, each preceded by a 0 bit, then print the table of $(n-1)$-bit numbers, each preceded by a 1-bit (see Exercise 5.25).

For the towers of Hanoi problem, the implication of the correspondence with n-bit numbers is a simple algorithm for the task. We can move the pile one peg to the right by iterating the following two steps until done:

- Move the small disk to the right if n is odd (left if n is even).
- Make the only legal move not involving the small disk.

That is, after we move the small disk, the other two pegs contain two disks, one smaller than the other. The only legal move not involving the small disk is to move the smaller one onto the larger one. Every other move involves the small disk for the same reason that every other number is odd and that every other mark on the rule is the shortest. Perhaps our monks *do* know this secret, because it is hard to imagine how they might be deciding which moves to make otherwise.

A formal proof by induction that every other move in the towers of Hanoi solution involves the small disk (beginning and ending with such moves) is instructive: For $n = 1$, there is just one move, involving the small disk, so the property holds. For $n > 1$, the assumption that the property holds for $n - 1$ implies that it holds for n by the recursive construction: The first solution for $n - 1$ begins with a small-disk move, and the second solution for $n - 1$ ends with a small-disk move,

0	0	0	0	1	
0	0	0	1	0	1
0	0	0	1	1	
0	0	1	0	0	2
0	0	1	0	1	
0	0	1	1	0	1
0	0	1	1	1	
0	1	0	0	0	3
0	1	0	0	1	
0	1	0	1	0	1
0	1	0	1	1	
0	1	1	0	0	2
0	1	1	0	1	
0	1	1	1	0	1
0	1	1	1	1	
1	0	0	0	0	4
1	0	0	0	1	
1	0	0	1	0	1
1	0	0	1	1	
1	0	1	0	0	2
1	0	1	0	1	
1	0	1	1	0	1
1	0	1	1	1	
1	1	0	0	0	3
1	1	0	0	1	
1	1	0	1	0	1
1	1	0	1	1	
1	1	1	0	0	2
1	1	1	0	1	
1	1	1	1	0	1
1	1	1	1	1	

Figure 5.9
Binary counting and the ruler function

Computing the ruler function is equivalent to counting the number of trailing zeros in the even N-bit numbers.

> ### Program 5.9 Nonrecursive program to draw a ruler
>
> In contrast to Program 5.8, we can also draw a ruler by first drawing all the marks of length 1, then drawing all the marks of length 2, and so forth. The variable t carries the length of the marks, and the variable j carries the number of marks in between two successive marks of length t. The outer for loop increments t and preserves the property $j = 2^{t-1}$. The inner for loop draws all the marks of length t.
>
> ```
> static void rule(int l, int r, int h)
>   {
>     for (int t = 1, j = 1; t <= h; j += j, t++)
>       for (int i = 0; l+j+i <= r; i += j+j)
>         mark(l+j+i, t);
>   }
> ```

so the solution for n begins and ends with a small-disk move. We put a move not involving the small disk in between two moves that do involve the small disk (the move ending the first solution for $n-1$ and the move beginning the second solution for $n-1$), so the property that every other move involves the small disk is preserved.

Program 5.9 is an alternate way to draw a ruler that is inspired by the correspondence to binary numbers (see Figure 5.10). We refer to this version of the algorithm as a *bottom-up* implementation. It is not recursive, but it is certainly suggested by the recursive algorithm. This correspondence between divide-and-conquer algorithms and the binary representations of numbers often provides insights for analysis and development of improved versions, such as bottom-up approaches. We consider this perspective to understand, and possibly to improve, each of the divide-and-conquer algorithms that we examine.

The bottom-up approach involves rearranging the *order* of the computation when we are drawing a ruler. Figure 5.11 shows another example, where we rearrange the order of the three method invocations in the recursive implementation. It reflects the recursive computation in the way that we first described it: Draw the middle mark, then draw the left half, then draw the right half. The pattern of drawing the marks is complex but is the result of simply exchanging two statements in Program 5.8. As we shall see in Section 5.6, the relationship between

Figure 5.10
Drawing a ruler in bottom-up order

To draw a ruler nonrecursively, we alternate drawing marks of length 1 and skipping positions, then alternate drawing marks of length 2 and skipping remaining positions, then alternate drawing marks of length 3 and skipping remaining positions, and so forth.

Figures 5.8 and 5.11 is akin to the distinction between postfix and prefix in arithmetic expressions.

Drawing the marks in order as in Figure 5.8 might be preferable to doing the rearranged computations contained in Program 5.9 and indicated in Figure 5.11, because we can draw an arbitrarily long ruler, if we imagine a drawing device that simply moves on to the next mark in a continuous scroll. Similarly, to solve the towers of Hanoi problem, we are constrained to produce the sequence of disk moves in the order that they are to be performed. In general, many recursive programs depend on the subproblems being solved in a particular order. For other computations (see, for example, Program 5.6), the order in which we solve the subproblems is irrelevant. For such computations, the only constraint is that we must solve the subproblems before we can solve the main problem. Understanding when we have the flexibility to reorder the computation is not only a secret to success in algorithm design but also has direct practical effects in many contexts. For example, this matter is critical when we consider implementing algorithms on parallel processors.

The bottom-up approach corresponds to the general method of algorithm design where we solve a problem by first solving trivial subproblems, then combining those solutions to solve slightly bigger subproblems, and so forth, until the whole problem is solved. This approach might be called *combine and conquer*.

It is a small step from drawing rulers to drawing two-dimensional patterns such as Figure 5.12. This figure illustrates how a simple recursive description can lead to a computation that appears to be complex (see Exercise 5.30).

Recursively defined geometric patterns such as Figure 5.12 are sometimes called *fractals*. If more complicated drawing primitives are used, and more complicated recursive invocations are involved (especially including recursively-defined functions on reals and in the complex plane), patterns of remarkable diversity and complexity can be developed. Another example, demonstrated in Figure 5.13, is the *Koch star*, which is defined recursively as follows: A Koch star of order 0 is the simple `hill` example of Figure 4.3, and a Koch star of order n is a Koch star of order $n - 1$ with each line segment replaced by the star of order 0, scaled appropriately.

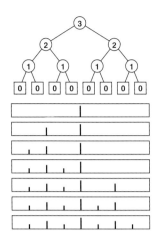

```
rule(0, 8, 3)
  mark(4, 3)
  rule(0, 4, 2)
    mark(2, 2)
    rule(0, 2, 1)
      mark(1, 1)
      rule(0, 1, 0)
      rule(1, 2, 0)
    rule(2, 4, 1)
      mark(3, 1)
      rule(2, 3, 0)
      rule(3, 4, 0)
  rule(4, 8, 2)
    mark(6, 2)
    rule(4, 6, 1)
      mark(5, 1)
      rule(4, 5, 0)
      rule(5, 6, 0)
    rule(6, 8, 1)
      mark(7, 1)
      rule(6, 7, 0)
      rule(7, 8, 0)
```

Figure 5.11
Ruler-drawing method invocations (preorder version)

This sequence indicates the result of drawing marks before the method invocations, instead of in between them.

Figure 5.12
Two-dimensional fractal star

This fractal is a two-dimensional version of Figure 5.10. The out-lined boxes in the bottom diagram highlight the recursive structure of the computation.

Table 5.1 Basic divide-and-conquer algorithms

Binary search (see Chapters 2 and 12) and mergesort (see Chapter 8) are prototypical divide-and-conquer algorithms that provide guaranteed optimal performance for searching and sorting, respectively. The recurrences indicate the nature of the divide-and-conquer computation for each algorithm. (See Sections 2.5 and 2.6 for derivations of the solutions in the rightmost column.) Binary search splits a problem in half, does 1 comparison, then makes a recursive call for one of the halves. Mergesort splits a problem in half, then works on both halves recursively, then does N comparisons. Throughout the book, we shall consider numerous other algorithms developed with these recursive schemes.

	recurrence	approximate solution
binary search		
comparisons	$C_N = C_{N/2} + 1$	$\lg N$
mergesort		
recursive calls	$A_N = 2A_{N/2} + 1$	N
comparisons	$C_N = 2C_{N/2} + N$	$N \lg N$

Like the ruler-drawing and the towers of Hanoi solutions, these algorithms are linear in the number of steps, but that number is exponential in the maximum depth of the recursion (see Exercises 5.29 and 5.33). They also can be directly related to counting in an appropriate number system (see Exercise 5.34).

The towers of Hanoi problem, ruler-drawing problem, and fractals are amusing, and the connection to binary numbers is surprising; but our primary interest in all of these topics is that they provide us with insights into understanding the basic algorithm design paradigm of divide in half and solve one or both halves independently, which is perhaps the most important such technique that we consider in this book. Table 5.1 includes details about binary search and mergesort, which are not only important and widely used practical algorithms but also exemplify the divide-and-conquer algorithm design paradigm.

Quicksort (see Chapter 7) and binary-tree search (see Chapter 12) represent a significant variation on the basic divide-and-conquer theme where the problem is split into subproblems of size $k - 1$ and $N - k$, for some value k, which is determined by the input. For random input, these algorithms divide a problem into subproblems that are half the size (as in mergesort or in binary search) *on the average*. We study the analysis of the effects of this difference when we discuss these algorithms.

Other variations on the basic theme that are worthy of consideration include these: divide into parts of varying size, divide into more than two parts, divide into overlapping parts, and do various amounts of work in the nonrecursive part of the algorithm. In general, divide-and-conquer algorithms involve doing work to split the input into pieces, or to merge the results of processing two independent solved portions of the input, or to help things along after half of the input has been processed. That is, there may be code before, after, or in between the two recursive calls. Naturally, such variations lead to algorithms more complicated and more difficult to analyze than are binary search and mergesort. We consider numerous examples in this book; we return to advanced applications and analysis in Part 8.

Exercises

5.16 Write a recursive program that finds the maximum element in an array, based on comparing the first element in the array against the maximum element in the rest of the array (computed recursively).

5.17 Write a recursive program that finds the maximum element in a linked list.

5.18 Modify the divide-and-conquer program for finding the maximum element in an array (Program 5.6) to divide an array of size N into one part of size $k = 2^{\lceil \lg N \rceil - 1}$ and another of size $N - k$ (so that the size of at least one of the parts is a power of 2).

5.19 Draw the tree corresponding to the recursive calls that your program from Exercise 5.18 makes when the array size is 11.

• **5.20** Prove by induction that the number of method invocations made by any divide-and-conquer algorithm that divides a problem into parts that constitute the whole and then solves the parts recursively is linear.

• **5.21** Prove that the recursive solution to the towers of Hanoi problem (Program 5.7) is optimal. That is, show that any solution *requires* at least $2^N - 1$ moves.

▷ **5.22** Write a recursive program that computes the length of the ith mark in a ruler with $2^n - 1$ marks.

•• **5.23** Examine tables of n-bit numbers, such as Figure 5.9, to discover a property of the ith number that determines the direction of the ith move

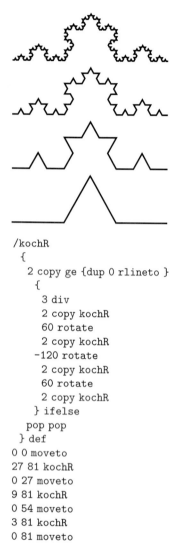

```
/kochR
  {
    2 copy ge {dup 0 rlineto }
      {
        3 div
        2 copy kochR
        60 rotate
        2 copy kochR
        -120 rotate
        2 copy kochR
        60 rotate
        2 copy kochR
      } ifelse
    pop pop
  } def
0 0 moveto
27 81 kochR
0 27 moveto
9 81 kochR
0 54 moveto
3 81 kochR
0 81 moveto
1 81 kochR
stroke
```

Figure 5.13
Recursive PostScript for Koch fractal

This modification to the PostScript program of Figure 4.3 transforms the output into a fractal (see text).

(indicated by the sign bit in Figure 5.7) for solving the towers of Hanoi problem.

5.24 Write a program that produces a solution to the towers of Hanoi problem by filling in an array that holds all the moves, as in Program 5.9.

○ **5.25** Write a recursive program that fills in an n-by-2^n array with 0s and 1s such that the array represents all the n-bit binary numbers, as depicted in Figure 5.9.

5.26 Draw the results of using the recursive ruler-drawing program (Program 5.8) for these unintended values of the arguments: `rule(0, 11, 4)`, `rule(4, 20, 4)`, and `rule(7, 30, 5)`.

5.27 Prove the following fact about the ruler-drawing program (Program 5.8): If the difference between its first two arguments is a power of 2, then both of its recursive calls have this property also.

○ **5.28** Write a method that computes efficiently the number of trailing 0s in the binary representation of an integer.

○ **5.29** How many squares are there in Figure 5.12 (counting the ones that are covered up by bigger squares)?

○ **5.30** Write a recursive Java program that outputs a PostScript program that draws the bottom diagram in Figure 5.12, in the form of a list of method invocations x y r box, which draws an r-by-r square at (x, y). Implement box in PostScript (see Section 4.3).

5.31 Write a bottom-up nonrecursive program (similar to Program 5.9) that draws the bottom diagram in Figure 5.12, in the manner described in Exercise 5.30.

• **5.32** Write a PostScript program that draws the bottom diagram in Figure 5.12.

▷ **5.33** How many line segments are there in a Koch star of order n?

•• **5.34** Drawing a Koch star of order n amounts to executing a sequence of commands of the form "rotate α degrees, then draw a line segment of length $\frac{1}{3^n}$." Find a correspondence with number systems that gives you a way to draw the star by incrementing a counter, then computing the angle α from the counter value.

• **5.35** Modify the Koch star program in Figure 5.13 to produce a different fractal based on a five-line figure for order 0, defined by 1-unit moves east, north, east, south, and east, in that order (see Figure 4.3).

5.36 Write a recursive divide-and-conquer method to draw an approximation to a line segment in an integer coordinate space, given the endpoints. Assume that all coordinates are between 0 and M. *Hint*: First plot a point close to the middle.

5.3 Dynamic Programming

An essential characteristic of the divide-and-conquer algorithms that we considered in Section 5.2 is that they partition the problem into independent subproblems. When the subproblems are not independent, the situation is more complicated, primarily because direct recursive implementations of even the simplest algorithms of this type can require unthinkable amounts of time. In this section, we consider a systematic technique for avoiding this pitfall for an important class of problems.

For example, Program 5.10 is a direct recursive implementation of the recurrence that defines the Fibonacci numbers (see Section 2.3). *Do not use this program*: It is spectacularly inefficient. Indeed, the number of recursive calls to compute F_N is exactly F_{N+1}. But F_N is about ϕ^N, where $\phi \approx 1.618$ is the golden ratio. The awful truth is that Program 5.10 is an *exponential-time* algorithm for this trivial computation. Figure 5.14, which depicts the recursive calls for a small example, makes plain the amount of recomputation that is involved.

By contrast, it is easy to compute F_N in *linear* (proportional to N) time, by computing the first N Fibonacci numbers and storing them in an array:

```
F[0] = 0; F[1] = 1;
for (i = 2; i <= N; i++)
  F[i] = F[i-1] + F[i-2];
```

The numbers grow exponentially, so the array is small—for example, $F_{45} = 1836311903$ is the largest Fibonacci number that can be represented as a 32-bit integer, so an array of size 46 will do.

This technique gives us an immediate way to get numerical solutions for any recurrence relation. In the case of Fibonacci numbers, we can even dispense with the array and keep track of just the previous two values (see Exercise 5.37); for many other commonly encountered recurrences (see, for example, Exercise 5.40), we need to maintain the array with all the known values.

A recurrence is a recursive function with integer values. Our discussion in the previous paragraph leads to the conclusion that we can evaluate any such function by computing all the function values in order starting at the smallest, using previously computed values at each step to compute the current value. We refer to this technique as

---

Program 5.10 Fibonacci numbers (recursive implementation)

This program, although compact and elegant, is not usable because it takes exponential time to compute F_N. The running time to compute F_{N+1} is $\phi \approx 1.6$ times as long as the running time to compute F_N. For example, since $\phi^9 > 60$, if we notice that our computer takes about a second to compute F_N, we know that it will take more than a minute to compute F_{N+9}, and more than an hour to compute F_{N+18}.

```
static int F(int i)
  {
    if (i < 1) return 0;
    if (i == 1) return 1;
    return F(i-1) + F(i-2);
  }
```

---

bottom-up dynamic programming. It applies to any recursive computation, *provided* that we can afford to save all the previously computed values. It is an algorithm-design technique that has been used successfully for a wide range of problems. We have to pay attention to a simple technique that can improve the running time of an algorithm from exponential to linear!

Top-down dynamic programming is an even simpler view of the technique that allows us to execute recursive methods at the same cost as (or less cost than) bottom-up dynamic programming, in an automatic way. We instrument the recursive program to save each value that it computes (as its final action) and to check the saved values to avoid recomputing any of them (as its first action). Program 5.11 is the mechanical transformation of Program 5.10 that reduces its running time to be linear via top-down dynamic programming. Figure 5.15 shows the drastic reduction in the number of recursive calls achieved by this simple automatic change. Top-down dynamic programming is also sometimes called *memoization.*

For a more complicated example, consider the *knapsack problem*: A thief robbing a safe finds it filled with N types of items of varying size and value but has only a small knapsack of capacity M to use to carry the goods. The knapsack problem is to find the combination of items which the thief should choose for the knapsack in order to maximize the total value of all the stolen items. For example, with

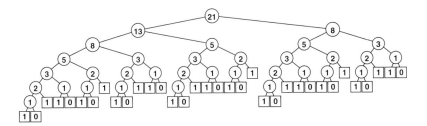

Figure 5.14
Structure of recursive algorithm for Fibonacci numbers

This picture of the recursive calls used to compute F_8 by the standard recursive algorithm illustrates how recursion with overlapping subproblems can lead to exponential costs. In this case, the second recursive call ignores the computations done during the first, which results in massive recomputation because the effect multiplies recursively. The recursive calls to compute $F_6 = 8$ (which are reflected in the right subtree of the root and the left subtree of the left subtree of the root) are listed below.

```
8 F(6)
  5 F(5)
    3 F(4)
      2 F(3)
        1 F(2)
          1 F(1)
          0 F(0)
        1 F(1)
      1 F(2)
        1 F(1)
        0 F(0)
    2 F(3)
      1 F(2)
        1 F(1)
        0 F(0)
      1 F(1)
  3 F(4)
    2 F(3)
      1 F(2)
        1 F(1)
        0 F(0)
      1 F(1)
    1 F(2)
      1 F(1)
      0 F(0)
```

the item types depicted in Figure 5.16, a thief with a knapsack of size 17 can take five A's (but not six) for a total take of 20, or a D and an E for a total take of 24, or one of many other combinations. Our goal is to find an efficient algorithm that somehow finds the maximum among all the possibilities, given any set of items and knapsack capacity.

There are many applications in which solutions to the knapsack problem are important. For example, a shipping company might wish to know the best way to load a truck or cargo plane with items for shipment. In such applications, other variants to the problem might arise as well: for example, there might be a limited number of each kind of item available, or there might be two trucks. Many such variants can be handled with the same approach that we are about to examine for solving the basic problem just stated; others turn out to be much more difficult. There is a fine line between feasible and infeasible problems of this type, which we shall examine in Part 8.

In a recursive solution to the knapsack problem we assume that we can (recursively) find an optimal way to pack the rest of the knapsack each time that we choose an item. For a knapsack of size cap, we determine, for each item i among the available item types, what total value we could carry by placing i in the knapsack with an optimal packing of other items around it. That optimal packing is simply the one we have discovered (or will discover) for the smaller knapsack of size cap-items[i].size. This solution exploits the principle that optimal decisions, once made, do not need to be changed. Once we know how to pack knapsacks of smaller capacities with optimal sets of items, we do not need to reexamine those problems, regardless of what the next items are.

Program 5.12 is a direct recursive solution based on this discussion. Again, this program is not feasible for use in solving actual

> **Program 5.11 Fibonacci numbers (dynamic programming)**
>
> By saving the values that we compute in a static array we explicitly avoid any recomputation. This program computes F_N in time proportional to N, in stark contrast to the $O(\phi^N)$ time used by Program 5.10.
>
> ```
> static final int maxN = 47;
> static int knownF[] = new int [maxN];
> static int F(int i)
>   {
>     if (knownF[i] != 0) return knownF[i];
>     int t = i;
>     if (i < 0) return 0;
>     if (i > 1) t = F(i-1) + F(i-2);
>     return knownF[i] = t;
>   }
> ```

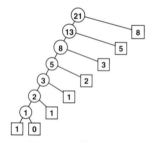

Figure 5.15
Top-down dynamic programming for computing Fibonacci numbers

This picture of the recursive calls used to compute F_8 by the top-down dynamic programming implementation of the recursive algorithm illustrates how saving computed values cuts the cost from exponential (see Figure 5.14) to linear.

problems, because it takes exponential time due to massive recomputation (see Figure 5.17), but we can automatically apply top-down dynamic programming to eliminate this problem, as shown in Program 5.13. As before, this technique eliminates all recomputation, as shown in Figure 5.18.

By design, dynamic programming eliminates all recomputation in *any* recursive program, subject only to the condition that we can afford to save the values of the function for arguments smaller than the call in question.

Property 5.3 *Dynamic programming reduces the running time of a recursive method to be at most the time required to evaluate the function for all arguments less than or equal to the given argument, treating the cost of a recursive invocation as constant.*

See Exercise 5.50. ∎

This property implies that the running time of the knapsack problem is proportional to NM. Thus, we can solve the knapsack problem easily when the capacity is not huge; for huge capacities, the time and space requirements may be prohibitively large.

Bottom-up dynamic programming applies to the knapsack problem as well. Indeed, we can use the bottom-up approach any time

Program 5.12 Knapsack problem (recursive implementation)

Our earlier warning about the recursive solution to the problem of computing the Fibonacci numbers maintains here: *do not use this program*, because it will take exponential time and therefore may not ever run to completion even for small problems. It does, however, represent a compact solution that we can improve easily (see Program 5.13). This code assumes that items have a size and a value, defined with

```
static class Item { int size; int val; }
```

and that we have an array of N items of type Item. For each possible item, we calculate (recursively) the maximum value that we could achieve by including that item, then take the maximum of all those values.

```
static int knap(int cap)
  { int i, space, max, t;
    for (i = 0, max = 0; i < N; i++)
      if ((space = cap-items[i].size) >= 0)
        if ((t = knap(space) + items[i].val) > max)
          max = t;
    return max;
  }
```

that we use the top-down approach, although we need to take care to ensure that we compute the function values in an appropriate order so that each value that we need has been computed when we need it. For methods with single integer arguments, such as the two that we have considered, we simply proceed in increasing order of the argument (see Exercise 5.53); for more complicated recursive methods, determining a proper order can be a challenge.

For example, we do not need to restrict ourselves to recursive functions with single integer arguments. When we have a function with multiple integer arguments, we can save solutions to smaller subproblems in multidimensional arrays, one for each argument. Other situations involve no integer arguments at all, but rather use an abstract discrete problem formulation that allows us to decompose problems into smaller ones. We shall consider examples of such problems in Parts 5 through 8.

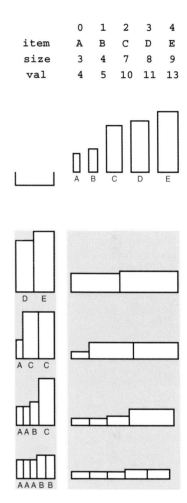

	0	1	2	3	4
item	A	B	C	D	E
size	3	4	7	8	9
val	4	5	10	11	13

Figure 5.16
Knapsack example

An instance of the knapsack problem (top) consists of a knapsack capacity and a set of items of varying size (horizontal dimension) and value (vertical dimension). This figure shows four different ways to fill a knapsack of size 17, two of which lead to the highest possible total value of 24.

Figure 5.17
Recursive structure of knap-
sack algorithm.

This tree represents the recursive
call structure of the simple recur-
sive knapsack algorithm in Pro-
gram 5.12. The number in each
node represents the remaining ca-
pacity in the knapsack. The algo-
rithm suffers the same basic prob-
lem of exponential performance
due to massive recomputation for
overlapping subproblems that we
considered in computing Fibonacci
numbers (see Figure 5.14).

In top-down dynamic programming, we save known values; in bottom-up dynamic programming, we precompute them. We generally prefer top-down to bottom-up dynamic programming, because

- It is a mechanical transformation of a natural problem solution.
- The order of computing the subproblems takes care of itself.
- We may not need to compute answers to all the subproblems.

Dynamic-programming applications differ in the nature of the subproblems and in the amount of information that we need to save regarding the subproblems.

A crucial point that we cannot overlook is that dynamic programming becomes ineffective when the number of possible function values that we might need is so high that we cannot afford to save (top-down) or precompute (bottom-up) all of them. For example, if M and the item sizes are 64-bit quantities or floating-point numbers in the knapsack problem, we will not be able to save values by indexing into an array. This distinction causes more than a minor annoyance—it poses a fundamental difficulty. No good solution is known for such problems; we will see in Part 8 that there is good reason to believe that no good solution exists.

Dynamic programming is an algorithm-design technique that is primarily suited for the advanced problems of the type that we shall consider in Parts 5 through 8. Most of the algorithms that we discuss in Parts 2 through 4 are divide-and-conquer methods with nonoverlapping subproblems, and we are focusing on subquadratic or sublinear, rather than subexponential, performance. However, top-down dynamic programming is a basic technique for developing efficient implementations of recursive algorithms that belongs in the toolbox of anyone engaged in algorithm design and implementation.

Exercises

▷ **5.37** Write a method that computes $F_N \bmod M$, using only a constant amount of space for intermediate calculations.

Program 5.13 Knapsack problem (dynamic programming)

This mechanical modification to the code of Program 5.12 reduces the running time from exponential to linear. We simply save any function values that we compute, then retrieve any saved values whenever we need them (using a sentinel value to represent unknown values), rather than making recursive calls. We save the index of the item so that, if we wish, we can reconstruct the contents of the knapsack after the computation: itemKnown[M] is in the knapsack, the remaining contents are the same as for the optimal knapsack of size M-itemKnown[M].size, so itemKnown[M-items[M].size] is in the knapsack, and so forth.

```
static int knap(int M)
  { int i, space, max, maxi = 0, t;
    if (maxKnown[M] != unknown) return maxKnown[M];
    for (i = 0, max = 0; i < N; i++)
      if ((space = M-items[i].size) >= 0)
        if ((t = knap(space) + items[i].val) > max)
          { max = t; maxi = i; }
    maxKnown[M] = max; itemKnown[M] = items[maxi];
    return max;
  }
```

5.38 What is the largest N for which F_N can be represented as a 64-bit integer?

∘ **5.39** Draw the tree corresponding to Figure 5.15 for the case where we exchange the recursive calls in Program 5.11.

5.40 Write a method that uses bottom-up dynamic programming to compute the value of P_N defined by the recurrence

$$P_N = \lfloor N/2 \rfloor + P_{\lfloor N/2 \rfloor} + P_{\lceil N/2 \rceil}, \qquad \text{for } N \geq 1 \text{ with } P_0 = 0.$$

Draw a plot of N versus $P_N - N \lg N/2$ for $0 \leq N \leq 1024$.

5.41 Write a method that uses top-down dynamic programming to solve Exercise 5.40.

∘ **5.42** Draw the tree corresponding to Figure 5.15 for your method from Exercise 5.41, when invoked for $N = 23$.

5.43 Draw a plot of N versus the number of recursive calls that your method from Exercise 5.41 makes to compute P_N, for $0 \leq N \leq 1024$. (For the purposes of this calculation, start your program from scratch for each N.)

Figure 5.18
Top-down dynamic program-
ming for knapsack algo-
rithm

As it did for the Fibonacci num-
bers computation, the technique
of saving known values reduces
the cost of the knapsack algorithm
from exponential (see Figure 5.17)
to linear.

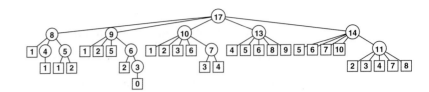

5.44 Write a method that uses bottom-up dynamic programming to compute the value of C_N defined by the recurrence

$$C_N = N + \frac{1}{N} \sum_{1 \le k \le N} (C_{k-1} + C_{N-k}), \qquad \text{for } N \ge 1 \text{ with } C_0 = 1.$$

5.45 Write a method that uses top-down dynamic programming to solve Exercise 5.44.

○ **5.46** Draw the tree corresponding to Figure 5.15 for your method from Exercise 5.45, when invoked for $N = 23$.

5.47 Draw a plot of N versus the number of recursive calls that your method from Exercise 5.45 makes to compute C_N, for $0 \le N \le 1024$. (For the purposes of this calculation, start your program from scratch for each N.)

▷ **5.48** Give the contents of the arrays `maxKnown` and `itemKnown` that are computed by Program 5.13 for the call `knap(17)` with the items in Figure 5.16.

▷ **5.49** Give the tree corresponding to Figure 5.18 under the assumption that the items are considered in decreasing order of their size.

● **5.50** Prove Property 5.3.

○ **5.51** Write a method that solves the knapsack problem using a bottom-up dynamic programming version of Program 5.12.

● **5.52** Write a method that solves the knapsack problem using top-down dynamic programming and a recursive solution that computes the optimal number of a particular item to include in the knapsack, based on (recursively) knowing the optimal way to pack the knapsack without that item.

○ **5.53** Write a method that solves the knapsack problem using a bottom-up dynamic programming version of the solution described in Exercise 5.52.

● **5.54** Use dynamic programming to solve Exercise 5.4. Keep track of the total number of method invocations that you save.

5.55 Write a program that uses top-down dynamic programming to compute the binomial coefficient $\binom{N}{k}$, based on the recursive rule

$$\binom{N}{k} = \binom{N-1}{k} + \binom{N-1}{k-1}$$

with $\binom{N}{0} = \binom{N}{N} = 1$.

5.4 Trees

Trees are a mathematical abstraction that play a central role in the design and analysis of algorithms because

- We use trees to describe dynamic properties of algorithms.
- We build and use explicit data structures that are concrete realizations of trees.

We have already seen examples of both of these uses. We designed algorithms for the connectivity problem that are based on tree structures in Chapter 1, and we described the call structure of recursive algorithms with tree structures in Sections 5.2 and 5.3.

We encounter trees frequently in everyday life—the basic concept is a familiar one. For example, many people keep track of ancestors or descendants with a family tree; as we shall see, much of our terminology is derived from this usage. Another example is found in the organization of sports tournaments; this usage was studied by Lewis Carroll, among others. A third example is found in the organizational chart of a large corporation; this usage is suggestive of the hierarchical decomposition that characterizes divide-and-conquer algorithms. A fourth example is a parse tree of an English sentence into its constituent parts; such trees are intimately related to the processing of computer languages, as discussed in Part 6. Figure 5.19 gives a typical example of a tree—one that describes the structure of this book. We touch on numerous other examples of applications of trees throughout the book.

In computer applications, one of the most familiar uses of tree structures is to organize file systems. We keep files in *directories* (which are also sometimes called *folders*) that are defined recursively as sequences of directories and files. This recursive definition again reflects a natural recursive decomposition and is identical to the definition of a certain type of tree.

There are many different types of trees, and it is important to understand the distinction between the abstraction and the concrete representation with which we are working for a given application. Accordingly, we shall consider the different types of trees and their representations in detail.

We begin our discussion by defining trees as abstract objects and by introducing most of the basic associated terminology. We shall

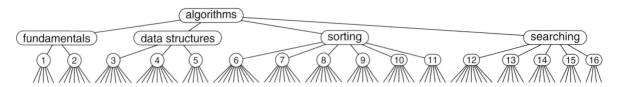

Figure 5.19
A tree

This tree depicts the parts, chapters, and sections in this book. There is a node for each entity. Each node is connected both to its constituent parts by links down to them and to the large part to which it belongs by a link up to that part.

discuss informally the different types of trees that we need to consider in decreasing order of generality:

- Trees
- Rooted trees
- Ordered trees
- M-ary trees and binary trees

After developing a context with this informal discussion, we move to formal definitions and consider representations and applications. Figure 5.20 illustrates many of the basic concepts that we consider.

A *tree* is a nonempty collection of vertices and edges that satisfies certain requirements. A *vertex* is a simple object (also referred to as a *node*) that can have a name and can carry other associated information; an *edge* is a connection between two vertices. A *path* in a tree is a list of distinct vertices in which successive vertices are connected by edges in the tree. The defining property of a tree is that there is precisely one path connecting any two nodes. If there is more than one path between some pair of nodes, or if there is no path between some pair of nodes, then we have a graph; we do not have a tree. A disjoint set of trees is called a *forest*.

A *rooted* tree is one where we designate one node as the *root* of a tree. In computer science, we normally reserve the term *tree* to refer to rooted trees and use the term *free tree* to refer to the more general structure described in the previous paragraph. In a rooted tree, any node is the root of a *subtree* consisting of it and the nodes below it.

There is exactly one path between the root and each of the other nodes in the tree. The definition implies no direction on the edges; we normally think of the edges as all pointing away from the root or all pointing towards the root, depending upon the application. We usually draw rooted trees with the root at the top (even though this convention seems unnatural at first), and we speak of node y as being *below* node x (and x as *above* y) if x is on the path from y to the root (that is, if y is below x as drawn on the page and is connected to x by a path that does not pass through the root). Each node (except

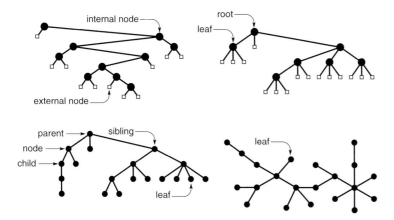

Figure 5.20
Types of trees

These diagrams show examples of a binary tree (top left), *a ternary tree* (top right), *a rooted tree* (bottom left), *and a free tree* (bottom right).

the root) has exactly one node above it, which is called its *parent*; the nodes directly below a node are called its *children*. We sometimes carry the analogy to family trees further and refer to the *grandparent* or the *sibling* of a node.

Nodes with no children are called *leaves*, or *terminal* nodes. To correspond to the latter usage, nodes with at least one child are sometimes called *nonterminal* nodes. We have seen an example in this chapter of the utility of distinguishing these types of nodes. In trees that we use to present the call structure of recursive algorithms (see, for example, Figure 5.14) the nonterminal nodes (circles) represent method invocations with recursive calls and the terminal nodes (squares) represent method invocations with no recursive calls.

In certain applications, the way in which the children of each node are ordered is significant; in other applications, it is not. An *ordered* tree is a rooted tree in which the order of the children at every node is specified. Ordered trees are a natural representation: for example, we place the children in some order when we draw a family tree. As we shall see, this distinction is also significant when we consider representing trees in a computer.

If each node *must* have a specific number of children appearing in a specific order, then we have an *M-ary tree*. In such a tree, it is often appropriate to define special external nodes that have no children. Then, external nodes can act as dummy nodes for reference by nodes that do not have the specified number of children. In particular, the simplest type of M-ary tree is the binary tree. A *binary tree* is an ordered tree consisting of two types of nodes: external nodes with no children and internal nodes with exactly two children. Since the two children of each internal node are ordered, we refer to the *left child* and the *right child* of internal nodes: every internal node must have both a left and a right child, although one or both of them might be an external node. A *leaf* in an M-ary tree is an internal node whose children are all external.

That is the basic terminology. Next, we shall consider formal definitions, representations, and applications of, in increasing order of generality:

- Binary trees and M-ary trees
- Ordered trees
- Rooted trees
- Free trees

That is, a binary tree is a special type of ordered tree, an ordered tree is a special type of rooted tree, and a rooted tree is a special type of free tree. The different types of trees arise naturally in various applications, and it is important to be aware of the distinctions when we consider ways of representing trees with concrete data structures. By starting with the most specific abstract structure, we shall be able to consider concrete representations in detail, as will become clear.

Definition 5.1   *A* **binary tree** *is either an external node or an internal node connected to a pair of binary trees, which are called the left subtree and the right subtree of that node.*

This definition makes it plain that the binary tree itself is an abstract mathematical concept. When we are working with a computer representation, we are working with just one concrete realization of that abstraction. The situation is no different from representing real numbers with `floats`, integers with `ints`, and so forth. When we draw a tree with a node at the root connected by edges to the left subtree on the left and the right subtree on the right, we are choosing a convenient concrete representation. There are many different ways to represent binary trees (see, for example, Exercise 5.62) that are surprising at first; upon reflection, they are to be expected, given the abstract nature of the definition.

The concrete representation that we use most often when implementing programs that use and manipulate binary trees is a structure

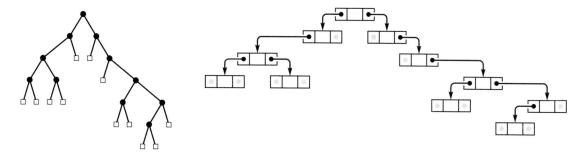

Figure 5.21
Binary-tree representation

The standard representation of a binary tree uses nodes with two links: a left link to the left subtree and a right link to the right subtree. Null links correspond to external nodes.

with two links (a left link and a right link) for internal nodes (see Figure 5.21). These structures are similar to linked lists, but they have two links per node, rather than one. Null links correspond to external nodes. Specifically, we add a link to our standard linked list representation from Section 3.3, as follows:

```
class Node
  { Item item; Node l; Node r;
    Node(Item v, Node l, Node r)
      { this.item = v; this.l = l; this.r = r; }
  }
```

which is nothing more than Java code for Definition 5.1. A node consists of an item and a pair of references to nodes (links). Thus, for example, we implement the abstract operation *move to the left subtree* with a reference assignment such as x = x.l.

This standard representation allows for efficient implementation of operations that call for moving *down* the tree from the root, but not for operations that call for moving *up* the tree from a child to its parent. For algorithms that require such operations, we might add a third link to each node, pointing to the parent. This alternative is analogous to a doubly linked list. As with linked lists (see Figure 3.8), we could keep tree nodes in an array and use indices instead of references as links, but we generally do not address such low-level optimizations (except to note their existence) because their effectiveness is system-dependent. We use other binary-tree representations for certain specific algorithms, most notably in Chapter 9.

Because of all the different possible representations, we might develop a binary-tree ADT that both encapsulates the important operations that we want to perform and separates the use and implementation of these operations. We do not take this approach in this book because

- We most often use the two-link representation.
- We use trees to implement higher-level ADTs and wish to focus on those.
- We work with algorithms whose efficiency depends on a particular representation—a fact that might be lost in an ADT.

These are the same reasons that we use familiar concrete representations for arrays and linked lists. The binary-tree representation depicted in Figure 5.21 is a fundamental tool that we are now adding to this short list.

For linked lists, we began by considering elementary operations for inserting and deleting nodes (see Figures 3.5 and 3.6). For the standard representation of binary trees, such operations are not necessarily elementary, because of the second link. If we want to delete a node from a binary tree, we have to reconcile the basic problem that we may have two children but only one parent to handle after the node is gone. There are three natural operations that do not have this difficulty: insert a new node at the bottom (replace a null link with a link to a new node), delete a leaf (replace the link to it by a null link), and combine two trees by creating a new root with a left link pointing to one tree and the right link pointing to the other one. We use these operations extensively when manipulating binary trees.

Definition 5.2 *An **M-ary tree** is either an external node or an internal node connected to an ordered sequence of M trees that are also M-ary trees.*

We normally represent nodes in M-ary trees either as structures with M named links (as in binary trees) or as arrays of M links. For example, in Chapter 15, we consider 3-ary (or *ternary*) trees where we use structures with three named links (left, middle, and right) each of which has specific meaning for associated algorithms. Otherwise, the use of arrays to hold the links is appropriate because the value of M is fixed although, as we shall see, we have to pay particular attention to excessive use of space when using such a representation.

Definition 5.3 *A **tree** (also called an **ordered tree**) is a node (called the root) connected to a sequence of disjoint trees. Such a sequence is called a **forest**.*

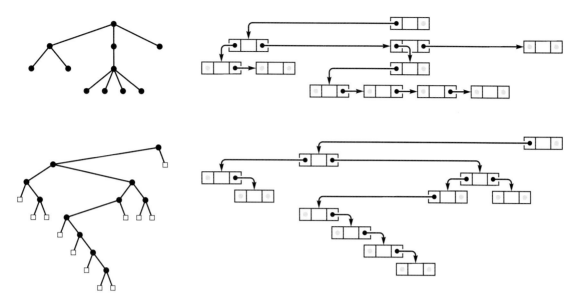

The distinction between ordered trees and M-ary trees is that nodes in ordered trees can have any number of children, whereas nodes in M-ary trees must have precisely M children. We sometimes use the term *general tree* in contexts where we want to distinguish ordered trees from M-ary trees.

Because each node in an ordered tree can have any number of links, it is natural to consider using a linked list, rather than an array, to hold the links to the node's children. Figure 5.22 is an example of such a representation. From this example, it is clear that each node then contains two links—one for the linked list connecting it to its siblings, the other for the linked list of its children.

Property 5.4 *There is a one-to-one correspondence between binary trees and ordered forests.*

The correspondence is depicted in Figure 5.22. We can represent any forest as a binary tree by making the left link of each node point to its leftmost child, and the right link of each node point to its sibling on the right. ■

Definition 5.4 *A* **rooted tree** *(or* **unordered tree***) is a node (called the root) connected to a multiset of rooted trees. (Such a multiset is called an unordered forest.)*

Figure 5.22
Tree representation

Representing an ordered tree by keeping a linked list of the children of each node is equivalent to representing it as a binary tree. The diagram on the right at the top shows a linked-list-of-children representation of the tree on the left at the top, with the list implemented in the right links of nodes, and each node's left link pointing to the first node in the linked list of its children. The diagram on the right at the bottom shows a slightly rearranged version of the diagram above it and clearly represents the binary tree at the left on the bottom. That is, we can consider the binary tree as representing the tree.

The trees that we encountered in Chapter 1 for the connectivity problem are unordered trees. Such trees may be defined as ordered trees where the order in which the children of a node are considered is not significant. We could also choose to define unordered trees as comprising a set of parent–child relationships among nodes. This choice would seem to have little relation to the recursive structures that we are considering, but it is perhaps the concrete representation that is most true to the abstract notion.

We could choose to represent an unordered tree in a computer with an ordered tree, recognizing that many different ordered trees might represent the same unordered tree. Indeed, the converse problem of determining whether or not two different ordered trees represent the same unordered tree (the *tree-isomorphism* problem) is a difficult one to solve.

The most general type of tree is one where no root node is distinguished. For example, the spanning trees resulting from the connectivity algorithms in Chapter 1 have this property. To define properly *unrooted, unordered trees*, or *free trees*, we start with a definition for *graphs*.

Definition 5.5 *A **graph** is a set of nodes together with a set of edges that connect pairs of distinct nodes (with at most one edge connecting any pair of nodes).*

We can envision starting at some node and following an edge to the constituent node for the edge, then following an edge from that node to another node, and so on. A sequence of edges leading from one node to another in this way with no node appearing twice is called a *simple path*. A graph is *connected* if there is a simple path connecting any pair of nodes. A path that is simple except that the first and final nodes are the same is called a *cycle*.

Every tree is a graph; which graphs are trees? We consider a graph to be a tree if it satisfies any of the following four conditions:
- G has $N - 1$ edges and no cycles.
- G has $N - 1$ edges and is connected.
- Exactly one simple path connects each pair of vertices in G.
- G is connected but does not remain connected if any edge is removed.

Any one of these conditions is necessary and sufficient to prove the other three. Formally, we should choose one of them to serve as a definition of a *free tree*; informally, we let them collectively serve as the definition.

We represent a free tree simply as a collection of edges. If we choose to represent a free tree as an unordered, ordered, or even a binary tree, we need to recognize that, in general, there are many different ways to represent each free tree.

The tree abstraction arises frequently, and the distinctions discussed in this section are important, because knowing different tree abstractions is often an essential ingredient in finding an efficient algorithm and corresponding data structure for a given problem. We often work directly with concrete representations of trees without regard to a particular abstraction, but we also often profit from working with the proper tree abstraction, then considering various concrete representations. We shall see numerous examples of this process throughout the book.

Before moving back to algorithms and implementations, we consider a number of basic mathematical properties of trees; these properties will be of use to us in the design and analysis of tree algorithms.

Exercises

▷ **5.56** Give representations of the free tree in Figure 5.20 as a rooted tree and as a binary tree.

● **5.57** How many different ways are there to represent the free tree in Figure 5.20 as an ordered tree?

▷ **5.58** Draw three ordered trees that are isomorphic to the ordered tree in Figure 5.20. That is, you should be able to transform the four trees to one another by exchanging children.

○ **5.59** Assume that trees contain items for which `equals()` is implemented. Write a recursive program that deletes all the leaves in a binary tree with items equal to a given item (see Program 5.5).

○ **5.60** Change the divide-and-conquer method for finding the maximum item in an array (Program 5.6) to divide the array into k parts that differ by at most 1 in size, recursively find the maximum in each part, and return the maximum of the maxima.

5.61 Draw the 3-ary and 4-ary trees corresponding to using $k = 3$ and $k = 4$ in the recursive construction suggested in Exercise 5.60, for an array of 11 elements (see Figure 5.6).

○ **5.62** Binary trees are equivalent to binary strings that have one more 0 bit than 1 bit, with the additional constraint that, at any position k, the number of 0 bits that appear strictly to the left of k is no larger than the number of

1 bits strictly to the left of k. A binary tree is either a 0 or two such strings concatenated together, preceded by a 1. Draw the binary tree that corresponds to the string

1 1 1 0 0 1 0 1 1 0 0 0 1 0 1 1 0 0 0.

○ **5.63** Ordered trees are equivalent to balanced strings of parentheses: An ordered tree either is null or is a sequence of ordered trees enclosed in parentheses. Draw the ordered tree that corresponds to the string

((( ) (( ) ( )) ( )) (( ) ( ) ( ))) .

•• **5.64** Write a program to determine whether or not two arrays of N integers between 0 and $N - 1$ represent isomorphic unordered trees, when interpreted (as in Chapter 1) as parent–child links in a tree with nodes numbered between 0 and $N - 1$. That is, your program should determine whether or not there is a way to renumber the nodes in one tree such that the array representation of the one tree is identical to the array representation of the other tree.

•• **5.65** Write a program to determine whether or not two binary trees represent isomorphic unordered trees.

▷ **5.66** Draw all the ordered trees that could represent the tree defined by the set of edges 0-1, 1-2, 1-3, 1-4, 4-5.

• **5.67** Prove that, if a connected graph of N nodes has the property that removing any edge disconnects the graph, then the graph has $N - 1$ edges and no cycles.

5.5 Mathematical Properties of Binary Trees

Before beginning to consider tree-processing algorithms, we continue in a mathematical vein by considering a number of basic properties of trees. We focus on binary trees, because we use them frequently throughout this book. Understanding their basic properties will lay the groundwork for understanding the performance characteristics of various algorithms that we will encounter—not only of those that use binary trees as explicit data structures, but also of divide-and-conquer recursive algorithms and other similar applications.

Property 5.5 *A binary tree with N internal nodes has $N + 1$ external nodes.*

We prove this property by induction: A binary tree with no internal nodes has one external node, so the property holds for $N = 0$. For $N > 0$, any binary tree with N internal nodes has k internal nodes in its left subtree and $N - 1 - k$ internal nodes in its right subtree for some k between 0 and $N - 1$, since the root is an internal node. By the inductive hypothesis, the left subtree has $k + 1$ external nodes and the right subtree has $N - k$ external nodes, for a total of $N + 1$. ∎

Property 5.6 *A binary tree with N internal nodes has $2N$ links: $N - 1$ links to internal nodes and $N + 1$ links to external nodes.*

In any rooted tree, each node, except the root, has a unique parent, and every edge connects a node to its parent, so there are $N - 1$ links connecting internal nodes. Similarly, each of the $N + 1$ external nodes has one link, to its unique parent. ∎

The performance characteristics of many algorithms depend not just on the number of nodes in associated trees, but on various structural properties.

Definition 5.6 *The **level** of a node in a tree is one higher than the level of its parent (with the root at level 0). The **height** of a tree is the maximum of the levels of the tree's nodes. The **path length** of a tree is the sum of the levels of all the tree's nodes. The **internal path length** of a binary tree is the sum of the levels of all the tree's internal nodes. The **external path length** of a binary tree is the sum of the levels of all the tree's external nodes.*

A convenient way to compute the path length of a tree is to sum, for all k, the product of k and the number of nodes at level k.

These quantities also have simple recursive definitions that follow directly from the recursive definitions of trees and binary trees. For example, the height of a tree is 1 greater than the maximum of the height of the subtrees of its root, and the path length of a tree with N nodes is the sum of the path lengths of the subtrees of its root plus $N - 1$. The quantities also relate directly to the analysis of recursive algorithms. For example, for many recursive computations, the height of the corresponding tree is precisely the maximum depth of the recursion, or the size of the stack needed to support the computation.

Property 5.7 *The external path length of any binary tree with N internal nodes is $2N$ greater than the internal path length.*

We could prove this property by induction, but an alternate proof (which also works for Property 5.6) is instructive. Any binary tree can be constructed by the following process: Start with the binary tree

Figure 5.23
**Three binary trees with 10
   internal nodes**

*The binary tree shown at the top
has height 7, internal path length
31, and external path length 51. A
fully balanced binary tree (center)
with 10 internal nodes has height
4, internal path length 19, and external path length 39 (no binary
tree with 10 nodes has smaller values for any of these quantities). A
degenerate binary tree (bottom)
with 10 internal nodes has height
10, internal path length 45, and
external path length 65 (no binary
tree with 10 nodes has larger values for any of these quantities).*

consisting of one external node. Then, repeat the following N times:
Pick an external node and replace it by a new internal node with two
external nodes as children. If the external node chosen is at level k,
the internal path length is increased by k, but the external path length
is increased by $k + 2$ (one external node at level k is removed, but two
at level $k + 1$ are added). The process starts with a tree with internal
and external path lengths both 0 and, for each of N steps, increases
the external path length by 2 more than the internal path length. ∎

Property 5.8 *The height of a binary tree with N internal nodes is at
least $\lg N$ and at most $N - 1$.*

The worst case is a degenerate tree with only one leaf, with $N - 1$ links
from the root to the leaf (see Figure 5.23). The best case is a balanced
tree with 2^i internal nodes at every level i except the bottom level (see
Figure 5.23). If the height is h, then we must have

$$2^{h-1} < N + 1 \leq 2^h,$$

since there are $N + 1$ external nodes. This inequality implies the
property stated: The best-case height is precisely equal to $\lg N$ rounded
up to the nearest integer. ∎

Property 5.9 *The internal path length of a binary tree with N internal
nodes is at least $N \lg(N/4)$ and at most $N(N - 1)/2$.*

The worst case and the best case are achieved for the same trees referred
to in the discussion of Property 5.8 and depicted in Figure 5.23. The
internal path length of the worst-case tree is $0 + 1 + 2 + \ldots + (N - 1) =
N(N - 1)/2$. The best case tree has $(N + 1)$ external nodes at height
no more than $\lfloor \lg N \rfloor$. Multiplying these and applying Property 5.7, we
get the bound $(N + 1)\lfloor \lg N \rfloor - 2N < N \lg(N/4)$. ∎

As we shall see, binary trees appear extensively in computer
applications, and performance is best when the binary trees are fully
balanced (or nearly so). For example, the trees that we use to describe
divide-and-conquer algorithms such as binary search and mergesort
are fully balanced (see Exercise 5.74). In Chapters 9 and 13, we shall
examine explicit data structures that are based on balanced trees.

These basic properties of trees provide the information that we
need to develop efficient algorithms for a number of practical problems. More detailed analyses of several of the specific algorithms

that we shall encounter require sophisticated mathematical analysis, although we can often get useful estimates with straightforward inductive arguments like the ones that we have used in this section. We discuss further mathematical properties of trees as needed in the chapters that follow. At this point, we are ready to move back to algorithmic matters.

Exercises

▷ **5.68** How many external nodes are there in an M-ary tree with N internal nodes? Use your answer to give the amount of memory required to represent such a tree, assuming that links and items require one word of memory each.

5.69 Give upper and lower bounds on the height of an M-ary tree with N internal nodes.

○ **5.70** Give upper and lower bounds on the internal path length of an M-ary tree with N internal nodes.

5.71 Give upper and lower bounds on the number of leaves in a binary tree with N nodes.

• **5.72** Show that if the levels of the external nodes in a binary tree differ by a constant, then the height is $O(\log N)$.

○ **5.73** A *Fibonacci tree* of height $n > 2$ is a binary tree with a Fibonacci tree of height $n - 1$ in one subtree and a Fibonacci tree of height $n - 2$ in the other subtree. A Fibonacci tree of height 0 is a single external node, and a Fibonacci tree of height 1 is a single internal node with two external children (see Figure 5.14). Give the height and external path length of a Fibonacci tree of height n, as a function of N, the number of nodes in the tree.

5.74 A *divide-and-conquer tree* of N nodes is a binary tree with a root labeled N, a divide-and-conquer tree of $\lfloor N/2 \rfloor$ nodes in one subtree, and a divide-and-conquer tree of $\lceil N/2 \rceil$ nodes in the other subtree. (Figure 5.6 depicts a divide-and-conquer tree.) Draw divide-and-conquer trees with 11, 15, 16, and 23 nodes.

○ **5.75** Prove by induction that the internal path length of a divide-and-conquer tree is between $N \lg N$ and $N \lg N + N$.

5.76 A *combine-and-conquer tree* of N nodes is a binary tree with a root labeled N, a combine-and-conquer tree of $\lfloor N/2 \rfloor$ nodes in one subtree, and a combine-and-conquer tree of $\lceil N/2 \rceil$ nodes in the other subtree (see Exercise 5.18). Draw combine-and-conquer trees with 11, 15, 16, and 23 nodes.

5.77 Prove by induction that the internal path length of a combine-and-conquer tree is between $N \lg N$ and $N \lg N + N$.

5.78 A *complete* binary tree is one with all levels filled, except possibly the final one, which is filled from left to right, as illustrated in Figure 5.24. Prove that the internal path length of a complete tree with N nodes is between $N \lg N$ and $N \lg N + N$.

Figure 5.24
Complete binary trees with 7 and 10 internal nodes

When the number of external nodes is a power of 2 (top), the external nodes in a complete binary tree are all at the same level. Otherwise (bottom), the external nodes appear on two levels, with the internal nodes to the left of the external nodes on the next-to-bottom level.

5.6 Tree Traversal

Before considering algorithms that construct binary trees and trees, we consider algorithms for the most basic tree-processing function: *tree traversal*: Given a (reference to) a tree, we want to process every node in the tree systematically. In a linked list, we move from one node to the next by following the single link; for trees, however, we have decisions to make, because there may be multiple links to follow.

We begin by considering the process for binary trees. For linked lists, we had two basic options (see Program 5.5): process the node and then follow the link (in which case we would visit the nodes in order), or follow the link and then process the node (in which case we would visit the nodes in reverse order). For binary trees, we have two links, and we therefore have three basic orders in which we might visit the nodes:

- *Preorder*, where we visit the node, then visit the left and right subtrees
- *Inorder*, where we visit the left subtree, then visit the node, then visit the right subtree
- *Postorder*, where we visit the left and right subtrees, then visit the node

We can implement these methods easily with a recursive program, as shown in Program 5.14, which is a direct generalization of the linked-list–traversal program in Program 5.5. To implement traversals in the other orders, we permute the method invocations in Program 5.14 in the appropriate manner. Figure 5.26 shows the order in which we visit the nodes in a sample tree for each order. Figure 5.25 shows the sequence of method invocations that is executed when we invoke Program 5.14 on the sample tree in Figure 5.26.

We have already encountered the same basic recursive processes on which the different tree-traversal methods are based, in divide-and-conquer recursive programs (see Figures 5.8 and 5.11), and in arithmetic expressions. For example, doing preorder traversal corresponds to drawing the marks on the ruler first, then making the recursive calls (see Figure 5.11); doing inorder traversal corresponds to moving the biggest disk in the towers of Hanoi solution in between recursive calls that move all of the others; doing postorder traversal corresponds to evaluating postfix expressions, and so forth. These correspondences

> **Program 5.14 Recursive tree traversal**
>
> This recursive method takes a link to a tree as an argument and calls visit with each of the nodes in the tree as argument. As is, the code implements a preorder traversal; if we move the call to visit between the recursive calls, we have an inorder traversal; and if we move the call to visit after the recursive calls, we have a postorder traversal.
>
> ```
> private void traverseR(Node h)
>   {
>     if (h == null) return;
>     h.item.visit();
>     traverseR(h.l);
>     traverseR(h.r);
>   }
> void traverse()
>   { traverseR(root); }
> ```

give us immediate insight into the mechanisms behind tree traversal. For example, we know that every other node in an inorder traversal is an external node, for the same reason that every other move in the towers of Hanoi problem involves the small disk.

It is also useful to consider nonrecursive implementations that use an explicit pushdown stack. For simplicity, we begin by considering an abstract stack that can hold items or trees, initialized with the tree to be traversed. Then, we enter into a loop, where we pop and process the top entry on the stack, continuing until the stack is empty. If the popped entity is an item, we visit it; if the popped entity is a tree, then we perform a sequence of push operations that depends on the desired ordering:

- For *preorder*, we push the right subtree, then the left subtree, and then the node.
- For *inorder*, we push the right subtree, then the node, and then the left subtree.
- For *postorder*, we push the node, then the right subtree, and then the left subtree.

We do not push null trees onto the stack. Figure 5.27 shows the stack contents as we use each of these three methods to traverse the sample

```
traverse E
  visit E
  traverse D
    visit D
    traverse B
      visit B
      traverse A
        visit A
        traverse *
        traverse *
      traverse C
        visit C
        traverse *
        traverse *
    traverse *
  traverse H
    visit H
    traverse F
      visit F
      traverse *
      traverse G
        visit G
        traverse *
        traverse *
    traverse *
```

**Figure 5.25
Preorder-traversal method invocations**

This sequence of method invocations constitutes preorder traversal for the example tree in Figure 5.26.

Figure 5.26
Tree-traversal orders

These sequences indicate the order in which we visit nodes for pre-order (left), *inorder* (center), *and postorder* (right) *tree traversal.*

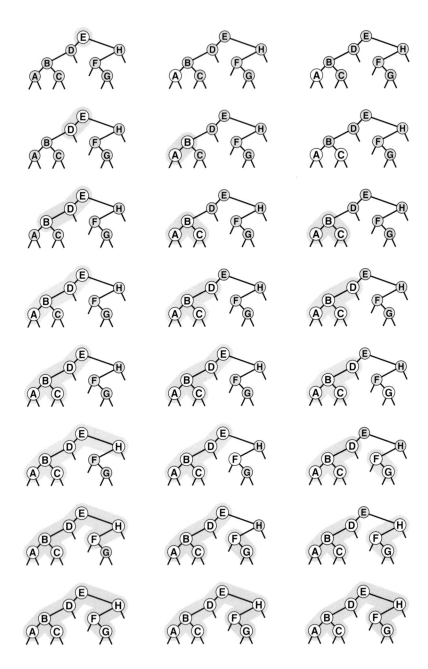

Program 5.15 Preorder traversal (nonrecursive)

This nonrecursive stack-based method is functionally equivalent to its recursive counterpart, Program 5.14.

```
private void traverseS(Node h)
  { NodeStack s = new NodeStack(max);
    s.push(h);
    while (!s.empty())
      {
        h = s.pop();
        h.item.visit();
        if (h.r != null) s.push(h.r);
        if (h.l != null) s.push(h.l);
      }
  }
void traverseS()
  { traverseS(root); }
```

---

tree in Figure 5.26. We can easily verify by induction that this method produces the same output as the recursive one for any binary tree.

The scheme described in the previous paragraph is a conceptual one that encompasses the three traversal methods, but the implementations that we use in practice are slightly simpler. For example, for preorder, we do not need to push nodes onto the stack (we visit the root of each tree that we pop), and we therefore can use a simple stack that contains only one type of item (tree link), as in the nonrecursive implementation in Program 5.15. The system stack that supports the recursive program contains return addresses and argument values, rather than items or nodes, but the actual sequence in which we do the computations (visit the nodes) is the same for the recursive and the stack-based methods.

A fourth natural traversal strategy is simply to visit the nodes in a tree as they appear on the page, reading down from top to bottom and from left to right. This method is called *level-order* traversal because all the nodes on each level appear together, in order. Figure 5.28 shows how the nodes of the tree in Figure 5.26 are visited in level order.

Figure 5.27
Stack contents for tree-traversal algorithms

These sequences indicate the stack contents for preorder (left), inorder (center), and postorder (right) tree traversal (see Figure 5.26), for an idealized model of the computation, similar to the one that we used in Figure 5.5, where we put the item and its two subtrees on the stack, in the indicated order.

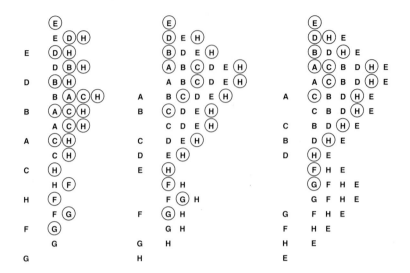

Remarkably, we can achieve level-order traversal by substituting a queue for the stack in Program 5.15, as shown in Program 5.16. For preorder, we use a LIFO data structure; for level order, we use a FIFO data structure. Otherwise, there is no difference at all between the two programs. These programs merit careful study, because they represent approaches to organizing work remaining to be done that differ in an essential way. In particular, level order does *not* correspond to a recursive implementation that relates to the recursive structure of the tree.

Preorder, postorder, and level order are well defined for forests as well. To make the definitions consistent, think of a forest as a tree with an imaginary root. Then, the preorder rule is "visit the root, then visit each of the subtrees," the postorder rule is "visit each of the subtrees, then visit the root." The level-order rule is the same as for binary trees. Direct implementations of these methods are straightforward generalizations of the stack-based preorder traversal programs (Programs 5.14 and 5.15) and the queue-based level-order traversal program (Program 5.16) for binary trees that we just considered. We omit consideration of implementations because we consider a more general procedure in Section 5.8.

> **Program 5.16 Level-order traversal**
>
> Switching the underlying data structure in preorder traversal (see Program 5.15) from a stack to a queue transforms the traversal into a level-order one.
>
> ```
> private void traverseQ(Node h)
>   { NodeQueue q = new NodeQueue(max);
>     q.put(h);
>     while (!q.empty())
>       {
>         h = q.get();
>         h.item.visit();
>         if (h.l != null) q.put(h.l);
>         if (h.r != null) q.put(h.r);
>       }
>   }
> void traverseQ()
>   { traverseQ(root); }
> ```

Exercises

▷ **5.79** Give preorder, inorder, postorder, and level-order traversals of the following binary trees:

▷ **5.80** Show the contents of the queue during the level order traversal (Program 5.16) depicted in Figure 5.28, in the style of Figure 5.27.

5.81 Show that preorder for a forest is the same as preorder for the corresponding binary tree (see Property 5.4), and that postorder for a forest is the same as inorder for the binary tree.

○ **5.82** Give a nonrecursive implementation of inorder traversal.

● **5.83** Give a nonrecursive implementation of postorder traversal.

● **5.84** Write a program that takes as input the preorder and inorder traversals of a binary tree and that produces as output the level-order traversal of the tree.

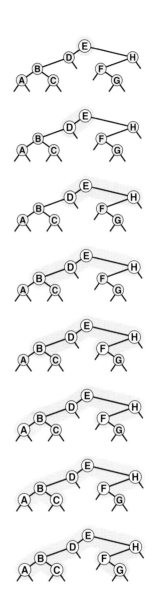

**Figure 5.28
Level-order traversal**

This sequence depicts the result of visiting nodes in order from top to bottom and left to right in the tree.

5.7 Recursive Binary-Tree Algorithms

The tree-traversal algorithms that we considered in Section 5.6 exemplify the basic fact that we are led to consider recursive algorithms for binary trees, because of these trees' very nature as recursive structures. Many tasks admit direct recursive divide-and-conquer algorithms, which essentially generalize the traversal algorithms. We process a tree by processing the root node and (recursively) its subtrees; we can do computation before, between, or after the recursive calls (or possibly all three).

We frequently need to find the values of various structural parameters for a tree, given only a link to the tree. For example, Program 5.17 comprises recursive methods for computing the number of nodes in and the height of a given tree. The methods follow immediately from Definition 5.6. Neither of these methods depends on the order in which the recursive calls are processed: they process all the nodes in the tree and return the same answer if we, for example, exchange the recursive

---

Program 5.17 Computation of tree parameters

We can use simple recursive methods such as these to learn basic structural properties of trees.

```
private static int count(Node h)
  {
    if (h == null) return 0;
    return count(h.l) + count(h.r) + 1;
  }
int count()
  { return count(root); }
private static int height(Node h)
  {
    if (h == null) return -1;
    int u = height(h.l), v = height(h.r);
    if (u > v) return u+1; else return v+1;
  }
int height()
  { return height(root); }
```

Program 5.18 Quick tree-print method

This recursive program keeps track of the tree height and uses that information for indentation in printing out a representation of the tree that we can use to debug tree-processing programs (see Figure 5.29). It assumes that items in nodes are of type Item.

```
static void printnode(Item x, int h)
  {
    for (int i = 0; i < h; i++)
      Out.print("   ");
    Out.println("[" + x + "]");
  }
private static void showR(Node t, int h)
  {
    if (t == null) { printnode(null, h); return; }
    showR(t.r, h+1);
    printnode(t.item, h);
    showR(t.l, h+1);
  }
void show()
  { showR(root, 0); }
```

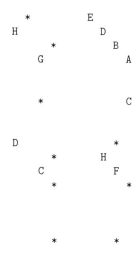

Figure 5.29
Printing a tree (inorder and preorder)

The output at the left results from using Program 5.18 on the sample tree in Figure 5.26 and exhibits the tree structure in a manner similar to the graphical representation that we have been using, rotated 90 degrees. The output at the right is from the same program with the print statement moved to the beginning; it exhibits the tree structure in a familiar outline format.

calls. Not all tree parameters are so easily computed: for example, a program to compute efficiently the internal path length of a binary tree is more challenging (see Exercises 5.88 through 5.90).

Another method that is useful whenever we write programs that process trees is one that prints out or draws the tree. For example, Program 5.18 is a recursive procedure that prints out a tree in the format illustrated in Figure 5.29. We can use the same basic recursive scheme to draw more elaborate representations of trees, such as those that we use in the figures in this book (see Exercise 5.85).

Program 5.18 is an inorder traversal—if we print the item before the recursive calls, we get a preorder traversal, which is also illustrated in Figure 5.29. This format is a familiar one that we might use, for example, for a family tree, or to list files in a tree-based file system, or to make an outline of a printed document. For example, doing a preorder traversal of the tree in Figure 5.19 gives a version of the table of contents of this book.

> **Program 5.19 Construction of a tournament**
>
> This recursive method divides an array a[1], ... , a[r] into the two parts a[1], ... , a[m] and a[m+1], ... , a[r], builds tournaments for the two parts (recursively), and makes a tournament for the whole array by setting links in a new node to the recursively built tournaments and setting its value to the larger of the values in the roots of the two recursively built tournaments.
>
> ```
> static class Node
>   { double val; Node l; Node r;
>     Node(double v, Node l, Node r)
>       { this.val = v; this.l = l; this.r = r; }
>   }
> static Node max(double a[], int l, int r)
>   { int m = (l+r)/2;
>     Node x = new Node(a[m], null, null);
>     if (l == r) return x;
>     x.l = max(a, l, m);
>     x.r = max(a, m+1, r);
>     double u = x.l.val, v = x.r.val;
>     if (u > v)
>       x.val = u; else x.val = v;
>     return x;
>   }
> ```

Our first example of a program that builds an explicit binary tree structure is associated with the find-the-maximum application that we considered in Section 5.2. Our goal is to build a *tournament*: a binary tree where the item in every internal node is a copy of the larger of the items in its two children. In particular, the item at the root is a copy of the largest item in the tournament. The items in the leaves (nodes with no children) constitute the data of interest, and the rest of the tree is a data structure that allows us to find the largest of the items efficiently.

Program 5.19 is a recursive program that builds a tournament from the items in an array. A modification of Program 5.6, it thus uses a divide-and-conquer recursive strategy: To build a tournament for a single item, we create (and return) a leaf containing that item. To build a tournament for $N > 1$ items, we use the divide-and-conquer

Figure 5.30
Explicit tree for finding the maximum (tournament)

This figure depicts the explicit tree structure that is constructed by Program 5.19 from the input A M P L E. The data items are in the leaves. Each internal node has a copy of the larger of the items in its two children; by induction, the largest item is at the root.

strategy: Divide the items in half, build tournaments for each half, and create a new node with links to the two tournaments and with an item that is a copy of the larger of the items in the roots of the two tournaments.

Figure 5.30 is an example of an explicit tree structure that might be built by Program 5.19. Building a recursive data structure such as this one is perhaps preferable in some situations to finding the maximum by scanning the data, as we did in Program 5.6, because the tree structure provides us with the flexibility to perform other operations. The very operation that we use to build the tournament is an important example: Given two tournaments, we can combine them into a single tournament in constant time by creating a new node, making its left link point to one of the tournaments and its right link point to the other, and taking the larger of the two items (at the roots of the two given tournaments) as the largest item in the combined tournament. We also can consider algorithms for adding items, removing items, and performing other operations. We shall not consider such operations in any further detail here because similar data structures with this flexibility are the topic of Chapter 9.

Indeed, tree-based implementations for several of the generalized queue ADTs that we discussed in Section 4.7 are a primary topic of discussion for much of this book. In particular, many of the algorithms in Chapters 12 through 15 are based on *binary search trees*, which are explicit trees that correspond to binary search, in a relationship analogous to the relationship between the explicit structure of Figure 5.30 and the recursive find-the-maximum algorithm (see Figure 5.6). The challenge in implementing and using such structures is to ensure that our algorithms remain efficient after a long sequence of *insert*, *remove*, and other operations.

Our second example of a program that builds a binary tree is a modification of our prefix-expression–evaluation program in Section 5.1 (Program 5.4) to construct a tree representing a prefix expression, instead of just evaluating it (see Figure 5.31). Program 5.20 uses the same recursive scheme as Program 5.4, but the recursive method returns a link to a tree, rather than a value. We create a new tree node for each character in the expression: Nodes corresponding to operators have links to their operands, and the leaf nodes contain the variables (or constants) that are inputs to the expression.

Translation programs such as compilers often use such internal tree representations for programs, because the trees are useful for many purposes. For example, we might imagine operands corresponding to variables that take on values, and we could generate machine code to evaluate the expression represented by the tree with a postorder traversal. Or, we could use the tree to print out the expression in infix with an inorder traversal or in postfix with a postorder traversal.

We considered the few examples in this section to introduce the concept that we can build and process explicit linked tree structures with recursive programs. To do so effectively, we need to consider the performance of various algorithms, alternate representations, non-recursive alternatives, and many other details. However, we shall defer consideration of tree-processing programs in further detail until Chapter 12, because we use trees primarily for descriptive purposes in Chapters 7 through 11. We return to explicit tree implementations in Chapter 12 because they form the basis of numerous algorithms that we consider in Chapters 12 through 15.

Exercises

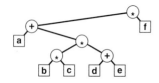

Figure 5.31
Parse tree

This tree is constructed by Program 5.20 for the prefix expression * + a * * b c + d e f. *It is a natural way to represent the expression: Each operand is in a leaf (which we draw here as an external node), and each operator is to be applied to the expressions represented by the left and right subtrees of the node containing the operator.*

∘ **5.85** Modify Program 5.18 to output a PostScript program that draws the tree, in a format like that used in Figure 5.23, but without the small boxes to represent the external nodes. Use moveto and lineto to draw lines, and the user-defined operator

    /node { newpath moveto currentpoint 4 0 360 arc fill} def

to draw nodes. After this definition, the call node draws a black dot at the coordinates on the stack (see Section 4.3).

▷ **5.86** Write a program that counts the leaves in a binary tree.

▷ **5.87** Write a program that counts the number of nodes in a binary tree that have one external and one internal child.

▷ **5.88** Write a recursive program that computes the internal path length of a binary tree, using Definition 5.6.

Program 5.20 Construction of a parse tree

To build a parse tree instead of just evaluating a prefix expression, we could use this recursive method instead of the `eval` method in Program 5.4. For simplicity, this code assumes that operands are single characters and that a `Node` class is defined like the one in Program 5.19, but with a `char` field for its data. Each call of the recursive method creates a new node with the next character from the input as the token. If the token is an operand, we return the new node; if it is an operator, we set the left and right pointers to the tree built (recursively) for the two arguments.

```
static Node parse()
   { char t = a[i++]; Node x = new Node(t);
     if ((t == '+') || (t == '*'))
       { x.l = parse(); x.r = parse(); }
     return x;
   }
```

5.89 Determine the number of method invocations made by your program when it is computing the internal path length of a binary tree. Prove your answer by induction.

• **5.90** Write a recursive program that computes the internal path length of a binary tree in time proportional to the number of nodes in the tree.

○ **5.91** Write a recursive program that deletes all the leaves with a given key from a tournament (see Exercise 5.59).

5.8 Graph Traversal

For our final example of a recursive program in this chapter, we consider one of the most important of all recursive programs: recursive graph traversal, or *depth-first search*. This method for systematically visiting all the nodes in a graph is a direct generalization of the tree-traversal methods that we considered in Section 5.6, and it serves as the basis for many basic algorithms for processing graphs (see Part 7). It is a simple recursive algorithm. Starting at any node v, we

- Visit v.
- (Recursively) visit each (*unvisited*) node attached to v.

If the graph is connected, we eventually reach all of the nodes. Program 5.21 is an implementation of this recursive procedure.

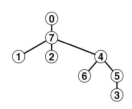

visit 0
  visit 7 (first on 0's list)
    visit 1 (first on 7's list)
      check 7 on 1's list
      check 0 on 1's list
    visit 2 (second on 7's list)
      check 7 on 2's list
      check 0 on 2's list
    check 0 on 7's list
    visit 4 (fourth on 7's list)
      visit 6 (first on 4's list)
        check 4 on 6's list
        check 0 on 6's list
      visit 5 (second on 4's list)
        check 0 on 5's list
        check 4 on 5's list
        visit 3 (third on 5's list)
          check 5 on 3's list
          check 4 on 3's list
      check 7 on 4's list
      check 3 on 4's list
  check 5 on 0's list
  check 2 on 0's list
  check 1 on 0's list
  check 6 on 0's list

Figure 5.32
Depth-first–search method in-vocations

This sequence of method invocations constitutes depth-first search for the example graph in Figure 3.16. The tree that depicts the recursive structure (top) is called the depth-first–search tree.

Program 5.21 Depth-first search

To visit all the nodes connected to node k in a graph, we mark it as *visited*, then (recursively) visit all the unvisited nodes on k's adjacency list.

```
private void dfs(int k)
  {
    visit(k); visited[k] = true;
    for (Node t = adj[k]; t != null; t = t.next)
      if (!visited[t.v]) dfs(t.v);
  }
```

For example, suppose that we use the adjacency-list representation depicted in the sample graph in Figure 3.16. Figure 5.32 shows the recursive calls made during the depth-first search of this graph, and the sequence on the left in Figure 5.33 depicts the way in which we follow the edges in the graph. We follow each edge in the graph, with one of two possible outcomes: if the edge takes us to a node that we have already visited, we ignore it; if it takes us to a node that we have not yet visited, we follow it there via a recursive call. The set of all edges that we follow in this way forms a spanning tree for the graph.

The difference between depth-first search and general tree traversal (see Program 5.14) is that we need to guard explicitly against visiting nodes that we have already visited. In a tree, we never encounter any such nodes. Indeed, if the graph is a tree, recursive depth-first search starting at the root is equivalent to preorder traversal.

Property 5.10 *Depth-first search requires time proportional to $V+E$ in a graph with V vertices and E edges, using the adjacency lists representation.*

In the adjacency-lists representation, there is one list node corresponding to each edge in the graph, and one list node reference corresponding to each vertex in the graph. Depth-first search touches all of them, at most once. ∎

Because it also takes time proportional to $V + E$ to build the adjacency lists representation from an input sequence of edges (see Program 3.17), depth-first search gives us a linear-time solution to the connectivity problem of Chapter 1. For huge graphs, however, the

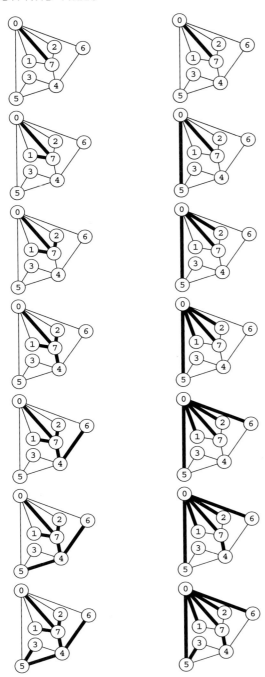

Figure 5.33
**Depth-first search and
breadth-first search**

Depth-first search (left) *moves from
node to node, backing up to the
previous node to try the next possibility whenever it has tried every possibility at a given node.
Breadth-first search* (right) *exhausts
all the possibilities at one node before moving to the next.*

Figure 5.34
Depth-first–search stack dynamics

We can think of the pushdown stack supporting depth-first search as containing a node and a reference to that node's adjacency list (indicated by a circled node) (left). Thus, we begin with node 0 on the stack, with reference to the first node on its list, node 7. Each line indicates the result of popping the stack, pushing a reference to the next node on the list for nodes that have been visited, and pushing an entry on the stack for nodes that have not been visited. Alternatively, we can think of the process as simply pushing all nodes adjacent to any unvisited node onto the stack (right).

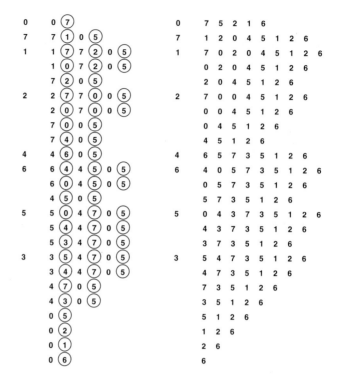

union–find solutions might still be preferable, because representing the whole graph takes space proportional to E, while the union–find solutions take space only proportional to V.

As we did with tree traversal, we can define a graph-traversal method that uses an explicit stack, as depicted in Figure 5.34. We can think of an abstract stack that holds dual entries: a node and a reference to some node in that node's adjacency list. With the stack initialized to the start node and the node reference initialized to the first node on that node's adjacency list, the depth-first search algorithm is equivalent to entering into a loop, where we visit the node at the top of the stack (if it has not already been visited); save the node referenced by the current adjacency-list node reference; update the adjacency-list reference to the next node (popping the entry if at the end of the adjacency list); and push a stack entry for the saved node, referencing the first node on its adjacency list.

Program 5.22 Breadth-first search

To visit all the nodes connected to node k in a graph, we put k onto a FIFO queue, then enter into a loop where we get the next node from the queue, and, if it has not been visited, visit it and push all the unvisited nodes on its adjacency list, continuing until the queue is empty.

```
void bfs(int k)
  { intQUEUE q = new intQUEUE(V*V);
    q.put(k);
    while (!q.empty())
      if (!visited[k = q.get()])
        { Node t;
          visit(k); visited[k] = true;
          for (t = adj[k]; t != null; t = t.next)
            if (!visited[t.v]) q.put(t.v);
        }
  }
```

Alternatively, as we did for tree traversal, we can consider the stack to contain links to nodes only. With the stack initialized to the start node, we enter into a loop where we visit the node at the top of the stack (if it has not already been visited), then push all the nodes adjacent to it onto the stack. Figure 5.34 illustrates that both of these methods are equivalent to depth-first search for our example graph, and the equivalence indeed holds in general.

The visit-the-top-node-and-push-all-its-neighbors algorithm is a simple formulation of depth-first search, but it is clear from Figure 5.34 that it suffers the disadvantage of possibly leaving multiple copies of each node on the stack. It does so even if we test whether each node that is about to go on the stack has been visited and refrain from putting the node in the stack if it has been. To avoid this problem, we can use a stack implementation that disallows duplicates by using a forget-the-old-item policy, because the copy nearest the top of the stack is always the first one visited, so the others are simply popped.

The stack dynamics for depth-first search that are illustrated in Figure 5.34 depend on the nodes on each adjacency list ending up on the stack in the same order that they appear in the list. To get this ordering for a given adjacency list when pushing one node at a time,

Figure 5.35
Breadth-first–search queue dynamics

We start with 0 on the queue, then get 0, visit it, and put the nodes on its adjacency list 7 5 2 1 6, in that order onto the queue. Then we get 7, visit it, and put the nodes on its adjacency list, and so forth. With duplicates disallowed with an ignore-the-new-item policy (right), we get the same result without any extraneous queue entries.

```
  0                          0
0   7 5 2 1 6              0   7 5 2 1 6
7   5 2 1 6 1 2 4         7   5 2 1 6 4
5   2 1 6 1 2 4 4 3       5   2 1 6 4 3
2   1 6 1 2 4 4 3         2   1 6 4 3
1   6 1 2 4 4 3           1   6 4 3
6   1 2 4 4 3 4           6   4 3
    2 4 4 3 4             4   3
    4 4 3 4               3
4   4 3 4 3
    3 4 3
3   4 3
    3
```

we would have to push the last node first, then the next-to-last node, and so forth. Moreover, to limit the stack size to the number of vertices while at the same time visiting the nodes in the same order as in depth-first search, we need to use a stack discipline with a forget-the-old-item policy. If visiting the nodes in the same order as depth-first search is not important to us, we can avoid both of these complications and directly formulate a nonrecursive stack-based graph-traversal method: With the stack initialized to the start node, we enter into a loop where we visit the node at the top of the stack, then proceed through its adjacency list, pushing each node onto the stack (if the node has not been visited already), using a stack implementation that disallows duplicates with an ignore-the-new-item policy. This algorithm visits all the nodes in the graph in a manner similar to depth-first-search, but it is not recursive.

The algorithm in the previous paragraph is noteworthy because we could use any generalized queue ADT and still visit each of the nodes in the graph (and generate a spanning tree). For example, if we use a queue instead of a stack, then we have *breadth-first search*, which is analogous to level-order traversal in a tree. Program 5.22 is an implementation of this method (assuming that we use a queue implementation like Program 4.17); an example of the algorithm in operation is depicted in Figure 5.35. In Part 5, we shall examine numerous graph algorithms based on more sophisticated generalized queue ADTs.

Breadth-first search and depth-first search both visit all the nodes in a graph, but their manner of doing so is dramatically different, as illustrated in Figure 5.36. Breadth-first search amounts to an army of searchers fanning out to cover the territory; depth-first search corresponds to a single searcher probing unknown territory as deeply as possible, retreating only when hitting dead ends. These are basic problem-solving paradigms of significance in many areas of computer science beyond graph searching.

Exercises

5.92 Show how recursive depth-first search visits the nodes in the graph built for the edge sequence 0-2, 1-4, 2-5, 3-6, 0-4, 6-0, and 1-3 (see Exercise 3.70), by giving diagrams corresponding to Figures 5.33 (left) and 5.34 (right).

5.93 Show how stack-based depth-first search visits the nodes in the graph built for the edge sequence 0-2, 1-4, 2-5, 3-6, 0-4, 6-0, and 1-3, by giving diagrams corresponding to Figures 5.33 (left) and 5.34 (right).

5.94 Show how (queue-based) breadth-first search visits the nodes in the graph built for the edge sequence 0-2, 1-4, 2-5, 3-6, 0-4, 6-0, and 1-3, by giving diagrams corresponding to Figures 5.33 (right) and 5.35 (left).

○ **5.95** Why is the running time in Property 5.10 quoted as $V + E$ and not simply E?

5.96 Show how stack-based depth-first search visits the nodes in the example graph in the text (Figure 3.16) when using a forget-the-old-item policy, by giving diagrams corresponding to Figures 5.33 (left) and 5.35 (right).

5.97 Show how stack-based depth-first search visits the nodes in the example graph in the text (Figure 3.16) when using an ignore-the-new-item policy, by giving diagrams corresponding to Figures 5.33 (left) and 5.35 (right).

▷ **5.98** Implement a stack-based depth-first search for graphs that are represented with adjacency lists.

○ **5.99** Implement a recursive depth-first search for graphs that are represented with adjacency lists.

5.9 Perspective

Recursion lies at the heart of early theoretical studies into the nature of computation. Recursive functions and programs play a central role in mathematical studies that attempt to separate problems that can be solved by a computer from problems that cannot be.

Figure 5.36
Graph-traversal trees

This diagram shows depth-first search (center) *and breadth-first search* (bottom), *halfway through searching in a large graph* (top). *Depth-first search meanders from one node to the next, so most nodes are connected to just two others. By contrast, breadth-first search sweeps through the graph, visiting all the nodes connected to a given node before moving on, so several nodes are connected to many others.*

It is certainly impossible to do justice to topics as far-reaching as trees and recursion in so brief a discussion. Many of the best examples of recursive programs will be our focus throughout the book—divide-and-conquer algorithms and recursive data structures that have been applied successfully to solve a wide variety of problems. For many applications, there is no reason to go beyond a simple, direct recursive implementation; for others, we will consider the derivation of alternate nonrecursive and bottom-up implementations.

In this book, our interest lies in the practical aspects of recursive programs and data structures. Our goal is to exploit recursion to produce elegant and efficient implementations. To meet that goal, we need to have particular respect for the dangers of simple programs that lead to an exponential number of method invocations or impossibly deep nesting. Despite this pitfall, recursive programs and data structures are attractive because they often provide us with inductive arguments that can convince us that our programs are correct and efficient.

We use trees throughout the book, both to help us understand the dynamic properties of programs and as dynamic data structures. Chapters 12 through 15 in particular are largely devoted to the manipulation of explicit tree structures. The properties described in this chapter provide us with the basic information that we need if we are to use explicit tree structures effectively.

Despite its central role in algorithm design, recursion is not a panacea. As we discovered in our study of tree- and graph-traversal algorithms, stack-based (inherently recursive) algorithms are not the only option when we have multiple computational tasks to manage. An effective algorithm-design technique for many problems is the use of generalized queue implementations other than stacks to give us the freedom to choose the next task according to some more subjective criteria than simply choosing the most recent. Data structures and algorithms that efficiently support such operations are a prime topic of Chapter 9, and we shall encounter many examples of their application when we consider graph algorithms in Part 5.

References for Part Two

There are numerous introductory textbooks on data structures. For example, the book by Standish covers linked structures, data abstraction, stacks and queues, memory allocation, and software engineering concepts at a more leisurely pace than here. The standard Java books by Arnold and Gosling, and by Gosling, Yellin and "The Java Team" both contain numerous examples of basic data structure implementations. Many of the basic data structures that we have discussed are implemented in standard Java libraries—we briefly discuss some of these implementations in the Appendix to this book.

The designers of PostScript perhaps did not anticipate that their language would be of interest to people learning basic algorithms and data structures. However, the language is not difficult to learn, and the reference manual is both thorough and accessible.

The client-interface-implementation paradigm is described in full detail, with numerous examples, in the book by Hanson. This book is an outstanding reference for programmers who want to write bugfree and portable code for large systems.

Knuth's books, particularly Volumes 1 and 3, remain the authoritative source on properties of elementary data structures. Baeza-Yates and Gonnet have more up-to-date information, backed by an extensive bibliography. Sedgewick and Flajolet cover mathematical properties of trees in detail.

Adobe Systems Incorporated, *PostScript Language Reference, third edition*, Addison-Wesley, Reading, MA, 1999.

K. Arnold and J. Gosling, *The Java Programming Language*, Addison-Wesley, Reading, MA, 1996.

R. Baeza-Yates and G. H. Gonnet, *Handbook of Algorithms and Data Structures*, second edition, Addison-Wesley, Reading, MA, 1984.

J. Gosling, F. Yellin, and The Java Team, *The Java Application Programming Interface. Volume 1: Core Packages*, Addison-Wesley, Reading, MA, 1996; *Volume 2: Window Toolkit and Applets*, Addison-Wesley, Reading, MA, 1996.

D. R. Hanson, *C Interfaces and Implementations: Techniques for Creating Reusable Software*, Addison-Wesley, Reading, MA, 1997.

D. E. Knuth, *The Art of Computer Programming. Volume 1: Fundamental Algorithms*, second edition, Addison-Wesley, Reading, MA, 1973; *Volume 2: Seminumerical Algorithms*, second edition, Addison-Wesley, Reading, MA, 1981; *Volume 3: Sorting and Searching*, third edition, Addison-Wesley, Reading, MA, 1998.

R. Sedgewick and P. Flajolet, *An Introduction to the Analysis of Algorithms*, Addison-Wesley, Reading, MA, 1996.

T. A. Standish, *Data Structures, Algorithms, and Software Principles in C*, Addison-Wesley, 1995.

Sorting

CHAPTER SIX

Elementary Sorting Methods

FOR OUR FIRST EXCURSION into the area of sorting algorithms, we shall study several elementary methods that are appropriate either for small files or for files that have a special structure. There are several reasons for studying these simple sorting algorithms in detail. First, they provide context in which we can learn terminology and basic mechanisms for sorting algorithms, and thus allow us to develop an adequate background for studying the more sophisticated algorithms. Second, these simple methods are actually more effective than the more powerful general-purpose methods in many applications of sorting. Third, several of the simple methods extend to better general-purpose methods or are useful in improving the efficiency of more sophisticated methods.

Our purpose in this chapter is not just to introduce the elementary methods but also to develop a framework within which we can study sorting in later chapters. We shall look at a variety of situations that may be important in applying sorting algorithms, examine different kinds of input files, and look at other ways of comparing sorting methods and learning their properties.

We begin by looking at a simple driver program for testing sorting methods, which provides a context for us to consider the conventions that we shall follow. We also consider the basic properties of sorting methods that are important for us to know when we are evaluating the utility of algorithms for particular applications. Next, we delve into the subject of developing data type interfaces and implementations, along the lines that we have discussed in Chapters 3 and 4, for extending our algorithms to sort the kinds of data files that arise in practice.

Then, we look closely at implementations of three elementary methods: selection sort, insertion sort, and bubble sort. Following that, we examine the performance characteristics of these algorithms in detail. Next, we look at shellsort, which is perhaps not properly characterized as elementary, but is easy to implement and is closely related to insertion sort. After a digression into the mathematical properties of shellsort, we consider linked-list sorting. The chapter concludes with a discussion of a specialized method that is appropriate when the key values are known to be restricted to a small range.

In numerous sorting applications, a simple algorithm may be the method of choice. First, we often use a sorting program only once, or just a few times. Once we have "solved" a sort problem for a set of data, we may not need the sort program again in the application manipulating those data. If an elementary sort is no slower than some other part of processing the data—for example, reading them in or printing them out—then there may be no point in looking for a faster way. If the number of items to be sorted is not too large (say, less than a few hundred elements), we might just choose to implement and run a simple method, rather than bothering with the interface to a system sort or with implementing and debugging a complicated method. Second, elementary methods are always suitable for small files (say, less than a few dozen elements)—sophisticated algorithms generally incur overhead that makes them slower than elementary ones for small files. This issue is not worth considering unless we wish to sort a huge number of small files, but applications with such a requirement are not unusual. Other types of files that are relatively easy to sort are ones that are already almost sorted (or already are sorted!) or ones that contain large numbers of duplicate keys. We shall see that several of the simple methods are particularly efficient when sorting such well-structured files.

As a rule, the elementary methods that we discuss here take time proportional to N^2 to sort N randomly arranged items. If N is small, this running time may be perfectly adequate. As just mentioned, the methods are likely to be even faster than more sophisticated methods for tiny files and in other special situations. But the methods that we discuss in this chapter are *not* suitable for large, randomly arranged files, because the running time will become excessive even on the fastest computers. A notable exception is shellsort (see Section 6.6), which takes many fewer than N^2 steps for large N and is arguably the sorting method of choice for midsize files and for a few other special applications.

6.1 Rules of the Game

Before considering specific algorithms, we will find it useful to discuss general terminology and basic assumptions for sorting algorithms. We shall be considering methods of sorting *files* of *items* containing *keys*. All these concepts are natural abstractions in modern programming environments. The keys, which are only part (often a small part) of the items, are used to control the sort. The objective of the sorting method is to rearrange the items such that their keys are ordered according to some well-defined ordering rule (usually numerical or alphabetical order). Specific characteristics of the keys and the items can vary widely across applications, but the abstract notion of putting keys and associated information into order is what characterizes the sorting problem.

If the file to be sorted will fit into memory, then the sorting method is called *internal*. Sorting files from tape or disk is called *external* sorting. The main difference between the two is that an internal sort can access any item easily, whereas an external sort must access items sequentially, or at least in large blocks. We shall look at a few external sorts in Chapter 11, but most of the algorithms that we consider are internal sorts.

We shall consider both arrays and linked lists. The problem of sorting arrays and the problem of sorting linked lists are both of interest: during the development of our algorithms, we shall also encounter some basic tasks that are best suited for sequential allocation and other tasks that are best suited for linked allocation. Some of the classical methods are sufficiently abstract that they can be implemented efficiently for either arrays or linked lists; others are particularly well suited to one or the other. Other types of access restrictions are also sometimes of interest.

We begin by focusing on array sorting. Program 6.1 illustrates many of the conventions that we shall use in our implementations. It consists of a driver that fills an array by generating random numbers,

Program 6.1 Example of array sort with driver program

This program illustrates our conventions for implementing basic array sorts. The main method is a driver that initializes an array of doubles with random values, calls a sort method to sort that array, then prints out the ordered result.

The sort method here is a version of insertion sort (see Section 6.4 for a detailed description, an example, and an improved implementation). It uses the methods less (compare two items), exch (exchange two items), and compExch (compare two items and exchange them if necessary to make the second not less than the first).

We can use this code to sort arrays of any primitive numeric type simply by replacing double with the type name everywhere. With an appropriate implementation of less, we can sort arrays of items of any reference type (see Section 6.2).

```
class ArraySortBasic
  { static int cnt = 0;
    static boolean less(double v, double w)
      { cnt++; return v < w; }
    static void exch(double[] a, int i, int j)
      { double t = a[i]; a[i] = a[j]; a[j] = t; }
    static void compExch(double[] a, int i, int j)
      { if (less(a[j], a[i])) exch (a, i, j); }
    static void sort(double[] a, int l, int r)
      { for (int i = l+1; i <= r; i++)
          for (int j = i; j > l; j--)
            compExch(a, j-1, j);
      }
    public static void main(String[] args)
      { int N = Integer.parseInt(args[0]);
        double a[] = new double[N];
        for (int i = 0; i < N; i++)
          a[i] = Math.random();
        sort(a, 0, N-1);
        if (N < 100)
          for (int i = 0; i < N; i++)
            Out.println(a[i] + "");
        Out.println("Compares used: " + cnt);
      }
  }
```

then calls a sort method to put the numbers in the array in order, then prints out the sorted result.

As we know from Chapters 3 and 4, there are numerous mechanisms available to us to arrange for our sort implementations to be useful for other types of data. We shall discuss the use of such mechanisms in detail in Section 6.2. The sort method in Program 6.1 refers to the items being sorted only through its first parameter and a few simple operations on the data. As usual, this approach allows us to use the same code to sort other types of items. For example, if code for generating, storing, and printing random keys in the main in Program 6.1 were changed to process integers instead of floating-point numbers, we would only have to change double to int in sort and its associated methods to have it sort arrays of integers. To provide such flexibility (while at the same time explicitly identifying those variables that hold items), our sort implementations will be implemented using a generic data type ITEM. For the moment, we can think of ITEM as int or double; in Section 6.2, we shall consider in detail data-type implementations that allow us to use our sort implementations for arbitrary items with floating-point numbers, strings, and other different types of keys, using mechanisms discussed in Chapters 3 and 4.

We can substitute for sort any of the array-sort implementations from this chapter or from Chapters 7 through 10. They all assume that items of type ITEM are to be sorted, and they all take three parameters: the array and the left and right bounds of the subarray to be sorted. They also all rely on less to compare keys in items and exch or compExch to exchange items. To differentiate sorting methods, we give our various sort routines different names. It is a simple matter to rename one of them or to change the driver in a program such as Program 6.1 without having to change any code in the sort implementation.

These conventions will allow us to examine natural and concise implementations of many array-sorting algorithms. In Section 6.2, we shall consider a driver that illustrates how to use the implementations in more general contexts, and numerous data type implementations. Although we are ever mindful of such packaging considerations, our focus will be on algorithmic issues, to which we now turn.

The example sort method in Program 6.1 is a variant of *insertion sort*, which we shall consider in detail in Section 6.4. Because it uses only compare–exchange operations, it is an example of a *nonadaptive* sort: The sequence of operations that it performs is independent of the order of the data. By contrast, an *adaptive* sort is one that performs different sequences of operations, depending on the outcomes of comparisons (invocations of less). Nonadaptive sorts are interesting because they are well suited for hardware implementation (see Chapter 11), but most of the general-purpose sorts that we consider are adaptive.

As usual, the primary performance parameter of interest is the running time of our sorting algorithms. The sort method in Program 6.1 always does exactly $N(N-1)/2$ comparisons (and exchanges), so it cannot be used when N is huge. The selection-sort, insertion-sort, and bubble-sort methods that we discuss in Sections 6.3 through 6.5 also require time proportional to N^2 to sort N items, as discussed in Section 6.6. The more advanced methods that we discuss in Chapters 7 through 10 can sort N items in time proportional to $N \log N$, but they are not always as good as the methods considered here for small N and in certain other special situations. In Section 6.8, we shall look at a more advanced method (shellsort) that can run in time proportional to $N^{3/2}$ or less, and, in Section 6.10, we shall see a specialized method (key-indexed sorting) that runs in time proportional to N for certain types of keys.

The analytic results described in the previous paragraph all follow from enumerating the basic operations (comparisons and exchanges) that the algorithms perform. As discussed in Section 2.2, we also must consider the costs of the operations, and we generally find it worthwhile to focus on the most frequently executed operations (the inner loop of the algorithm). Our goal is to develop efficient and reasonable implementations of efficient algorithms. In pursuit of this goal, we will not just avoid gratuitous additions to inner loops but will also look for ways to remove instructions from inner loops when possible. Generally, the best way to reduce costs in an application is to switch to a more efficient algorithm; the second best way is to tighten the inner loop. We shall consider both options in detail for sorting algorithms.

The amount of extra memory used by a sorting algorithm is the second important factor that we shall consider. Basically, the methods divide into three types: those that sort in place and use no extra memory except perhaps for a small stack or table; those that use a linked-list representation or otherwise refer to data through references or array indices and so need extra memory for N references or indices, and those that need enough extra memory to hold another copy of the array to be sorted.

We frequently use sorting methods for items with multiple keys— we may even need to sort one set of items using different keys at different times. In such cases, it may be important for us to be aware whether or not the sorting method that we use has the following property:

Definition 6.1 *A sorting method is said to be* **stable** *if it preserves the relative order of items with duplicated keys in the file.*

For example, if an alphabetized list of students and their year of graduation is sorted by year, a stable method produces a list in which people in the same class are still in alphabetical order, but a nonstable method is likely to produce a list with no vestige of the original alphabetic order. Figure 6.1 shows an example. Often, people who are unfamiliar with stability are surprised by the way an unstable algorithm seems to scramble the data when they first encounter the situation.

Several (but not all) of the simple sorting methods that we consider in this chapter are stable. On the other hand, many (but not all) of the sophisticated algorithms that we consider in the next several chapters are not. If stability is vital, we can force it by appending a small index to each key before sorting or by lengthening the sort key in some other way. Doing this extra work is tantamount to using both keys for the sort in Figure 6.1; using a stable algorithm would be preferable. It is easy to take stability for granted; actually, few of the sophisticated methods that we see in later chapters achieve stability without using significant extra time or space.

As we have mentioned, sorting programs normally access items in one of two ways: either keys are accessed for comparison, or entire items are accessed to be moved. If the items to be sorted are large, it is wise to avoid shuffling them around by doing an *indirect sort*: we rearrange not the items themselves, but rather an array of references such that the first entry refers to the smallest item, the second entry refers to the next smallest item, and so forth. We could rearrange the items after the sort, but that is often unnecessary, because we do have the capability to refer to them in sorted order (indirectly, through the

Adams	1
Black	2
Brown	4
Jackson	2
Jones	4
Smith	1
Thompson	4
Washington	2
White	3
Wilson	3

Adams	1
Smith	1
Washington	2
Jackson	2
Black	2
White	3
Wilson	3
Thompson	4
Brown	4
Jones	4

Adams	1
Smith	1
Black	2
Jackson	2
Washington	2
White	3
Wilson	3
Brown	4
Jones	4
Thompson	4

Figure 6.1
Stable-sort example

A sort of these records might be appropriate on either key. Suppose that they are sorted initially by the first key (top). A nonstable sort on the second key does not preserve the order in records with duplicate keys (center), but a stable sort does preserve the order (bottom).

references). In Java, indirect sorting is actually the norm, as we shall see in the next section, where we address the process of sorting files of items that are not just simple numeric types.

Exercises

▷ **6.1** A child's sorting toy has i cards that fit on a peg in position i for i from 1 to 5. Write down the method that you use to put the cards on the pegs, assuming that you cannot tell from the card whether it fits on a peg (you have to try fitting it on).

6.2 A card trick requires that you put a deck of cards in order by suit (in the order spades, hearts, clubs, diamonds) and by rank within each suit. Ask a few friends to do this task (shuffling in between!) and write down the method(s) that they use.

6.3 Explain how you would sort a deck of cards with the restriction that the cards must be laid out face down in a row, and the only allowed operations are to check the values of two cards and (optionally) to exchange them.

○ **6.4** Explain how you would sort a deck of cards with the restriction that the cards must be kept stacked in the deck, and the only allowed operations are to look at the value of the top two cards, to exchange the top two cards, and to move the top card to the bottom of the deck.

6.5 Give all sequences of three compare–exchange operations that will sort three elements (see Program 6.1).

○ **6.6** Give a sequence of five compare–exchange operations that will sort four elements.

6.7 Checking that the array is sorted after `sort` provides no guarantee that the sort works. Why not?

● **6.8** Write a performance driver that runs `sort` multiple times on files of various sizes, measures the time taken for each run, and prints out or plots the average running times.

● **6.9** Write an exercise driver that runs `sort` on difficult or pathological cases that might turn up in practical applications. Examples include files that are already in order, files in reverse order, files where all keys are the same, files consisting of only two distinct values, and files of size 0 or 1.

6.2 Generic Sort Implementations

Although it is reasonable to learn most sorting algorithms by thinking of them as simply putting arrays of numbers into numerical order or characters into alphabetical order, it is also worthwhile to recognize that the algorithms are largely independent of the type of items being

---

Program 6.2 Item interface

Any class of items to be sorted must include a method that gives an object from the class the capability to determine whether it is less than another object from the class, or not.

```
interface ITEM
  { boolean less(ITEM v); }
```

---

sorted, and that is not difficult to move to a more general setting. In this section, we discuss the conventions that we shall follow so as to make our sort implementations useful in a variety of contexts. By treating this topic in detail at the outset, we can significantly expand the applicability of our code and the ease of using it.

Program 6.2 defines the most essential convention: to sort items, we need to be able to compare them. In Java, we express such a requirement by defining an interface that includes the method that we need and requiring that any class that defines an item to be sorted implement this interface. Such implementations are not difficult to develop (we will consider three detailed examples later in this section, in Programs 6.8 through 6.11); the net result is that we can use the method `less` for comparisons in our implementations and still use them to sort all types of items. This interface is very similar to the `Comparable` interface in Java, which requires implementations to include a `compareTo` method.

Beyond this fundamental step, the path towards developing generic implementations constitutes a digression from the algorithmics of sorting, and you may safely skip the rest of this section and refer or return to it while learning the basic algorithms and their properties in Sections 6.3 through 6.6, Section 6.8, and Chapters 7 through 9. You can understand any of those implementations as substitutions for the `sort` method in Program 6.1 that use the primitive type `double` instead of the generic type `ITEM`.

Program 6.3 shows our convention for packaging sort implementations as a method in the class `Sort`. Any client with an array of objects from a class that implements the `ITEM` interface (and therefore defines a `less` method) can sort the array by invoking `Sort.sort`. In this book, we are going to consider numerous implementations of `sort`. To avoid confusion, we give each implementation a different

---

Program 6.3 Class for sort methods

We keep our actual sort code as a static method in a separate class so that any client can use it to sort any array of objects of any type that implements the less function, as specified in the ITEM interface.

This class is also a convenient place to put the static utility methods less, exch, and compExch, for use by any of our sort implementations.

```
class Sort
  {
    static boolean less(ITEM v, ITEM w)
      { return v.less(w); }
    static void exch(ITEM[] a, int i, int j)
      { ITEM t = a[i]; a[i] = a[j]; a[j] = t; }
    static void compExch(ITEM[] a, int i, int j)
      { if (less(a[j], a[i])) exch (a, i, j); }
    static void sort(ITEM[] a, int l, int r)
      { example(a, l, r); }
    static void example(ITEM[] a, int l, int r)
      {
        for (int i = l+1; i <= r; i++)
          for (int j = i; j > l; j--)
            compExch(a, j-1, j);
      }
  }
```

---

name so that clients can just call sort but we can substitute a different implementation, either by substituting its code for the example method in this Sort.java file or by using Java's class path mechanism (see Section 4.6).

Our sort implementations generally use a two-parameter static method less to compare items. When items are a primitive type, we can use the < operator, as in Program 6.1. When items are of a class that implements ITEM, then we can define less in terms of the class method less for that class, as shown in Program 6.3. Some of our sort implementations also use the exch and compExch methods, whose implementations for primitive items are given in Program 6.1 and for reference items in Program 6.3. Alternatively, we could add less to our item class and the exchange operations to our array class; or, since

---

Program 6.4 Item ADT interface

This ADT interface illustrates how to define generic operations that we might want to perform on the items that we sort: compare each item with another, read an item from standard input, generate a random item, and compute a string representation for each item (so as to be able to print it out). Every implementation must include `less` (to implement the `ITEM` interface) and may include `toString` (otherwise, the default from `Object` will be taken).

```
class myItem implements ITEM // ADT interface
  { // implementations and private members hidden
    public boolean less(ITEM)
    void read()
    void rand()
    public String toString()
  }
```

---

they are one-liners, we can just include them as private methods in sorts. Using these methods provides us the flexibility, for example, to instrument our sorts to count comparisons, as in Program 6.1, or to animate them, as in Program 6.16.

We have talked in detail about breaking our programs into independent modules to implement data types and abstract data types (see Chapters 3 and 4); in this section, we consider ways in which we can apply the concepts discussed there to build implementations, interfaces, and client programs for sorting algorithms. Specifically, we consider ADTs for

- *Items*, or generic objects to be sorted
- *Arrays* of items

The item data type provides us with a way to use our sort code for any type of data for which certain basic operations are defined. The approach is effective both for primitive types and for reference types, and we shall consider numerous implementations. The array interface is less critical to our mission; we include it as a useful example of generic programming in Java.

To work with particular types of items and keys, we declare all the relevant operations on them in an explicit interface, then provide application-specific implementations of the operations defined in the

---

Program 6.5 Sortable-array ADT interface

This ADT interface illustrates methods that we might want to provide for clients that sort arrays: initialize with random values, initialize with values read from standard input, show the contents, and sort the contents. We do not need to refer to the type of the items being sorted to define any of these operations.

```
class myArray // ADT interface
  { // implementations and private members hidden
    myArray(int)
    void rand()
    void read()
    void show(int, int)
    void sort(int, int)
  }
```

---

interface. Program 6.4 is an example of such an interface. We add to the required less method the capability to generate a random item, to read an item, and to convert an item to a string (so, for example, we can print it).

Our sorting algorithms work not just with items, but with arrays of items. Accordingly, Program 6.5 is an ADT interface that defines a *sortable array* abstraction. The operations defined in this interface refer to arrays, not to items, and are intended to support clients that test or exercise sorting algorithms. (It is easy to arrange for a client that needs to sort a single array to just directly invoke the sort method (see Exercise 6.11).) The methods in Program 6.5 are but a few examples of operations that we might want to perform on arrays. In a particular application, we might want to define various other operations (the Vector class in the java.util package is one approach to providing a general interface of this kind). The ADT of Program 6.5 focuses on sortable arrays. As usual, we can substitute different implementations of the various operations without having to change client programs that use the interface.

For example, Program 6.6 is a simple driver that has the same general functionality of the main program in Program 6.1. It either reads an array or generates a random one, sorts it, and prints the result. This program demonstrates that we can define such a computation

---

Program 6.6 Sort driver for sortable arrays

This driver for array sorts fills a generic array with generic items, sorts
it, and shows the result. It interprets the first command-line argument
to be the number of items to be sorted and the existence of the second
command-line argument to be a switch indicating whether to generate
random items or read them from the standard input stream. Since it
uses the ADT from Program 6.5, this code does not refer to the type of
item being sorted.

   This arrangement not only allows us to both use each sort implementation to sort various types of data without changing any code but
also to develop methods for arrays independently (perhaps to develop
various different drivers).

```
class ArraySort
{
  public static void main(String[] args)
    { int N = Integer.parseInt(args[0]);
      myArray A = new myArray(N);
      if (args.length < 2) A.rand(); else A.read();
      A.sort(0, N-1);
      A.show(0, N-1);
    }
}
```

---

without reference to the type of items being sorted: it is generic. We
can use the same ADT to define drivers that perform more complicated
tasks and then arrange to use them for arrays of various types of items,
without changing any implementation code (see Exercise 6.12).

   Program 6.7 is an implementation of the sortable array ADT of
Program 6.5, which is a client of the generic item ADT of Program 6.4.
To read an array from standard input, we read items; to generate a
random array, we generate random items; to print an array, we print
its items; and to sort an array, we use Sort.sort. The modular
organization allows us to substitute other implementations, depending
on the application. For example, we might use an implementation
where show prints out only part of the array when testing sorts on
huge arrays.

   Finally, we consider the ADT implementations that we need to
sort various types of items (the point of the exercise). For example, Pro-

---

Program 6.7 Sample implementation of sortable-array ADT

This implementation uses the generic item interface of Program 6.4 to maintain a private array of items. It uses the `rand`, `read`, and `toString` methods for items to implement the corresponding methods for arrays. For greater flexibility, the `sort` method is kept in a static class `Sort`. Implementations of `sort` use the `less` method from the `myItem` implementation.

```
class myArray
  {
    private myItem[] a;
    private int N;
    myArray(int N)
      {
        this.N = N;
        a = new myItem[N];
        for (int i = 0; i < N; i++)
          a[i] = new myItem();
      }
    void rand()
      { for (int i = 0; i < N; i++) a[i].rand(); }
    void read()
      { for (int i = 0; i < N; i++)
          if (!In.empty()) a[i].read(); }
    void show(int l, int r)
      { for (int i = l; i <= r; i++)
          Out.println(a[i] + ""); }
    void sort(int l, int r)
      { Sort.sort(a, l, r); }
  }
```

---

gram 6.8 is an implementation of the `myItem` ADT that we could use to have Program 6.6 sort arrays of integers. This implementation can be used with any sort client, any sort implementation, and any array implementation, without changing any other client or implementation code at all.

Developing implementations that are similar to Program 6.8 for other types of records and keys is straightforward, so this mechanism

---

Program 6.8 ADT implementation for integer items

This code implements the generic myItem ADT Program 6.4 for records that are integer keys.

```
class myItem implements ITEM
  { private int key;
    public boolean less(ITEM w)
      { return key < ((myItem) w).key; }
    void read()
      { key = In.getInt(); }
    void rand()
      { key = (int) (1000 * Math.random()); }
    public String toString() { return key + ""; }
  }
```

---

makes our sort implementations broadly applicable. For primitive types, this flexibility comes at the usual price of an extra level of indirection, as discussed later in this section. In most practical situations, however, we work not with primitive types but with records that have all manner of information associated with keys, and the advantages of working with a generic item type outweigh the costs. We conclude this section with two more examples that show how easily such applications can be handled.

Consider an accounting application, where we might have a key corresponding to a customer's account number, a string with the customer's name, and a floating-point number corresponding to that customer's account balance. Program 6.9 is an implementation of a class for such records. Now, suppose that we wish to process the records in sorted order. Sometimes, we might want to see them in alphabetic order by name; other times, we might want to see them in order of account number or in order of the size of the balance. Program 6.10 shows how we can arrange to do any of these sorts by deriving a class from Record that implements the ITEM interface that includes a method for specifying the sort key.

For example, if Program 6.10 is the file myItem.java (perhaps in a directory indicated as appropriate by the class path mechanism) then Program 6.6 sorts records on the account number field. If we

> **Program 6.9 Sample record class**
>
> This example illustrates a typical class for records in a data processing application. It has three fields: a string, an integer, and a floating-point number. These might hold, for example, a customer's name, account number, and account balance, respectively.
>
> ```
> class Record
>   {
>     int id;
>     double balance;
>     String who;
>     static int SortKeyField = 0;
>     public String toString()
>       { return id + " " + balance + " " + who; }
>   }
> ```

want records to appear in order of the size of the balance, we simply set the sort key field value to 1, as follows:

```
Record.SortKeyField = 1;
```

Similarly, if we set the sort key field value to 2, then we get a sort on the name field. We also could invoke sort multiple times with multiple sort key field values in order to sort the records multiple times, using different keys for each sort. Implementing and invoking this mechanism requires no change at all in the sort code itself.

The approach for deriving a class that implements the ITEM interface that is illustrated in Program 6.10 is a general one that is useful in many applications. We can imagine a large body of software based on processing such records; with this approach, we can add the capability of sorting them without much extra expense and without changing any of the other software.

We can use the same approach to put our sorts to use for all types of data—such as complex numbers (see Exercise 6.13), vectors (see Exercise 6.18), or polynomials (see Exercise 6.19)—without changing the sort code at all. For more complicated types of items, the ADT implementations have to be more complicated, but this implementation work is completely separated from the algorithm-design questions that we have been considering. We can use these same mechanisms with

---

Program 6.10 ADT implementation for record items

This example shows how we can implement the ITEM interface and the
myItem ADT by extending another class, in this case the data-processing
records of Program 6.9. The implementation of the rand method is
omitted. The less implementation allows clients to change the field
used for sorting.

```java
class myItem extends Record implements ITEM
  {
    public boolean less(ITEM w)
      { myItem r = (myItem) w;
        switch (SortKeyField)
          {
            case 2: return who.compareTo(r.who) < 0;
            case 1: return balance < r.balance;
            default: return id < r.id;
          }
      }
    void read()
      {
        id = In.getInt();
        balance = In.getDouble();
        who = In.getString();
      }
  }
```

---

most of the sorting methods that we consider in this chapter and
with those that we shall study in Chapters 7 through 9 as well. We
consider in detail one important exception in Section 6.10—it leads
to a whole family of important sorting algorithms that have to be
packaged differently, which is the subject of Chapter 10.

The approach just described is known in the classical literature
as *pointer* sorting, so called because we process references to items
and do not move the data itself. In programming languages such
as C and C++, programmers explicitly manipulate pointers; in Java,
pointer manipulation is implicit. Except for primitive numeric types,
we *always* manipulate references to objects (pointers), not the objects
themselves.

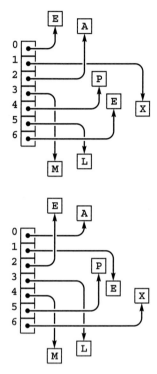

Figure 6.2
Pointer sort

The typical situation in Java is that we sort a group of objects by re-arranging references (pointers) to them instead of moving the objects. The top diagram illustrates a typical array to be sorted, with references to objects having the keys E X A M P L E, in that order. The bottom diagram illustrates the result of a sort, leaving the references such that the array refers to the objects in the order A E E L M P X.

For example, consider the difference between sorting chars (say, by changing all the doubles in Program 6.1 to chars) and using a myItem implementation like Program 6.8, except with a char key, as illustrated in Figure 6.2. In the former case, we exchange the characters themselves and put them in order in the array; in the latter, we exchange references to myItems, which contain the character values. If we are doing nothing more than sorting a huge file of characters, we are paying the cost of an equal number of references plus the extra cost of accessing the characters through the references. Note that if we were to use a Character object as the key field in the myItem implementation, we would add still another level of references.

For large records, which we typically encounter in practical applications, the extra space required for the references is small compared to the space required for the records themselves, and the extra time required to follow the references is more than offset by the time saved because the records do not have to be moved around. On the other hand, for small records, Java offers no good solution, except encoding records in a primitive numeric type, an approach recommended only for experts.

For another look at the issues involved, consider the problem of sorting strings. Program 6.11 illustrates the most natural way to proceed in Java: a direct implementation of the myItem ADT for String objects, using a String field for the key. This implementation (which works for any kind of object) adds a level of references: the array contains references to myItem objects, which contain Strings, which are references to sequences of characters. There are various ways to remove this second level of indirection in Java if necessary, but, in Java, it is common for programmers to accept extra levels of indirection in favor of the easily understood reference model. Since Java has automatic memory management, programmers do not have to face many of the serious issues that bedevil people who program in other languages.

We are faced with memory-management choices of this kind any time that we modularize a program. Who should be responsible for managing the memory corresponding to the concrete realization of an object: the client, the data-type implementation, or the system? Who should be responsible for decided which memory is unused and then

---

Program 6.11 ADT implementation for string items

This code implements the generic myItem ADT of Program 6.4 for records that are string keys.

```
class myItem implements ITEM
  { String key;
    public boolean less(ITEM w)
      { return key.compareTo(((myItem) w).key)<0; }
    void read()
      { key = In.getString(); }
    void rand()
      { int a = (int)('a'); key = "";
        for (int i = 0; i < 1+9*Math.random(); i++)
          key += (char) (a + 26*Math.random());
      }
    public String toString() { return key; }
  }
```

---

reclaiming it? In many languages, there is no hard-and-fast answer to these questions; In Java, the system takes responsibility.

There are certainly many benefits of the Java approach. In the context of sorting, the primary advantage of using references is that we avoid intruding on the data being sorted. We can "sort" a file even if read-only access is all that is available. Moreover, with multiple reference arrays, we can have two different sorted representations of a single body of data. This flexibility to manipulate the data without actually changing them is very useful in many applications. A full discussion of the issues involved is beyond the scope of this book, but we do need to be mindful of the impact on performance so that we can improve things when critical in applications. We will return to this issue in Section 6.6.

Another advantage of using references is that we avoid the cost of moving full records. The cost savings is significant for files with large records (and small keys), because the comparison needs to access just a small part of the record, and most of the record is not even touched during the sort. The reference approach makes the cost of an exchange roughly equal to the cost of a comparison for general situations involving arbitrarily large records (at the cost of the extra space for the references). Indeed, if the keys are long, the exchanges might even wind up being less costly than the comparisons. When we estimate the running times of methods that sort files of integers, we are often making the assumption that the costs of comparisons and exchanges are not much different. Conclusions based on this assumption are likely to apply to a broad class of applications, when we are sorting reference objects.

The approach that we have discussed in this section is a middle road between Program 6.1 and an industrial-strength fully abstract set of implementations complete with error checking, management of external storage, and even more general capabilities. Packaging issues of this sort are of increasing importance in some modern programming and applications environments. We will necessarily leave some questions unanswered. Our primary purpose is to demonstrate, through the relatively simple mechanisms that we have examined, that the sorting implementations that we are studying are widely applicable.

Exercises

▷ **6.10** Write a `myItem` ADT implementation for use in sorting `doubles`.

▷ **6.11** Suppose that you have clients who simply need the capability to sort a single array of objects of type `String`. Write an implementation like Program 6.3 for this purpose and describe how the clients should use it.

6.12 Modify your performance and exercise drivers from Exercises 6.8 and 6.9 to use `Sort.sort`. Add public methods to Program 6.3 to return the number of comparisons and exchanges used by the most recent sort, so that you can study those quantities in addition to the running time.

○ **6.13** Write classes to support having the sorting methods sort complex numbers $x + iy$ using the magnitude $\sqrt{x^2 + y^2}$ for the key. *Note:* Ignoring the square root is likely to improve efficiency.

▷ **6.14** Add a method `check` to the array ADT in Program 6.5 and provide an implementation for Program 6.7 that returns `true` if the array is in sorted order, `false` otherwise.

○ **6.15** Provide an implementation of the `check` method from Exercise 6.14 that returns `true` if the array is in sorted order *and* the set of items in the array is the same as the set of items that were in the array when `sort` was invoked, `false` otherwise.

○ **6.16** Design and implement a checking capability in the spirit of Exercises 6.14 and 6.15 that returns `true` if the most recent invocation of `sort` was stable, `false` otherwise.

● **6.17** Extend the rand method in your implementation of myItem for doubles (see Exercise 6.10) so that it generates test data according to distributions similar to those illustrated in Figure 6.15. Provide an integer parameter for the client to use to specify the distribution.

○ **6.18** Write classes for use in having the sorting methods sort multidimensional vectors of d integers, putting the vectors in order by first component, those with equal first component in order by second component, those with equal first and second components in order by third component, and so forth.

6.19 Write classes for use in having the sorting methods sort polynomials (see Section 4.10). Part of your task is to define an appropriate ordering.

6.3 Selection Sort

One of the simplest sorting algorithms works as follows: First, find the smallest element in the array, and exchange it with the element in the first position. Then, find the second smallest element and exchange it with the element in the second position. Continue in this way until the entire array is sorted. This method is called *selection sort* because it works by repeatedly selecting the smallest remaining element. Figure 6.3 shows the method in operation on a sample file.

Program 6.12 is an implementation of selection sort that adheres to our conventions. The inner loop is just a comparison to test a current element against the smallest element found so far (plus the code necessary to increment the index of the current element and to check that it does not exceed the array bounds); it could hardly be simpler. The work of moving the items around falls outside the inner loop: each exchange puts an element into its final position, so the number of exchanges is $N - 1$ (no exchange is needed for the final element). Thus the running time is dominated by the number of comparisons. In Section 6.6, we show this number to be proportional to N^2 and examine more closely how to predict the total running time and how to compare selection sort with other elementary sorts.

A disadvantage of selection sort is that its running time depends only slightly on the amount of order already in the file. The process of finding the minimum element on one pass through the file does not seem to give much information about where the minimum might be on the next pass through the file. For example, the user of the sort might be surprised to realize that it takes about as long to run selection sort for a file that is already in order, or for a file with all keys equal, as it

Figure 6.3
Selection sort example

The first pass has no effect in this example, because there is no element in the array smaller than the A at the left. On the second pass, the other A is the smallest remaining element, so it is exchanged with the S in the second position. Then, the E near the middle is exchanged with the O in the third position on the third pass; then, the other E is exchanged with the R in the fourth position on the fourth pass; and so forth.

Program 6.12 Selection sort

For each i from 1 to r-1, exchange a[i] with the minimum element in a[i], ..., a[r]. As the index i travels from left to right, the elements to its left are in their final position in the array (and will not be touched again), so the array is fully sorted when i reaches the right end.

As discussed in detail in Section 6.2, we use the keyword ITEM to denote the type of item being sorted in this code. To use it in Program 6.1, we replace ITEM by double; we would do the same to sort arrays of any primitive type. To use this code for reference types, we implement the ITEM interface of Program 6.2, replace the example method in Program 6.3 by this method, and change the example invocation to an invocation of this method. We will use this same convention for all of our sorting algorithm implementations.

```
static void selection(ITEM[] a, int l, int r)
  {
    for (int i = l; i < r; i++)
      { int min = i;
        for (int j = i+1; j <= r; j++)
          if (less(a[j], a[min])) min = j;
        exch(a, i, min);
      }
  }
```

---

does for a randomly ordered file! As we shall see, other methods are better able to take advantage of order in the input file.

Despite its simplicity and evident brute-force approach, selection sort outperforms more sophisticated methods in one important application: it is the method of choice for sorting files with huge items and small keys. For such applications, the cost of moving the data dominates the cost of making comparisons, and no algorithm can sort a file with substantially less data movement than selection sort (see Property 6.5 in Section 6.6).

Exercises

▷ **6.20** Show, in the style of Figure 6.3, how selection sort sorts the sample file EASYQUESTION.

6.21 What is the maximum number of exchanges involving any particular element during selection sort? What is the average number of exchanges involving an element?

6.22 Give an example of a file of N elements that maximizes the number of times the test a[j] < a[min] fails (and, therefore, min gets updated) during the operation of selection sort.

○ **6.23** Is selection sort stable?

6.4 Insertion Sort

The method that people often use to sort bridge hands is to consider the cards one at a time, inserting each into its proper place among those already considered (keeping them sorted). In a computer implementation, we need to make space for the element being inserted by moving larger elements one position to the right, and then inserting the element into the vacated position. The sort method in Program 6.1 is an implementation of this method, which is called *insertion sort*.

As in selection sort, the elements to the left of the current index are in sorted order during the sort, but they are not in their final position, as they may have to be moved to make room for smaller elements encountered later. The array is, however, fully sorted when the index reaches the right end. Figure 6.4 shows the method in operation on a sample file.

The implementation of insertion sort in Program 6.1 is straightforward, but inefficient. We shall now consider three ways to improve it in order to illustrate a recurrent theme throughout many of our implementations: We want code to be succinct, clear, and efficient, but these goals sometimes conflict, so we must often strike a balance. We do so by developing a natural implementation, then seeking to improve it by a sequence of transformations, checking the effectiveness (and correctness) of each transformation.

Program 6.13 is an implementation of insertion sort that is more efficient than the one given in Program 6.1 (in Section 6.6, we shall see that it is nearly twice as fast). In this book, we are interested *both* in elegant and efficient algorithms *and* in elegant and efficient implementations of them. In this case, the underlying algorithms do differ slightly—we should properly refer to the sort method in Program 6.1 as a *nonadaptive insertion sort*. A good understanding of the properties of an algorithm is the best guide to developing an implementation that can be used effectively in an application.

Figure 6.4
Insertion sort example

During the first pass of insertion sort, the S in the second position is larger than the A, so it does not have to be moved. On the second pass, when the O in the third position is encountered, it is exchanged with the S to put A O S in sorted order, and so forth. Unshaded elements that are not circled are those that were moved one position to the right.

Program 6.13 Insertion sort

This code is an improvement over the implementation of sort in Program 6.1 because (*i*) it first puts the smallest element in the array into the first position so that that element can serve as a sentinel; (*ii*) it does a single assignment, rather than an exchange, in the inner loop; and (*iii*) it terminates the inner loop when the element being inserted is in position. For each i, it sorts the elements a[1], ... , a[i] by moving one position to the right elements in the sorted list a[1], ... , a[i-1] that are larger than a[i], then putting a[i] into its proper position.

```
static void insertion(ITEM[] a, int l, int r)
  { int i;
    for (i = r; i > l; i--) compExch(a, i-1, i);
    for (i = l+2; i <= r; i++)
      { int j = i; ITEM v = a[i];
        while (less(v, a[j-1]))
          { a[j] = a[j-1]; j--; }
        a[j] = v;
      }
  }
```

First, we can stop doing compExch operations when we encounter a key that is not larger than the key in the item being inserted, because the subarray to the left is sorted. Specifically, we can break out of the inner for loop in sort in Program 6.1 when the condition a[j-1] < a[j] is true. This modification changes the implementation into an adaptive sort and speeds up the program by about a factor of 2 for randomly ordered keys (see Property 6.2).

With the improvement described in the previous paragraph, we have two conditions that terminate the inner loop—we could recode it as a while loop to reflect that fact explicitly. A more subtle improvement of the implementation follows from noting that the test j>l is usually extraneous: indeed, it succeeds *only* when the element inserted is the smallest seen so far and reaches the beginning of the array. A commonly used alternative is to keep the keys to be sorted in a[1] to a[N] and to put a *sentinel key* in a[0], making it at least as small as the smallest key in the array. Then, the test whether a smaller key has been encountered simultaneously tests both conditions of interest, making the inner loop smaller and the program faster.

Sentinels are sometimes inconvenient to use: perhaps the smallest possible key is not easily defined, or perhaps the calling routine has no room to include an extra key. Program 6.13 illustrates one way around these two problems for insertion sort: We make an explicit first pass over the array that puts the item with the smallest key in the first position. Then, we sort the rest of the array, with that first and smallest item now serving as sentinel. We generally shall avoid sentinels in our code, because it is often easier to understand code with explicit tests, but we shall note situations where sentinels might be useful in making programs both simpler and more efficient.

The third improvement in Program 6.13 involves removing extraneous instructions from the inner loop. It follows from noting that successive exchanges involving the same element are inefficient. If there are two or more exchanges, we have

```
t = a[j]; a[j] = a[j-1]; a[j-1] = t;
```

followed by

```
t = a[j-1]; a[j-1] = a[j-2]; a[j-2] = t;
```

and so forth. The value of t does not change between these two sequences, and we waste time storing it, then reloading it for the next exchange. Program 6.13 moves larger elements one position to the right instead of using exchanges, and thus avoids wasting time in this way.

Unlike that of selection sort, the running time of insertion sort primarily depends on the initial order of the keys in the input. For example, if the file is large and the keys are already in order (or even are nearly in order), then insertion sort is quick and selection sort is slow. We compare the algorithms in more detail in Section 6.6.

Exercises

▷ **6.24** Show, in the style of Figure 6.4, how insertion sort sorts the sample file E A S Y Q U E S T I O N.

6.25 Give an implementation of insertion sort with the inner loop coded as a while loop that terminates on one of two conditions, as described in the text.

6.26 For each of the conditions in the while loop in Exercise 6.25, describe a file of N elements where that condition is always false when the loop terminates.

○ **6.27** Is insertion sort stable?

6.28 Give a nonadaptive implementation of selection sort based on finding the minimum element with code like the first `for` loop in Program 6.13.

6.5 Bubble Sort

The first sort that many people learn, because it is so simple, is *bubble sort*: Keep passing through the file, exchanging adjacent elements that are out of order, continuing until the file is sorted. Bubble sort's prime virtue is that it is easy to implement, but whether it is actually easier to implement than insertion or selection sort is arguable. Bubble sort generally will be slower than the other two methods, but we consider it briefly for the sake of completeness.

Suppose that we always move from right to left through the file. Whenever the minimum element is encountered during the first pass, we exchange it with each of the elements to its left, eventually putting it into position at the left end of the array. Then on the second pass, the second smallest element will be put into position, and so forth. Thus, N passes suffice, and bubble sort operates as a type of selection sort, although it does more work to get each element into position. Program 6.14 is an implementation, and Figure 6.5 shows an example of the algorithm in operation.

We can speed up Program 6.14 by carefully implementing the inner loop, in much the same way as we did in Section 6.3 for insertion sort (see Exercise 6.34). Indeed, comparing the code, Program 6.14 appears to be virtually identical to the nonadaptive insertion sort in Program 6.1. The difference between the two is that the inner `for` loop moves through the left (sorted) part of the array for insertion sort and through the right (not necessarily sorted) part of the array for bubble sort.

Program 6.14 uses only `compExch` instructions and is therefore nonadaptive, but we can improve it to run more efficiently when the file is nearly in order by testing whether no exchanges at all are performed on one of the passes (and therefore the file is in sorted order, so we can `break` out of the outer loop). Adding this improvement will make bubble sort faster on some types of files, but it is generally not as effective as is changing insertion sort to break out of the inner loop, as discussed in detail in Section 6.6.

Figure 6.5
Bubble sort example

Small keys percolate over to the left in bubble sort. As the sort moves from right to left, each key is exchanged with the one on its left until a smaller one is encountered. On the first pass, the E is exchanged with the L, the P, and the M before stopping at the A on the right; then the A moves to the beginning of the file, stopping at the other A, which is already in position. The ith smallest key reaches its final position after the ith pass, just as in selection sort, but other keys are moved closer to their final position as well.

> **Program 6.14 Bubble sort**
>
> For each i from 1 to r-1, the inner (j) loop puts the minimum element among the elements in a[i], ..., a[r] into a[i] by passing from right to left through the elements, compare–exchanging successive elements. The smallest one moves on all such comparisons, so it "bubbles" to the beginning. As in selection sort, as the index i travels from left to right through the file, the elements to its left are in their final position in the array.
>
> ```
> static void bubble(ITEM[] a, int l, int r)
>   { for (int i = l; i < r; i++)
>       for (int j = r; j > i; j--)
>         compExch(a, j-1, j);
>   }
> ```

Exercises

▷ **6.29** Show, in the style of Figure 6.5, how bubble sort sorts the sample file E A S Y Q U E S T I O N.

6.30 Give an example of a file for which the number of exchanges done by bubble sort is maximized.

∘ **6.31** Is bubble sort stable?

6.32 Explain how bubble sort is preferable to the nonadaptive version of selection sort described in Exercise 6.28.

● **6.33** Do experiments to determine how many passes are saved, for random files of N elements, when you add to bubble sort a test to terminate when the file is sorted.

6.34 Develop an efficient implementation of bubble sort, with as few instructions as possible in the inner loop. Make sure that your "improvements" do not slow down the program!

6.6 Performance Characteristics of Elementary Sorts

Selection sort, insertion sort, and bubble sort are all quadratic-time algorithms both in the worst and in the average case, and none requires extra memory. Their running times thus differ by only a constant factor, but they operate quite differently, as illustrated in Figures 6.6 through 6.8.

Generally, the running time of a sorting algorithm is proportional to the number of comparisons that the algorithm uses, to the number of times that items are moved or exchanged, or to both. For random input, comparing the methods involves studying constant-factor differences in the numbers of comparisons and exchanges and constant-factor differences in the lengths of the inner loops. For input with special characteristics, the running times of the methods may differ by more than a constant factor. In this section, we look closely at the analytic results in support of this conclusion.

Property 6.1 *Selection sort uses about $N^2/2$ comparisons and N exchanges.*

We can verify this property easily by examining the sample run in Figure 6.3, which is an N-by-N table in which unshaded letters correspond to comparisons. About one-half of the elements in the table are unshaded—those above the diagonal. The $N - 1$ (not the final one) elements on the diagonal each correspond to an exchange. More precisely, examination of the code reveals that, for each i from 1 to $N - 1$, there is one exchange and $N - i$ comparisons, so there is a total of $N - 1$ exchanges and $(N-1) + (N-2) + \cdots + 2 + 1 = N(N-1)/2$ comparisons. These observations hold no matter what the input data are; the only part of selection sort that does depend on the input is the number of times that min is updated. In the worst case, this quantity could also be quadratic; in the average case, however, it is just $O(N \log N)$ (*see reference section*), so we can expect the running time of selection sort to be insensitive to the input. ∎

Property 6.2 *Insertion sort uses about $N^2/4$ comparisons and $N^2/4$ half-exchanges (moves) on the average, and twice that many at worst.*

As implemented in Program 6.13, the number of comparisons and of moves is the same. Just as for Property 6.1, this quantity is easy to visualize in the N-by-N diagram in Figure 6.4 that gives the details of the operation of the algorithm. Here, the elements below the diagonal are counted—all of them, in the worst case. For random input, we expect each element to go about halfway back, on the average, so one-half of the elements below the diagonal should be counted. ∎

Property 6.3 *Bubble sort uses about $N^2/2$ comparisons and $N^2/2$ exchanges on the average and in the worst case.*

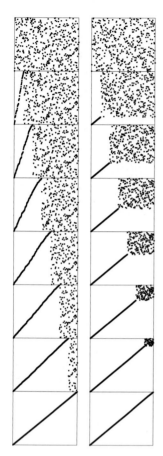

**Figure 6.6
Dynamic characteristics of insertion and selection sorts**

These snapshots of insertion sort (left) and selection sort (right) in action on a random permutation illustrate how each method progresses through the sort. We represent an array being sorted by plotting i vs. a[i] for each i. Before the sort, the plot is uniformly random; after the sort, it is a diagonal line from bottom left to top right. Insertion sort never looks ahead of its current position in the array; selection sort never looks back.

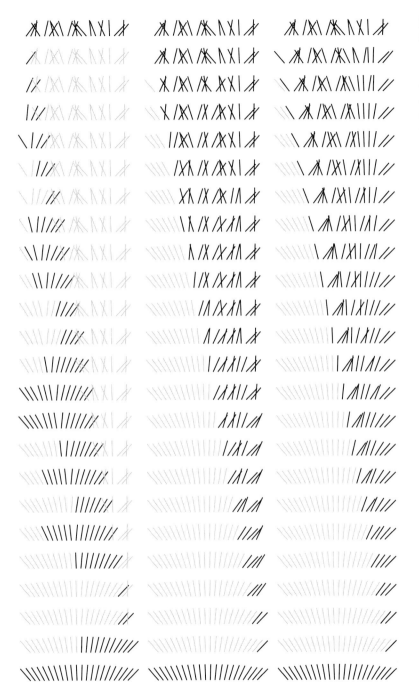

Figure 6.7
Comparisons and exchanges in elementary sorts

This diagram highlights the differences in the ways that insertion sort, selection sort, and bubble sort bring a file into order. The file to be sorted is represented by lines that are to be sorted according to their angles. Black lines correspond to the items accessed during each pass of the sort; gray lines correspond to items not touched. For insertion sort (left), the element to be inserted goes about halfway back through the sorted part of the file on each pass. Selection sort (center) and bubble sort (right) both go through the entire unsorted part of the array to find the next smallest element there for each pass. The difference between the methods is that bubble sort exchanges any adjacent out-of-order elements that it encounters, whereas selection sort just exchanges the minimum into position. The effect of this difference is that the unsorted part of the array becomes more nearly sorted as bubble sort progresses.

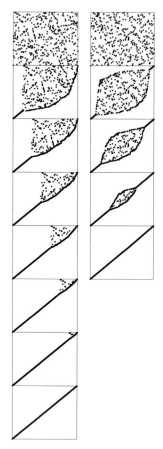

Figure 6.8
Dynamic characteristics of two bubble sorts

Standard bubble sort (left) operates in a manner similar to selection sort in that each pass brings one element into position, but it also brings some order into other parts of the array, in an asymmetric manner. Changing the scan through the array to alternate between beginning to end and end to beginning gives a version of bubble sort called shaker sort *(right), which finishes more quickly (see Exercise 6.40).*

The ith bubble sort pass requires $N - i$ compare–exchange operations, so the proof goes as for selection sort. When the algorithm is modified to terminate when it discovers that the file is sorted, the running time depends on the input. Just one pass is required if the file is already in order, but the ith pass requires $N - i$ comparisons *and* exchanges if the file is in reverse order. The average-case performance is not significantly better than the worst case, as stated, although the analysis that demonstrates this fact is complicated (*see reference section*). ∎

Although the concept of a partially sorted file is necessarily rather imprecise, insertion sort and bubble sort work well for certain types of nonrandom files that often arise in practice. General-purpose sorts are commonly misused for such applications. For example, consider the operation of insertion sort on a file that is already sorted. Each element is immediately determined to be in its proper place in the file, and the total running time is linear. The same is true for bubble sort, but selection sort is still quadratic.

Definition 6.2 *An* **inversion** *is a pair of keys that are out of order in the file.*

To count the number of inversions in a file, we can add up, for each element, the number of elements to its left that are greater (we refer to this quantity as the number of inversions corresponding to the element). But this count is precisely the distance that the elements have to move when inserted into the file during insertion sort. A file that has some order will have fewer inversions than will one that is arbitrarily scrambled.

In one type of partially sorted file, each item is close to its final position in the file. For example, some people sort their hand in a card game by first organizing the cards by suit in order to put their cards close to their final position, and then by considering the cards one by one. We shall be considering a number of sorting methods that work in much the same way—they bring elements close to final positions in early stages to produce a partially sorted file with every element not far from where it ultimately must go. Insertion sort and bubble sort (but not selection sort) are efficient methods for sorting such files.

Property 6.4 *Insertion sort and bubble sort use a linear number of comparisons and exchanges for files with at most a constant number of inversions corresponding to each element.*

As just mentioned, the running time of insertion sort is directly proportional to the number of inversions in the file. For bubble sort (here, we are referring to Program 6.14, modified to terminate when the file is sorted), the proof is more subtle (see Exercise 6.39). Each bubble sort pass reduces the number of smaller elements to the right of any element by precisely 1 (unless the number was already 0), so bubble sort uses at most a constant number of passes for the types of files under consideration and therefore does at most a linear number of comparisons and exchanges. ∎

In another type of partially sorted file, we perhaps have appended a few elements to a sorted file or have edited a few elements in a sorted file to change their keys. This kind of file is prevalent in sorting applications. Insertion sort is an efficient method for such files; bubble sort and selection sort are not.

Property 6.5 *Insertion sort uses a linear number of comparisons and exchanges for files with at most a constant number of elements having more than a constant number of corresponding inversions.*

The running time of insertion sort depends on the total number of inversions in the file and not on the way in which the inversions are distributed. ∎

To draw conclusions about running time from Properties 6.1 through 6.5, we need to analyze the relative cost of comparisons and exchanges, a factor that in turn depends on the size of the items and keys (see Table 6.1). For example, if the items are one-word keys, then an exchange (four array accesses) should be about twice as expensive as a comparison. In such a situation, the running times of selection and insertion sort are roughly comparable, but bubble sort is slower. But if the items are large in comparison to the keys, then selection sort will be best.

Property 6.6 *Selection sort runs in linear time for files with large items and small keys.*

Let M be the ratio of the size of the item to the size of the key. Then we can assume the cost of a comparison to be 1 time unit and the cost of an exchange to be M time units. Selection sort takes about $N^2/2$ time units for comparisons and about NM time units for exchanges. If M is larger than a constant multiple of N, then the NM term dominates

Table 6.1 Empirical study of elementary sorting algorithms

Insertion sort and selection sort are about twice as fast as bubble sort for small files, but running times grow quadratically (when the file size grows by a factor of 2, the running time grows by a factor of 4). None of the methods are useful for large randomly ordered files—for example, the numbers corresponding to those in this table are less than 1 for the shellsort algorithm in Section 6.8. When comparisons are expensive—for example, when the keys are objects or strings—then insertion sort is much faster than the other two because it uses many fewer comparisons. Not included here is the case where exchanges are expensive; then selection sort is best.

	int *items*				Integer *keys*			String *keys*		
N	S	I*	I	B	S	I	B	S	I	B
1000	14	54	8	54	100	55	130	129	65	170
2000	54	218	33	221	436	229	569	563	295	725
4000	212	848	129	871	1757	986	2314	2389	1328	3210

Key:
- S   Selection sort (Program 6.12)
- I*   Insertion sort, exchange-based (Program 6.1)
- I   Insertion sort (Program 6.13)
- B   Bubble sort (Program 6.14)

the N^2 term, so the running time is proportional to NM, which is proportional to the amount of time that would be required to move all the data. ∎

For example, if we have to sort 1000 items that consist of 1-word keys and 1000 words of data each, and we actually have to rearrange the items, then we cannot do better than selection sort, since the running time will be dominated by the cost of moving all 1 million words of data.

Exercises

▷ **6.35** Which of the three elementary methods (selection sort, insertion sort, or bubble sort) runs fastest for a file with all keys identical?

6.36 Which of the three elementary methods runs fastest for a file in reverse order?

○ **6.37** Run empirical tests for selection, insertion, and bubble sorts and print a table of the average and standard deviation of the numbers of comparisons and exchanges used, for $N = 10$, 100, and 1000(see Exercise 6.12).

6.38 Give an example of a file of 10 elements (use the keys A through J) for which bubble sort uses fewer comparisons than insertion sort, or prove that no such file exists.

• **6.39** Show that each bubble sort pass reduces by precisely 1 the number of elements to the left of each element that are greater (unless that number was already 0).

6.40 Implement a version of bubble sort that alternates left-to-right and right-to-left passes through the data. This (faster but more complicated) algorithm is called *shaker sort* (see Figure 6.8).

• **6.41** Show that Property 6.5 does not hold for shaker sort (see Exercise 6.40).

6.7 Algorithm Visualization

Sorting algorithms are especially amenable to pictorial representations that make plain their dynamic characteristics. We have already seen, in figures throughout this chapter, several examples that illustrate this point. Visual representations are both so useful in understanding the operation sorting algorithms and so easy to create, that we digress briefly to discuss the topic.

Perhaps the simplest way to create visualizations of sorting algorithms is to use PostScript (see Section 4.3), as illustrated in Figure 6.9. Little could be more straightforward than to plot an array of points, given their coordinates. Similarly, implementing a Java program that creates PostScript programs like this is not much more difficult than implementing one that prints out the contents of the array periodically, as shown in Program 6.15.

Of course, Java also has a Graphics object with associated drawing methods, and we might simply use those directly for creating a visualization (see Exercise 6.42). We leave that for an exercise because in Java it is more interesting and not much more difficult to consider *dynamic* visual respresentations, where we can watch the items move through the array as it is sorted.

Programs 6.16 and 6.17 implement a sample Java sorting animation in a Java applet. The implementation is based on instrumenting

```
/w 72 def /h 72 def /N 12 def
/dot
  {
    moveto currentpoint
    2 0 360 arc fill
  } def
0 .91 dot
1 .49 dot
2 .10 dot
3 .05 dot
4 .74 dot
5 .53 dot
6 .25 dot
7 .13 dot
8 .41 dot
9 .92 dot
10 .19 dot
11 .96 dot
```

Figure 6.9
PostScript visualization of array contents

This PostScript program plots the contents of an array of numbers between 0 and 1 by calling the function dot, *with the index and value of each array entry as arguments. The values* w *and* h *are the width and height of the frame, respectively, and* N *is the number of values in the array. The* dot *function scales the index to be an x coordinate between 0 and* w *by multiplying by* w *and dividing by* N, *and the value to be a y coordinate between 0 and* h *by multiplying by* h. *It then draws a filled circle of radius 2 at (x, y).*

Program 6.15 Visualizing a sorting algorithm

This program prints out a PostScript program like the one in Figure 6.9. The constants h and w give the height and width (respectively) of the frames (in points), and the constant cuts gives the number of frames. The show method prints the code that plots the values in the array, and the sort is instrumented to call show at appropriate intervals.

```
class Visualize
{ private static final int cuts = 5, h = 72, w = 72;
  static int N;
  static void sort(double a[], int l, int r)
    { double t;
      for (int i = l; i <= r; i++)
        { for (int j = i; j > l; j--)
            if (a[j] < a[j-1]) exch(a, j-1, j);
          if (i*cuts % N == 0) show(a, l, r);
        }
    }
  static void show(double[] a, int l, int r)
    {
      for (int i = l; i <= r; i++)
        { float x = h*((float) i) / ((float) N);
          float y = w*((float) a[i]);
          Out.println(x + " " + y + " dot");
        }
      Out.println(1.1*w + " 0 translate");
    }
  public static void main(String[] args)
    { N = Integer.parseInt(args[0]);
      double a[] = new double[N];
      for (int i = 0; i < N; i++)
        a[i] = Math.random();
      Out.print("72 72 translate ");
      Out.print("/dot {moveto currentpoint");
      Out.println(" 2 0 360 arc fill} def");
      sort(a, 0, N-1);
    }
}
```

the exch method to change the visual representation every time the sorting algorithm does an exchange.

While some details vary, you usually can run the animation by starting an appletviewer or a browser with an .html file containing the following HTML code:

```
<applet code=SortAnimate.class width=640 height=480>
<param name=N value="200">
</applet>
```

In many Java implementations, this simple strategy provides a very effective animation; in others, the animation may not run smoothly depending on the system load, buffering strategies and other factors.

It is beyond the scope of this book to examine all of the issues involved in developing effective animations; on the other hand, getting a basic animation like this one working is well worth the effort. For example, we can get an effective animation for any exchange-based sorting algorithm in Program 6.17 without changing the sort code at all.

It is important to bear in mind that we should not draw conclusions about performance from visualizations and animations unless we have been careful in building them. For example, if we animate selection sort with Program 6.16, the animation finishes far faster than for insertion sort, simply because, as we have already noted, selection sort does so few exchanges. If we were to instrument comparisons as well as exchanges in the animation, then the relative performance of the animations would be more representative of the relative performance of the algorithms.

Worse, we often find ourselves watching performance properties of a graphics system rather than our algorithms. For example, one way to make the animation in Programs 6.16 and 6.17 operate more smoothly for small examples is to use the repaint() operation periodically. But repaint() can be overly expensive: for example, if we want to animate an algorithm that does millions of exchanges, the approach of repainting on each exchange will collapse because of the time required to do millions (or even thousands) of repaint() operations.

Such pitfalls aside, visual representations can play a critical role in helping us understand how algorithms work, and we shall be using them liberally in figures throughout the book. We could also have

Program 6.16 Animating a sorting algorithm

This abstract class provides basic methods in support of animating sorting algorithms (see Program 6.17).

```java
import java.applet.Applet;
import java.awt.*;
abstract public class Animate
  extends Applet implements Runnable
  { Graphics g;
    Thread animatorThread;
    int N; double[] a;
    public void start()
      { g = getGraphics();
        new Thread(this).start();
      }
    public void stop() { animatorThread = null; }
    public void run()
      { N = Integer.parseInt(getParameter("N"));
        a = new double[N];
        for (int i = 0; i < N; i++)
          { a[i] = Math.random();
            dot(X(i), Y(a[i]), Color.black); }
        sort(a, 0, N-1);
      }
    int X(int i)
      { return (i*getSize().width)/N; }
    int Y(double v)
      { return (1.0 - v)*getSize().height; }
    void dot(int x, int y, Color c)
      { g.setColor(c); g.fillOval(x, y, 5, 5); }
    void exch(double [] a, int i, int j)
      { double t = a[i]; a[i] = a[j]; a[j] = t;
        dot(X(i), Y(a[j]), Color.red);
        dot(X(j), Y(a[i]), Color.red);
        dot(X(i), Y(a[i]), Color.black);
        dot(X(j), Y(a[j]), Color.black);
      }
    abstract void sort(double a[], int l, int r);
  }
```

Program 6.17 Animating a sorting algorithm

This class, which extends Program 6.16, animates the insertion sort in Program 6.6, producing a visual represenation on the screen like the ones in Figures 6.6 and 6.8, but with the dots moving into place. The dots also leave tracks, so the resulting display gives a history of the sort. Since the implementation is based on instrumenting the exch method, it is immediately effective for any exchange-based sort. Similar instrumentation of less is advisable (see Exercise 6.44).

```
import java.awt.*;
public class SortAnimate extends Animate
  {
    void sort(double a[], int l, int r)
      {
        for (int i = l+1; i <= r; i++)
          for (int j = i; j > l; j--)
            if (a[j] < a[j-1]) exch(a, j-1, j);
      }
  }
```

exercises for each algorithm asking you to visualize and animate it, because each algorithm, each visual representaion, and each animation can be augmented in all sorts of interesting ways. We refrain from doing so because most readers are likely to be drawn into working with visual representations when they are appropriate, particularly for sorting algorithms. Once you have used a program such as Program 6.15 or Programs 6.16 and 6.17, you are likely to enjoy using programs like them them to visualize other algorithms, and you are certainly encouraged to do so.

Exercises

6.42 Write a version of Program 6.15 that uses appropriate methods from the Java Graphics2D class to draw the visualization on your display.

• **6.43** Implement insertion, selection, and bubble sort in PostScript, and use your implementation to draw figures like Figures 6.6 through 6.8. You may either try a recursive implementation or read the manual to learn about loops and arrays in PostScript.

○ **6.44** Modify the sort in Program 6.17 to call less to compare keys, and add an implementation of less to Program 6.16 that makes it give a dynamic visual representation of compares as well as exchanges. Animate both insertion sort and selection sort.

● **6.45** Develop an interactive animation program that allows a user to select from a list of algorithms to animate, specify the number of items to sort, and specify the model used to generate random items (see Exercise 6.17).

●● **6.46** Add to your program from Exercise 6.45 the capability to save a script of all animated events; then implement the capability for users to replay algorithms and to run them backwards.

Figure 6.10
Interleaving 4-sorts

The top part of this diagram shows the process of 4-sorting a file of 15 elements by first insertion sorting the subfile at positions 0, 4, 8, 12, then insertion sorting the subfile at positions 1, 5, 9, 13, then insertion sorting the subfile at positions 2, 6, 10, 14, then insertion sorting the subfile at positions 3, 7, 11. But the four subfiles are independent, so we can achieve the same result by inserting each element into position into its subfile, going back four at a time (bottom). Taking the first row in each section of the top diagram, then the second row in each section, and so forth, gives the bottom diagram.

6.8 Shellsort

Insertion sort is slow because the only exchanges it does involve adjacent items, so items can move through the array only one place at a time. For example, if the item with the smallest key happens to be at the end of the array, N steps are needed to get it where it belongs. *Shellsort* is a simple extension of insertion sort that gains speed by allowing exchanges of elements that are far apart.

The idea is to rearrange the file to give it the property that taking every hth element (starting anywhere) yields a sorted file. Such a file is said to be *h-sorted*. Put another way, an h-sorted file is h independent sorted files, interleaved together. By h-sorting for some large values of h, we can move elements in the array long distances and thus make it easier to h-sort for smaller values of h. Using such a procedure for any sequence of values of h that ends in 1 will produce a sorted file: that is the essence of shellsort.

One way to implement shellsort would be, for each h, to use insertion sort independently on each of the h subfiles. Despite the apparent simplicity of this process, we can use an even simpler approach, precisely because the subfiles are independent. When h-sorting the file, we simply insert it among the previous elements in its h-subfile by moving larger elements to the right (see Figure 6.10). We accomplish this task by using the insertion-sort code, but modified to increment or decrement by h instead of 1 when moving through the file. This observation reduces the shellsort implementation to nothing more than an insertion-sort–like pass through the file for each increment, as in Program 6.18. The operation of this program is illustrated in Figure 6.11.

How do we decide what increment sequence to use? In general, this question is a difficult one to answer. Properties of many different increment sequences have been studied in the literature, and some

---

Program 6.18 Shellsort

If we do not use sentinels and then replace every occurrence of "1" by "h" in insertion sort, the resulting program *h*-sorts the file. Adding an outer loop to change the increments leads to this compact shellsort implementation, which uses the increment sequence 1 4 13 40 121 364 1093 3280 9841 . . . .

```
static void shell(ITEM[] a, int l, int r)
  { int h;
    for (h = 1; h <= (r-l)/9; h = 3*h+1);
    for ( ; h > 0; h /= 3)
      for (int i = l+h; i <= r; i++)
        { int j = i; ITEM v = a[i];
          while (j >= l+h && less(v, a[j-h]))
            { a[j] = a[j-h]; j -= h; }
          a[j] = v;
        }
  }
```

```
A S O R T I N G E X A M P L E
A S O R T I N G E X A M P L E
A E O R T I N G E X A M P L S

A E O R T I N G E X A M P L S
A E O R T I N G E X A M P L S
A E N R T I O G E X A M P L S
A E N G T I O R E X A M P L S
A E N G E I O R T X A M P L S
A E N G E I O R T X A M P L S
A E A G E I N R T X O M P L S
A E A G E I N M T X O R P L S
A E A G E I N M P X O R T L S
A E A G E I N M P L O R T X S
A E A G E I N M P L O R T X S

A E A G E I N M P L O R T X S
A A E G E I N M P L O R T X S
A A E G E I N M P L O R T X S
A A E E G I N M P L O R T X S
A A E E G I N M P L O R T X S
A A E E G I N M P L O R T X S
A A E E G I M N P L O R T X S
A A E E G I M N P L O R T X S
A A E E G I L M N P O R T X S
A A E E G I L M N O P R T X S
A A E E G I L M N O P R T X S
A A E E G I L M N O P R T X S
A A E E G I L M N O P R S T X
A A E E G I L M N O P R S T X
```

Figure 6.11
Shellsort example

Sorting a file by 13-sorting (top), then 4-sorting (center), then 1-sorting (bottom) does not involve many comparisons (as indicated by the unshaded elements). The final pass is just insertion sort, but no element has to move far because of the order in the file due to the first two passes.

have been found that work well in practice, but no provably best sequence has been found. In practice, we generally use sequences that decrease roughly geometrically, so the number of increments is logarithmic in the size of the file. For example, if each increment is about one-half of the previous, then we need only about 20 increments to sort a file of 1 million elements; if the ratio is about one-quarter, then 10 increments will suffice. Using as few increments as possible is an important consideration that is easy to respect—we also need to consider arithmetical interactions among the increments such as the size of their common divisors and other properties.

The practical effect of finding a good increment sequence is limited to perhaps a 25 percent speedup, but the problem presents an intriguing puzzle that provides a good example of the inherent complexity in an apparently simple algorithm.

The increment sequence 1 4 13 40 121 364 1093 3280 9841 . . . that is used in Program 6.18, with a ratio between increments of about one-third, was recommended by Knuth in 1969 (*see reference section*). It is easy to compute (start with 1, generate the next increment by

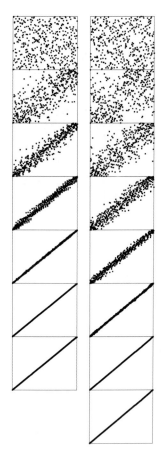

Figure 6.12
Dynamic characteristics of shellsort (two different increment sequences)

In this representation of shellsort in operation, it appears as though a rubber band, anchored at the corners, is pulling the points toward the diagonal. Two increment sequences are depicted: 121 40 13 4 1 *(left) and* 209 109 41 19 5 1 *(right). The second requires one more pass than the first, but is faster because each pass is more efficient.*

multiplying by 3 and adding 1) and leads to a relatively efficient sort, even for moderately large files, as illustrated in Figures 6.12 and 6.13.

Many other increment sequences lead to a more efficient sort but it is difficult to beat the sequence in Program 6.18 by more than 20 percent even for relatively large N. One increment sequence that does so is 1 8 23 77 281 1073 4193 16577 . . . , the sequence $4^{i+1}+3\cdot2^i+1$ for $i > 0$, which has provably faster worst-case behavior (see Property 6.10). Figure 6.12 shows that this sequence and Knuth's sequence—and many other sequences—have similar dynamic characteristics for large files. The possibility that even better increment sequences exist is still real. A few ideas on improved increment sequences are explored in the exercises.

On the other hand, there are some bad increment sequences: for example 1 2 4 8 16 32 64 128 256 512 1024 2048 . . . (the original sequence suggested by Shell when he proposed the algorithm in 1959 (*see reference section*)) is likely to lead to bad performance because elements in odd positions are not compared against elements in even positions until the final pass. The effect is noticeable for random files and is catastrophic in the worst case: The method degenerates to require quadratic running time if, for example, the half of the elements with the smallest values are in even positions and the half of the elements with the largest values are in the odd positions (See Exercise 6.50.)

Program 6.18 computes the next increment by dividing the current one by 3, after initializing to ensure that the same sequence is always used. Another option is just to start with h = N/3 or with some other function of N. It is best to avoid such strategies, because bad sequences of the type described in the previous paragraph are likely to turn up for some values of N.

Our description of the efficiency of shellsort is necessarily imprecise, because no one has been able to analyze the algorithm. This gap in our knowledge makes it difficult not only to evaluate different increment sequences, but also to compare shellsort with other methods analytically. Not even the functional form of the running time for shellsort is known (furthermore, the form depends on the increment sequence). Knuth found that the functional forms $N(\log N)^2$ and $N^{1.25}$ both fit the data reasonably well, and later research suggests that a more complicated function of the form $N^{1+1/\sqrt{\lg N}}$ is involved for some sequences.

Figure 6.13
Shellsorting a random permutation

The effect of each of the passes in Shellsort is to bring the file as a whole closer to sorted order. The file is first 40-sorted, then 13-sorted, then 4-sorted, then 1-sorted. Each pass brings the file closer to sorted order.

We conclude this section by digressing into a discussion of several facts about the analysis of shellsort that *are* known. Our primary purpose in doing so is to illustrate that even algorithms that are apparently simple can have complex properties, and that the analysis of algorithms is not just of practical importance but also can be intellectually challenging. Readers intrigued by the idea of finding a new and improved shellsort increment sequence may find the information that follows useful; other readers may wish to skip to Section 6.9.

Property 6.7 *The result of h-sorting a file that is k-ordered is a file that is both h- and k-ordered.*

This fact seems obvious, but is tricky to prove (see Exercise 6.61). ∎

Property 6.8 *Shellsort does less than $N(h-1)(k-1)/g$ comparisons to g-sort a file that is h- and k-ordered, provided that h and k are relatively prime.*

The basis for this fact is illustrated in Figure 6.14. No element farther than $(h-1)(k-1)$ positions to the left of any given element x can be greater than x, if h and k are relatively prime (see Exercise 6.57). When g-sorting, we examine at most one out of every g of those elements. ∎

Property 6.9 *Shellsort does less than $O(N^{3/2})$ comparisons for the increments* 1 4 13 40 121 364 1093 3280 9841 ....

For large increments, there are h subfiles of size about N/h, for a worst-case cost about N^2/h. For small increments, Property 6.8 implies that the cost is about Nh. The result follows if we use the better of these bounds for each increment. It holds for any relatively prime sequence that grows exponentially. ∎

**Figure 6.14
A 4- and 13- ordered file.**

The bottom row depicts an array, with shaded boxes depicting those items that must be smaller than or equal to the item at the far right, if the array is both 4- and 13-ordered. The four rows at top depict the origin of the pattern. If the item at right is at array position i, then 4-ordering means that items at array positions $i-4$, $i-8$, $i-12$, ... are smaller or equal (top); 13-ordering means that the item at $i-13$, and, therefore, because of 4-ordering, the items at $i-17$, $i-21$, $i-25$, ... are smaller or equal (second from top); also, the item at $i-26$, and, therefore, because of 4-ordering, the items at $i-30$, $i-34$, $i-38$, ... are smaller or equal (third from top); and so forth. The white squares remaining are those that could be larger than the item at left; there are at most 18 such items (and the one that is farthest away is at $i-36$). Thus, at most $18N$ comparisons are required for an insertion sort of a 13-ordered and 4-ordered file of size N.

39 26 13 8 4

Property 6.10 *Shellsort does less than $O(N^{4/3})$ comparisons for the increments* 1 8 23 77 281 1073 4193 16577 ....

The proof of this property is along the lines of the proof of Property 6.9. The property analogous to Property 6.8 implies that the cost for small increments is about $Nh^{1/2}$. Proof of this property requires number theory that is beyond the scope of this book (*see reference section*). ∎

The increment sequences that we have discussed to this point are effective because successive elements are relatively prime. Another family of increment sequences is effective precisely because successive elements are *not* relatively prime.

In particular, the proof of Property 6.8 implies that, in a file that is 2-ordered and 3-ordered, each element moves at most one position during the final insertion sort. That is, such a file can be sorted with one bubble-sort pass (the extra loop in insertion sort is not needed). Now, if a file is 4-ordered and 6-ordered, then it also follows that each element moves at most one position when we are 2-sorting it (because each subfile is 2-ordered and 3-ordered); and if a file is 6-ordered and 9-ordered, each element moves at most one position when we are 3-sorting it. Continuing this line of reasoning, we are led to the following triangle of increments:

$$1$$
$$2 \quad 3$$
$$4 \quad 6 \quad 9$$
$$8 \quad 12 \quad 18 \quad 27$$
$$16 \quad 24 \quad 36 \quad 54 \quad 81$$
$$32 \quad 48 \quad 72 \quad 108 \quad 162 \quad 243$$
$$64 \quad 96 \quad 144 \quad 216 \quad 324 \quad 486 \quad 729$$

Each number in the triangle is two times the number above and to the right of it and also three times the number above and to the left of it. If we use these numbers from bottom to top and right to left as a shellsort increment sequence, then every increment x after the bottom row is preceded by $2x$ and $3x$, so every subfile is 2-ordered and 3-ordered, and no element moves more than one position during the entire sort!

Property 6.11 *Shellsort does less than $O(N(\log N)^2)$ comparisons for the increments* 1 2 3 4 6 9 8 12 18 27 16 24 36 54 81 . . . .

The number of increments in the triangle that are less than N is certainly less than $(\log_2 N)^2$. ∎

This set of increments was developed by V. Pratt in 1971 (*see reference section*). Pratt's increments tend not to work as well as the others in practice, because there are too many of them. But we can use the same principle to build an increment sequence from *any* two relatively prime numbers h and k. Such sequences do well in practice because the worst-case bounds corresponding to Property 6.11 overestimate the cost for random files.

The problem of designing good increment sequences for shellsort provides an excellent example of the complex behavior of a simple algorithm. We certainly will not be able to focus at this level of detail on all the algorithms that we encounter (not only do we not have the space, but also, as we did with shellsort, we might encounter mathematical analysis beyond the scope of this book, or even open research problems). However, many of the algorithms in this book are the product of extensive analytic and empirical studies by many researchers over the past several decades, and we can benefit from this work. This research illustrates that the quest for improved performance can be both intellectually challenging and practically rewarding, even for simple algorithms. Table 6.2 gives empirical results that show that several approaches to designing increment sequences work well in practice; the relatively short sequence 1 8 23 77 281 1073 4193 16577 . . . is among the simplest to use in a shellsort implementation.

Figure 6.15 shows that shellsort performs reasonably well on a variety of kinds of files, rather than just on random ones. Indeed, constructing a file for which shellsort runs slowly for a given increment sequence is a challenging exercise (see Exercise 6.56). As we have mentioned, there are some bad increment sequences for which shellsort may require a quadratic number of comparisons in the worst case (see

---

Table 6.2 Empirical study of shellsort increment sequences

Shellsort is many times faster than the other elementary methods, even when the increments are powers of 2, but some increment sequences can speed it up by another factor of 5 or more. The three best sequences in this table are totally different in design. Shellsort is a practical method even for large files, particularly by contrast with selection sort, insertion sort, and bubble sort (see Table 6.1).

N	O	K	G	S	P	I
12500	68	28	29	29	33	28
25000	117	40	42	38	53	40
50000	280	92	97	75	114	82
100000	1039	217	185	171	252	186
200000	2853	488	468	388	592	418

Key:

O   1 2 4 8 16 32 64 128 256 512 1024 2048 ...
K   1 4 13 40 121 364 1093 3280 9841 ... (Property 6.9)
G   1 2 4 10 23 51 113 249 548 1207 2655 5843 ... (Exercise 6.54)
S   1 8 23 77 281 1073 4193 16577 ... (Property 6.10)
P   1 7 8 49 56 64 343 392 448 512 2401 2744 ... (Exercise 6.58)
I   1 5 19 41 109 209 505 929 2161 3905 ... (Exercise 6.59)

Exercise 6.50), but much lower bounds have been shown to hold for a wide variety of sequences.

Shellsort is the method of choice for many sorting applications because it has acceptable running time even for moderately large files and requires a small amount of code that is easy to get working. In the next few chapters, we shall see methods that are more efficient, but they are perhaps only twice as fast (if that much) except for large N, and they are significantly more complicated. In short, if you need a quick solution to a sorting problem, and do not want to bother with interfacing to a system sort, you can use shellsort, then determine sometime later whether the extra work required to replace it with a more sophisticated method will be worthwhile.

Exercises

▷ **6.47**   Is shellsort stable?

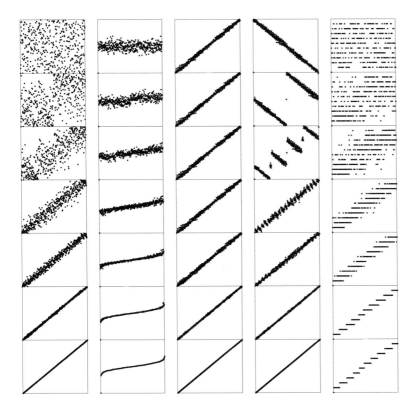

Figure 6.15
Dynamic characteristics of shellsort for various types of files

These diagrams show shellsort, with the increments 209 109 41 19 5 1, in operation on files that are random, Gaussian, nearly ordered, nearly reverse-ordered, and randomly ordered with 10 distinct key values (left to right, on the top). The running time for each pass depends on how well ordered the file is when the pass begins. After a few passes, these files are similarly ordered; thus, the running time is not particularly sensitive to the input.

6.48 Show how to implement a shellsort with the increments 1 8 23 77 281 1073 4193 16577 . . . , with direct calculations to get successive increments in a manner similar to the code given for Knuth's increments.

▷ **6.49** Give diagrams corresponding to Figures 6.10 and 6.11 for the keys E A S Y Q U E S T I O N.

6.50 Find the running time when you use shellsort with the increments 1 2 4 8 16 32 64 128 256 512 1024 2048 . . . to sort a file consisting of the integers $1, 2, \ldots, N$ in the odd positions and $N+1, N+2, \ldots, 2N$ in the even positions.

6.51 Write a driver to compare increment sequences for shellsort. Read the sequences from standard input, one per line, then use them all to sort 10 random files of size N for $N = 100, 1000,$ and $10,000$. Count comparisons, or measure actual running times.

• **6.52** Run experiments to determine whether adding or deleting an increment can improve the increment sequence 1 8 23 77 281 1073 4193 16577 . . . for $N = 10,000$.

• **6.53** Run experiments to determine the value of x that leads to the lowest running time for random files when the 13 is replaced by x in the increment sequence 1 4 13 40 121 364 1093 3280 9841 ... used for $N = 10,000$.

6.54 Run experiments to determine the value of α that leads to the lowest running time for random files for the increment sequence 1, $\lfloor\alpha\rfloor$, $\lfloor\alpha^2\rfloor$, $\lfloor\alpha^3\rfloor$, $\lfloor\alpha^4\rfloor$, ...; for $N = 10,000$.

• **6.55** Find the three-increment sequence that uses as small a number of comparisons as you can find for random files of 1000 elements.

•• **6.56** Construct a file of 100 elements for which shellsort, with the increments 1 8 23 77, uses as large a number of comparisons as you can find.

• **6.57** Prove that any number greater than or equal to $(h-1)(k-1)$ can be expressed as a linear combination (with nonnegative coefficients) of h and k, if h and k are relatively prime. *Hint*: Show that, if any two of the first $h-1$ multiples of k have the same remainder when divided by h, then h and k must have a common factor.

6.58 Run experiments to determine the values of h and k that lead to the lowest running times for random files when a Pratt-like sequence based on h and k is used for sorting $10,000$ elements.

6.59 The increment sequence 1 5 19 41 109 209 505 929 2161 3905 ... is based on merging the sequences $9\cdot4^i - 9\cdot2^i + 1$ and $4^i - 3\cdot2^i + 1$ for $i > 0$. Compare the results of using these sequences individually and using the merged result, for sorting $10,000$ elements.

6.60 We derive the increment sequence 1 3 7 21 48 112 336 861 1968 4592 13776 ... by starting with a base sequence of relatively prime numbers, say 1 3 7 16 41 101, then building a triangle, as in Pratt's sequence, this time generating the ith row in the triangle by multiplying the first element in the $i-1$st row by the ith element in the base sequence; and multiplying every element in the $i-1$st row by the $i+1$st element in the base sequence. Run experiments to find a base sequence that improves on the one given for sorting $10,000$ elements.

• **6.61** Complete the proofs of Properties 6.7 and 6.8.

• **6.62** Implement a shellsort that is based on the shaker sort algorithm of Exercise 6.40, and compare with the standard algorithm. *Note*: Your increment sequences should be substantially different from those for the standard algorithm.

6.9 Sorting of Linked Lists

As we know from Chapter 3, arrays and linked lists provide two of the most basic ways to structure data, and we considered an implementation of insertion sort for linked lists as a list-processing example in Section 3.4 (Program 3.10). The sort implementations that we have considered to this point all assume that the data to be sorted is in an array and are not directly applicable if we are working within a system that uses linked lists to organize data. In some cases, the *algorithms* may be useful, but only if they process data in the essentially sequential manner that we can support efficiently for linked lists.

Program 3.10 is a driver program that is similar to Program 6.1 for testing linked-list sorts. As for the array driver, it initializes the list, sorts it, and shows its contents. As discussed in Chapter 3, it is possible to work with linked lists at a higher level of abstraction, but the low-level approach that we are using makes it easier to concentrate on the link manipulations that characterize the algorithms and data structures, our prime focus in this book. It is a straightforward matter to define an interface for lists and build generic implementations like those that we built for arrays in Section 6.2 (see Exercise 6.66).

There is a ground rule for manipulating linked structures that is critical in many applications but not always evident from our code. In a more complex environment, it could be the case that references to the list nodes that we are manipulating are maintained by other parts of the applications system (that is, they are in multilists). The possibility that nodes could be accessed through references that are maintained outside the sort means that our programs should *change only links in nodes, and should not alter keys or other information.* For example, when we want to do an exchange, it would seem simplest just to exchange items (as we did when sorting arrays). But then any reference to either node through some other link would find the value changed and probably will not have the desired effect. We need to change the links themselves such that the nodes appear in sorted order when the list is traversed via the links we have access to, without affecting their order when accessed via any other links. Doing so makes the implementations more difficult but usually is necessary.

We can adapt insertion, selection, and bubble sort to linked-list implementations, although each one presents amusing challenges. Selection sort is straightforward: We maintain an input list (which initially has the data) and an output list (which collects the sorted result). It is a straightforward exercise in linked-list manipulation to scan through the list to find the maximum element in the input list, remove it from the list, and add it to the front of the output

Program 6.19 Linked-list selection sort

Selection sort of a linked list is straightforward, but differs slightly from
the array version because it is easier to insert at the front of a list. We
maintain an input list (pointed to by h.next), and an output list (pointed
to by out). While it is nonempty, we scan the input list to find the
maximum remaining element, then remove that element from the input
list and insert it at the front of the output list. This implementation uses
a private method findMax, which returns a link to the node whose link
points to the maximum element on a list.

```
private static Node findMax(Node h)
  {
    for (Node t = h; t.next != null; t = t.next)
      if (h.next.item < t.next.item) h = t;
    return h;
  }
static Node sort(Node h)
  { Node head = new Node(-1, h), out = null;
    while (head.next != null)
      { Node max = findMax(head);
        Node t = max.next; max.next = t.next;
        t.next = out; out = t;
      }
    return out;
  }
```

list (see Figure 6.16). An implementation is given in Program 6.19.
Program 3.10 gives an implementation of insertion sort for linked lists,
and Exercise 6.68 addresses bubble sort. These methods can be useful
for sorting short lists, with the same kinds of performance tradeoffs
that we found for their array-based counterparts.

In some list-processing situations, we may not need to explicitly
implement a sort at all. For example, we could choose to keep the list
in order at all times, inserting new nodes into the list as in insertion
sort. This approach comes at little extra cost if insertions are relatively
rare, or the list is small, and in certain other situations. For example,
we might need to scan the whole list for some reason before inserting
new nodes (perhaps to check for duplicates). We shall discuss an
algorithm that uses ordered linked lists in Chapter 14, and we shall see

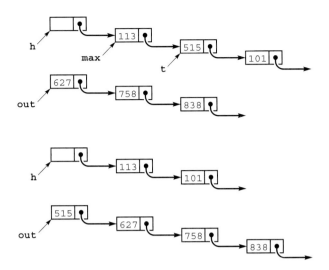

Figure 6.16
Linked-list selection sort

This diagram depicts one step of selection sort for linked lists. We maintain an input list, pointed to by h.next, and an output list, pointed to by out (top). We scan through the input list to make max point to the node before (and t point to) the node containing the maximum item. These are the pointers we need to remove t from the input list (reducing its length by 1) and put it at the front of the output list (increasing its length by 1), keeping the output list in order (bottom). Iterating, we eventually exhaust the input list and have the nodes in order in the output list.

numerous data structures that gain efficiency from order in the data in Chapters 12 and 14.

Exercises

▷ **6.63** Give the contents of the input list and output list as Program 6.19 is used for the keys A S O R T I N G E X A M P L E.

6.64 Implement a performance-driver client program for linked-list sorts (see Exercise 6.8).

6.65 Implement an exercise-driver client program for linked-list sorts that tests pathological cases (see Exercise 6.9).

6.66 Design a sortable linked-list ADT that includes a method for random initialization, a method for initialization from the standard input stream, a sort method, and an output method. All should take a node reference as a parameter and provide one as a return value in order to support the functional programming style of Program 3.10.

6.67 Write a class that extends your abstract class from Exercise 6.66 to implement linked lists with records that are double keys.

6.68 Implement bubble sort for a linked list. *Caution*: Exchanging two adjacent elements on a linked list is more difficult than it might seem at first.

6.69 The insertion-sort method used in Program 3.10 makes the linked-list insertion sort run significantly slower than the array version for some input files. Describe one such file, and explain the problem.

• **6.70** Implement a linked-list version of shellsort that does not use significantly more time or space than the array version for large random files. *Hint*: Use bubble sort.

• **6.71** Develop a linked-list implementation for the array ADT interface in Program 6.5 so that, for example, you can use Program 6.6 to debug linked-list sort implementations.

6.10 Key-Indexed Counting

A number of sorting algorithms gain efficiency by taking advantage of special properties of keys. For example, consider the following problem: Sort a file of N items whose keys are distinct integers between 0 and $N-1$. We can solve this problem immediately, using a temporary array b, with the statement

```
for (i = 0; i < N; i++) b[a[i]] = a[i];
```

That is, we sort by using the keys as *indices*, rather than as abstract items that are compared. In this section, we consider an elementary method that uses key indexing in this way to sort efficiently when the keys are integers in a small range.

If all the keys are 0, sorting is trivial; but now suppose that there are two distinct key values 0 and 1. Such a sorting problem might arise when we want to separate out the items in a file that satisfy some (perhaps complicated) acceptance test: we take the key 0 to mean "accept" and the key 1 to mean "reject." One way to proceed is to count the number of 0s, then to make a second pass through the input a to distribute its items to the temporary array b, using an array of two counters, as follows: We start with 0 in cnt[0] and the number of 0 keys in the file cnt[1] in order to indicate that there are no keys that are less than 0 and cnt[1] keys that are less than 1 in the file. Clearly, we can fill in the b array by putting 0s at the beginning (starting at b[[cnt[0]], or b[0]) and 1s starting at b[cnt[1]]. That is, the code

```
for (i = 0; i < N; i++) b[cnt[a[i]]++] = a[i];
```

serves to distribute the items from a to b. Again, we get a fast sort by using the keys as indices (to pick between cnt[0] and cnt[1]).

This approach generalizes immediately. A more realistic problem in the same spirit is this: Sort a file of N items whose keys are integers between 0 and $M-1$. We can extend the basic method in the previous

Program 6.20 Key-indexed counting

The first for loop initializes the counts to 0; the second for loop sets the second counter to the number of 0s, the third counter to the number of 1s, and so forth. Then, the third for loop simply adds these numbers to produce counts of the number of keys less than or equal to the one corresponding to the count. These numbers now give the indices of the end of the part of the file where keys belong. The fourth for loop moves the keys into an auxiliary array b according to these indices, and the final loop moves the sorted file back into a. The keys must be integers less than M for this code to work, although we can easily modify it to extract such keys from more complex items (see Exercise 6.75).

```
static void distCount(int a[], int l, int r)
  { int i, j, cnt[] = new int[M];
    int b[] = new int[a.length];
    for (j = 0; j < M; j++) cnt[j] = 0;
    for (i = 1; i <= r; i++) cnt[a[i]+1]++;
    for (j = 1; j < M; j++) cnt[j] += cnt[j-1];
    for (i = 1; i <= r; i++) b[cnt[a[i]]++] = a[i];
    for (i = 1; i <= r; i++) a[i] = b[i-1];
  }
```

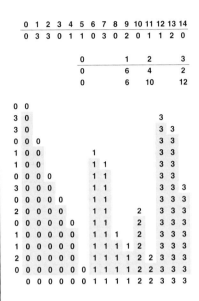

Figure 6.17
Sorting by key-indexed counting.

First, we determine how many keys of each value there are in the file: In this example there are six 0s, four 1s, two 2s, and three 3s. Then, we take partial sums to find the number of keys less than each key: 0 keys are less than 0, 6 keys are less than 1, 10 keys are less than 2, and 12 keys are less than 3 (table in middle). Then, we use the partial sums as indices in placing the keys into position: The 0 at the beginning of the file is put into location 0; we then increment the pointer corresponding to 0, to point to where the next 0 should go. Then, the 3 from the next position on the left in the file is put into location 12 (since there are 12 keys less than 3); its corresponding count is incremented; and so forth.

paragraph to an algorithm called *key-indexed counting*, which solves this problem effectively if M is not too large. Just as with two key values, the idea is to count the number of keys with each value and then to use the counts to move the items into position on a second pass through the file. First, we count the number of keys of each value, then we compute partial sums to get counts of the number of keys less than or equal to each value. Then, again just as we did when we had two key values, we use these counts as indices for the purpose of distributing the keys. For each key, we view its associated count as an index pointing to the end of the block of keys with the same value, use the index to distribute the key into b, and decrement. This process is illustrated in Figure 6.17. An implementation is given in Program 6.20.

Property 6.12 *Key-indexed counting is a linear-time sort, provided that the range of distinct key values is within a constant factor of the file size.*

Each item is moved twice, once for the distribution and once to be moved back to the original array; and each key is referenced twice, once to do the counts and once to do the distribution. The two other for loops in the algorithm involve building the counts and will contribute insignificantly to the running time unless the number of counts becomes significantly larger than the file size. ∎

If huge files are to be sorted, the auxiliary array b can present memory-allocation problems. It is possible to modify Program 6.20 to complete the sort in place (avoiding the need for an auxiliary array). This operation is closely related to basic methods that we shall be discussing in later chapters, so we defer it to Exercises 10.19 and 10.20 in Section 10.3. As we shall see in Chapter 10, this space savings comes at the cost of the stability property of the algorithm and thus limits the algorithm's utility because applications involving large numbers of duplicate keys often have other associated keys, whose relative order should be preserved. We shall see a particularly important example of such an application in Chapter 10.

Exercises

○ **6.72** Give a specialized version of key-indexed counting for sorting files, where elements can take on only one of three values (a, b, or c).

6.73 Suppose that we use insertion sort on a randomly ordered file where elements have only one of three values. Is the running time linear, quadratic, or something in between?

▷ **6.74** Show how key-indexed counting sorts the file A B R A C A D A B R A.

6.75 Implement key-indexed counting for items that are potentially large records with integer keys from a small range.

6.76 Give a key-indexed counting implementation that does not move the items in the input array a, but rather computes a second array b such that b[0] is the index of the item in a that would appear first in a sort, b[1] is the index of the item in a that would appear second, and so forth.

CHAPTER SEVEN

Quicksort

THE SUBJECT OF THIS CHAPTER is the sorting algorithm that is probably used more widely than any other, *quicksort*. The basic algorithm was invented in 1960 by C. A. R. Hoare, and it has been studied by many people since that time (*see reference section*). Quicksort is popular because it is not difficult to implement, works well for a variety of different kinds of input data, and consumes fewer resources than any other sorting method in many situations.

The quicksort algorithm's desirable features are that it is in-place (uses only a small auxiliary stack), requires time only proportional to $N \log N$ on the average to sort N items, and has an extremely short inner loop. Its drawbacks are that it is not stable, takes about N^2 operations in the worst case, and is fragile in the sense that a simple mistake in the implementation can go unnoticed and can cause it to perform badly for some files.

The performance of quicksort is well understood. The algorithm has been subjected to a thorough mathematical analysis, and we can make precise statements about its performance. The analysis has been verified by extensive empirical experience, and the algorithm has been refined to the point where it is the method of choice in a broad variety of practical sorting applications. It is therefore worthwhile for us to look more carefully than for other algorithms at ways of implementing quicksort efficiently. Similar implementation techniques are appropriate for other algorithms; with quicksort, we can use them with confidence, because we know precisely how they will affect performance.

It is tempting to try to develop ways to improve quicksort: A faster sorting algorithm is computer science's "better mousetrap," and quicksort is a venerable method that seems to invite tinkering. Almost from the moment Hoare first published the algorithm, improved versions have been appearing in the literature. Many ideas have been tried and analyzed, but it is easy to be deceived, because the algorithm is so well balanced that the effects of improvements in one part of the program can be more than offset by the effects of bad performance in another part of the program. We examine in detail three modifications that do improve quicksort substantially.

A carefully tuned version of quicksort is likely to run significantly faster on most computers than will any other sorting method, and quicksort is widely used as a library sort utility and for other serious sorting applications. Indeed, the the standard Java library's sort is an implementation of quicksort. Despite its deserved reputation as a fast algorithm, the running time of quicksort does depend on the input and ranges from linear to quadratic in the number of items to be sorted. People are sometimes surprised by undesirable and unexpected effects for some inputs, particularly in highly tuned versions of the algorithm. When an application does not justify the work required to be sure that a quicksort implementation is not flawed, some programmers turn to shellsort as a safer choice that will perform well for less implementation investment. For huge files, however, quicksort is likely to run 5 to 10 times as fast as shellsort, and it can adapt to be even more efficient for other types of files that might occur in practice.

7.1 The Basic Algorithm

Quicksort is a divide-and-conquer method for sorting. It works by *partitioning* an array into two parts, then sorting the parts independently. As we shall see, the precise position of the partition depends on the initial order of the elements in the input file. The crux of the method is the partitioning process, which rearranges the array to make the following three conditions hold:

- The element a[i] is in its final place in the array for some i.
- None of the elements in a[l], ... , a[i-1] is greater than a[i].
- None of the elements in a[i+1], ... , a[r] is less than a[i].

Program 7.1 Quicksort

If the array has one or fewer elements, do nothing. Otherwise, the array is processed by a partition procedure (see Program 7.2), which puts a[i] into position for some i between 1 and r inclusive and rearranges the other elements such that the recursive calls properly finish the sort.

```
static void quicksort(ITEM[] a, int l, int r)
  {
    if (r <= l) return;
    int i = partition(a, l, r);
    quicksort(a, l, i-1);
    quicksort(a, i+1, r);
  }
```

We achieve a complete sort by partitioning, then recursively applying the method to the subfiles, as depicted in Figure 7.1. Because the partitioning process always puts at least one element into position, a formal proof by induction that the recursive method constitutes a proper sort is not difficult to develop. Program 7.1 is a recursive program that implements this idea.

We use the following general strategy to implement partitioning. First, we arbitrarily choose a[r] to be the *partitioning element*—the one that will go into its final position. Next, we scan from the left end of the array until we find an element greater than the partitioning element, and we scan from the right end of the array until we find an element less than the partitioning element. The two elements that stopped the scans are obviously out of place in the final partitioned array, so we exchange them. Continuing in this way, we ensure that no array elements to the left of the left index are greater than the partitioning element, and no array elements to the right of the right index are less than the partitioning element, as depicted in the following diagram.

less than or equal to v		greater than or equal to v	v

↑ 　　　　　 ↑ 　　 ↑ 　　　　　 ↑
l 　　　　　 i 　　 j 　　　　　 r

Figure 7.1
Quicksort example

Quicksort is a recursive partitioning process: We partition a file by putting some element (the partitioning element) in place and rearranging the array such that smaller elements are to the left of the partitioning element and larger elements to its right. Then, we sort the left and right parts of the array recursively. Each line in this diagram depicts the result of partitioning the displayed subfile using the circled element. The end result is a fully sorted file.

Here, v refers to the value of the partitioning element, i to the left index, and j to the right index. As indicated in this diagram, it is best to stop the left scan for elements greater than *or equal to* the partitioning element and the right scan for elements less than *or equal to* the partitioning element, even though this policy might seem to create unnecessary exchanges involving elements equal to the partitioning element (we shall examine the reasons for this policy later in this section). When the scan indices cross, all that we need to do to complete the partitioning process is to exchange a[r] with the leftmost element of the right subfile (the element pointed to by the left index). Program 7.2 is an implementation of this process, and Figures 7.2 and 7.3 depict examples.

The inner loop of quicksort increments an index and compares an array element against a fixed value. This simplicity is what makes quicksort quick: It is hard to envision a shorter inner loop in a sorting algorithm.

Program 7.2 uses an explicit test to stop the scan if the partitioning element is the smallest element in the array. It might be worthwhile to use a sentinel to avoid this test: The inner loop of quicksort is so small that this one superfluous test could have a noticeable effect on performance. A sentinel is not needed for this implementation when the partitioning element is the largest element in the file, because the partitioning element itself is at the right end of the array to stop the scan. Other implementations of partitioning discussed later in this section and elsewhere in this chapter do not necessarily stop the scan on keys equal to the partitioning element—we might need to add a test to stop the index from running off the right end of the array in such an implementation. On the other hand, the improvement to quicksort that we discuss in Section 7.5 has the side benefit of needing neither the test nor a sentinel at either end.

The partitioning process is not stable, because any key might be moved past a large number of keys equal to it (which have not even been examined yet) during any exchange. No easy way to make an array-based quicksort stable is known.

The partitioning procedure must be implemented carefully. Specifically, the most straightforward way to guarantee that the recursive program terminates is that it (*i*) does not call itself for files of size 1 or less; and (*ii*) calls itself *only* for files that are strictly smaller

Figure 7.2
Quicksort partitioning

Quicksort partitioning begins with the (arbitrary) choice of a partitioning element. Program 7.2 uses the rightmost element E. Then, it scans from the left over smaller elements and from the right over larger elements, exchanges the elements that stop the scans, continuing until the scan indices meet. First, we scan from the left and stop at the S, then we scan from the right and stop at the A, and then we exchange the S and the A. Next, we continue the scan from the left until we stop at the O, and continue the scan from the right until we stop at the E, then exchange the O and the E. Next, our scanning indices cross: We continue the scan from the left until we stop at the R, then continue the scan from the right (past the R) until we stop at the E. To finish the process, we exchange the partitioning element (the E at the right) with the R.

Program 7.2 Partitioning

The variable v holds the value of the partitioning element a[r], and i and j are the left and right scan indices, respectively. The partitioning loop increments i and decrements j, while maintaining the invariant property that no elements to the left of i are greater than v and no elements to the right of j are smaller than v. Once the indices meet, we complete the partitioning by exchanging a[i] and a[r], which puts v into a[i], with no larger elements to v's right and no smaller elements to its left.

The partitioning loop is implemented as an infinite loop, with a break when the indices cross. The test j == 1 protects against the case that the partitioning element is the smallest element in the file.

```
static int partition(ITEM a[], int l, int r)
  { int i = l-1, j = r; ITEM v = a[r];
    for (;;)
      {
        while (less(a[++i], v)) ;
        while (less(v, a[--j])) if (j == 1) break;
        if (i >= j) break;
        exch(a, i, j);
      }
    exch(a, i, r);
    return i;
  }
```

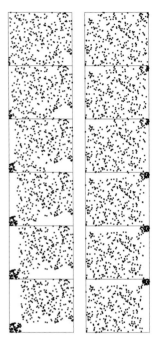

Figure 7.3
Dynamic characteristics of quicksort partitioning

The partitioning process divides a file into two subfiles that can be sorted independently. None of the elements to the left of the left scan index is larger, so there are no dots above and to its left; and none of the elements to the right of the right scan index is smaller, so there are no dots below and to its right. As shown in these two examples, partitioning a random array divides it into two smaller random arrays, with one element (the partitioning element) ending up on the diagonal.

than given as input. These policies may seem obvious, but it is easy to overlook a property of the input that can lead to a spectacular failure. For instance, a common mistake in implementing quicksort is not ensuring that one element is always put into position, then falling into an infinite recursive loop when the partitioning element happens to be the largest or smallest element in the file.

When duplicate keys are present in the file, the index crossing is subtle. We could improve the partitioning process slightly by terminating the scans when i < j, and then using j, rather than i-1, to delimit the right end of the left subfile for the first recursive call. Letting the loop iterate one more time in this case is an improvement, because whenever the scanning loops terminate with j and i referring to the same element, we end up with *two* elements in their final positions: the element that stopped both scans, which must therefore be equal to the partitioning element, and the partitioning element itself. This case would occur, for example, if R were E in Figure 7.2. This change is probably worth making, because, in this particular case, the program as given leaves a record with a key equal to the partitioning key in a[r], and that makes the first partition in the call quicksort(a, i+1, r) degenerate, because its rightmost key is its smallest. The partitioning implementation in Program 7.2 is a bit easier to understand, however, so we refer to it as the basic quicksort partitioning method. If significant numbers of duplicate keys might be present, other factors come into play. We consider them next.

There are three basic strategies that we could adopt with respect to keys equal to the partitioning element: have both indices stop on such keys (as in Program 7.2); have one index stop and the other scan over them; or have both indices scan over them. The question of which of these strategies is best has been studied in detail mathematically, and results show that it is best to have both indices stop, primarily because this strategy tends to balance the partitions in the presence of many duplicate keys, whereas the other two can lead to badly unbalanced partitions for some files. We also consider a slightly more complicated and much more effective method for dealing with duplicate keys in Section 7.6.

Ultimately, the efficiency of the sort depends on how well the partitioning divides the file, which in turn depends on the value of the partitioning element. Figure 7.2 shows that partitioning divides a large randomly ordered file into two smaller randomly ordered files, but that the actual split could be anywhere in the file. We would prefer to choose an element that would split the file near the middle, but we do not have the necessary information to do so. If the file is randomly ordered, choosing a[r] as the partitioning element is the same as choosing any other specific element and will give us a split near the middle *on the average*. In Section 7.4 we consider the analysis of the algorithm that allows us to see how this choice compares to the ideal choice. In Section 7.5 we see how the analysis guides us in considering choices of the partitioning element that make the algorithm more efficient.

Exercises

▷ 7.1   Show, in the style of the example given here, how quicksort sorts the file E A S Y Q U E S T I O N.

7.2   Show how the file 1 0 0 1 1 1 0 0 0 0 0 1 0 1 0 0 is partitioned, using both Program 7.2 and the minor modifications suggested in the text.

7.3   Implement partitioning without using a `break` statement or a `goto` statement.

● 7.4   Develop a stable quicksort for linked lists.

○ 7.5   What is the maximum number of times during the execution of quicksort that the largest element can be moved, for a file of N elements?

7.2 Performance Characteristics of Quicksort

Despite its many assets, the basic quicksort program has the definite liability that it is extremely inefficient on some simple files that can arise in practice. For example, if it is called with a file of size N that is already sorted, then all the partitions will be degenerate, and the program will call itself N times, removing just one element for each call.

Property 7.1   *Quicksort uses about $N^2/2$ comparisons in the worst case.*

By the argument just given, the number of comparisons used for a file that is already in order is

$$N + (N - 1) + (N - 2) + \ldots + 2 + 1 = (N + 1)N/2.$$

All the partitions are also degenerate for files in reverse order, as well as for other kinds of files that are less likely to occur in practice (see Exercise 7.6). ∎

This behavior means not only that the time required will be about $N^2/2$ but also that the space required to handle the recursion will be about N (see Section 7.3), which is unacceptable for large files. Fortunately, there are relatively easy ways to reduce drastically the likelihood that this worst case will occur in typical applications of the program.

The best case for quicksort is when each partitioning stage divides the file exactly in half. This circumstance would make the number of comparisons used by quicksort satisfy the divide-and-conquer recurrence

$$C_N = 2C_{N/2} + N.$$

The $2C_{N/2}$ covers the cost of sorting the two subfiles; the N is the cost of examining each element, using one partitioning index or the other. From Chapter 5, we know that this recurrence has the solution

$$C_N \approx N \lg N.$$

Although things do not always go this well, it is true that the partition falls in the middle *on the average*. Taking into account the precise probability of each partition position makes the recurrence more complicated and more difficult to solve, but the final result is similar.

Property 7.2 *Quicksort uses about $2N \ln N$ comparisons on the average.*

The precise recurrence formula for the number of comparisons used by quicksort for N randomly ordered distinct elements is

$$C_N = N + 1 + \frac{1}{N} \sum_{1 \leq k \leq N} (C_{k-1} + C_{N-k}) \quad \text{for } N \geq 2,$$

with $C_1 = C_0 = 0$. The $N + 1$ term covers the cost of comparing the partitioning element with each of the others (two extra for where the indices cross); the rest comes from the observation that each element k is likely to be the partitioning element with probability $1/k$, after which we are left with random files of size $k - 1$ and $N - k$.

Although it looks rather complicated, this recurrence is actually easy to solve, in three steps. First, $C_0 + C_1 + \cdots + C_{N-1}$ is the same as $C_{N-1} + C_{N-2} + \cdots + C_0$, so we have

$$C_N = N + 1 + \frac{2}{N} \sum_{1 \leq k \leq N} C_{k-1}.$$

Second, we can eliminate the sum by multiplying both sides by N and subtracting the same formula for $N - 1$:

$$NC_N - (N - 1)C_{N-1} = N(N + 1) - (N - 1)N + 2C_{N-1}.$$

This formula simplifies to the recurrence

$$NC_N = (N + 1)C_{N-1} + 2N.$$

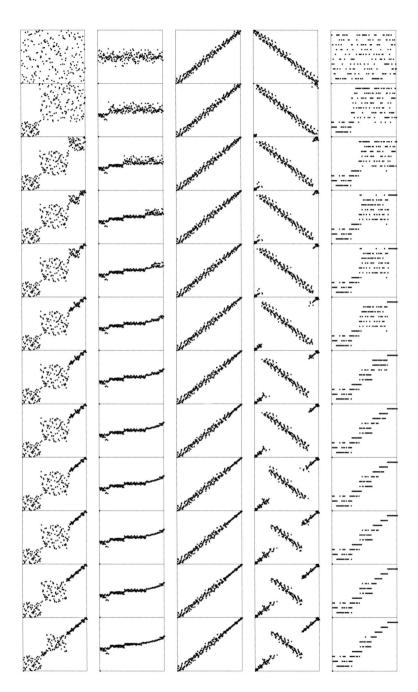

Figure 7.4
Dynamic characteristics of quicksort on various types of files

The choice of an arbitrary partitioning element in quicksort results in differing partitioning scenarios for different files. These diagrams illustrate the initial portions of scenarios for files that are random, Gaussian, nearly ordered, nearly reverse ordered, and randomly ordered with 10 distinct key values (left to right), using a relatively large value of the cutoff for small subfiles. Elements not involved in partitioning end up close to the diagonal, leaving an array that could be handled easily by insertion sort. The nearly ordered files require an excessive number of partitions.

Third, dividing both sides by $N(N + 1)$ gives a recurrence that telescopes:

$$\frac{C_N}{N + 1} = \frac{C_{N-1}}{N} + \frac{2}{N + 1}$$
$$= \frac{C_{N-2}}{N - 1} + \frac{2}{N} + \frac{2}{N + 1}$$
$$= \vdots$$
$$= \frac{C_2}{3} + \sum_{3 \leq k \leq N} \frac{2}{k + 1}.$$

This exact answer is nearly equal to a sum that is easily approximated by an integral (see Section 2.3):

$$\frac{C_N}{N + 1} \approx 2 \sum_{1 \leq k < N} \frac{1}{k} \approx 2 \int_1^N \frac{1}{x} dx = 2 \ln N,$$

which implies the stated result. Note that $2N \ln N \approx 1.39 N \lg N$, so the average number of comparisons is only about 39 percent higher than in the best case. ∎

This analysis assumes that the file to be sorted comprises randomly ordered records with distinct keys, but the implementation in Programs 7.1 and 7.2 can run slowly in some cases when the keys are not necessarily distinct and not necessarily in random order, as illustrated in Figure 7.4. If the sort is to be used a great many times or if it is to be used to sort a huge file (or, in particular, if it is to be used as a general-purpose library sort that will be used to sort files of unknown characteristics), then we need to consider several of the improvements discussed in Sections 7.5 and 7.6 that can make it much less likely that a bad case will occur in practice, while also reducing the average running time by 20 percent.

Exercises

7.6 Give six files of 10 elements for which quicksort (Program 7.1) uses the same number of comparisons as the worst-case file (when all the elements are in order).

7.7 Write a program to compute the exact value of C_N, and compare the exact value with the approximation $2N \ln N$, for $N = 10^3$, 10^4, 10^5, and 10^6.

○ **7.8** About how many comparisons will quicksort (Program 7.1) make when sorting a file of N equal elements?

7.9 About how many comparisons will quicksort (Program 7.1) make when sorting a file consisting of N items that have just two different key values (k items with one value, $N - k$ items with the other)?

• **7.10** Write a program that produces a best-case file for quicksort: a file of N distinct elements with the property that every partition will produce subfiles that differ in size by at most 1.

7.3 Stack Size

As in Chapter 3, we can use an explicit pushdown stack for quicksort, thinking of the stack as containing work to be done in the form of subfiles to be sorted. Any time that we need a subfile to process, we pop the stack. When we partition, we create two subfiles to be processed and push both on the stack. In the recursive implementation in Program 7.1, the stack maintained by the system holds this same information.

For a random file, the maximum size of the stack is proportional to $\log N$ (*see reference section*), but the stack can grow to size proportional to N for a degenerate case, as illustrated in Figure 7.5. Indeed, the very worst case is when the input file is already sorted. The potential for stack growth proportional to the size of the original file is a subtle but real difficulty with a recursive implementation of quicksort: There is always an underlying stack, and a degenerate case on a large file could cause the program to terminate abnormally because of lack of memory—behavior obviously undesirable for a library sorting routine. (Actually, we likely would run out of time before running out of space.) It is difficult to provide a *guarantee* against this behavior, but we shall see in Section 7.5 that it is not difficult to provide safeguards that make such degenerate cases extremely unlikely to occur.

Program 7.3 is a nonrecursive implementation that addresses this problem by checking the sizes of the two subfiles and putting the larger of the two on the stack first. Figure 7.6 illustrates this policy. Comparing this example with the one in Figure 7.1, we see that the subfiles are not changed by this policy; only the order in which they are processed is changed. Thus, we save on space costs without affecting time costs.

The policy of putting the larger of the small subfiles on the stack ensures that each entry on the stack is no more than one-half of the

Figure 7.5
Stack size for quicksort

The recursive stack for quicksort does not grow large for random files but can take excessive space for degenerate files. The stack sizes for two random files (left, center) and that for a partially ordered file (right) are plotted here.

Figure 7.6
Quicksort example (sorting the smaller subfile first)

The order in which the subfiles are processed does not affect the correct operation of the quicksort algorithm, or the time taken, but might affect the size of the push-down stack underlying the recursive structure. Here the smaller of the two subfiles is processed first after each partition.

Program 7.3 Nonrecursive quicksort

This nonrecursive implementation (see Chapter 5) of quicksort uses an explicit pushdown stack, replacing recursive calls with stack pushes (of the parameters) and the procedure call/exit with a loop that pops parameters from the stack and processes them as long as the stack is nonempty. We put the larger of the two subfiles on the stack first to ensure that the maximum stack depth for sorting N elements is $\lg N$ (see Property 7.3).

```
static void quicksort(ITEM[] a, int l, int r)
  { intStack S = new intStack(50);
    S.push(l); S.push(r);
    while (!S.empty())
      {
        r = S.pop(); l = S.pop();
        if (r <= l) continue;
        int i = partition(a, l, r);
        if (i-1 >  r-i) { S.push(l); S.push(i-1); }
        S.push(i+1); S.push(r);
        if (r-i >= i-1) { S.push(l); S.push(i-1); }
      }
  }
```

size of the one below it, so that the stack needs to contain room for only about $\lg N$ entries. This maximum stack usage occurs when the partition always falls at the center of the file. For random files, the actual maximum stack size is much lower; for degenerate files it is likely to be small.

Property 7.3 *If the smaller of the two subfiles is sorted first, then the stack never has more than $\lg N$ entries when quicksort is used to sort N elements.*

The worst-case stack size must be less than T_N, where T_N satisfies the recurrence $T_N = T_{\lfloor N/2 \rfloor} + 1$ with $T_1 = T_0 = 0$. This recurrence is a standard one of the type that is considered in Chapter 5 (see Exercise 7.13). ∎

This technique does not necessarily work in a truly recursive implementation, because it depends on *end-* or *tail-recursion removal*. If the last action of a procedure is to call another procedure, some programming environments will arrange things such that local variables are cleared from the stack *before*, rather than after, the call. Without end-recursion removal, we cannot guarantee that the stack size will be small for quicksort. For example, a call to quicksort for a file of size N that is already sorted will result in a recursive call to such a file of size $N - 1$, in turn resulting in a recursive call for such a file of size $N - 2$, and so on, ultimately resulting in a stack depth proportional to N. This observation would seem to suggest using a nonrecursive implementation to guard against excessive stack growth. On the other hand, some Java compilers automatically remove end recursion, and many machines have direct hardware support for function calls—the nonrecursive implementation in Program 7.3 might therefore actually be slower than the recursive implementation in Program 7.1 in such environments.

Figure 7.7 further illustrates the point that the nonrecursive method processes the same subfiles (in a different order) as does the recursive method for any file. It shows a tree structure with the partitioning element at the root and the trees corresponding to the left and right subfiles as left and right children, respectively. Using the recursive implementation of quicksort corresponds to visiting the nodes of this tree in preorder; the nonrecursive implementation corresponds to a visit-the-smaller-subtree-first traversal rule.

When we use an explicit stack, as we did in Program 7.3, we avoid some of the overhead implicit in a recursive implementation, although modern programming systems do not incur much overhead for such simple programs. Program 7.3 can be further improved. For example, it puts both subfiles on the stack, only to have the top one immediately popped off; we could change it to set the variables l and r directly. Also, the test for r <= l is done as subfiles come off the stack, whereas it would be more efficient never to put such subfiles on the stack (see Exercise 7.14). This case might seem insignificant, but the recursive nature of quicksort actually ensures that a large fraction of the subfiles during the course of the sort are of size 0 or 1. Next, we examine an important improvement to quicksort that gains efficiency by expanding upon this idea, handling all small subfiles in as efficient a manner as possible.

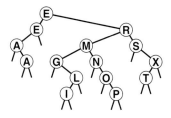

Figure 7.7
Quicksort partitioning tree

If we collapse the partitioning diagrams in Figures 7.1 and 7.6 by connecting each partitioning element to the partitioning element used in its two subfiles, we get this static representation of the partitioning process (in both cases). In this binary tree, each subfile is represented by its partitioning element (or by itself, if it is of size 1), and the subtrees of each node are the trees representing the subfiles after partitioning. For clarity, null subfiles are not shown here, although our recursive versions of the algorithm do make recursive calls with r < l when the partitioning element is the smallest or largest element in the file. The tree itself does not depend on the order in which the subfiles are partitioned. Our recursive implementation of quicksort corresponds to visiting the nodes of this tree in preorder; our nonrecursive implementation corresponds to a visit-the-smaller-subtree-first rule.

Exercises

▷ **7.11** Give, in the style of Figure 5.5, the stack contents after each pair of *push* and *pop* operations, when Program 7.3 is used to sort a file with the keys E A S Y Q U E S T I O N.

▷ **7.12** Answer Exercise 7.11 for the case where we always push the right subfile, then the left subfile (as is the case in the recursive implementation).

7.13 Complete the proof of Property 7.3, by induction.

7.14 Revise Program 7.3 such that it never puts on the stack subfiles with r <= 1.

▷ **7.15** Give the maximum stack size required by Program 7.3 when $N = 2^n$.

7.16 Give the maximum stack sizes required by Program 7.3 when $N = 2^n - 1$ and $N = 2^n + 1$.

○ **7.17** Would it be reasonable to use a queue instead of a stack for a nonrecursive implementation of quicksort? Explain your answer.

7.18 Determine and report whether your programming environment implements end-recursion removal.

• **7.19** Run empirical studies to determine the average stack size used by the basic recursive quicksort algorithm for random files of N elements, for $N = 10^3$, 10^4, 10^5, and 10^6.

•• **7.20** Find the average number of subfiles of size 0, 1, and 2 when quicksort is used to sort a random file of N elements.

7.4 Small Subfiles

A definite improvement to quicksort arises from the observation that a recursive program is guaranteed to call itself for many small subfiles, so it should use as good a method as possible when it encounters small subfiles. One obvious way to arrange for it to do so is to change the test at the beginning of the recursive routine from a `return` to a call on insertion sort, as follows:

```
if (r-l <= M) insertion(a, l, r);
```

Here, M is some parameter whose exact value depends upon the implementation. We can determine the best value for M either through analysis or with empirical studies. It is typical to find in such studies that the running time does not vary much for M in the range from about 5 to about 25, with the running time for M in this range on the order of 10 percent less than for the naive choice $M = 1$ (see Figure 7.8).

A slightly easier way to handle small subfiles, which is also slightly more efficient than insertion sorting them as they are encountered, is just to change the test at the beginning to

```
if (r-l <= M) return;
```

That is, we simply ignore small subfiles during partitioning. In a nonrecursive implementation, we could do so by not putting any files of size less than M on the stack or, alternatively, by ignoring all files of size less than M that are found on the stack. After partitioning, what is left is a file that is almost sorted. As discussed in Section 6.6, however, insertion sort is the method of choice for such files. That is, insertion sort will work about as well for such a file as for the collection of little files that it would get if it were being used directly. This method should be used with caution, because insertion sort is likely to work even if quicksort has a bug that causes it not to sort at all. Excessive cost may be the only sign that something went wrong.

Figure 7.9 illustrates this process for a larger file. Even with a relatively large cutoff for small subfiles, the quicksort part of the process runs quickly because relatively few elements are involved in partitioning steps. The insertion sort that finishes the job also runs quickly because it starts with a file that is nearly in order.

This technique can be used to good advantage whenever we are dealing with a recursive algorithm. Because of their very nature, we can be sure that *all* recursive algorithms will be processing small problem instances for a high percentage of the time; we generally do have available a low-overhead brute-force algorithm for small cases; and we therefore generally can improve overall timings with a hybrid algorithm.

Exercises

7.21 Are sentinel keys needed if insertion sort is called directly from within quicksort?

7.22 Instrument Program 7.1 to give the percentage of the comparisons used in partitioning files of size less than 10, 100, and 1000, and print out the percentages when you sort random files of N elements, for $N = 10^3, 10^4, 10^5$, and 10^6.

∘**7.23** Implement a recursive quicksort with a cutoff to insertion sort for subfiles with less than M elements, and empirically determine the value of M

Figure 7.8
Cutoff for small subfiles

Choosing the optimal value for the cutoff for small subfiles results in about a 10 percent improvement in the average running time. Choosing the value precisely is not critical; values from a broad range (from about 5 to about 20) will work about as well for most implementations. The thick line (top) was obtained empirically; the thin line (bottom) was derived analytically.

**Figure 7.9
Comparisons in quicksort**

*Quicksort subfiles are processed
independently. This picture shows
the result of partitioning each subfile during a sort of 200 elements
with a cutoff for files of size 15 or
less. We can get a rough idea of
the total number of comparisons
by counting the number of marked
elements by column vertically. In
this case, each array position is involved in only six or seven subfiles
during the sort.*

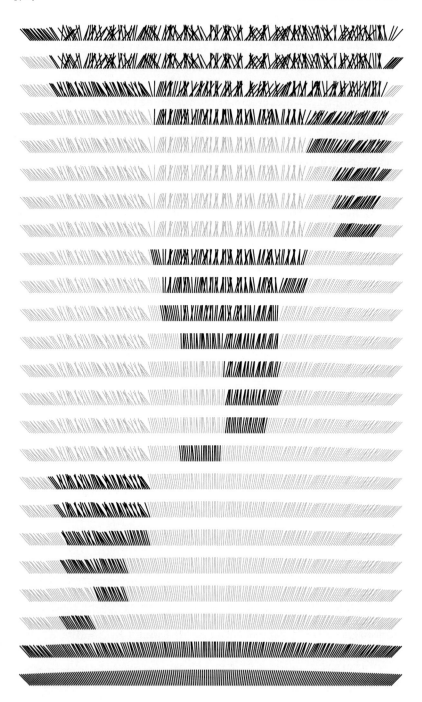

for which Program 7.4 runs fastest in your computing environment to sort random files of N integers, for $N = 10^3$, 10^4, 10^5, and 10^6.

7.24 Solve Exercise 7.23 using a nonrecursive implementation.

7.25 Solve Exercise 7.23, for the case when the records to be sorted are the data-processing records of Program 6.7. Give the best value of M corresponding to each of the three possible sort keys (see also Program 6.8).

• **7.26** Write a program that plots a histogram (see Program 3.7) of the subfile sizes left for insertion sort when you run quicksort for a file of size N with a cutoff for subfiles of size less than M. Run your program for $M = 10$, 100, and 1000 and $N = 10^3$, 10^4, 10^5, and 10^6.

7.27 Run empirical studies to determine the average stack size used by quicksort with cutoff for files of size M, when sorting random files of N elements, for $M = 10$, 100, and 1000 and $N = 10^3$, 10^4, 10^5, and 10^6.

7.5 Median-of-Three Partitioning

Another improvement to quicksort is to use a partitioning element that is more likely to divide the file near the middle. There are several possibilities here. A safe choice to avoid the worst case is to use a random element from the array for a partitioning element. Then, the worst case will happen with negligibly small probability. This method is a simple example of a *probabilistic algorithm*—one that uses randomness to achieve good performance with high probability, regardless of the arrangement of the input. We will see numerous examples later in the book of the utility of randomness in algorithm design, particularly when bias in the input is suspected. For quicksort, it may be overkill in practice to put in a full random-number generator just for this purpose: simple arbitrary choices can also be effective.

Another well-known way to find a better partitioning element is to take a sample of three elements from the file, then to use the median of the three for the partitioning element. By choosing the three elements from the left, middle, and right of the array, we can incorporate sentinels into this scheme as well: sort the three elements (using the three-exchange method in Chapter 6), then exchange the one in the middle with a[r-1], and then run the partitioning algorithm on a[l+1], ..., a[r-2]. This improvement is called the *median-of-three* method.

The median-of-three method helps quicksort in three ways. First, it makes the worst case much more unlikely to occur in any actual

---

Program 7.4 Improved quicksort

Choosing the median of the first, middle, and final elements as the partitioning element and cutting off the recursion for small subfiles can significantly improve the performance of quicksort. This implementation partitions on the median of the first, middle, and final elements in the array (otherwise leaving these elements out of the partitioning process). Files of size 11 or smaller are ignored during partitioning; then, insertion from Chapter 6 is used to finish the sort.

```
private final static int M = 10;
static void quicksort(ITEM[] a, int l, int r)
  {
    if (r-l <= M) return;
    exch(a, (l+r)/2, r-1);
    compExch(a, l, r-1);
      compExch(a, l, r);
        compExch(a, r-1, r);
    int i = partition(a, l+1, r-1);
    quicksort(a, l, i-1);
    quicksort(a, i+1, r);
  }
static void hybridsort(ITEM a[], int l, int r)
  { quicksort(a, l, r); insertion(a, l, r); }
```

---

sort. For the sort to take N^2 time, two out of the three elements examined must be among the largest or among the smallest elements in the file, and this event must happen consistently through most of the partitions. Second, it eliminates the need for a sentinel key for partitioning, because this function is served by one of the three elements that are examined before partitioning. Third, it reduces the total average running time of the algorithm by about 5 percent.

The combination of using the median-of-three method with a cutoff for small subfiles can improve the running time of quicksort over the naive recursive implementation by 20 to 25 percent. Program 7.4 is an implementation that incorporates all these improvements.

We might consider continuing to improve the program by removing recursion, replacing the subroutine calls by inline code, using sentinels, and so forth. However, on modern machines, such proce-

Table 7.1 Empirical study of basic quicksort algorithms

Quicksort (Program 7.1) is nearly three times faster than shellsort (Program 6.15) for large randomly ordered files. A cutoff for small subfiles and the median-of-three improvement (Program 7.4) further lower the running time.

N	shellsort	Basic quicksort			Median-of-three quicksort		
		$M = 3$	$M = 10$	$M = 20$	$M = 3$	$M = 15$	$M = 30$
12500	31	22	10	9	14	8	9
25000	42	19	19	19	21	19	19
50000	94	41	39	40	45	40	42
100000	214	88	85	90	97	84	88
200000	516	194	189	188	204	187	192
400000	1159	420	417	404	435	397	409
800000	2678	908	870	876	939	866	887

dure calls are normally efficient, and they are not in the inner loop. More important, the use of the cutoff for small subfiles tends to compensate for any extra overhead that may be involved (outside the inner loop). The primary reason to use a nonrecursive implementation with an explicit stack is to be able to provide guarantees on limiting the stack size (see Figure 7.10).

Further algorithmic improvements are possible (for example, we could use the median of five or more elements), but the amount of time gained will be marginal for random files. We *can* realize significant time savings by coding the inner loops (or the whole program) in assembly or machine language. These observations have been validated on numerous occasions by experts with serious sorting applications (*see reference section*).

For randomly ordered files, the first exchange in Program 7.4 is superfluous. We include it not just because it leads to optimal partitioning for files already in order but also because it protects against anomalous situations that might occur in practice (see, for example, Exercise 7.33).

Figure 7.10
Stack size for improved versions of quicksort

Sorting the smaller subfile first guarantees that the stack size will be logarithmic at worst. Plotted here are the stack sizes for the same files as in Figure 7.5, with the smaller of the subfiles sorted first during the sort (left) and with the median-of-three modification added (right). These diagrams are not indicative of running time; that variable depends on the size of the files on the stack, rather than only their number. For example, the third file (partially sorted) does not require much stack space, but leads to a slow sort because the subfiles being processed are usually large.

Figure 7.11
Dynamic characteristics of median-of-three quicksort on various types of files

The median-of three modification (particularly, using the middle element of the file) does a good job of making the partitioning process more robust. The degenerate types of files shown in Figure 7.4 are handled particularly well. Another option that achieves this same goal is to use a random partitioning element.

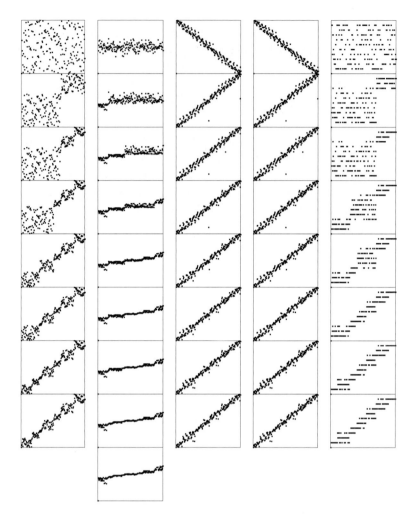

Figure 7.11 illustrates the effectiveness of involving the middle element in the partitioning decision, for files drawn from various distributions.

The median-of-three method is a special case of the general idea that we can sample an unknown file and use properties of the sample to estimate properties of the whole file. For quicksort, we want to estimate the median to balance the partitioning. It is the nature of the algorithm that we do not need a particularly good estimate (and may not want one if such an estimate is expensive to compute); we just want

to avoid a particularly bad estimate. If we use a random sample of just
one element, we get a randomized algorithm that is virtually certain to
run quickly, no matter what the input. If we randomly choose three
or five elements from the file, then use the median of that sample for
partitioning, we get a better partition, but the improvement is offset
by the cost of taking the sample.

Quicksort is widely used because it runs well in a variety of situations. Other methods might be more appropriate for particular cases
that might arise, but quicksort handles more types of sorting problems
than are handled by many other methods, and it is often significantly
faster than alternative approaches. Table 7.1 gives empirical results in
support of some of these comments.

Exercises

7.28 Our implementation of the median-of-three method is careful to ensure
that the sampled elements do not participate in the partitioning process. One
reason is that they can serve as sentinels. Give another reason.

7.29 Implement a quicksort based on partitioning on the median of a random
sample of five elements from the file. Make sure that the elements of the
sample do not participate in partitioning (see Exercise 7.28). Compare the
performance of your algorithm with the median-of-three method for large
random files.

7.30 Run your program from Exercise 7.29 on large nonrandom files—for
example, sorted files, files in reverse order, or files with all keys equal. How
does its performance for these files differ from its performance for random
files?

•• **7.31** Implement a quicksort based on using a sample of size $2^k - 1$. First,
sort the sample, then arrange to have the recursive routine partition on the
median of the sample and to move the two halves of the rest of the sample to
each subfile, such that they can be used in the subfiles, without having to be
sorted again. This algorithm is called *samplesort*.

•• **7.32** Run empirical studies to determine the best value of the sample size in
samplesort (see Exercise 7.31), for $N = 10^3, 10^4, 10^5$, and 10^6. Does it matter
whether quicksort or samplesort is used to sort the sample?

• **7.33** Show that Program 7.4, if changed to omit the first exchange and to
scan over keys equal to the partitioning element, runs in quadratic time on a
file that is in reverse order.

7.6 Duplicate Keys

Files with large numbers of duplicate sort keys arise frequently in applications. For example, we might wish to sort a large personnel file by year of birth, or even to use a sort to separate females from males.

When there are many duplicate keys present in the file to be sorted, the quicksort implementations that we have considered do not have unacceptably poor performance, but they can be substantially improved. For example, a file that consists solely of keys that are equal (just one value) does not need to be processed further, but our implementations so far keep partitioning down to small subfiles, no matter how big the file is (see Exercise 7.8). In a situation where there are large numbers of duplicate keys in the input file, the recursive nature of quicksort ensures that subfiles consisting solely of items with a single key value will occur often, so there is potential for significant improvement.

One straightforward idea is to partition the file into *three* parts, one each for keys smaller than, equal to, and larger than the partitioning element:

less than v	equal to v	greater than v

```
↑                    ↑                ↑              ↑
l                    j                i              r
```

Accomplishing this partitioning is more complicated than the two-way partitioning that we have been using, and various different methods have been suggested for the task. It was a classical programming exercise popularized by Dijkstra as the *Dutch National Flag problem*, because the three possible key categories might correspond to the three colors on the flag (*see reference section*). For quicksort, we add the constraint that a single pass through the file must do the job—an algorithm that involves two passes through the data would slow down quicksort by a factor of two, even if there are no duplicate keys at all.

A clever method invented by Bentley and McIlroy in 1993 for three-way partitioning works by modifying the standard partitioning scheme as follows: Keep keys equal to the partitioning element that are encountered in the left subfile at the left end of the file, and keep keys equal to the partitioning element that are encountered in the right subfile at the right end of the file. During the partitioning process, we maintain the following situation:

equal	less		greater	equal	v
↑	↑	↑ ↑	↑	↑
1	p	i j	q	r

Then, when the indices cross and the precise location for the equal keys is known, we swap into position all the items with keys equal to the partitioning element. This scheme does not quite meet the requirement that three-way partitioning be accomplished in one pass through the file, but the extra overhead for duplicate keys is proportional to only the number of duplicate keys found. This fact has two implications: First, the method works well even if there are no duplicate keys, since there is no extra overhead. Second, the method is linear time when there is only a constant number of key values: Each partitioning phase removes from the sort all the keys with the same value as the partitioning element, so each key can be involved in at most a constant number of partitions.

Figure 7.12 illustrates the three-way partitioning algorithm on a sample file, and Program 7.5 is a quicksort implementation based on the method. The implementation requires the addition of just two if statements in the exchange loop, and just two for loops to complete partitioning by putting the keys equal to the partitioning element into position. It seems to require less code than other alternatives for maintaining three partitions. More important, it not only handles duplicate keys in as efficient a manner as possible but also incurs a minimal amount of extra overhead in the case that there are no duplicate keys.

Exercises

▷ **7.34** Explain what happens when Program 7.5 is run on a randomly ordered file with (*i*) two distinct key values, and (*ii*) three distinct key values.

7.35 Modify Program 7.1 to return if all keys in the subfile are equal. Compare the performance of your program to Program 7.1 for large random files with keys having t distinct values for $t = 2, 5$, and 10.

7.36 Suppose that we scan over keys equal to the partitioning element in Program 7.2 instead of stopping the scans when we encounter them. Show that the running time of Program 7.1 would be quadratic in this case.

Figure 7.12
Three-way partitioning

This diagram depicts the process of putting all keys equal to the partitioning element into position. As in Figure 7.2, we scan from the left to find an element that is not smaller than the partitioning element and from the right to find an element that is not larger than the partitioning element, then exchange them. If the element on the left after the exchange is equal to the partitioning element, we exchange it to the left end of the array; we proceed similarly on the right. When the indices cross, we put the partitioning element into position as before (next-to-bottom line), then exchange all the keys equal to it into position on either side of it (bottom line).

Program 7.5 Quicksort with three-way partitioning

This program is based on partitioning the array into three parts: elements smaller than the partitioning element (in a[l], ... , a[j]); elements equal to the partitioning element (in a[j+1], ... , a[i-1]); and elements larger than the partitioning element (in a[i], ... , a[r]). Then the sort can be completed with two recursive calls.

To accomplish the objective, the program keeps keys equal to the partitioning element on the left between l and p and on the right between q and r. In the partitioning loop, after the scan indices stop and the items at i and j are exchanged, it checks each of those items to see whether it is equal to the partitioning element. If the one now on the left is equal to the partitioning element, it is exchanged into the left part of the array; if the one now on the right is equal to the partitioning element, it is exchanged into the right part of the array.

After the indices cross, the elements equal to the partitioning element are exchanged from the ends of the array into position. Then those keys can be excluded from the subfiles for the recursive calls.

If there are large numbers of equal keys anywhere in the file, one will eventually be chosen as a partitioning element and those keys will not be processed further once they are in position.

```
static void quicksort(ITEM a[], int l, int r)
  {
    if (r <= l) return;
    ITEM v = a[r];
    int i = l-1, j = r, p = l-1, q = r, k;
    for (;;)
      {
        while (less(a[++i], v)) ;
        while (less(v, a[--j])) if (j == l) break;
        if (i >= j) break;
        exch(a, i, j);
        if (equal(a[i], v)) { p++; exch(a, p, i); }
        if (equal(v, a[j])) { q--; exch(a, q, j); }
      }
    exch(a, i, r); j = i-1; i = i+1;
    for (k = l  ; k <= p; k++,j--) exch(a, k, j);
    for (k = r-1; k >= q; k--,i++) exch(a, k, i);
    quicksort(a, l, j);
    quicksort(a, i, r);
  }
```

● **7.37** Prove that the running time of the program in Exercise 7.36 is quadratic for all files with $O(1)$ distinct key values.

7.38 Write a program to determine the number of distinct keys that occur in a file. Use your program to count the distinct keys in random files of N integers in the range 0 to $M - 1$, for $M = 10, 100$, and 1000, and for $N = 10^3$, 10^4, 10^5, and 10^6.

7.7 Strings and Vectors

As discussed in Section 6.2, we can write an `ITEM` interface implementation to use the quicksort implementations in this chapter to sort records with string keys. This approach provides a correct and efficient implementation (faster than any other method we have seen so far, for large files), but there is a hidden cost that is interesting to consider.

The problem lies in the cost of comparing strings. The standard way to compares two strings is by proceeding from left to right, comparing the strings character by character, taking time proportional to the number of leading characters that match in the two strings. For the later partitioning stages of quicksort, when keys are close together, this match might be relatively long. As usual, because of the recursive nature of quicksort, nearly all the cost of the algorithm is incurred in the later stages, so examining improvements there is worthwhile.

For example, consider a subfile of size 5 containing the keys `discreet`, `discredit`, `discrete`, `discrepancy`, and `discretion`. All the comparisons used for sorting these keys examine at least seven characters, when it would suffice to start at the seventh character, if the extra information that the first six characters are equal were available.

The three-way partitioning procedure that we considered in Section 7.6 provides an elegant way to take advantage of this observation. At each partitioning stage, we examine just one character (say the one at position d), assuming that the keys to be sorted are equal in positions 0 through d-1. We do a three-way partition with keys whose dth character is smaller than the dth character of the partitioning element on the left, those whose dth character is equal to the dth character of the partitioning element in the middle, and those whose dth character is larger than the dth character of the partitioning element on the right. Then, we proceed as usual, *except* that we sort the middle sub-

---

Table 7.2 Empirical study of quicksort variants

This table gives relative costs for several different versions of quicksort on the task of sorting the first N words of *Moby Dick*. Using insertion sort directly for small subfiles, or ignoring them and insertion sorting the same file afterward, are equally effective strategies, but the cost savings is slightly more than for integer keys (see Table 7.1) because comparisons are more expensive for strings. If we do not stop on duplicate keys when partitioning, then the time to sort a file with all keys equal is quadratic; the effect of this inefficiency is noticeable on this example, because there are numerous words that appear with high frequency in the data. For the same reason, three-way partitioning is effective; it is 30 to 35 percent faster than Program 7.1.

N	V	I	M	X	T
12500	84	59	59	55	60
25000	146	117	130	136	107
50000	354	273	311	341	264
100000	916	756	772	975	626

Key:
  V   Quicksort (Program 7.1)
  I   Insertion sort for small subfiles
  M   Ignore small subfiles, insertion sort afterward
  X   Scan over duplicate keys (goes quadratic when keys all equal)
  T   Three-way partitioning (Program 7.5)

---

file, starting at character d+1. It is not difficult to see that this method leads to a proper sort on strings, which turns out to be very efficient (see Table 7.2). We have here a convincing example of the power of thinking (and programming) recursively.

To implement the sort, we need a more general abstract type that allows access to characters of keys. The way in which strings are handled in Java makes the implementation of this method particularly straightforward. However, we defer considering the implementation in detail until Chapter 10, where we consider a variety of techniques for sorting that take advantage of the fact that sort keys can often be easily decomposed into smaller pieces.

This approach generalizes to handle multidimensional sorts, where the sort keys are vectors and the records are to be rearranged such that the first components of the keys are in order, then those with first component equal are in order by second component, and so forth. If the components do not have duplicate keys, the problem reduces to sorting on the first component; in a typical application, however, each of the components may have only a few distinct values, and three-way partitioning (moving to the next component for the middle partition) is appropriate. This case was discussed by Hoare in his original paper and is an important application.

Exercises

7.39 Discuss the possibility of improving selection, insertion, bubble, and shell sorts for strings.

○ **7.40** How many characters are examined by the standard quicksort algorithm (Program 7.1, using a StringITEM class like Program 6.4, but with a String field for the key) when sorting a file consisting of N strings of length t, all of which are equal? Answer the same question for the modification proposed in the text.

7.8 Selection

An important application related to sorting but for which a full sort is not required is the operation of finding the median of a set of numbers. This operation is a common computation in statistics and in various other data-processing applications. One way to proceed would be to sort the numbers and to look at the middle one, but we can do better, using the quicksort partitioning process.

The operation of finding the median is a special case of the operation of *selection*: finding the kth smallest of a set of numbers. Because an algorithm cannot guarantee that a particular item is the kth smallest without having examined and identified the $k - 1$ elements that are smaller and the $N - k$ elements that are larger, most selection algorithms can return all the k smallest elements of a file without a great deal of extra calculation.

Selection has many applications in the processing of experimental and other data. The use of the median and other *order statistics* to divide a file into smaller groups is common. Often, only a small part of a large file is to be saved for further processing; in such cases, a

---

Program 7.6 Selection

This procedure partitions an array about the (k-1)th smallest element (the one in a[k]): It rearranges the array to leave a[1], ..., a[k-1] less than or equal to a[k], and a[k+1], ..., a[r] greater than or equal to a[k].

For example, we could call select(a, 0, N-1, N/2) to partition the array on the median value, leaving the median in a[N/2].

```
static void select(ITEM[] a, int l, int r, int k)
  {
    if (r <= l) return;
    int i = partition(a, l, r);
    if (i > k) select(a, l, i-1, k);
    if (i < k) select(a, i+1, r, k);
  }
```

```
A S O R T I N G E X A M P L E
A A E Ⓔ T I N G O X S M P L R
    L I N G O P M Ⓡ X T S
    L I G Ⓜ O P N
A A E E L I G Ⓜ O P N R X T S
```

Figure 7.13
Selection of the median

For the keys in our sorting example, partitioning-based selection uses only three recursive calls to find the median. On the first call, we seek the eighth smallest in a file of size 15, and partioning gives the fourth smallest (the E); so on the second call, we seek the fourth smallest in a file of size 11, and partitioning gives the eighth smallest (the R); so on the third call, we seek the fourth smallest in a file of size 7, and find it (the M). The file is rearranged such that the median is in place, with smaller elements to the left and larger elements to the right (equal elements could be on either side), but it is not fully sorted.

program that can select, say, the top 10 percent of the elements of the file might be more appropriate than a full sort. Another important example is the use of partitioning about the median as a first step in many divide-and-conquer algorithms.

We have already seen an algorithm that we can adapt directly to selection. If k is extremely small, then selection sort (see Chapter 6) will work well, requiring time proportional to Nk: first find the smallest element, then find the second smallest by finding the smallest of the remaining items, and so forth. For slightly larger k, we shall see methods in Chapter 9 that we could adapt to run in time proportional to $N \log k$.

A selection method that runs in linear time on the average for all values of k follows directly from the partitioning procedure used in quicksort. Recall that quicksort's partitioning method rearranges an array a[1], ..., a[r] and returns an integer i such that a[1] through a[i-1] are less than or equal to a[i], and a[i+1] through a[r] are greater than or equal to a[i]. If k is equal to i, then we are done. Otherwise, if k < i, then we need to continue working in the left subfile; if k > i, then we need to continue working in the right subfile. This approach leads immediately to the recursive program for selection that is Program 7.6. An example of this procedure in operation on a small file is given in Figure 7.13.

Program 7.7 Nonrecursive selection

A nonrecursive implementation of selection simply does a partition, then moves the left index in if the partition fell to the left of the position sought, or moves the right index in if the partition fell to the right of the position sought.

```
static void select(ITEM[] a, int l, int r, int k)
  {
    while (r > l)
      { int i = partition(a, l, r);
        if (i >= k) r = i-1;
        if (i <= k) l = i+1;
      }
  }
```

Program 7.7 is a nonrecursive version that follows directly from the recursive version in Program 7.6. Since that program always ends with a single call on itself, we simply reset the parameters and go back to the beginning. That is, we remove the recursion without needing a stack, also eliminating the calculations involving k by keeping k as an array index.

Property 7.4 *Quicksort-based selection is linear time on the average.*

As we did for quicksort, we can argue (roughly) that, on an extremely large file, each partition should roughly split the array in half, so the whole process should require about $N + N/2 + N/4 + N/8 + \ldots = 2N$ comparisons. And, as it was for quicksort, this rough argument is not far from the truth. An analysis similar to, but significantly more complex than, that given in Section 7.2 for quicksort (*see reference section*) leads to the result that the average number of comparisons is about

$$2N + 2k \ln(N/k) + 2(N - k) \ln(N/(N - k)),$$

which is linear for any allowed value of k. For $k = N/2$, this formula evaluates to give the result that about $(2 + 2 \ln 2)N$ comparisons are required to find the median. ∎

An example showing how this method finds the median in a large file is depicted in Figure 7.14. There is only one subfile, which is cut

Figure 7.14
Selection of the median by partitioning

The selection process involves partitioning the subfile that contains the element sought, moving the left index to the right or the right index to the left depending on where the partition falls.

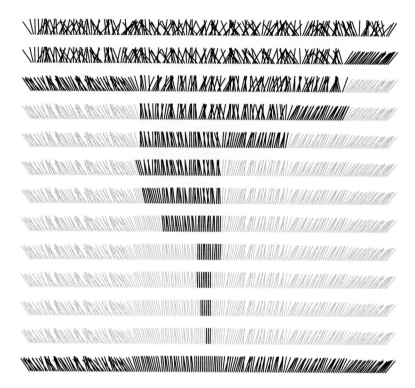

down in size by a constant factor on each call, so the procedure finishes in $O(\log N)$ steps. We can speed up the program with sampling, but we need to exercise care in doing so (see Exercise 7.45).

The worst case is about the same as for quicksort—using this method to find the smallest element in a file that is already in sorted order would result in a quadratic running time. It is possible to modify this quicksort-based selection procedure such that its running time is *guaranteed* to be linear. These modifications, although theoretically important, are extremely complex and not at all practical.

Exercises

7.41 About how many comparisons are required, on the average, to find the smallest of N elements using select?

7.42 About how many comparisons are required, on the average, to find the αNth smallest element using select, for $\alpha = 0.1, 0.2, \ldots, 0.9$?

7.43 How many comparisons are required in the worst case to find the median of N elements using select?

7.44 Write an efficient program to rearrange a file such that all the elements with keys equal to the median are in place, with smaller elements to the left and larger elements to the right.

•• **7.45** Investigate the idea of using sampling to improve selection. *Hint*: Using the median may not always be helpful.

• **7.46** Implement a selection algorithm based on three-way partitioning for large random files with keys having t distinct values for $t = 2$, 5, and 10.

CHAPTER EIGHT

Merging and Mergesort

T HE QUICKSORT FAMILY of algorithms that we studied in
Chapter 7 are based on the *selection* operation—finding the kth
smallest element in a file. We saw that performing selection is akin to
dividing a file into two parts, the k smallest elements and the $N - k$
largest elements. In this chapter, we examine a family of sorting algorithms based on a complementary process, *merging*—combining two
ordered files to make one larger ordered file. Merging is the basis
for a straightforward divide-and-conquer (see Section 5.2) sorting algorithm and for a bottom-up counterpart, both of which are easy to
implement.

Selection and merging are complementary operations in the sense
that selection splits a file into two independent files, whereas merging
joins two independent files to make one file. The contrast between
these operations also becomes evident when we apply the divide-and-
conquer paradigm to create a sorting method. We can rearrange the
file such that, when two parts are sorted, the whole file is ordered;
alternatively, we can break the file into two parts to be sorted and then
combine the ordered parts to make the whole ordered file. We have
already seen what happens in the first instance: that is quicksort, which
consists of a selection procedure followed by two recursive calls. In this
chapter, we shall look at *mergesort*, which is quicksort's complement in
that it consists of two recursive calls followed by a merging procedure.

One of mergesort's most attractive properties is that it sorts a file
of N elements in time proportional to $N \log N$, no matter what the
input. In Chapter 9, we shall see another algorithm that is guaranteed
to finish in time proportional to $N \log N$; it is called *heapsort*. The

prime disadvantage of mergesort is that extra space proportional to N is needed in straightforward implementations. We can overcome this handicap, but doing so is sufficiently complicated and costly that it is generally not worthwhile in practice, particularly in light of the heapsort alternative. Mergesort is no more difficult to code than is heapsort, and the length of the inner loop is between those of quicksort and heapsort, so mergesort is worth considering if speed is of the essence, bad worst-case performance cannot be tolerated, and extra space is available.

A guaranteed $N \log N$ running time can be a liability. For example, in Chapter 6, we saw that there are methods that can adapt to run in linear time in certain special situations, such as when there is a significant amount of order in the file, or when there are only a few distinct keys. By contrast, the running time of mergesort depends primarily on only the number of input keys and is virtually insensitive to their order.

Mergesort is a stable sort, and this feature tips the balance in its favor for applications where stability is important. Competitive methods such as quicksort and heapsort are not stable. Various techniques to make such methods stable tend to require extra space; mergesort's extra-space requirement thus becomes less significant if stability is a prime consideration.

Another feature of mergesort that is important in certain situations is that mergesort is normally implemented such that it accesses the data primarily sequentially (one item after the other). For example, mergesort is the method of choice for sorting a linked list, where sequential access is the only kind of access available. For similar reasons, as we shall see in Chapter 11, merging is often chosen as the basis for sorting on special-purpose and high-performance machines, because it is often the case that sequential access to data is fastest in such environments.

8.1 Two-Way Merging

Given two ordered input files, we can combine them into one ordered output file simply by keeping track of the smallest element in each file and entering a loop where the smaller of the two elements that are smallest in their files is moved to the output, continuing until both

Program 8.1 Merging

To combine two ordered arrays a and b into an ordered array c, we use a for loop that puts an element into c at each iteration. If a is exhausted, the element comes from b; if b is exhausted, the element comes from a; and if items remain in both, the smallest of the remaining elements in a and b goes to c. Beyond the implicit assumptions that the arrays are ordered and sufficiently large to be indexed as indicated, this implementation assumes that the array c is disjoint from (that is, does not overlap or share storage with) a and b.

```
static void mergeAB(ITEM[] c, int cl,
                    ITEM[] a, int al, int ar,
                    ITEM[] b, int bl, int br )
  { int i = al, j = bl;
    for (int k = cl; k < cl+ar-al+br-bl+1; k++)
      {
        if (i > ar) { c[k] = b[j++]; continue; }
        if (j > br) { c[k] = a[i++]; continue; }
        c[k] = less(a[i], b[j]) ? a[i++] : b[j++];
      }
  }
```

input files are exhausted. We shall look at several implementations of this basic abstract operation in this and the next section. The running time is linear in the number of elements in the output, as long as we can perform the operation of finding the next smallest element in a file in constant time, which is certainly the case for files that are in sorted order and represented with a data structure that supports constant-time sequential access, such as an array or a linked list. This procedure is *two-way merging*; in Chapter 11, we shall look in detail at *multiway merging*, when more than two files are involved. The most important application of multiway merging is external sorting, which is discussed in detail in that chapter.

To begin, let us suppose that we have two disjoint ordered arrays a[0], ..., a[N-1] and b[0], ..., b[M-1] of integers that we wish to merge into a third array c[0], ... , c[N+M-1]. The obvious strategy, which is easily implemented, is to choose successively for c the smallest remaining element from a and b, as shown in Program 8.1. This implementation is simple, but it has two important characteristics that we shall now examine.

First, the implementation assumes that the arrays are disjoint. In particular, if a and b are huge arrays, then a third (also huge) array c is needed to hold the output. Instead of using extra space proportional to the size of the merged file, it would be desirable to have an in-place method so that, for example, we could combine the ordered files a[1], ..., a[m] and a[m+1], ..., a[r] into a single ordered file by moving the elements around within a[1], ..., a[r], without using a significant amount of other extra space. It is a worthwhile exercise to pause momentarily to consider how we might do that. This problem seems to be one that must be simple to solve; actually, however, the solutions that are known are complicated, especially by comparison to Program 8.1. Indeed, it is not easy to develop an algorithm for in-place merging that can outperform the alternative of using an in-place *sort*. We shall return to this issue in Section 8.2.

Merging has specific applications in its own right. For example, in a typical data-processing environment, we might need to maintain a large (ordered) data file, to which we will need to regularly add new entries. One approach is to *batch* each group of new entries—append them to the (much larger) main file, then resort the whole file. This situation is tailor-made for merging: A much more efficient strategy is to sort the (small) batch of new entries, then merge the resulting small file with the large main file. Merging has many other similar applications that make its study worthwhile. Our prime interest in this chapter will be the sorting methods that are based on merging.

Exercises

8.1   Suppose that an ordered file of size N is to be combined with an unordered file of size M, with M much smaller than N. Assume that you have a sorting program that takes about $c_1 N \lg N$ seconds to sort a file of size N and a merging program that takes about $c_2(N + M)$ seconds to merge a file of size N with one of size M, with $c_1 \approx c_2$. How many times faster than resorting is the suggested merge-based method, as a function of M, for $N = 10^3$, 10^6, and 10^9?

8.2   How does the strategy of using insertion sort for the whole file compare with the two methods postulated in Exercise 8.1? Assume that the small file is random, so each insertion goes about halfway into the large file, and the running time is about $c_3 M N/2$, with c_3 approximately the same as the other constants.

8.3   Describe what happens if you try to use Program 8.1 for an in-place merge, by using the call merge(a, 0, a, 0, N/2, a, (N/2)+1, N) for the keys A E Q S U Y E I N O S T.

○ **8.4**   Does Program 8.1, called as described in Exercise 8.3, produce proper output if and only if the two input subarrays are in sorted order? Prove your answer, or provide a counterexample.

8.2 Abstract In-Place Merge

Although implementing a merge seems to require extra space, we still find the *abstraction* of an in-place merge useful in the implementations of sorting methods that we examine here. In our next implementation of merging, we shall emphasize this point by using the method signature merge(a, l, m, r) to indicate that the merge subroutine will put the result of merging a[l], ..., a[m] and a[m+1], ..., a[r] into a single ordered file, leaving the result in a[l], ..., a[r]. We could implement this merge routine by first copying everything to an auxiliary array and then using the basic method of Program 8.1; instead we shall consider an improvement to that approach. Although the extra *space* for the auxiliary array seems to be a fixed practical cost, we shall consider in Section 8.4 further improvements that allow us to avoid the extra *time* required to copy the array.

The second characteristic of the basic merge that is worthy of note is that the inner loop includes two tests to determine whether the ends of the two input arrays have been reached. Of course, these two tests usually fail, and the situation thus cries out for the use of sentinel keys to allow the tests to be removed. That is, if elements with a key value larger than those of all the other keys are added to the ends of the a and aux arrays, the tests can be removed, because when the a (b) array is exhausted, the sentinel causes the next elements for the c array to be taken from the b (a) array until the merge is complete.

As we saw in Chapters 6 and 7, however, it is not always easy to use sentinels, either because it might not be easy to know the largest key value or because space might not be available conveniently. For merging, there is a simple remedy, which is illustrated in Figure 8.1. The method is based on the following idea: Given that we are resigned to copying the arrays to implement the in-place abstraction, we simply put the second array in reverse order when it is copied (at no extra cost),

Figure 8.1
Merging without sentinels

To merge two ascending files, we copy into an auxiliary array, with the second file in reverse order immediately following the first. Then, we follow this simple rule: Move the left or right item, whichever has the smaller key, to the output. The largest key serves as a sentinel for the other file, no matter in which file the key is. This figure illustrates how the files A R S T and G I N are merged.

Program 8.2 Abstract in-place merge

This program merges without using sentinels by copying the second
array into the auxiliary array aux in reverse order back to back with the
first (putting aux in *bitonic* order). The first for loop moves the first
array and leaves i at l, ready to begin the merge. The second for loop
moves the second array, and leaves j at r. Then, in the merge (the third
for loop), the largest element serves as the sentinel in whichever array
it is. The inner loop of this program is short (move to aux, compare,
move back to a, increment i or j, increment and test k).

```
static void merge(ITEM[] a, int l, int m, int r)
  { int i, j;
    for (i = m+1; i > l; i--) aux[i-1] = a[i-1];
    for (j = m; j < r; j++) aux[r+m-j] = a[j+1];
    for (int k = l; k <= r; k++)
      if (less(aux[j], aux[i]))
          a[k] = aux[j--]; else a[k] = aux[i++];
  }
```

---

so that its associated index moves from right to left. This arrangement
leads to the largest element—in whichever array it is—serving as sentinel for the other array. Program 8.2 is an efficient implementation
of the abstract in-place merge based on this idea; it serves as the basis
for the sorting algorithms that we discuss later in this chapter. It still
uses an auxiliary array of size proportional to the merge output, but
it is more efficient than the straightforward implementation because it
avoids the tests for the ends of the arrays.

A sequence of keys that increases, then decreases (or decreases,
then increases) is referred to as a *bitonic* sequence. Sorting bitonic
sequences is equivalent to merging, but it is sometimes convenient to
cast a merging problem as a bitonic sorting problem; this method of
avoiding sentinel tests is a simple example.

An important property of Program 8.1 is that the merge is stable:
It preserves the relative order of duplicate keys. This characteristic is
easy to verify, and it is often worth making sure that stability is maintained when we implement an abstract in-place merge, because a stable
merge leads immediately to stable *sorting* methods, as we shall see in
Section 8.3. It is not always easy to maintain stability: for example,

Program 8.2 is not stable (see Exercise 8.6). This consideration further complicates the problem of developing a true in-place merge.

Exercises

▷ **8.5** Show how the keys A E Q S U Y E I N O S T are merged using Program 8.2, in the style of the example diagrammed in Figure 8.1.

○ **8.6** Explain why Program 8.2 is not stable, and develop a version that is stable.

8.7 What is the result when Program 8.2 is used for the keys E A S Y Q U E S T I O N?

○ **8.8** Does Program 8.2 produce proper output if and only if the two input subarrays are in sorted order? Prove your answer, or provide a counterexample.

8.3 Top-Down Mergesort

Once we have a merging procedure, it is not difficult to use that procedure as the basis for a recursive sorting procedure. To sort a given file, we divide it in half, recursively sort the two halves, and then merge them. An implementation is given in Program 8.3; an example is depicted in Figure 8.2. As mentioned in Chapter 5, this algorithm is one of the best-known examples of the utility of the *divide-and-conquer* paradigm for efficient algorithm design.

Top-down mergesort is analogous to a top-down management style, where a manager gets an organization to take on a big task by dividing it into pieces to be solved independently by underlings. If each manager operates by simply dividing the given task in half, then putting together the solutions that the subordinates develop and passing the result up to a superior, the result is a process like mergesort. Not much real work gets done until someone with no subordinates gets a task (in this case, merging two files of size 1); but management does much of the work, putting together solutions.

Mergesort is important because it is a straightforward optimal sorting method (it runs in time proportional to $N \log N$) that can be implemented in a stable manner. These facts are relatively easy to prove.

As we have seen in Chapter 5 (and, for quicksort, in Chapter 7), we can use tree structures to help us to visualize the recursive call

A S O R T I N G E X A M P L E
A S
    O R
A O R S
      I T
        G N
      G I N T
A G I N O R S T
          E X
            A M
          A E M X
              L P
              E L P
          A E E L M P X
A A E E G I L M N O P R S T X

Figure 8.2
Top-down mergesort example

Each line shows the result of a call on merge *during top-down merge- sort. First, we merge A and S to get A S; then, we merge O and R to get O R; then, we merge O R with A S to get A O R S. Later, we merge I T with G N to get G I N T, then merge this result with A O R S to get A G I N O R S T, and so on. The method recursively builds up small sorted files into larger ones.*

Program 8.3 Top-down mergesort

This basic mergesort implementation is a prototypical divide-and-conquer recursive program. It sorts the array a[l], ..., a[r] by dividing it into two parts a[l], ..., a[m] and a[m+1], ..., a[r], sorting them independently (via recursive calls), and merging the resulting ordered subfiles to produce the final ordered result.

It is convenient to consider the merge operation as an abstract in-place merge (see text) that is implemented, for example, by Program 8.2. To avoid excessive allocation costs, the auxiliary array aux that is used by Program 8.2 should be a private member of a class that includes these methods (such as, for example, Program 6.3).

```
static void mergesort(ITEM[] a, int l, int r)
  { if (r <= l) return;
    int m = (r+l)/2;
    mergesort(a, l, m);
    mergesort(a, m+1, r);
    merge(a, l, m, r);
  }
```

structure of a recursive algorithm, to help us to understand variants of the algorithm, and to expedite the analysis of the algorithm. For mergesort, the recursive call structure depends only upon the size of the input. For any given N, we define a tree, called a *divide-and-conquer tree*, that describes the sizes of the subfiles that are processed during the operation of Program 8.3 (see Exercise 5.73): If N is 1, the tree is a single node with label 1; otherwise, the tree is a node containing the file size N as the root, the tree for $\lfloor N/2 \rfloor$ as the left subtree, and the tree for $\lceil N/2 \rceil$ as the right subtree. Each node in the tree thus corresponds to a call on mergesort, with the label giving the problem size corresponding to the recursive call. When N is a power of 2, this construction leads to a complete balanced tree with powers of 2 in all the nodes and 1s in all the external nodes. When N is not a power of 2, the tree is more complicated. Examples of both cases are illustrated in Figure 8.3. We have enountered such trees before, when considering an algorithm with the same recursive call structure as mergesort, in Section 5.2.

Structural properties of divide-and-conquer trees are directly relevant to the analysis of mergesort. For example, the total number of

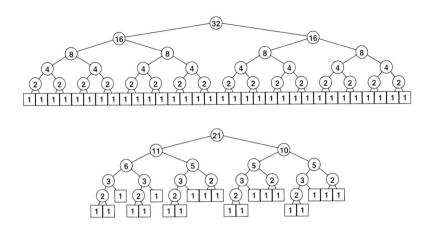

Figure 8.3
Divide-and-conquer trees

These tree diagrams depict the sizes of the subproblems created by top-down mergesort. Unlike the trees corresponding to quicksort, for example, these patterns are dependent on only the initial file size, rather than on the values of the keys in the file. The top diagram shows how a file of 32 elements is sorted. We (recursively) sort two files of 16 elements, then merge them. We sort the files of 16 elements by (recursively) sorting files of 8 elements, and so forth. For file sizes that are not a power of 2, the pattern is more intricate, as indicated by the bottom diagram.

comparisons used by the algorithm is precisely the sum of all the node labels.

Property 8.1 *Mergesort requires about $N \lg N$ comparisons to sort any file of N elements.*

In the implementations in Sections 8.1 and 8.2, each $(N/2)$-by-$(N/2)$ merge will require N comparisons (this amount could vary by 1 or 2, depending on how sentinels are used). The total number of comparisons for the full sort is therefore described by the standard divide-and-conquer recurrence: $M_N = M_{\lfloor N/2 \rfloor} + M_{\lceil N/2 \rceil} + N$, with $M_1 = 0$. The recurrence also describes the sum of the node labels and the external path length of a divide-and-conquer tree with N nodes (see Exercise 5.73). The stated result is easy to verify when N is a power of 2 (see Formula 2.4) and to prove by induction for general N. Exercises 8.12 through 8.14 describe a direct proof. ∎

Property 8.2 *Mergesort uses extra space proportional to N.*

This fact is clear from the discussion in Section 8.2. We can take some steps to reduce the extra space used at the expense of making the algorithm considerably more complicated (for example, see Exercise 8.21). As we shall see in Section 8.7, mergesort is also effective when the file to be sorted is organized as a linked list. In this case, the property still holds, but the extra space is used for the links. For arrays, as we noted in Section 8.2 and shall discuss in Section 8.4, it is possible to do merges in place, although this strategy is unlikely to be worthwhile in practice. ∎

Property 8.3 *Mergesort is stable, if the underlying merge is stable.*

This fact is easy to verify by induction. For merge implementations such as Program 8.1, it is easy to show that the relative position of duplicate keys is undisturbed by merging. However, the more intricate the algorithm, the higher the chance that stability is disturbed (see Exercise 8.6). ∎

Property 8.4 *The resource requirements of mergesort are insensitive to the initial order of its input.*

In our implementations, the input determines only the order in which elements are processed in the merges. Each pass requires space and a number of steps proportional to the subfile size, because of the costs of moving to the auxiliary array. The two branches of `if` statements may take slightly different amounts of time in the compiled code, which could lead to a slight input-dependent variation in running time, but the number of comparisons and other operations on the input is not dependent on how it is ordered. Note that this is *not* the same as saying that the algorithm is nonadaptive (see Section 6.1)—the sequence of comparisons does depend on the input order. ∎

Exercises

▷ **8.9** Show, in the style of Figure 8.2, the sequence of merges that Program 8.3 does to sort the keys E A S Y Q U E S T I O N.

8.10 Draw divide-and-conquer trees for $N = 16, 24, 31, 32, 33$, and 39.

• **8.11** Implement a recursive mergesort on arrays, using the idea of doing *three-way*, rather than two-way, merges.

○ **8.12** Prove that all the nodes labeled 1 in a divide-and-conquer tree are on the bottom two levels.

○ **8.13** Prove that the labels on the nodes on each level in the divide-and-conquer tree of size N sum to N, except possibly for the bottom level.

○ **8.14** Using Exercises 8.12 and 8.13, prove that the number of comparisons required by mergesort is between $N \lg N$ and $N \lg N + N$.

• **8.15** Find and prove a relationship between the number of comparisons used by mergesort and the number of bits in the $\lceil \lg N \rceil$-bit positive numbers less than N.

8.4 Improvements to the Basic Algorithm

As we saw with quicksort, we can improve most recursive algorithms by handling small cases differently. The recursion guarantees that the method will be used often for small cases, so improvements in handling them lead to improvements in the whole algorithm. Thus, just as it did with quicksort, switching to insertion sort for small subfiles will improve the running time of a typical mergesort implementation by 10 to 15 percent.

A second improvement that is reasonable to consider for mergesort is to eliminate the time taken to copy to the auxiliary array used for merging. To do so, we arrange the recursive calls such that the computation switches the roles of the input array and the auxiliary array at each level. One way to proceed is to implement two versions of the routines—one taking its input in aux and its output in a, and the other taking its input in a and its output in aux—then have the two versions call each other. A different approach is shown in Program 8.4, which makes one copy of the array at the beginning, then uses Program 8.1 and switches arguments in the recursive calls to eliminate the explicit array copy operation. Instead, we switch back and forth between putting the merged output in the auxiliary array and putting it in the input array. (This program is a tricky one.)

This technique eliminates the array copy at the expense of putting back into the inner loop the tests for whether the input arrays are exhausted. (Recall that our technique for eliminating those tests in Program 8.2 involved making the array bitonic during the copy.) That loss can be regained via a recursive implementation of the same idea: We implement routines for both merge and mergesort, one each for putting arrays in increasing order and in decreasing order. With this strategy, it is possible to bring back the bitonic strategy and thus to arrange that the inner loop for the merge never needs sentinels.

Given that it uses up to four copies of the basic routines and some mindbending recursive argument switchery, this superoptimization is only recommended for experts (or students!), but it does speed up mergesort considerably. The experimental results that we discuss in Section 8.6 indicate that the combination of all these improvements speeds up mergesort by a factor of about 40 percent but still leaves mergesort about 25 percent slower than quicksort. These numbers

---

Program 8.4 Mergesort with no copying

This recursive program is set up to sort b, leaving the result in a. Thus, the recursive calls are written to leave their result in b, and we use Program 8.1 to merge those files from b into a. In this way, all the data movement is done during the course of the merges.

```
static ITEM[] aux;
static void mergesortABr
              (ITEM[] a, ITEM[] b, int l, int r)
  { if (r <= l) return;
    int m = (r+l)/2;
    mergesortABr(b, a, l, m);
    mergesortABr(b, a, m+1, r);
    mergeAB(a, l, b, l, m, b, m+1, r);
  }
static void mergesortAB(ITEM[] a, int l, int r)
  {
    aux = new ITEM[a.length];
    for (int i = l; i <= r; i++) aux[i] = a[i];
    mergesortABr(a, aux, l, r);
  }
```

---

are dependent on the implementation and on the machine, but similar results are likely in a variety of situations.

Other implementations of merging that involve an explicit test for the first file being exhausted may lead to a greater (but not much) variation of running time depending on the input. In random files, the size of the other subfile when the first subfile exhausts will be small, and the cost of moving to the auxiliary array still will be proportional to the subfile size. We might consider improving the performance of mergesort when a great deal of order is present in the file by skipping the call on merge when the file is already in sorted order, but this strategy is not effective for many types of files.

Exercises

8.16 Implement an abstract in-place merge that uses extra space proportional to the size of the smaller of the two arrays to be merged. (Your method should cut in half the space requirement for mergesort.)

8.17 Run mergesort for large random files, and make an empirical determination of the average length of the other subfile when the first subfile exhausts, as a function of N (the sum of the two subfile sizes for a given merge).

8.18 Suppose that Program 8.3 is modified to skip the call on `merge` when `a[m]<a[m+1]`. How many comparisons does this alternative save when the file to be sorted is already in sorted order?

8.19 Run the modified algorithm suggested in Exercise 8.18 for large random files. Determine empirically the average number of times the merge is skipped, as a function of N (the original file size for the sort).

8.20 Suppose that mergesort is to be run on h-sorted files for small h. How would you change the `merge` routine to take advantage of this property of the input? Experiment with shellsort–mergesort hybrids based on this routine.

8.21 Develop a merge implementation that reduces the extra space requirement to $\max(M, N/M)$, based on the following idea. Divide the array into N/M blocks of size M (for simplicity in this description, assume that N is a multiple of M). Then, (i) considering the blocks as records with their first key as the sort key, sort them using selection sort; and (ii) run through the array merging the first block with the second, then the second block with the third, and so forth.

8.22 Prove that the method of Exercise 8.21 runs in linear time.

8.23 Implement bitonic mergesort with no copying.

8.5 Bottom-Up Mergesort

As we discussed in Chapter 5, every recursive program has a non-recursive analog that, although equivalent, may perform computations in a different order. As prototypes of the divide-and-conquer algorithm-design philosophy, nonrecursive implementations of mergesort are worth studying in detail.

Consider the sequence of merges done by the recursive algorithm. In the example given in Figure 8.2, we saw that a file of size 15 is sorted by the following sequence of merges:

1-by-1	1-by-1	2-by-2	1-by-1	1-by-1	2-by-2	4-by-4
1-by-1	1-by-1	2-by-2	1-by-1	2-by-1	4-by-3	8-by-7

This order of the merges is determined by the recursive structure of the algorithm. However, the subfiles are processed independently, and merges can be done in different sequences. Figure 8.4 shows

> **Program 8.5 Bottom-up mergesort**
>
> Bottom-up mergesort consists of a sequence of passes over the whole file doing m-by-m merges, doubling m on each pass. The final subfile is of size m only if the file size is an even multiple of m, so the final merge is an m-by-x merge, for some x less than or equal to m.
>
> ```
> static int min(int A, int B)
>   { return (A < B) ? A : B; }
> static void mergesort(ITEM[] a, int l, int r)
>   { if (r <= l) return;
>     aux = new ITEM[a.length];
>     for (int m = 1; m <= r-l; m = m+m)
>       for (int i = l; i <= r-m; i += m+m)
>         merge(a, i, i+m-1, min(i+m+m-1, r));
>   }
> ```

A S O R T I N G E X A M P L E
A S
    O R
        I T
            G N
                E X
                    A M
                        L P
A O R S
        G I N T
            A E M X
                    E L P
A G I N O R S T
                A E E L M P X
A A E E G I L M N O P R S T X

Figure 8.4
Bottom-up mergesort example

Each line shows the result of a call on merge *during bottom-up merge-sort. The 1-by-1 merges are done first: A and S are merged to give A S; then, O and R are merged to give O R; and so forth. Since the file size is odd, the last E is not involved in a merge. On the second pass, the 2-by-2 merges are done: We merge A S with O R to get A O R S, and so forth, finishing with a 2-by-1 merge. The sort is completed with a 4-by-4 merge, a 4-by-3 merge, and, finally, an 8-by-7 merge.*

the bottom-up strategy for the same example, where the sequence of merges is

1-by-1	1-by-1	1-by-1	1-by-1	1-by-1	1-by-1	1-by-1
2-by-2	2-by-2	2-by-2	2-by-1	4-by-4	4-by-3	8-by-7

In both cases, there are seven 1-by-1 merges, three 2-by-2 merges, a 2-by-1 merge, a 4-by-4 merge, a 4-by-3 merge, and an 8-by-7 merge, but the merges are done in different orders. The bottom-up strategy is to merge the smallest remaining files, passing from left to right through the array.

The sequence of merges done by the recursive algorithm is determined by the divide-and-conquer tree shown in Figure 8.3: We simply traverse the tree in postorder. As we saw in Chapter 3, a nonrecursive algorithm using an explicit stack can be developed that gives the same sequence of merges. But there is no need to restrict to postorder: *Any* tree traversal that traverses the subtrees of a node before it visits the node itself will give a proper algorithm. The only restriction is that files to be merged must have been sorted first. For mergesort, it is convenient to do all the 1-by-1 merges first, then all the 2-by-2 merges, then all the 4-by-4 merges, and so forth. This sequence corresponds to a level-order traversal, working up from the bottom of the recursion tree.

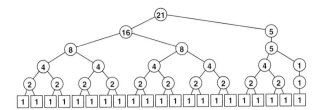

Figure 8.5
Bottom-up mergesort file sizes

The merging patterns for bottom-up mergesort are completely different from those for top-down mergesort (Figure 8.3) when the file size is not a power of 2. For bottom-up mergesort, all file sizes except possibly the final one are a power of 2. These differences are of interest in understanding the basic structure of the algorithms, but have little influence on performance.

We saw in several examples in Chapter 5 that, when we are thinking in a bottom-up fashion, it is worthwhile to reorient our thinking towards a combine-and-conquer strategy, where we take solutions to small subproblems and combine them to get a solution to a larger problem. Specifically, we get the combine-and-conquer nonrecursive version of mergesort in Program 8.5 as follows: We view all the elements in a file as ordered sublists of size 1. Then, we scan through the list performing 1-by-1 merges to produce ordered sublists of size 2; then, we scan through the list performing 2-by-2 merges to produce ordered sublists of size 4; then, we do 4-by-4 merges to get ordered sublists of size 8; and so on, until the whole list is ordered. The final sublist will not always be the same size as all of the others unless the file size is a power of 2, but we can still merge it in.

If the file size is a power of 2, the *set* of merges done by bottom-up mergesort is precisely the same as that done by the recursive mergesort, but the *sequence* of merges is different. Bottom-up mergesort corresponds to a *level-order* traversal of the divide-and-conquer tree, from bottom to top. By contrast, we have referred to the recursive algorithm as *top-down mergesort* because the postorder traversal works from the top of the tree down.

If the file size is not a power of 2, the bottom-up algorithm does a different set of merges, as shown in Figure 8.5. The bottom-up algorithm corresponds to a combine-and-conquer tree (see Exercise 5.75), which is different from the divide-and-conquer tree related to the top-down algorithm. It is possible to arrange for the sequence of merges made by a recursive method to be the same as that for a nonrecursive method, but there is no particular reason to do so, because differences in cost are slight relative to total cost.

Properties 8.1 through 8.4 hold for bottom-up mergesort, and we have the following additional properties.

Figure 8.6
Bottom-up mergesort

We need to do only seven passes to sort a file of 200 elements using bottom-up mergesort. Each pass halves the number of sorted subfiles and doubles the subfiles' lengths (except possibly that of the final one).

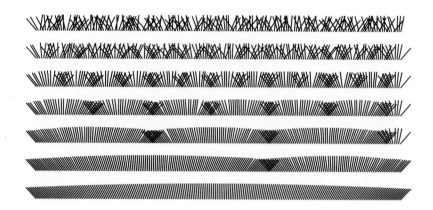

Property 8.5 *All the merges in each pass of a bottom-up mergesort involve file sizes that are a power of 2, except possibly the final file size.*

This fact is easy to prove by induction. ∎

Property 8.6 *The number of passes in a bottom-up mergesort of N elements is precisely the number of bits in the binary representation of N (ignoring leading 0 bits).*

Each pass in a bottom-up mergesort doubles the size of the ordered subfiles, so the size of the sublists after k passes is 2^k. Thus, the number of passes to sort a file of N elements is the smallest k for which $2^k \geq N$, which is precisely $\lceil \lg N \rceil$, the number of bits in the binary representation of N. We could also prove this result by induction or by analyzing structural properties of combine-and-conquer trees. ∎

The operation of bottom-up mergesort on a larger file is illustrated in Figure 8.6. We can sort 1 million elements in 20 passes through the data, 1 billion elements in 30 passes through the data, and so forth.

In summary, bottom-up and top-down mergesort are two straightforward sorting algorithms that are based upon the operation of merging two ordered subfiles into a combined ordered output file. The algorithms are closely related and indeed perform the same set of merges when the file size is a power of 2, but they are certainly not identical. Figure 8.7 is an illustration of their differing dynamic performance characteristics on a large file. Either algorithm might be used for practical applications when space is not at premium and a guaranteed worst-case running time is desirable. Both algorithms are of interest as prototypes of the general *divide-and-conquer* and *combine-and-conquer* algorithm design paradigms.

Exercises

8.24 Show the merges that bottom-up mergesort (Program 8.5) does for the keys E A S Y Q U E S T I O N.

8.25 Implement a bottom-up mergesort that starts by sorting blocks of M elements with insertion sort. Determine empirically the value of M for which your program runs fastest to sort random files of N elements, for $N = 10^3$, 10^4, 10^5, and 10^6.

8.26 Draw trees that summarize the merges that Program 8.5 performs, for $N = 16, 24, 31, 32, 33,$ and 39.

8.27 Write a recursive mergesort that performs the same merges that bottom-up mergesort does.

8.28 Write a bottom-up mergesort that performs the same merges that top-down mergesort does. (This exercise is much more difficult than is Exercise 8.27.)

8.29 Suppose that the file size is a power of 2. Remove the recursion from top-down mergesort to get a nonrecursive mergesort that performs the same *sequence* of merges.

8.30 Prove that the number of passes taken by top-down mergesort is *also* the number of bits in the binary representation of N (see Property 8.6).

8.6 Performance Characteristics of Mergesort

Table 8.1 shows the relative effectiveness of the various improvements that we have examined. As is often the case, these studies indicate that we can cut the running time by half or more when we focus on improving the inner loop of the algorithm.

In addition to netting the improvements discussed in Section 8.2, a good Java VM implementation might avoid unnecessary array accesses to reduce the inner loop of mergesort to a comparison (with conditional branch), two index increments (k and either i or j), and a test with conditional branch for loop completion. The total number of instructions in such an inner loop is slightly higher than that for quicksort, but the instructions are executed only $N \lg N$ times, where quicksort's are executed 39 percent more often (or 29 percent with the

Figure 8.7
Bottom-up versus top-down mergesort

Bottom-up mergesort (left) consists of a series of passes through the file that merge together sorted subfiles, until just one remains. Every element in the file, except possibly a few at the end, is involved in each pass. By contrast, top-down mergesort (right) sorts the first half of the file before proceeding to the second half (recursively), so the pattern of its progress is decidedly different.

Table 8.1 Empirical study of mergesort algorithms

These relative timings for various sorts on random files of integers indicate that standard quicksort is about twice as fast as standard mergesort; that adding a cutoff for small files lowers the running times of both bottom-up and top-down mergesort by about 15 percent; that top-down mergesort is about 10 percent faster than bottom-up mergesort for these file sizes; and that even eliminating the cost of the file copy (the method used in the Java system sort) leaves mergesort substantially slower than quicksort for randomly ordered files.

N	Q	top-down			bottom-up		S
		T	T*	O	B	B*	
12500	23	27	16	19	30	20	19
25000	20	43	34	27	42	36	28
50000	45	91	79	52	92	77	56
100000	95	199	164	111	204	175	117
200000	201	421	352	244	455	396	256
400000	449	904	764	520	992	873	529
800000	927	1910	1629	1104	2106	1871	1119

Key:
- Q Quicksort, standard (Program 7.1)
- T Top-down mergesort, standard (Program 8.1)
- T* Top-down mergesort with cutoff for small files
- O Top-down mergesort with cutoff and no array copy
- B Bottom-up mergesort, standard (Program 8.5)
- B* Bottom-up mergesort with cutoff for small files
- S `java.util.Arrays.sort`

median-of-three modification). Careful implementation and detailed analysis are required for more precise comparison of the algorithms in particular environments; nonetheless, we do know that mergesort has an inner loop that is slightly longer than that of quicksort.

As usual, we must add the caveat that pursuit of improvements of this nature, although irresistible to many programmers, can sometimes lead to marginal gains and should be taken on only after more important considerations have been resolved. In this case, mergesort

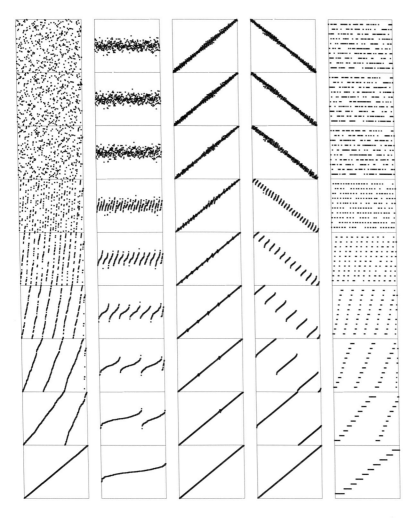

Figure 8.8
Sorting of various types of files with bottom-up mergesort

The running time for mergesort is insensitive to the input. These diagrams illustrate that the number of passes taken by bottom-up mergesort for files that are random, Gaussian, nearly ordered, nearly reverse ordered, and randomly ordered with 10 distinct key values (left to right) *depends only on the file size, no matter what the input values are. This behavior is in sharp contrast to that of quicksort and to that of many other algorithms.*

has the clear advantages over quicksort that it is stable and is guaranteed to run fast (no matter what the input), and the clear disadvantage that it uses extra space proportional to the size of the array. If these factors point to the use of mergesort (and speed is important), then the improvements that we have suggested may be worth considering, along with careful study of VM performance, the use of native C code, special properties of the machine architecture, and so forth.

On the other hand, we must also add the usual caveat that programmers should always have one eye on performance in order to avoid costs that are completely unnecessary. All programmers (and authors!) have suffered the embarrassment of having a simple unnoticed characteristic of an implementation dominate all that implementation's other sophisticated mechanisms. It is not unusual for a factor-of-2 improvement in running time to be found when implementations are examined carefully in this way. Frequent testing is the most effective defense against last-minute surprises of this type.

We discussed these points at length in Chapter 5, but the allure of premature optimization is so strong that it is worthwhile to reinforce them each time that we study techniques for performance improvement at this level of detail. For mergesort, we are comfortable with optimizing because Properties 8.1 through 8.4 essentially characterize the performance and hold for all the implementations that we have examined: Their running time is proportional to $N \log N$ and is insensitive to the input (see Figure 8.8); they use extra space; and they can be implemented in a stable manner. Maintaining these while improving the running time is generally not difficult.

Exercises

8.31 Implement bottom-up mergesort with no array copy.

8.32 Develop a three-level hybrid sort that uses quicksort, mergesort, and insertion sort to get a method that is as fast as the most efficient quicksort (even on small files) but can guarantee better than quadratic performance in the worst case.

8.7 Linked-List Implementations of Mergesort

Extra space appears to be required for a practical implementation of mergesort, so we may as well consider a linked-list implementation. In other words, rather than use the extra space for an auxiliary array, we can use it for links. We can build a general-purpose sort along these lines, or we might well be presented with the problem of sorting a linked list in the first place (see Section 6.9). In fact, mergesort turns out to be well-suited to linked lists. A full implementation of the merge method for linked lists is given in Program 8.6. Note that the code for the actual merge is just about as simple as the code for array-based merge (Program 8.2).

Given this merge method, a top-down mergesort is easy to derive. Program 8.7 is a direct recursive implementation of a method that takes

---

Program 8.6 Linked-list merge

This program merges the list referenced by a with the list referenced by
b, with the help of an auxiliary reference variable c. The key comparison
in merge includes equality, so that the merge will be stable, if the b list is
considered to follow the a list. For simplicity, we adopt the convention
that all lists end with 0. Other conventions for ending the list would
work as well (see Table 3.1). More important, we do *not* use list head
nodes, in order to avoid proliferation of them.

```
static Node merge(Node a, Node b)
  { Node dummy = new Node();
    Node head = dummy, c = head;
    while ((a != null) && (b != null))
      if (less(a.item, b.item))
        { c.next = a; c = a; a = a.next; }
      else
        { c.next = b; c = b; b = b.next; }
    c.next = (a == null) ? b : a;
    return head.next;
  }
```

---

as input a reference to an unordered list and returns a reference to a
list comprising the same elements, in sorted order. The program does
its work by rearranging the nodes of the list: No temporary nodes or
lists need to be allocated. Program 8.7 uses a trick to find the middle
of the list: alternative implementations might do so either by passing
the list length as a parameter to the recursive program or by storing
the length with the list. This program is simple to understand in a
recursive formulation, even though it is a sophisticated algorithm.

We can also use a bottom-up combine-and-conquer approach
for linked-list mergesort, although details of keeping track of links
make this implementation more challenging than it might seem. As
we discussed when considering bottom-up array-based methods in
Section 8.5, there is no particular reason to adhere precisely to the set
of merges performed by the recursive or array-based versions when we
are developing a bottom-up list mergesort.

An amusing version of bottom-up linked-list mergesort suggests
itself that is simple to explain: Put the items in a *circular* list, then

Program 8.7 Top-down list mergesort

This program sorts by splitting the list referenced by c into two halves referenced by a and b, sorting the two halves recursively, and then using merge (Program 8.6) to produce the final result. The input list must end with null (and therefore so does the b list), and the explicit instruction c.next = null puts null at the end of the a list.

```
static Node mergesort(Node c)
  {
    if (c == null || c.next == null) return c;
    Node a = c, b = c.next;
    while ((b != null) && (b.next != null))
      { c = c.next; b = (b.next).next; }
    b = c.next; c.next = null;
    return merge(mergesort(a), mergesort(b));
  }
```

proceed through the list, merging together pairs of ordered subfiles until done. This method is conceptually simple, but (as with most low-level programs involving linked lists) it can be tricky to implement (see Exercise 8.36). Another version of bottom-up linked-list mergesort that is based on the same idea is given in Program 8.8: keep all the lists to be merged on a queue ADT. This method is also conceptually simple, but (as with many high-level programs involving ADTs) it can *also* be tricky to implement. But it does offer an excellent example of the use of an ADT abstraction to support a higher-level computation.

One important feature of this method is that it method takes advantage of any order that might be already present in the file. Indeed, the number of passes through the list is not $\lceil \lg N \rceil$, but rather is $\lceil \lg S \rceil$, where S is the number of ordered subfiles in the original array. Mergesorts with this property are sometimes called *natural* mergesorts. For random files, natural mergesorts offer no great advantage, because only a pass or two is likely to be saved (in fact, the method is likely to be slower than the top-down method, because of the extra cost of checking for order in the file), but it is not uncommon for a file to consist of blocks of ordered subfiles, and this method will be effective in such situations.

Program 8.8 Bottom-up list mergesort

This program uses a queue ADT (Program 4.18) to implement a bottom-up mergesort. Queue elements are ordered linked lists. After initializing the queue with lists of length 1, the program simply removes two lists from the queue, merges them, and puts the result back on the queue, continuing until there is only one list. This corresponds to a sequence of passes through all the elements, doubling the length of the ordered lists on each pass, as in bottom-up mergesort.

```
static Node mergesort(Node t)
  {
    NodeQueue Q = new NodeQueue();
    if (t == null || t.next == null) return t;
    for (Node u = null; t != null; t = u)
      { u = t.next; t.next = null; Q.put(t); }
    t = Q.get();
    while (!Q.empty())
      { Q.put(t); t = merge(Q.get(), Q.get()); }
    return t;
  }
```

Exercises

• **8.33** Develop an implementation of top-down list mergesort that carries the list length as a parameter to the recursive procedure and uses it to determine how to split the lists.

• **8.34** Develop an implementation of top-down list mergesort that works with lists that carry their length in header nodes and uses the lengths to determine how to split the lists.

8.35 Add a cutoff for small subfiles to Program 8.7. Determine the extent to which proper choice of the cutoff value speeds up the program.

○ **8.36** Implement bottom-up mergesort using a circular linked list, as described in the text.

8.37 Add a cutoff for small subfiles to your bottom-up circular-list mergesort from Exercise 8.36. Determine the extent to which proper choice of the cutoff value speeds up the program.

8.38 Add a cutoff for small subfiles to Program 8.8. Determine the extent to which proper choice of the cutoff value speeds up the program.

○ **8.39** Draw combine-and-conquer trees that summarize the merges that Program 8.8 performs, for $N = 16, 24, 31, 32, 33,$ and 39.

8.40 Draw combine-and-conquer trees that summarize the merges that circular-list mergesort (Exercise 8.38) performs, for $N = 16$, 24, 31, 32, 33, and 39.

8.41 Run empirical studies to develop a hypothesis about the number of ordered subfiles in an array of N random 32-bit integers.

• **8.42** Empirically determine the number of passes needed in a natural mergesort for random 64-bit keys with $N = 10^3$, 10^4, 10^5, and 10^6. *Hint*: You do not need to implement a sort (or even generate full 64-bit keys) to complete this exercise.

• **8.43** Convert Program 8.8 into a natural mergesort, by initially populating the queue with the ordered subfiles that occur in the input.

○ **8.44** Implement an array-based natural mergesort.

8.8 Recursion Revisited

The programs of this chapter, and quicksort from the previous chapter, are typical of implementations of divide-and-conquer algorithms. We shall see several algorithms with similar structure in later chapters, so it is worthwhile to take a more detailed look at basic characteristics of these implementations.

Quicksort might perhaps more properly be called a *conquer-and-divide* algorithm: In a recursive implementation, most of the work for a particular activation is done *before* the recursive calls. On the other hand, the recursive mergesort has more the spirit of divide and conquer: First, the file is divided into two parts; then, each part is conquered individually. The first problem for which mergesort does processing is a small one; at the finish, the largest subfile is processed. Quicksort starts with processing on the largest subfile and finishes up with the small ones. It is amusing to contrast the algorithms in the context of the management analogy mentioned at the beginning of this chapter: quicksort corresponds to each manager investing effort to make the right decision on how to divide up the task, so the job is complete when the subtasks are done, whereas mergesort corresponds to each manager making a quick arbitrary choice to divide the task in half, then needing to work to cope with the consequences after the subtasks are done.

This difference is manifest in the nonrecursive implementations. Quicksort must maintain a stack, because it has to save large subproblems that are divided up in a data-dependent manner. Mergesort admits a simple nonrecursive version because the way in which it divides the file is independent of the data, so we can rearrange the order in which it processes subproblems to give a simpler program.

We might argue that quicksort is more naturally thought of as a top-down algorithm, because it does work at the top of the recursion tree, then proceeds down to finish the sort. We could contemplate a nonrecursive quicksort that traverses the recursion tree in level order from top to bottom. Thus, a sort makes multiple passes through the array, partitioning files into smaller subfiles. For arrays, this method is not practical, because of the bookkeeping cost of keeping track of the subfiles; for linked lists, it is analogous to bottom-up mergesort.

We have noted that mergesort and quicksort differ on the issue of stability. For mergesort, if we assume that the subfiles have been sorted stably, then we need be sure only that the merge is done in a stable manner, which is easy to arrange. The recursive structure of the algorithm leads immediately to an inductive proof of stability. For an array-based implementation of quicksort, no easy way of doing the partitioning in a stable manner suggests itself, so the possibility of stability is foreclosed even before the recursion comes into play. The straightforward implementation of quicksort for linked lists is, however, stable (see Exercise 7.4).

As we saw in Chapter 5, algorithms with one recursive call reduce to a loop, but algorithms with two recursive calls, like mergesort and quicksort, open up the world of divide-and-conquer algorithms and tree structures, where many of our best algorithms are found. Mergesort and quicksort are worthy of careful study, not just because of their practical importance as sorting algorithms but also because of the insights they give into the nature of recursion, which can serve us well in developing and understanding other recursive algorithms.

Exercises

• **8.45** Suppose that mergesort is implemented to split the file at a *random* position, rather than exactly in the middle. How many comparisons are used by such a method to sort N elements, on the average?

• **8.46** Study the performance of mergesort when it is sorting strings. How many character comparisons are involved when a large file is sorted, on the average?

• **8.47** Run empirical studies to compare the performance of quicksort for linked lists (see Exercise 7.4) and top-down mergesort for linked lists (Program 8.7).

CHAPTER NINE

Priority Queues and Heapsort

MANY APPLICATIONS REQUIRE that we process records with keys in order, but not necessarily in full sorted order and not necessarily all at once. Often, we collect a set of records, then process the one with the largest key, then perhaps collect more records, then process the one with the current largest key, and so forth. An appropriate data structure in such an environment supports the operations of inserting a new element and deleting the largest element. Such a data structure is called a *priority queue*. Using priority queues is similar to using queues (remove the oldest) and stacks (remove the newest), but implementing them efficiently is more challenging. The priority queue is the most important example of the generalized queue ADT that we discussed in Section 4.7. In fact, the priority queue is a proper generalization of the stack and the queue, because we can implement these data structures with priority queues, using appropriate priority assignments (see Exercises 9.3 and 9.4).

Definition 9.1   A **priority queue** *is a data structure of items with keys which supports two basic operations: insert a new item, and remove the item with the largest key.*

Applications of priority queues include simulation systems, where the keys might correspond to event times, to be processed in chronological order; job scheduling in computer systems, where the keys might correspond to priorities indicating which users are to be served first; and numerical computations, where the keys might be computational errors, indicating that the largest should be dealt with first.

We can use any priority queue as the basis for a sorting algorithm by inserting all the records, then successively removing the largest to get the records in reverse order. Later on in this book, we shall see how to use priority queues as building blocks for more advanced algorithms. In Part 5, we shall see how priority queues are an appropriate abstraction for helping us understand the relationships among several fundamental graph-searching algorithms; and in Part 6, we shall develop a file-compression algorithm using routines from this chapter. These are but a few examples of the important role played by the priority queue as a basic tool in algorithm design.

In practice, priority queues are more complex than the simple definition just given, because there are several other operations that we may need to perform to maintain them under all the conditions that might arise when we are using them. Indeed, one of the main reasons that many priority-queue implementations are so useful is their flexibility in allowing client application programs to perform a variety of different operations on sets of records with keys. We want to build and maintain a data structure containing records with numerical keys (*priorities*) that supports some of the following operations:

- *Construct* a priority queue from N given items.
- *Insert* a new item.
- *Remove the maximum* item.
- *Change the priority* of an arbitrary specified item.
- *Remove* an arbitrary specified item.
- *Join* two priority queues into one large one.

If records can have duplicate keys, we take "maximum" to mean "any record with the largest key value." As with many data structures, we also need to add a standard *test if empty* operation and perhaps a *copy* (clone) operation to this set.

There is overlap among these operations, and it is sometimes convenient to define other, similar operations. For example, certain clients may need frequently to *find the maximum* item in the priority queue, without necessarily removing it. Or, we might have an operation to *replace the maximum* item with a new item. We could implement operations such as these using our two basic operations as building blocks: *Find the maximum* could be *remove the maximum* followed by *insert*, and *replace the maximum* could be either *insert* followed by *remove the maximum* or *remove the maximum* followed by *insert*. We

---

Program 9.1 Basic priority-queue ADT

This interface defines operations for the simplest type of priority queue: initialize, test if empty, add a new item, remove the largest item. Elementary implementations of these methods using arrays and linked lists can require linear time in the worst case, but we shall see implementations in this chapter where all operations are guaranteed to run in time at most proportional to the logarithm of the number of items in the queue. The constructor's parameter specifies the maximum number of items expected in the queue and may be ignored by some implementations.

```
class PQ // ADT interface
  { // implementations and private members hidden
    PQ(int)
    boolean empty()
    void insert(ITEM)
    ITEM getmax()
  };
```

---

normally get more efficient code, however, by implementing such operations directly, provided that they are needed and precisely specified. Precise specification is not always as straightforward as it might seem. For example, the two options just given for *replace the maximum* are quite different: the former always makes the priority queue grow temporarily by one item, and the latter always puts the new item on the queue. Similarly, the *change priority* operation could be implemented as a *remove* followed by an *insert*, and *construct* could be implemented with repeated uses of *insert*.

For some applications, it might be slightly more convenient to switch around to work with the *minimum*, rather than with the maximum. We stick primarily with priority queues that are oriented toward accessing the maximum key. When we do need the other kind, we shall refer to it (a priority queue that allows us to *remove the minimum* item) as a *minimum-oriented* priority queue.

The priority queue is a prototypical *abstract data type (ADT)* (see Chapter 4): It represents a well-defined set of operations on data, and it provides a convenient abstraction that allows us to separate applications programs (clients) from various implementations that we will consider in this chapter. The interface given in Program 9.1 defines the most basic priority-queue operations; we shall consider a more complete interface in Section 9.5. Strictly speaking, different subsets of the various operations that we might want to include lead to different abstract data structures, but the priority queue is essentially characterized by the *remove-the-maximum* and *insert* operations, so we shall focus on them.

Different implementations of priority queues afford different performance characteristics for the various operations to be performed, and different applications need efficient performance for different sets of operations. Indeed, performance differences are, in principle, the *only* differences that can arise in the abstract-data-type concept. This situation leads to cost tradeoffs. In this chapter, we consider a variety of ways of approaching these cost tradeoffs, nearly reaching the ideal of being able to perform the *remove the maximum* operation in logarithmic time and all the other operations in constant time.

First, in Section 9.1, we illustrate this point by discussing a few elementary data structures for implementing priority queues. Next, in Sections 9.2 through 9.4, we concentrate on a classical data structure called the *heap*, which allows efficient implementations of all the operations but *join*. In Section 9.4, we also look at an important sorting algorithm that follows naturally from these implementations. In Sections 9.5 and 9.6, we look in more detail at some of the problems involved in developing complete priority-queue ADTs. Finally, in Section 9.7, we examine a more advanced data structure, called the *binomial queue*, that we use to implement all the operations (including *join*) in worst-case logarithmic time.

During our study of all these various data structures, we shall bear in mind both the basic tradeoffs dictated by linked versus sequential memory allocation (as introduced in Chapter 3) and the problems involved with making packages usable by applications programs. In particular, some of the advanced algorithms that appear later in this book are client programs that make use of priority queues.

Exercises

▷ **9.1** A letter means *insert* and an asterisk means *remove the maximum* in the sequence

P R I O * R * * I * T * Y * * * Q U E * * * U * E.

Give the sequence of values returned by the *remove the maximum* operations.

▷ **9.2** Add to the conventions of Exercise 9.1 a plus sign to mean *join* and parentheses to delimit the priority queue created by the operations within them. Give the contents of the priority queue after the sequence

$$(((P R I O *) + (R * I T * Y *)) * * *) + (Q U E * * * U * E).$$

∘ **9.3** Explain how to use a priority queue ADT to implement a stack ADT.

∘ **9.4** Explain how to use a priority queue ADT to implement a queue ADT.

9.1 Elementary Implementations

The basic data structures that we discussed in Chapter 3 provide us with numerous options for implementing priority queues. Program 9.2 is an implementation that uses an unordered array as the underlying data structure. The *find the maximum* operation is implemented by scanning the array to find the maximum, then exchanging the maximum item with the last item and decrementing the queue size. Figure 9.1 shows the contents of the array for a sample sequence of operations. This basic implementation corresponds to similar implementations that we saw in Chapter 4 for stacks and queues (see Programs 4.7 and 4.17) and is useful for small queues. The significant difference has to do with performance. For stacks and queues, we were able to develop implementations of all the operations that take constant time; for priority queues, it is easy to find implementations where *either* the *insert* or the *remove the maximum* operations takes constant time, but finding an implementation where *both* operations will be fast is a more difficult task, and it is the subject of this chapter.

We can use unordered or ordered sequences, implemented as linked lists or as arrays. The basic tradeoff between leaving the items unordered and keeping them in order is that maintaining an ordered sequence allows for constant-time *remove the maximum* and *find the maximum* but might mean going through the whole list for *insert*, whereas an unordered sequence allows a constant-time *insert* but might mean going through the whole sequence for *remove the maximum* and *find the maximum*. The unordered sequence is the prototypical *lazy* approach to this problem, where we defer doing work until necessary (to find the maximum); the ordered sequence is the prototypical *eager* approach to the problem, where we do as much work as we can up front (keep the list sorted on insertion) to make later operations efficient. We can use an array or linked-list representation in either case, with the basic tradeoff that the (doubly) linked list allows a

```
B       B
E       B E
*   E   B
S       B S
T       B S T
I       B S T I
*   T   B S I
N       L S I N
*   S   B N I
F       B N I F
I       B N I F I
R       B N I F I R
*   R   B N I F I
S       B N I F I S
T       B N I F I S T
*   T   B N I F I S
*   S   B N I F I
O       B N I F I O
U       B N I F I O U
*   U   B N I F I O
T       B N I F I O T
*   T   B N I F I O
*   O   B N I F I
*   N   B I I F
*   I   B F I
*   I   B F
*   F   B
*   B
```

Figure 9.1
Priority-queue example (unordered array representation)

This sequence shows the result of the sequence of operations in the left column (top to bottom), where a letter denotes insert *and an asterisk denotes* remove the maximum. *Each line displays the operation, the letter removed for the remove-the-maximum operations, and the contents of the array after the operation.*

Program 9.2 Array implementation of a priority queue

This implementation, which may be compared with the array implementations for stacks and queues that we considered in Chapter 4 (see Programs 4.7 and 4.17), keeps the items in an unordered array. Items are added to and removed from the end of the array, as in a stack.

```
class PQ
  {
    static boolean less(ITEM v, ITEM w)
      { return v.less(w); }
    static void exch(ITEM[] a, int i, int j)
      { ITEM t = a[i]; a[i] = a[j]; a[j] = t; }
    private ITEM[] pq;
    private int N;
    PQ(int maxN)
      { pq = new ITEM[maxN]; N = 0; }
    boolean empty()
      { return N == 0; }
    void insert(ITEM item)
      { pq[N++] = item; }
    ITEM getmax()
      { int max = 0;
        for (int j = 1; j < N; j++)
          if (less(pq[max], pq[j])) max = j;
        exch(pq, max, N-1);
        return pq[--N];
      }
  };
```

constant-time *remove* (and, in the unordered case, *join*), but requires more space for the links.

The worst-case costs of the various operations (within a constant factor) on a priority queue of size N for various implementations are summarized in Table 9.1.

Developing a full implementation requires paying careful attention to the interface—particularly to how client programs access nodes for the *remove* and *change priority* operations, and how they access priority queues themselves as data types for the *join* operation. These

Table 9.1 Worst-case costs of priority-queue operations

Implementations of the priority queue ADT have widely varying performance characteristics, as indicated in this table of the worst-case time
(within a constant factor for large N) for various methods. Elementary
methods (first four lines) require constant time for some operations and
linear time for others; more advanced methods guarantee logarithmic-
or constant-time performance for most or all operations.

	insert	remove maximum	remove	find maximum	change priority	join
ordered array	N	1	N	1	N	N
ordered list	N	1	1	1	N	N
unordered array	1	N	1	N	1	N
unordered list	1	N	1	N	1	1
heap	$\lg N$	$\lg N$	$\lg N$	1	$\lg N$	N
binomial queue	$\lg N$	$\lg N$	$\lg N$	$\lg N$	$\lg N$	$\lg N$
best in theory	1	$\lg N$	$\lg N$	1	1	1

issues are discussed in Sections 9.4 and 9.7, where two full implementations are given: one using doubly linked unordered lists, and another
using binomial queues.

The running time of a client program using priority queues depends not just on the keys but also on the mix of the various operations.
It is wise to keep in mind the simple implementations because they
often can outperform more complicated methods in many practical
situations. For example, the unordered-list implementation might be
appropriate in an application where only a few *remove the maximum*
operations are performed, as opposed to a huge number of insertions,
whereas an ordered list would be appropriate if a huge number of *find
the maximum* operations are involved, or if the items inserted tend to
be larger than those already in the priority queue.

Exercises

▷ **9.5** Criticize the following idea: To implement *find the maximum* in constant time, why not keep track of the maximum value inserted so far, then
return that value for *find the maximum*?

▷ **9.6** Give the contents of the array after the execution of the sequence of operations depicted in Figure 9.1.

9.7 Provide an implementation for the basic priority-queue interface that uses an ordered array for the underlying data structure.

9.8 Provide an implementation for the basic priority-queue interface that uses an unordered linked list for the underlying data structure. *Hint*: See Programs 4.8 and 4.16.

9.9 Provide an implementation for the basic priority-queue interface that uses an ordered linked list for the underlying data structure. *Hint*: See Program 3.11.

○ **9.10** Consider a lazy implementation where the list is ordered only when a *remove the maximum* or a *find the maximum* operation is performed. Insertions since the previous sort are kept on a separate list, then are sorted and merged in when necessary. Discuss advantages of such an implementation over the elementary implementations based on unordered and ordered lists.

• **9.11** Write a performance driver client program that uses `insert` to fill a priority queue, then uses `getmax` to remove half the keys, then uses `insert` to fill it up again, then uses `getmax` to remove all the keys, doing so multiple times on random sequences of keys of various lengths ranging from small to large; measures the time taken for each run; and prints out or plots the average running times.

• **9.12** Write a performance driver client program that uses `insert` to fill a priority queue, then does as many `getmax` and `insert` operations as it can do in 1 second, doing so multiple times on random sequences of keys of various lengths ranging from small to large; and prints out or plots the average number of `getmax` operations it was able to do.

9.13 Use your client program from Exercise 9.12 to compare the unordered-array implementation in Program 9.2 with your unordered-list implementation from Exercise 9.8.

9.14 Use your client program from Exercise 9.12 to compare your ordered-array and ordered-list implementations from Exercises 9.7 and 9.9.

• **9.15** Write an exercise driver client program that uses the methods in our priority-queue interface Program 9.1 on difficult or pathological cases that might turn up in practical applications. Simple examples include keys that are already in order, keys in reverse order, all keys the same, and sequences of keys having only two distinct values.

9.16 (This exercise is 24 exercises in disguise.) Justify the worst-case bounds for the four elementary implementations that are given in Table 9.1, by reference to the implementation in Program 9.2 and your implementations from Exercises 9.7 through 9.9 for *insert* and *remove the maximum*; and by informally describing the methods for the other operations. For *remove*, *change priority*, and *join*, assume that you have a handle that gives you direct access to the referent.

9.2 Heap Data Structure

The main topic of this chapter is a simple data structure called the *heap* that can efficiently support the basic priority-queue operations. In a heap, the records are stored in an array such that each key is guaranteed to be larger than the keys at two other specific positions. In turn, each of those keys must be larger than two more keys, and so forth. This ordering is easy to see if we view the keys as being in a binary tree structure with edges from each key to the two keys known to be smaller.

Definition 9.2 *A tree is* **heap-ordered** *if the key in each node is larger than or equal to the keys in all of that node's children (if any). Equivalently, the key in each node of a heap-ordered tree is smaller than or equal to the key in that node's parent (if any).*

Property 9.1 *No node in a heap-ordered tree has a key larger than the key at the root.*

We could impose the heap-ordering restriction on any tree. It is particularly convenient, however, to use a *complete binary tree*. Recall from Chapter 3 that we can draw such a structure by placing the root node and then proceeding down the page and from left to right, connecting two nodes beneath each node on the previous level until N nodes have been placed. We can represent complete binary trees sequentially within an array by simply putting the root at position 1, its children at positions 2 and 3, the nodes at the next level in positions 4, 5, 6 and 7, and so on, as illustrated in Figure 9.2.

Definition 9.3 *A* **heap** *is a set of nodes with keys arranged in a complete heap-ordered binary tree, represented as an array.*

We could use a linked representation for heap-ordered trees, but complete trees provide us with the opportunity to use a compact array representation where we can easily get from a node to its parent and children without needing to maintain explicit links. The parent of the node in position i is in position $\lfloor i/2 \rfloor$, and, conversely, the two children of the node in position i are in positions $2i$ and $2i + 1$. This arrangement makes traversal of such a tree even easier than if the tree were implemented with a linked representation, because, in a linked representation, we would need to have three links associated with each key to allow travel up and down the tree (each element would have

```
 1 2 3 4 5 6 7 8 9 10 11 12
 X T O G S M N A E R  A  I
```

Figure 9.2
Array representation of a heap-ordered complete binary tree

Considering the element in position $\lfloor i/2 \rfloor$ in an array to be the parent of the element in position i, for $2 \le i \le N$ (or, equivalently, considering the ith element to be the parent of the $2i$th element and the $(2i + 1)$st element), corresponds to a convenient representation of the elements as a tree. This correspondence is equivalent to numbering the nodes in a complete binary tree (with nodes on the bottom as far left as possible) in level order. A tree is heap-ordered if the key in any given node is greater than or equal to the keys of that node's children. A heap is an array representation of a complete heap-ordered binary tree. The ith element in a heap is larger than or equal to both the $2i$th and the $(2i + 1)$st elements.

one pointer to its parent and one to each child). Complete binary trees represented as arrays are rigid structures, but they have just enough flexibility to allow us to implement efficient priority-queue algorithms.

We shall see in Section 9.3 that we can use heaps to implement all the priority-queue operations (except *join*) such that they require logarithmic time in the worst case. The implementations all operate along some path inside the heap (moving from parent to child toward the bottom or from child to parent toward the top, but not switching directions). As we discussed in Chapter 3, all paths in a complete tree of N nodes have about $\lg N$ nodes on them: there are about $N/2$ nodes on the bottom, $N/4$ nodes with children on the bottom, $N/8$ nodes with grandchildren on the bottom, and so forth. Each generation has about one-half as many nodes as the next, and there are at most $\lg N$ generations.

We can also use explicit linked representations of tree structures to develop efficient implementations of the priority-queue operations. Examples include triply linked heap-ordered complete trees (see Section 9.5), tournaments (see Program 5.19), and binomial queues (see Section 9.7). As with simple stacks and queues, one important reason to consider linked representations is that they free us from having to know the maximum queue size ahead of time, as is required with an array representation. In certain situations, we also can make use of the flexibility provided by linked structures to develop efficient algorithms. Readers who are inexperienced with using explicit tree structures are encouraged to read Chapter 12 to learn basic methods for the even more important symbol-table ADT implementation before tackling the linked tree representations discussed in the exercises in this chapter and in Section 9.7. However, careful consideration of linked structures can be reserved for a second reading, because our primary topic in this chapter is the heap (linkless array representation of the heap-ordered complete tree).

Exercises

▷ **9.17** Is an array that is sorted in descending order a heap?

○ **9.18** The largest element in a heap must appear in position 1, and the second largest element must be in position 2 or position 3. Give the list of positions in a heap of size 15 where the kth largest element (*i*) can appear, and (*ii*) cannot appear, for $k = 2, 3, 4$ (assuming the values to be distinct).

● **9.19** Answer Exercise 9.18 for general k, as a function of N, the heap size.

• **9.20** Answer Exercises 9.18 and 9.19 for the *k*th *smallest* element.

9.3 Algorithms on Heaps

The priority-queue algorithms on heaps all work by first making a simple modification that could violate the heap condition, then traveling through the heap, modifying the heap as required to ensure that the heap condition is satisfied everywhere. This process is sometimes called *heapifying*, or just *fixing* the heap. There are two cases. When the priority of some node is increased (or a new node is added at the bottom of a heap), we have to travel *up* the heap to restore the heap condition. When the priority of some node is decreased (for example, if we replace the node at the root with a new node), we have to travel *down* the heap to restore the heap condition. First, we consider how to implement these two basic methods; then, we see how to use them to implement the various priority-queue operations.

If the heap property is violated because a node's key becomes larger than that node's parent's key, then we can make progress toward fixing the violation by exchanging the node with its parent. After the exchange, the node is larger than both its children (one is the old parent, and the other is smaller than the old parent because it was a child of that node) but may still be larger than its parent. We can fix that violation in the same way, and so forth, moving up the heap until we reach a node with a larger key, or the root. An example of this process is shown in Figure 9.3. The code is straightforward, based on the notion that the parent of the node at position k in a heap is at position k/2. Program 9.3 is an implementation of a method that restores a possible violation due to increased priority at a given node in a heap by moving up the heap.

If the heap property is violated because a node's key becomes smaller than one or both of that node's childrens' keys, then we can make progress toward fixing the violation by exchanging the node with the larger of its two children. This switch may cause a violation at the child; we fix that violation in the same way, and so forth, moving down the heap until we reach a node with both children smaller, or the bottom. An example of this process is shown in Figure 9.4. The code again follows directly from the fact that the children of the node at position k in a heap are at positions 2k and 2k+1. Program 9.4 is an

Program 9.3 Bottom-up heapify

To restore the heap condition when an item's priority is increased, we move up the heap, exchanging the item at position k with its parent (at position k/2) if necessary, continuing as long as the item at position k/2 is less than the node at position k or until we reach the top of the heap. The methods less and exch compare and exchange (respectively) the items at the heap indices specified by their parameters (see Program 9.5 for implementations).

```
private void swim(int k)
  {
    while (k > 1 && less(k/2, k))
      { exch(k, k/2); k = k/2; }
  }
```

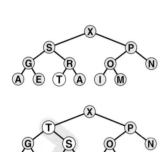

Figure 9.3
Bottom-up heapify (swim)

The tree depicted on the top is heap-ordered except for the node T on the bottom level. If we exchange T with its parent, the tree is heap-ordered, except possibly that T may be larger than its new parent. Continuing to exchange T with its parent until we encounter the root or a node on the path from T to the root that is larger than T, we can establish the heap condition for the whole tree. We can use this procedure as the basis for the insert *operation on heaps in order to reestablish the heap condition after adding a new element to a heap (at the rightmost position on the bottom level, starting a new level if necessary).*

implementation of a method that restores a possible violation due to increased priority at a given node in a heap by moving down the heap. This method needs to know the size of the heap (N) in order to be able to test when it has reached the bottom.

These two operations are independent of the way that the tree structure is represented, as long as we can access the parent (for the bottom-up method) and the children (for the top-down method) of any node. For the bottom-up method, we move up the tree, exchanging the key in the given node with the key in its parent until we reach the root or a parent with a larger (or equal) key. For the top-down method, we move down the tree, exchanging the key in the given node with the largest key among that node's children, moving down to that child, and continuing down the tree until we reach the bottom or a point where no child has a larger key. Generalized in this way, these operations apply not just to complete binary trees but also to any tree structure. Advanced priority-queue algorithms usually use more general tree structures but rely on these same basic operations to maintain access to the largest key in the structure, at the top.

If we imagine the heap to represent a corporate hierarchy, with each of the children of a node representing subordinates (and the parent representing the immediate superior), then these operations have amusing interpretations. The bottom-up method corresponds to a promising new manager arriving on the scene, being promoted up

Program 9.4 Top-down heapify

To restore the heap condition when a node's priority is decreased, we move down the heap, exchanging the node at position k with the larger of that node's two children if necessary and stopping when the node at k is not smaller than either child or the bottom is reached. Note that if N is even and k is N/2, then the node at k has only one child—this case must be treated properly!

The inner loop in this program has two distinct exits: one for the case that the bottom of the heap is hit, and another for the case that the heap condition is satisfied somewhere in the interior of the heap. It is a prototypical example of the need for the break construct.

```
private void sink(int k, int N)
  {
    while (2*k <= N)
      { int j = 2*k;
        if (j < N && less(j, j+1)) j++;
        if (!less(k, j)) break;
        exch(k, j); k = j;
      }
  }
```

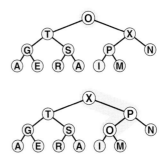

**Figure 9.4
Top-down heapify (sink)**

The tree depicted on the top is heap-ordered, except at the root. If we exchange the O with the larger of its two children (X), the tree is heap-ordered, except at the sub-tree rooted at O. Continuing to exchange O with the larger of its two children until we reach the bottom of the heap or a point where O is larger than both its children, we can establish the heap condition for the whole tree. We can use this procedure as the basis for the remove the maximum *operation on heaps in order to reestablish the heap condition after replacing the key at the root with the rightmost key on the bottom level.*

the chain of command (by exchanging jobs with any lower-qualified boss) until the new person encounters a higher-qualified boss. Mixing methaphors, we also think about the new arrival having to *swim* to the surface. The top-down method is analogous to the situation when the president of the company is replaced by someone less qualified. If the president's most powerful subordinate is stronger than the new person, they exchange jobs, and we move down the chain of command, demoting the new person and promoting others until the level of competence of the new person is reached, where there is no higher-qualified subordinate (this idealized scenario is rarely seen in the real world). Again mixing metaphors, we also think about the new person having to *sink* to the bottom.

These two basic operations allow efficient implementation of the basic priority-queue ADT, as given in Program 9.5. With the priority queue represented as a heap-ordered array, using the *insert* operation amounts to adding the new element at the end and moving that element up through the heap to restore the heap condition; the *remove the*

Figure 9.5
Top-down heap construction

This sequence depicts the insertion of the keys A S O R T I N G into an initially empty heap. New items are added to the heap at the bottom, moving from left to right on the bottom level. Each insertion affects only the nodes on the path between the insertion point and the root, so the cost is proportional to the logarithm of the size of the heap in the worst case.

Program 9.5 Heap-based priority queue

To implement insert, we increment N, add the new element at the end, then use swim to restore the heap condition. For getmax we take the value to be returned from pq[1], then decrement the size of the heap by moving pq[N] to pq[1] and using sink to restore the heap condition. The first position in the array, pq[0], is not used.

```
class PQ
  {
    private boolean less(int i, int j)
      { return pq[i].less(pq[j]); }
    private void exch(int i, int j)
      { ITEM t = pq[i]; pq[i] = pq[j]; pq[j] = t; }
    private void swim(int k)
      // Program 9.3
    private void sink(int k, int N)
      // Program 9.4
    private ITEM[] pq;
    private int N;
    PQ(int maxN)
      { pq = new ITEM[maxN+1]; N = 0; }
    boolean empty()
      { return N == 0; }
    void insert(ITEM v)
      { pq[++N] = v; swim(N); }
    ITEM getmax()
      { exch(1, N); sink(1, N-1); return pq[N--]; }
  };
```

maximum operation amounts to taking the largest value off the top, then putting in the item from the end of the heap at the top and moving it down through the array to restore the heap condition.

Property 9.2 *The insert and remove the maximum operations for the priority queue abstract data type can be implemented with heap-ordered trees such that insert requires no more than lg N comparisons and remove the maximum no more than 2 lg N comparisons, when performed on an N-item queue.*

Both operations involve moving along a path between the root and the bottom of the heap, and no path in a heap of size N includes more than $\lg N$ elements (see, for example, Property 5.8 and Exercise 5.77). The *remove the maximum* operation requires two comparisons for each node: one to find the child with the larger key, the other to decide whether that child needs to be promoted. ∎

Figures 9.5 and 9.6 show an example in which we construct a heap by inserting items one by one into an initially empty heap. In the array representation that we have been using for the heap, this process corresponds to heap ordering the array by moving sequentially through the array, considering the size of the heap to grow by 1 each time that we move to a new item, and using swim to restore the heap order. The process takes time proportional to $N \log N$ in the worst case (if each new item is the largest seen so far, it travels all the way up the heap), but it turns out to take only linear time on the average (a random new item tends to travel up only a few levels). In Section 9.4 we shall see a way to construct a heap (to heap order an array) in linear worst-case time.

The basic swim and sink operations in Programs 9.3 and 9.4 also allow direct implementation for the *change priority* and *remove* operations. To change the priority of an item somewhere in the middle of the heap, we use swim to move up the heap if the priority is increased, and sink to go down the heap if the priority is decreased. Full implementations of such operations, which refer to specific data items, make sense only if a handle is maintained for each item to that item's place in the data structure. In order to do so, we need to define an ADT for that purpose. We shall consider such an ADT and corresponding implementations in detail in Sections 9.5 through 9.7.

Property 9.3 *The* **change priority, remove,** *and* **replace the maximum** *operations for the priority queue abstract data type can be implemented with heap-ordered trees such that no more than* $2 \lg N$ *comparisons are required for any operation on an N-item queue.*

Since they require handles to items, we defer considering implementations that support these operations to Section 9.6 (see Program 9.12 and Figure 9.14). They all involve moving along one path in the heap, perhaps all the way from top to bottom or from bottom to top in the worst case. ∎

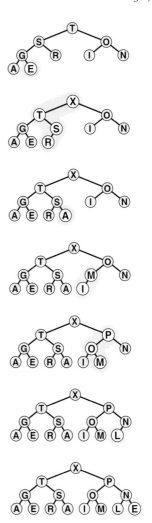

Figure 9.6
Top-down heap construction (continued)

This sequence depicts insertion of the keys E X A M P L E into the heap started in Figure 9.5. The total cost of constructing a heap of size N is less than

$$\lg 1 + \lg 2 + \ldots + \lg N,$$

which is less than $N \lg N$.

Figure 9.7
Sorting from a heap

After replacing the largest element in the heap by the rightmost element on the bottom level, we can restore the heap order by sifting down along a path from the root to the bottom.

Program 9.6 Sorting with a priority queue

This class uses our priority-queue ADT to implement the standard Sort class that was introduced in Program 6.3.

To sort a subarray a[1], ..., a[r], we construct a priority queue with enough capacity to hold all of its items, use insert to put all the items on the priority queue, and then use getmax to remove them, in decreasing order. This sorting algorithm runs in time proportional to $N \lg N$ but uses extra space proportional to the number of items to be sorted (for the priority queue).

```
class Sort
  {
    static void sort(ITEM[] a, int l, int r)
      { PQsort(a, l, r); }
    static void PQsort(ITEM[] a, int l, int r)
      { int k;
        PQ pq = new PQ(r-l+1);
        for (k = 1; k <= r; k++)
          pq.insert(a[k]);
        for (k = r; k >= 1; k--)
          a[k] = pq.getmax();
      }
  }
```

Note carefully that the *join* operation is not included on this list. Combining two priority queues efficiently seems to require a much more sophisticated data structure. We shall consider such a data structure in detail in Section 9.7. Otherwise, the simple heap-based method given here suffices for a broad variety of applications. It uses minimal extra space and is guaranteed to run efficiently *except in the presence of frequent and large join operations.*

As we have mentioned, we can use any priority queue to develop a sorting method, as shown in Program 9.6. We insert all the keys to be sorted into the priority queue, then repeatedly use *remove the maximum* to remove them all in decreasing order. Using a priority queue represented as an unordered list in this way corresponds to doing a selection sort; using an ordered list corresponds to doing an insertion sort.

Figures 9.5 and 9.6 give an example of the first phase (the construction process) when a heap-based priority-queue implementation is used; Figures 9.7 and 9.8 show the second phase (which we refer to as the *sortdown* process) for the heap-based implementation. For practical purposes, this method is comparatively inelegant, because it unnecessarily makes an extra copy of the items to be sorted (in the priority queue). Also, using N successive insertions is not the most efficient way to build a heap from N given elements. Next, we address these two points and derive the classical heapsort algorithm.

Exercises

▷ **9.21** Give the heap that results when the keys E A S Y Q U E S T I O N are inserted into an initially empty heap.

▷ **9.22** Using the conventions of Exercise 9.1, give the sequence of heaps produced when the operations

P R I O * R * * I * T * Y * * * Q U E * * * U * E

are performed on an initially empty heap.

9.23 Because the exch primitive is used in the heapify operations, the items are loaded and stored twice as often as necessary. Give more efficient implementations that avoid this problem, à la insertion sort.

9.24 Why do we not use a sentinel to avoid the j<N test in sink?

○ **9.25** Add the *replace the maximum* operation to the heap-based priority-queue implementation of Program 9.5. Be sure to consider the case when the value to be added is larger than all values in the queue. *Note*: Use of pq[0] leads to an elegant solution.

9.26 What is the minimum number of keys that must be moved during a *remove the maximum* operation in a heap? Give a heap of size 15 for which the minimum is achieved.

9.27 What is the minimum number of keys that must be moved during three successive *remove the maximum* operations in a heap? Give a heap of size 15 for which the minimum is achieved.

9.4 Heapsort

We can adapt the basic idea in Program 9.6 to sort an array without needing any extra space, by maintaining the heap within the array to be sorted. That is, focusing on the task of sorting, we abandon the notion of hiding the representation of the priority queue, and rather

**Figure 9.8
Sorting from a heap
(continued)**

This sequence depicts removal of the rest of the keys from the heap in Figure 9.7. Even if every element goes all the way back to the bottom, the total cost of the sorting phase is less than

$$\lg N + \ldots + \lg 2 + \lg 1,$$

which is less than $N \log N$.

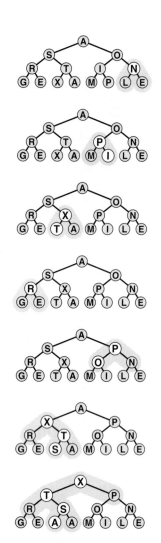

Figure 9.9
Bottom-up heap construction

Working from right to left and bottom to top, we construct a heap by ensuring that the subtree below the current node is heap ordered. The total cost is linear in the worst case, because most nodes are near the bottom.

than being constrained by the interface to the priority-queue ADT, we use swim and sink directly.

Using Program 9.5 directly in Program 9.6 corresponds to proceeding from left to right through the array, using swim to ensure that the elements to the left of the scanning pointer make up a heap-ordered complete tree. Then, during the sortdown process, we put the largest element into the place vacated as the heap shrinks. That is, the sortdown process is like selection sort, but it uses a more efficient way to find the largest element in the unsorted part of the array.

Rather than constructing the heap via successive insertions as shown in Figures 9.5 and 9.6, it is more efficient to build the heap by going backward through it, making little subheaps from the bottom up, as shown in Figure 9.9. That is, we view every position in the array as the root of a small subheap and take advantage of the fact that sink works as well for such subheaps as it does for the big heap. If the two children of a node are heaps, then calling sink on that node makes the subtree rooted there a heap. By working backward through the heap, calling sink on each node, we can establish the heap property inductively. The scan starts halfway back through the array because we can skip the subheaps of size 1.

A full implementation is given in Program 9.7, the classical *heapsort* algorithm. Although the loops in this program seem to do different tasks (the first constructs the heap, and the second destroys the heap for the sortdown), they are both built around the swim method, which restores order in a tree that is heap-ordered except possibly at the root, using the array representation of a complete tree. Figure 9.10 illustrates the contents of the array for the example corresponding to Figures 9.7 through 9.9.

Property 9.4 *Bottom-up heap construction takes linear time.*

This fact follows from the observation that most of the heaps processed are small. For example, to build a heap of 127 elements, we process 32 heaps of size 3, 16 heaps of size 7, 8 heaps of size 15, 4 heaps of size 31, 2 heaps of size 63, and 1 heap of size 127, so $32 \cdot 1 + 16 \cdot 2 + 8 \cdot 3 + 4 \cdot 4 + 2 \cdot 5 + 1 \cdot 6 = 120$ promotions (twice as many comparisons) are required in the worst case. For $N = 2^n - 1$, an upper bound on

Program 9.7 Heapsort

This code sorts a[1], ..., a[N], using the sink method of Program 9.4 (with exch and less implementations that exchange and compare, respectively, the items in a specified by their parameters). The for loop constructs the heap; then, the while loop exchanges the largest element (a[1]) with a[N] and repairs the heap, continuing until the heap is empty. This implementation depends on the first element of the array being at index 1 so that it can treat the array as representing a complete tree and compute implicit indices (see Figure 9.2); it is not difficult to shift indices to implement our standard interface to sort a subarray a[1], ..., a[r] (see Exercise 9.30).

```
for (int k = N/2; k >= 1; k--)
  sink(k, N);
while (N > 1)
  { exch(1, N); sink(1, --N); }
```

the number of promotions is

$$\sum_{1 \le k < n} k 2^{n-k-1} = 2^n - n - 1 < N.$$

A similar proof holds when $N + 1$ is not a power of 2. ∎

This property is not of particular importance for heapsort, because its time is still dominated by the $N \log N$ time for the sortdown, but it is important for other priority-queue applications, where a linear-time *construct* operation can lead to a linear-time algorithm. As noted in Figure 9.6, constructing a heap with N successive *insert* operations requires a total of $N \log N$ steps in the worst case (even though the total turns out to be linear on the average for random files).

Property 9.5 *Heapsort uses fewer than $2N \lg N$ comparisons to sort N elements.*

The slightly higher bound $3N \lg N$ follows immediately from Property 9.2. The bound given here follows from a more careful count based on Property 9.4. ∎

Property 9.5 and the in-place property are the two primary reasons that heapsort is of practical interest: It is *guaranteed* to sort N elements in place in time proportional to $N \log N$, no matter what the

```
A S O R T I N G E X A M P L E
A S O R T I N G E X A M P L E
A S O R T P N G E X A M I L E
A S O R X P N G E T A M I L E
A S O R X P N G E T A M I L E
A S P R X O N G E T A M I L E
A X P R T O N G E S A M I L E
X T P R S O N G E A A M I L E

T S P R E O N G E A A M I L X
S R P L E O N G E A A M I T X
R L P I E O N G E A A M S T X
P L O I E M N G E A A R S T X
O L N I E M A G E A P R S T X
N L M I E A A G E O P R S T X
M L E I E A A G N O P R S T X
L I E G E A A M N O P R S T X
I G E A E A L M N O P R S T X
G E E A A I L M N O P R S T X
E A E A G I L M N O P R S T X
E A A E G I L M N O P R S T X
A A E E G I L M N O P R S T X
A A E E G I L M N O P R S T X
```

Figure 9.10
Heapsort example

Heapsort is an efficient selection-based algorithm. First, we build a heap from the bottom up, in-place. The top eight lines in this figure correspond to Figure 9.9. Next, we repeatedly remove the largest element in the heap. The unshaded parts of the bottom lines correspond to Figures 9.7 and 9.8; the shaded parts contain the growing sorted file.

input. There is no worst-case input that makes heapsort run significantly slower (unlike quicksort), and heapsort does not use any extra space (unlike mergesort). This guaranteed worst-case performance does come at a price: for example, the algorithm's inner loop (cost per comparison) has more basic operations than quicksort's, and it uses more comparisons than quicksort for random files, so heapsort is likely to be slower than quicksort for typical or random files.

Heaps are also useful for solving the *selection* problem of finding the k largest of N items (see Chapter 7), particularly if k is small. We simply stop the heapsort algorithm after k items have been taken from the top of the heap.

Property 9.6   *Heap-based selection allows the kth largest of N items to be found in time proportional to N when k is small or close to N, and in time proportional to N log N otherwise.*

One option is to build a heap, using fewer than $2N$ comparisons (by Property 9.4), then to remove the k largest elements, using $2k \lg N$ or fewer comparisons (by Property 9.2), for a total of $2N + 2k \lg N$. Another method is to build a minimum-oriented heap of size k, then to perform k *replace the minimum* (*insert* followed by *remove the minimum*) operations with the remaining elements for a total of at most $2k + 2(N - k) \lg k$ comparisons (see Exercise 9.36). This method uses space proportional to k, so is attractive for finding the k largest of N elements when k is small and N is large (or is not known in advance). For random keys and other typical situations, the $\lg k$ upper bound for heap operations in the second method is likely to be $O(1)$ when k is small relative to N (see Exercise 9.37). ∎

Various ways to improve heapsort further have been investigated. One idea, developed by Floyd, is to note that an element reinserted into the heap during the sortdown process usually goes all the way to the bottom. Thus, we can save time by avoiding the check for whether the element has reached its position, simply promoting the larger of the two children until the bottom is reached, then moving back up the heap to the proper position. This idea cuts the number of comparisons by a factor of 2 asymptotically—close to the $\lg N! \approx N \lg N - N/\ln 2$ that is the absolute minimum number of comparisons needed by any sorting algorithm (see Part 8). The method requires extra bookkeeping, and it is useful in practice only when the cost of comparisons is relatively high (for example, when we are sorting records with strings or other types of long keys).

Another idea is to build heaps based on an array representation of complete heap-ordered *ternary* trees, with a node at position k larger than or equal to nodes at positions $3k - 1$, $3k$, and $3k + 1$ and smaller than or equal to nodes at position $\lfloor (k + 1)/3 \rfloor$, for positions between 1 and N in an array of N elements. There is a tradeoff between the lower cost from the reduced tree height and the higher cost of finding the largest of the three children at each node. This tradeoff is dependent on details of the implementation (see Exercise 9.31) and on the expected relative frequency of *insert*, *remove the maximum*, and *change priority* operations.

Figure 9.11 shows heapsort in operation on a randomly ordered file. At first, the process seems to do anything but sort, because large elements are moving to the beginning of the file as the heap is being constructed. But then the method looks more like a mirror image of selection sort, as expected. Figure 9.12 shows that different types of input files can yield heaps with peculiar characteristics, but they look more like random heaps as the sort progresses.

Naturally, we are interested in how to choose among heapsort, quicksort, and mergesort for a particular application. The choice between heapsort and mergesort essentially reduces to a choice between a sort that is not stable (see Exercise 9.28) and one that uses extra memory; the choice between heapsort and quicksort reduces to a choice between average-case speed and worst-case speed. Having dealt extensively with improving the inner loops of quicksort and mergesort, we leave this activity for heapsort as exercises in this chapter. Making heapsort faster than quicksort is typically not in the cards—as indicated by the empirical studies in Table 9.2—but people interested in fast sorts on their machines will find the exercise instructive. As usual, various specific properties of machines and programming environments can play an important role. For example, quicksort and mergesort have a locality property that gives them a further advantage on certain machines. When comparisons are extremely expensive, Floyd's version is the method of choice, as it is nearly optimal in terms of time and space costs in such situations.

Exercises

9.28 Show that heapsort is not stable.

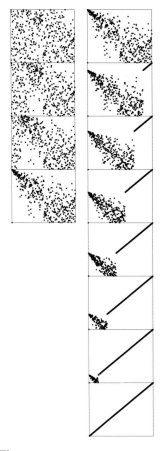

Figure 9.11
Dynamic characteristics of heapsort

The construction process (left) seems to unsort the file, putting large elements near the beginning. Then, the sortdown process (right) works like selection sort, keeping a heap at the beginning and building up the sorted array at the end of the file.

Figure 9.12
**Dynamic characteristics of
heapsort on various
types of files**

*The running time for heapsort is
not particularly sensitive to the
input. No matter what the input
values are, the largest element is
always found in less than $\lg N$
steps. These diagrams show files
that are random, Gaussian, nearly
ordered, nearly reverse-ordered,
and randomly ordered with 10 distinct key values (at the top, left to
right). The second diagrams from
the top show the heap constructed
by the bottom-up algorithm, and
the remaining diagrams show the
sortdown process for each file. The
heaps somewhat mirror the initial
file at the beginning, but all become more like the heaps for a
random file as the process contin-
ues.*

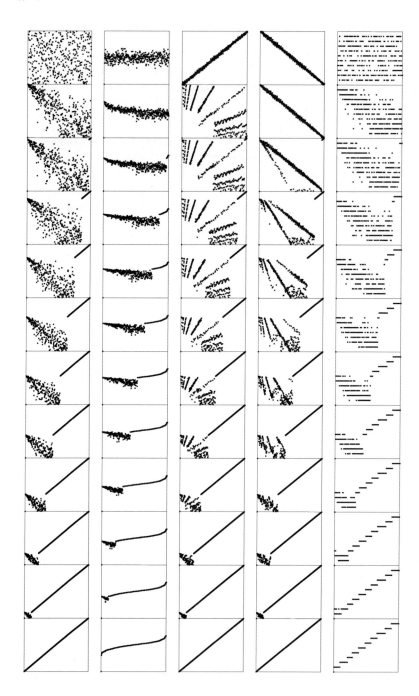

Table 9.2 Empirical study of heapsort algorithms

The relative timings for various sorts on files of random integers in the left part of the table confirm our expectations from the lengths of the inner loops that heapsort is slower than quicksort but competitive with mergesort. The timings for the first N words of *Moby Dick* in the right part of the table show that Floyd's method is an effective improvement to heapsort when comparisons are expensive.

N	32-bit integer keys					string keys		
	Q	M	PQ	H	F	Q	H	F
12500	22	21	53	23	24	106	141	109
25000	20	32	75	34	34	220	291	249
50000	42	70	156	71	67	518	756	663
100000	95	152	347	156	147	1141	1797	1584
200000	194	330	732	352	328			
400000	427	708	1690	818	768			
800000	913	1524	3626	1955	1851			

Key:
Q Quicksort with cutoff for small files
M Mergesort with cutoff for small files
PQ Priority-queue–based heapsort (Program 9.6)
H Heapsort, standard implementation (Program 9.7)
F Heapsort with Floyd's improvement

● 9.29 Empirically determine the percentage of time heapsort spends in the construction phase for $N = 10^3$, 10^4, 10^5, and 10^6.

9.30 Write a heapsort-based implementation of our standard `sort` method, which sorts the subarray `a[l], ..., a[r]`.

● 9.31 Implement a version of heapsort based on complete heap-ordered ternary trees, as described in the text. Compare the number of comparisons used by your program empirically with the standard implementation, for $N = 10^3$, 10^4, 10^5, and 10^6.

● 9.32 Continuing Exercise 9.31, determine empirically whether or not Floyd's method is effective for ternary heaps.

○ 9.33 Considering the cost of comparisons only, and assuming that it takes t comparisons to find the largest of t elements, find the value of t that minimizes the coefficient of $N \log N$ in the comparison count when a t-ary heap is used in heapsort. First, assume a straightforward generalization of Program 9.7; then, assume that Floyd's method can save one comparison in the inner loop.

○ **9.34** For $N = 32$, give an arrangement of keys that makes heapsort use as many comparisons as possible.

•• **9.35** For $N = 32$, give an arrangement of keys that makes heapsort use as few comparisons as possible.

9.36 Prove that building a priority queue of size k then doing $N - k$ *replace the minimum* (*insert* followed by *remove the minimum*) operations leaves the k largest of the N elements in the heap.

9.37 Implement both of the versions of heapsort-based selection referred to in the discussion of Property 9.6, using the method described in Exercise 9.25. Compare the number of comparisons they use empirically with the quicksort-based method from Chapter 7, for $N = 10^6$ and $k = 10, 100, 1000, 10^4, 10^5$, and 10^6.

• **9.38** Implement a version of heapsort based on the idea of representing the heap-ordered tree in preorder rather than in level order. Empirically compare the number of comparisons used by this version with the number used by the standard implementation, for randomly ordered keys with $N = 10^3, 10^4, 10^5$, and 10^6.

9.5 Priority-Queue ADT

For most applications of priority queues, we want to arrange to have the priority-queue method, instead of returning values for *remove the maximum*, tell us *which* of the records has the largest key, and to work in a similar fashion for the other operations. That is, we assign priorities and use priority queues for only the purpose of accessing other information in an appropriate order. This arrangement is akin to use of the *indirect-sort* or the *pointer-sort* concepts described in Chapter 6. In particular, this approach is required for operations such as *change priority* or *remove* to make sense. We examine an implementation of this idea in detail here, both because we shall be using priority queues in this way later in the book and because this situation is prototypical of the problems we face when we design interfaces and implementations for ADTs.

When we want to *remove* an item from a priority queue, how do we specify which item? When we want to maintain multiple priority queues, how do we organize the implementations so that we can manipulate priority queues in the same way that we manipulate other

Program 9.8 Full priority-queue ADT

This interface for a priority-queue ADT allows client programs to delete items and to change priorities (using object handles provided by the implementation) and to merge priority queues together.

```
class PQfull // ADT interface
  { // implementations and private members hidden
    boolean empty()
    Object insert(ITEM)
    ITEM getmax()
    void change(Object, ITEM)
    void remove(Object)
    void join(PQfull)
  };
```

types of data? Questions such as these are the topic of Chapter 4. Program 9.8 gives a general interface for priority queues along the lines that we discussed in Section 4.9. It supports a situation where a client has keys and associated information and, while primarily interested in the operation of accessing the information associated with the highest key, may have numerous other data-processing operations to perform on the objects, as we discussed at the beginning of this chapter. All operations refer to a particular priority queue through a handle (a pointer to an object whose class is not specified). The *insert* operation returns a handle for each object added to the priority queue by the client program. In this arrangement, client programs are responsible for keeping track of handles, which they may later use to specify which objects are to be affected by *remove* and *change priority* operations, and which priority queues are to be affected by all of the operations.

This arrangement places restrictions on both the client and the implementation. The client is not given a way to access information through handles except through this interface. It has the responsibility to use the handles properly: for example, there is no good way for an implementation to check for an illegal action such as a client using a handle to an item that is already removed. For its part, the implementation cannot move around information freely, because clients have handles that they may use later. This point will become clearer when we examine details of implementations. As usual, whatever level of detail we choose in our implementations, an abstract interface such as Program 9.8 is a useful starting point for making tradeoffs between the needs of applications and the needs of implementations.

Implementations of the basic priority-queue operations, using an unordered doubly linked-list representation, are given in Programs 9.9 and 9.10. Most of the code is based on elementary linked list operations from Section 3.3, but the implementation of the client handle abstraction is noteworthy in the present context: the insert method returns an Object, which the client can only take to mean "a reference to an object of some unspecified class" since Node, the actual type of the object, is private. So the client can do little else with the reference but keep it in some data structure associated with the item that it provided as a parameter to insert. But if the client needs to *change priority* the item's key or to *remove* the item from the priority queue, this object is precisely what the implementation needs to be able to accomplish the task: the appropriate methods can cast the type to Node and make the necessary modifications. It is easy to develop other, similarly straight-forward, implementations using other elementary representations (see, for example, Exercise 9.40).

As we discussed in Section 9.1, the implementation given in Programs 9.9 and 9.10 is suitable for applications where the priority queue is small and *remove the maximum* or *find the maximum* operations are infrequent; otherwise, heap-based implementations are preferable. Implementing swim and sink for heap-ordered trees with explicit links while maintaining the integrity of the handles is a challenge that we leave for exercises, because we shall be considering two alternative approaches in detail in Sections 9.6 and 9.7.

A full ADT such as Program 9.8 has many virtues, but it is sometimes advantageous to consider other arrangements, with different restrictions on the client programs and on implementations. In Section 9.6 we consider an example where the client program keeps the responsibility for maintaining the records and keys, and the priority-queue routines refer to them indirectly.

Slight changes in the interface also might be appropriate. For example, we might want a method that returns the value of the highest priority key in the queue, rather than just a way to reference that key and its associated information. Also, the issues that we considered in Sections 4.9 and 4.10 associated with memory management and

Program 9.9 Unordered doubly linked list priority queue

This implementation includes the *construct*, *test if empty*, and *insert* methods from the interface of Program 9.8 (see Program 9.10 for implementations of the other four methods). It maintains a simple unordered list, with head and tail nodes. We specify the class `Node` to be a doubly linked list node (with an item and two links). The private data fields are just the list's head and tail links.

```
class PQfull
  {
    private static class Node
      { ITEM key; Node prev, next;
        Node(ITEM v)
          { key = v; prev = null; next = null; }
      }
    private Node head, tail;
    PQfull()
      {
        head = new Node(null);
        tail = new Node(null);
        head.prev = tail; head.next = tail;
        tail.prev = head; tail.next = head;
      }
    boolean empty()
      { return head.next.next == head; }
    Object insert(ITEM v)
      { Node t = new Node(v);
        t.next = head.next; t.next.prev = t;
        t.prev = head; head.next = t;
        return t;
      }
    ITEM getmax()
      // See Program 9.10
    void change(Object x, ITEM v)
      // See Program 9.10
    void remove(Object x)
      // See Program 9.10
    void join(PQfull p)
      // See Program 9.10
  }
```

copy semantics come into play. We are not considering the *copy* operation and have chosen just one out of several possibilities for *join* (see Exercises 9.44 and 9.45).

It is easy to add such procedures to the interface in Program 9.8, but it is much more challenging to develop an implementation where logarithmic performance for all operations is guaranteed. In applications where the priority queue does not grow to be large, or where the mix of *insert* and *remove the maximum* operations has some special properties, a fully flexible interface might be desirable. But in applications where the queue will grow to be large, and where a tenfold or a hundredfold increase in performance might be noticed or appreciated, it might be worthwhile to restrict to the set of operations where efficient performance is assured. A great deal of research has gone into the design of priority-queue algorithms for different mixes of operations; the binomial queue described in Section 9.7 is an important example.

Exercises

9.39 Which priority-queue implementation would you use to find the 100 smallest of a set of 10^6 random numbers? Justify your answer.

9.40 Provide implementations similar to Programs 9.9 and 9.10 that use *ordered* doubly linked lists. *Note*: Because the client has handles into the data structure, your programs can change only links (rather than keys) in nodes.

9.41 Provide implementations for *insert* and *remove the maximum* (the priority-queue interface in Program 9.1) using complete heap-ordered trees represented with explicit nodes and links. *Note*: Because the client has no handles into the data structure, you can take advantage of the fact that it is easier to exchange information fields in nodes than to exchange the nodes themselves.

• **9.42** Provide implementations for *insert*, *remove the maximum*, *change priority*, and *remove* (the priority-queue interface in Program 9.8) using heap-ordered trees with explicit links. *Note*: Because the client has handles into the data structure, this exercise is more difficult than Exercise 9.41, not just because the nodes have to be triply linked, but also because your programs can change only links (rather than keys) in nodes.

9.43 Add a (brute-force) implementation of the *join* operation to your implementation from Exercise 9.42.

○ **9.44** Suppose that we add a `clone` method to Program 9.8 (and specify that every implementation `implements Cloneable`). Add an implementation of `clone` to Programs 9.9 and 9.10, and write a driver program that tests your interface and implementation.

Program 9.10 Doubly linked list priority queue (continued)

These method implementations complete the priority queue implementation of Program 9.9. The *remove the maximum* operation requires scanning through the whole list, but the overhead of maintaining doubly linked lists is justified by the fact that the *change priority*, *remove*, and *join* operations all are implemented in constant time, using only elementary operations on the lists (see Chapter 3 for more details on doubly linked lists).

The change and remove methods take an Object reference as a parameter, which must reference an object of (private) type Node—a client can only get such a reference from insert.

We might make this class Cloneable and implement a clone method that makes a copy of the whole list (see Section 4.9), but client object handles would be invalid for the copy. The join implementation appropriates the list nodes from the parameter to be included in the result, but it does *not* make copies of them, so client handles remain valid.

```
ITEM getmax()
  { ITEM max; Node x = head.next;
    for (Node t = x; t.next != head; t = t.next)
      if (Sort.less(x.key, t.key)) x = t;
    max = x.key;
    remove(x);
    return max;
  }
void change(Object x, ITEM v)
  { ((Node) x).key = v; }
void remove(Object x)
  { Node t = (Node) x;
    t.next.prev = t.prev;
    t.prev.next = t.next;
  }
void join(PQfull p)
  {
    tail.prev.next = p.head.next;
    p.head.next.prev = tail.prev;
    head.prev = p.tail;
    p.tail.next = head;
    tail = p.tail;
  }
```

- **9.45** Change the interface and implementation for the *join* operation in Programs 9.9 and 9.10 such that it returns a PQfull (the result of joining the parameters).

9.46 Provide a priority-queue interface and implementation that supports *construct* and *remove the maximum*, using tournaments (see Section 5.7). Program 5.19 will provide you with the basis for *construct*.

- **9.47** Add *insert* to your solution to Exercise 9.46.

9.6 Priority Queues for Client Arrays

Suppose that the records to be processed in a priority queue are in an existing array. In this case, it makes sense to have the priority-queue routines refer to items through the array index. Moreover, we can use the array index as a handle to implement all the priority-queue operations. An interface along these lines is illustrated in Program 9.11. Figure 9.13 shows how this approach might apply for a small example. Without copying or making special modifications of records, we can keep a priority queue containing a subset of the records.

Using indices into an existing array is a natural arrangement, but it leads to implementations with an orientation opposite to that of Program 9.8. Now it is the client program that cannot move around information freely, because the priority-queue routine is maintaining indices into data maintained by the client. For its part, the priority queue implementation must not use indices without first being given them by the client.

To develop an implementation, we use precisely the same approach as we did for index sorting in Section 6.8. We manipulate indices and define less such that comparisons reference the client's array. There are added complications here, because the priority-queue routine must keep track of the objects so that it can find them when the client program refers to them by the handle (array index). To this end, we add a second index array to keep track of the position of the keys in the priority queue. To localize the maintenance of this array, we move data only with the exch operation and define exch appropriately.

Program 9.12 is a heap-based implementation of this approach that differs only slightly from Program 9.5 but is well worth studying because it is so useful in practice. We refer to the data structure built by this program as an *index heap*. We shall use this program as a

Program 9.11 Priority-queue ADT interface for index items

Instead of building a data structure from the items themselves, this interface provides for building a priority queue using indices into a client array. The constructor takes a reference to an array as a parameter, and the *insert*, *remove the maximum*, *change priority*, and *remove* methods all use indices into that array and compare array entries with ITEM's less method. For example, the client program might define less so that less(i, j) is the result of comparing data[i].grade and data[j].grade.

```
class PQi // ADT interface
  { // implementations and private members hidden
    PQi(Array)
    boolean empty()
    void insert(int)
    int getmax()
    void change(int)
    void remove(int)
  };
```

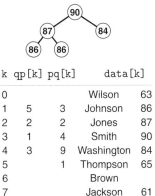

k	qp[k]	pq[k]	data[k]	
0			Wilson	63
1	5	3	Johnson	86
2	2	2	Jones	87
3	1	4	Smith	90
4	3	9	Washington	84
5	1		Thompson	65
6			Brown	
7			Jackson	61
8			White	76
9	4		Adams	86
10			Black	71

**Figure 9.13
Index heap data structures**

By manipulating indices, rather than the records themselves, we can build a priority queue on a subset of the records in an array. Here, a heap of size 5 in the array pq contains the indices to those students with the top five grades. Thus, data[pq[1]].name contains Smith, the name of the student with the highest grade, and so forth. An inverse array qp allows the priority-queue routines to treat the array indices as handles. For example, if we need to change Smith's grade to 85, we change the entry in data[3].grade, then call PQchange(3). The priority-queue implementation accesses the record at pq[qp[3]] (or pq[1], because qp[3]=1) and the new key at data[pq[1]].name (or data[3].name, because pq[1]=3).

building block for other algorithms in Parts 5 through 7. As usual, we do no error checking, and we assume (for example) that indices are always in the proper range and that the user does not try to insert anything on a full queue or to remove anything from an empty one. Adding code for such checks is straightforward.

We can use the same approach for any priority queue that uses an array representation (for example, see Exercises 9.50 and 9.51). The main disadvantage of using indirection in this way is the extra space used. The size of the index arrays has to be the size of the data array, when the maximum size of the priority queue could be much less.

Other approaches to building a priority queue on top of existing data in an array are either to have the client program make records consisting of a key with its array index as associated information or to use a class for index keys with its own less method. Then, if the implementation uses a linked-allocation representation such as the one in Programs 9.9 and 9.10 or Exercise 9.42, then the space used by the priority queue would be proportional to the maximum number of elements on the queue at any one time. Such approaches would

Program 9.12 Index-heap–based priority queue

This implementation of Program 9.11 maintains pq as an array of indices into a client array.

We keep the heap position corresponding to index value k in qp[k], which allows us to implement *change priority* (see Figure 9.14) and *remove* (see Exercise 9.49). We maintain the invariant pq[qp[k]]=qp[pq[k]]=k for all k in the heap (see Figure 9.13). The methods less and exch are the key to the implementation—they allow us to use the same sink and swim code as for standard heaps.

```
class PQi
  {
    private boolean less(int i, int j)
      { return a[pq[i]].less(pq[j]); }
    private void exch(int i, int j)
      { int t = pq[i]; pq[i] = pq[j]; pq[j] = t;
        qp[pq[i]] = i; qp[pq[j]] = j;
      }
    private void swim(int k)
      // Program 9.3
    private void sink(int k, int N)
      // Program 9.4
    private ITEM[] a;
    private int[] pq, qp;
    private int N;
    PQi(ITEM[] items)
      { a = items; N = 0;
        pq = new int[a.length+1];
        qp = new int[a.length+1];
      }
    boolean empty()
      { return N == 0; }
    void insert(int v)
      { pq[++N] = v; qp[v] = N; swim(N); }
    int getmax()
      { exch(1, N); sink(1, N-1); return pq[N--]; }
    void change(int k)
      { swim(qp[k]); sink(qp[k], N); }
  };
```

be preferred over Program 9.12 if space must be conserved and if the priority queue involves only a small fraction of the data array.

Contrasting this approach to providing a complete priority-queue implementation to the approach in Section 9.5 exposes essential differences in ADT design. In the first case (Programs 9.9 and 9.10, for example), it is the responsibility of the priority-queue implementation to allocate and deallocate the memory for the keys, to change key values, and so forth. The ADT supplies the client with handles to items, and the client accesses items only through calls to the priority-queue routines, using the handles as parameters. In the second case (Program 9.12, for example), the client is responsible for the keys and records, and the priority-queue routines access this information only through handles provided by the user (array indices, in the case of Program 9.12). Both uses require cooperation between client and implementation.

Note that, in this book, we are normally interested in cooperation beyond that encouraged by programming language support mechanisms. In particular, we want the performance characteristics of the implementation to match the dynamic mix of operations required by the client. One way to ensure that match is to seek implementations with provable worst-case performance bounds, but we can solve many problems more easily by matching their performance requirements with simpler implementations.

Exercises

9.48 Suppose that an array is filled with the keys E A S Y Q U E S T I O N. Give the contents of the pq and qp arrays after these keys are inserted into an initially empty heap using Program 9.12.

○ **9.49** Add a *remove* operation to Program 9.12.

9.50 Implement the priority-queue ADT for index items (see Program 9.11) using an ordered-array representation for the priority queue.

9.51 Implement the priority-queue ADT for index items (see Program 9.11) using an unordered-array representation for the priority queue.

○ **9.52** Given an array a of N elements, consider a complete binary tree of $2N$ elements (represented as an array pq) containing indices from the array with the following properties: (*i*) for i from 0 to N-1, we have pq[N+i]=i; and (*ii*) for i from 1 to N-1, we have pq[i]=pq[2*i] if a[pq[2*i]]>a[pq[2*i+1]], and we have pq[i]=pq[2*i+1] otherwise. Such a structure is called an *index heap tournament* because it combines the features of index heaps and tournaments

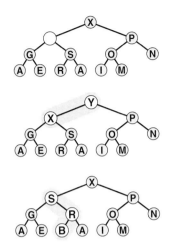

Figure 9.14
Changing of the priority of a node in a heap

The top diagram depicts a heap that is heap-ordered, except possibly at one given node. If the node is larger than its parent, then it must move up, just as depicted in Figure 9.3. This situation is illustrated in the middle diagram, with Y moving up the tree (in general, it might stop before hitting the root). If the node is smaller than the larger of its two children, then it must move down, just as depicted in Figure 9.4. This situation is illustrated in the bottom diagram, with B moving down the tree (in general, it might stop before hitting the bottom). We can use this procedure in two ways: as the basis for the change priority operation on heaps in order to reestablish the heap condition after changing the key in a node, or as the basis for the remove operation on heaps in order to reestablish the heap condition after replacing the key in a node with the rightmost key on the bottom level.

(see Program 5.19). Give the index heap tournament corresponding to the keys E A S Y Q U E S T I O N.

○ **9.53** Implement the priority-queue ADT for index items (see Program 9.11) using an index heap tournament (see Exercise 9.46).

9.7 Binomial Queues

None of the implementations that we have considered admit implementations of *join*, *remove the maximum*, and *insert* that are all efficient in the worst case. Unordered linked lists have fast *join* and *insert*, but slow *remove the maximum*; ordered linked lists have fast *remove the maximum*, but slow *join* and *insert*; heaps have fast *insert* and *remove the maximum*, but slow *join*; and so forth. (See Table 9.1.) In applications where frequent or large *join* operations play an important role, we need to consider more advanced data structures.

In this context, we mean by "efficient" that the operations should use no more than logarithmic time in the worst case. This restriction would seem to rule out array representations, because we can join two large arrays apparently only by moving all the elements in at least one of them. The unordered doubly linked-list representation of Program 9.9 does the *join* in constant time but requires that we walk through the whole list for *remove the maximum*. Use of a doubly linked ordered list (see Exercise 9.40) gives a constant-time *remove the maximum* but requires linear time to merge lists for *join*.

Numerous data structures have been developed that can support efficient implementations of all the priority-queue operations. Most of them are based on direct linked representation of heap-ordered trees. Two links are needed for moving down the tree (either to both children in a binary tree or to the first child and next sibling in a binary tree representation of a general tree), and one link to the parent is needed for moving up the tree. Developing implementations of the heap-ordering operations that work for any (heap-ordered) tree shape with explicit nodes and links or other representation is generally straightforward. The difficulty lies in dynamic operations such as *insert*, *remove*, and *join*, which require us to modify the tree structure. Different data structures are based on different strategies for modifying the tree structure while still maintaining balance in the tree. The algorithms use trees that are both more flexible than are complete trees and keep the trees sufficiently balanced to ensure a logarithmic time bound.

The overhead of maintaining a triply linked structure—ensuring that a particular implementation correctly maintains three pointers in all circumstances—can be burdensome (see Exercise 9.41). Moreover, in many practical situations, it is difficult to demonstrate that efficient implementations of *all* the operations are required, so we might pause before taking on such an implementation. On the other hand, it is also difficult to demonstrate that efficient implementations are *not* required, and the investment to guarantee that all the priority-queue operations will be fast may be justified. Regardless of such considerations, the next step from heaps to a data structure that allows for efficient implementation of *join*, *insert*, and *remove the maximum* is fascinating and worthy of study in its own right.

Even with a linked representation for the trees, the heap condition and the condition that the heap-ordered binary tree be complete are too strong to allow efficient implementation of the *join* operation. Given two heap-ordered trees, how do we merge them together into just one tree? For example, if one of the trees has 1023 nodes and the other has 255 nodes, how can we merge them into a tree with 1278 nodes, without touching more than 10 or 20 nodes? It seems impossible to merge heap-ordered trees in general if the trees are to be heap ordered and complete, but various advanced data structures have been devised that weaken the heap-order and balance conditions to get the flexibility that we need to devise an efficient *join*. Next, we consider an ingenious solution to this problem, called the *binomial queue*, that was developed by Vuillemin in 1978.

To begin, we note that the *join* operation is trivial for one particular type of tree with a relaxed heap-ordering restriction.

Definition 9.4   *A binary tree comprising nodes with keys is said to be* **left-heap-ordered** *if the key in each node is larger than or equal to all the keys in that node's left subtree (if any).*

Definition 9.5   *A* **power-of-2 heap** *is a left-heap-ordered tree consisting of a root node with an empty right subtree and a complete left subtree. The tree corresponding to a power-of-2 heap by the left-child, right-sibling correspondence is called a* **binomial tree**.

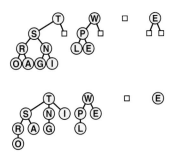

Figure 9.15
A binomial queue of size 13

A binomial queue of size N is a list of left-heap-ordered power-of-2 heaps, one for each bit in the binary representation of N. Thus, a binomial queue of size $13 = 1101_2$ consists of an 8-heap, a 4-heap, and a 1-heap. Shown here are the left-heap-ordered power-of-2 heap representation (top) and the heap-ordered binomial-tree representation (bottom) of the same binomial queue.

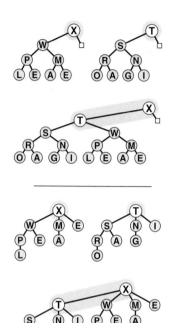

Figure 9.16
Joining of two equal-sized power-of-2 heaps.

We join two power-of-two heaps (top) by putting the larger of the roots at the root, with that root's (left) subtree as the right subtree of the other original root. If the operands have 2^n nodes, the result has 2^{n+1} nodes. If the operands are left-heap-ordered, then so is the result, with the largest key at the root. The heap-ordered binomial-tree representation of the same operation is shown below the line.

Program 9.13 Joining of two equal-sized power-of-2 heaps

We need to change only a few links to combine two equal-sized power-of-2 heaps into one power-of-2 heap that is twice that size. This method, which we define as a private method in the implementation, is one key to the efficiency of the binomial queue algorithm.

```
static Node pair(Node p, Node q)
  {
    if (p.item.less(q.item))
      { p.r = q.l; q.l = p; return q; }
    else { q.r = p.l; p.l = q; return p; }
  }
```

Binomial trees and power-of-2 heaps are equivalent. We work with both representations because binomial trees are slightly easier to visualize, whereas the simple representation of power-of-2 heaps leads to simpler implementations. In particular, we depend upon the following facts, which are direct consequences of the definitions:

- The number of nodes in a power-of-2 heap is a power of 2.
- No node has a key larger than the key at the root.
- Binomial trees are heap-ordered.

The trivial operation upon which binomial-queue algorithms are based is that of joining two power-of-2 heaps that have an equal number of nodes. The result is a heap with twice as many nodes which is easy to create, as illustrated in Figure 9.16. The root node with the larger key becomes the root of the result (with the other original root as the result root's left child), with its left subtree becoming the right subtree of the other root node. Given a linked representation for the trees, the join is a constant-time operation: We simply adjust two links at the top. An implementation is given in Program 9.13. This basic operation is at the heart of Vuillemin's general solution to the problem of implementing priority queues with no slow operations.

Definition 9.6 *A* **binomial queue** *is a set of power-of-2 heaps, no two of the same size. The structure of a binomial queue is determined by that queue's number of nodes, by correspondence with the binary representation of integers.*

A binomial queue of N elements has one power-of-2 heap for
each 1 bit in the binary representation of N. For example, a binomial
queue of 13 nodes comprises an 8-heap, a 4-heap, and a 1-heap, as
illustrated in Figure 9.15. There are at most $\lg N$ power-of-2 heaps in
a binomial queue of size N, all of height no greater than $\lg N$.

In accordance with Definitions 9.5 and 9.6, we represent power-
of-2 heaps (and handles to items) as links to nodes containing keys and
two links (like the explicit tree representation of tournaments in Figure 5.10); and we represent binomial queues as arrays of power-of-2
heaps, by including the following private members in our implementation of Program 9.8:

```
private static class Node
  { ITEM item; Node l, r;
    Node(ITEM v)
      { item = v; l = null; r = null; }
  }
private Node[] bq;
```

The arrays are not large and the trees are not high; and this representation is sufficiently flexible to allow implementation of all the
priority-queue operations in less than $\lg N$ steps, as we shall now see.

Each link in the array bq is a link to a power-of-2 heap: bq[i] is
either null or a link to a 2^i-heap. As the queue grows and shrinks, the
length of the array increases and decreases, but much less frequently:
for example, the array length increases by 1 only after the queue size
doubles. It will be convenient to always have the last link null, so we
begin with an array of size 1, a null link:

```
PQfull()
  { bq = new Node[1]; bq[0] = null; }
```

thus adopting the convention that a queue is empty if and only if the
array is of length 1.

Now, let us consider the *insert* operation. The process of inserting a new item into a binomial queue mirrors precisely the process
of incrementing a binary number. To increment a binary number, we
move from right to left, changing 1s to 0s because of the carry associated with $1 + 1 = 10_2$, until finding the rightmost 0, which we change
to 1. In the analogous way, to add a new item to a binomial queue, we
move from right to left, merging heaps corresponding to 1 bits with a

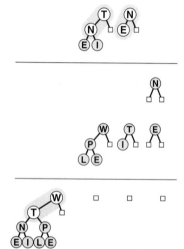

Figure 9.17
Insertion of a new element
into a binomial queue

Adding an element to a binomial queue of 7 nodes is analogous to performing the binary addition $111_2 + 1 = 1000_2$, with carries at each bit. The result is the binomial queue at the bottom, with an 8-heap and null 4-, 2-, and 1-heaps.

Program 9.14 Insertion into a binomial queue

To insert a node into a binomial queue, we first make the node into a 1-heap, identify it as a carry 1-heap, and then iterate the following process starting at i = 0. If the binomial queue has no 2^i-heap, we put the carry 2^i-heap into the queue. If the binomial queue has a 2^i-heap, we combine that with the new one (using the pair method from Program 9.13) to make a 2^{i+1}-heap, increment i, and iterate until finding an empty heap position in the binomial queue. When we carry in to the null link at the end of the array, we call grow to increase the size of the array by 1 and put a null link in the new position (*see text*).

```
Object insert(ITEM v)
  { Node t = new Node(v), c = t;
    for (int i = 0; i < bq.length+1; i++)
      {
        if (c == null) break;
        if (i == bq.length-1) bq = grow(bq);
        if (bq[i] == null) { bq[i] = c; break; }
        c = pair(c, bq[i]); bq[i] = null;
      }
    return t;
  }
```

carry heap, until finding the rightmost empty position to put the carry heap.

Specifically, to insert a new item into a binomial queue, we make the new item into a 1-heap. Then, if N is even (rightmost bit 0), we just put this 1-heap in the empty rightmost position of the binomial queue. If N is odd (rightmost bit 1), we join the 1-heap corresponding to the new item with the 1-heap in the rightmost position of the binomial queue to make a carry 2-heap. If the position corresponding to 2 in the binomial queue is empty, we put the carry heap there; otherwise, we merge the carry 2-heap with the 2-heap from the binomial queue to make a carry 4-heap, and so forth, continuing until we get to an empty position in the binomial queue. This process is depicted in Figure 9.17; Program 9.14 is an implementation.

When we add an element to a binomial queue with $2^k - 1$ items to make one with 2^k items, we carry into the null link at the end of the array, replacing it with a binomial tree of size 2^k (the rest of the

> **Program 9.15 Removal of the maximum in a binomial queue**
>
> We first scan the root nodes to find the maximum and remove the power-of-2 heap containing the maximum from the binomial queue. We then remove the root node containing the maximum from its power-of-2 heap and temporarily build a binomial queue that contains the remaining constituent parts of the power-of-2 heap. Finally, we use the *join* operation to merge this binomial queue back into the original binomial queue.
>
> ```
> ITEM getmax()
>   { int i, max; ITEM v = null;
>     for (i = 0, max = -1; i < bq.length; i++)
>       if (bq[i] != null)
>         if ((max == -1) || v.less(bq[i].item))
>           { max = i; v = bq[max].item; }
>     Node[] temp = new Node[max+1]; temp[max] = null;
>     Node x = bq[max].l; bq[max] = null;
>     for (i = max-1; i >= 0; i--)
>       { temp[i] = x; x = x.r; temp[i].r = null; }
>     bq = BQjoin(bq, temp);
>     return v;
>   }
> ```

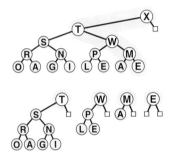

**Figure 9.18
Removal of the maximum in a power-of-2 heap**

Taking away the root gives a forest of power-of-2 heaps, all left-heap ordered, with roots from the right spine of the tree. This operation leads to a way to remove the maximum element from a binomial queue: Take away the root of the power-of-2 heap that contains the largest element, then use the join operation to merge the resulting binomial queue with remaining power-of-2 heaps in the original binomial queue.

links are all null). To adhere to our convention in this case, we need to add a null link at the end, which necessitates increasing the size of the array by 1. The method grow that Program 9.14 invokes for this task is simple to implement (see Exercise 9.62).

Other binomial-queue operations are also best understood by analogy with binary arithmetic. As we shall see, implementing *join* corresponds to implementing addition for binary numbers.

For the moment, assume that we have an (efficient) method for *join* that is organized to merge the priority-queue reference in its second operand with the priority-queue reference in its first operand (leaving the result in the first operand). Using this method, we could implement the *insert* operation with a call to the *join* method where one of the operands is a binomial queue of size 1 (see Exercise 9.66).

We can also implement the *remove the maximum* operation with one call to *join*. To find the maximum item in a binomial queue, we scan the queue's power-of-2 heaps. Each of these heaps is left-heap-ordered, so it has its maximum element at the root. The largest of the items in the roots is the largest element in the binomial queue. Because there are no more than $\lg N$ heaps in the binomial queue, the total time to find the maximum element is less than $\lg N$.

To perform the *remove the maximum* operation, we note that removing the root of a left-ordered 2^k-heap leaves k left-ordered power-of-2 heaps—a 2^{k-1}-heap, a 2^{k-2}-heap, and so forth—which we can easily restructure into a binomial queue of size $2^k - 1$, as illustrated in Figure 9.18. Then, we can use the *join* operation to combine this binomial queue with the rest of the original queue in order to complete the *remove the maximum* operation. This implementation is given in Program 9.15.

How do we join two binomial queues? First, we note that the operation is trivial if they do not contain two power-of-2 heaps of the same size, as illustrated in Figure 9.19: we simply merge the heaps from the two binomial queues to make one binomial queue. A queue of size 10 (consisting of an 8-heap and a 2-heap) and a queue of size 5 (consisting of a 4-heap and a 1-heap) simply merge together to make a queue of size 15 (consisting of an 8-heap, a 4-heap, a 2-heap, and a 1-heap). The more general case follows by direct analogy with performing addition on two binary numbers, complete with carry, as illustrated in Figure 9.20.

For example, when we add a queue of size 7 (consisting of a 4-heap, a 2-heap, and a 1-heap) to a queue of size 3 (consisting of a 2-heap and a 1-heap), we get a queue of size 10 (consisting of an 8-heap and a 2-heap); to do the addition, we need to merge the 1-heaps and carry a 2-heap, then merge the 2-heaps and carry a 4-heap, then merge the 4-heaps to get an 8-heap result, in a manner precisely analogous to the binary addition $011_2 + 111_2 = 1010_2$. The example of Figure 9.19 is simpler than Figure 9.20 because it is analogous to $1010_2 + 0101_2 = 1111_2$, with no carry.

This direct analogy with binary arithmetic carries through to give us a natural implementation for the *join* operation (see Program 9.16). For each bit, there are eight cases to consider, based on all the possible different values for the 3 bits involved (carry and 2 bits in the operands). The code is more complicated than that for plain addition, because we are dealing with distinguishable heaps, rather than with

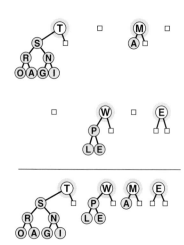

Figure 9.19
Joining of two binomial queues (no carry)

When two binomial queues to be joined do not have any power-of-2 heaps of the same size, the join operation is a simple merge. Doing this operation is analogous to adding two binary numbers without ever encountering $1 + 1$ (no carry). Here, a binomial queue of 10 nodes is merged with one of 5 nodes to make one of 15 nodes, corresponding to $1010_2 + 0101_2 = 1111_2$.

indistinguishable bits, but each case is straightforward. For example, if all 3 bits are 1, we need to leave a heap in the result binomial queue and to join the other two heaps for the carry into the next position. Indeed, this operation brings us full cycle on abstract data types: we (barely) resist the temptation to cast Program 9.16 as a purely abstract binary addition procedure, with the binomial-queue implementation nothing more than a client program using the more complicated bit addition procedure in Program 9.13.

We do a *join* operation after reducing the size of the binomial queue by 1. If the next-to-last link in the result is null, then we can shrink the size of the array by 1, since the last link in the result will be null. The method shrink that Program 9.16 invokes for this task is simple to implement (see Exercise 9.62).

Property 9.7 *All the operations for the priority-queue ADT can be implemented with binomial queues such that $O(\lg N)$ steps are required for any operations performed on an N-item queue.*

These performance bounds are the goal of the design of the data structure. They are direct consequences of the fact that the implementations all have only one or two loops that iterate through the roots of the trees in the binomial queue. ∎

Another option, which leads to a slightly simpler implementation, is to keep the number of trees in the queue constant (see Exercise 9.64) so that the running time of all the methods is proportional to this number (the logarithm of the maximum size of the binomial queue).

Property 9.8 *Construction of a binomial queue with N insert operations on an initially empty queue requires $O(N)$ comparisons in the worst case.*

For one-half the insertions (when the queue size is even and there is no 1-heap), no comparisons are required; for one-half the remaining insertions (when there is no 2-heap), only 1 comparison is required; when there is no 4-heap, only 2 comparisons are required; and so forth. Thus, the total number of comparisons is less than $0 \cdot N/2 + 1 \cdot N/4 + 2 \cdot N/8 + \ldots < N$. ∎

Binomial queues provide guaranteed fast performance, but data structures have been designed with even better theoretical performance

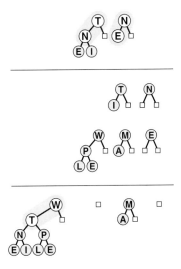

Figure 9.20
Joining of two binomial queues

Adding a binomial queue of 3 nodes to one of 7 nodes gives one of 10 nodes through a process that mimics the binary addition $011_2 + 111_2 = 1010_2$. Adding N to E gives an empty 1-heap in the result with a carry 2-heap containing N and E. Then, adding the three 2-heaps leaves a 2-heap in the result with a carry 4-heap containing T N E I. This 4-heap is added to the other 4-heap, producing the binomial queue at the bottom. Few nodes are touched in the process.

Program 9.16 Joining (merging) of two binomial queues

This code mimics the operation of adding two binary numbers. Proceeding from right to left with an initial carry bit of 0, we treat the eight possible cases (all possible values of the operands and carry bits) in a straightforward manner. For example, case 3 corresponds to the operand bits being both 1 and the carry 0. Then, the result is 0, but the carry is 1 (the result of adding the operand bits).

We exchange the references if necessary to make a reference the queue with the larger array representation, and we increase or decrease the size of a's array for the result, if warranted. If there is a carry into the last (null) link in case 4, it invokes grow; if the next-to-last link is null after the operation is complete, it invokes shrink.

Like pair, this method is a private method in the implementation, which is called by getmax and join. The implementation of the ADT method join(PQfull p) is the invocation BQjoin(bq, p.bq).

```java
static int bit(Node x)
  { return x == null ? 0 : 1; }
static int bits(Node C, Node B, Node A)
  { return 4*bit(C) + 2*bit(B) + 1*bit(A); }
static Node[] BQjoin(Node[] a, Node[] b)
  { Node c = null;
    if (a.length < b.length)
      { Node[] t = a; a = b; b = t; }
    for (int i = 0; i < b.length; i++)
      switch(bits(c, b[i], a[i]))
        {
          case 2: a[i] = b[i]; break;
          case 3: c = pair(a[i], b[i]);
                  a[i] = null; break;
          case 4: if (i == a.length-1) a = grow(a);
                  a[i] = c; c = null; break;
          case 5: c = pair(c, a[i]);
                  a[i] = null; break;
          case 6:
          case 7: c = pair(c, b[i]); break;
        }
    if (a[a.length-1] == null) a = shrink(a);
    return a;
  }
```

characteristics, providing guaranteed constant-time performance for certain operations. This problem is an interesting and active area of data-structure design. On the other hand, the practical utility of many of these esoteric structures is dubious. Before delving into complex data-structure solutions, we need to be certain that performance bottlenecks exist that we can relieve only by reducing the running time of some priority-queue operation. Indeed, for practical applications, we should prefer a trivial structure for debugging and for small queues; then, we should use heaps to speed up the operations unless fast *join* operations are required; finally, we should use binomial queues to guarantee loga   performance for all operations. All things considered, howe   package based on binomial queues is a valuable

Exercises

▷ **9.54** Dra   l-tree representation.

• **9.55** W   ation of a binomial queue, g   o keys).

9.56   ys E A S Y Q U E S T I O N ar

9.57 into wh qu g

'   the sequence of binomial queues

          F   L***U*E

are performed on an initially empty   queue.

9.59 Using the conventions of Exercise 9.2, give the sequence of binomial queues produced when the operations

$$(((P R I O *) + (R * I T * Y *)) * * *) + (Q U E * * * U * E)$$

are performed on an initially empty binomial queue.

9.60 Prove that a binomial tree with 2^n nodes has $\binom{n}{i}$ nodes at level i for $0 \leq i \leq n$. (This fact is the origin of the name *binomial tree*.)

▷ **9.61** Give an implementation for empty() that is appropriate for the binomial-queue implementation given in the text.

9.62 Implement the `grow` and `shrink` methods that increase by one and decrease by one, respectively, the size of a `Node` array leaving a `null` link in the last array position (`shrink` should throw an exception if that is not the case).

9.63 Change the binomial-queue implementation in the text to represent the queues with Java `Vector` objects instead of arrays.

○ **9.64** Develop a binomial-queue implementation that uses a fixed-size array of representation so that `grow` and `shrink` are not needed, but the operations all take time proportional to the array size.

○ **9.65** Modify your solution such that Property 9.7 holds, by maintaining a sentinel pointer to mark the point where the loops should terminate.

● **9.66** Implement *insert* for binomial queues by just using the *join* operation explicitly.

●● **9.67** Implement *change priority* and *remove* for binomial queues. *Note:* You will need to add a third link, which points up the tree, to the nodes.

● **9.68** Add an implementation of `clone` to the binomial-queue implementations (Programs 9.13 through 9.16) in the text, and test your implementation with your driver program from Exercise 9.44.

● **9.69** Empirically compare binomial queues against heaps as the basis for sorting, as in Program 9.6, for randomly ordered keys with $N = 1000$, 10^4, 10^5, and 10^6.

● **9.70** Develop an in-place sorting method like heapsort, but based on binomial queues. *Hint*: See Exercise 9.38.

CHAPTER TEN

Radix Sorting

F OR MANY SORTING applications, the keys used to define the
order of the records for files can be complicated. For example,
consider the complex nature of the keys used in a telephone book or
a library catalog. To separate this complication from essential properties of the sorting methods that we have been studying, we have used
just the basic operations of comparing two keys and exchanging two
records (hiding all the details of manipulating keys in these methods)
as the abstract interface between sorting methods and applications for
most of the methods in Chapters 6 through 9. In this chapter, we
examine a different abstraction for sort keys. For example, processing
the full key at every step is often unnecessary: to look up a person's
number in a telephone book, we often just check the first few letters
in the name to find the page containing the number. To gain similar efficiencies in sorting algorithms, we shall shift from the abstract
operation where we compare keys to an abstraction where we decompose keys into a sequence of fixed-sized pieces. Binary numbers are
sequences of bits, strings are sequences of characters, decimal numbers are sequences of digits, and many other (but not all) types of keys
can be viewed in this way. Sorting methods built on processing keys
one piece at a time are called *radix sorts*. These methods do not just
compare keys: They process and compare pieces of keys.

In radix-sorting algorithms, the pieces of the keys are of fixed
size, so there is a fixed number of different values each piece could
have. It is usually the case that the R different possible values for each
piece are the integers $0, 1, \ldots, R - 1$. Accordingly, our algorithms treat

the keys as numbers represented as base-R numbers, for various values of R (the *radix*), and work with individual digits of the numbers.

For example, when a machine at the post office processes a pile of packages that have on them 5-digit decimal numbers, it distributes the packages into ten piles: one having numbers beginning with 0, one having numbers beginning with 1, one having numbers beginning with 2, and so forth. The piles can then be processed individually, by using the same method on the next digit or by using some easier method if there are not many packages. If we were to pick up the packages in the piles in order from 0 to 9 and in order within each pile after they have been processed, we would get them in sorted order. This procedure is a radix sort with $R = 10$, and it is the method of choice in sorting applications where keys are 5- to 10-digit decimal numbers, such as postal codes, telephone numbers, or social-security numbers. We shall examine the method in detail in Section 10.3.

Different values of the radix R are appropriate in various applications. In this chapter, we focus primarily on keys that are integers (in Java, data of one of the primitive types `byte`, `char`, `short`, `int`, or `long`) or strings (in Java, `String` objects), where radix sorts are widely used. For integers, because they are represented as binary numbers in computers, we most often work with either $R = 2$ or some power of 2, because this choice allows us to decompose keys into independent pieces. For keys that involve strings of characters, we use $R = 2^8$ or $R = 2^{16}$, aligning the radix with the byte size. Beyond such direct applications, we can ultimately treat virtually *anything* that is represented inside a digital computer as a binary number, and we can recast many sorting applications using other types of keys to make feasible the use of radix sorts operating on keys that are binary numbers.

Radix-sorting algorithms are based on the abstract operation "extract the ith digit from a key." Fortunately, Java provides low-level operators that make it possible to implement such an operation in a straightforward and efficient manner. This fact is significant because some languages in the past (for example, Pascal), in order to encourage us to write machine-independent programs, intentionally made it difficult to write a program that depends on the way that a particular machine represents numbers. In such languages, it was difficult to implement many types of bit-by-bit manipulation techniques that actually suit most computers well. Radix sorting in particular was, for a time, a casualty of this "progressive" philosophy. But the designers of C, C++, and Java recognized that direct manipulation of bits is often useful, and we shall be able to take advantage of low-level language facilities to implement radix sorts.

Good hardware support also is required, and it cannot be taken for granted. Some machines provide efficient ways to get at small data, but some other machines slow down significantly when such operations are used. Whereas radix sorts are simply expressed in terms of the extract-the-digit operation, the task of getting peak performance out of a radix-sorting algorithm can be a fascinating introduction to our hardware and software environment.

There are two, fundamentally different, basic approaches to radix sorting. The first class of methods involves algorithms that examine the digits in the keys in a left-to-right order, working with the most significant digits first. These methods are generally referred to as *most-significant-digit (MSD) radix sorts*. MSD radix sorts are attractive because they examine the minimum amount of information necessary to get a sorting job done (see Figure 10.1). MSD radix sorts generalize quicksort, because they partition the file to be sorted according to the leading digits of the keys, then recursively apply the same method to the subfiles. Indeed, when the radix is 2, we implement MSD radix sorting in a manner similar to that for quicksort. The second class of radix-sorting methods is different: They examine the digits in the keys in a right-to-left order, working with the least significant digits first. These methods are generally referred to as *least-significant-digit (LSD) radix sorts*. LSD radix sorts are somewhat counterintuitive, since they spend processing time on digits that cannot affect the result, but it is easy to ameliorate this problem, and this venerable approach is the method of choice for many sorting applications.

10.1 Bits, Bytes, and Words

The key to understanding radix sorts is to recognize that (*i*) computers generally are built to process bits in groups called *machine words*, which are often grouped into smaller pieces call *bytes*; (*ii*) sort keys also are commonly organized as byte sequences; and (*iii*) byte values can also serve as array indices or machine addresses. Therefore, it will be convenient for us to work with the following abstractions.

.396465048	.015583409	.0
.353336658	.159072306	.1590
.318693642	.159369371	.1593
.015583409	.269971047	.2
.159369371	.318693642	.31
.691004885	.353336658	.35
.899854354	.396465048	.39
.159072306	.538069659	.5
.604144269	.604144269	.60
.269971047	.691004885	.69
.538069659	.899854354	.8

Figure 10.1
MSD radix sorting

Even though the 11 numbers between 0 and 1 on this list (left) *each have 9 digits for a total of 99 digits, we can put them in order* (center) *by just examining 22 of the digits* (right).

Definition 10.1 *A* **byte** *is a fixed-length sequence of bits; a* **string** *is a variable-length sequence of bytes; a* **word** *is a fixed-length sequence of bytes.*

In radix sorting, depending on the context, a *key* may be a word or a string. Some of the algorithms that we consider in this chapter depend on the keys being fixed length (words); others are designed to adapt to the situation when the keys are variable length (strings).

A typical machine might have 8- or 16-bit bytes and 32- or 64-bit words, and Java has built-in primitive data types whose numbers of bits are explicitly specified, but we use the terms *byte*, *string*, and *word* in a generic sense in this chapter, because it will be convenient for us to consider various other byte and word sizes as well (generally small integer multiples or fractions of built-in machine sizes).

Thus, we use machine- and application-dependent defined constants for the number of bits per word and the number of bits per byte; for example,

```
static final int bitsword = 32;
static final int bitsbyte = 8;
static final int bytesword = bitsword/bitsbyte;
static final int R = 1 << bitsbyte;
```

Also included in these definitions for use when we begin looking at radix sorts is the constant R, which is the number of different byte values. When using these definitions, we generally assume that bitsword is a multiple of bitsbyte, that the number of bits per machine word is not less than (typically, is equal to) bitsword, and that bytes are individually addressable.

Most computers have bitwise *and* and *shift* operations, which we can use to extract bytes from words. In Java, we can directly express the operation of extracting the Bth byte of an integer key as follows:

```
static int digit(int key, int B)
{ return (key >> bitsbyte*(bytesword-B-1)) & (R-1); }
```

For example, this method would extract byte 2 (the third byte) of a 32-bit number by shifting right $32 - 3*8 = 8$ bit positions, then using the mask 00000000000000000000000011111111 to zero out all the bits except those of the desired byte, in the 8 bits at the right.

Different computers have different conventions for referring to their bits and bytes—we are considering the bits in a word to be numbered, left to right, from 0 to `bitsword-1`, and the bytes in a word to be numbered, left to right, from 0 to `bytesword-1`. In both cases, we assume the numbering to also be from most significant to least significant.

Another option is to arrange things such that the radix is aligned with the byte size, and therefore a single access will get the right bits quickly. This operation is supported directly for `String` objects in Java: We take R to be 2^{16} (since `String` objects are sequences of 16-bit Unicode characters) and can access the Bth character of a `String` st either with the single method invocation `st.charAt(B)` or (after initially using `toCharArry` to convert each string to a key that is a character array) a single array access. In Java this approach could be used for numbers as well, because we are guaranteed that numbers will be represented the same way in all virtual machines. We also need to be aware that byte-access operations of this type might be implemented with underlying shift-and-mask operations similar to the ones in the previous paragraph in some implementations.

At a slightly different level of abstraction, we can think of keys as numbers and bytes as digits. Given a (key represented as a) number, the fundamental operation needed for radix sorts is to extract a digit from the number. When we choose a radix that is a power of 2, the digits are groups of bits, which we can easily access directly using one of the macros just discussed. Indeed, the primary reason that we use radices that are powers of 2 is that the operation of accessing groups of bits is inexpensive. In some computing environments, we can use other radices as well. For example, if a is a positive integer, the bth digit of the radix-R representation of a is

$$\lfloor a/R^b \rfloor \bmod R.$$

On a machine built for high-performance numerical calculations, this computation might be as fast for general R as for $R = 2$.

Yet another viewpoint is to think of keys as numbers between 0 and 1 with an implicit decimal point at the left, as shown in Figure 10.1. In this case, the bth digit of a is

$$\lfloor aR^b \rfloor \bmod R.$$

If we are using a machine where we can do such operations efficiently, then we can use them as the basis for our radix sort. This model also applies when keys are variable length (strings).

Thus, for the remainder of this chapter, we view keys as radix-R numbers (with `bitsword`, `bitsbyte`, and R not specified) and use a `digit` method to access digits of keys, with confidence that we will be able to develop appropriate implementations of `digit` for particular applications. As we have been doing with `less`, we might want to implement `digit` as a single-parameter class method in our `myItem` class, then implement a two-parameter static `digit` which invokes that method; or, for primitive-type items, we can substitute the primitive type name for item type names in our code and use a direct implementation of `digit` like the one given earlier in this section. For clarity, we use the name `bit` instead of `digit` when R is 2.

Definition 10.2 *A* **key** *is a radix-R number, with digits numbered from the left (starting at 0).*

In light of the examples that we just considered, it is safe for us to assume that this abstraction will admit efficient implementations for many applications on most computers, although we must be careful that a particular implementation is efficient within a given hardware and software environment.

We assume that the keys are not short, so it is worthwhile to extract their bits. If the keys are short, then we can use the key-indexed counting method of Chapter 6. Recall that this method can sort N keys known to be integers between 0 and $R - 1$ in linear time, using one auxiliary table of size R for counts and another of size N for rearranging records. Thus, if we can afford a table of size 2^w, then w-bit keys can easily be sorted in linear time. Indeed, key-indexed counting lies at the heart of the basic MSD and LSD radix-sorting methods. Radix sorting comes into play when the keys are sufficiently long (say, $w = 64$) that using a table of size 2^w is not feasible.

Exercises

▷ **10.1** How many digits are there when a 32-bit quantity is viewed as a radix-256 number? Describe how to extract each of the digits. Answer the same question for radix 2^{16}.

▷ **10.2** For $N = 10^3$, 10^6, and 10^9, give the smallest byte size that allows any number between 0 and N to be represented in a 4-byte word.

▷ **10.3** Implement a class `wordItem` that extends the `myItem` ADT of Section 6.2 to include a `digit` method as described in the text (and the constants `bitsword`, `bitsbyte`, `bytesword`, and R), for 64-bit keys and 8-bit bytes.

▷ 10.4 Implement a class `bitsItem` that extends the `myItem` ADT of Section 6.2 to include a `bit` method as described in the text (and the constants `bitsword`, `bitsbyte`, `bytesword`, and `R`), for 10-bit keys and 1-bit bytes.

○ 10.5 Implement a comparison method `less` using the `digit` abstraction (so that, for example, we could run empirical studies comparing the algorithms in Chapters 6 and 9 with the methods in this chapter, using the same data).

○ 10.6 Design and carry out an experiment to compare the cost of extracting digits using bit-shifting and arithmetic operations on your machine. How many digits can you extract per second, using each of the two methods? *Note:* Be wary; your compiler might convert arithmetic operations to bit-shifting ones, or vice versa!

• 10.7 Write a program that, given a set of N random decimal numbers ($R = 10$) uniformly distributed between 0 and 1, will compute the number of digit comparisons necessary to sort them, in the sense illustrated in Figure 10.1. Run your program for $N = 10^3$, 10^4, 10^5, and 10^6.

• 10.8 Answer Exercise 10.7 for $R = 2$, using random 32-bit quantities.

• 10.9 Answer Exercise 10.7 for the case where the numbers are distributed according to a Gaussian distribution.

10.2 Binary Quicksort

Suppose that we can rearrange the records of a file such that all those whose keys begin with a 0 bit come before all those whose keys begin with a 1 bit. Then, we can use a recursive sorting method that is a variant of quicksort (see Chapter 7): Partition the file in this way, then sort the two subfiles independently. To rearrange the file, scan from the left to find a key that starts with a 1 bit, scan from the right to find a key that starts with a 0 bit, exchange, and continue until the scanning pointers cross. This method is often called *radix-exchange sort* in the literature (including in earlier editions of this book); here, we shall use the name *binary quicksort* to emphasize that it is a simple variant of the algorithm invented by Hoare, even though it was actually discovered before quicksort was (*see reference section*).

Program 10.1 is a full implementation of this method. The partitioning process is essentially the same as Program 7.2, except that the number 2^b, instead of some key from the file, is used as the partitioning element. Because 2^b may not be in the file, there can be no guarantee that an element is put into its final place during partitioning. The algorithm also differs from normal quicksort because the recursive calls

```
A S O R T I N G E X A M P L E
A E O L M I N G E A X T P R S
                    S T P R X
                    S R P T
                    P R S
                      R S
A E A E G I N M L O
        I N M L O
        L M N O
              N O
          L M
A A E E G
    E E G
    E E
    E E
A A
A A
A A
A A E E G I L M N O P R S T X
```

Figure 10.2
Binary quicksort example

Partitioning on the leading bit does not guarantee that one value will be put into place; it guarantees only that all keys with leading 0 bits come before all keys with leading 1 bits. We can compare this diagram with Figure 7.1 for quicksort, although the operation of the partitioning method is completely opaque without the binary representation of the keys. Figure 10.3 gives the details that explain the partition positions precisely.

Program 10.1 Binary quicksort

This program sorts objects of type `bitsItem`, a class which allows access to the bits of the keys (see Exercise 10.4). It is a recursive method that partitions a file on the leading bits of the keys, and then sorts the subfiles recursively. The variable d keeps track of the bit being examined, starting at 0 (leftmost). The partitioning stops with j equal to i, and all elements to the right of a[i] having 1 bits in the dth position and all elements to the left of a[i] having 0 bits in the dth position. The element a[i] itself will have a 1 bit *unless* all keys in the file have a 0 in position d. An extra test just after the partitioning loop covers this case.

```
static void
quicksortB(bitsItem[] a, int l, int r, int d)
  { int i = l, j = r;
    if (r <= l || d > bitsItem.bitsword) return;
    while (j != i)
      {
        while (bit(a[i], d) == 0 && (i < j)) i++;
        while (bit(a[j], d) == 1 && (j > i)) j--;
        exch(a, i, j);
      }
    if (bit(a[r], d) == 0) j++;
    quicksortB(a, l, j-1, d+1);
    quicksortB(a, j, r, d+1);
  }
```

are for keys with 1 fewer bit. This difference has important implications for performance. For example, when a degenerate partition occurs for a file of N elements, a recursive call for a subfile of size N will result, for keys with 1 fewer bit. Thus, the number of such calls is limited by the number of bits in the keys. By contrast, consistent use of partitioning values not in the file in a standard quicksort could result in an infinite recursive loop.

As with standard quicksort, various options are available in implementing the inner loop. In Program 10.1, tests for whether the pointers have crossed are included in both inner loops. This arrangement results in an extra exchange for the case $i = j$, which could be avoided with a break, as is done in Program 7.2, although in this case

A 00001	A 00001	A 00001	A 00001	A 00001	A 00001	A 00001
S 10011	E 00101	E 00101	A 00001	A 00001	A 00001	A 00001
O 01111	O 01111	A 00001	E 00101	E 00101	E 00101	E 00101
R 10010	L 01100	E 00101	E 00101	E 00101	E 00101	E 00101
T 10100	M 01101	G 00111	G 00111	G 00111	G 00111	G 00111
I 01001	I 01001	I 01001	I 01001	I 01001	I 01001	I 01001
N 01110	N 01110	N 01110	N 01110	L 01100	L 01100	L 01100
G 00111	G 00111	M 01101	M 01101	M 01101	M 01101	M 01101
E 00101	E 00101	L 01100	L 01100	N 01110	N 01110	N 01110
X 11000	A 00001	O 01111	O 01111	O 01111	O 01111	O 01111
A 00001	X 11000	S 10011	S 10011	P 10000	P 10000	P 10000
M 01101	T 10100	T 10100	T 10100	R 10010	R 10010	R 10010
P 10000	P 10000	P 10000	R 10010	S 10011	S 10011	S 10011
L 01100	R 10010	R 10010	P 10000	T 10100	T 10100	T 10100
E 00101	S 10011	X 11000	X 11000	X 11000	X 11000	X 11000

Figure 10.3
Binary quicksort example (key bits exposed)

We derive this figure from Figure 10.2 by translating the keys to their binary encoding, compressing the table such that the independent subfile sorts are shown as though they happen in parallel, and transposing rows and columns. The first stage splits the file into a subfile with all keys beginning with 0, and a subfile with all keys beginning with 1. Then, the first subfile is split into one subfile with all keys beginning with 00, and another with all keys beginning with 01; independently, at some other time, the other subfile is split into one subfile with all keys beginning with 10, and another with all keys beginning with 11. The process stops when the bits are exhausted (for duplicate keys, in this example) or the subfiles are of size 1.

the exchange of a[i] with itself is harmless. Another alternative is to use sentinel keys.

Figure 10.2 depicts the operation of Program 10.1 on a small sample file, for comparison with Figure 7.1 for quicksort. This figure shows what the data movement is, but not *why* the various moves are made—that depends on the binary representation of the keys. A more detailed view for the same example is given in Figure 10.3. This example assumes that the letters are encoded with a simple 5-bit code, with the ith letter of the alphabet represented by the binary representation of the number i. This encoding is a simplified version of real character codes, which use more bits (7, 8, or even 16) to represent more characters (uppercase or lowercase letters, numbers, and special symbols).

For full-word keys consisting of random bits, the starting point in Program 10.1 should be the leftmost bit of the words, or bit 0. In general, the starting point that should be used depends in a straightforward way on the application, on the number of bits per word in the machine, and on the machine representation of integers and negative numbers. For the one-letter 5-bit keys in Figures 10.2 and 10.3, the starting point on a 32-bit machine would be bit 27.

This example highlights a potential problem with binary quicksort in practical situations: Degenerate partitions (partitions with all keys having the same value for the bit being used) can happen frequently. It is not uncommon to sort small numbers (with many leading zeros) as in our examples. The problem also occurs in keys comprising characters: for example, suppose that we make up 64-bit keys from four characters by encoding each in 16-bit Unicode and then putting them together. Then, degenerate partitions are likely to occur at the beginning of each character position, because, for example, lowercase letters all begin with the same bits. This problem is typical of the effects that we need to address when sorting encoded data, and similar problems arise in other radix sorts.

Once a key is distinguished from all the other keys by its left bits, no further bits are examined. This property is a distinct advantage in some situations; it is a disadvantage in others. When the keys are truly random bits, only about $\lg N$ bits per key are examined, and that could be many fewer than the number of bits in the keys. This fact is discussed in Section 10.6; see also Exercise 10.7 and Figure 10.1. For example, sorting a file of 1000 records with random keys might involve examining only about 10 or 11 bits from each key (even if the keys are, say, 64-bit keys). On the other hand, all the bits of equal keys are examined. Radix sorting simply does not work well on files that contain huge numbers of duplicate keys that are not short. Binary quicksort and the standard method are both fast if keys to be sorted comprise truly random bits (the difference between them is primarily determined by the difference in cost between the bit-extraction and comparison operations), but the standard quicksort algorithm can adapt better to nonrandom sets of keys, and 3-way quicksort is ideal when duplicate keys predominate.

As it was with quicksort, it is convenient to describe the partitioning structure with a binary tree (as depicted in Figure 10.4): The root corresponds to a subfile to be sorted, and its two subtrees correspond to the two subfiles after partitioning. In standard quicksort, we know that at least one record is put into position by the partitioning process, so we put that key into the root node; in binary quicksort, we know that keys are in position only when we get to a subfile of size 1 or we have exhausted the bits in the keys, so we put the keys at the bottom of the tree. Such a structure is called a *binary trie*—properties of tries are covered in detail in Chapter 15. For example, one important property of interest is that the structure of the trie is completely determined by the key values, rather than by their order.

Partitioning divisions in binary quicksort depend on the binary representation of the range and number of items being sorted. For example, if the files are random permutations of the integers less than

Figure 10.4
Binary quicksort partitioning trie

This tree describes the partitioning structure for binary quicksort, corresponding to Figures 10.2 and 10.3. Because no item is necessarily put into position, the keys correspond to external nodes in the tree. The structure has the following property: Following the path from the root to any key, taking 0 for left branches and 1 for right branches, gives the leading bits of the key. These are precisely the bits that distinguish the key from other keys during the sort. The small black squares represent the null partitions (when all the keys go to the other side because their leading bits are the same). This happens only near the bottom of the tree in this example, but could happen higher up in the tree: For example, if I or X were not among the keys, their node would be replaced by a null node in this drawing. Note that duplicated keys (A and E) cannot be partitioned (the sort puts them in the same subfile only after all their bits are exhausted).

$171 = 10101011_2$, then partitioning on the first bit is equivalent to partitioning about the value 128, so the subfiles are unequal (one of size 128 and the other of size 43). The keys in Figure 10.5 are random 8-bit values, so this effect is absent there, but the effect is worthy of note now, lest it come as a surprise when we encounter it in practice.

We can improve the basic recursive implementation in Program 10.1 by removing recursion and treating small subfiles differently, just as we did for standard quicksort in Chapter 7.

Exercises

▷ **10.10** Draw the trie in the style of Figure 10.2 that corresponds to the partitioning process in radix quicksort for the key E A S Y Q U E S T I O N.

10.11 Compare the number of exchanges used by binary quicksort with the number used by the normal quicksort for the file of 3-bit binary numbers 001, 011, 101, 110, 000, 001, 010, 111, 110, 010.

○ **10.12** Why is it not as important to sort the smaller of the two subfiles first in binary quicksort as it was for normal quicksort?

○ **10.13** Describe what happens on the second level of partitioning (when the left subfile is partitioned and when the right subfile is partitioned) when we use binary quicksort to sort a random permutation of the nonnegative integers less than 171.

10.14 Write a program that, in one preprocessing pass, identifies the number of leading bit positions where all keys are equal, then calls a binary quicksort that is modified to ignore those bit positions. Compare the running time of your program with that of the standard implementation for $N = 10^3, 10^4, 10^5$, and 10^6 when the input is 32-bit words of the following format: The rightmost 16 bits are uniformly random, and the leftmost 16 bits are all 0 except with a 1 in position i if there are i 1s in the right half.

10.15 Modify binary quicksort to check explicitly for the case that all keys are equal. Compare the running time of your program with that of the standard implementation for $N = 10^3, 10^4, 10^5$, and 10^6 with the input described in Exercise 10.14.

10.3 MSD Radix Sort

Using just 1 bit in radix quicksort amounts to treating keys as radix-2 (binary) numbers and considering the most significant digits first. Generalizing, suppose that we wish to sort radix-R numbers by considering the most significant bytes first. Doing so requires partitioning the array into R, rather than just two, different parts. Traditionally we

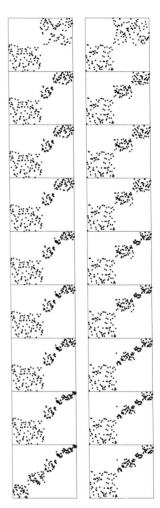

Figure 10.5
Dynamic characteristics of binary quicksort on a large file

Partitioning divisions in binary quicksort are less sensitive to key order than they are in standard quicksort. Here, two different random 8-bit files lead to virtually identical partitioning profiles.

refer to the partitions as *bins* or *buckets* and think of the algorithm as using a group of R bins, one for each possible value of the first digit, as indicated in the following diagram:

keys with first byte 0	keys with first byte 1	keys with first byte 2	· · ·	keys with first byte M-1
↑ bin 0	↑ bin 1	↑ bin 2		↑ bin M-1

We pass through the keys, distributing them among the bins, then recursively sort the bin contents on keys with 1 fewer byte.

Figure 10.6 shows an example of MSD radix sorting on a random permutation of integers. By contrast with binary quicksort, this algorithm can bring a file nearly into order rather quickly, even on the first partition, if the radix is sufficiently large.

As mentioned in Section 10.2, one of the most attractive features of radix sorting is the intuitive and direct manner in which it adapts to sorting applications where keys are strings of characters. This observation is especially true in Java and other programming environments that provide direct support for processing strings (`String` objects). For MSD radix sorting, we simply use a radix corresponding to the byte size. To extract a digit, we load a byte; to move to the next digit, we increment an index into a character array. For the moment, we consider fixed-length keys; we shall see shortly that variable-length string keys are easy to handle with the same basic mechanisms.

Figure 10.7 shows an example of MSD radix sorting on three-letter words. For simplicity, this figure assumes that the radix is 26, although in most applications we would use a larger radix corresponding to the standard Java Unicode character encodings. First, the words are partitioned so all those that start with a appear before those that start with b, and so forth. Then, the words that start with a are sorted recursively, then the words that start with b are sorted, and so forth. As is obvious from the example, most of the work in the sort lies in partitioning on the first letter; the subfiles that result from the first partition are small.

As we saw for quicksort in Chapter 7 and Section 10.2 and for mergesort in Chapter 8, we can improve the performance of most recursive programs by using a simple algorithm for small cases. Using a different method for small subfiles (bins containing a small number of elements) is essential for radix sorting, because there are so many of

Figure 10.6
Dynamic characteristics of MSD radix sort

Just one stage of MSD radix sort can nearly complete a sort task, as shown in this example with random 8-bit integers. The first stage of an MSD sort, on the leading 2 bits (left), divides the file into four subfiles. The next stage divides each of those into four subfiles. An MSD sort on the leading 3 bits (right) divides the file into eight subfiles, in just one distribution-counting pass. At the next level, each of those subfiles is divided into eight parts, leaving just a few elements in each.

them! Moreover, we can tune the algorithm by adjusting the value of R because there is a clear tradeoff: If R is too large, the cost of initializing and checking the bins dominates; if it is too small, the method does not take advantage of the potential gain available by subdividing into as many pieces as possible. We return to these issues at the end of this section and in Section 10.6.

To implement MSD radix sort, we need to generalize the methods for partitioning an array that we studied in relation to quicksort implementations in Chapter 7. These methods, which are based on pointers that start from the two ends of the array and meet in the middle, work well when there are just two or three partitions, but such methods do not immediately generalize. Fortunately, the *key-indexed counting* method from Chapter 6 for sorting files with key values in a small range suits our needs perfectly. We use a table of counts and an auxiliary array; on a first pass through the array, we count the number of occurrences of each leading digit value. These counts tell us where the partitions will fall. Then, on a second pass through the array, we use the counts to move items to the appropriate position in the auxiliary array.

Program 10.2 implements this process. Its recursive structure generalizes quicksort's, so the same issues that we considered in Section 7.3 need to be addressed. Should we do the largest of the subfiles last to avoid excessive recursion depth? Probably not, because the recursion depth is limited by the length of the keys. Should we sort small subfiles with a simple method such as insertion sort? Certainly, because there are huge numbers of them.

To do the partitioning, Program 10.2 uses an auxiliary array of size equal to the size of the array to be sorted. Alternatively, we could choose to use in-place key-indexed counting (see Exercises 10.19 and 10.20). We need to pay particular attention to space, because the recursive calls might use excessive space for local variables. In Program 10.2, the temporary buffer for moving keys (aux) can be global, but the array that holds the counts and the partition positions (count) must be local.

Extra space for the auxiliary array is not a major concern in many practical applications of radix sorting that involve long keys and records, because we normally are manipulating references to such data. Therefore, the extra space is for rearranging references and

now	ace	ace	ace
for	ago	ago	ago
tip	and	and	and
ilk	bet	bet	bet
dim	cab	cab	cab
tag	caw	caw	caw
jot	cue	cue	cue
sob	dim	dim	dim
nob	dug	dug	dug
sky	egg	egg	egg
hut	for	few	fee
ace	fee	fee	few
bet	few	for	for
men	gig	gig	gig
egg	hut	hut	hut
few	ilk	ilk	ilk
jay	jam	jay	jam
owl	jay	jam	jay
joy	jot	jot	jot
rap	joy	joy	joy
gig	men	men	men
wee	now	now	nob
was	nob	nob	now
cab	owl	owl	owl
wad	rap	rap	rap
caw	sob	sky	sky
cue	sky	sob	sob
fee	tip	tag	tag
tap	tag	tap	tap
ago	tap	tar	tar
tar	tar	tip	tip
jam	wee	wad	wad
dug	was	was	was
and	wad	wee	wee

Figure 10.7
MSD radix sort example

We divide the words into 26 bins according to the first letter. Then, we sort all the bins by the same method, starting at the second letter.

> **Program 10.2 MSD radix sort**
>
> This program sorts objects of type wordItem, a class which allows access
> to the bytes of the keys (see Exercise 10.3). It is a recursive method that
> is derived from Program 6.20 (key-indexed-counting sort) by changing
> key references to key-digit references and adding a loop at the end that
> does recursive calls for each subfile of keys starting with the same digit.
> This code assumes the keys to be of fixed length; it is easily adapted
> to handle variable-length keys (*see text*). As for Program 8.3, the aux
> array is a private member of Sort, allocated in sort before this method
> is invoked.
>
> ```
> private final static int M = 10;
> static void
> radixMSD(wordItem[] a, int l, int r, int d)
>   { int i, j, cnt[] = new int[wordItem.R+1];
>     if (d > wordItem.bytesword) return;
>     if (r-l <= M) { insertion(a, l, r); return; }
>     for (j = 0; j < wordItem.R; j++) cnt[j] = 0;
>     for (i = l; i <= r; i++)
>       cnt[digit(a[i], d) + 1]++;
>     for (j = 1; j < wordItem.R; j++)
>       cnt[j] += cnt[j-1];
>     for (i = l; i <= r; i++)
>       aux[cnt[digit(a[i], d)]++] = a[i];
>     for (i = l; i <= r; i++) a[i] = aux[i-l];
>     radixMSD(a, l, l+cnt[0]-1, d+1);
>     for (j = 0; j < wordItem.R-1; j++)
>       radixMSD(a, l+cnt[j], l+cnt[j+1]-1, d+1);
>   }
> ```

is small compared to the space for the keys and records themselves
(although still not insignificant). If space is available and speed is of
the essence (a common situation when we use radix sorts), we can also
eliminate the time required for the array copy by recursive argument
switchery, in the same manner as we did for mergesort in Section 8.4.

For random keys, the number of keys in each bin (the size of the
subfiles) after the first pass will be N/R on the average. In practice,
the keys may not be random (for example, when the keys are String
objects representing English-language words, we know that few start

with x and none start with xx, not to mention all the Unicode characters that we do not use), so many bins will be empty and some of the nonempty ones will have many more keys than others do (see Figure 10.8). Despite this effect, the multiway partitioning process will generally be effective in dividing a large file to be sorted into many smaller ones.

Another natural way to implement MSD radix sorting is to use linked lists. We keep one linked list for each bin: On a first pass through the items to be sorted, we insert each item into the appropriate linked list, according to its leading digit value. Then, we sort the sublists and stitch together all the linked lists to make a sorted whole. This approach presents a challenging programming exercise (see Exercise 10.42). Stitching together the lists requires keeping track of the beginning and the end of all the lists, and, of course, coping with the fact that many of the lists are likely to be empty.

To achieve good performance using radix sort for a particular application, we need to limit the number of empty bins encountered by choosing appropriate values both for the radix size and for the cutoff for small subfiles. As a concrete example, suppose that 2^{24} (about sixteen million) 64-bit integers are to be sorted. To keep the table of counts small by comparison with the file size, we might choose a radix of $R = 2^{16}$, corresponding to checking 16 bits of the keys. But after the first partition, the average file size is only 2^8, and a radix of 2^{16} for such small files is overkill. To make matters worse, there can be huge numbers of such files: about 2^{16} of them in this case. For each of those 2^{16} files, the sort sets 2^{16} counters to zero, then checks that all but about 2^8 of them are nonzero, and so forth, for a cost of *at least* 2^{32} arithmetic operations. Program 10.2, which is implemented on the assumption that most bins are nonempty, does more than a few arithmetic operations for each empty bin (for example, it does recursive calls for all the empty bins), so its running time would be huge for this example. A more appropriate radix for the second level might be 2^8 or 2^4. In short, we should be certain not to use large radices for small files in a MSD radix sort. We shall consider this point in detail in Section 10.6, when we look carefully at the performance of the various methods.

It is not difficult to modify Program 10.2 to handle variable-length keys. One particularly easy approach applies when we can use

Figure 10.8
MSD radix sort example (with empty bins)

Excessive numbers of empty bins are encountered, even in the second stage, for small files.

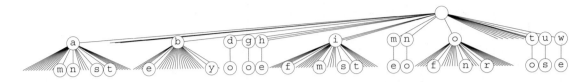

Figure 10.9
Recursive structure of MSD radix sort.

This tree corresponds to the operation of the recursive MSD radix sort in Program 10.2 on the two-letter MSD sorting example in Figure 10.8. If the file size is 1 or 0, there are no recursive calls. Otherwise, there are 26 calls: one for each possible value of the current byte.

the digit value 0 to serve to mark the end of a key (and we know that 0 can appear nowhere else in any key), as in C-style strings (see Section 3.6). Then we can remove the test on having reached the last byte at the beginning of Program 10.2 and just skip the recursive call corresponding to bin 0. Another approach is to include a `length()` method in `wordItem`, reserve bin 0 for keys with d not less than the key length, add 1 to all the other bin numbers, and skip the recursive call corresponding to bin 0.

To use Program 10.2 to sort Java `String` objects, we can use a `wordItem` implementation based on implementing the `digit` abstract operation as a single array access (as discussed in Section 10.1) and adopt either of the approaches described in the previous paragraph to handle the variable-length keys (see Exercises 10.21 and 10.22). By adjusting R and `bytesword` (and testing their values), we can easily make further modifications to handle string keys built from nonstandard alphabets or in nonstandard formats involving length restrictions or other conventions.

String sorting again illustrates the importance of managing empty bins properly. Figure 10.8 shows the partitioning process for an example like Figure 10.7, but with two-letter words and with the empty bins shown explicitly. In this example, we radix sort two-letter words using radix 26, so there are 26 bins at every stage. In the first stage, there are not many empty bins; in the second stage, however, most bins are empty.

An MSD radix-sorting method divides the file on the first digit of the keys, then recursively calls itself for subfiles corresponding to each value. Figure 10.9 shows this recursive-call structure for MSD radix sorting for the example in Figure 10.8. The call structure corresponds to a *multiway trie*, a direct generalization of the trie structure for binary quicksort in Figure 10.4. Each node corresponds to a recursive call on the MSD sort for some subfile. For example, the subtree of the root with root labeled o corresponds to sorting the subfile consisting of the three keys of, on, and or.

These figures make obvious the presence of significant numbers of empty bins in MSD sorting with strings. In Section 10.4, we study one way to cope with this problem; in Chapter 15, we examine explicit uses of trie structures in string-processing applications. Generally, we work with compact representations of the trie structures that do not include the nodes corresponding to the empty bins and that have the labels moved from the edges to the nodes below, as illustrated in Figure 10.10, the structure that corresponds to the recursive call structure (ignoring empty bins) for the three-letter MSD radix-sorting example of Figure 10.7. For example, the subtree of the root with root labeled j corresponds to sorting the bin containing the four keys jam, jay, jot, and joy. We examine properties of such tries in detail in Chapter 15.

The main challenge in getting maximum efficiency in a practical MSD radix sort for keys that are long strings is to deal with lack of randomness in the data. Typically, keys may have long stretches of equal or unnecessary data, or parts of them might fall in only a narrow range. For example, an information-processing application for student data records might have keys with fields corresponding to graduation year (4 bytes, but one of four different values), state names (perhaps 10 bytes, but one of 50 different values), and gender (1 byte with one of two given values), as well as to a person's name (more similar to random strings, but probably not short, with nonuniform letter distributions, and with trailing blanks in a fixed-length field). All these various restrictions lead to large numbers of empty bins during the MSD radix sort (see Exercise 10.27).

One practical way to cope with this problem is to develop a more complex implementation of the abstract operation of accessing bytes that takes into account any specialized knowledge that we might have about the strings being sorted. Another method that is easy to implement, which is called the *bin-span heuristic*, is to keep track of the high and low ends of the range of nonempty bins during the counting phase, then to use only bins in that range (perhaps also including special cases for a few special key values, such as 0 or blank). This arrangement is attractive for the kind of situation described in the previous paragraph. For example, with radix-256 alphanumeric data, we might be working with numbers in one section of the keys and thus have only 10 nonempty bins corresponding to the digits, while

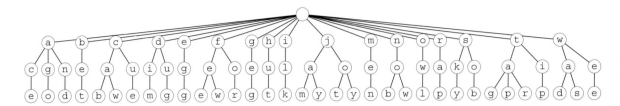

Figure 10.10
Recursive structure of MSD radix sort (null subfiles ignored)

This representation of the recursive structure of MSD radix sort is more compact than the one in Figure 10.9. Each node in this tree is labeled with the value of the $(i-1)$st digit of certain keys, where i is the distance from the node to the root. Each path from the root to the bottom of the tree corresponds to a key; putting the node labels together gives the key. This tree corresponds to the three-letter MSD sorting example in Figure 10.7.

we might be working with uppercase letters in another section of the keys and thus have only 26 nonempty bins corresponding to them.

There are various alternatives that we might try for extending the bin-span heuristic (*see reference section*). For example, we could consider keeping track of the nonempty bins in an auxiliary data structure, and only keep counters and do the recursive calls for those. Doing so (and even the bin-span heuristic itself) is probably overkill for this situation, however, because the cost savings is negligible unless the radix is huge or the file size is tiny, in which case we should be using a smaller radix or sorting the file with some other method. We might achieve some of the same cost savings that we could achieve by adjusting the radix or switching to a different method for small files by using an ad hoc method, but we could not do so as easily. In Section 10.4, we shall consider yet another version of quicksort that does handle the empty-bin problem gracefully.

Exercises

▷ **10.16** Draw the compact trie strucure (with no empty bins and with keys in nodes, as in Figure 10.10) corresponding to Figure 10.9.

▷ **10.17** How many nodes are there in the full trie corresponding to Figure 10.10?

▷ **10.18** Show how the set of keys `now is the time for all good people to come the aid of their party` is partitioned with MSD radix sort.

• **10.19** Write a program that does four-way partitioning in place, by counting the frequency of occurrence of each key as in key-indexed counting, then using a method like Program 11.5 to move the keys.

•• **10.20** Write a program to solve the general R-way partitioning problem, using the method sketched in Exercise 10.19.

○ **10.21** Implement a `stringItem` class for C-style strings. Use `String` keys with Unicode value 0 as a virtual end-of-string marker. (Implement `digit` such that it returns 0 when d is not less than the string length.)

∘ **10.22** Modify Program 10.2 so that it sorts Java `String` objects, by using the `length()` method to assign keys whose characters have all been examined to bin 0 and adjusting the other bins as appropriate.

10.23 Develop a `wordItem` implementation based on a key generator that generates random 80-byte keys. Use this implementation to generate N random keys, then sort them with MSD radix sort, for $N = 10^3$, 10^4, 10^5, and 10^6. Instrument your program to print out the total number of key bytes examined for each sort.

∘ **10.24** What is the rightmost key byte position that you would expect the program in Exercise 10.23 to access for each of the given values of N? If you have done that exercise, instrument your program to keep track of this quantity, and compare your theoretical result with empirical results.

10.25 Develop a `wordItem` implementation based on a key generator that generates keys by shuffling a random 80-byte sequence. Use your implementation to generate N random keys, then sort them with MSD radix sort, for $N = 10^3$, 10^4, 10^5, and 10^6. Compare your performance results with those for the random case (see Exercise 10.23).

10.26 What is the rightmost key byte position that you would expect the program in Exercise 10.25 to access for each value of N? If you have done that exercise, compare your theoretical result with empirical results from your program.

10.27 Develop a `wordItem` implementation based on a key generator that generates 30-byte random objects made up of three fields: a 4-byte field with one of a set of 10 given strings; a 10-byte field with one of a set of 50 given strings; a 1-byte field with one of two given values; and a 15-byte field with random left-justified strings of letters equally likely to be 4 through 15 characters long. Use your key generator to generate N random keys, then sort them with MSD radix sort, for $N = 10^3$, 10^4, 10^5, and 10^6. Instrument your program to print out the total number of key bytes examined. Compare your performance results with those for the random case (see Exercise 10.23).

10.28 Modify Program 10.2 to implement the bin-span heuristic. Test your program on the data of Exercise 10.27.

10.4 Three-Way Radix Quicksort

Another way to adapt quicksort for MSD radix sorting is to use three-way partitioning on the leading byte of the keys, moving to the next byte on only the middle subfile (keys with leading byte equal to that of the partitioning element). This method is not difficult to implement (the one-sentence description plus the three-way partitioning code in Program 7.5 suffices, essentially), and it adapts well to a variety of situations.

Program 10.3 is an implementation of this method for Java String objects. The less and equal methods that are used in this code are supposed to compare the d+1st character of two String objects whose first d characters are known to match. They may be implemented as follows:

```
static boolean less(String s, String t, int d)
  {
    if (t.length() <= d) return false;
    if (s.length() <= d) return true;
    return s.charAt(d) < t.charAt(d);
  }
static boolean equal(String s, String t, int d)
  { return !less(s, t, d) && !less(t, s, d); }
```

These methods are invoked only for strings that both have at least d characters (which are known to match). If both strings have more than d characters, less simply compares the indicated characters. Otherwise, if t has d characters, then s cannot be less than t—either s has d characters (in which case s and t are equal) or s has more than d characters (in which case t is less than s).

With slight modification, Program 10.3 can also be adapted for use with fixed-length keys (see Exercise 10.30) or with C-style strings (see Exercise 10.31). In both cases, the implementation of less is much simpler than the one above. This fact is significant because the inner loop of the algorithm is nothing more than a pointer increment and a less invocation, so speeding up less speeds up the whole program.

In essence, doing three-way radix quicksort amounts to sorting the file on the leading characters of the keys (using quicksort), then applying the method recursively on the remainder of the keys. For sorting strings, the method compares favorably with normal quicksort and with MSD radix sort. Indeed, it might be viewed as a hybrid of these two algorithms.

To compare three-way radix quicksort to standard MSD radix sort, we note that it divides the file into only three parts, so it does not get the benefit of the quick multiway partition, especially in the early stages of the sort. On the other hand, for later stages, MSD radix sort involves large numbers of empty bins, whereas three-way radix quicksort adapts well to handle duplicate keys, keys that fall into a small range, small files, and other situations where MSD radix sort

Program 10.3 Three-way radix quicksort

This MSD radix sort for Java String objects is essentially the same code as quicksort with three-way partitioning (Program 7.5), but with the following changes: (*i*) key references become key-character references, (*ii*) the current character position is a parameter to the recursive routine, and (*iii*) the recursive calls for the middle subfile move to the next character. We avoid moving past the ends of keys by checking whether d is equal to the length of v before recursive calls that move to the next byte. When d is equal to the length of v, the left subfile is empty, the middle subfile corresponds to the keys that the program has found to be equal, and the right subfile corresponds to longer strings that need to be processed further. For fixed-length keys, remove the tests guarding the recursive calls for d+1 and add a statement at the beginning that returns if d exceeds key length, as in Program 10.2.

```java
static void StrSort(String a[], int l, int r, int d)
{
  if (r <= l) return;
  String v = a[r];
  int i = l-1, j = r, p = l-1, q = r, k;
  while (i < j)
    {
      while (less(a[++i], v, d)) ;
      while (less(v, a[--j], d)) if (j == l) break;
      if (i > j) break;
      exch(a, i, j);
      if (equal(a[i], v, d)) exch(a, ++p, i);
      if (equal(v, a[j], d)) exch(a, --q, j);
    }
  if (p == q)  // first d+1 chars of all keys equal
    if (v.length() > d) StrSort(a, l, r, d+1);
  if (p == q) return;
  if (less(a[i], v, d)) i++;
  for (k = l; k <= p; k++, j--) exch(a, k, j);
  for (k = r; k >= q; k--, i++) exch(a, k, i);
  StrSort(a, l, j, d);
  if ((i == r) && (equal(a[i], v, d))) i++;
  if (v.length() >= d) StrSort(a, j+1, i-1, d+1);
  StrSort(a, i, r, d);
}
```

```
now gig ace ago  ago
for for bet bet  ace
tip dug dug and  and

ilk ilk cab ace  bet

dim dim dim cab
tag ago ago caw
jot and and cue

sob fee egg egg
nob cue cue dug
sky caw caw dim

hut hut fee
ace ace for
bet bet few

men cab ilk
egg egg gig
few few hut

jay jay jam
owl jot jay

joy joy joy
rap jam jot

gig owl owl  men

wee wee now owl
was was nob nob
cab men men now

wad wad rap

caw sky sky sky  sky
cue nob was tip  sob

fee sob sob sob tip  tar
tap tap tap tap tap  tap
ago tag tag tag tag  tag

tar tar tar tar tar  tip

dug tip tip was
and now wee wee
jam rap wad wad
```

Figure 10.11
Three-way radix quicksort

We divide the file into three parts: words beginning with a *through* i, *words begininning with* j, *and words beginning with* k *through* z. *Then, we sort recursively.*

might run slowly. Of particular importance is that the partitioning adapts to different types of nonrandomness in different parts of the key. Furthermore, no auxiliary array is required. Balanced against all these advantages is that extra exchanges are required to get the effect of the multiway partition via a sequence of three-way partitions when the number of subfiles is large.

Figure 10.11 shows an example of the operation of this method on the three-letter-word sorting problem of Figure 10.7. Figure 10.12 depicts the recursive-call structure. Each node corresponds to precisely three recursive calls: for keys with a smaller first byte (left child), for keys with first byte equal (middle child), and for keys with first byte larger (right child).

Even when the sort keys fit the abstraction of Section 10.2, standard quicksort and all the other sorts in Chapters 6 through 9 can be viewed as MSD radix sorts, because the compare method has to access the most significant part of the key first (see Exercise 10.5). For example, if the keys are strings, the compare method should access only the leading bytes if they are different, the leading 2 bytes if the first bytes are the same and the second different, and so forth. The standard algorithm thus automatically realizes some of the same performance gain that we seek in MSD radix sorting (see Section 7.7). The essential difference is that the standard algorithm cannot take special action when the leading bytes are equal. Indeed, one way to think of Program 10.3 is as a way for quicksort to keep track of what it knows about leading digits of items after they have been involved in multiple partitions. In the small subfiles, where most of the comparisons in the sort are done, the keys are likely to have many equal leading bytes. The standard algorithm has to scan over all those bytes for each comparison; the three-way algorithm avoids doing so.

Consider a case where the keys are long (and are fixed length, for simplicity), but most of the leading bytes are all equal. In such a situation, the running time of normal quicksort would be proportional to the word length *times* $2N \ln N$, whereas the running time of the radix version would be proportional to N times the word length (to discover all the leading equal bytes) *plus* $2N \ln N$ (to do the sort on the remaining short keys). That is, this method could be up to a factor of $\ln N$ faster than normal quicksort, counting just the cost of comparisons. It is not unusual for keys in practical sorting appli-

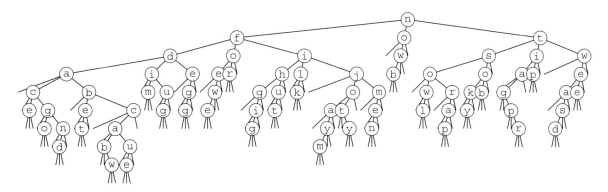

cations to have characteristics similar to this artificial example (see Exercise 10.29).

Another interesting property of three-way radix quicksort is that it has no direct dependencies on the size of the radix. For other radix-sorting methods, we have to maintain an auxiliary array indexed by radix value, and we need to ensure that the size of this array is not appreciably larger than the file size. For this method, there is no such table. Taking the radix to be extremely large (larger than the word size) reduces the method to normal quicksort, and taking the radix to be 2 reduces it to binary quicksort, but intermediate values of the radix give us an efficient way to deal with equal stretches among pieces of keys.

For many practical applications, we can develop a hybrid method with excellent performance by using standard MSD radix sort for large files, in order to get the advantage of multiway partitioning, and a three-way radix quicksort with a smaller radix for smaller files, in order to avoid the negative effects of large numbers of empty bins.

Three-way radix quicksort is also applicable when the keys to be sorted are *vectors* (either in the mathematical sense or in the sense of Java Vector objects). That is, if the keys are made up of independent components (each an abstract key), we might wish to reorder records such that they are in order according to the first components of the keys, *and* in order according to the second component of the keys if the first components are equal, and so forth. We can think of vector sorting as a generalization of radix sorting where we take R to be

Figure 10.12
Recursive structure of three-way radix quicksort

This tree-trie combination corresponds to a substitution of the 26-way nodes in the trie in Figure 10.10 by ternary binary search trees, as illustrated in Figure 10.13. Any path from the root to the bottom of the tree that ends in a middle link defines a key in the file, given by the characters in the nodes left by middle links in the path. Figure 10.10 has 1035 null links that are not depicted; all the 155 null links in this tree are shown here. Each null link corresponds to an empty bin, so this difference illustrates how three-way partitioning can cut dramatically the number of empty bins encountered in MSD radix sorting.

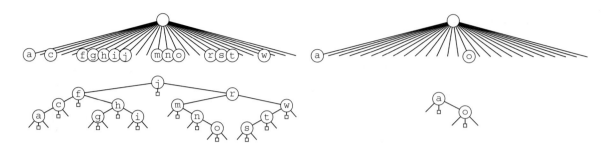

Figure 10.13
Example of trie nodes for three-way radix quicksort

Three-way radix quicksort addresses the empty-bin problem for MSD radix sort by doing three-way partitioning to eliminate 1 byte value and (recursively) to work on the others. This action corresponds to replacing each M-way node in the trie that describes the recursive call structure of MSD radix sort (see Figure 10.9) by a ternary tree with an internal node for each nonempty bin. For full nodes (left), this change costs time without saving much space, but for empty nodes (right), the time cost is minimal and the space savings is considerable.

arbitrarily large. When we adapt Program 10.3 to this application, we refer to it as *multikey quicksort*.

Exercises

10.29 For $d > 4$, suppose that keys consist of d bytes, with the final 4 bytes having random values and all the other bytes having value 0. Estimate the number of bytes examined when you sort the file using three-way radix quicksort (Program 10.3) and normal quicksort (Program 7.1) for files of size N for large N, and calculate the ratio of the running times.

10.30 Modify Program 10.3 so that it sorts objects with fixed-length keys, using type wordItem (see Exercise 10.3), as in Program 10.2.

10.31 Modify Program 10.3 so that it sorts objects with keys that are C-style strings, using type stringItem (see Exercise 10.21).

10.32 Empirically determine the byte size for which three-way radix quicksort runs fastest, for random 64-bit keys with $N = 10^3$, 10^4, 10^5, and 10^6.

• **10.33** Develop an implementation of three-way radix quicksort for linked lists.

10.34 Develop an implementation of multikey quicksort for the case where the keys are vectors of t floating-point numbers, using Vector objects and an implementation of equals that cconsiders two floating-point numbers to be equal if they differ in absolute value by less than 10^{-6}.

10.35 Using the key generator of Exercise 10.23, run three-way radix quicksort for $N = 10^3$, 10^4, 10^5, and 10^6. Compare its performance with that of MSD radix sort.

10.36 Using the key generator of Exercise 10.25, run three-way radix quicksort for $N = 10^3$, 10^4, 10^5, and 10^6. Compare its performance with that of MSD radix sort.

10.37 Using the key generator of Exercise 10.27, run three-way radix quicksort for $N = 10^3$, 10^4, 10^5, and 10^6. Compare its performance with that of MSD radix sort.

10.5 LSD Radix Sort

An alternative radix-sorting method is to examine the bytes from right to left. Figure 10.14 shows how our three-letter word sorting task is accomplished in just three passes through the file. We sort the file according to the final letter (using key-indexed counting), then according to the middle letter, then according to the first letter.

It is not easy, at first, to be convinced that the method works; in fact, it does not work at all unless the sort method used is *stable* (see Definition 6.1). Once stability has been identified as being significant, a simple proof that LSD radix sorting works is easy to articulate: After putting keys into order on their i trailing bytes (in a stable manner), we know that any two keys appear in proper order (considering just those bytes) in the file either because the first of their i trailing bytes are different, in which case the sort on that byte put them in the proper order, or because the first of their ith trailing bytes are the same, in which case they are in proper order because of stability. Stated another way, if the $w - i$ bytes that have not been examined for a pair of keys are identical, any difference between the keys is restricted to the i bytes already examined so the keys have been properly ordered and will remain so because of stability. If, on the other hand, the $w - i$ bytes that have not been examined are different, the i bytes already examined do not matter, and a later pass will correctly order the pair based on the more-significant differences.

The stability requirement means, for example, that the partitioning method used for binary quicksort could not be used for a binary version of this right-to-left sort. On the other hand, key-indexed counting *is* stable and immediately leads to a classic and efficient algorithm. Program 10.4 is an implementation of this method. An auxiliary array for the distribution seems to be required—the technique of Exercises 10.19 and 10.20 for doing the distribution in place sacrifices stability to avoid using the auxiliary array.

LSD radix sorting is the method used by old computer-card–sorting machines. Such machines had the capability of distributing a deck of cards among 10 bins, according to the pattern of holes punched in the selected columns. If a deck of cards had numbers punched in a particular set of columns, an operator could sort the cards by running them through the machine on the rightmost digit,

now	sob	cab	ace
for	nob	wad	ago
tip	cab	tag	and
ilk	wad	jam	bet
dim	and	rap	cab
tag	ace	tap	caw
jot	wee	tar	cue
sob	cue	was	dim
nob	fee	caw	dug
sky	tag	raw	egg
hut	egg	jay	fee
ace	gig	ace	few
bet	dug	wee	for
men	ilk	fee	gig
egg	owl	men	hut
few	dim	bet	ilk
jay	jam	few	jam
owl	men	egg	jay
joy	ago	ago	jot
rap	tip	gig	joy
gig	rap	dim	men
wee	tap	tip	nob
was	for	sky	now
cab	tar	ilk	owl
wad	was	and	rap
tap	jot	sob	raw
caw	hut	nob	sky
cue	bet	for	sob
fee	you	jot	tag
raw	now	you	tap
ago	few	now	tar
tar	caw	joy	tip
jam	raw	cue	wad
dug	sky	dug	was
you	jay	hut	wee
and	joy	owl	you

Figure 10.14
LSD radix sort example

Three-letter words are sorted in three passes (left to right) *with LSD radix sorting.*

Program 10.4 LSD radix sort

As does Program 10.2, this program implements key-indexed counting on the bytes in wordItem keys, but moving right to left. The key-indexed counting implementation must be stable. If R is 2 (and therefore bytesword and bitsword are the same), this program is *straight radix sort*—a right-to-left bit-by-bit radix sort (see Figure 10.15).

```
static void radixLSD(wordItem[] a, int l, int r)
  {
    for (int d = wordItem.bytesword-1; d >=0; d--)
      { int i, j, cnt[] = new int[wordItem.R+1];
        for (j = 0; j < wordItem.R; j++) cnt[j] = 0;
        for (i = l; i <= r; i++)
          cnt[digit(a[i], d) + 1]++;
        for (j = 1; j < wordItem.R; j++)
          cnt[j] += cnt[j-1];
        for (i = l; i <= r; i++)
          aux[cnt[digit(a[i], d)]++] = a[i];
        for (i = l; i <= r; i++) a[i] = aux[i-l];
      }
  }
```

then picking up and stacking the output decks in order, then running them through the machine on the next-to-rightmost digit, and so forth, until getting to the first digit. The physical stacking of the cards is a stable process, which is mimicked by key-indexed counting sort. Not only was this version of LSD radix sorting important in commercial applications in the 1950s and 1960s, but it was also used by many cautious programmers, who would punch sequence numbers in the final few columns of a program deck so as to be able to put the deck back in order mechanically if it were accidentally dropped.

Figure 10.15 depicts the operation of binary LSD radix sort on our sample keys, for comparison with Figure 10.3. For these 5-bit keys, the sort is completed in five passes, moving right to left through the keys. Sorting records with single-bit keys amounts to partitioning the file such that all the records with 0 keys appear before all the records with 1 keys. As just mentioned, we cannot use the partitioning strategy that we discussed at the beginning of this chapter in Pro-

A	00001	R	10010	T	10100	X	11000	P	10000	A	00001
S	10011	T	10100	X	11000	P	10000	A	00001	A	00001
O	01111	N	01110	P	10000	A	00001	A	00001	E	00101
R	10010	X	11000	L	01100	I	01001	R	10010	E	00101
T	10100	P	10000	A	00001	A	00001	S	10011	G	00111
I	01001	L	01110	I	01001	R	10010	T	10100	I	01001
N	01110	A	00001	E	00101	S	10011	E	00101	L	01100
G	00111	S	10011	A	00001	T	10100	E	00101	L	01101
E	00101	O	01111	M	01101	L	01100	X	11000	M	01101
X	11000	I	01001	E	00101	E	00101	I	01001	N	01110
A	00001	G	00111	R	10010	M	01101	L	01100	O	01111
M	01101	E	00101	N	01110	E	00101	M	01101	P	10000
P	10000	A	00001	S	10011	N	01110	N	01110	R	10010
L	01100	M	01101	O	01111	O	01111	O	01111	S	10011
E	00101	E	00101	G	00111	G	00111	G	00111	T	10100
										X	11000

Figure 10.15
LSD (binary) radix sort example (key bits exposed)

This diagram depicts a right-to-left bit-by-bit radix sort working on our file of sample keys. We compute the ith column from the $(i-1)$st column by extracting (in a stable manner) all the keys with a 0 in the ith bit, then all the keys with a 1 in the ith bit. If the $(i-1)$st column is in order on the trailing $(i-1)$ bits of the keys before the operation, then the ith column is in order on the trailing i bits of the keys after the operation. The movement of the keys in the third stage is indicated explicitly.

gram 10.1, even though it seems to solve this same problem, because it is not stable. It is worthwhile to look at radix-2 sorting, because it is often appropriate for high-performance machines and special-purpose hardware (see Exercise 10.44). In software, we use as many bits as we can to reduce the number of passes, limited only by the size of the array for the counts (see Figure 10.16).

It is typically difficult to apply the LSD approach to a string-sorting application because of variable-length keys. For MSD sorting, it is simple enough to distinguish keys according to their leading bytes, but LSD sorting is based on a fixed-length key, with the leading keys getting involved for only the final pass. Even for (long) fixed-length keys, LSD radix sorting would seem to be doing unnecessary work on the right parts of the keys since, as we have seen, only the left parts of the keys are typically used in the sort. We shall see a way to address this problem in Section 10.7, after we have examined the properties of radix sorts in detail.

Exercises

10.38 Using the key generator of Exercise 10.23, run LSD radix sort for $N = 10^3, 10^4, 10^5$, and 10^6. Compare its performance with that of MSD radix sort.

10.39 Using the key generators of Exercises 10.25 and 10.27, run LSD radix sort for $N = 10^3, 10^4, 10^5$, and 10^6. Compare its performance with that of MSD radix sort.

10.40 Show the (unsorted) result of trying to use an LSD radix sort based on the binary quicksort partitioning method for the example of Figure 10.15.

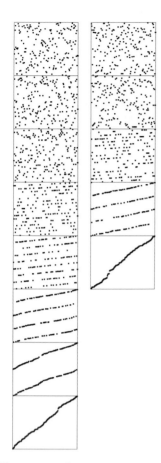

Figure 10.16
Dynamic characteristics of LSD radix sort

This diagram shows the stages of LSD radix sort on random 8-bit keys, for both radix 2 (left) and radix 4, which comprises every other stage from the radix-2 diagram (right). For example, when 2 bits remain (second-to-last stage on the left, next-to-last stage on the right), the file consists of four intermixed sorted subfiles consisting of the keys beginning with 00, 01, 10, and 11.

▷ 10.41 Show the result of using LSD radix sort on the leading two characters for the set of keys `now is the time for all good people to come the aid of their party`.

• 10.42 Develop an implementation of LSD radix sort using linked lists.

• 10.43 Find an efficient method that (*i*) rearranges the records of a file such that all those whose keys begin with a 0 bit come before all those whose keys begin with a 1 bit, (*ii*) uses extra space proportional to the square root of the number of records (or less), and (*iii*) is stable.

• 10.44 Implement a method that sorts an array of 32-bit words using only the following abstract operation: Given a bit position i and a pointer into the array `a[k]`, rearrange `a[k]`, `a[k+1]`, . . ., `a[k+63]` in a stable manner such that those words with a 0 bit in position i appear before those words with a 1 bit in position i.

10.6 Performance Characteristics of Radix Sorts

The running time of LSD radix sort for sorting N records with w-byte keys is proportional to Nw, because the algorithm makes w passes over all N keys. This analysis does not depend on the input, as illustrated in Figure 10.17.

For long keys and short bytes, this running time is comparable to $N \lg N$: For example, if we are using a binary LSD radix sort to sort 1 billion 32-bit keys, then w and $\lg N$ are both about 32. For shorter keys and longer bytes this running time is comparable to N: For example, if a 16-bit radix is used on 64-bit keys, then w will be 4, a small constant.

To compare properly the performance of radix sort with the performance of comparison-based algorithms, we need to account carefully for the bytes in the keys, rather than for only the number of keys.

Property 10.1 *The worst case for radix sorting is to examine all the bytes in all the keys.*

In other words, the radix sorts are *linear* in the sense that the time taken is at most proportional to the number of digits in the input. This observation follows directly from examination of the programs: No digit is examined more than once. This worst case is achieved, for all the programs we have examined, when all the keys are equal. ■

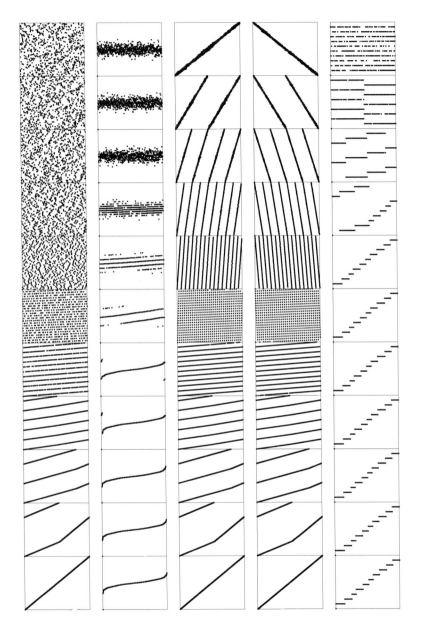

Figure 10.17
Dynamic characteristics of LSD radix sort on various types of files

These diagrams illustrate the stages of LSD radix sort for files of size 700 that are random, Gaussian, nearly ordered, nearly reverse ordered, and randomly ordered with 10 distinct key values (left to right). The running time is insensitive to the initial order of the input. The three files that contain the same set of keys (the first, third, and fourth all are a permutation of the integers from 1 to 700) have similar characteristics near the end of the sort.

As we have seen, for random keys and for many other situations, the running time of MSD radix sorting can be *sublinear* in the total number of data bits, because the whole key does not necessarily have to be examined. The following classical result holds for arbitrarily long keys:

Property 10.2 *Binary quicksort examines about $N \lg N$ bits, on average, when sorting keys composed of random bits.*

If the file size is a power of 2 and the bits are random, then we expect one-half of the leading bits to be 0 and one-half to be 1, so the recurrence $C_N = 2C_{N/2} + N$ should describe the performance, as we argued for quicksort in Chapter 7. Again, this description of the situation is not entirely accurate, because the partition falls in the center only on the average (and because the number of bits in the keys is finite). However, the partition is much more likely to be near the center for binary quicksort than for standard quicksort, so the leading term of the running time is the same as it would be were the partitions perfect. The detailed analysis that proves this result is a classical example in the analysis of algorithms, first done by Knuth before 1973 (*see reference section*). ∎

This result generalizes to apply to MSD radix sort. However, since our interest is generally in the total running time, rather than in only the key characters examined, we have to exercise caution, because part of the running time of MSD radix sort is proportional to the size of the radix R and has nothing to do with the keys.

Property 10.3 *MSD radix sort with radix R on a file of size N requires at least $2N + 2R$ steps.*

MSD radix sort involves at least one key-indexed counting pass, and key-indexed counting consists of at least two passes through the records (one for counting and one for distributing), accounting for at least $2N$ steps, and two passes through the counters (one to initialize them to 0 at the beginning and one to determine where the subfiles are at the end), accounting for at least $2R$ steps. ∎

This property almost seems too obvious to state, but it is essential to our understanding of MSD radix sort. In particular, it tells us that we cannot conclude that the running time will be low from the fact that N is small, because R could be much larger than N. In short, *some other method should be used for small files.* This observation is a solution to the empty-bins problem that we discussed at the end of Section 10.3. For example, if R is 256 and N is 2, MSD radix sort will be up to 128 times slower than the simpler method of just comparing elements. The recursive structure of MSD radix sort ensures that the recursive program will call itself for large numbers of small files. Therefore, ignoring the empty-bins problem could make the whole radix sort up to 128 times slower than it could be for this example. For intermediate situations (for example, suppose that R is 256 and N is 64), the cost is not so catastrophic, but is still significant. Using insertion sort is not wise, because its expected cost of $N^2/4$ comparisons is too high; ignoring the empty bins is not wise, because there are significant numbers of them. The simplest way to cope with this problem is to use a radix that is less than the file size.

Property 10.4 *If the radix is always less than the file size, the number of steps taken by MSD radix sort is within a small constant factor of $N \log_R N$ on the average (for keys comprising random bytes) and within a small constant factor of the number of bytes in the keys in the worst case.*

The worst-case result follows directly from the preceding discussion, and the analysis cited for Property 10.2 generalizes to give the average-case result. For large R, the factor $\log_R N$ is small, so the total time is proportional to N for practical purposes. For example, if $R = 2^{16}$, then $\log_R N$ is less than 3 for all $N < 2^{48}$, which value certainly encompasses all practical file sizes. ∎

As in Property 10.2, we have from Property 10.4 the important practical implication that MSD radix sorting is actually a *sublinear* function of the total number of bits for random keys that are not short. For example, sorting 1 million 64-bit random keys will require examining only the leading 20 to 30 bits of the keys, or less than one-half of the data.

Property 10.5 *Three-way radix quicksort uses $2N \ln N$ byte comparisons, on the average, to sort N (arbitrarily long) keys.*

There are two instructive ways to understand this result. First, considering the method to be equivalent to quicksort partitioning on the leading byte, then (recursively) using the same method on the sub-files, we should not be surprised that the total number of operations is about the same as for normal quicksort—but they are single-byte comparisons, not full-key comparisons. Second, considering the method from the point of view depicted in Figure 10.13, we expect that the $N \log_R N$ running time from Property 10.3 should be multiplied by a factor of $2 \ln R$ because it takes quicksort $2R \ln R$ steps to sort R bytes, as opposed to the R steps for the same bytes in the trie. We omit the full proof (*see reference section*). ∎

Property 10.6 *LSD radix sort can sort N records with w-bit keys in $w/\lg R$ passes, using extra space for R counters (and a buffer for rearranging the file).*

Proof of this fact is straightforward from the implementation. In particular, if we take $R = 2^{w/4}$, we get a four-pass linear sort. ∎

Exercises

10.45 Suppose that an input file consists of 1000 copies of each of the numbers 1 through 1000, each in a 32-bit word. Describe how you would take advantage of this knowledge to get a fast radix sort.

10.46 Suppose that an input file consists of 1000 copies of each of a thousand different 32-bit numbers. Describe how you would take advantage of this knowledge to get a fast radix sort.

10.47 What is the total number of bytes examined by three-way radix quicksort when sorting fixed-length bytestrings, in the worst case?

10.48 Empirically compare the number of bytes examined by three-way radix quicksort for long strings with $N = 10^3$, 10^4, 10^5, and 10^6 with the number of comparisons used by standard quicksort for the same files.

○ **10.49** Give the number of bytes examined by MSD radix sort and three-way radix quicksort for a file of N keys A, AA, AAA, AAAA, AAAAA, AAAAAA, ...

10.7 Sublinear-Time Sorts

The primary conclusion that we can draw from the analytic results of Section 10.6 is that the running time of radix sorts can be sublinear in the total amount of information in the keys. In this section, we consider practical implications of this fact.

The LSD radix-sort implementation given in Section 10.5 makes `bytesword` passes through the file. By making R large, we get an efficient sorting method, as long as N is also large and we have space for R counters. As mentioned in the proof of Property 10.5, a reasonable choice is to make $\lg R$ (the number of bits per byte) about one-quarter of the word size so that the radix sort is four key-indexed counting passes. Each byte of each key is examined, but there are only four digits per key. This example corresponds directly to the architectural organization of many computers: one typical organization has 32-bit words, each consisting of four 8-bit bytes. We extract bytes, rather than bits, from words, which approach is likely to be much more efficient on many computers. Now, each key-indexed–counting pass is linear, and, because there are only four of them, the entire sort is linear—certainly the best performance we could hope for in a sort.

In fact, it turns out that we can get by with only two key-indexed counting passes. We do so by taking advantage of the fact that the file will be *almost* sorted if only the leading $w/2$ bits of the w-bit keys are used. As with quicksort, we can complete the sort efficiently by using insertion sort on the whole file afterward. This method is a trivial modification to Program 10.4. To do a right-to-left sort using the leading one-half of the keys, we simply start the outer `for` loop at `bytesword/2-1`, rather than `bytesword-1`. Then, we use a conventional insertion sort on the nearly ordered file that results. Figures 10.3 and 10.18 provide convincing evidence that a file sorted on its leading bits is well ordered. Insertion sort would use only six exchanges to sort the file in the fourth column of Figure 10.3, and Figure 10.18 shows that a larger file sorted on only the leading one-half of its bits also could be sorted efficiently by insertion sort.

For some file sizes, it might make sense to use the extra space that would otherwise be used for the auxiliary array to try to get by with just *one* key-indexed–counting pass, doing the rearrangement in place. For example, sorting 1 million random 32-bit keys could be done with one key-indexed–counting sort on the leading 20 bits, then an insertion sort. To do that, we need space just for the (1 million) counters—significantly less than would be needed for an auxiliary array. Using this method is equivalent to using standard MSD radix sort with $R = 2^{20}$, although it is essential that a small radix be used for small files for such a sort (see the discussion after Property 10.4).

The LSD approach to radix sorting is widely used, because it involves extremely simple control structures and its basic operations

Figure 10.18
Dynamic characteristics of LSD radix sort on MSD bits

When keys are random bits, sorting the file on the leading bits of the keys brings it nearly into order. This diagram compares a six-pass LSD radix sort (left) on a file of random 6-bit keys with a three-pass LSD radix sort, which can be followed by an insertion-sort pass (right). The latter strategy is nearly twice as fast.

Table 10.1 Empirical study of radix sorts (integer keys)

These relative timings for radix sorts on random files of N 32-bit integers (all with a cutoff to insertion sort for N less than 16) indicate that, when used with care, radix sorts can be among the fastest sorts available. If we use a huge radix for tiny files, we ruin the performance of MSD radix sort, but adapting the radix to be less than the file size cures this problem. The fastest method for integer keys is LSD radix sort on the leading one-half of the bits, which we can speed up further by paying careful attention to the inner loop (see Exercise 10.51).

		4-bit bytes		8-bit bytes			16-bit bytes		
N	Q	M	L	M	L	L*	M	L	M*
12500	53	29	35	13	14	18	21	15	2
25000	49	22	40	19	20	16	26	23	5
50000	73	50	84	32	42	24	35	38	12
100000	91	99	170	66	89	51	61	74	64
200000	192	202	373	130	195	119	202	158	82
400000	410	457	784	515	413	274	62506	346	153
800000	892	1003	1587	2452	847	637	588076	726	1039

Key:
    Q   Quicksort, standard (Program 7.1)
    M   MSD radix sort, standard (Program 10.2)
    L   LSD radix sort (Program 10.4)
    M* MSD radix sort, radix adapting to file size
    L* LSD radix sort on MSD bits

are suitable for machine-language implementation, which can directly adapt to special-purpose high-performance hardware. In such an environment, it might be fastest to run a full LSD radix sort. We need to have space for just N extra references (and R counters) to use LSD radix sort, and this investment yields a method that can sort random files with only three or four passes.

In conventional programming environments, the inner loop of the key-indexed–counting program on which the radix sorts are based contains a substantially higher number of instructions than do the inner loops of quicksort or mergesort. This property of the implementations

Table 10.2 Empirical study of radix sorts (string keys)

These relative timings for various sorts on the first N words of *Moby Dick* (all, except heapsort, with a cutoff to insertion sort for N less than 16) indicate that the MSD-first approach is effective for string data. The cutoff for small subfiles is not effective unless we modify the insertion sort to avoid going through the leading parts of the keys (see Exercise 10.52). Three-way partitioning benefits from the large numbers of equal keys in the file and MSD radix sort benefits from the assumption that all characters are lower-case letters—in more general situations, three-way radix quicksort is likely to outperform the other methods.

N	Q	T	M	F	R	X	X*
12500	75	59	68	74	69	64	43
25000	129	107	145	169	127	115	102
50000	313	257	341	418	237	283	267
100000	819	603	757	986	500	681	649

Key:
- Q Quicksort, standard (Program 7.1)
- T Quicksort with three-way partitioning (Program 7.5)
- M Mergesort (Program 8.3)
- F Heapsort with Floyd's improvement (see Section 9.4)
- R MSD radix sort (Program 10.2)
- X Three-way radix quicksort (Program 10.3)
- X* Three-way radix quicksort (with cutoff)

implies that the sublinear methods that we have been describing may not be as much faster than quicksort (say) as we might expect in many situations.

General-purpose algorithms such as quicksort are more widely used than radix sort, because they adapt to a broader variety of applications. The primary reason for this state of affairs is that the key abstraction on which radix sort is built is less general than the one that we used in Chapters 6 through 9. Our use of the ITEM interface to specify that items to be sorted must have a less method (and Java's use of Comparable and compareTo for the same purpose) is to have the client provide the comparison method. This arrangement not only handles situations where the client can use specialized knowledge about complex keys to implement a fast comparison but also allows us to sort using an ordering relation that may not involve keys at all. Radix sorting may not be applicable in such situations.

When any of them could be used, the choice among quicksort and the various radix sort algorithms (and related versions of quicksort!) that we have considered in this chapter will depend not only on features of the application (such as key, record, and file size) but also on features of the programming and machine environment that relate to the efficiency of access and use of individual bits and bytes. Tables 10.1 and 10.2 give empirical results in support of the conclusion that the linear- and sublinear-time performance results that we have discussed for various applications of radix sorts make these sorting methods an attractive choice for a variety of suitable applications.

Exercises

▷ **10.50** What is the major drawback of doing LSD radix sorting on the leading bits of the keys, then cleaning up with insertion sort afterward?

• **10.51** Develop an implementation of LSD radix sort for 32-bit keys with as few instructions as possible in the inner loop.

10.52 Implement three-way radix quicksort such that the insertion sort for small files does not use leading bytes that are known to be equal in comparisons.

10.53 Given 1 million random 32-bit keys, find the choice of byte size that minimizes the total running time when we use the method of using LSD radix sort on the first 2 bytes, then using insertion sort to clean up.

10.54 Answer Exercise 10.53 for 1 billion 64-bit keys.

10.55 Answer Exercise 10.54 for *three-pass* LSD radix sort.

CHAPTER ELEVEN

Special-Purpose Sorting Methods

SORTING METHODS ARE critical components of many applications systems, and it is not unusual for special measures to be taken to make a sort as fast as possible or capable of handling huge files. We might encounter high-performance enhancements to a computer system, or special-purpose hardware specifically designed for sorting, or simply a new computer system based on some new architectural design. In such cases, the implicit assumptions that we have been making about the relative costs of operations on the data to be sorted may not be valid. In this chapter, we examine examples of sorting methods that are designed to run efficiently on various different kinds of machines. We consider several different examples of the restrictions imposed by high-performance hardware, and several methods that are useful in practice for implementing high-performance sorts.

Any new computer architecture is eventually going to need to support an efficient sorting method. Indeed, sorting has historically served as one testbed for evaluating new architectures, because it is so important and so well understood. We want to learn not just which known algorithms run best on a new machine and why, but also whether specific characteristics of a new machine can be exploited in some new algorithm. To develop a new algorithm, we define an abstract machine that encapsulates the essential properties of the real machine; design and analyze algorithms for the abstract machine; then implement, test, and refine both the best algorithms and the model. We draw on our past experience, including the many methods for general-purpose machines that we have seen in Chapters 6 through 10, but the abstract machines impose limitations that help us to focus on the true costs and make it clear that different algorithms are appropriate for different machines.

At one end of the spectrum, we shall consider low-level models where the only allowed operation is the compare–exchange operation. At the other end of the spectrum, we shall consider high-level models where we read and write large blocks of data to a slow external medium or among independent parallel processors.

First, we examine a version of mergesort known as *Batcher's odd–even mergesort*. It is based on a divide-and-conquer merge algorithm that uses only compare–exchange operations, with *perfect-shuffle* and *perfect-unshuffle* operations for data movement. These are of interest in their own right and apply to many problems other than sorting. Next, we examine Batcher's method as a sorting network. A *sorting network* is a simple abstraction for low-level sorting hardware. Networks consist of interconnected *comparators*, which are modules capable of performing compare–exchange operations.

Another important abstract sorting problem is the *external-sorting* problem, where the file to be sorted is far too large to fit in memory. The cost of accessing individual records can be prohibitive, so we shall use an abstract model, where records are transferred to and from external devices in large blocks. We consider two algorithms for external sorting and use the model to compare them.

Finally, we consider *parallel sorting*, for the case when the file to be sorted is distributed among independent parallel processors. We define a simple parallel-machine model, then examine how Batcher's method provides an effective solution. Our use of the same basic algorithm to solve a high-level problem and a low-level problem is a convincing example of the power of abstraction.

The different abstract machines in this chapter are simple but are worthy of study because they encapsulate specific constraints that can be critical in particular sorting applications. Low-level sorting hardware has to consist of simple components; external sorts generally require access to huge data files in blocks, with sequential access more efficient than random access; and parallel sorting involves communications constraints among processors. On the one hand, we cannot do justice to detailed machine models that fully correspond to particular real machines; on the other hand, the abstractions that we do consider lead us not only to theoretical formulations that provide information about essential limitations on performance but also to interesting algorithms that are of direct practical utility.

11.1 Batcher's Odd–Even Mergesort

To begin, we shall consider a sorting method that is based on just two abstract operations: the *compare–exchange* operation and the *perfect shuffle* operation (along with its inverse, the *perfect unshuffle*). The algorithm, developed by Batcher in 1968, is known as *Batcher's odd-even mergesort*. It is a simple task to implement the algorithm using shuffles, compare–exchanges, and double recursion, but it is more challenging to understand why the algorithm works and to untangle the shuffles and recursion to see how it operates at a low level.

We encountered the compare–exchange operation briefly in Chapter 6, where we noted that some of the elementary sort methods discussed there could be expressed more concisely in terms of this abstract operation. Now, we are interested in methods that examine the data *exclusively* with compare–exchange operations. Standard comparisons are ruled out: The compare–exchange operation does not return a result, so there is no way for a program to take action that depends on data values.

Definition 11.1 *A* **nonadaptive** *sorting algorithm is one where the sequence of operations performed depends on only the number of the inputs, rather than on the values of the keys.*

In this section, we do allow operations that unilaterally rearrange the data, such as exchanges and perfect shuffles, but they are not essential, as we shall see in Section 11.2. Nonadaptive methods are equivalent to *straight-line programs* for sorting: They can be expressed simply as a list of the compare–exchange operations to be performed. For example, the sequence

```
compexch(a[0], a[1])
compexch(a[1], a[2])
compexch(a[0], a[1])
```

is a straight-line program for sorting three elements. We use loops, shuffles, and other high-level operations for convenience and economy in expressing algorithms, but our goal in developing an algorithm is to define, for each N, a fixed sequence of compexch operations that

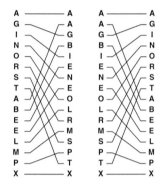

Figure 11.1
Perfect shuffle and perfect unshuffle

To perform a perfect shuffle (left), we take the first element in the file, then the first element in the second half, then the second element in the file, then the second element in the second half, and so forth. Consider the elements to be numbered starting at 0, top to bottom. Then, elements in the first half go to even-numbered positions, and elements in the second half go to odd-numbered positions. To perform a perfect unshuffle (right), we do the opposite: Elements in even-numbered positions go to the first half, and elements in odd-numbered positions go to the second half.

Program 11.1 Perfect shuffle and perfect unshuffle

The shuffle function rearranges a subarray a[1], ..., a[r] by splitting that subarray in half, then alternating elements from each half: Elements in the first half go in the even-numbered positions in the result, and elements in the second half go in the odd-numbered positions in the result. The unshuffle function does the opposite: Elements in the even-numbered positions go in the first half of the result, and elements in the odd-numbered positions go in the second half of the result.

We use these functions only for subarrays with an even number of elements. Also, while both use an auxiliary array, initialized as for mergesort (see Program 8.3), it is not difficult to do these permutations without using such an array (see Exercise 11.42).

```
static ITEM[] aux;
static void shuffle(ITEM a[], int l, int r)
  { int i, j, m = (l+r)/2;
    for (i = l, j = 0; i <= r; i+=2, j++)
      { aux[i] = a[l+j]; aux[i+1] = a[m+1+j]; }
    for (i = l; i <= r; i++) a[i] = aux[i];
  }
static void unshuffle(ITEM a[], int l, int r)
  { int i, j, m = (l+r)/2;
    for (i = l, j = 0; i <= r; i+=2, j++)
      { aux[l+j] = a[i]; aux[m+1+j] = a[i+1]; }
    for (i = l; i <= r; i++) a[i] = aux[i];
  }
```

---

can sort any set of N keys. We can assume without loss of generality that the key values are the integers 1 through N (see Exercise 11.4); to know that a straight-line program is correct, we have to prove that it sorts each possible permutation of these values (see, for example, Exercise 11.5).

Few of the sorting algorithms that we considered in Chapters 6 through 10 are nonadaptive—they all use less or examine the keys in other ways, then take differing actions depending on key values. One exception is bubble sort (see Section 6.5), which uses only compare–exchanges. Pratt's version of shellsort (see Section 6.8) is another nonadaptive method.

Program 11.1 gives an implementation of the other abstract operations that we shall be using—the perfect shuffle and the perfect unshuffle—and Figure 11.1 gives an example of each. The perfect shuffle rearranges an array in a manner corresponding to the way that a deck of cards might be rearranged when shuffled by an expert: It is split precisely in half, then the cards are taken alternately from each half to make the shuffled deck. We always take the first card from the top half of the deck. If the number of cards is even, the two halves have the same number of cards; if the number of cards is odd, the extra card ends up in the top half. The perfect unshuffle does the opposite: We make the unshuffled deck by putting cards alternately in the top half and the bottom half.

Batcher's sort is exactly the top-down mergesort of Section 8.3; the difference is that instead of one of the adaptive merge implementations from Chapter 8, it uses Batcher's odd-even merge, a nonadaptive top-down recursive merge. Program 8.3 itself does not access the data at all, so our use of a nonadaptive merge implies that the whole sort is nonadaptive.

We shall implicitly assume in the text throughout this section and Section 11.2 that the number of items to be sorted is a power of 2. Then, we can always refer to "$N/2$" without a caveat about N being odd, and so forth. This assumption is impractical, of course—our programs and examples involve other file sizes—but it simplifies the discussion considerably. We shall return to this issue at the end of Section 11.2.

Batcher's merge is itself a divide-and-conquer recursive method. To do a 1-by-1 merge, we use a single compare–exchange operation. Otherwise, to do an N-by-N merge, we unshuffle to get two $N/2$-by-$N/2$ merging problems, and then solve them recursively to get two sorted files. Shuffling these files, we get a file that is nearly sorted—all that is needed is a single pass of $N/2 - 1$ independent compare–exchange operations: between elements $2i$ and $2i + 1$ for i from 1 to $N/2 - 1$. An example is depicted in Figure 11.2. From this description, the implementation in Program 11.2 is immediate.

Why does this method sort all possible input permutations? The answer to this question is not at all obvious—the classical proof is an indirect one that depends on a general characteristic of nonadaptive sorting programs.

Figure 11.2
Top-down Batcher's odd–even merge example

To merge A G I N O R S T with A E E L M P X Y, we begin with an unshuffle operation, which creates two independent merging problems of about one-half the size (shown in the second line): we have to merge A I O S with A E M X (in the first half of the array) and G N R T with E L P Y (in the second half of the array). After solving these subproblems recursively, we shuffle the solutions to these problems (shown in the next-to-last line) and complete the sort by compare–exchanging E with A, G with E, L with I, N with M, P with O, R with S, and T with X.

Program 11.2 Batcher's odd–even merge (recursive version)

This recursive program implements an abstract inplace merge, using the
`shuffle` and `unshuffle` operations from Program 11.1, although they
are not essential—Program 11.3 is a bottom-up nonrecursive version
of this program with shuffling removed. Our primary interest here is
that this implementation provides a compact description of Batcher's
algorithm, when the file size is a power of 2.

```
static void merge(ITEM[] a, int l, int m, int r)
  {
    if (r == l+1) compExch(a, l, r);
    if (r < l+2) return;
    unshuffle(a, l, r);
    merge(a, l, (l+m)/2, m);
    merge(a, m+1, (m+1+r)/2, r);
    shuffle(a, l, r);
    for (int i = l+1; i < r; i+=2)
      compExch(a, i, i+1);
  }
```

Property 11.1 (*0–1 principle*) *If a nonadaptive program produces
sorted output when the inputs are all either 0 or 1, then it does so
when the inputs are arbitrary keys.*

See Exercise 11.7. ∎

Property 11.2 *Batcher's odd–even merge (Program 11.2) is a valid
merging method.*

Using the 0–1 principle, we check only that the method properly merges
when the inputs are all either 0 or 1. Suppose that there are i 0s in the
first subfile and j 0s in the second subfile. The proof of this property
involves checking four cases, depending on whether i and j are odd or
even. If they are both even, then the two merging subproblems each
involve one file with $i/2$ 0s and one file with $j/2$ 0s, so both results
have $(i + j)/2$ 0s. Shuffling, we get a sorted 0–1 file. The 0–1 file
is also sorted after shuffling in the case that i is even and j is odd
and the case that i is odd and j is even. But if both i and j are odd,
then we end up shuffling a file with $(i + j)/2 + 1$ 0s with a file with
$(i + j)/2 - 1$ 0s, so the 0–1 file after shuffling has $i + j - 1$ 0s, a 1, a

0, then $N - i - j - 1$ 1s (see Figure 11.3), and one of the comparators in the final stage completes the sort. ∎

We do not need actually to shuffle the data. Indeed, we can use Programs 11.2 and 8.3 to output a straight-line sorting program for any N, by changing the implementations of compexch and shuffle to maintain indices and to refer to the data indirectly (see Exercise 11.12). Or, we can have the program output the compare–exchange instructions to use on the original input (see Exercise 11.13). We could apply these techniques to any nonadaptive sorting method that rearranges the data with exchanges, shuffles, or similar operations. For Batcher's merge, the structure of the algorithm is so simple that we can develop a bottom-up implementation directly, as we shall see in Section 11.2.

Exercises

▷ **11.1** Give the result of shuffling and unshuffling the keys E A S Y Q U E S T I O N.

11.2 Generalize Program 11.1 to implement h-way shuffle and unshuffle. Defend your strategy for the case that the file size is not a multiple of h.

● **11.3** Implement the shuffle and unshuffle operations without using an auxiliary array.

● **11.4** Show that a straight-line program that sorts N distinct keys will sort N keys that are not necessarily distinct.

▷ **11.5** Show how the straight-line program given in the text sorts each of the six permutations of the integers 1, 2, and 3.

○ **11.6** Give a straight-line program that sorts four elements.

● **11.7** Prove Property 11.1. *Hint:* Show that if the program does not sort some input array with arbitrary keys, then there is some 0–1 sequence that it does not sort.

▷ **11.8** Show how the keys A E Q S U Y E I N O S T are merged using Program 11.2, in the style of the example diagrammed in Figure 11.2.

▷ **11.9** Answer Exercise 11.8 for the keys A E S Y E I N O Q S T U.

○ **11.10** Answer Exercise 11.8 for the keys 1 0 0 1 1 1 0 0 0 0 0 1 0 1 0 0.

11.11 Empirically compare the running time of Batcher's mergesort with that of standard top-down mergesort (Programs 8.3 and 8.2) for $N = 10^3$, 10^4, 10^5, and 10^6.

11.12 Give implementations of compexch, shuffle, and unshuffle that cause Programs 11.2 and 8.3 to compute, given N, an array p such that p[i] is the index of the ith smallest element, for $0 \le i < N$.

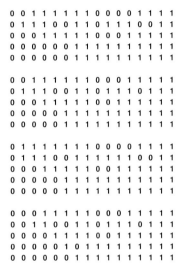

Figure 11.3
Four cases for 0-1 merging

These four examples consist of five lines each: a 0-1 merging problem; the result of an unshuffle operation, which gives two merging problems; the result of recursively completing the merges; the result of a shuffle; and the result of the final odd–even compares. The last stage performs an exchange only when the number of 0s in both input files is odd.

○ **11.13** Give implementations of `compexch`, `shuffle`, and `unshuffle` that cause Programs 11.2 and 8.3 to print, given N, a straight-line program for sorting N elements.

11.14 If we put the second file for the merge in reverse order, we have a *bitonic* sequence, as defined in Section 8.2. Changing the final loop in Program 11.2 to start at 1 instead of l+1 turns the program into one that sorts bitonic sequences. Show how the keys A E S Q U Y T S O N I E are merged using this method, in the style of the example diagrammed in Figure 11.2.

● **11.15** Prove that the modified Program 11.2 described in Exercise 11.14 sorts any bitonic sequence.

11.2 Sorting Networks

The simplest model for studying nonadaptive sorting algorithms is an abstract machine that can access the data *only* through compare–exchange operations. Such a machine is called a *sorting network*. A sorting network comprises atomic *compare–exchange modules*, or *comparators*, which are wired together so as to implement the capability to perform fully general sorting.

Figure 11.4 shows a simple sorting network for four keys. Customarily, we draw a sorting network for N items as a sequence of N horizontal lines, with comparators connecting pairs of lines. We imagine that the keys to be sorted pass from right to left through the network, with a pair of numbers exchanged if necessary to put the smaller on top whenever a comparator is encountered.

Many details must be worked out before an actual sorting machine based on this scheme could be built. For example, the method of encoding the inputs is left unspecified. One approach would be to think of each wire in Figure 11.4 as a group of lines, each holding 1 bit of data, so that all the bits of a key flow through a line simultaneously. Another approach would be to have the comparators read their inputs 1 bit at a time along a single line (most significant bit first). Also left unspecified is the timing: mechanisms must be included to ensure that no comparator performs its operation before its input is ready. Sorting networks are a good abstraction because they allow us to separate such implementation considerations from higher-level design considerations, such as minimizing the number of comparators. Moreover, as we shall see in Section 11.6, the sort network abstraction is useful for applications other than direct circuit realizations.

Figure 11.4
A sorting network

The keys move from left to right on the lines in the network. The comparators that they encounter exchange the keys if necessary to put the smaller one on the higher line. In this example, B and C are exchanged on the top two lines, then A and D are exchanged on the bottom two, then A and B, and so forth, leaving the keys in sorted order from top to bottom at the end. In this example, all the comparators do exchanges except the fourth one. This network sorts any permutation of four keys.

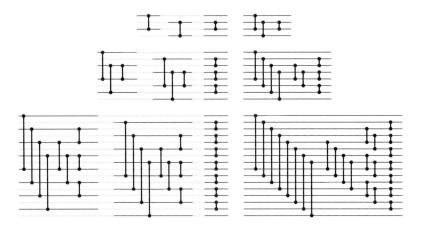

Figure 11.5
Batcher's odd–even merging
networks

*These different representations of
the networks for 4 (top), 8 (center),
and 16 (bottom) lines expose the
network's basic recursive structure.
On the left are direct representations of the construction of the networks of size N with two copies of
the networks of size $N/2$ (one for
the even-numbered lines and one
for the odd-numbered lines), plus a
stage of comparators between lines
1 and 2, 3 and 4, 5 and 6, and so
forth. On the right are simpler networks that we derive from those on
the left by grouping comparators of
the same length; grouping is possible because we can move comparators on odd lines past those on
even lines without interference.*

Another important application of sorting networks is as a model
for parallel computation. If two comparators do not use the same
input lines, we assume that they can operate at the same time. For
example, the network in Figure 11.4 shows that four elements can
be sorted in three parallel steps. The 0–1 comparator and the 2–
3 comparator can operate simultaneously in the first step, then the
0–2 comparator and the 1–3 comparator can operate simultaneously
in the second step, and then the 2–3 comparator finishes the sort in
the third step. Given any network, it is not difficult to classify the
comparators into a sequence of *parallel stages* that consist of groups
of comparators that can operate simultaneously (see Exercise 11.17).
For efficient parallel computation, our challenge is to design networks
with as few parallel stages as possible.

Program 11.2 corresponds directly to a merging network for
each N, but it is also instructive for us to consider a direct bottom-
up construction, which is illustrated in Figure 11.5. To construct a
merging network of size N, we use two copies of the network of size
$N/2$; one for the even-numbered lines and one for the odd-numbered
lines. Because the two sets of comparators do not interfere, we can
rearrange them to interleave the two networks. Then, at the end, we
complete the network with comparators between lines 1 and 2, 3 and
4, and so forth. The odd–even interleaving replaces the perfect shuffle
in Program 11.2. The proof that these networks merge properly is
the same as that given for Properties 11.1 and 11.2, using the 0–1
principle. Figure 11.6 shows an example of the merge in operation.

Figure 11.6
Bottom-up Batcher's merge example

When all the shuffling is removed, Batcher's merge for our example amounts to the 25 compare-exchange operations depicted here. They divide into four phases of independent compare-exchange operations at a fixed offset for each phase.

Program 11.3 Batcher's odd-even merge (nonrecursive version)

This implementation of Batcher's odd–even merge (which assumes that the file size N is a power of 2) is compact but mysterious. We can understand how it accomplishes the merge by examining how it corresponds to the recursive version (see Program 11.2 and Figure 11.5). It accomplishes the merge in $\lg N$ passes consisting of uniform and independent compare–exchange instructions.

```
static void merge(ITEM[] a, int l, int m, int r)
  { int N = r-l+1;  // assuming N/2 is m-l+1
    for (int k = N/2; k > 0; k /= 2)
      for (int j = k % (N/2); j+k < N; j += k+k)
        for (int i = 0; i < k; i++)
          compExch(a, l+j+i, l+j+i+k);
  }
```

Program 11.3 is a bottom-up implementation of Batcher's merge, with no shuffling, that corresponds to the networks in Figure 11.5. This program is a compact and elegant in-place merging method that is perhaps best understood as just an alternate representation of the networks, although direct proofs that it accomplishes the merging task correctly are also interesting to contemplate. We shall examine one such proof at the end of this section.

Figure 11.7 shows Batcher's odd–even sorting network, built from the merging networks in Figure 11.5 using the standard recursive mergesort construction. The construction is doubly recursive: once for the merging networks and once for the sorting networks. Although they are not optimal—we shall discuss optimal networks shortly—these networks are efficient.

Property 11.3 *Batcher's odd–even sorting networks have about $N(\lg N)^2/4$ comparators and can run in $(\lg N)^2/2$ parallel steps.*

The merging networks need about $\lg N$ parallel steps, and the sorting networks need $1 + 2 + \ldots + \lg N$, or about $(\lg N)^2/2$ parallel steps. Comparator counting is left as an exercise (see Exercise 11.23). ∎

Using the merge method in Program 11.3 within the standard recursive mergesort in Program 8.3 gives a compact in-place sorting method that is nonadaptive and uses $O(N(\lg N)^2)$ compare–exchange

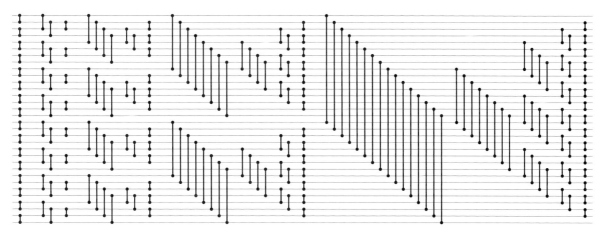

operations. Alternatively, we can remove the recursion from the merge-sort and implement a bottom-up version of the whole sort directly, as shown in Program 11.4. As was Program 11.3, this program is perhaps best understood as an alternate representation of the network in Figure 11.7. The implementation involves adding one loop and adding one test in Program 11.3, because the merge and the sort have similar recursive structure. To perform the bottom-up pass of merging a sequence of sorted files of length 2^k into a sequence of sorted files of length 2^{k+1}, we use the full merging network, but include only those comparators that fall completely within subfiles. This program perhaps wins the prize as the most compact nontrivial sort implementation that we have seen, and it is likely to be the method of choice when we want to take advantage of high-performance architectural features to develop a high-speed sort for small files (or to build a sorting network). Understanding how and why the program sorts would be a formidable task if we did not have the perspective of the recursive implementations and network constructions that we have been considering.

As usual with divide-and-conquer methods, we have two basic choices when N is not a power of 2 (see Exercises 11.24 and 11.21). We can divide in half (top-down) or divide at the largest power of 2 less than N (bottom-up). The latter is somewhat simpler for sorting networks, because it is equivalent to building a full network for the smallest power of 2 greater than or equal to N, then using only the first N lines and only comparators with both ends connected to those

Figure 11.7
Batcher's odd–even sorting networks

This sorting network for 32 lines contains two copies of the network for 16 lines, four copies of the network for 8 lines, and so forth. Reading from right to left, we see the structure in a top-down manner: A sorting network for 32 lines consists of a 16-by-16 merging network following two copies of the sorting network for 16 lines (one for the top half and one for the bottom half). Each network for 16 lines consists of an 8-by-8 merging network following two copies of the sorting network for 8 lines, and so forth. Reading from left to right, we see the structure in a bottom-up manner: The first column of comparators creates sorted subfiles of size 2; then, we have 2-by-2 merging networks that create sorted subfiles of size 4; then, 4-by-4 merging networks that create sorted subfiles of size 8, and so forth.

Program 11.4 Batcher's odd–even sort (nonrecursive version)

This implementation of Batcher's odd–even sort corresponds directly to the network representation in Figure 11.7. It divides into phases, indexed by the variable p. The last phase, when p is N, is Batcher's odd–even merge. The next-to-last phase, when p is N/2, is the odd–even merge with the first stage and all comparators that cross N/2 eliminated; the third-to-last phase, when p is N/4, is the odd–even merge with the first two stages and all comparators that cross any multiple of N/4 eliminated, and so forth.

```
static void batchersortNR(ITEM a[], int l, int r)
  { int N = r-l+1;
    for (int p = 1; p < N; p += p)
      for (int k = p; k > 0; k /= 2)
        for (int j = k%p; j+k < N; j += (k+k))
          for (int i = 0; i < N-j-k; i++)
            if ((j+i)/(p+p) == (j+i+k)/(p+p))
              compExch(a, l+j+i, l+j+i+k);
  }
```

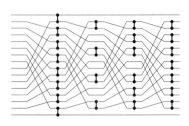

Figure 11.8
Shuffling in Batcher's odd–even merge

A direct implementation of Program 11.2 as a sorting network gives a network replete with recursive unshuffling and shuffling (top). *An equivalent implementation* (bottom) *involves only full shuffles.*

lines. The proof that this construction is valid is simple. Suppose that the lines that are not used have sentinel keys that are greater than any other keys on the network. Then, comparators on those lines never exchange, so removing them has no effect. Indeed, we could use *any* contiguous set of N lines from the larger network: Consider ignored lines at the top to have small sentinels and ignored lines at the bottom to have large sentinels. All these networks have about $N(\lg N)^2/4$ comparators.

The theory of sorting networks has an interesting history (*see reference section*). The problem of finding networks with as few comparators as possible was posed by Bose before 1960 and is called the *Bose–Nelson* problem. Batcher's networks were the first good solution to the problem, and for some time people conjectured that they were optimal. Batcher's *merging* networks *are* optimal, so any sorting network with substantially fewer comparators has to be constructed with an approach other than recursive mergesort. The problem of finding optimal sorting networks eluded researchers until, in 1983, Ajtai, Komlos, and Szemeredi proved the existence of networks with $O(N \log N)$ comparators. However, the AKS networks are a mathematical construction that is not at all practical, and Batcher's networks are still among the best available for practical use.

The connection between perfect shuffling and Batcher's networks makes it amusing to complete our study of sorting networks by considering yet another version of the algorithm. If we shuffle the lines in Batcher's odd–even merge, we get networks where all the comparators connect adjacent lines. Figure 11.8 illustrates a network that corresponds to the shuffling implementation corresponding to Program 11.2. This interconnection pattern is sometimes called a *butterfly network*. Also shown in the figure is another representation of the same straight-line program that provides an even more uniform pattern; it involves only full shuffles.

Figure 11.9 shows yet another interpretation of the method that illustrates the underlying structure. First, we write one file below the other; then, we compare those elements that are vertically adjacent and exchange them if necessary to put the larger one below the smaller one. Next, we split each row in half and interleave the halves, then perform the same compare–exchange operations on the numbers in the second and third lines. Comparisons involving other pairs of rows are not necessary because of the previous sorting. The split-interleave operation keeps both the rows and the columns of the table sorted. This property is preserved in general by the same operation: Each step doubles the number of rows, halves the number of columns, and still keeps the rows and the columns sorted; eventually we end up with 1 column of N rows, which is therefore completely sorted. The connection between the tableaux in Figure 11.9 and the network at the bottom in Figure 11.8 is that, when we write down the tables in column-major order (the elements in the first column followed by the elements in the second column, and so forth), we see that the permutation required to go from one step to the next is none other than the perfect shuffle.

Now, with an abstract parallel machine that has the perfect-shuffle interconnection built in, as shown in Figure 11.10, we would be able to implement directly networks like the one at the bottom of Figure 11.8. At each step, the machine does compare–exchange operations between some pairs of adjacent processors, as indicated by the algorithm, then performs a perfect shuffle of the data. Programming

Figure 11.9
Split-interleave merging

Starting with two sorted files in 1 row, we merge them by iterating the following operation: split each row in half and interleave the halves (left), and do compare-exchanges between items now vertically adjacent that came from different rows (right). At the beginning we have 16 columns and 1 row, then 8 columns and 2 rows, then 4 columns and 4 rows, then 2 columns and 8 rows, and finally 16 rows and 1 column, which is sorted.

Figure 11.10
A perfect shuffling machine

A machine with the interconnec-
tions drawn here could perform
Batcher's algorithm (and many oth-
ers) efficiently. Some parallel com-
puters have connections like these.

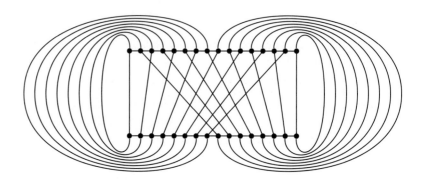

the machine amounts to specifying which pairs of processors should do compare–exchange operations at each cycle.

Figure 11.11 shows the dynamic characteristics of both the bottom-up method and this full-shuffling version of Batcher's odd-even merge.

Shuffling is an important abstraction for describing data movement in divide-and-conquer algorithms, and it arises in a variety of problems other than sorting. For example, if a 2^n-by-2^n square matrix is kept in row-major order, then n perfect shuffles will transpose the matrix (convert the matrix to column-major order). More important examples include the fast Fourier transform and polynomial evaluation (see Part 8). We can solve each of these problems using a cycling perfect-shuffle machine like the one shown in Figure 11.10 but with more powerful processors. We might even contemplate having general-purpose processors that can shuffle and unshuffle (some real machines of this type have been built); we return to the discussion of such parallel machines in Section 11.6.

Exercises

11.16 Give sorting networks for four (see Exercise 11.6), five, and six elements. Use as few comparators as possible.

○ **11.17** Write a program to compute the number of parallel steps required for any given straight-line program. *Hint*: Use the following labeling strategy. Label the input lines as belonging to stage 0, then do the following for each comparator: Label both output lines as inputs to stage $i + 1$ if the label on one of the input lines is i and the label on the other is not greater than i.

11.18 Compare the running time of Program 11.4 with that of Program 8.3, for randomly ordered keys with $N = 10^3$, 10^4, 10^5, and 10^6.

▷ 11.19 Draw Batcher's network for doing a 10-by-11 merge.

•• 11.20 Prove the relationship between recursive unshuffling and shuffling that is suggested by Figure 11.8.

○ 11.21 From the argument in the text, there are 11 networks for sorting 21 elements hidden in Figure 11.7. Draw the one among these that has the fewest comparators.

11.22 Give the number of comparators in Batcher's odd–even sorting networks for $2 \leq N \leq 32$, where networks when N is not a power of 2 are derived from the first N lines of the network for the next largest power of 2.

○ 11.23 For $N = 2^n$, derive an exact expression for the number of comparators used in Batcher's odd–even sorting networks. *Note*: Check your answer against Figure 11.7, which shows that the networks have 1, 3, 9, 25, and 65 comparators for N equal to 2, 4, 8, 16, and 32, respectively.

○ 11.24 Construct a sorting network for sorting 21 elements using a top-down recursive style, where a network of size N is a composition of networks of sizes $\lfloor N/2 \rfloor$ and $\lceil N/2 \rceil$ followed by a merging network. (Use your answer from Exercise 11.19 as the final part of the network.)

11.25 Use recurrence relations to compute the number of comparators in sorting networks constructed as described in Exercise 11.24 for $2 \leq N \leq 32$. Compare your results with those that you obtained in Exercise 11.22.

• 11.26 Find a 16-line sorting network that uses fewer comparators than Batcher's network does.

11.27 Draw the merging networks corresponding to Figure 11.8 for bitonic sequences, using the scheme described in Exercise 11.14.

11.28 Draw the sorting network corresponding to shellsort with Pratt's increments (see Section 6.8), for $N = 32$.

11.29 Give a table containing the number of comparators in the networks described in Exercise 11.28 and the number of comparators in Batcher's networks, for $N = 16, 32, 64, 128,$ and 256.

11.30 Design sorting networks that will sort files of N elements that are 3- and 4-sorted.

• 11.31 Use your networks from Exercise 11.30 to design a Pratt-like scheme based on multiples of 3 and 4. Draw your network for $N = 32$, and answer Exercise 11.29 for your networks.

• 11.32 Draw a version of Batcher's odd–even sorting network for $N = 16$ that has perfect shuffles between stages of independent comparators connecting adjacent lines. (The final four stages of the network should be those from the merging network at the bottom of Figure 11.8.)

○ 11.33 Write a merging program for the machine in Figure 11.10, using the following conventions. An instruction is a sequence of 15 bits, where the ith

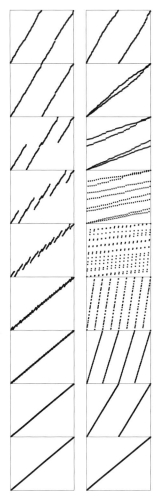

Figure 11.11
Dynamic characteristics of odd–even merging

The bottom-up version of the odd–even merge (left) involves a sequence of stages where we compare–exchange the large half of one sorted subfile with the small half of the next. With full shuffling (right), the algorithm has an entirely different appearance.

bit, for $1 \leq i \leq 15$, indicates (if it is 1) that processor i and processor $i - 1$ should do a compare–exchange. A program is a sequence of instructions, and the machine executes a perfect shuffle between each instruction.

○ 11.34 Write a sorting program for the machine in Figure 11.10, using the conventions described in Exercise 11.33.

11.3 Sorting In Place

The following amusing problem is a useful model for a variety of sorting applications. Suppose that a single driver is given the task of rearranging a sequence of trucks, which are parked in a single line, into some specified order. For example, we might imagine that the trucks arrive at a distribution center in some arbitrary order in the evening, but they need to go out in a specific order in the morning. If there is another place to park all the trucks, the task is easy: the driver just finds the first truck, drives it to the first position, finds the second truck, drives it to the second position, and so forth. However, we can easily imagine that extra space for parking all the trucks is not available. How is the driver to proceed?

Figure 11.12 illustrates a way to solve this problem that uses just one extra parking place. The driver moves the first truck to the extra place, then finds the truck that goes into the place vacated, and so forth, continuing until vacating the place where the first truck belongs, whereupon the driver gets that truck and puts it in the space. This process may not get all the trucks moved, but the driver can find any truck that needs to be moved and repeat the same procedure, continuing until all the trucks have been moved.

Problems like this arise frequently in sorting applications. For example, many external storage devices have the property that accessing data sequentially is far more efficient than random access, so we often find ourselves rearranging data so that it may be more efficiently accessed. To fix ideas, suppose that we have a disk with a large number of large blocks of data and that we know we have to rearrange the blocks because we want to scan through them repeatedly in some specific order. If the disk is filled with the data and we do not have another one available, we have no choice but to rearrange the blocks "'in place." Reading a block from disk into memory corresponds to parking a truck in the extra space, and reading one block and writing

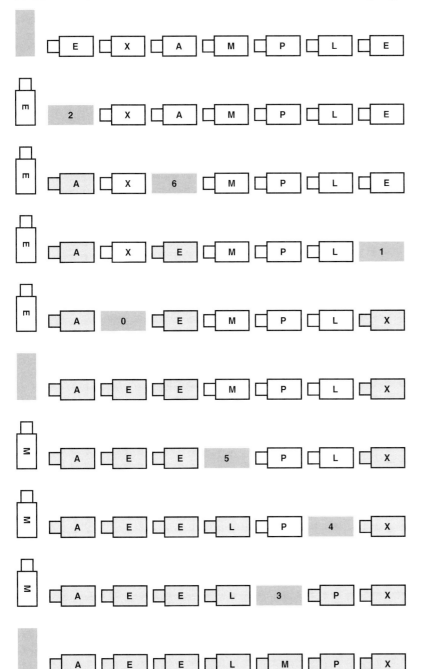

Figure 11.12
Rearranging in place

This sequence shows how a single driver might rearrange a row of trucks so that they are in order, using a single extra parking place. The first step is to move the first truck (the first one labeled E, in parking place 0) to the extra place, leaving an empty space at parking place 0 (second from top). In the figure, this space is labeled with the number of the space where the truck that belongs there can be found: in this case, the truck labeled A is in parking place 2. Next, the driver moves that truck from place 2 to place 0, leaving an empty space at 2. All trucks that have been moved are marked as such (shaded gray in the figure). Now, place 2 has a label telling the driver to go to place 6 to get the other truck labeled E and bring it to place 2 and so forth. After that, the driver moves the truck labeled X from place 1 to place 6 and finds that place 1 is to be filled with the truck that was at 0, which is the truck in the extra space (the driver knows to go to the extra space because the truck at 0 is marked as already having been moved). Next, the driver finds the leftmost truck that has not been moved, moves it to the extra space, and follows the same procedure. All trucks move in and out of their places just once; some of them spend time in the extra parking place.

0	10	9	Wilson	63
1	4	2	Johnson	86
2	5	1	Jones	87
3	6	0	Smith	90
4	8	4	Washington	84
5	7	8	Thompson	65
6	2	3	Brown	82
7	3	10	Jackson	61
8	9	6	White	76
9	0	5	Adams	86
10	1	7	Black	71

Figure 11.13
Index sorting example

By manipulating indices rather than the records themselves, we can sort an array simultaneously on several keys. For this sample data that might represent students' names and grades, the second column is the result of an index sort on the name, and the third column is the result of an index sort on the grade. For example, Wilson *is last in alphabetic order and has the tenth highest grade, while* Adams *is first in alphabetic order and has the sixth highest grade.*

A rearrangement of the N distinct nonnegative integers less than N is called a permutation in mathematics: an index sort computes a permutation. In mathematics, permutations are normally defined as rearrangements of the integers 1 through N; we shall use 0 through N − 1 to emphasize the direct relationship between permutations and Java array indices.

its contents at another position corresponds to moving a truck from one parking place to another.

To implement this process, we will use Disk and Block abstractions whose implementation, while straightforward, depend on characteristics of particular devices and are omitted. We assume that a Disk is an indexed sequence of N disk blocks whose contents are Blocks, and that the Disk class has a member method read that takes an integer index parameter and returns a Block with the contents of the indexed disk block and a member method write that takes an index and a Block as parameters and writes the contents of the Block to the indexed disk block. We also assume that the Block class has a member method key that returns a sort key for the block.

As already noted in Section 6.6, one way to solve this problem is to use selection sort. This would correspond to our driver moving the truck in the first parking place to the extra place, then moving the truck with the smallest key to the first place, then moving the truck in the extra place to the place vacated, and so forth. This method is less attractive than the one depicted in Figure 11.12 because it requires substantially more driving, since every move involves driving a new truck to the extra place, while we expect to move relatively few trucks to the extra place in the method depicted in Figure 11.12 (see Exercise 11.44). More important, we have not discussed how the driver finds the truck that he needs. For selection sort, with a very long line of trucks, we might imagine that the driver will be spending a substantial amount of time walking down the row of trucks looking for the one with the smallest key. In our disk-sorting problem, this corresponds to a running time quadratic in the number of blocks, which may be unacceptable.

The sorting process divides into two steps: first we must compute, for each place, the index of the block that belongs there; then we must actually do the specified rearrangement.

We can use any of our sorting algorithms for the first task, as follows: Define a class Item that implements our ITEM interface (see Section 6.2) with two fields: an index and a key. Then, create an array p of N items and initialize it (by scanning through all the blocks on the disk) by setting the index field of p[i] to i and the key field of p[i] to the key of the ith disk block. We assume that we have enough room in memory for such an array; if not, then the external sorting methods introduced in Section 11.4 apply. Now, if we define the less method to be

```
boolean less(ITEM w)
  { return this.key < ((Item) w).key; }
```

we can use any of the sorting methods that we have discussed (quicksort, for example) to sort the index items. After the sort, the index field of p[0] is the index of the disk block with the smallest key, p[1] gives the index of the data item with the second smallest key, and so on. That is, these index numbers are none other than the numbers shown in Figure 11.12, which tell the driver where to put each truck.

For some applications, this process is all that we need, since we can achieve the effect of sorting by accessing the keys through the indices, as we do for any Java sort where we rearrange references to objects. Also, we have the flexibility to maintain multiple different sorted index arrays on the same data base, as illustrated in Figure 11.13.

The cost of the sort is the space for the array of index items, the time to scan through the N records to get the keys, and the time proportional to $N \log N$ to do the index sort. The sort cost is typically dwarfed by the cost of scanning through all the disk blocks, so the process amounts to a linear-time sort. If the keys are huge, we might use an ITEM implementation that goes to disk for every key access, but this would increase the number of disk reads by a factor of $\log N$, which is substantial (see Exercise 11.40).

Now, back to the problem at hand: How do we rearrange a file that has been sorted with an index sort? We cannot blindly copy the contents of the block at position p[i] into position i, because that would prematurely overwrite the block currently at position i. In our truck-parking scenario, this observation just amounts to noting that we cannot move a truck from position p[i] to position i without first moving the truck out of position i. If we have extra room sufficient for another copy of all the data (say, for example, on another disk), then the task is simple; if not, we need to implement a method that imitates the process depicted in Figure 11.12.

Program 11.5 is such an implementation. It uses a single pass through the file, and just enough space to save the contents of one block. The main loop scans to find the next position i that a block needs to be moved to (from position p[i], which is not equal to i). Then it saves the contents of block i in B and works through the cycle,

```
0  1  2  3  4  5  6  7  8  9 10 11 12 13 14
A  S  O  R  T  I  N  G  E  X  A  M  P  L  E
0 10  8 14  7  5 13 11  6  2 12  3  1  4  9
```

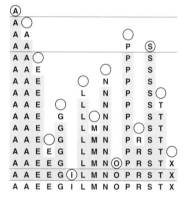

Figure 11.14
In-place rearrangement

To rearrange an array in place, we move from left to right, moving elements that need to be moved in cycles. Here, there are four cycles: The first and last are single-element degenerate cases. The second cycle starts at 1. The S goes into a temporary variable, leaving a hole at 1. Moving the second A there leaves a hole at 10. This hole is filled by P, which leaves a hole at 12. That hole is to be filled by the element at position 1, so the reserved S goes into that hole, completing the cycle 1 10 12 that puts those elements in position. Similarly, the cycle 2 8 6 13 4 7 11 3 14 9 completes the sort.

Program 11.5 In-place rearrangement

This function rearranges a set of N abstract `Block`s on an abstract `Disk` in place, as directed by the index array `p[0]`, ... , `p[N-1]`, using `read` and `write` member functions that are supposed to manage the transfer of block contents from and to the disk. For all indices `i`, the block that is in position `p[i]` at the beginning of the process is moved (by reading and then writing its contents) to be in position `i` at the end of the process. Each time that we make such a move, we set `p[i]` to `i`, which means that the block is in place and does not need to be touched again.

Starting at the left, the outer loop scans through the array to find a block `i` that needs to be moved (with `p[i]` not equal to `i`). For the inner loop, it saves the contents of the `i`th block, initializes an index variable `k` to `i` and then finds the block to fill the hole in position `k` (which changes each time through the loop). That block is the one at position `p[k]`—in other words, reading block `p[k]` and writing to position `k` puts block `k` into position `p[k]` (so we set `p[k]` to `k`) and moves the hole to `p[k]` (so we set `k` to the old value of `p[k]`). Iterating, the inner loop is finished when it gets to a situation where the hole needs to be filled by the block at position `i`, which was saved.

```java
public static void insitu(Disk D, int[] p, int N)
  { for (int i = 0; i < N; i++)
     { Block B = D.read(i);
       int j, k;
       for (k = i; p[k] != i; k = p[j], p[j] = j)
         { j = k; D.write(k, D.read(p[k])); }
       D.write(k, B); p[k] = k;
     }
  }
```

moving the block in position `p[i]` to position `i`, moving the block in position `p[p[i]]` to position `p[i]`, moving the block in position `p[p[p[i]]]` to position `p[p[i]]`, until reaching the index `i` again, when B can be written into the place vacated by the last block moved. Continuing in this way, the entire file is rearranged in place, reading and writing each block only once (see Figure 11.14).

This process is called *in situ permutation*, or *in-place rearrangement* of the file. Although the algorithm is unnecessary in many applications (because accessing the data indirectly through references often suffices), it is a fundamental computation that is not difficult to implement in applications where we want to move things into sorted order without wasting space. For example, we can use the same basic idea to implement, without an auxiliary array, the shuffling and unshuffling operations of Section 11.1 (see Exercise 11.42) and the rearrangement step in key-indexed counting that underlies the radix sorts of Chapter 10 (see Exercise 11.43).

The method described in this section is flexible, easy to implement, and useful in a wide variety of sorting applications, whenever space to hold the index array is available. If the blocks are huge relative to their number, it is slightly more efficient to rearrange them with a conventional selection sort (see Property 6.6). If the number of records is truly huge and we cannot afford to manipulate references to all of them, we are led to a different family of algorithms, which we consider next.

Exercises

▷ **11.35** Give the index array that results when the keys E A S Y Q U E S T I O N are index sorted.

▷ **11.36** Give the sequence of data moves required to permute the keys E A S Y Q U E S T I O N in place after an index sort (see Exercise 11.35).

11.37 Give examples that minimize and maximize the number of times the driver has to drive a truck to the extra space. (Describe permutations of size N (a set of values for the array p) that maximize and minimize the number of times that the body of the for loop is entered during Program 11.5).

○ **11.38** We could eliminate the extra parking place in Figure 11.12 by using the following process to move trucks: Find a truck to be moved, and drive it to where it is to go. Then (leaving the truck in the road momentarily), drive the the truck in that place out and (leaving that truck in the road momentarily) park the first truck. Then, drive the second truck to the place where that truck is to be moved, and so on, continuing until getting to the place vacated by the first truck. Show how the trucks in Figure 11.12 are moved when this method is used, and give an implementation that corresponds to Program 11.5.

▷ **11.39** Use the Disk and Block abstractions described in this section to implement a selection-sort–based disk sort.

▷ **11.40** Give an implementation of less for an implementation of the ITEM interface that keeps only the index as a field and has to go to the disk to get keys.

11.41 Prove that we are guaranteed to return to the key with which we started when moving keys and leaving holes in Program 11.5.

○ **11.42** Give implementations of the shuffle and unshuffle methods of Program 11.1 that do not use an auxiliary array.

○ **11.43** Give an implementation of distribution counting (Program 6.20) that does not use an auxiliary array.

○ **11.44** Suppose that the trucks in Figure 11.12 are randomly arranged. What is the expected number of trucks that are taken to the extra parking place? (This problem is equivalent to finding the average number of cycles in a random permutation, a famous elementary problem in combinatorics.)

11.4 External Sorting

We move next to another kind of abstract sorting problem, which applies when the file to be sorted is much too large to fit in the random-access memory of the computer and has much too many records for us to contemplate manipulating references to them all. We use the term *external sorting* to describe this situation. There are many different types of external sorting devices, which can place a variety of different restrictions on the atomic operations used to implement the sort. Still, it is useful to consider sorting methods that use two basic primitive operations: *read* data from external storage into main memory, and *write* data from main memory onto external storage. We assume that the cost of these two operations is so much larger than the cost of primitive computational operations that we ignore the latter entirely. For example, in this abstract model, we ignore the cost of sorting the main memory! For huge memories or poor sorting methods, this assumption may not be justified; but it is generally possible to factor in an estimate of the true cost in practical situations if necessary.

The wide variety of types and costs of external storage devices makes the development of external sorting methods highly dependent on current technology. These methods can be complicated, and many parameters affect their performance; that a clever method might go unappreciated or unused because of a simple change in the technology is certainly a possibility in the study of external sorting. For this reason, we shall concentrate on reviewing general methods rather than on developing specific implementations in this section.

Over and above the high read–write cost for external devices, there are often severe restrictions on access, depending on the device. For example, for most types of devices, read and write operations between main memory and external storage are generally done most efficiently in large contiguous blocks of data. Also, external devices with huge capacities are often designed such that peak performance is achieved when we access the blocks in a *sequential* manner. For example, we cannot read items at the end of a magnetic tape without first scanning through items at the beginning—for practical purposes, our access to items on the tape is restricted to those appearing somewhere close to the items most recently accessed. Several modern technologies have this same property. Accordingly, in this section, we concentrate on methods that read and write large blocks of data sequentially, making the implicit assumption that fast implementations of this type of data access can be achieved for the machines and devices that are of interest.

When we are in the process of reading or writing a number of different files, we assume that they are all on different external storage devices. On ancient machines, where files were stored on externally mounted magnetic tapes, this assumption was an absolute requirement. When working with disks, it is possible to implement the algorithms that we consider using only a single external device, but it generally will be much more efficient to use multiple devices.

A first step for someone planning to implement an efficient program to sort a huge file might be to implement an efficient program to make a copy of the file. A second step might be to implement a program to reverse the order of the file. Whatever difficulties arise in solving these tasks certainly need to be addressed in implementing an external sort. (The sort might have to do either one of them.) The purpose of using an abstract model is to allow us to separate such implementation issues from algorithm design issues.

The sorting algorithms that we examine are organized as a number of passes over all the data, and we usually measure the cost of an external sorting method by simply counting the number of such passes. Typically, we need relatively few passes—perhaps ten or fewer. This fact implies that eliminating even a single pass can significantly improve performance. Our basic assumption is that the running time of an external sorting method is dominated by input and output; thus, we can estimate the running time of an external sort by multiplying the number of passes it uses by the time required to read and write the whole file.

In summary, the abstract model that we shall use for external sorting involves a basic assumption that the file to be sorted is far too large for us to even fit a reference to each record in main memory, and it accounts for two other resources: running time (number of passes through the data) and the number of external devices available for use. We assume that we have

- N records to be sorted, on an external device
- space in the main memory to hold M records and
- $2P$ external devices for use during the sort.

We assign the label 0 to the external device containing the input, and the labels 1, 2, ..., $2P - 1$ to the others. The goal of the sort is to put the records back onto device 0, in sorted order. As we shall see, there is a tradeoff between P and the total running time—we are interested in quantifying that tradeoff so that we can compare competing strategies.

There are many reasons why this idealized model may not be realistic. Still, like any good abstract model, it does capture the essential aspects of the situation, and it does provide a precise framework within which we can explore algorithmic ideas, many of which are of direct utility in practical situations.

Most external sorting methods use the following general strategy: Make a first pass through the file to be sorted, breaking it up into blocks about the size of the internal memory, and *sort* these blocks. Then, *merge* the sorted blocks together, if necessary by making several passes through the file, creating successively larger sorted blocks until the whole file is sorted. This approach is called *sort–merge*, and it has been used effectively since computers first found widespread use in commercial applications in the 1950s.

The simplest sort–merge strategy, which is called *balanced multiway merging*, is illustrated in Figure 11.15. The method consists of an *initial distribution* pass, followed by several *multiway merging passes*.

In the initial distribution pass, we distribute the input among external devices P, $P + 1$, ..., $2P - 1$, in sorted blocks of M records each (except possibly the final block, which is smaller, if N is not a multiple of M). This distribution is easy to do—we read the first M records from the input, sort them, and write the sorted block onto device P; then read the next M records from the input, sort them, and write the sorted block onto device $P + 1$; and so forth. If, after reaching device $2P - 1$ we still have more input (that is, if $N > PM$), we put a second sorted block on device P, then a second sorted block on device $P + 1$, and so forth. We continue in this way until the input

```
A S O R T I N G A N D M E R G I N G E X A M P L E W I T H F O R T Y F I V E R E C O R D S • $

A O S • D M N • A E X • F H T • E R V • $
I R T • E G R • L M P • O R T • C E O • $
A G N • G I N • E I W • F I Y • D R S • $

A A G I N O R S T • F F H I O R T T Y • $
D E G G I M N N R • C D E E O R R S V • $
A E E I L M P W X • $

A A A D E E G G G I I I L M M N N N O P R R S T W X • $
C D E E F F H I O O R R R S T T V Y • $
• $

A A A C D D E E E E E F F G G G H I I I I L M M N N N O O O P R R R R R S S T T T V W X Y • $
```

Figure 11.15
**Three-way balanced merge
  example**

*In the initial distribution pass, we
take the elements A S O from the
input, sort them, and put the sorted
run A O S on the first output device. Next, we take the elements R
T I from the input, sort them, and
put the sorted run I R T on the second output device. Continuing in
this way, cycling through the output devices, we end with 15 runs:
5 on each output device. In the
first merging phase, we merge A
O S, I R T, and A G N to get A A
G I N O R S T, which we put on
the first output device; then, we
merge the second runs on the input devices to get D E G G I M N
N R, which we put on the second
output device; and so forth; again
ending up with the data distributed
in a balanced manner on three devices. We complete the sort with
two additional merging passes.*

is exhausted. After the distribution, the number of sorted blocks on
each device is N/M rounded up or down to the next integer. If N is a
multiple of M, then all the blocks are of size N/M (otherwise, all but
the final one are of size N/M). For small N, there may be fewer than
P blocks, and one or more of the devices may be empty.

In the first multiway merging pass, we regard devices P through
$2P - 1$ as input devices, and devices 0 through $P - 1$ as output devices.
We do P-way merging to merge the sorted blocks of size M on the
input devices into sorted blocks of size PM, then distribute them onto
the output devices in as balanced a manner as possible. First, we
merge together the first block from each of the input devices and put
the result onto device 0; then, we put the result of merging the second
block on each input device onto device 1; and so forth. After reaching
device $P - 1$, we put a second sorted block on device 0, then a second
sorted block on device 1, and so forth. We continue in this way until
the inputs are exhausted. After the distribution, the number of sorted
blocks on each device is $N/(PM)$ rounded up or down to the next
integer. If N is a multiple of PM, then all the blocks are of size PM
(otherwise, the final block is smaller). If N is not larger than PM,
there is just one sorted block left (on device 0), and we are finished.

Otherwise, we iterate the process and do a second multiway
merging pass, regarding devices 0, 1, …, $P - 1$ as the input devices,
and devices P, $P + 1$, …, $2P - 1$ as the output devices. We do P-way
merging to make the sorted blocks of size PM on the input devices
into sorted blocks of size P^2M, then distribute them back onto the

output devices. We are finished after the second pass (with the result on device P) if N is not larger than $P^2 M$.

Continuing in this way, back and forth between devices 0 through $P - 1$ and devices P through $2P - 1$, we increase the size of the blocks by a factor of P through P-way merges until we eventually have just one block, on device 0 or on device P. The final merge in each pass may not be a full P-way merge; otherwise, the process is well balanced. Figure 11.16 depicts the process using only the numbers and relative sizes of the runs. We measure the cost of the merge by performing the indicated multiplications in this table, summing the results (not including the entry in the bottom row), and dividing by the initial number of runs. This calculation gives cost in terms of the number of *passes* over the data.

To implement P-way merging, we can use a priority queue of size P. We want to output repeatedly the smallest of the elements not yet output from each of the P sorted blocks to be merged, then to replace the element output with the next element from the block from which it came. To accomplish this action, we keep device indices in the priority queue, with a `less` method that reads the value of the key of the next record to be read from the indicated device (and provides a sentinel larger than all keys in records when the end of a block is reached). The merge is then a simple loop that reads the next record from the device having the smallest key and writes that record to the output, then replaces that record on the priority queue with the next record from the same device, continuing until a sentinel key is the smallest in the priority queue. We could use a heap implementation to make the time required for the priority queue proportional to $\log P$, but P is normally so small that this cost is dwarfed by the cost of writing to external storage. In our abstract model, we ignore priority-queue costs and assume that we have efficient sequential access to data on external devices so that we can measure running time by counting the number of passes through the data. In practice, we might use an elementary priority-queue implementation and focus our programming on making sure that the external devices run at maximum efficiency.

Property 11.4 *With $2P$ external devices and internal memory sufficient to hold M records, a sort–merge that is based on a P-way balanced merge takes about $1 + \lceil \log_P(N/M) \rceil$ passes.*

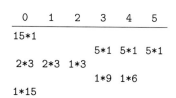

	0	1	2	3	4	5
	15*1					
				5*1	5*1	5*1
	2*3	2*3	1*3			
				1*9	1*6	
	1*15					

Figure 11.16
Run distribution for balanced 3-way merge

In the initial distribution for a balanced three-way sort–merge of a file 15 times the size of the internal memory, we put five runs of relative size 1 on devices 3, 4, and 5, leaving devices 0, 1, and 2 empty. In the first merging phase, we put two runs of size 3 on devices 0 and 1, and one run of size 3 on device 2, leaving devices 3, 4, and 5 empty. Then, we merge the runs on devices 0, 1, and 2, and distribute them back to devices 3, 4, and 5, and so forth, continuing until only one run remains, on device 0. The total number of records processed is 60: four passes over all 15 records.

One pass is required for distribution. If $N = MP^k$, the blocks are all of size MP after the first merge, MP^2 after the second, MP^3 after the third; and so forth. The sort is complete after $k = \log_P(N/M)$ passes. Otherwise, if $M^{P^{k-1}} < N < M^{P^k}$, the effect of incomplete and empty blocks makes the blocks vary in size near the end of the process, but we are still finished after $k = \lceil \log_P(N/M) \rceil$ passes. ∎

For example, if we want to sort 1 billion records using six devices and enough internal memory to hold 1 million records, we can do so with a three-way sort–merge with a total of eight passes through the data—one for distribution and $\lceil \log_3 1000 \rceil = 7$ merging passes. We will have sorted runs of 1 million records after the distribution pass, 3 million records after the first merge, 9 million records after the second merge, 27 million records after the third merge, and so forth. We can estimate that it should take about nine times as long to sort the file as it does to copy the file.

The most important decision to be made in a practical sort–merge is the choice of the value of P, the order of the merge. In our abstract model, we are restricted to sequential access, which implies that P has to be one-half the number of external devices available for use. This model is a realistic one for many external storage devices. For many other devices, however, nonsequential access is possible—it is just more expensive than sequential access. If only a few devices are available for the sort, nonsequential access might be unavoidable. In such cases, we can still use multiway merging, but we will have to take into account the basic tradeoff that increasing P will decrease the number of passes but increase the amount of (slow) nonsequential access.

Exercises

▷ **11.45** Show how the keys E A S Y Q U E S T I O N W I T H P L E N T Y O F K E Y S are sorted using 3-way balanced merging, in the style of the example diagrammed in Figure 11.15.

▷ **11.46** What would be the effect on the number of passes used in multiway merging if we were to double the number of external devices in use?

▷ **11.47** What would be the effect on the number of passes used in multiway merging if we were to increase by a factor of 10 the amount of internal memory available?

• **11.48** Develop an interface for external input and output that involves sequential transfer of blocks of data from external devices that operate asynchronously (or learn details about an existing one on your system). Use the interface to implement P-way merging, with P as large as you can make it while still arranging for the P input files and the input file to be on different output devices. Compare the running time of your program with the time required to copy the files to the output, one after another.

- � 11.49 Use the interface from Exercise 11.48 to write a program to reverse the order of as large a file as is feasible on your system.

- �)11.50 How would you do a perfect shuffle of all the records on an external device?

- ▸11.51 Develop a cost model for multiway merging that encompasses algorithms that can switch from one file to another on the same device, at a fixed cost that is much higher than the cost of a sequential read.

- ▸▸ 11.52 Develop an external sorting approach that is based on partitioning à la quicksort or MSD radix sort, analyze it, and compare it with multiway merge. You may use a high level of abstraction, as we did in the description of sort–merge in this section, but you should strive to be able to predict the running time for a given number of devices and a given amount of internal memory.

11.53 How would you sort the contents of an external device if no other devices (except main memory) were available for use?

11.54 How would you sort the contents of an external device if only one extra device (and main memory) was available for use?

11.5 Sort–Merge Implementations

The general sort–merge strategy outlined in Section 11.4 is effective in practice. In this section, we consider two improvements that can lower the costs. The first technique, *replacement selection*, has the same effect on the running time as does increasing the amount of internal memory that we use; the second technique, *polyphase merging*, has the same effect as does increasing the number of devices that we use.

In Section 11.4, we discussed the use of priority queues for P-way merging but noted that P is so small that fast algorithmic improvements are unimportant. During the initial distribution pass, however, we can make good use of fast priority queues to produce sorted runs that are longer than could fit in internal memory. The idea is to pass the (unordered) input through a large priority queue, always writing out the smallest element on the priority queue as before and always replacing it with the next element from the input, with one additional proviso: If the new element is smaller than the one output most recently, then, because it could not possibly become part of the current sorted block, we mark it as a member of the next block and treat it as greater than all elements in the current block. When a marked element makes it to the top of the priority queue, we begin a new block. Figure 11.17 depicts the method in operation.

Property 11.5 *For random keys, the runs produced by replacement selection are about twice the size of the heap used.*

If we were to use heapsort to produce initial runs, we would fill the memory with records, then write them out one by one, continuing until the heap is empty. Then, we would fill the memory with another batch of records and repeat the process, again and again. On the average, the heap occupies only one-half the memory during this process. By contrast, replacement selection keeps the memory filled with the same data structure, so it is not surprising that it does twice as well. The full proof of this property requires a sophisticated analysis (*see reference section*), although the property is easy to verify experimentally (see Exercise 11.57). ■

For random files, the practical effect of replacement selection is to save perhaps one merging pass: Rather than starting with sorted runs about the size of the internal memory, then taking a merging pass to produce longer runs, we can start right off with runs about twice the size of the internal memory. For $P = 2$, this strategy would save precisely one merging pass; for larger P, the effect is less important. However, we know that practical sorts rarely deal with random files, and, if there is some order in the keys, then using replacement selection could result in huge runs. For example, if no key has more than M larger keys before it in the file, the file will be completely sorted by the replacement-selection pass, and no merging will be necessary! This possibility is the most important practical reason to use replacement selection.

The major weakness of balanced multiway merging is that only about one-half the devices are actively in use during the merges: the P input devices and whichever device is collecting the output. An alternative is always to do $(2P - 1)$-way merges with all output onto device 0, then distribute the data back to the other tapes at the end of each merging pass. But this approach is not more efficient, because

Figure 11.17
Replacement selection

This sequence shows how we can produce the two runs A I N O R S T X and A E E G L M P, which are of length 8 and 7, respectively, from the sequence A S O R T I N G E X A M P L E using a heap of size 5.

```
A S O R T I N G A N D M E R G I N G E X A M P L E W I T H F O R T Y F I V E R E C O R D S • $

A O S • D M N • A E X • F H T • $
I R T • E G R • L M P • O R T • E R V • D R S • $
A G N • G I N • E I W • F I Y • C E O • • • $

A A G I N O R S T • D E G G I M N N R • A E E I L M P W X • F F H I O R T T Y • $
E R V • D R S • $
C E O • • • $

A A C E E G I N O O R R S T V • D D E G G I M N N R R S • $
A E E I L M P W X • F F H I O R T T Y • $
• $

D D E G G I M N N R R S • $
F F H I O R T T Y • $
A A A C E E E E G I I L M N O O P R R S T V W X • $

A A A C D D E E E E E F F G G G H I I I I L M M N N N O O O P R R R R R S S T T T V W X Y • $
```

Figure 11.18
Polyphase merge example

In the initial distribution phase, we put the different numbers of runs on the tapes according to a prearranged scheme, rather than keeping the numbers of runs balanced, as we did in Figure 11.15. Then, we do three-way merges at every phase until the sort is complete. There are more phases than for the balanced merge, but the phases do not involve all the data.

it effectively doubles the number of passes, for the distribution. Balanced multiway merging seems to require either an excessive number of tape units or excessive copying. Several clever algorithms have been invented that keep all the external devices busy by changing the way in which the small sorted blocks are merged together. The simplest of these methods is called *polyphase merging*.

The basic idea behind polyphase merging is to distribute the sorted blocks produced by replacement selection somewhat unevenly among the available tape units (leaving one empty) and then to apply a *merge-until-empty* strategy: Since the tapes being merged are of unequal length, one will run out sooner than the rest, and it then can be used as output. That is, we switch the roles of the output tape (which now has some sorted blocks on it) and the now-empty input tape, continuing the process until only one block remains. Figure 11.18 depicts an example.

The merge-until-empty strategy works for an arbitrary number of tapes, as shown in Figure 11.19. The merge is broken up into many *phases* (not all of which involve all of the data) which involve no extra copying. Figure 11.19 shows how to compute the initial run distribution. We compute the *number* of runs on each device by working backward.

For the example depicted in Figure 11.19, we reason as follows: We want to finish the merge with 1 run, on device 0. Therefore, just before the last merge, we want device 0 to be empty, and we want to have 1 run on each of devices 1, 2, and 3. Next, we deduce the run distribution that we would need just before the next-to-last merge for that merge to produce this distribution. One of devices 1, 2, or 3 has to be empty (so that it can be the output device for the next-to-last merge)—we pick 3 arbitrarily. That is, the next-to-last merge merges together 1 run from each of devices 0, 1, and 2, and puts the result on device 3. Since the next-to-last merge *leaves* 0 runs on device 0 and 1 run on each of devices 1 and 2, it must have begun with 1 run on device 0 and 2 runs on each of devices 1 and 2. Similar reasoning tells us that the merge prior to that must have begun with 2, 3, and 4 runs on devices 3, 0, and 1, respectively. Continuing in this fashion, we can build the table of run distributions: Take the largest number in each row, make it zero, and add it to each of the other numbers to get the previous row. This convention corresponds to defining for the previous row the highest-order merge that could give the present row. This technique works for any number of tapes (at least three): The numbers that arise are *generalized Fibonacci numbers*, which have many interesting properties. If the number of runs is not a generalized Fibonacci number, we assume the existence of dummy runs to make the number of initial runs exactly what is needed for the table. The main challenge in implementing a polyphase merge is to determine how to distribute the initial runs (see Exercise 11.64).

Given the run distribution, we can compute the relative lengths of the runs by working forward, keeping track of the run lengths produced by the merges. For example, the first merge in the example in Figure 11.19 produces 4 runs of relative size 3 on device 1, leaving 2 runs of size 1 on device 0 and 1 run of size 1 on device 3, and so forth. As for balanced multiway merging, we can perform the indicated multiplications, sum the results (not including the bottom row), and divide by the number of initial runs to get a measure of the cost as a multiple of the cost of making a full pass over all the data. For simplicity, we include the dummy runs in the cost calculation, which gives us an upper bound on the true cost.

Property 11.6 *With three external devices and internal memory sufficient to hold M records, a sort–merge that is based on replacement selection followed by a two-way polyphase merge takes about $1 + \lceil \log_\phi(N/2M) \rceil / \phi$ effective passes, on the average.*

0	1	2	3
	17*1		
7*1		4*1	6*1
3*1	4*3		2*1
1*1	2*3	2*5	
	1*3	1*5	1*9
1*17			

Figure 11.19
Run distribution for polyphase three-way merge

In the initial distribution for a polyphase three-way merge of a file 17 times the size of the internal memory, we put 7 runs on device 0, 4 runs on device 2, and 6 runs on device 3. Then, in the first phase, we merge until device 2 is empty, leaving 3 runs of size 1 on device 0, 2 runs of size 1 on device 3, and creating 4 runs of size 3 on device 1. For a file 15 times the size of the internal memory, we put 2 dummy runs on device 0 at the beginning (see Figure 11.18). The total number of blocks processed for the whole merge is 59, one fewer than for our balanced merging example (see Figure 11.16), but we use two fewer devices (see also Exercise 11.60).

The general analysis of polyphase merging, done by Knuth and other researchers in the 1960s and 1970s, is complicated, extensive, and beyond the scope of this book. For $P = 3$, the Fibonacci numbers are involved—hence the appearance of ϕ. Other constants arise for larger P. The factor $1/\phi$ accounts for the fact that each phase involves only that fraction of the data. We count the number of "effective passes" as the amount of data read divided by the total amount of data. Some of the general research results are surprising. For example, the optimal method for distributing dummy runs among the tapes involves using extra phases and more dummy runs than would seem to be needed, because some runs are used in merges much more often than are others (*see reference section*). ∎

For example, if we want to sort 1 billion records using three devices and enough internal memory to hold 1 million records, we can do so with a two-way polyphase merge with $\lceil\log_\phi 500\rceil/\phi = 8$ passes. Adding the distribution pass, we incur a slightly higher cost (one pass) than a balanced merge that uses *twice* as many devices. That is, we can think of the polyphase merge as enabling us to do the same job with half the amount of hardware. For a given number of devices, polyphase is always more efficient than balanced merging, as indicated in Figure 11.20.

As we discussed at the beginning of Section 11.4, our focus on an abstract machine with sequential access to external devices has allowed us to separate algorithmic issues from practical issues. While developing practical implementations, we need to test our basic assumptions and to take care that they remain valid. For example, we depend on efficient implementations of the input–output functions that transfer data between the processor and the external devices and other systems software. Modern systems generally have well-tuned implementations of such software.

Taking this point of view to an extreme, note that many modern computer systems provide a large *virtual memory* capability—a more general abstract model for accessing external storage than the one we have been using. In a virtual memory, we have the ability to address a huge number of records, leaving to the system the responsibility of making sure that the addressed data are transferred from external to internal storage when needed; our access to the data is seemingly as convenient as is direct access to the internal memory. But the illusion

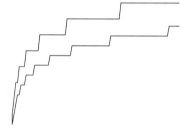

Figure 11.20
Balanced and polyphase merge cost comparisons

The number of passes used in balanced merging with 4 tapes (top) is always larger than the number of effective passes used in polyphase merging with 3 tapes (bottom). These plots are drawn from the functions in Properties 11.4 and 11.6, for N/M from 1 to 100. Because of dummy runs, the true performance of polyphase merging is more complicated than indicated by this step function.

is not perfect: As long as a program references memory locations that are relatively close to other recently referenced locations, then transfers from external to internal storage are needed infrequently, and the performance of virtual memory is good. (For example, programs that access data sequentially fall in this category.) If a program's memory accesses are scattered, however, the virtual memory system may *thrash* (spend all its time accessing external memory), with disastrous results.

Virtual memory should not be overlooked as a possible alternative for sorting huge files. We could implement sort–merge directly, or, even simpler, could use an internal sorting method such as quicksort or mergesort. These internal sorting methods deserve serious consideration in a good virtual-memory environment. Methods such as heapsort or a radix sort, where the the references are scattered throughout the memory, are not likely to be suitable, because of thrashing.

On the other hand, using virtual memory can involve excessive overhead, and relying instead on our own, explicit methods (such as those that we have been discussing) may be the best way to get the most out of high-performance external devices. One way to characterize the methods that we have been examining is that they are designed to make as many independent parts of the computer system as possible work at full efficiency, without leaving any part idle. When we consider the independent parts to be processors themselves, we are led to parallel computing, the subject of Section 11.6.

Exercises

▷ **11.55** Give the runs produced by replacement selection with a priority queue of size 4 for the keys E A S Y Q U E S T I O N.

○ **11.56** What is the effect of using replacement selection on a file that was produced by using replacement selection on a given file?

● **11.57** Empirically determine the average number of runs produced using replacement selection with a priority queue of size 1000, for random files of size $N = 10^3$, 10^4, 10^5, and 10^6.

11.58 What is the *worst-case* number of runs when you use replacement selection to produce initial runs in a file of N records, using a priority queue of size M with $M < N$?

▷ **11.59** Show how the keys E A S Y Q U E S T I O N W I T H P L E N T Y O F K E Y S are sorted using polyphase merging, in the style of the example diagrammed in Figure 11.18.

○ 11.60 In the polyphase merge example of Figure 11.18, we put two dummy runs on the tape with 7 runs. Consider the other ways of distributing the dummy runs on the tapes, and find the one that leads to the lowest-cost merge.

11.61 Draw a table corresponding to Figure 11.16 to determine the largest number of runs that could be merged by balanced three-way merging with five passes through the data (using six devices).

11.62 Draw a table corresponding to Figure 11.19 to determine the largest number of runs that could be merged by polyphase merging at the same cost as five passes through all the data (using six devices).

○ 11.63 Write a program to compute the number of passes used for multiway merging and the effective number of passes used for polyphase merging for a given number of devices and a given number of initial blocks. Use your program to print a table of these costs for each method, for $P = 3, 4, 5, 10$, and 100, and $N = 10^3, 10^4, 10^5$, and 10^6.

•• 11.64 Write a program to assign initial runs to devices for P-way polyphase merging, sequentially. Whenever the number of runs is a generalized Fibonacci number, the runs should be assigned to devices as required by the algorithm; your task is to find a convenient way to distribute the runs, one at a time.

• 11.65 Implement replacement selection using the interface defined in Exercise 11.48.

•• 11.66 Combine your solutions to Exercise 11.48 and Exercise 11.65 to make a sort–merge implementation. Use your program to sort as large a file as is feasible on your system, using polyphase merging. If possible, determine the effect on the running time of increasing the number of devices.

11.67 How should small files be handled in a quicksort implementation to be run on a huge file in a virtual-memory environment?

• 11.68 If your computer has a suitable virtual memory system, empirically compare quicksort, LSD radix sort, MSD radix sort, and heapsort for huge files. Use as large a file size as is feasible.

• 11.69 Develop an implementation for recursive multiway mergesort based on k-way merging that would be suitable for sorting huge files in a virtual-memory environment (see Exercise 8.11).

• 11.70 If your computer has a suitable virtual memory system, empirically determine the value of k that leads to the lowest running time for your implementation for Exercise 11.69. Use as large a file size as is feasible.

11.6 Parallel Sort–Merge

How do we get several independent processors to work together on the same sorting problem? Whether the processors control external memory devices or are complete computer systems, this question is at the heart of algorithm design for high-performance computing systems. The subject of parallel computing has been studied widely in recent years. Many different types of parallel computers have been devised, and many different models for parallel computation have been proposed. The sorting problem is a test case for the effectiveness of both.

We have already discussed low-level parallelism, in our discussion of sorting networks in Section 11.2, where we considered doing a number of compare–exchange operations at the same time. Now, we discuss a high-level parallel model, where we have a large number of independent general-purpose processors (rather than just comparators) that have access to the same data. Again, we ignore many practical issues, but can examine algorithmic questions in this context.

The abstract model that we use for parallel processing involves a basic assumption that the file to be sorted is distributed among P independent processors. We assume that we have

- N records to be sorted and
- P processors, each capable of holding N/P records

We assign the processors the labels $0, 1, \ldots, P-1$, and assume that the file to be input is in the local memories of the processors (that is, each processor has N/P of the records). The goal of the sort is to rearrange the records to put the smallest N/P records in processor 0's memory, the next smallest N/P records in processor 1's memory, and so forth, in sorted order. As we shall see, there is a tradeoff between P and the total running time—we are interested in quantifying that tradeoff so that we can compare competing strategies.

This model is one of many possible ones for parallelism, and it has many of the same liabilities with respect to practical applicability as did our model for external sorting (Section 11.4). Indeed, it does not address one of the most important issues to be faced in parallel computing: constraints on communication between the processors.

We shall assume that such communication is far more costly than references to local memory and that it is most efficiently done sequentially, in large blocks. In a sense, processors treat other processors' memory as external storage devices. Again, this high-level abstract model can be regarded as unsatisfactory from a practical standpoint, because it is an oversimplification; it can be regarded as unsatisfactory from a theoretical standpoint, because it is not fully specified. Still, it provides a framework within which we can develop useful algorithms.

Indeed, this problem (with these assumptions) provides a convincing example of the power of abstraction, because we can use the same sorting networks that we discussed in Section 11.2, by modifying the compare–exchange abstraction to operate on large blocks of data.

Definition 11.2 *A* **merging comparator** *takes as input two sorted files of size M and produces as output two sorted files: one containing the M smallest of the $2M$ inputs, and the other containing the M largest of the $2M$ inputs.*

Such an operation is easy to implement: Merge the two input files, and output the first half and the second half of the merged result.

Property 11.7 *We can sort a file of size N by dividing it into N/M blocks of size M, sorting each file, then using a sorting network built with merging comparators.*

Establishing this fact from the 0–1 principle is tricky (see Exercise 11.71), but tracing through an example, such as the one in Figure 11.21, is a persuasive exercise. ∎

We refer to the method described in Property 11.7 as *block sorting*. We have a number of design parameters to consider before we use the method on a particular parallel machine. Our interest in the method concerns the following performance characteristic:

Property 11.8 *Block sorting on P processors, using Batcher's sort with merging comparators, can sort N records in about $(\lg P)^2/2$ parallel steps.*

By *parallel step* in this context, we mean a set of disjoint merging comparators. Property 11.8 is a direct consequence of Properties 11.3 and 11.7. ∎

To implement a merging comparator on two processors, we can have them exchange copies of their blocks of data, have both do the merge (in parallel), and have one keep the small half of the keys and the other keep the large half of the keys. If block transfer is slow compared to the individual processor speeds, then we can estimate the total time required for the sort by multiplying the cost of one block transfer by $(\lg P)^2/2$. This estimate embodies a large number

Figure 11.21
Block sorting example

This figure shows how we can use the network in Figure 11.4 to sort blocks of data. The comparators put the small half of the elements in the two input lines out onto the top line and the large half out onto the bottom line. Three parallel steps suffice.

of assumptions; for example, it assumes that multiple block transfers can be done in parallel without penalty, a rarely achieved goal in real parallel computers. Still, it provides a starting point for understanding what we can expect in a practical implementation.

If the block-transfer cost is comparable to individual processor speeds (another ideal goal that is only approached in real machines), then we have to account for the time to do the initial sorts. The processors each do about $(N/P)\lg(N/P)$ comparisons (in parallel) to sort the N/P blocks initially, and about $P^2(\lg P)/2$ stages with (N/P)-by-(N/P) merges. If the cost of a comparison is α and the cost per record for a merge is β, then the total running time is about

$$\alpha(N/P)\lg(N/P) + \beta(N/P)P^2(\lg P)/2.$$

For huge N and small P, this performance is the best that we can hope for in any comparison-based parallel sorting method, because the cost in that case is about $\alpha(N\lg N)/P$, which is optimal: Any sort requires $N\lg N$ comparisons, and the best that we could do is to do P of them at once. For large P, the second term dominates, and the cost is about $\beta N(P\lg P)/2$, which is suboptimal but still perhaps is competitive. For example, the second term contributes about $256\beta N/P$ to the cost of sorting 1 billion elements on 64 processors, as compared to the contribution of $32\alpha N/P$ from the first term.

When P is large, the communication among all the processors might create a bottleneck on some machines. If so, using a perfect shuffle as in Figure 11.8 might provide a way to control such costs. For precisely this reason, some parallel machines have built-in low-level interconnections that allow us to implement shuffles efficiently.

This example shows that we *can* get a large number of processors to work efficiently on a huge sort problem, under certain circumstances. To find the best way to do so, we certainly would need to consider many other algorithms for this kind of parallel machine, to learn many other characteristics of a real parallel machine, and to consider many variations on the machine model that we are using.

Moreover, we might need to take a completely different approach to parallelism. Still, the idea that increasing the number of processors increases the costs of communicating among them is fundamental to parallel computing, and Batcher's networks provide an effective way of controlling these costs, as we have seen at a low level in Section 11.2 and at a high level in this section.

The sorting methods described in this section and elsewhere in this chapter have a flavor different from those of the methods that we have discussed in Chapters 6 through 10, because they involve coping with constraints that we do not consider in ordinary programming. In Chapters 6 through 10, simple assumptions about the nature of our data were sufficient to allow us to compare a large number of different methods for the same basic problem. By contrast, in this chapter we have focused on articulating a variety of problems and have been able to discuss just a few solutions for each. These examples illustrate that changes in real-world constraints can provide new opportunities for algorithmic solutions; a critical part of the process is to develop useful abstract formulations of problems.

Sorting is essential in many practical applications, and the design of an efficient sort is often one of the first problems to be addressed on new computer architectures and in new programming environments. To the extent that new developments build on past experience, the array of techniques that we have discussed here and in Chapters 6 through 10 is important to know; to the extent that radical new departures are invented, the kind of abstract thinking discussed here will be necessary if we are to develop fast sorting procedures on new machines.

Exercises

∘ **11.71** Use the 0–1 principle (Property 11.1) to prove Property 11.7.

• **11.72** Implement a sequential version of block sorting with Batcher's odd–even merge: (*i*) use standard mergesort (Programs 8.3 and 8.2) to sort the blocks, (*ii*) use the standard abstract in-place merge (Program 8.2) to implement the merging comparators, and (*iii*) use bottom-up Batcher's odd–even merge (Program 11.3) to implement the block sort.

11.73 Estimate the running time of the program described in Exercise 11.72, as a function of N and M, for large N.

• **11.74** Do Exercises 11.72 and 11.73, but substitute bottom-up Batcher's odd–even merge (Program 11.3) for Program 8.2 in both instances.

11.75 Give the values of P for which $(N/P)\lg N = NP\lg P$, for $N = 10^3$, 10^6, 10^9, and 10^{12}.

11.76 Give approximate expressions of the form $c_1 N \lg N + c_2 N$ for the number of comparisons between data items used by a parallel Batcher's block sort, for $P = 1, 4, 16, 64,$ and 256.

11.77 How many parallel steps would be required to sort 10^{15} records that are distributed on 1000 disks, using 100 processors?

References for Part Three

The primary reference for this section is Volume 3 of Knuth's series, on sorting and searching. Further information on virtually every topic that we have touched upon can be found in this book. In particular, the results discussed here on performance characteristics of the various algorithms are backed up there by complete mathematical analyses.

There is a vast literature on sorting. Knuth and Rivest's 1973 bibliography contains hundreds of references to articles that give insight into the development of many of the classic methods that we have considered. A more up-to-date reference, with an extensive bibliography covering recent work, is the book by Baeza-Yates and Gonnet. A survey of the state of our knowledge about shellsort may be found in Sedgewick's 1996 paper.

For quicksort, the best reference is Hoare's original 1962 paper, which suggests all the important variants, including the use for selection discussed in Chapter 7. Many more details on the mathematical analysis and the practical effects of many of the modifications and embellishments suggested as the algorithm came into widespread use may be found in Sedgewick's 1978 paper. Bentley and McIlroy give a modern treatment of the subject. The material on three-way partitioning in Chapter 7 and three-way radix quicksort in Chapter 10 is based on that paper and the 1997 article by Bentley and Sedgewick. The earliest partitioning-style algorithm (binary quicksort, or radix-exchange sort) appears in the 1959 article by Hildebrandt and Isbitz.

Vuillemin's binomial queue data structure, as implemented and analyzed by Brown, supports all the priority queue operations in an elegant and efficient manner. The pairing heap described by Fredman, Sedgewick, Sleator, and Tarjan is a refinement that is of practical interest.

The 1993 article by McIlroy, Bostic, and McIlroy presents the state of the art in radix sort implementations.

The book by Stone provides some of the background needed to actually put methods like those described in Chapter 11 into practical use. The fundamental ideas described by Stone and the basic methods described in Chapter 11 are only an introduction to this subject, because the onslaught of new devices and new methods of storing and moving information make this subject a volatile one.

R. Baeza-Yates and G. H. Gonnet, *Handbook of Algorithms and Data Structures*, second edition, Addison-Wesley, Reading, MA, 1984.

J. L. Bentley and M. D. McIlroy, "Engineering a sort function," *Software—Practice and Experience* **23**, 1 (January, 1993).

J. L. Bentley and R. Sedgewick, "Sorting and searching strings," Eighth Symposium on Discrete Algorithms, New Orleans, January, 1997.

M. R. Brown, "Implementation and analysis of binomial queue algorithms," *SIAM Journal of Computing* **7**, 3 (August, 1978).

M. L. Fredman, R. Sedgewick, D. D. Sleator, and R. E. Tarjan, "The pairing heap: a new form of self-adjusting heap," *Algorithmica* **1**, 1 (1986).

P. Hildebrandt and H. Isbitz, "Radix exchange — an internal sorting method for digital computers," *Journal of the ACM*, **6**, 2 (1959).

C. A. R. Hoare, "Quicksort," *Computer Journal*, **5**, 1 (1962).

D. E. Knuth, *The Art of Computer Programming. Volume 3*: *Sorting and Searching*, second edition, Addison-Wesley, Reading, MA, 1997.

P. M. McIlroy, K. Bostic, and M. D. McIlroy, "Engineering radix sort," *Computing Systems* **6**, 1 (1993).

R. L. Rivest and D. E. Knuth, "Bibliography 26: Computing Sorting," *Computing Reviews*, **13** 6 (June, 1972).

R. Sedgewick, "Implementing quicksort programs," *Communications of the ACM* **21**, 10 (October 1978).

R. Sedgewick, "Analysis of shellsort and related algorithms," Fourth European Symposium on Algorithms, Barcelona, September, 1996.

H. Stone, *High Performance Computer Architecture* Addison-Wesley, Reading, MA, 1993.

J. Vuillemin, "A data structure for manipulating priority queues," *Communications of the ACM* **21**, 4 (April 1978).

PART FOUR

Searching

CHAPTER TWELVE

Symbol Tables and Binary Search Trees

THE RETRIEVAL OF a particular piece or pieces of information from large volumes of previously stored data is a fundamental operation, called *search*, that is intrinsic to a great many computational tasks. As with sorting algorithms in Chapters 6 through 11 and, in particular, priority queues in Chapter 9, we work with data divided into records or *items*, each item having a *key* for use in searching. The goal of the search is to find the items with keys matching a given *search key*. The purpose of the search is usually to access information within the item (not merely the key) for processing.

Applications of search are widespread and involve a variety of different operations. For example, consider a bank that needs to keep track of all its customers' account information and to search through these records to check account balances and to perform transactions. Another example is an airline that needs to keep track of reservations on all its flights and to search through them to find empty seats or to cancel or otherwise modify the reservations. A third example is a search engine on a network software interface that looks for all documents in the network containing a given keyword. The demands of these applications are similar in some ways (the bank and the airline both demand accuracy and reliability) and different in others (the bank's data have a long life, compared to the data in the others); all need good search algorithms.

Definition 12.1   *A* **symbol table** *is a data structure of items with keys that supports two basic operations: insert a new item, and return an item with a given key.*

Symbol tables are also sometimes called *dictionaries*, by analogy with the time-honored system of providing definitions for words by listing them alphabetically in a reference book. In an English-language dictionary, the "keys" are the words and the "items" are the entries associated with the words that contain the definition, pronunciation, and other information. People use search algorithms to find information in a dictionary, usually depending on the fact that the entries appear in alphabetical order. Telephone books, encyclopedias, and other reference books are organized in essentially the same way, and some of the search methods that we shall discuss (for example, the binary search algorithm in Sections 2.6 and 12.4) also depend upon the entries being kept in order.

An advantage of computer-based symbol tables is that they can be much more dynamic than a dictionary or a telephone book, so most of the methods that we shall discuss build data structures that not only enable efficient search algorithms but also support efficient implementations of operations to add new items, to remove or modify items, to combine two symbol tables into one, and so forth. In this chapter, we shall revisit many of the issues related to such operations that we considered for priority queues in Chapter 9. The development of dynamic data structures to support search is one of the oldest and most widely studied problems in computer science; it will be our main focus in this chapter and in Chapters 13 through 16. As we shall see, many ingenious algorithms have been (and are still being) invented to solve the symbol-table implementation problem.

Beyond basic applications of the type just mentioned, symbol tables have been studied intensively by computer scientists and programmers because they are indispensable aids in organizing software on computer systems. A symbol table is the dictionary for a program: The keys are the symbolic names used in the program, and the items contain information describing the object named. From the early days of computing, when symbol tables allowed programmers to move from using numeric addresses in machine code to using symbolic names in assembly language, to modern applications of the new millennium, when symbolic names have meaning across worldwide computer networks, fast search algorithms have played and will play an essential role in computation.

Symbol tables are also frequently encountered in low-level abstractions, occasionally at the hardware level. The term *associative memory* is sometimes used to describe the concept. We shall focus on software implementations, but some of the methods that we consider are also appropriate for hardware implementation.

As with our study of sorting methods in Chapter 6, we shall begin our study of search methods in this chapter by looking at some elementary methods that are useful for small tables and in other special situations and that illustrate fundamental techniques exploited by more advanced methods. Then, for much of the remainder of the chapter, we shall focus on the *binary search tree (BST)*, a fundamental and widely used data structure that admits fast search algorithms.

We considered two search algorithms in Section 2.6 as an illustration of the effectiveness of mathematical analysis in helping us to develop effective algorithms. For completeness in this chapter, we repeat some of the information that we considered in Section 2.6, though we refer back to that section for some proofs. Later in the chapter, we also refer to the basic properties of binary trees that we considered in Sections 5.4 and 5.5.

12.1 Symbol-Table Abstract Data Type

As with priority queues, we think of search algorithms as belonging to interfaces declaring a variety of generic operations that can be separated from particular implementations so that we can easily substitute alternative implementations. The operations of interest include

- *Insert* a new item.
- *Search* for an item (or items) having a given key.
- *Remove* a specified item.
- *Select* the kth largest item in a symbol table.
- *Sort* the symbol table (show all the items in order of their keys).
- *Join* two symbol tables.

As we do with many data types, we also need to add a *construct* operation (constructor), a *test if empty* operation, and perhaps a *copy* (clone) operation to this set. In addition, we often consider other practical modifications of the basic interface. For example, a *search-and-insert* operation is an attractive alternative for implementations

> ### Program 12.1 ADT for symbol-table items
>
> These ADT interfaces illustrate how to define symbol-table items, similar to the way that we defined items to be sorted in Section 6.2. Here, to emphasize the distinction between items and their keys, we define separately the key abstraction.
>
> Our symbol-table implementations are KEY clients that use the methods equals and less to compare keys and also ITEM clients that use the method key to access keys in items, so they work with any implementations of ITEM and KEY (*see text*). The methods read, rand and toString are for use by clients.
>
> ```
> class myItem implements ITEM // ADT interface
>   { // implementations and private members hidden
>     public KEY key()
>     void read()
>     void rand()
>     public String toString()
>   }
> class myKey implements KEY  // ADT interface
>   { // implementations and private members hidden
>     public boolean less(myKey)
>     public boolean equals(myKey)
>     void read()
>     void rand()
>     public String toString()
>   }
> ```

where the search for a key, even if unsuccessful, nevertheless gives precisely the information needed to insert a new item with that key.

We commonly use the term "search algorithm" to mean "symbol-table ADT implementation," although the latter more properly implies defining and building an underlying data structure for the symbol table and implementing ADT operations in addition to search. Symbol tables are so important to so many computer applications that they are available as high-level abstractions in many programming environments. Java has the Dictionary class as a standard utility, and the Hashtable class that extends it, using the approach that we shall cover in Chapter 14. As usual, it is difficult for a general-purpose implementation to meet the demanding performance needs of diverse

Program 12.2 Symbol-table key implementation example

This class implements the interface of Program 12.1 for records whose keys have integer values. It uses a constant M to specify an upper bound on key values, whose value is application-dependent and is omitted.

```
class myKey implements KEY
  {
    private int val;
    public boolean less(KEY w)
      { return val < ((myKey) w).val; }
    public boolean equals(KEY w)
      { return val == ((myKey) w).val; }
    public void read()
      { val = In.getInt(); }
    public void rand()
      { val = (int) (M * Math.random()); }
    public String toString()
      { return val + ""; }
  }
```

applications. Our study of many of the ingenious methods that have been developed to implement the symbol-table abstraction will set a context to help us understand the characteristics of prepackaged implementations and to help us decide when to develop an implementation that is tailored to a particular application.

As we did with sorting, we will consider the methods without specifying the types of the items being processed, in the same manner that we discussed in detail in Section 6.2. But to emphasize the separate roles played by items and keys in search, we modify the approach that we used in Chapters 6 through 11 to define the item and key abstractions separately. For example, the myItem and myKey ADTs shown in Program 12.1 define the basic abstract operations that we want to perform. Using ADTs like these gives us the flexibility to implement and test various symbol-table implementations on various types of items and keys. The methods rand, read, and toString in Program 12.1 are for use by symbol-table clients, and the methods key, less, and equals are for use by symbol-table implementations.

Program 12.3 Symbol-table item implementation example

This class implements the `myItem` interface of Program 12.1 for records whose associated information is a floating-point number. The type of the key is determined by the implementation of `myKey` (see, for example, Program 12.2).

```
class myItem implements ITEM
  {
    private myKey val;
    private float info;
    myItem()
      { val = new myKey(); }
    public KEY key() { return val; }
    void read()
      { val.read(); info = In.getFloat(); }
    void rand()
      { val.rand(); info = (float) Math.random(); }
    public String toString()
      { return "(" + key() + " " + info + ")"; }
  }
```

Since symbol-table clients and symbol-table implementations both need to use classes like `myItem` and `myKey`, it is useful to distinguish their needs, we use the Java `interface` mechanism in the same way as we did in Section 6.2. Specifically, we define the interface

```
interface ITEM
  { KEY key(); }
```

so that search implementations can use ITEM types and the key method to access keys; and we define the interface

```
interface KEY
  {
    boolean less(KEY v);
    boolean equals(KEY v);
  }
```

so that search implementations can use KEY types and the methods `less` and `equals` to compare them. Indeed, our symbol-table implementations *only* access items and keys through these methods—to use one

of them, you only need to define appropriate classes that implement
ITEM and KEY.

Program 12.2 is an example implementation for integer keys: it
uses a constant M to specify the largest key value; in practice we might
choose a more complicated interface to allow clients to specify this
value. If, for example, keys are 9-digit social security numbers, we
might use $M = 10^9$. Program 12.3 is an example implementation for
items that can associate any type of key with a floating-point number.
We might also use an object type instead of a primitive type for the
associated information. Developing implementations like these for
specific types of items and keys needed in practice is straightforward.
For example, we could upgrade the item data type implementations for
records and strings from Section 6.2 in order to use myKey in myItem
for the key type, implement key() and change accesses to the key field
to invoke key() instead, and implement a myKey class with appropriate
less and equals methods.

We define less and equals as separate methods because several
basic algorithms are naturally expressed in terms of these two separate
primitives. Some of our implementations invoke less and equals
successively for the same pair of keys, which might be wasteful if the
comparisons are costly to perform. In such cases, it is worthwhile
to switch to a three-way comparison method that returns -1 if the
first key is less than the second, 0 if the two keys are equal, and 1 if
the first key is greater than the second. Some other implementations
do not use less or equals at all: for example, the first symbol-table
implementation that we consider, in Section 12.2, uses integer keys
as array indices but never explicitly compares them. In Chapters 14
and 15, our search algorithms are based on extracting pieces of keys
using the basic radix operations that we used in Chapter 10. In all
such cases, we omit or modify KEY and ITEM as appropriate.

As usual, defining classes for each abstraction leads to extra levels of indirection, so we might wish to avoid using the KEY interface or
the myKey type, by replacing KEY in our code with the type name, as
illustrated in Program 12.4. For primitive types, we can use the built-
in operators < and == to compare keys. As for sorting algorithms,
our implementations generally are written in terms of two-parameter
static methods less and equals to compare two keys; this convention
makes it easy to use either primitive or class types for keys. In some ap-

---

Program 12.4 Symbol-table item with integer keys

When we want to use keys that are of a primitive type, we replace
KEY in our code by the typename to avoid the use of an extra level of
referencing, as illustrated in this implementation.

```
class intkeyItem
  {
    private int val;
    private float info;
    public int key() { return val; }
    void read()
      { val = In.getInt(); info = In.getFloat(); }
    void rand()
      { val = (int) (M * Math.random());
        info = (float) Math.random(); }
    public String toString()
      { return "(" + key() + " " + info + ")"; }
  }
```

---

plications, we may wish to make further adjustments to accommodate
items that are primitive types.

Program 12.5 is an interface that defines the basic symbol-table
operations (except *join*), in terms of the item and key abstractions that
we just discussed. We shall use this interface between client programs
and all the search implementations in this and the next several chapters.

We could define a version of the interface in Program 12.5 to manipulate handles (Object references) to items in a manner similar to
Program 9.8 (see Exercise 12.7). In principle, the use of handles should
obviate the need to *search* before removing, and so can admit faster algorithms. In practice, typical implementations do not retain sufficient
structure to support efficient removal. For example, some implementations put items on linked lists—the lists would need to be doubly
linked to support removal by reference. To avoid unnecessarily complicated code, we use removal by key and leave removal-by-reference
implementations for exercises. The interface does not specify how we
determine which item to *remove*, when duplicate keys are present. One
reasonable interpretation would be "remove all items with the given

---

Program 12.5 Symbol-table ADT

This interface defines operations for a simple symbol table: initialize, return the item count, find an item with a given key, add a new item, remove an item with a given key, select the kth smallest item, and compute a string representation of the list of items in the table.

```
class ST // ADT interface
  { // implementations and private members hidden
    ST(int)
    int count()
    void insert(ITEM)
    ITEM search(KEY)
    void remove(KEY)
    ITEM select(int)
    public String toString()
  }
```

---

key." Instead, most of our implementations use the interpretation "remove any item with the given key," with an implied *search*.

Some algorithms do not assume any implied ordering among the keys and therefore use only equals (and not less) to compare keys, but many of the symbol-table implementations use the ordering relationship among keys implied by less to structure the data and to guide the search. Also, the *select* and *sort* abstract operations explicitly refer to key order. The *sort* operation is packaged as a method that sends all the items in order to the output stream, without necessarily rearranging them. We can easily generalize *sort* implementations to make a method that visits the items in order of their keys, perhaps applying a method in an object passed as a parameter to each. Typically, we include toString implementations for symbol tables when they show the contents of the symbol table in sorted order (implement *sort*). Algorithms that do not use less do not require that keys be comparable to one another, and they do not necessarily support efficient implementations of *select* and *sort*, so we omit implementatons of select and toString in such cases.

As already noted with regard to the *remove* operation, the possibility of items with duplicate keys needs special consideration in symbol-table implementations. Some applications disallow duplicate keys so that keys can be used as handles. An example of this situation is the use of social security numbers as keys in personnel files. Other applications may involve numerous items with duplicate keys: for example, a bank may need to search its database for all transactions involving a particular customer. We can handle items with duplicate keys in one of several ways. One approach is to insist that the primary search data structure contain only items with distinct keys, and to maintain, for each key, a link to a list of items with duplicate keys. That is, we use items that contain a key and a link in our primary data structures and do not have items with duplicate keys. This arrangement is convenient in some applications, since all the items with a given search key are returned with one *search* or can be removed with one *remove*. From the point of view of the implementation, this arrangement is equivalent to leaving duplicate-key management to the client. The Java `Dictionary` interface uses this convention.

A second possibility is to leave items with equal keys in the primary search data structure and to return *any* item with the given key for a *search*. This convention is simpler for applications that process one item at a time, where the order in which items with duplicate keys are processed is not important. It may be inconvenient in terms of the algorithm design, because the interface might have to be extended to include a mechanism to retrieve all items with a given key or to call a specified method for each item with the given key.

A third possibility is to assume that each item has a unique identifier (apart from the key) and to require that a *search* find the item with a given identifier, given the key. Or, a more complicated mechanism might be necessary. These considerations apply to all the symbol-table operations in the presence of duplicate keys. Do we want to *remove* all items with the given key, or any item with the key, or a specific item (which requires an implementation that provides handles to items)? When describing symbol-table implementations, we indicate informally how items with duplicate keys might be handled, without necessarily considering each mechanism for each implementation.

Program 12.6 is a sample client that illustrates some of these conventions for symbol-table implementations. It uses a symbol table to find the distinct values in a sequence of keys (randomly generated or read from standard input), then prints them in sorted order.

Program 12.6 Example of a symbol-table client

This program is a client of our item, key, and symbol-table ADTs (see Programs 12.1 and 12.5) that uses a symbol table to omit items with duplicate keys from a sequence generated randomly or read from standard input. For each item, it uses search to check whether the key has been seen before. If not, it prints the item and inserts it into the symbol table.

```
class DeDup
  {
    public static void main(String[] args)
      { int i, N = Integer.parseInt(args[0]),
             sw = Integer.parseInt(args[1]);
        ST st = new ST(N);
        for (i = 0; i < N; i++)
          { myItem v = new myItem();
            if (sw == 1) v.rand(); else v.read();
            if (st.search(v.key()) == null)
              { st.insert(v); Out.println(v + ""); }
          }
        Out.print(N + " keys, ");
        Out.println(N-st.count() + " dups");
      }
  }
```

As usual, we have to be aware that differing implementations of the symbol-table operations have differing performance characteristics, which may depend on the mix of operations. One application might use *insert* relatively infrequently (perhaps to build a table), then follow up with a huge number of *search* operations; another application might use *insert* and *remove* a huge number of times on relatively small tables, intermixed with *search* operations. Not all implementations will support all operations, and some implementations might provide efficient support of certain operations at the expense of others, with an implicit assumption that the expensive operations are performed rarely. Each of the fundamental operations in the symbol table interface has important applications, and many basic organizations have been suggested to support efficient use of various combinations of the operations. In this and the next few chapters, we shall concentrate on implementations of the fundamental operations *construct*, *insert*, and *search*, with some comment on *remove*, *select*, *sort*, and *join* when appropriate. The wide variety of algorithms to consider stems from differing performance characteristics for various combinations of the basic operations, and perhaps also from constraints on key values, or item size, or other considerations.

In this chapter, we shall see implementations where *search*, *insert*, *remove*, and *select* take time proportional to the logarithm of the number of items in the dictionary, on the average, for random keys, and *sort* runs in linear time. In Chapter 13, we shall examine ways to guarantee this level of performance, and we shall see one implementation in Section 12.2 and several in Chapters 14 and 15 with constant-time performance under certain circumstances.

Many other operations on symbol tables have been studied. Examples include *finger search*, where a search can begin from the point where a previous search ended; *range search*, where we want to count or show all the nodes falling within a specified interval; and, when we have a concept of *distance* between keys, *near-neighbor* search, where we want to find items with keys closest to a given key. In Part 7 we consider such operations in the context of geometric algorithms.

Exercises

▷ **12.1** Write a `myKey` class implementation (similar to Program 12.2) to support having the symbol-table implementations process items with `String` keys.

○ **12.2** Write an `myItem` class implementation that extends the `Record` class of Program 6.9 such that clients can build three symbol tables and search on any of the three keys.

▷ **12.3** Use the symbol-table ADT defined by the interface Program 12.5 to implement stack and queue ADTs.

▷ **12.4** Use the symbol-table ADT defined by the interface Program 12.5 to implement a priority-queue ADT that supports *both* remove-the-maximum *and* remove-the-minimum operations.

12.5 Use the symbol-table ADT defined by the interface Program 12.5 to implement an array sort compatible with those in Chapters 6 through 10.

▷ **12.6** Add a `clone` method operator to Program 12.5 and make it `Cloneable`. (see Section 4.9).

12.7 Define an interface for a symbol-table ADT that allows client programs to remove specific items via handles and to change keys (see Section 9.5).

▷ 12.8 Give an implementation of the `myItem` and `myKey` interfaces for items with two fields: a 16-bit integer key and a `String` object that contains information associated with the key.

● 12.9 Give the average number of distinct keys that our example driver program (Program 12.6) will find among N random positive integers less than 1000, for $N = 10, 10^2, 10^3, 10^4$, and 10^5. Determine your answer empirically, or analytically, or both.

12.2 Key-Indexed Search

Suppose that the keys are small integers (as is the case, for example, with Programs 12.6 and 12.4). In this case, the simplest search algorithm is based on storing the items in an array, indexed by the keys, as in the implementation given in Program 12.7. The code is straightforward: Operator `new[]` initializes all the entries with `null`; then we *insert* an item with key value k simply by storing it in `st[k]`, and *search* for an item with key value k by looking in `st[k]`. To *remove* an item with key value k, we put `null` in `st[k]`. The *select*, *sort*, and *count* implementations in Program 12.7 use a linear scan through the array, skipping null items. The implementation leaves to the client the tasks of handling items with duplicate keys and checking for conditions such as specifying *remove* for a key not in the table.

This implementation does not implement the interface of Program 12.5 because it requires that keys be integers (it uses `intkeyItem`, not `ITEM` and `KEY`). We start with this implementation because it a simple one that exemplifies all of the symbol-table implementations that we consider in this chapter and in Chapters 13 through 15. The indexing operation upon which key-indexed search is based is the same as the basic operation in the key-indexed counting sort method that we examined in Section 6.10. When it is applicable, key-indexed search is the method of choice, because *search* and *insert* could hardly be implemented more efficiently.

If there are no items at all (just keys), we can use a table of bits. The symbol table in this case is called an *existence table*, because we may think of the kth bit as signifying whether k exists among the set of keys in the table. (The Java `BitSet` class implements such a symbol table.) For example, we could use this method to determine quickly whether a given 4-digit number in a telephone exchange has already

Program 12.7 Key-indexed-array–based symbol table

This implementation uses integer keys and further assumes that keys are positive and less than the constructor's parameter so that it can use them as indices into an array. The primary costs to watch are both the amount of space required when the array is large and the amount of time required for new to initialize all the array entries to null when the number of keys in the array is small relative to its size.

```
class ST
  {
    private intkeyItem[] st;
    ST(int M)
      { st = new intkeyItem[M]; }
    int count()
      { int N = 0;
        for (int i = 0; i < st.length; i++)
          if (st[i] != null) N++;
        return N;
      }
    void insert(intkeyItem x)
      { st[x.key()] = x; }
    void remove(int key)
      { st[key] = null; }
    intkeyItem search(int key)
      { return st[key]; }
    intkeyItem select(int k)
      {
        for (int i = 0; i < st.length; i++)
          if (st[i] != null && k-- == 0)
            return st[i];
        return null;
      }
    public String toString()
      { String s = "";
        for (int i = 0; i < st.length; i++)
          if (st[i] != null) s += st[i] + "\n";
        return s;
      }
  }
```

been assigned, using a table of 313 words on a 32-bit computer (see Exercise 12.15).

Property 12.1   *If key values are positive integers less than M and items have distinct keys, then the symbol-table data type can be implemented with key-indexed arrays of items such that* **insert**, **search**, *and* **remove** *require constant time; and* **initialize**, **select**, *and* **sort** *require time proportional to M, whenever any of the operations are performed on an N-item table.*

This fact is immediate from inspection of the code. Note that the conditions on the keys imply that $N \leq M$. ∎

Program 12.7 does not handle duplicate keys, and it assumes that the key values are between 0 and M-1. We could use linked lists or one of the other approaches mentioned in Section 12.1 to store any items with duplicate keys, and we could do simple transformations of the keys before using them as indices (see Exercise 12.14); but we defer considering these cases in detail to Chapter 14, when we consider *hashing*, which uses this same approach to implement symbol tables for general keys, by transforming keys from a potentially large range such that they fall within a small range, then taking appropriate action for items with duplicate keys. For the moment, we assume that an old item with a key value equal to the key in an item to be inserted can be either silently ignored (as in Program 12.7) or treated as an error condition.

The implementation of *count* in Program 12.7 is a lazy approach where we do work only when the method count is called. An alternative (eager) approach is to maintain the count of nonempty table positions in a local variable, incrementing the variable if insert is into a table position that contains null, and decrementing it if remove is for a table position that does not contain null (see Exercise 12.11). The lazy approach is the better of the two if the *count* operation is used rarely (or not at all) and the number of possible key values is small; otherwise, the eager approach is better. For a library routine, the eager approach is preferred, because it provides optimal worst-case performance at the cost of a small constant factor for *insert* and *remove*; for the inner loop in an application with a huge number of *insert* and *remove* operations but few *count* operations, the lazy approach is preferred, because it gives the fastest implementation of the common operations. This type of tradeoff is common in the design of ADTs that must support a varying mix of operations, as we have seen on several occasions.

There are various other design decisions that we also need to make in developing a general-purpose interface. For example, should the key range be the same for all objects, or be different for different objects? If the latter option is chosen, then it may be necessary to add parameters to the constructor and to have methods giving the client access to the key range.

Key-indexed arrays are useful for many applications, but they do not apply if keys do not fall into a small range. Indeed, we might think of this and the next several chapters as being concerned with designing solutions for the case where the keys are from such a large range that it is not feasible to have an indexed table with one potential place for each key.

Exercises

▷ 12.10 Modify Programs 12.5 and 12.6 to be an interface and a client corresponding to the implementation of Program 12.7.

▷ 12.11 Modify the implementation of Program 12.7 to provide an eager implementation of count (by keeping track of the number of nonnull entries).

12.12 Implement a clonable symbol-table ADT (see Exercise 12.6) that uses key-indexed arrays.

12.13 Modify your implementation from Exercise 12.12 to provide an eager implementation of count (see Exercise 12.11).

12.14 Develop a version of Program 12.7 that assumes that KEY has a method h that converts keys to nonnegative integers less than M, with no two keys mapping to the same integer. (This improvement makes the implementation useful whenever keys are in a small range (not necessarily starting at 0) and in other simple cases.)

12.15 Develop a version of Program 12.7 for the case when items are keys that are positive integers less than M (no associated information). In the implementation, use an array of about M/32 integers.

12.16 Use your implementation from Exercise 12.15 for experiments to determine empirically the average and standard deviation for the number of distinct integers in a random sequence of N nonnegative integers less than N, for N close to the memory available to a program on your computer, expressed as a number of bits (see Program 12.6).

12.17 Develop a solution to Exercise 12.15 that uses a boolean array and compare its performance with your original solution for the task posed in Exercise 12.16.

12.3 Sequential Search

For general key values from too large a range for them to be used as indices, one simple approach for a symbol-table implementation is to store the items contiguously in an array, in order. When a new item is to be inserted, we put it into the array by moving larger elements over one position as we did for insertion sort; when a search is to be performed, we look through the array sequentially. Because the array is in order, we can report a search miss when we encounter a key larger than the search key. Moreover, since the array is in order, both *select* and *sort* are trivial to implement. Program 12.8 is a symbol-table implementation that is based on this approach.

It is worthwhile to revisit the issue of item and key representation. While we do so in the context of this specific implementation, the same issues arise in most other implementations. To be specific, suppose that we have a symbol table whose records are integer keys with associated floating-point numbers (as in our example in Program 12.3). When we use the ADTs of Program 12.1, we need two references to access each key, as depicted at the bottom in Figure 12.1. These references may be no problem in an application that involves thousands of searches on thousands of keys but may represent excessive cost in an application that involves billions of searches on millions of keys. As discussed in Section 12.1, it is not difficult to use a primitive type instead of KEY, which saves one reference per item, as depicted in the center in Figure 12.1. When the associated information is also primitive (or there is none), we can use parallel arrays, with no references, as depicted at the top in Figure 12.1. This arrangement would involve changing our interfaces and implementations to accept primitive-type parameters for both keys and associated information (see Exercise 12.20). Such improvements can have substantial effects in performance-critical applications, and they apply to most of the symbol-table implementations that we will consider. We use the separate ITEM and KEY abstractions to express our algorithms with more precision and because they are quite useful in practical situations that involve complicated records and keys, which are common.

We could slightly improve the inner loop in the implementation of *search* in Program 12.8 by using a sentinel to eliminate the test for running off the end of the array in the case that no item in the table

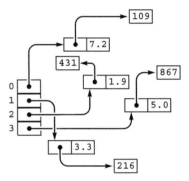

Figure 12.1
Item and key object representations

This diagram depicts Java representations for ordered-array symbol tables of records with integer keys and floating-point associated information, using three different representations for the records: parallel arrays (top); an item class with two primitive-type fields (center); and an item class that uses a key class (bottom). A fourth option, where the associated information is also an object type, is not shown.

Program 12.8 Array-based symbol table (ordered)

Like Program 12.7, this implementation uses an array of items, but it does not require the keys to be small integers. We keep the array in order when inserting a new item by moving larger items to make room, in the same manner as insertion sort. Then, the search method can scan through the array to look for an item with the specified key, returning null when encountering an item with a larger key. The select method is trivial, and the implementations of remove and toString are left as an exercise (see Exercise 12.18).

```
class ST
  {
    private boolean less(KEY v, KEY w)
      { return v.less(w); }
    private boolean equals(KEY v, KEY w)
      { return v.equals(w); }
    private ITEM[] st;
    private int N = 0;
    ST(int maxN)
      { st = new ITEM[maxN]; }
    int count()
      { return N; }
    void insert(ITEM x)
      { int i = N++; KEY v = x.key();
        while (i > 0 && less(v, st[i-1].key()))
          { st[i] = st[i-1]; i--; }
        st[i] = x;
      }
    ITEM search(KEY key)
      { int i = 0;
        for ( ; i < N; i++)
          if (!less(st[i].key(), key)) break;
        if (i == N) return null;
        if (equals(key, st[i].key())) return st[i];
        return null;
      }
    ITEM select(int k)
      { return st[k]; }
  }
```

has the search key. Specifically, we could reserve the position after the end of the array as a sentinel, then fill its key field with the search key before a search. Then the search loop will always terminate with an item containing the search key, and we can determine whether or not the key was in the table by checking whether that item is the sentinel.

Alternatively, we could develop an implementation where we do not insist that the items in the array be kept in order. When a new item is to be inserted, we put it at the end of the array; when a search is to be performed, we look through the array sequentially. The characteristic property of this approach is that *insert* is fast but *select* and *sort* require substantially more work (they each require one of the methods in Chapters 7 through 10). We can *remove* an item with a specified key by doing a search for it, then moving the final item in the array to its position and decrementing the size by 1; and we can *remove* all items with a specified key by iterating this operation. If a handle giving the index of an item in the array is available, the search is unnecessary and *remove* takes constant time.

Another straightforward option for a symbol-table implementation is to use a linked list. Again, we can choose to keep the list in order, to be able to easily support the *sort* operation, or to leave it unordered, so that *insert* can be fast. Program 12.9 is an implementation of the latter. As usual, the advantage of using linked lists over arrays is that we do not have to predict the maximum size of the table in advance; the disadvantages are that we need extra space (for the links) and we cannot support *select* efficiently.

The unordered-array and ordered-list approaches are left for exercises (see Exercise 12.24 and Exercise 12.25). These four implementation approaches (array or list, ordered or unordered) could be used interchangeably in applications, differing only (we expect) in time and space requirements. In this and the next several chapters, we will examine numerous different approaches to the symbol-table–implementation problem.

Keeping the items in order is an illustration of the general idea that symbol-table implementations generally use the keys to structure the data in some way to provide for fast search. The structure might allow fast implementations of some of the other operations, but this savings has to be balanced against the cost of maintaining the structure, which might be slowing down other operations. We shall see many

Program 12.9 Linked-list–based symbol table (unordered)

This implementation of *construct*, *count*, *search*, and *insert* uses a singly linked list with each node containing an item with a key and a link. The `insert` method puts the new item at the beginning of the list and takes constant time. The `search` member method uses a private recursive method `searchR` to scan through the list.

 The private `equals` method is the same as in Program 12.8 and is omitted. Implementations of the *select* and *sort* operations are also omitted because this data structure does not support efficient implementations of those operations, and *remove* is left as an exercise (see Exercise 12.22).

```
class ST
  {
    private class Node
      { ITEM item; Node next;
        Node(ITEM x, Node t) { item = x; next = t; }
      }
    private Node head;
    private int N;
    ST(int maxN) { head = null; N = 0; }
    int count() { return N; }
    void insert(ITEM x)
      { head = new Node(x, head); N++; }
    private ITEM searchR(Node t, KEY key)
      {
        if (t == null) return null;
        if (equals(t.item.key(), key))
          return t.item;
        return searchR(t.next, key);
      }
    ITEM search(KEY key)
      { return searchR(head, key); }
    public String toString()
      { Node h = head; String s = "";
        while (h != null)
          { s += h.item + "\n"; h = h.next; }
        return s;
      }
  }
```

examples of this phenomenon. For example, in an application where the *sort* operation is needed frequently, we would choose an ordered (array or list) representation because the chosen structure of the table makes the *sort* operation trivial, as opposed to it needing a full sort implementation. In an application where we know that the *select* operation might be performed frequently, we would choose an ordered array representation because this structure of the table makes *select* constant-time. By contrast, *select* takes linear time in a linked list, even an ordered one.

To analyze the performance of sequential search for random keys in more detail, we begin by considering the cost of inserting new keys and by considering separately the costs of *successful* and *unsuccessful* searches. We often refer to the former as a *search hit*, and to the latter as a *search miss*. We are interested in the costs for both hits and misses, on the average and in the worst case. Strictly speaking, our ordered-array implementation (see Program 12.8) uses two comparisons for each item examined (one equal and one `less`). For the purposes of analysis, we regard such a pair as a single comparison throughout Chapters 12 through 16, since we normally can effectively combine them into a three-way comparison (see, for example, Program 12.14).

Property 12.2 *Sequential search in a symbol table with N items uses about $N/2$ comparisons for search hits (on the average).*

See Property 2.1. The argument applies for arrays or linked lists, ordered or unordered. ■

Property 12.3 *Sequential search in a symbol table of N unordered items uses a constant number of steps for inserts and N comparisons for search misses (always).*

These facts are true for both the array and linked-list representations and are immediate from the implementations (see Exercise 12.24 and Program 12.9). ■

Property 12.4 *Sequential search in a symbol table of N ordered items uses about $N/2$ comparisons for insertion, search hits, and search misses (on the average).*

See Property 2.2. Again, these facts are true for both the array and linked-list representations and are immediate from the implementations (see Program 12.8 and Exercise 12.25). ■

Building an ordered table by successive insertion is essentially equivalent to running the insertion-sort algorithm of Section 6.4. The total running time to build the table is quadratic, so we would not use this method for large tables. If we have a huge number of *search* operations in a small table, then keeping the items in order is worthwhile, because Properties 12.3 and 12.4 tell us that this policy can save a factor of 2 in the time for search misses. If items with duplicate keys are not to be kept in the table, the extra cost of keeping the table in order is not as burdensome as it might seem, because an insertion happens only after a search miss, so the time for insertion is proportional to the time for search. On the other hand, if items with duplicate keys may be kept in the table, we can have a constant-time *insert* implementation with an unordered table. The use of an unordered table is preferred for applications where we have a huge number of *insert* operations and relatively few *search* operations.

Beyond these differences, we have the standard tradeoff that linked-list implementations use space for the links, whereas array implementations require that the maximum table size be known ahead of time or that the table undergo amortized growth (see Section 14.5). Also, as discussed in Section 12.9, a linked-list implementation has the flexibility to allow efficient implementation of other operations such as *join* and *remove*.

Table 12.1 summarizes these results and puts them in context with other search algorithms discussed later in this chapter and in Chapters 13 and 14. In Section 12.4, we consider *binary search*, which brings the search time down to $\lg N$ and is therefore widely used for static tables (when insertions are relatively infrequent).

In Sections 12.5 through 12.9, we consider *binary search trees*, which have the flexibility to admit search and insertion in time proportional to $\lg N$, but only on the average. In Chapter 13, we shall consider *red-black trees* and *randomized binary search trees*, which guarantee logarithmic performance or make it extremely likely, respectively. In Chapter 14, we shall consider *hashing*, which provides constant-time search and insertion, on the average, but does not efficiently support *sort* and some other operations. In Chapter 15, we shall consider the radix search methods that are analogous to the radix sorting methods of Chapter 10; in Chapter 16, we shall consider methods that are appropriate for files that are stored externally.

Table 12.1 Costs of insertion and search in symbol tables

The entries in this table are running times within a constant factor as a function of N, the number of items in the table, and M, the size of the table (if different from N), for implementations where we can *insert* new items without regard to whether items with duplicate keys are in the table. Elementary methods (first four lines) require constant time for some operations and linear time for others; more advanced methods yield guaranteed logarithmic or constant-time performance for most or all operations. The $N \lg N$ entries in the column for *select* represent the cost of sorting the items—a linear-time *select* for an unordered set of items is possible in theory but is not practical (see Section 7.8). Starred entries indicate worst-case events that are extremely unlikely.

	worst case			average case		
	insert	search	select	insert	search hit	search miss
key-indexed array	1	1	M	1	1	1
ordered array	N	N	1	$N/2$	$N/2$	$N/2$
ordered linked list	N	N	N	$N/2$	$N/2$	$N/2$
unordered array	1	N	$N \lg N$	1	$N/2$	N
unordered linked list	1	N	$N \lg N$	1	$N/2$	N
binary search	N	$\lg N$	1	$N/2$	$\lg N$	$\lg N$
binary search tree	N	N	N	$\lg N$	$\lg N$	$\lg N$
red–black tree	$\lg N$	$\lg N$	$\lg N$	$\lg N$	$\lg N$	$\lg N$
randomized tree	N^*	N^*	N^*	$\lg N$	$\lg N$	$\lg N$
hashing	1	N^*	$N \lg N$	1	1	1

Exercises

▷ **12.18** Complete our ordered-array–based symbol-table implementation (Program 12.8) by adding implementations of `remove` and `toString`. (Since the table is ordered, `toString` can put the items in order of their keys.)

▷ **12.19** Implement `searchinsert` methods for our list-based (Program 12.9) and array-based (Program 12.8) symbol-table implementations. They should search the symbol table for items with the same key as a given item, then insert the item if there is none.

12.20 Write a symbol-table ADT interface for an application that needs to associate floating-point numbers with integer keys.

12.21 Write an implementation of your interface from Exercise 12.20 that uses two arrays (an ordered array of ints and a parallel array of doubles) and no references.

12.22 Implement a *remove* (by key) operation for our list-based symbol-table implementation (Program 12.9).

12.23 Give the number of comparisons required to put the keys E A S Y Q U E S T I O N into an initially empty table using ADTs that are implemented with each of the four elementary approaches: ordered or unordered array or list. Assume that a search is performed for each key, then an insertion is done for search misses, as in Exercise 12.19.

12.24 Implement the *construct*, *search*, and *insert* operations for the symbol-table interface in Program 12.5, using an unordered array to represent the symbol table. Your program should match the performance characteristics set forth in Table 12.1.

∘ **12.25** Implement the *construct*, *search*, *insert*, *select*, and *sort* operations for the symbol-table interface in Program 12.5, using an ordered linked list to represent the symbol table. Your program should meet the performance characteristics set forth in Table 12.1.

∘ **12.26** Change our list-based symbol-table implementations (Program 12.9) to use doubly linked lists so that they can support client item handles (see Exercise 12.7); add an implementation of a clone (see Exercise 12.6); and write a driver program that tests your interface and implementation.

12.27 Write a performance driver program that uses insert to fill a symbol table, then uses select and remove to empty it, doing so multiple times on random sequences of keys of various lengths ranging from small to large; measures the time taken for each run; and prints out or plots the average running times.

12.28 Write a performance driver program that uses insert to fill a symbol table, then uses search such that each item in the table is hit an average of 10 times and there is about the same number of misses, doing so multiple times on random sequences of keys of various lengths ranging from small to large; measures the time taken for each run; and prints out or plots the average running times.

12.29 Write an exercise driver program that uses the methods in our symbol-table interface Program 12.5 on difficult or pathological cases that might turn up in practical applications. Simple examples include files that are already in order, files in reverse order, files where all keys are the same, and files consisting of only two distinct values.

∘ **12.30** Which symbol-table implementation would you use for an application that does 10^2 *insert* operations, 10^3 *search* operations, and 10^4 *select* operations, randomly intermixed? Justify your answer.

∘ **12.31** (This exercise is five exercises in disguise.) Answer Exercise 12.30 for the other five possibilities of matching up operations and frequency of use.

12.32 A *self-organizing* search algorithm is one that rearranges items to make those that are accessed frequently likely to be found early in the search. Modify your *search* implementation for Exercise 12.24 to perform the following action on every search hit: move the item found to the beginning of the list, moving all items between the beginning of the list and the vacated position to the right one position. This procedure is called the *move-to-front* heuristic.

▷ **12.33** Give the order of the keys after items with the keys E A S Y Q U E S T I O N have been put into an initially empty table with *search*, then *insert* on search miss, using the move-to-front self-organizing search heuristic (see Exercise 12.32).

12.34 Write a driver program for self-organizing search methods that uses *insert* to fill a symbol table with N keys, then does $10N$ searches to hit items according to a predefined probability distribution.

12.35 Use your solution to Exercise 12.34 to compare the running time of your implementation from Exercise 12.24 with your implementation from Exercise 12.32, for $N = 10$, 100, and 1000, using the probability distribution where *search* hits the ith largest key with probability $1/2^i$ for $1 \leq i \leq N$.

12.36 Do Exercise 12.35 for the probability distribution where *search* hits the ith largest key with probability $1/(iH_N)$ for $1 \leq i \leq N$. This distribution is called *Zipf's law*.

12.37 Compare the move-to-front heuristic with the optimal arrangement for the distributions in Exercises 12.35 and 12.36, which is to keep the keys in increasing order (decreasing order of their expected frequency). That is, use Program 12.8, instead of your solution to Exercise 12.24, in Exercise 12.35.

12.4 Binary Search

In the array implementation of sequential search, we can reduce significantly the total search time for a large set of items by using a search procedure based on applying the standard divide-and-conquer paradigm (see Section 5.2): Divide the set of items into two parts, determine to which of the two parts the search key belongs, then concentrate on that part. A reasonable way to divide the sets of items into parts is to keep the items sorted, then to use indices into the sorted array to delimit the part of the array being worked on. This search technique is called *binary search*. Program 12.10 is a recursive implementation of this fundamental strategy. Program 2.2 is a nonrecursive implementation of the method—no stack is needed because the recursive method in Program 12.10 ends in a recursive call.

Figure 12.2 shows the subfiles examined by binary search when a small table is searched; Figure 12.3 depicts a larger example. Each iteration eliminates slightly more than one-half of the table, so the number of iterations required is small.

Property 12.5 *Binary search never uses more than* $\lfloor \lg N \rfloor + 1$ *comparisons for a search (hit or miss).*

See Property 2.3. It is amusing to note that the maximum number of comparisons used for a binary search in a table of size N is precisely the number of bits in the binary representation of N, because the operation of shifting 1 bit to the right converts the binary representation of N into the binary representation of $\lfloor N/2 \rfloor$ (see Figure 2.6). ∎

Keeping the table sorted as we do in insertion sort leads to a running time that is a quadratic function of the number of *insert* operations, but this cost might be tolerable or even negligible if the number of *search* operations is huge. In the typical situation where all the items (or even a large number of them) are available before the search begins, we might *construct* the symbol table by having a constructor that takes an array as its parameter and uses one of the standard sorting methods from Chapters 6 through 10 to sort the table during initialization. After doing so, we could handle updates to the table in various ways. For example, we could maintain order during insert, as in Program 12.8 (see also Exercise 12.25), or we could batch them, sort, and merge (as discussed in Exercise 8.1). Any update could involve an item with a smaller key than those of any item in the table, so every item in the table might have to be moved to make room. This potential for a high cost of updating the table is the biggest liability of using binary search. On the other hand, there are a great many applications where a static table can be presorted and the fast access provided by implementations like Program 12.10 makes binary search the method of choice.

If we need to insert new items dynamically, it seems that we need a linked structure, but a singly linked list does not lead to an efficient implementation, because the efficiency of binary search depends on our ability to get to the middle of any subarray quickly via indexing, and the only way to get to the middle of a singly linked list is to follow links. To combine the efficiency of binary search with the flexibility of linked structures, we need more complicated data structures, which we shall begin examining shortly.

A A A C E E E Ⓖ H I L M N P R
              H I L Ⓜ N P R
              H Ⓘ L
                Ⓛ

Figure 12.2
Binary search

Binary search uses only three iterations to find a search key L in this sample file. On the first call, the algorithm compares L to the key in the middle of the file, the G. Since L is larger, the next iteration involves the right half of the file. Then, since L is less than the M in the middle of the right half, the third iteration involves the subfile of size 3 containing H, I, and L. After one more iteration, the subfile size is 1, and the algorithm finds the L.

> **Program 12.10 Binary search (for array-based symbol table)**
>
> This implementation of search uses a recursive binary-search proce-
> dure. To find whether a given key v is in an ordered array, it first
> compares v with the element at the middle position. If v is smaller, then
> it must be in the first half of the array; if v is greater, then it must be in
> the second half of the array.
>
>   The array must be in sorted order. This method could replace
> search in Program 12.8, which maintains the order dynamically dur-
> ing insertion. We could also include a symbol-table constructor that
> takes an array as a parameter, then builds a symbol table from items in
> the parameter array and uses a standard sort routine to prepare it for
> searching (see Program 12.14).
>
> ```
>     private ITEM searchR(int l, int r, KEY v)
>       {
>         if (l > r) return null;
>         int m = (l+r)/2;
>         if (equals(v, st[m].key())) return st[m];
>         if (less(v, st[m].key()))
>              return searchR(l, m-1, v);
>         else return searchR(m+1, r, v);
>       }
>     ITEM search(KEY v)
>       { return searchR(0, N-1, v); }
> ```

If duplicate keys are present in the table, then we can extend binary search to support symbol-table operations for counting the number of items with a given key or returning them as a group. Multiple
items with keys equal to the search key in the table form a contiguous
block in the table (because it is in order), and a successful search in
Program 12.10 will end somewhere within this block. If an application
requires access to all such items, we can add code to scan both directions from the point where the search terminated and to return two
indices delimiting the items with keys equal to the search key. In this
case, the running time for the search will be proportional to $\lg N$ plus
the number of items found. A similar approach solves the more general *range-search* problem of finding all items with keys falling within
a specified interval. We shall consider such extensions to the basic set
of symbol-table operations in Part 6.

Figure 12.3
Binary search

With binary search, we need only seven iterations to find a record in a file of 200 elements. The subfile sizes follow the sequence 200, 99, 49, 24, 11, 5, 2, 1; each is slightly less than one-half of the previous.

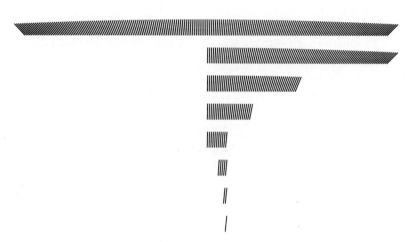

The sequence of comparisons made by the binary search algorithm is predetermined: The specific sequence used depends on the value of the search key and on the value of N. The comparison structure can be described by a binary-tree structure such as the one illustrated in Figure 12.4. This tree is similar to the tree that we used in Chapter 8 to describe the subfile sizes for mergesort (Figure 8.3). For binary search, we take one path through the tree; for mergesort, we take all paths through the tree. This tree is static and implicit; in Section 12.6, we shall see algorithms that use a dynamic, explicitly constructed binary-tree structure to guide the search.

One improvement that is possible for binary search is to guess where the search key falls within the current interval of interest with more precision (rather than blindly testing it against the middle element at each step). This tactic mimics the way we look up a name in the telephone directory or a word in a dictionary: If the entry that we are seeking begins with a letter near the beginning of the alphabet, we look near the beginning of the book, but if it begins with a letter near the end of the alphabet, we look near the end of the book. To implement this method, called *interpolation search*, we modify Program 12.10 to mimic this process. To this end, note that the expression $(l + r)/2$ that we use in binary search is shorthand for $l + \frac{1}{2}(r - l)$: We compute the middle of the interval by adding one-half of the size of the interval to the left endpoint. Using interpolation search amounts to replacing $\frac{1}{2}$ in this formula by an estimate of where the key might be—specifically

$(v-k_l)/(k_r-k_l)$, where k_l and k_r denote the values of a[1].key() and a[r].key(), respectively. Thus, to implement interpolation search, we replace the statement

    m = (l+r)/2;

in binary search by

    m = l+(v-a[l].key())*(r-l)/(a[r].key()-a[l].key());

This calculation is based on the assumption that the key values are numerical and evenly distributed.

For files of random keys, it is possible to show that interpolation search uses fewer than $\lg\lg N+1$ comparisons for a search (hit or miss). That proof is quite beyond the scope of this book. This function grows very slowly and can be thought of as a constant for practical purposes: If N is 1 billion, $\lg\lg N<5$. Thus, we can find any item using only a few accesses (on the average)—a substantial improvement over binary search. For keys that are more regularly distributed than random, the performance of interpolation search is even better. Indeed, the limiting case is the key-indexed search method of Section 12.2.

Interpolation search, however, does depend heavily on the assumption that the keys are well distributed over the interval—it can be badly fooled by poorly distributed keys, which do commonly arise in practice. Also, it requires extra computation. For small N, the $\lg N$ cost of straight binary search is close enough to $\lg\lg N$ that the cost of interpolating is not likely to be worthwhile. On the other hand, interpolation search certainly should be considered for large files, for applications where comparisons are particularly expensive, and for external methods where high access costs are involved.

Exercises

▷ **12.38** Give a nonrecursive implementation of the search method in Program 12.10 (see Program 2.2).

12.39 Draw trees that correspond to Figure 12.4 for $N = 17$ and $N = 24$.

○ **12.40** Find the values of N for which binary search in a symbol table of size N becomes 10, 100, and 1000 times faster than sequential search. Predict the values with analysis and verify them experimentally.

12.41 Suppose that insertions into a dynamic symbol table of size N are implemented as in insertion sort, but that we use binary search for *search*. Assume that searches are 1000 times more frequent than insertions. Estimate the percentage of the total time that is devoted to insertions, for $N = 10^3$, 10^4, 10^5, and 10^6.

Figure 12.4
Comparison sequence in binary search

These divide-and-conquer tree diagrams depict the index sequence for the comparisons in binary search. The patterns are dependent on only the initial file size, rather than on the values of the keys in the file. They differ slightly from the trees corresponding to mergesort and similar algorithms (Figures 5.6 and 8.3) because the element at the root is not included in the subtrees.

The top diagram shows how a file of 15 elements, indexed from 0 to 14, is searched. We look at the middle element (index 7), then (recursively) consider the left subtree if the element sought is less, and the right subtree if the element sought is greater. Each search corresponds to a path from top to bottom in the tree; for example, a search for an element that falls between the elements 10 and 11 would involve the sequence 7, 11, 9, 10. For file sizes that are not 1 less than a power of 2, the pattern is not quite as regular, as indicated by the bottom diagram, for 12 elements.

12.42 Develop a symbol-table implementation using binary search and lazy insertion that supports the *construct, count, search, insert,* and *sort* operations, using the following strategy. Keep a large sorted array for the main symbol table and an unordered array for recently inserted items. When search is called, sort the recently inserted items (if there are any), merge them into the main table, then use binary search.

12.43 Add lazy removal to your implementation for Exercise 12.42.

12.44 Answer Exercise 12.41 for your implementation for Exercise 12.42.

○ **12.45** Implement a method similar to binary search (Program 12.10) that returns the number of items in the symbol table with keys equal to a given key.

12.46 Write a program that, given a value of N, produces a sequence of N macro instructions, indexed from 0 to N-1, of the form compare(1, h), where the ith instruction on the list means "compare the search key with the value at table index i; then report a search hit if equal, do the lth instruction next if less, and do the hth instruction next if greater" (reserve index 0 to indicate search miss). The sequence should have the property that any search will do the same comparisons as would binary search on the same data.

● **12.47** Develop an expansion of the macro in Exercise 12.46 such that your program produces machine code that can do binary search in a table of size N with as few machine instructions per comparison as possible.

12.48 Suppose that a[i] == 10*i for i between 1 and N. How many table positions are examined by interpolation search during the unsuccessful search for $2k - 1$?

● **12.49** Find the values of N for which interpolation search in a symbol table of size N becomes 1, 2, and 10 times faster than binary search, assuming the keys to be random. Predict the values with analysis, and verify them experimentally.

12.5 Index Implementations with Symbol Tables

For many applications we want a search structure simply to help us find items, without moving them around. For example, we might have an array of items with keys, and we might want the search method to give us the index into that array of the item matching a certain key. Or we might want to remove the item with a given index from the search structure but still keep it in the array for some other use. An important feature of this approach is that it allows the client to maintain extra arrays (extra information associated with each node) to be added without the symbol-table code being changed at all. When the search routine returns the index for an item, it gives a way to access

---

Program 12.11 String-index ADT

This ADT describes an essential operation for strings: build an index (preprocess a text string) such that, given a query string, we can quickly search the text for the query. We normally specify that search should return -1 if the query string is not found in the text; otherwise it should return the text index where it found a match.

```
class TI // ADT interface
  { // implementations and private members hidden
    TI(String)
    int search(String)
  }
```

```
           0 1 2 3 4 5 6 7 8 9
index  27 0 42 8 46 5 37 31 16 21

   0 call me ishmael some...
   5 me ishmael some year...
   8 ishmael some years a...
  16 some years ago never...
  21 years ago never mind...
  27 ago never mind how l...
  31 never mind how long...
  37 mind how long...
  42 how long...
  46 long...
     ...
```

Figure 12.5
Text string index

In this example of a string index, we define a string key to begin with each word in a text; then, we build a table with the indices appearing in order of the keys that they reference. The first entry, string index 27, refers to the string key that begins ago ...; *the second entry refers to* call ...; *the third entry to* how ...; *and so forth. The we can use binary search on this table. For example, to find out whether the phrase* never mind *appears in this text, we compare with* long... *in the middle (string index 46 at position 4 in the middle of the index array), then we find a match in the middle of the right half (string index 31 at position 7 in the middle of the right half of the index array). We use word boundaries for clarity; our implementations typically define a new key starting at each character position. The keys are arbitrarily long in principle, but only a few leading characters are generally examined, in practice.*

immediately all the information associated with that item, by using the index to access an appropriate array.

In Section 9.6, we considered the advantages of processing index items in priority queues, referring to data in a client array indirectly. For symbol tables, the same concept leads to the familiar *index*: a search structure external to a set of items that provides quick access to items with a given key. In Chapter 16, we shall consider the case where the items and perhaps even the index are in external storage; in this section, we briefly consider the case when both the items and the index fit in memory.

We can adapt any symbol-table implementation to build indices in precisely the same manner as we provided indirection for heaps in Section 9.6: pass an array of items to the constructor and redefine less and equals to refer to items through their indices. This solution is straightforward and useful, but leave it for exercises (see Exercises 12.50 through 12.52).

We consider instead an important special case: implementing an ADT to provide keyword searching in a string of text, as specified in Program 12.11. Given a text string, we want to support queries of the form: "Is this query string found in the text string?" We will be considering several versions and implementations of this kind of ADT in Part 6; for this section, we assume that the text is huge and that we are willing to spend some time preprocessing it (in the constructor) so as to be able to quickly respond to queries (see Figure 12.5).

Program 12.12 String-index client

This client uses an index to search in a text string for a sequence of strings from standard input. The main program reads the text from a specified file, puts it in a (potentially huge) `String` and builds an index from the substrings defined by starting at each character in the text string. Then, it reads query strings from standard input and prints a position where the query is found in the text (or prints `not found`). A naive index implementation would take time proportional to the length of the text, but we can use a symbol table to make the search fast, even for huge strings.

```
import java.io.*;
class TextSearch
  {
    public static void main(String[] args)
      throws IOException
      { FileReader f = new FileReader(args[0]);
        BufferedReader b = new BufferedReader(f);
        String text = "", line = "";
        while ((line = b.readLine()) != null)
          text += line + " ";
        TI ti = new TI(text);
        In.init(); String q; int i;
        while ((q = In.getString()) != null)
          if ((i = ti.search(q)) < 0)
                Out.println(q + " not found");
          else Out.println(q + " " + i );
      }
  }
```

Program 12.12 is an example of a client. It reads a text string from an external file, builds an index, then reads a series of query strings from standard input and uses `search` to print the position in the text of some occurrence of each query (or an indication that the query does not occur in the text).

The first step in developing an implementation is to consider each position in the text string to define a string key starting at that position and going to the end of the string. In the abstract, these keys can be quite long, but we will take pains in our implementations to represent each key only with an index, and we will look at only enough of their characters to decide how to compare them. No two keys are equal (for example, they are all of different lengths), but if we consider two strings to be equal if one is a prefix of the other, we can use our standard symbol-table implementations to decide whether a given query string is in the text.

One approach to doing so is to develop appropriate implementations of `myItem` and `myKey` (see Exercise 12.1). The advantage of this approach is that it enables use of any of our symbol-table implementations and provides the flexibility to handle multiple text strings or to extend the basic ADT in a variety of ways. We leave that for an exercise because it leads to an excessive number of references when we have a huge text string (since we have one reference per key). We might ameliorate this cost by indexing the string only on word boundaries or some similar scheme.

Programs 12.13 and 12.14 illustrate a direct implementation that is based on binary search. We construct a symbol table that is made up of an ordered array of keys, except that we keep in that array not the key, but an index into the text string that points to the first character of the key. We start with the keys in the order in which they appear in the text string (with the ith entry in the index equal to i, the position in the text of the ith key) and rearrange them to be in sorted order (with the ith entry in the index equal to position in the text of the ith smallest key). As in Section 11.3, the key to the implementation is the definition of the `less` method. When we are to compare key i with key j, we actually want to compare the substring of the text beginning at i with the substring of the text beginning at j. If `less` is implemented to do so, we can think of the keys residing in the array, when actually it is their indices. Any of our sort implementations can be used (with `int` item type) to perform the sort.

If the text is in a `String s`, we might compare key i with key j with the Java code

```
s.substring(i).compareTo(s.substring(j))
```

but we avoid using these methods because they carry no performance guarantees. In particular, `substring` might take time or space proportional to the length of the substring, which would be disastrous for this application. We *are* assuming that `charAt` is a constant-time operation, which may not be true in some implementations. If that is

Program 12.13 String-index implementation (constructor)

This code uses binary search to build an index for a given text string, using an indirect sort. The constructor creates an array `index`, initializes it so that `index[i] = i`, and uses quicksort to rearrange the entries such that `index[i]` is the position in the text of the *i*th lexicographically smallest substring. We do not need to change the quicksort code at all to accomplish this result—we just define `less` so that `less(i, j)` compares the substring of the text starting at `i` with the substring of the text starting at `j`.

```
class TI
  {
    private String text;
    private int[] index;
    private int N;
    TI(String s)
      { text = s; N = text.length();
        index = new int[N+1]; index[N] = -1;
        for (int i = 0; i < N; i++)
          index[i] = i;
        quicksort(index, 0, N-1);
      }
    private char s(int i)
      { return text.charAt(i); }
    private boolean less(int v, int w)
      {
        if (v == w) return false;
        for (int i = 0; ; i++)
          if (w+i >= N) return false;
          else if (v+i >= N) return true;
          else if (s(v+i) < s(w+i)) return true;
          else if (s(v+i) > s(w+i)) return false;
      }
    private void exch(int[] a, int i, int j)
      { int t = a[i]; a[i] = a[j]; a[j] = t; }
    private void quicksort(int[] a, int l, int r)
      // Program 7.1 with int for ITEM
    int search(String v)
      // Program 12.14
  }
```

Program 12.14 String-index implementation (search)

To search in the text using the index array constructed in Program 12.13, we again redefine the comparison methods to refer to the text through the index array. Since comparisons may be expensive, we avoid doing both less and equals at every step by using a modified version of Program 12.10 based on a three-way comparison (*see text*).

```
private int compare(String s, int v)
  { char[] key = s.toCharArray();
    int t = index[v];
    for (int i = 0; i < key.length; i++)
      if (t+i >= N) return 1;
      else if (key[i] > text(t+i)) return 1;
      else if (key[i] < text(t+i)) return -1;
    return 0;
  }
private int searchR(int l, int r, String v)
  { int m = (l+r)/2;
    if (l > r) return N;
    switch (compare(v, m))
      {
        case -1: return searchR(l, m-1, v);
        case  1: return searchR(m+1, r, v);
      }
    return m; // case 0
  }
int search(String v)
  { return index[searchR(0, N-1, v)]; }
```

---

the case, it is not difficult to modify Programs 12.13 and 12.14 to use character arrays rather than Strings (see Section 3.6). An additional point to note is that compareTo is carefully implemented so as to provide proper ordering of Unicode strings, but that feature is irrelevant to this application, where we are only using the ordering to structure an efficient search for equal substrings.

Once the constructor builds the sorted key index array, then it is a simple matter to use it for a binary search, again by implementing an appropriate comparison method, as shown in Program 12.14. We could implement `less` and `equals` methods and use our binary search code from Program 12.10, but, as mentioned in Section 12.1, it is simpler and more efficient to use a three-way comparison method like the Java `compareTo` method for strings, since our binary search implementation always follows an `equals` text with a `less` test on the same keys. The `compare` method in Program 12.14 compares a given string with a given substring of the text and returns −1 if less, 0 if equal (the whole substring is found in the text), and 1 if greater.

Since the symbol table is implemented with binary search, then we expect from Property 2.3 that the search will involve about $\lg N$ comparisons. For example, once the index is built, we could find any phrase in a text consisting of about 1 million characters (such as *Moby Dick*) with about 20 string comparisons.

There are other issues for us to consider when we are building indices in practical applications, many of which we consider in the context of particular implementations (see, for example, Exercises 12.54 and 12.81). As we shall see in Chapter 15, there are also many ways that we can take particular advantage of the properties of string keys to speed up our algorithms. More sophisticated methods for string search and for providing indices with useful capabilities for string keys will be primary topics in Part 6.

Exercises

▷ **12.50** Give an ADT interface similar to Program 9.11 for building a symbol table using indices into a client array that supports the *search* and *select* operations.

○ **12.51** Provide an implementation of your interface from Exercise 12.50 that uses class `Sort` (see Program 6.3)—so that you can use any sort implementation—and binary search.

12.52 Write a driver program that tests your interface from Exercise 12.50 and the performance of your implementation from Exercise 12.51.

12.53 Give the index array that is constructed by Program 12.13 for the text string `abracadabra`, and then the the index values that are returned by Program 12.14 for the query strings `cad`, `abra` and `a`.

○ **12.54** Modify the ADT interface of Program 12.11 such that `search` returns an array with *all* the text indices that match the query, and modify Program 12.14 to implement your interface.

○ **12.55** Give an example of a text string where the number of character comparisons for the index-construction part of Program 12.12 is quadratic in the length of the string.

12.56 Modify our string index implementation (Program 12.12) to use only the keys that start on word boundaries to build the index (see Figure 12.5). (For *Moby Dick*, this change cuts the size of the index by more than a factor of five.)

12.6 Binary Search Trees

Insertions into ordered lists and searches in unordered lists are both expensive, so neither data structure is useful when we have a mix of such operations. In this section, we see that using an explicit tree structure as the basis for a symbol-table implementation allows us to develop algorithms with fast average-case performance for the *search*, *insert*, *select*, and *sort* symbol-table operations. It is the method of choice for many applications and qualifies as one of the most fundamental algorithms in computer science.

We discussed trees at some length, in Chapter 5, but it will be useful to review the terminology. We are working with data structures comprised of nodes that contain links that either point to other nodes or to *external nodes*, which have no links. In a (rooted) *tree*, we have the restriction that every node is pointed to by just one other node, which is called its parent. In a *binary tree*, we have the further restriction that each node has exactly two links, which are called its left and right links. Nodes with two links are also referred to as *internal nodes*. For search, each internal node also has an item with a key value, and we refer to links to external nodes as *null links*. The key values in internal nodes are compared with the search key, and control the progress of the search.

Definition 12.2 *A* **binary search tree (BST)** *is a binary tree that has a key associated with each of its internal nodes, with the additional property that the key in any node is larger than (or equal to) the keys in all nodes in that node's left subtree and smaller than (or equal to) the keys in all nodes in that node's right subtree.*

Program 12.15 uses BSTs to implement the symbol-table *search*, *insert*, and *construct* operations. It defines nodes in BSTs as each containing an item (with a key), a left link, and a right link. The left link points to a BST for items with smaller (or equal) keys, and the right link points to a BST for items with larger (or equal) keys.

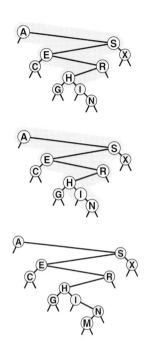

Figure 12.6
BST search and insertion

In a successful search for H in this sample tree (top), we move right at the root (since H is larger than A), then left at the right subtree of the root (since H is smaller than S), and so forth, continuing down the tree until we encounter the H. In an unsuccessful search for M in this sample tree (center), we move right at the root (since M is larger than A), then left at the right subtree of the root (since M is smaller than S), and so forth, continuing down the tree until we encounter an external link at the left of N at the bottom. To insert M after the search miss, we simply replace the link that terminated the search with a link to M (bottom).

Program 12.15 BST-based symbol table

The search and insert methods in this implementation use the private recursive methods searchR and insertR that directly mirror the recursive definition of BSTs. The link head points to the root of the tree. The less and equals methods are the same as in Program 12.8 and are omitted.

```
class ST
  {
    private class Node
      { ITEM item; Node l, r;
        Node(ITEM x) { item = x; }
      }
    private Node head;
    ST(int maxN)
      { head = null; }
    private Node insertR(Node h, ITEM x)
      {
        if (h == null)
            return new Node(x);
        if (less(x.key(), h.item.key()))
            h.l = insertR(h.l, x);
        else h.r = insertR(h.r, x);
        return h;
      }
    void insert(ITEM x)
      { head = insertR(head, x); }
    private ITEM searchR(Node h, KEY v)
      {
        if (h == null) return null;
        if (equals(v, h.item.key())) return h.item;
        if (less(v, h.item.key()))
            return searchR(h.l, v);
        else return searchR(h.r, v);
      }
    ITEM search(KEY key)
      { return searchR(head, key); }
```

Given this structure, a recursive algorithm to search for a key in a BST follows immediately: If the tree is empty, we have a search miss; if the search key is equal to the key at the root, we have a search hit. Otherwise, we search (recursively) in the appropriate subtree. The searchR method in Program 12.15 implements this algorithm directly. We invoke a recursive method that takes a tree as first parameter and a key as second parameter, starting with the root of the tree and the search key. At each step, we are guaranteed that no parts of the tree other than the current subtree can contain items with the search key. Just as the size of the interval in binary search shrinks by a little more than half on each iteration, the current subtree in binary-tree search is smaller than the previous (by about half, ideally). The procedure stops either when an item with the search key is found (search hit) or when the current subtree becomes empty (search miss).

The diagram at the top in Figure 12.6 illustrates the search process for a sample tree. Starting at the top, the search procedure at each node involves a recursive invocation for one of that node's children, so the search defines a path through the tree. For a search hit, the path terminates at the node containing the key. For a search miss, the path terminates at an external node, as illustrated in the middle diagram in Figure 12.6.

Program 12.15 uses null links to represent external nodes, and a private data member head that is a link to the root of the tree. To construct an empty BST, we set head to null. We could also use a dummy node at the root and another to represent all external nodes, in various combinations analogous to those we considered for linked lists in Table 3.1 (see Exercise 12.67).

The search method in Program 12.15 is as simple as binary search; an essential feature of BSTs is that *insert* is as easy to implement as *search*. A recursive method insertR to insert a new item into a BST follows from logic similar to that we used to develop searchR: If the tree is empty, we return a new node containing the item; if the search key is less than the key at the root, we set the left link to the result of inserting the item into the left subtree; otherwise, we set the right link to the result of inserting the key into the right subtree. For the simple BSTs that we are considering, resetting the link after the recursive call is usually unnecessary, because the link changes only if the subtree was empty, but it is as easy to set the link as to test to avoid setting it. In

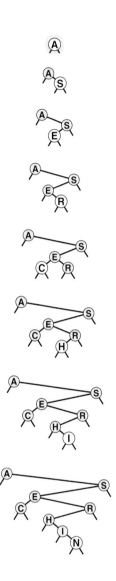

Figure 12.7
BST construction

This sequence depicts the result of inserting the keys A S E R C H I N into an initially empty BST. Each insertion follows a search miss at the bottom of the tree.

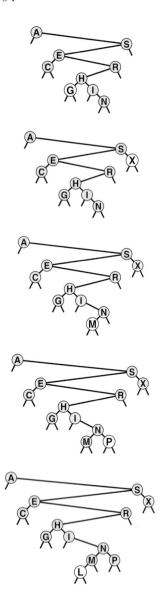

Figure 12.8
BST construction (continued)

*This sequence depicts insertion
of the keys* G X M P L *to the BST
started in Figure 12.7.*

Program 12.16 Counting nodes and sorting in BSTs

An inorder traversal of a BST visits all the items in order of their keys, and therefore can serve as the basis for implementing the *count* and *sort* operations, as in these methods. This lazy count implementation of *count* is appropriate only when counts are infrequent; to implement an eager count, we could maintain a field in each node giving the number of nodes in its subtree (see Exercise 12.60).

```
private int countR(Node h)
  { if (h == null) return 0;
    return 1 + countR(h.l) + countR(h.r);
  }
int count() { return countR(head); }
private String toStringR(Node h)
  { if (h == null) return "";
    String s = toStringR(h.l);
    s += h.item.toString() + "\n";
    s += toStringR(h.r);
    return s;
  }
public String toString()
  { return toStringR(head); }
```

Section 12.8 and in Chapter 13, we shall study more advanced tree structures that are naturally expressed with this same recursive scheme but that more often actually change the link.

Figures 12.7 and 12.8 show how we construct a sample BST by inserting a sequence of keys into an initially empty tree. New nodes are attached to null links at the bottom of the tree; the tree structure is not otherwise changed. Because each node has two links, the tree tends to grow out, rather than down.

The *sort* operation for symbol tables is available with little extra work when BSTs are used. Constructing a binary search tree amounts to sorting the items, since a binary search tree represents a sorted file when we look at it the right way. In our figures, the keys appear in order if read from left to right on the page (ignoring their height and the links). A program has only the links with which to work, but a simple inorder traversal does the job, by definition, as shown by the

Program 12.17 Insertion in BSTs (nonrecursive)

Inserting an item into a BST is equivalent to doing an unsuccessful search for it, then attaching a new node for the item in place of the null link where the search terminates. Attaching the new node requires that we keep track of the parent p of the current node q as we proceed down the tree. When we reach the bottom of the tree, p points to the node whose link we must change to point to the new node inserted.

```
public void insert(ITEM x)
  { KEY key = x.key();
    if (head == null)
      { head = new Node(x); return; }
    Node p = head, q = p;
    while (q != null)
      if (less(key, q.item.key()))
          { p = q; q = q.l; }
      else { p = q; q = q.r; }
    if (less(key, p.item.key()))
        p.l = new Node(x);
    else p.r = new Node(x);
  }
```

recursive implementation toStringR in Program 12.16. To show the items in a BST in order of their keys, we show the items in the left subtree in order of their keys (recursively), then show the root, then show the items in the right subtree in order of their keys (recursively).

As discussed in Section 12.1, we shall refer on occasion to a generic *visit* operation for symbol tables, where we want to visit each of the items in the symbol table in a systematic manner. For BSTs, we can visit items in order of their keys by replacing "show" by "visit" in the description just given and perhaps arranging to pass an object that has a method to visit an item as a parameter (see Section 5.6).

Thinking nonrecursively when contemplating search and insert in BSTs is also instructive. In a nonrecursive implementation, the search process consists of a loop where we compare the search key against the key at the root, then move left if the search key is less and right if it is greater. Insertion consists of a search miss (ending in an empty link), then replacement of the empty link with a pointer to a new node. This process corresponds to manipulating the links explicitly along a path down the tree (see Figure 12.6). In particular, to be able to insert a new node at the bottom, we need to maintain a link to the parent of the current node, as in the implementation in Program 12.17. As usual, the recursive and nonrecursive versions are essentially equivalent, but understanding both points of view enhances our understanding of the algorithm and data structure.

The BST methods in Program 12.15 do not explicitly check for items with duplicate keys. When a new node whose key is equal to some key already in the tree is inserted, it falls to the right of the node already in the tree. One side effect of this convention is that nodes with duplicate keys do not appear contiguously in the tree (see Figure 12.9). However, we can find them by continuing the search from the point where search finds the first match, until we encounter a null link. There are several other options for dealing with items that have duplicate keys, as mentioned in Section 12.1.

BSTs are dual to quicksort. The node at the root of the tree corresponds to the partitioning element in quicksort (no keys to the left are larger, and no keys to the right are smaller). In Section 12.6, we shall see how this observation relates to the analysis of properties of the trees.

Exercises

▷ **12.57** Draw the BST that results when you insert items with the keys E A S Y Q U T I O N, in that order, into an initially empty tree.

▷ **12.58** Draw the BST that results when you insert items with the keys E A S Y Q U E S T I O N, in that order, into an initially empty tree.

▷ **12.59** Give the number of comparisons required to put the keys E A S Y Q U E S T I O N into an initially empty symbol table using a BST. Assume that a *search* is performed for each key, followed by an *insert* for each search miss, as in Program 12.6.

12.60 Add an integer field N to Node and modify the BST code in Programs 12.15 and 12.16 to implement an eager *count* operation that takes constant time.

○ **12.61** Inserting the keys in the order A S E R H I N G C into an initially empty tree also gives the top tree in Figure 12.8. Give ten other orderings of these keys that produce the same result.

○ **12.62** Write an implementation of your interface from Exercise 12.20 that uses a BST with an int field and a double field in each node.

Figure 12.9
Duplicate keys in BSTs

When a BST has records with duplicate keys (top), they appear scattered throughout the tree, as illustrated by the three highlighted A's. Duplicate keys do all appear on the search path for the key from the root to an external node, so they can readily be accessed. However, to avoid confusing usages such as "the A below the C," we use distinct keys in our examples (bottom).

▷ **12.63** Draw a diagram like Figure 12.1 that depicts three representations of the 4-key BST in Figure 12.7: one with primitive fields in the nodes (as in Exercise 12.62), one with `int` keys, and one with `myKey` keys.

12.64 Implement a `searchinsert` method for BSTs (Program 12.15). It should search the symbol table for an item with the same key as a given item, then insert the item if it finds none.

▷ **12.65** Write a method that returns the number of items in a BST with keys equal to a given key.

12.66 Suppose that we have an estimate ahead of time of how often search keys are to be accessed in a binary tree. Should the keys be inserted into the tree in increasing or decreasing order of likely frequency of access? Explain your answer.

○ **12.67** Simplify the search and insertion code in the BST implementation in Program 12.15 by using two dummy nodes: a node `head` that contains an item with a sentinel key smaller than all others and whose right link points to the root of the tree; and a node `z` that contains an item with a sentinel key larger than all others whose left and right links point to itself and that represents all external nodes (external nodes are links to `z`). (*See Table 3.1.*)

12.68 Modify the BST implementation in Program 12.15 to keep items with duplicate keys in linked lists hanging from tree nodes. Change the interface to have *search* operate like *sort* (for all the items with the search key).

12.69 The nonrecursive insertion procedure in Program 12.17 uses a redundant comparison to determine which link of p to replace with the new node. Give an implementation that avoids this comparison.

12.7 Performance Characteristics of BSTs

The running times of algorithms on binary search trees are dependent on the shapes of the trees. In the best case, the tree could be perfectly balanced, with about $\lg N$ nodes between the root and each external node, but in the worst case there could be N nodes on the search path.

We might expect the search times also to be logarithmic in the average case, because the first element inserted becomes the root of the tree: If N keys are to be inserted at random, then this element would divide the keys in half (on the average), which would yield logarithmic search times (using the same argument on the subtrees). Indeed, it could happen that a BST would lead to precisely the same comparisons as binary search (see Exercise 12.72). This case would be the best for this algorithm, with guaranteed logarithmic running time for all searches. In a truly random situation, the root is equally likely

Figure 12.10
Example of a binary search tree

In this BST, which was built by inserting about 200 random keys into an initially empty tree, no search uses more than 12 comparisons. The average cost for a search hit is about 7.

to be any key, so such a perfectly balanced tree is extremely rare, and we cannot easily keep the tree perfectly balanced after every insertion. However, highly unbalanced trees are also extremely rare for random keys, so the trees are rather well balanced on the average. In this section, we shall quantify this observation.

Specifically, the path-length and height measures of binary trees that we considered in Section 5.5 relate directly to the costs of searching in BSTs. The height is the worst-case cost of a search, the internal path length is directly related to the cost of search hits, and external path length is directly related to the cost of search misses.

Property 12.6   *Search hits require about* $2 \ln N \approx 1.39 \lg N$ *comparisons, on the average, in a BST built from N random keys.*

We regard successive `equals` and `less` operations as a single comparison, as discussed in Section 12.3. The number of comparisons used for a search hit ending at a given node is 1 plus the distance from that node to the root. Adding these distances for all nodes, we get the internal path length of the tree. Thus, the desired quantity is 1 plus the average internal path length of the BST, which we can analyze with a familiar argument: If C_N denotes the average internal path length of a binary search tree of N nodes, we have the recurrence

$$C_N = N - 1 + \frac{1}{N} \sum_{1 \le k \le N} (C_{k-1} + C_{N-k}),$$

with $C_1 = 1$. The $N - 1$ term takes into account that the root contributes 1 to the path length of each of the other $N - 1$ nodes in the tree; the rest of the expression comes from observing that the key at the root (the first inserted) is equally likely to be the kth largest, leaving random subtrees of size $k - 1$ and $N - k$. This recurrence is nearly identical to the one that we solved in Chapter 7 for quicksort, and we can solve it in the same way to derive the stated result. ∎

Property 12.7 *Insertions and search misses require about* $2 \ln N \approx 1.39 \lg N$ *comparisons, on the average, in a BST built from N random keys.*

A search for a random key in a tree of N nodes is equally likely to end at any of the $N + 1$ external nodes on a search miss. This property, coupled with the fact that the difference between the external path length and the internal path length in any tree is merely $2N$ (see Property 5.7), establishes the stated result. In any BST, the average number of comparisons for an insertion or a search miss is about 1 greater than the average number of comparisons for a search hit. ∎

 Property 12.6 says that we should expect the search cost for BSTs to be about 39 percent higher than that for binary search for random keys, but Property 12.7 says that the extra cost is well worthwhile, because a new key can be inserted at about the same cost—flexibility not available with binary search. Figure 12.10 shows a BST built from a long random permutation. Although it has some short paths and some long paths, we can characterize it as well balanced: Any search requires less than 12 comparisons, and the average number of comparisons for a random search hit is 7.06, as compared to 5.55 for binary search.

 Properties 12.6 and 12.7 are results on average-case performance that depend on the keys being randomly ordered. If the keys are not randomly ordered, the algorithm can perform badly.

Property 12.8 *In the worst case, a search in a binary search tree with N keys can require N comparisons.*

Figures 12.11 and 12.12 depict two examples of worst-case BSTs. For these trees, binary-tree search is no better than sequential search using singly linked lists. ∎

 Thus, good performance of the basic BST implementation of symbol tables is dependent on the keys being sufficiently similar to random keys that the tree is not likely to contain many long paths. Furthermore, this worst-case behavior is not unlikely in practice—it arises when we insert keys in order or in reverse order into an initially empty tree using the standard algorithm, a sequence of operations that

**Figure 12.11
A worst-case BST**

If the keys arrive in increasing order at a BST, it degenerates to a form equivalent to a singly linked list, leading to quadratic tree-construction time and linear search time.

we certainly might attempt without any explicit warnings to avoid doing so. In Chapter 13, we shall examine techniques for making this worst case extremely unlikely and for eliminating it entirely, making all trees look more like best-case trees, with all path lengths guaranteed to be logarithmic.

None of the other symbol-table implementations that we have discussed can be used for the task of inserting a huge number of random keys into a table, then searching for each of them—the running time of each of the methods that we discussed in Sections 12.3 through 12.4 goes quadratic for this task. Furthermore, the analysis tells us that the average distance to a node in a binary tree is proportional to the logarithm of the number of nodes in the tree, which gives us the flexibility to efficiently handle intermixed searches, insertions, and other symbol-table ADT operations, as we shall soon see.

Table 12.2 gives empirical results that support the analytic results that we have been examining and demonstrates the utility of BSTs for dynamic symbol tables with random keys.

Exercises

▷ **12.70** Write a recursive program that computes the maximum number of comparisons required by any search in a given BST (the height of the tree).

▷ **12.71** Write a recursive program that computes the average number of comparisons required by a search hit in a given BST (the internal path length of the tree divided by N).

12.72 Give an insertion sequence for the keys E A S Y Q U E S T I O N into an initially empty BST such that the tree produced is equivalent to binary search, in the sense that the sequence of comparisons done in the search for any key in the BST is the same as the sequence of comparisons used by binary search for the same set of keys.

○ **12.73** Write a program that inserts a set of keys into an initially empty BST such that the tree produced is equivalent to binary search, in the sense described in Exercise 12.72.

12.74 Draw all the structurally different BSTs that can result when N keys are inserted into an initially empty tree, for $2 \leq N \leq 5$.

● **12.75** Find the probability that each of the trees in Exercise 12.74 is the result of inserting N random distinct elements into an initially empty tree.

● **12.76** How many binary trees of N nodes are there with height N? How many different ways are there to insert N distinct keys into an initially empty tree that result in a BST of height N?

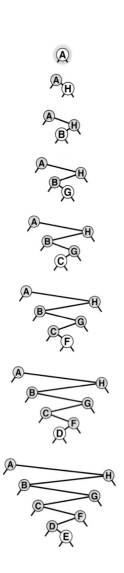

Figure 12.12
Another worst-case BST

Many other key insertion orders, such as this one, lead to degenerate BSTs. Still, a BST built from randomly ordered keys is likely to be well balanced.

Table 12.2 Empirical study of symbol-table implementations

This table gives relative times for constructing a symbol table, then doing a (successful) search for each of the keys in the table. BSTs provide fast implementations of both search and insertion; all the other methods require quadratic time for one of the two tasks and therefore cannot be used for huge problems. Binary search is generally slightly faster than BST search and is therefore the method of choice for applications where the number of searches far exceeds the number of entries in the table. The price for using binary search is the cost of presorting the table (and linear-time insertion cost afterwards); the price for using BSTs is the space for the links.

N	construction				search hits			
	A	L	B	T	A	L	B	T
1250	0	81	90	4	123	250	5	6
2500	0	291	356	8	457	977	9	11
5000	1	1260	1445	19	1853	4077	18	24
12500	2	10848	10684	53	12749	34723	54	69
25000				169				174
50000				407				431
100000				900				995
200000				2343				2453

Key:
  A Unordered array (Exercise 12.24)
  L Ordered linked list (Exercise 12.25)
  B Binary search (Program 12.10)
  T Binary search tree (Program 12.15)

---

o **12.77** Prove by induction that the difference between the external path length and the internal path length in any binary tree is $2N$ (see Property 5.7).

12.78 Run empirical studies to compute the average and standard deviation of the number of comparisons used for search hits and for search misses in a binary search tree built by inserting N random keys into an initially empty tree, for $N = 10^3, 10^4, 10^5$, and 10^6.

12.79 Write a program that builds t BSTs by inserting N random keys into an initially empty tree, and that computes the maximum tree height (the maximum number of comparisons involved in any search miss in any of the t trees), for $N = 10^3$, 10^4, 10^5, and 10^6 with $t = 10$, 100, and 1000.

12.80 Suppose that items are primitive types that are keys. Develop a BST implementation that represents the BST with three arrays (preallocated to the maximum size given in the constructor): one with the keys, one with array indices corresponding to left links, and one with array indices corresponding to right links. Compare the performance of your program with that of the standard implementation, using one of the drivers in Exercise 12.27 or Exercise 12.28.

12.81 Modify our BST implementation (Program 12.15) to implement your interface from Exercise 12.50 for using indices into client arrays (see Exercise 12.7). Compare the performance of your program with that of the standard implementation, using one of the drivers in Exercise 12.27 or Exercise 12.28.

∘ **12.82** Develop a text-string index implementation that uses binary search trees with index keys.

12.83 Compare the running time of your implementation from Exercise 12.82 with Programs 12.13 and 12.14 for the task of constructing an index for a random text string of N characters and then doing 100000 (unsuccessful) searches for random keys, for $N = 10^3$, 10^4, 10^5, and 10^6.

Figure 12.13
Right rotation in a BST

This diagram shows the result (bottom) of a right rotation at S in an example BST (top). The node containing S moves down in the tree, becoming the right child of its former left child.

We accomplish the rotation by getting the link to the new root E from the left link of S, setting the left link of S by copying the right link of E, setting the right link of E to S, and setting the link to S from A to point to E instead.

The effect of the rotation is to move E and its left subtree up one level, and to move S and its right subtree down one level. The rest of the tree is not affected at all.

12.8 Insertion at the Root in BSTs

In the standard implementation of BSTs, every new node inserted goes somewhere at the bottom of the tree, replacing some external node. This state of affairs is not an absolute requirement; it is just an artifact of the natural recursive insertion algorithm. In this section, we consider an alternative insertion method, where we insist that each new item be inserted at the root so that recently inserted nodes are at the *top* of the tree. Trees built in this way have some interesting properties, but our main reason for considering this method is that it plays a crucial role in two of the improved BST algorithms that we consider in Chapter 13.

Suppose that the key of the item to be inserted is larger than the key at the root. We might start to make a new tree by putting the new item into a new root node, with the old root as the left subtree and the right subtree of the old root as the right subtree. However, the right subtree may contain some smaller keys, so we need to do more work to complete the insertion. Similarly, if the key of the item to be inserted is smaller than the key at the root and is larger than all the keys in the left subtree of the root, we can again make a new tree with

---

Program 12.18 Rotations in BSTs

These twin routines perform the *rotation* operation on a BST. A *right rotation* makes the old root the right subtree of the new root (the old left subtree of the root); a *left rotation* makes the old root the left subtree of the new root (the old right subtree of the root).

For implementations that maintain a field with the subtree size in each node, perhaps to support *select* (see Section 14.9) or an eager *count* implementation (see Exercise 12.60), we need also to update these fields in the nodes involved in the rotation (see Exercise 12.86).

```
private Node rotR(Node h)
  { Node x = h.l; h.l = x.r; x.r = h; return x; }
private Node rotL(Node h)
  { Node x = h.r; h.r = x.l; x.l = h; return x; }
```

---

the new item at the root, but more work is needed if the left subtree contains some larger keys. To move all nodes with smaller keys to the left subtree and all nodes with larger keys to the right subtree seems a complicated transformation in general, since the nodes that have to be moved can be scattered along the search path for the node to be inserted.

Fortunately, there is a simple recursive solution to this problem, which is based on *rotation*, a fundamental transformation on trees. Essentially, a rotation allows us to interchange the role of the root and one of the root's children in a tree while still preserving the BST ordering among the keys in the nodes. A *right rotation* involves the root and the left child (see Figure 12.13). The rotation puts the root on the right, essentially reversing the direction of the left link of the root: Before the rotation, it points from the root to the left child; after the rotation, it points from the old left child (the new root) to the old root (the right child of the new root). The tricky part, which makes the rotation work, is to copy the right link of the left child to be the left link of the old root. This link points to all the nodes with keys *between* the two nodes involved in the rotation. Finally, the link *to* the old root has to be changed to point to the new root. The description of a *left rotation* is identical to the description just given, with "right" and "left" interchanged everywhere (see Figure 12.14).

A rotation is a local change, involving only three links and two nodes, that allows us to move nodes around in trees without changing

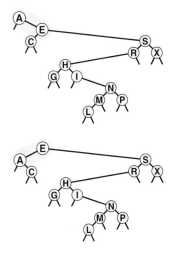

Figure 12.14
Left rotation in a BST

This diagram shows the result (bottom) of a left rotation at A in an example BST (top). The node containing A moves down in the tree, becoming the left child of its former right child.

We accomplish the rotation by getting the link to the new root E from the right link of A, setting the right link of A by copying the left link of E, setting the left link of E to A, and setting the link to A (the head link of the tree) to point to E instead.

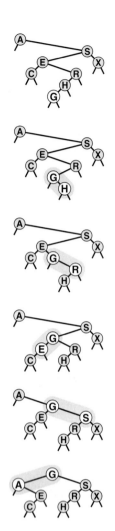

Figure 12.15
BST root insertion

This sequence depicts the result of inserting G into the BST at the top, with (recursive) rotation after insertion to bring the newly inserted node G to the root. The process is equivalent to inserting G, then performing a sequence of rotations to bring it to the root.

Program 12.19 Root insertion in BSTs

With the rotation methods in Program 12.18, a recursive method that inserts a new node at the root of a BST is immediate: Insert the new item at the root in the appropriate subtree, then perform the appropriate rotation to bring it to the root of the main tree.

```
private Node insertT(Node h, ITEM x)
  { if (h == null) return new Node(x);
    if (less(x.key(), h.item.key()))
         { h.l = insertT(h.l, x); h = rotR(h); }
    else { h.r = insertT(h.r, x); h = rotL(h); }
    return h;
  }
public void insert(ITEM x)
  { head = insertT(head, x); }
```

the global ordering properties that make BSTs useful for search (see Program 12.18). We use rotations to move specific nodes through a tree and to keep the trees from becoming unbalanced. In Section 12.9 we implement *remove*, *join*, and other ADT operations with rotations; in Chapter 13 we use them to help us build trees that afford near-optimal performance.

The rotation operations provide a straightforward recursive implementation of root insertion: Recursively insert the new item into the appropriate subtree (leaving it, when the recursive operation is complete, at the root of that tree), then rotate to make it the root of the main tree. Figure 12.15 depicts an example, and Program 12.19 is a direct implementation of this method. This program is a persuasive example of the power of recursion—any reader not so persuaded is encouraged to try Exercise 12.87.

Figures 12.16 and 12.17 show how we construct a BST by inserting a sequence of keys into an initially empty tree, using the root insertion method. If the key sequence is random, a BST built in this way has precisely the same stochastic properties as does a BST built by the standard method. For example, Properties 12.6 and 12.7 hold for BSTs built by root insertion.

In practice, an advantage of the root insertion method is that recently inserted keys are near the top. The cost for search hits on recently inserted keys therefore is likely to be lower than that for the standard method. This property is significant, because many applications have precisely this kind of dynamic mix among their *search* and *insert* operations. A symbol table might contain a great many items, but a large fraction of the searches might refer to the items that were most recently inserted. For example, in a commercial transaction processing system, active transactions could remain near the top and be processed quickly, without access to old transactions being lost. The root insertion method gives the data structure this and similar properties automatically.

If we also change the *search* method to bring the node found to the root when we have a search hit, then we have a self-organizing search method (see Exercise 12.32) that keeps frequently accessed nodes near the top of the tree. In Chapter 13, we shall see a systematic application of this idea to provide a symbol-table implementation that has guaranteed fast performance characteristics.

As is true of several other methods that we have mentioned in this chapter, it is difficult to make precise statements about the performance of the root insertion method versus the standard insertion method for practical applications, because the performance depends on the mixture of symbol-table operations in a way that is difficult to characterize analytically. Our inability to analyze the algorithm should not necessarily dissuade us from using root insertion when we know that the preponderance of searches are for recently inserted data, but we always seek precise performance guarantees—in Chapter 13, we focus on methods for constructing BSTs such that these guarantees can be provided.

Exercises

▷ 12.84 Draw the BST that results when you insert items with the keys E A S Y Q U E S T I O N into an initially empty tree, using the root insertion method.

12.85 Give a sequence of 10 keys (use the letters A through J) that, when inserted into an initially empty tree via the root insertion method, requires a maximal number of comparisons to build the tree. Give the number of comparisons used.

12.86 Suppose that Program 12.18 is to be used with an implementation that maintains a field in each node with its subtree size (see Exercise 12.60). Add the code necessary to have Program 12.18 properly maintain these fields.

○ 12.87 Develop a nonrecursive implementation for BST root insertion (see Program 12.19).

Figure 12.16
BST construction with root insertion

This sequence depicts the result of inserting the keys A S E R C H I into an initially empty BST, using the root insertion method. Each new node is inserted at the root, with links along its search path changed to make a proper BST.

12.88 Run empirical studies to compute the average and standard deviation of the number of comparisons used for search hits and for search misses in a BST built by inserting N random keys into an initially empty tree, then performing a sequence of N random searches for the $N/10$ most recently inserted keys, for $N = 10^3$, 10^4, 10^5, and 10^6. Run your experiment both for the standard insertion method and for the root insertion method; then, compare the results.

12.9 BST Implementations of Other ADT Operations

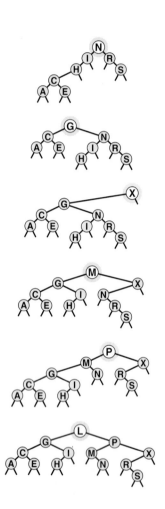

Figure 12.17
BST construction with root insertion (continued)

This sequence depicts insertion of the keys N G X M P L to the BST started in Figure 12.16.

The recursive implementations given in Section 12.5 for the fundamental *search*, *insert*, and *sort* operations using binary tree structures are straightforward. In this section, we consider implementations of *select*, *join*, and *remove*. One of these, *select*, also has a natural recursive implementation, but the others can be cumbersome to implement and can lead to performance problems. The *select* operation is important to consider because the ability to support *select* and *sort* efficiently is one reason that BSTs are preferred over competing structures for many applications. Some programmers even avoid using BSTs so that they need not deal with the *remove* operation; in this section, we shall see a compact implementation that ties together these operations and uses the rotation-to-the-root technique of Section 12.8.

Generally, the operations involve moving down a path in the tree; so, for random BSTs, we expect the costs to be logarithmic. However, we cannot take for granted that BSTs will stay random when multiple operations are performed on the trees. We shall return to this issue at the end of this section.

To implement *select*, we can use a recursive procedure that is analogous to the quicksort-based selection method that is described in Section 7.8. In this discussion, as in Section 7.8, we use zero-based indexing so that, for example, we choose $k = 3$ to get the item with the *fourth* smallest key because that one would be in a[3] if the items were in sorted order in the array a. To find the item with the $(k+1)$st smallest key in a BST, we check the number of nodes in the left subtree. If there are k nodes there, then we return the item at the root. Otherwise, if the left subtree has more than k nodes, we (recursively) look for the item with the $(k + 1)$st smallest key there. If neither of these conditions holds, then the left subtree has t items with $t < k$, and the item with the $(k + 1)$st smallest key in the BST is the item with the $(k - t)$th smallest key in the right subtree. Program 12.20 is a direct

---

Program 12.20 Selection with a BST

This recursive procedure finds the item with the $(k + 1)$st smallest key in a BST, assuming an eager *count* implementation where the subtree size is maintained for each tree node (see Exercise 12.60). Compare the program with quicksort-based selection in an array (Program 9.6).

```
private ITEM selectR(Node h, int k)
  { if (h == null) return null;
    int t = (h.l == null) ? 0 : h.l.N;
    if (t > k) return selectR(h.l, k);
    if (t < k) return selectR(h.r, k-t-1);
    return h.item;
  }
ITEM select(int k)
  { return selectR(head, k); }
```

---

implementation of this method. As usual, since each execution of the method ends with at most one recursive call, a nonrecursive version is immediate (see Exercise 12.89).

The *select* implementation in Program 12.20 is the primary algorithmic motivation for maintaining a subtree-size field in each BST node. We also use this field to support a trivial eager *count* implementation (see Exercise 12.60), and we shall see another use in Chapter 13. The drawbacks to having the subtree-size field are twofold: it uses extra space in every node, and every method that changes the tree needs to update the field. Maintaining the subtree-size field may not be worth the trouble in some applications where *insert* and *search* are the primary operations, but it is a small price to pay in applications where it is important to support the *select* operation in a dynamic symbol table.

We can change this implementation of the *select* operation into a *partition* operation, which rearranges the tree to put the kth smallest element at the root, with precisely the same recursive technique that we used for root insertion in Section 12.8: If we (recursively) put the desired node at the root of one of the subtrees, we can then make it the root of the whole with a single rotation. Program 12.21 gives an implementation of this method. Like rotations, partitioning is not an ADT operation because it is a method that transforms a particu-

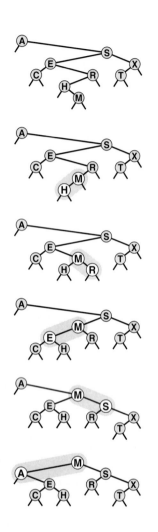

Figure 12.18
Partitioning of a BST

This sequence depicts the result (bottom) of partitioning an example BST (top) about the median key, using (recursive) rotation in the same manner as for root insertion.

Program 12.21 Partitioning of a BST

Adding rotations after the recursive calls transforms the selection method of Program 12.20 into a method that puts the item with the $(k+1)$st smallest key in the BST at the root.

```
Node partR(Node h, int k)
  { int t = (h.l == null) ? 0 : h.l.N;
    if (t > k)
      { partR(h.l, k); h = rotR(h); }
    if (t < k)
      { partR(h.r, k-t-1); h = rotL(h); }
    return h;
  }
```

lar symbol-table representation and should be transparent to clients. Rather, it is an auxiliary routine that we can use to implement ADT operations or to make them run more efficiently. Figure 12.18 depicts an example showing how, in the same way as in Figure 12.15, this process is equivalent to proceeding down the path from the root to the desired node in the tree, then climbing back up, performing rotations to bring the node up to the root.

To *remove* a node with a given key from a BST, we first check whether the node is in one of the subtrees. If it is, we replace that subtree with the result of (recursively) removing the node from it. If the node to be removed is at the root, we replace the tree with the result of combining the two subtrees into one tree. Several options are available for accomplishing the combination. One approach is illustrated in Figure 12.19, and an implementation is given in Program 12.22. To combine two BSTs with all keys in the second known to be larger than all keys in the first, we apply the *partition* operation on the second tree in order to bring the smallest element in that tree to the root. At this point, the left subtree of the root must be empty (otherwise, there would be a smaller element than the one at the root—a contradiction), and we can finish the job by replacing that link with a link to the first tree. Figure 12.20 shows a series of removals in an example tree, which illustrate some of the situations that can arise.

This approach is asymmetric and is *ad hoc* in one sense: Why use the smallest key in the second tree as the root for the new tree, rather than the largest key in the first tree? That is, why do we choose to replace the node that we are removing with the *next* node in the inorder traversal of the tree, rather than the *previous* node? We also might want to consider other approaches. For example, if the node to be removed has a null left link, why not just make its right child the new root, rather than using the node with smallest key in the right subtree? Various similar modifications to the basic remove procedure have been suggested. Unfortunately, they all suffer from a similar flaw: The tree remaining after removal is not random, even if the tree was random beforehand. Moreover, it has been shown that Program 12.22 tends to leave a tree slightly unbalanced (average height proportional to $\sqrt{N}$) if the tree is subjected to a large number of random remove–insert pairs (see Exercise 12.95).

These differences may not be noticed in practical applications unless N is huge. Still, this combination of an inelegant algorithm with undesirable performance characteristics is unsatisfying. In Chapter 13, we shall examine two different ways to address this situation.

It is typical of search algorithms to require significantly more complicated implementations for removal than for search. The key values play an integral role in shaping the structure, so removal of a key can involve complicated repairs. One alternative is to use a lazy removal strategy, leaving removed nodes in the data structure but marking them as "removed" so that they can be ignored in searches. In the search implementation in Program 12.15, we can implement this strategy by skipping the equality test for such nodes. We must make sure that large numbers of marked nodes do not lead to excessive waste of time or space; but if removals are infrequent, the extra cost may not be significant. We could reuse the marked nodes on future insertions when convenient (for example, it would be easy to do so for nodes at the bottom of the tree). Or we could periodically rebuild the entire data structure, leaving out the marked nodes. These considerations apply to *any* data structure involving insertions and removals—they are not peculiar to symbol tables.

We conclude this chapter by considering the implementation of *remove* with handles and *join* for symbol-table ADT implementations that use BSTs. We assume that handles are links and omit further discussion about packaging issues so that we can concentrate on the two basic algorithms.

Figure 12.19
Removal of the root in a BST

This diagram shows the result (bottom) of removing the root of an example BST (top). First, we remove the node, leaving two subtrees (second from top). Then, we partition the right subtree to put its smallest element at the root (third from top), leaving the left link pointing to an empty subtree. Finally, we replace this link with a link to the left subtree of the original tree (bottom).

The primary challenge in implementing a method to *remove* a node with a given handle (link) is the same as it was for linked lists: We need to change the pointer in the structure that points *to* the node being removed. There are at least four ways to address this problem. First, we could add a third link in each tree node, pointing to its parent. The disadvantage of this arrangement is that it is cumbersome to maintain extra links, as we have noted before on several occasions. Second, we could use the key in the item to search in the tree, stopping when we find a matching pointer. This approach suffers from the disadvantage that the average position of a node is near the bottom of the tree, and this approach therefore requires an unnecessary trip through the tree. Third, in a low-level language such as C, we could use a pointer to the pointer to the node as the handle. This method is difficult to implement directly in Java. Fourth, we could adopt a lazy approach, marking removed nodes and periodically rebuilding the data structure, as just described.

The last operation for symbol-table ADTs that we need to consider is the *join* operation. In a BST implementation, this amounts to merging two trees. How do we join two BSTs into one?

Various algorithms present themselves to do the job, but each has certain disadvantages. For example, we could traverse the first BST, inserting each of its nodes into the second BST (this algorithm is a one-liner: wrap `insert` into the second BST in an object used as a parameter to a traversal of the first BST). This solution does not have linear running time, since each insertion could take linear time. Another idea is to traverse both BSTs, put the items into an array, merge them, and then build a new BST. This operation can be done in linear time, but it also uses a potentially large array.

Program 12.23 is a compact linear-time recursive implementation of the *join* operation. First, we insert the root of the first BST into the second BST, using root insertion. This operation gives us two subtrees with keys known to be smaller than this root, and two subtrees with keys known to be larger than this root, so we get the result by (recursively) combining the former pair to be the left subtree of the root and the latter to be the right subtree of the root (!). Each node can be the root node on a recursive call at most once, so the total time is linear.

Program 12.22 **Removal of a node with a given key in a BST**

This implementation of the *remove* operation removes the first node with key v encountered in the BST. Working top down, it makes recursive calls for the appropriate subtree until the node to be removed is at the root. Then, it replaces the node with the result of combining its two subtrees—the smallest node in the right subtree becomes the root, then its left link is set to point to the left subtree.

```
private Node joinLR(Node a, Node b)
  { if (b == null) return a;
    b = partR(b, 0); b.l = a;
    return b;
  }
private Node removeR(Node h, KEY v)
  { if (h == null) return null;
    KEY w = h.item.key();
    if (less(v, w)) removeR(h.l, v);
    if (less(w, v)) removeR(h.r, v);
    if (equals(v, w)) h = joinLR(h.l, h.r);
    return h;
  }
void remove(KEY v)
  { removeR(head, v); }
```

An example is shown in Figure 12.21. Like removal, this process is asymmetric and can lead to trees that are not well balanced, but randomization provides a simple fix, as we shall see in Chapter 13. Note that the number of comparisons used for *join* must be at least linear in the worst case; otherwise, we could develop a sorting algorithm that uses fewer than $N \lg N$ comparisons, using an approach such as bottom-up mergesort (see Exercise 12.99).

We have not included the code necessary to maintain the count field in BST nodes during the transformations for *join* and *remove*, which is necessary for applications where we want to support *select* (Program 12.20) as well. This task is conceptually simple, but requires some care. One systematic way to proceed is to implement a small utility method that sets the count field in a node with a value one greater than the sum of the count fields of its children, then call that

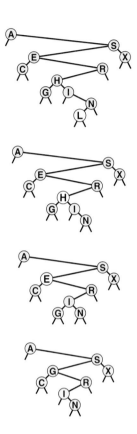

Figure 12.20
BST node removal

This sequence depicts the result of removing the nodes with keys L, H, and E from the BST at the top. First, the L is simply removed, since it is at the bottom. Second, the H is replaced with its right child, the I, since the left child of I is empty. Finally, the E is replaced with its successor in the tree, the G.

Figure 12.21
Joining of two BSTs

This diagram shows the result (bottom) of combining two example BSTs (top). First, we insert the root G of the first tree into the second tree, using root insertion (second from top). We are left with two subtrees with keys less than G and two subtrees with keys greater than G. Combining both pairs (recursively) gives the result (bottom).

Program 12.23 Joining of two BSTs

If either BST is empty, the other is the result. Otherwise, we combine the two BSTs by (arbitrarily) choosing the root of the first as the root, root inserting that root into the second, then (recursively) combining the pair of left subtrees and the pair of right subtrees.

```
private Node joinR(Node a, Node b)
  { if (b == null) return a;
    if (a == null) return b;
    insertT(b, a.item);
    b.l = joinR(a.l, b.l);
    b.r = joinR(a.r, b.r);
    return b;
  }
public void join(ST b)
  { head = joinR(head, b.head); }
```

routine for every node whose links are changed. Specifically, we can do so for both nodes in rotL and rotR in Program 12.18, which suffices for the transformations in Program 12.19 and Program 12.21, since they transform trees solely with rotations. For joinLR and removeR in Program 12.22 and join in Program 12.23, it suffices to call the node-count update routine for the node to be returned, just before the return statement.

The basic *search*, *insert*, and *sort* operations for BSTs are easy to implement and perform well with even a modicum of randomness in the sequence of operations, so BSTs are widely used for dynamic symbol tables. They also admit simple recursive solutions to support other kinds of operations, as we have seen for *select*, *remove*, and *join* in this chapter, and as we shall see for many examples later in the book.

Despite their utility, there are two primary drawbacks to using BSTs in applications. The first is that they require a substantial amount of space for links. We often think of links and records as being about the same size (say, one machine word)—if that is the case, then a BST implementation uses two-thirds of its allocated memory for links and only one-third for keys. Our use of myKey and myItem objects adds two or three more references per item (see Exercise 12.63). This effect is less important in applications with large records and more important in environments where pointers are large. If memory is at a premium, we may prefer one of the open-addressing hashing methods of Chapter 14 to using BSTs.

The second drawback of using BSTs is the distinct possibility that the trees could become poorly balanced and lead to slow performance. In Chapter 13, we examine several approaches to providing performance guarantees. If memory space for links is available, these algorithms make BSTs an attractive choice to serve as the basis for implementation of symbol-table ADTs, because they lead to guaranteed fast performance for a large set of useful ADT operations.

Exercises

▷ **12.89** Implement a nonrecursive BST *select* method (see Program 12.20).

▷ **12.90** Draw the BST that results when you insert items with the keys E A S Y Q U T I O N into an initially empty tree, then remove the Q.

▷ **12.91** Draw the binary search tree that results when you insert items with the keys E A S Y into one initially empty tree, and insert items with the keys Q U E S T I O N into another initially empty tree, then combine the result.

12.92 Implement a nonrecursive BST *remove* method (see Program 12.22).

12.93 Implement a version of *remove* for BSTs (Program 12.22) that removes *all* nodes in the tree that have keys equal to the given key.

o **12.94** Change our BST-based symbol-table implementations to support client item handles (see Exercise 12.7); add an implementation of a clone method (see Exercise 12.6); and write a driver program that tests your interface and implementation.

12.95 Run experiments to determine how the height of a BST grows in response to a long sequence of alternating random insertions and removals in a random tree of N nodes, for $N = 10$, 100, and 1000, and for up to N^2 insertion–removal pairs for each N.

12.96 Implement a version of remove (see Program 12.22) that makes a random decision whether to replace the node to be removed with that node's predecessor or successor in the tree. Run experiments as described in Exercise 12.95 for this version.

o **12.97** Implement a version of remove that uses a recursive method to move the node to be removed to the bottom of the tree through rotations, in the manner of root insertion (Program 12.19). Draw the tree produced when your program removes the root from a complete tree of 31 nodes.

o **12.98** Run experiments to determine how the height of a BST grows as you repeatedly reinsert the item at the root into the tree that results when you combine the subtrees of the root in a random tree of N nodes, for $N = 10$, 100, and 1000.

○ 12.99 Implement a version of bottom-up mergesort based on the *join* operation: Start by putting keys into N 1-node trees, then combine the 1-node trees in pairs to get $N/2$ 2-node trees, then combine the 2-node trees in pairs to get $N/4$ 4-node trees, and so forth.

12.100 Implement a version of join (see Program 12.23) that makes a random decision whether to use the root of the first tree or the root of the second tree for root of the result tree. Run experiments as described in Exercise 12.98 for this version.

CHAPTER THIRTEEN

Balanced Trees

THE BST ALGORITHMS in the previous chapter work well for a wide variety of applications, but they do have the problem of bad worst-case performance. What is more, it is embarrassingly true that the bad worst case for the standard BST algorithm, like that for quicksort, is one that is likely to occur in practice if the user of the algorithm is not watching for it. Files already in order, files with large numbers of duplicate keys, files in reverse order, files with alternating large and small keys, or files with any large segment having a simple structure can all lead to quadratic BST construction times and linear search times.

In the ideal case, we could keep our trees perfectly balanced, like the tree depicted in Figure 13.1. This structure corresponds to binary search and therefore allows us to guarantee that all searches can be completed in less than $\lg N + 1$ comparisons, but it is expensive to maintain for dynamic insertions and deletions. The search performance guarantee holds for any BST for which all the external nodes are on the bottom one or at most two levels; there are many such BSTs, so we have some flexibility in arranging for our tree to be balanced. If we are satisfied with near-optimal trees, then we can have even more flexibility. For example, there are a great many BSTs of height less than $2\lg N$. If we relax our standard but can guarantee that our algorithms build only such BSTs, then we can provide the protection against bad worst-case performance which we would like to have in practical applications in a dynamic data structure. As a side benefit, we get better average-case performance as well.

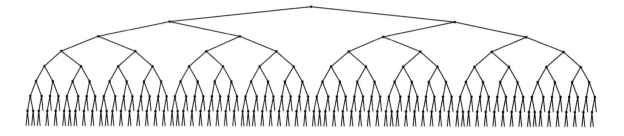

Figure 13.1
A large BST that is perfectly balanced

The external nodes in this BST all fall on one of two levels, and the number of comparisons for any search is the same as the number of comparisons that would be used by binary search for the same key (if the items were in an ordered array). The goal of a balanced-tree algorithm is to keep a BST as close as possible to being as well balanced as this one, while still supporting efficient dynamic insertion, deletion, and other dictionary ADT operations.

One approach to producing better balance in BSTs is periodically to rebalance them explicitly. Indeed, we can balance most BSTs completely in linear time, using the recursive method shown in Program 13.1 (see Exercise 13.4). Such rebalancing is likely to improve performance for random keys but does not provide guarantees against quadratic worst-case performance in a dynamic symbol table. On the one hand, the insertion time for a sequence of keys between rebalancing operations can grow quadratic in the length of the sequence; on the other hand, we do not want to rebalance huge trees frequently, because each rebalancing operation costs at least linear time in the size of the tree. This tradeoff makes it difficult to use global rebalancing to guarantee fast performance in dynamic BSTs. All the algorithms that we will consider, as they walk through the tree, do incremental, local operations that collectively improve the balance of the whole tree, yet they never have to walk through all the nodes in the way that Program 13.1 does.

The problem of providing guaranteed performance for symbol-table implementations based on BSTs gives us an excellent forum for examining precisely what we mean when we ask for performance guarantees. We shall see solutions to this problem that are prime examples of each of the three general approaches to providing performance guarantees in algorithm design: we can *randomize*, *amortize*, or *optimize*. We now consider each of these approaches briefly, in turn.

A *randomized* algorithm introduces random decision making into the algorithm itself in order to reduce dramatically the chance of a worst-case scenario (no matter what the input). We have already seen a prime example of this arrangement when we used a random element as the partitioning element in quicksort. In Sections 13.1 and 13.5, we shall examine *randomized BSTs* and *skip lists*—two sim-

> **Program 13.1 Balancing a BST**
>
> This recursive method puts a BST into perfect balance in linear time, using the partitioning method partR from Program 12.21. We partition to put the median node at the root, then (recursively) do the same for the subtrees.
>
> ```
> private Node balanceR(Node h)
>   {
>     if ((h == null) || (h.N == 1)) return h;
>     h = partR(h, h.N/2);
>     h.l = balanceR(h.l);
>     h.r = balanceR(h.r);
>     fixN(h.l); fixN(h.r); fixN(h);
>     return h;
>   }
> ```

ple ways to use randomization in symbol-table implementations to give efficient implementations of all the symbol-table ADT operations. These algorithms are simple and broadly applicable but went undiscovered for decades (*see reference section*). The analysis that proves these algorithms to be effective is not elementary, but the algorithms are simple to understand, implement, and put to practical use.

An *amortization* approach does extra work at one time to avoid more work later in order to be able to provide guaranteed upper bounds on the average per-operation cost (the total cost of all operations divided by the number of operations). In Section 13.2, we shall examine *splay BSTs*, a variant of BSTs that we can use to provide such guarantees for symbol-table implementations. The development of this method was one impetus for the development of the concept of amortization (*see reference section*). The algorithm is a straightforward extension of the root insertion method that we discussed in Chapter 12, but the analysis that proves the performance bounds is sophisticated.

An *optimization* approach takes the trouble to provide performance guarantees for every operation. Various methods have been developed that take this approach, some dating back to the 1960s. These methods require that we maintain some structural information in the trees; programmers typically find the algorithms cumbersome to implement. In this chapter, we shall examine two simple abstractions that not only make the implementation straightforward but also lead to near-optimal upper bounds on the costs.

After examining implementations of symbol-table ADTs with guaranteed fast performance using each of these three approaches, we conclude the chapter with a comparison of performance characteristics. Beyond the differences suggested by the differing natures of the performance guarantees that each of the algorithms provides, the methods each carry a (relatively slight) cost in time or space to provide those guarantees; the development of a truly optimal balanced-tree ADT is still a research goal. Still, the algorithms that we consider in this chapter are all important ones that can provide fast implementations of *search* and *insert* (and several other symbol-table ADT operations) in dynamic symbol tables for a variety of applications.

Exercises

∘ **13.1** Implement an efficient method that rebalances BSTs that do not have a count field in their nodes.

13.2 Modify the standard BST insertion method in Program 12.15 to use Program 13.1 to rebalance the tree each time that the number of items in the symbol table reaches a power of 2. Compare the running time of your program with that of Program 12.15 for the tasks of (*i*) building a tree from N random keys and (*ii*) searching for N random keys in the resulting tree, for $N = 10^3, 10^4, 10^5$, and 10^6.

13.3 Estimate the number of comparisons used by your program from Exercise 13.2 when inserting an increasing sequence of N keys into a symbol table.

●● **13.4** Show that Program 13.1 runs in time proportional to $N \log N$ for a degenerate tree. Then give as weak a condition on the tree as you can that implies that the program runs in linear time.

13.5 Modify the standard BST insertion method in Program 12.15 to partition about the median any node encountered that has less than one-quarter of its nodes in one of its subtrees. Compare the running time of your program with that of Program 12.15 for the tasks of (*i*) building a tree from N random keys and (*ii*) searching for N random keys in the resulting tree, for $N = 10^3, 10^4, 10^5$, and 10^6.

13.6 Estimate the number of comparisons used by your program from Exercise 13.5 when inserting an increasing sequence of N keys into a symbol table.

● **13.7** Extend your implementation in Exercise 13.5 to rebalance in the same way while performing the *remove* operation. Run experiments to determine whether the height of the tree grows as a long sequence of alternating random insertions and deletions are made in a random tree of N nodes, for $N = 10$, 100, and 1000, and for N^2 insertion–deletion pairs for each N.

13.1 Randomized BSTs

To analyze the average-case performance costs for binary search trees, we made the assumption that the items are inserted in random order (see Section 12.7). The primary consequence of this assumption in the context of the BST algorithm is that each node in the tree is equally likely to be the one at the root, and this property also holds for the subtrees. Remarkably, it is possible to introduce randomness into the algorithm so that this property holds without *any* assumptions about the order in which the items are inserted. The idea is simple: When we insert a new node into a tree of N nodes, the new node should appear at the root with probability $1/(N + 1)$, so we simply make a randomized decision to use root insertion with that probability. Otherwise, we recursively use the method to insert the new record into the left subtree if the record's key is less than the key at the root, and into the right subtree if the record's key is greater. Program 13.2 is an implementation of this method.

Viewed nonrecursively, doing randomized insertion is equivalent to performing a standard search for the key and making a randomized decision at every step whether to continue the search or to terminate it and do root insertion. Thus, the new node could be inserted anywhere on its search path, as illustrated in Figure 13.2. This simple probabilistic combination of the standard BST algorithm with the root insertion method gives guaranteed performance in a probabilistic sense.

Property 13.1 *Building a randomized BST is equivalent to building a standard BST from a random initial permutation of the keys. We use about $2N \ln N$ comparisons to construct a randomized BST with N items (no matter in what order the items are presented for insertion), and about $2 \ln N$ comparisons for searches in such a tree.*

Each element is equally likely to be the root of the tree, and this property holds for both subtrees, as well. The first part of this statement is true by construction, but a careful probabilistic argument is needed to show that the root insertion method preserves randomness in the subtrees (*see reference section*). ∎

Figure 13.2
Insertion into a randomized BST

The final position of a new record in a randomized BST may be anywhere on the record's search path, depending on the outcome of randomized decisions made during the search. This figure shows each of the possible final positions for a record with key F when the record is inserted into a sample tree (top).

Program 13.2 Randomized BST insertion

This method makes a randomized decision whether to use the root insertion method of Program 12.19 or the standard insertion method of Program 12.15. In a random BST, each of the nodes is at the root with equal probability; so we get random trees by putting a new node at the root of a tree of size N with probability $1/(N+1)$.

```
private Node insertR(Node h, ITEM x)
  { if (h == null) return new Node(x);
    if (Math.random()*h.N < 1.0)
      return insertT(h, x);
    if (less(x.key(), h.item.key()))
        h.l = insertR(h.l, x);
    else h.r = insertR(h.r, x);
    h.N++;
    return h;
  }
void insert(ITEM x)
  { head = insertR(head, x); }
```

The distinction between average-case performance for randomized BSTs and for standard BSTs is subtle, but essential. The average costs are the same (though the constant of proportionality is slightly higher for randomized trees), but for standard trees the result depends on the *assumption* that the items are presented for insertion in a random ordering of their keys (all orderings equally likely). This assumption is not valid in many practical applications, and therefore the significance of the randomized algorithm is that it allows us to remove the assumption and to depend instead on the laws of probability and randomness in the random-number generator. If the items are inserted with their keys in order, or in reverse order, or *any order whatever*, the BST will still be random.

Figure 13.3 depicts the construction of a randomized tree for an example set of keys. Since the decisions made by the algorithm are randomized, the sequence of trees is likely to be different each time that we run the algorithm. Figure 13.4 shows that a randomized tree constructed from a set of items with keys in increasing order looks to have the same properties as a standard BST constructed from randomly ordered items (cf. Figure 12.8).

There is still a chance that the random number generator could lead to the wrong decision at every opportunity and thus leave us with poorly balanced trees, but we can analyze this chance mathematically and prove it to be vanishingly small.

Property 13.2   *The probability that the construction cost of a randomized BST is more than a factor of α times the average is less than $e^{-\alpha}$.*

This result and similar ones with the same character are implied by a general solution to probabilistic recurrence relations that was developed by Karp in 1995 (*see reference section*). ■

For example, it takes about 2.3 million comparisons to build a randomized BST of 100,000 nodes, but the probability that the number of comparisons will be more than 23 million is much less than 0.01 percent. Such a performance guarantee is more than adequate for meeting the practical requirements of processing real data sets of this size. When using a standard BST for such a task, we cannot provide such a guarantee: for example, we are subject to performance problems if there is significant order in the data, which is unlikely in random data, but certainly would not be unusual in real data, for a host of reasons.

A result analogous to Property 13.2 also holds for the running time of quicksort, by the same argument. But the result is more important here, because it also implies that the cost of *searching* in the tree is close to the average. Regardless of any extra costs in constructing the trees, we can use the standard BST implementation to perform *search* operations, with costs that depend only on the shape of the trees, and no extra costs at all for balancing. This property is important in typical applications, where *search* operations are far more numerous than are any others. For example, the 100,000-node BST described in the previous paragraph might hold a telephone directory and might be used for millions of searches. We can be nearly certain that each search will be within a small constant factor of the average cost of about 23 comparisons, and, for practical purposes, we do not have to worry about the possibility that a large number of searches would cost close

**Figure 13.3
Construction of a randomized BST**

This sequence depicts the insertion of the keys A B C D E F G H I into an initially empty BST, with randomized insertion. The tree at the bottom appears to have been built with the standard BST algorithm, with the same keys inserted in random order.

Program 13.3 Randomized BST combination

This method uses the same approach as Program 12.23, except that it makes a randomized, rather than an arbitrary, decision about which node to use for the root in a combined tree, using probabilities that ensure that each node is equally likely to be the root.

As with all randomized BST code, the code assumes that the rotation implementations (see Program 12.18) properly update the counts in the nodes such that each node's N field has the number of nodes in its subtree (see Exercise 12.86).

```
private Node joinR(Node a, Node b)
  { if (b == null) return a;
    if (a == null) return b;
    insertT(b, a.item);
    b.l = joinR(a.l, b.l);
    b.r = joinR(a.r, b.r);
    return b;
  }
public void join(ST b)
  { int N = head.N;
    if (Math.random()*(N+b.count()) < 1.0*N)
         head = joinR(head, b.head);
    else head = joinR(b.head, head);
  }
```

---

to 100,000 comparisons, whereas with standard BSTs, we would need to be concerned.

One of the main drawbacks to randomized insertion is the cost of generating random numbers at every node during every insertion. A high-quality system-supported random number generator might work hard to produce pseudo-random numbers with more randomness than randomized BSTs require, so constructing a randomized BST might be slower than constructing a standard BST in certain practical situations (for example, if the assumption that the items are in random order *is* valid). As we did with quicksort, we can reduce this cost by using numbers that are less than perfectly random but that are cheap to generate and sufficiently similar to random numbers that they achieve the goal of avoiding the bad worst case for BSTs for key insertion sequences that are likely to arise in practice (see Exercise 13.14).

Program 13.4 Deletion in a randomized BST

We use the same `remove` method as we did for standard BSTs (see Program 12.22) but replace the `joinLR` method with the one shown here, which makes a randomized rather than an arbitrary decision about whether to replace the deleted node with the predecessor or the successor, using probabilities that ensure that each node in the resulting tree is equally likely to be the root.

```
private Node joinLR(Node a, Node b)
  { int N = a.N + b.N;
    if (a == null) return b;
    if (b == null) return a;
    if (Math.random()*N < 1.0*a.N)
        { a.r = joinLR(a.r, b); return a; }
    else { b.l = joinLR(a, b.l); return b; }
  }
```

Another potential drawback of randomized BSTs is that they need to have a field in each node for the number of nodes in that node's subtree. The extra space required for this field may be a liability for large trees. On the other hand, as we discussed in Section 12.9, this field may be needed for other reasons—for example, to support the *select* operation or to provide a check on the integrity of the data structure. In such cases, randomized BSTs incur no extra space cost and are an attractive choice.

The basic guiding principle of preserving randomness in the trees also leads to efficient implementations of the *remove*, *join*, and other symbol-table ADT operations, still producing random trees.

To *join* an N-node tree with an M-node tree, we use the basic method from Chapter 12, except that we make a randomized decision to choose the root based on reasoning that the root of the combined tree must come from the N-node tree with probability $N/(M+N)$ and from the M-node tree with probability $M/(M+N)$. Program 13.3 is an implementation of this operation.

In the same way, we replace the arbitrary decision in the *remove* algorithm by a randomized one, as shown in Program 13.4. This method corresponds to an option that we did not consider for deleting

Figure 13.4
A large randomized BST

This BST is the result of inserting 200 keys in increasing order into an initially empty tree, using randomized insertion. The tree appears to have been built from randomly ordered keys (see Figure 12.8).

nodes in standard BSTs because it would seem—in the absence of randomization—to lead to unbalanced trees (see Exercise 13.21).

Property 13.3 *Making a tree with an arbitrary sequence of randomized insert, remove, and join operations is equivalent to building a standard BST from a random permutation of the keys in the tree.*

As it is for Property 13.1, a careful probabilistic argument is needed to establish this fact (*see reference section*). ∎

Proving facts about probabilistic algorithms requires having a good understanding of probability theory, but understanding these proofs is not necessarily a requirement for programmers using the algorithms. A careful programmer will check claims such as Property 13.3 no matter how they are proved (to check, for example, the quality of the random-number generator or other properties of the implementation) and therefore can use these methods with confidence. Randomized BSTs are perhaps the easiest way to support a full symbol-table ADT with near-optimal performance guarantees; they are therefore useful for many practical applications.

Exercises

▷ **13.8** Draw the randomized BST that results when you insert items with the keys E A S Y Q U T I O N in that order into an initially empty tree, assuming a bad randomization method that results in the root insertion option being taken whenever the tree size is odd.

13.9 Write a driver program that performs the following experiment 1000 times, for $N = 10$ and 100: Insert items with keys 0 through $N - 1$ (in that order) into an initially empty randomized BST using Program 13.2. Then print, for each N, the χ^2 statistic for the hypothesis that each key falls at the root with probability $1/N$ (see Exercise 14.5).

○ **13.10** Give the probability that F lands in each of the positions depicted in Figure 13.2.

13.11 Write a program to compute the probability that a randomized insertion ends at one of the internal nodes in a given tree, for each of the nodes on the search path.

13.12 Write a program to compute the probability that a randomized insertion ends at one of the external nodes of a given tree.

○ **13.13** Implement a nonrecursive version of the randomized insertion method in Program 13.2.

13.14 Draw the randomized BST that results when you insert items with the keys E A S Y Q U T I O N in that order into an initially empty tree, using a version of Program 13.2 where you replace the expression involving rand() with the test (111 % h.N) == 3 to decide to switch to root insertion.

13.15 Do Exercise 13.9 for a version of Program 13.2 where you replace the expression involving rand() with the test (111 % h.N) == 3 to decide to switch to root insertion.

13.16 Show the sequence of randomized decisions that would result in the keys E A S Y Q U T I O N being built into a degenerate tree (keys in order, left links null). What is the probability that this event will happen?

13.17 Could *every* BST containing the keys E A S Y Q U T I O N be constructed by *some* sequence of randomized decisions when those keys are inserted in that order into an initially empty tree? Explain your answer.

13.18 Run empirical studies to compute the average and standard deviation of the number of comparisons used for search hits and for search misses in a randomized BST built by inserting N random keys into an initially empty tree, for $N = 10^3$, 10^4, 10^5, and 10^6.

▷ **13.19** Draw the BST that results from using Program 13.4 to delete the Q from your tree in Exercise 13.14, using the test (111 % (a.N + b.N)) < a.N to decide to join with a at the root.

13.20 Draw the BST that results when you insert items with the keys E A S Y into one initially empty tree, and items with the keys Q U E S T I O N into another initially empty tree, then combine the result, using Program 13.3 with the test described in Exercise 13.19.

13.21 Draw the BST that results when you insert items with the keys E A S Y Q U T I O N in that order into an initially empty tree, then use Program 13.4 to delete the Q, assuming a bad randomization method that always returns 0.

13.22 Run experiments to determine how the height of a BST grows as a long sequence of alternating random insertions and deletions using Programs 13.2 and 13.3 is made in a tree of N nodes, for $N = 10$, 100, and 1000, and for N^2 insertion–deletion pairs for each N.

○ **13.23** Compare your results from Exercise 13.22 with the result of deleting and reinserting the largest key in a random tree of N nodes using Programs 13.2 and 13.3, for $N = 10$, 100, and 1000, and for N^2 insertion–deletion pairs for each N.

13.24 Instrument your program from Exercise 13.22 to determine the average number of calls to `rand()` which it makes per item deleted.

13.2 Splay BSTs

In the root-insertion method of Section 12.8, we accomplished our primary objective of bringing the newly inserted node to the root of the tree by using left and right rotations. In this section, we examine how we can modify root insertion such that the rotations balance the tree in a certain sense as well.

Rather than considering (recursively) the single rotation that brings the newly inserted node to the top of the tree, we consider the *two* rotations that bring the node from a position as one of the grandchildren of the root up to the top of the tree. First, we perform one rotation to bring the node to be a child of the root. Then, we perform another rotation to bring it to the root. There are two essentially different cases, depending on whether or not the two links from the root to the node being inserted are oriented in the same way. Figure 13.5 shows the case where the orientations are different; Figure 13.6 shows the case where the orientations are the same. Splay BSTs are based on the observation that there is an alternative way to proceed when the links from the root to the node being inserted are oriented in the same way: Simply perform two rotations at the root, as shown at the right in Figure 13.6.

Splay insertion brings newly inserted nodes to the root using the transformations shown in Figure 13.5 (standard root insertion when the links from the root to the grandchild on the search path have different orientation) and on the right in Figure 13.6 (two rotations at the root when the links from the root to the grandchild on the search path have the same orientation). The BSTs built in this way are *splay BSTs*. Program 13.5 is a recursive implementation of splay insertion; Figure 13.7 depicts an example of a single insertion, and Figure 13.8 shows the construction process for a sample tree. The difference between splay insertion and standard root insertion may

Figure 13.5
Double rotation in a BST (orientations different)

In this sample tree (top), a left rotation at G followed by a right rotation at L brings I to the root (bottom). These rotations might complete a standard or splay BST root-insertion process.

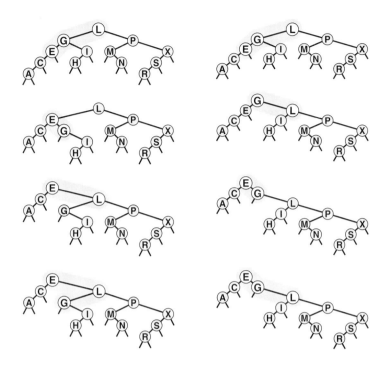

Figure 13.6
Double rotation in a BST (orientations alike)

We have two options when both links in a double rotation are oriented in the same direction. With the standard root-insertion method, we perform the lower rotation first (left); with splay insertion, we perform the higher rotation first (right).

seem inconsequential, but it is quite significant: the splay operation eliminates the quadratic worst case that is the primary liability of standard BSTs.

Property 13.4 *The number of comparisons used when a splay BST is built from N insertions into an initially empty tree is $O(N \lg N)$.*

This bound is a consequence of Property 13.5, a stronger property that we will consider shortly. ∎

The constant implied in the O-notation is 3. For example, it always takes less than 5 million comparisons to build a BST of 100,000 nodes using splay insertion. This result does not guarantee that the resulting search tree will be well-balanced, or that each operation will be efficient, but the implied guarantee on the total running time is significant, and the actual running time that we observe in practice is likely to be lower still.

Program 13.5 Splay insertion in BSTs

This method differs from the root-insertion algorithm of Program 12.13 in just one essential detail: If the search path goes left-left or right-right, the node is brought to the root with a double rotation from the top, rather than from the bottom (see Figure 13.6).

The program checks the four possibilities for two steps of the search path from the root and performs the appropriate rotations:

left-left: Rotate right at the root twice.
left-right: Rotate left at the left child, then right at the root.
right-right: Rotate left at the root twice.
right-left: Rotate right at the right child, then left at the root.

```
private Node splay(Node h, ITEM x)
  {
    if (h == null) return new Node(x);
    if (less(x.key(), h.item.key()))
    {
      if (h.l == null)
        { h.l = new Node(x); return rotR(h); }
      if (less(x.key(), h.l.item.key()))
        { h.l.l = splay(h.l.l, x); h = rotR(h); }
      else
        { h.l.r = splay(h.l.r, x); h.l = rotL(h.l);}
      return rotR(h);
    }
    else
    {
      if (h.r == null)
        { h.r = new Node(x); return rotL(h); }
      if (less(h.r.item.key(), x.key()))
        { h.r.r = splay(h.r.r, x); h = rotL(h); }
      else
        { h.r.l = splay(h.r.l, x); h.r = rotR(h.r);}
      return rotL(h);
    }
  }
void insert(ITEM x)
  { head = splay(head, x); }
```

When we insert a node into a BST using splay insertion, we not only bring that node to the root but also bring the other nodes that we encounter (on the search path) closer to the root. Precisely, the rotations that we perform cut in half the distance from the root to any node that we encounter. This property also holds if we implement the *search* operation such that it performs the splay transformations during the search. Some paths in the trees do get longer: If we do not access nodes on those paths, that effect is of no consequence to us. If we do access nodes on a long path, it becomes one-half as long after we do so; thus, no one path can build up high costs.

Property 13.5 *The number of comparisons required for any sequence of M insert or search operations in an N-node splay BST is $O\big((N + M)\lg(N + M)\big)$.*

The proof of this result, by Sleator and Tarjan in 1985, is a classic example of amortized analysis of algorithms (*see reference section*). We will examine it in detail in Part 8. ∎

Property 13.5 is an amortized performance guarantee: We guarantee not that each operation is efficient but rather that the *average* cost of all the operations performed is efficient. This average is not a probabilistic one; rather, we are stating that the *total* cost is guaranteed to be low. For many applications, this kind of guarantee suffices, but it may not be adequate for some other applications. For example, we cannot provide guaranteed response times for each operation when using splay BSTs, because some operations could take linear time. If an operation does take linear time, then we are guaranteed that other operations will be that much faster, but that may be no consolation to the customer who had to wait.

The bound given in Property 13.5 is a worst-case bound on the total cost of all operations: As is typical with worst-case bounds, it may be much higher than the actual costs. The splaying operation brings recently accessed elements closer to the top of the tree; therefore, this method is attractive for search applications with nonuniform access patterns—particularly applications with a relatively small, even if slowly changing, working set of accessed items.

Figure 13.9 gives two examples that show the effectiveness of the splay-rotation operations in balancing the trees. In these figures, a degenerate tree (built via insertion of items in order of their keys)

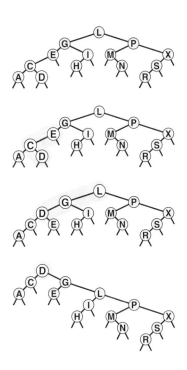

Figure 13.7
Splay insertion

This figure depicts the result (bottom) of inserting a record with key D into the sample tree at top, using splay root insertion. In this case, the insertion process consists of a left-right double rotation followed by a right-right double rotation (from the top).

Figure 13.8
Splay BST construction

This sequence depicts the insertion of records with keys A S E R C H I N G *into an initially empty tree using splay insertion.*

is brought into relatively good balance by a small number of *search* operations.

If duplicate keys are maintained in the tree, then the splay operation can cause items with keys equal to the key in a given node to fall on both sides of that node (see Exercise 13.38). This observation tells us that we cannot find all items with a given key as easily as we can for standard binary search trees. We must either check for duplicates in both subtrees or use some alternative method to work with duplicate keys, as discussed in Chapter 12.

Exercises

▷ **13.25** Draw the splay BST that results when you insert items with the keys E A S Y Q U T I O N in that order into an initially empty tree, using splay insertion.

▷ **13.26** How many tree links must be changed for a double rotation? How many are actually changed for each of the double rotations in Program 13.5?

13.27 Add an implementation of *search*, with splaying, to Program 13.5.

○ **13.28** Implement a nonrecursive version of the splay insertion method in Program 13.5.

13.29 Use your driver program from Exercise 12.33 to determine the effectiveness of splay BSTs as self-organizing search structures by comparing them with standard BSTs for the search query distributions defined in Exercises 12.34 and 12.35.

○ **13.30** Draw all the structurally different BSTs that can result when you insert N keys into an initially empty tree using splay insertion, for $2 \leq N \leq 7$.

● **13.31** Find the probability that each of the trees in Exercise 13.30 is the result of inserting N random distinct elements into an intially empty tree.

○ **13.32** Run empirical studies to compute the average and standard deviation of the number of comparisons used for search hits and for search misses in a BST built by insertion of N random keys into an initially empty tree with splay insertion, for $N = 10^3$, 10^4, 10^5, and 10^6. You do not need to do any searches: Just build the trees and compute their path lengths. Are splay BSTs more nearly balanced than random BSTs, less so, or the same?

13.33 Extend your program for Exercise 13.32 to do N random searches (they most likely will be misses) with splaying in each tree constructed. How does splaying affect the average number of comparisons for a search miss?

13.34 Instrument your programs for Exercises 13.32 and 13.33 to measure running time, rather than just to count comparisons. Run the same experiments. Explain any changes in the conclusions that you draw from the empirical results.

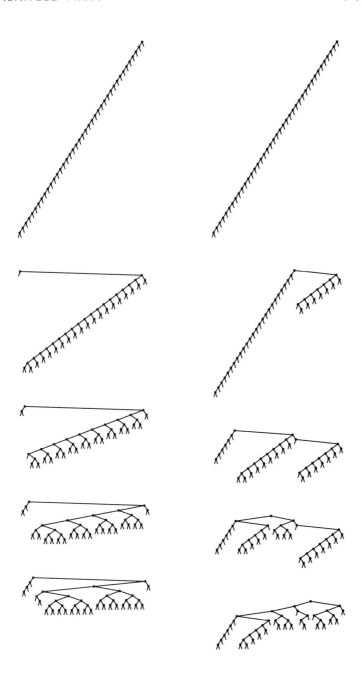

Figure 13.9
Balancing of a worst-case splay tree with searches

Inserting keys in sorted order into an initially empty tree using splay insertion takes only a constant number of steps per insertion but leaves an unbalanced tree, shown at the top on the left and on the right. The sequence on the left shows the result of searching (with splaying) for the smallest, second-smallest, third-smallest, and fourth-smallest keys in the tree. Each search halves the length of the path to the search key (and most other keys in the tree). The sequence on the right shows the same worst-case starting tree being balanced by a sequence of random search hits. Each search halves the number of nodes on its path, reducing the length of search paths for many other nodes in the tree. Collectively, a small number of searches improves the tree balance substantially.

13.35 Compare splay BSTs with standard BSTs for the task of building an index from a piece of real-world text that has at least 1 million characters. Measure the time taken to build the index and the average path lengths in the BSTs.

13.36 Empirically determine the average number of comparisons for search hits in a splay BST built by inserting random keys, for $N = 10^3$, 10^4, 10^5, and 10^6.

13.37 Run empirical studies to test the idea of using splay insertion, instead of standard root insertion, for randomized BSTs.

▷ **13.38** Draw the splay BST that results when you insert items with the keys 0 0 0 0 0 0 0 0 0 0 0 0 1 in that order into an initially empty tree.

13.3 Top-Down 2-3-4 Trees

Despite the performance guarantees that we can provide with random-ized BSTs and with splay BSTs, both still admit the possibility that a particular search operation could take linear time. They therefore do not help us answer the fundamental question for balanced trees: Is there a type of BST for which we can guarantee that each and every *insert* and *search* operation will be logarithmic in the size of the tree? In this section and Section 13.4, we consider an abstract generalization of BSTs and an abstract representation of these trees as a type of BST that allows us to answer this question in the affirmative.

To guarantee that our BSTs will be balanced, we need flexibility in the tree structures that we use. To get this flexibility, let us assume that the nodes in our trees can hold more than one key. Specifically, we will allow *3-nodes* and *4-nodes*, which can hold two and three keys, respectively. A 3-node has three links coming out of it: one for all items with keys smaller than both its keys, one for all items with keys in between its two keys, and one for all items with keys larger than both its keys. Similarly, a 4-node has four links coming out of it: one for each of the intervals defined by its three keys. The nodes in a standard BST could thus be called *2-nodes*: one key, two links. Later, we shall see efficient ways to define and implement the basic operations on these extended nodes; for now, let us assume that we can manipulate them conveniently and see how they can be put together to form trees.

Definition 13.1 *A* **2-3-4 search tree** *is a tree that either is empty or comprises three types of nodes:* **2-nodes,** *with one key, a left link to*

Figure 13.10
A 2-3-4 tree

This figure depicts a 2-3-4 tree that contains the keys A S R C H I N G E X M P L. We can find a key in such a tree by using the keys in the node at the root to find a link to a subtree, then continuing re-cursively. For example, to search for P in this tree, we would fol-low the right link from the root, since P is larger than I, follow the middle link from the right child of the root, since P is between N and R, then terminate the successful search at the 2-node containing the P.

a tree with smaller keys, and a right link to a tree with larger keys;
3-nodes, *with two keys, a left link to a tree with smaller keys, a middle link to a tree with key values between the node's keys and a right link to a tree with larger keys; and* **4-nodes,** *with three keys and four links to trees with key values defined by the ranges subtended by the node's keys.*

Definition 13.2 *A* **balanced 2-3-4 search tree** *is a 2-3-4 search tree with all links to empty trees at the same distance from the root.*

In this chapter, we shall use the term *2-3-4 tree* to refer to balanced 2-3-4 search trees (it denotes a more general structure in other contexts). Figure 13.10 depicts an example of a 2-3-4 tree. The search algorithm for keys in such a tree is a generalization of the search algorithm for BSTs. To determine whether a key is in the tree, we compare it against the keys at the root: If it is equal to any of them, we have a search hit; otherwise, we follow the link from the root to the subtree corresponding to the set of key values containing the search key, and then recursively search in that tree. There are a number of ways to represent 2-, 3-, and 4-nodes and to organize the mechanics of finding the proper link; we defer discussing these solutions until Section 13.4, where we shall discuss a particularly convenient arrangement.

　　To insert a new node in a 2-3-4 tree, we could do an unsuccessful search and then hook on the node, as we did with BSTs, but the new tree would not be balanced. The primary reason that 2-3-4 trees are important is that we can do insertions and still maintain perfect balance in the tree, in every case. For example, it is easy to see what to do if the node at which the search terminates is a 2-node: We just turn the node into a 3-node. Similarly, if the search terminates at a 3-node, we just turn the node into a 4-node. But what should we do if the search terminates at a 4-node? The answer is that we can make room for the new key while maintaining the balance in the tree, by first splitting the 4-node into two 2-nodes, and then passing the middle key up to the node's parent. These three cases are illustrated in Figure 13.11.

　　Now, what do we do if we need to split a 4-node whose parent is also a 4-node? One method would be to split the parent also, but the grandparent could also be a 4-node, and so could its parent, and so forth—we could wind up splitting nodes all the way back up the tree. An easier approach is to make sure that the search path will not end at a 4-node, by splitting any 4-node we see on the way *down* the tree.

Figure 13.11
Insertion into a 2-3-4 tree

A 2-3-4 tree consisting only of 2-nodes is the same as a BST (top). We can insert C by converting the 2-node where the search for C terminates into a 3-node (second from top). Similarly, we can insert H by converting the 3-node where the search for it terminates into a 4-node (third from top). We need to do more work to insert I, because the search for it terminates at a 4-node. First, we split up the 4-node, pass its middle key up to its parent, and convert that node into a 3-node (fourth from top, high-lighted). This transformation gives a valid 2-3-4 tree containing the keys, one that has room for I at the bottom. Finally, we insert I into the 2-node that now terminates the search, converting that node into a 3-node (bottom).

Specifically, as shown in Figure 13.12, every time we encounter a 2-node connected to a 4-node, we transform the pair into a 3-node connected to two 2-nodes, and every time we encounter a 3-node connected to a 4-node, we transform the pair into a 4-node connected to two 2-nodes. Splitting 4-nodes is possible because of the way not only the keys but also the *links* can be moved around. Two 2-nodes have the same number (four) of links as a 4-node, so we can execute the split without having to propagate any changes below (or above) the split node. A 3-node is not changed to a 4-node just by the addition of another key; another link is needed also (in this case, the extra link provided by the split). The crucial point is that these transformations are purely local: No part of the tree needs to be examined or modified other than the part shown in Figure 13.12. Each of the transformations passes up one of the keys from a 4-node to that node's parent in the tree, and then restructures links accordingly.

On our way down the tree, we do not need to worry explicitly about the parent of the current node being a 4-node, because our transformations ensure that, as we pass through each node in the tree, we come out on a node that is not a 4-node. In particular, when we reach the bottom of the tree, we are not on a 4-node, and we can insert the new node directly by transforming either a 2-node to a 3-node or a 3-node to a 4-node. We can think of the insertion as a split of an imaginary 4-node at the bottom that passes up the new key.

One final detail: Whenever the root of the tree becomes a 4-node, we just split it into a triangle of three 2-nodes, as we did for our first node split in the preceding example. Splitting the root after an insertion is slightly more convenient than is the alternative of waiting until the next insertion to do the split, because we never need to worry about the parent of the root. Splitting the root (and only this operation) makes the tree grow one level higher.

Figure 13.13 depicts the construction of a 2-3-4 tree for a sample set of keys. Unlike standard BSTs, which grow down from the top, these trees grow up from the bottom. Because the 4-nodes are split on the way from the top down, the trees are called top-down 2-3-4 trees. The algorithm is significant because it produces search trees that are nearly perfectly balanced, yet it makes only a few local transformations as it walks through the tree.

Figure 13.12
Splitting 4-nodes in a 2-3-4 tree

In a 2-3-4 tree, we can split any 4-node that is not the child of a 4-node into two 2-nodes, passing its middle record up to its parent. A 2-node attached to a 4-node (top left) becomes a 3-node attached to two 2-nodes (top right), and a 3-node attached to a 4-node (bottom left) becomes a 4-node attached to two 2-nodes (bottom right).

Property 13.6 *Searches in N-node 2-3-4 trees visit at most* $\lg N + 1$ *nodes.*

Every external node is the same distance from the root: The transformations that we perform have no effect on the distance from any node to the root, except when we split the root (in this case the distance from all nodes to the root is increased by 1). If all the nodes are 2-nodes, the stated result holds, since the tree is like a full binary tree; if there are 3-nodes and 4-nodes, the height can only be lower. ■

Property 13.7 *Insertions into N-node 2-3-4 trees require fewer than* $\lg N + 1$ *node splits in the worst case and seem to require less than one node split on the average.*

The worst that can happen is that all the nodes on the path to the insertion point are 4-nodes, all of which will be split. But in a tree built from a random permutation of N elements, not only is this worst case unlikely to occur, but also few splits seem to be required on the average, because there are not many 4-nodes in the trees. For example, in the large tree depicted in Figure 13.14, all but two of the 4-nodes are on the bottom level. Precise analytic results on the average-case performance of 2-3-4 trees have so far eluded the experts, but it is clear from empirical studies that very few splits are used to balance the trees. The worst case is only $\lg N$, and that is not approached in practical situations. ■

The preceding description is sufficient to define an algorithm for searching using 2-3-4 trees that has guaranteed good worst-case performance. However, we are only half of the way to an implementation. Although it would be possible to write algorithms which actually perform transformations on distinct data types representing 2-, 3-, and 4-nodes, most of the tasks that are involved are inconvenient to implement in this direct representation. As in splay BSTs, the overhead incurred in manipulating the more complex node structures could make the algorithms slower than standard BST search. The primary purpose of balancing is to provide insurance against a bad worst case, but we would prefer the overhead cost for that insurance to be low and we also would prefer to avoid paying the cost on every run of the algorithm. Fortunately, as we will see in Section 13.4, there is a relatively simple representation of 2-, 3-, and 4-nodes that allows

Figure 13.13
2-3-4 search tree construction

This sequence depicts the result of inserting items with keys A S E R C H I N G X into an initially empty 2-3-4 tree. We split each 4-node that we encounter on the search path, thus ensuring that there is room for the new item at the bottom.

Figure 13.14
A large 2-3-4 tree

This 2-3-4 tree is the result of 200 random insertions into an initially empty tree. All search paths in the trees have six or fewer nodes.

the transformations to be done in a uniform way with little overhead beyond the costs incurred by standard binary-tree search.

The algorithm that we have described is just one possible way to maintain balance in 2-3-4 search trees. Several other methods that achieve the same goals have been developed.

For example, we can balance from the bottom up. First, we do a search in the tree to find the bottom node where the item to be inserted belongs. If that node is a 2-node or a 3-node, we grow it to a 3-node or a 4-node, just as before. If it is a 4-node, we split it as before (inserting the new item into one of the resulting 2-nodes at the bottom) and insert the middle item into the parent, if the parent is a 2-node or a 3-node. If the parent is a 4-node, we split that node (inserting the middle node from the bottom into the appropriate 2-node) and insert the middle item into its parent, if the parent is a 2-node or a 3-node. If the grandparent is also a 4-node, we continue up the tree in the same way, splitting 4-nodes until we encounter a 2-node or a 3-node on the search path.

We can do this kind of bottom-up balancing in trees that have only 2- or 3-nodes (no 4-nodes). This approach leads to more node splitting during the execution of the algorithm, but it is easier to code because there are fewer cases to consider. In another approach, we seek to reduce the amount of node splitting by looking for siblings that are not 4-nodes when we are ready to split a 4-node.

Implementations of all these methods involve the same basic recursive scheme, as we shall see in Section 13.4. We shall also discuss generalizations, in Chapter 16. The primary advantage of the top-down insertion approach that we are considering over other methods is that it can achieve the necessary balancing in one top-down pass through the tree.

Exercises

▷ **13.39** Draw the balanced 2-3-4 search tree that results when you insert items with the keys E A S Y Q U T I O N in that order into an initially empty tree, using the top-down insertion method.

▷ **13.40** Draw the balanced 2-3-4 search tree that results when you insert items with the keys E A S Y Q U T I O N in that order into an initially empty tree, using the bottom-up insertion method.

○ **13.41** What are the minimum and maximum heights possible for balanced 2-3-4 trees with N nodes?

○ **13.42** What are the minimum and maximum heights possible for balanced 2-3-4 BSTs with N keys?

○ **13.43** Draw all the structurally different balanced 2-3-4 BSTs with N keys for $2 \leq N \leq 12$.

● **13.44** Find the probability that each of the trees in Exercise 13.43 is the result of the insertion of N random distinct elements into an initially empty tree.

13.45 Make a table showing the number of trees for each N from Exercise 13.43 that are isomorphic, in the sense that they can be transformed to one another by exchanges of subtrees in nodes.

▷ **13.46** Describe algorithms for search and insertion in balanced 2-3-4-5-6 search trees.

▷ **13.47** Draw the unbalanced 2-3-4 search tree that results when you insert items with the keys E A S Y Q U T I O N in that order into an initially empty tree, using the following method. If the search ends in a 2-node or a 3-node, change it to a 3-node or a 4-node, as in the balanced algorithm; if the search ends in a 4-node, replace the appropriate link in that 4-node with a new 2-node.

13.4 Red–Black Trees

The top-down 2-3-4 insertion algorithm described in the previous section is easy to understand, but implementing it directly is cumbersome because of all the different cases that can arise. We need to maintain three different types of nodes, in order to compare search keys against each of the keys in the nodes, copy links and other information from one type of node to another, create and destroy nodes, and so forth. In this section, we examine a simple abstract representation of 2-3-4 trees that leads us to a natural implementation of the symbol-table algorithms with near-optimal worst-case performance guarantees.

The basic idea is to represent 2-3-4 trees as standard BSTs (2-nodes only) but to add one extra bit of information per node to encode 3-nodes and 4-nodes. We think of the links as being of two different types: *red* links, which bind together small binary trees comprising 3-nodes and 4-nodes, and *black* links, which bind together the 2-3-4 tree. Specifically, as illustrated in Figure 13.15, we represent 4-nodes

Figure 13.15
3-nodes and 4-nodes in red-black trees

The use of two types of links provides us with an efficient way to represent 3-nodes and 4-nodes in 2-3-4 trees. We use red links (thick lines in our diagrams) for internal connections in nodes, and black links (thin lines in our diagrams) for 2-3-4 tree links. A 4-node (top left) is represented by a balanced subtree of three 2-nodes connected by red links (top right). Both have three keys and four black links. A 3-node (bottom left) is represented by one 2-node connected to another (either on the right or the left) with a single red link (bottom right). All have two keys and three black links.

as three 2-nodes connected by red links, and 3-nodes as two 2-nodes connected by a single red link. The red link in a 3-node may be a left link or a right link, so there are two ways to represent each 3-node.

In any tree, each node is pointed to by one link, so *coloring the links is equivalent to coloring the nodes*. Accordingly, we use one extra bit per node to store the color of the link pointing *to* that node. We refer to 2-3-4 trees represented in this way as *red–black BSTs*. The orientation of each 3-node is determined by the dynamics of the algorithm that we shall describe. It would be possible to enforce a rule that 3-nodes all slant the same way, but there is no reason to do so. Figure 13.16 shows an example of a red–black tree. If we eliminate the red links and collapse together the nodes they connect, the result is the 2-3-4 tree in Figure 13.10.

Red–black trees have two essential properties: (*i*) the standard *search* method for BSTs works without modification and (*ii*) they correspond directly to 2-3-4 trees, so we can implement the balanced 2-3-4 tree algorithm by maintaining the correspondence. We get the best of both worlds: the simple search method from the standard BST and the simple insertion–balancing method from the 2-3-4 search tree.

The search method never examines the field that represents node color, so the balancing mechanism adds no overhead to the time taken by the fundamental search procedure. Since each key is inserted just once, but may be searched for many times in a typical application, the end result is that we get improved search times (because the trees are balanced) at relatively little cost (because no work for balancing is done during the searches). Moreover, the overhead for insertion is small: we have to take action for balancing only when we see 4-nodes, and there are not many 4-nodes in the tree because we are always breaking them up. The inner loop of the insert procedure is the code that walks down the tree (the same as for the search or search-and-insert operations in standard BSTs), with one extra test added: If a node has two red children, it is a part of a 4-node. This low overhead is a primary reason for the efficiency of red–black BSTs.

Now, let us consider the red–black representation for the two transformations that we might need to perform when we do encounter a 4-node: If we have a 2-node connected to a 4-node, then we should convert the pair into a 3-node connected to two 2-nodes; if we have a 3-node connected to a 4-node, then we should convert the pair into a

Figure 13.16
A red–black tree

This figure depicts a red–black tree that contains the keys A S R C H I N G E X M P L. We can find a key in such a tree with standard BST search. Any path from the root to an external node in this tree has three black links. If we collapse the nodes connected by red links in this tree, we get the 2-3-4 tree of Figure 13.10.

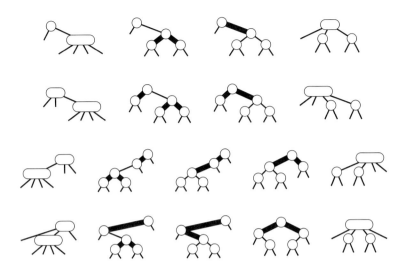

Figure 13.17
Splitting 4-nodes in a red–black tree

In a red–black tree, we implement the operation of splitting a 4-node that is not the child of a 4-node by changing the node colors in the three nodes comprising the 4-node, then possibly doing one or two rotations. If the parent is a 2-node (top) or a 3-node that has a convenient orientation (second from top), no rotations are needed. If the 4-node is on the center link of the 3-node (bottom), a double rotation is needed; otherwise, a single rotation suffices (third from top).

4-node connected to two 2-nodes. When a new node is added at the bottom, we imagine it to be a 4-node that has to be split and its middle node passed up to be inserted into the bottom node where the search ends, which is guaranteed by the top-down process to be either a 2-node or a 3-node. The transformation required when we encounter a 2-node connected to a 4-node is easy, and the same transformation works if we have a 3-node connected to a 4-node in the "right" way, as shown in the first two cases in Figure 13.17.

We are left with the two other situations that can arise if we encounter a 3-node connected to a 4-node, as shown in the second two cases in Figure 13.17. (There are actually four situations, because the mirror images of these two can also occur for 3-nodes of the other orientation.) In these cases, the naive 4-node split leaves two red links in a row—the tree that results does not represent a 2-3-4 tree in accordance with our conventions. The situation is not too bad, because we do have three nodes connected by red links: all we need to do is to transform the tree such that the red links point down from the same node.

Fortunately, the rotation operations that we have been using are precisely what we need to achieve the desired effect. Let us begin with the easier of the two remaining cases: the third case in Figure 13.17, where a 4-node attached to a 3-node has split, leaving two red links in

Program 13.6 Insertion in red–black BSTs

This method implements insertion in 2-3-4 trees using the red–black representation. We add a boolean field `cbit` to the `Node` class (and extend its constructor accordingly) to represent the color, with `true` signifying that the node is red and `false` signifying that it is black. On the way down the tree (before the recursive call), we check for 4-nodes and split them by flipping the color bits in all three nodes. When we reach the bottom, we create a new red node for the item to be inserted and return a pointer to it. On the way up the tree (after the recursive call), we check whether a rotation is needed. If the search path has two red links with the same orientation, we do a single rotation from the top node, then flip the color bits to make a proper 4-node. If the search path has two red links with different orientations, we do a single rotation from the bottom node, reducing to the other case for the next step up.

```
private static final boolean R = true;
private static final boolean B = false;
private boolean red(Node x)
  { if (x == null) return false; return x.cbit; }
private Node insertR(Node h, ITEM x, boolean sw)
  {
    if (h == null) { return new Node(x, R); }
    if (red(h.l) && red(h.r))
      { h.cbit = R; h.l.cbit = B; h.r.cbit = B; }
    if (less(x.key(), h.item.key()))
      {
        h.l = insertR(h.l, x, false);
        if (red(h) && red(h.l) && sw) h = rotR(h);
        if (red(h.l) && red(h.l.l))
          { h = rotR(h); h.cbit = B; h.r.cbit = R; }
      }
    else
      {
        h.r = insertR(h.r, x, true);
        if (red(h) && red(h.r) && !sw) h = rotL(h);
        if (red(h.r) && red(h.r.r))
          { h = rotL(h); h.cbit = B; h.l.cbit = R; }
      }
    return h;
  }
void insert(ITEM x)
  { head = insertR(head, x, B); head.cbit = B; }
```

a row that are oriented the same way. This situation would not have arisen if the 3-node had been oriented the other way: Accordingly, we restructure the tree to switch the orientation of the 3-node and thus reduce this case to be the same as the second case, where the naive 4-node split was sufficient. Restructuring the tree to reorient a 3-node is a single rotation with the additional requirement that the colors of the two nodes have to be switched.

Finally, to handle the case where a 4-node attached to a 3-node has split leaving two red links in a row that are oriented differently, we rotate to reduce immediately to the case where the links are oriented the same way, which we then handle as before. This transformation amounts to the same operations as the left-right and right-left double rotations that we used for splay BSTs in Section 13.2, although we have to do slightly more work to maintain the colors properly. Figures 13.18 and 13.19 depict examples of red–black insertion operations.

Program 13.6 is an implementation of *insert* for red–black trees that performs the transformations that are summarized in Figure 13.17. The recursive implementation makes it possible to perform the color flips for 4-nodes on the way down the tree (before the recursive calls), and then to perform rotations on the way up the tree (after the recursive calls). This program would be difficult to understand without the two layers of abstraction that we have developed to implement it. We can check that the recursive trickery implements the rotations depicted in Figure 13.17; then, we can check that the program implements our high-level algorithm on 2-3-4 trees—break up 4-nodes on the way down the tree, then insert the new item into the 2- or 3-node where the search path ends at the bottom of the tree.

Figure 13.20 (which we can think of as a more detailed version of Figure 13.13) shows how Program 13.6 constructs the red–black trees that represent balanced 2-3-4 trees as a sample set of keys is inserted. Figure 13.21 shows a tree built from the larger example that we have been using; the average number of nodes visited during a search for a random key in this tree is just 5.81, as compared to 7.00 for the tree built from the same keys in Chapter 12, and to 5.74, the best possible for a perfectly balanced tree. At a cost of only a few rotations, we get a tree that has far better balance than any of the others that we have seen in this chapter for the same keys. Program 13.6 is an efficient, relatively compact algorithm for insertion using a binary tree structure

**Figure 13.18
Insertion into a red–black tree**

This figure depicts the result (bottom) of inserting a record with key I into the sample red–black tree at the top. In this case, the insertion process consists of splitting the 4-node at C with a color flip (center), then adding the new node at the bottom, converting the node containing H from a 2-node to a 3-node.

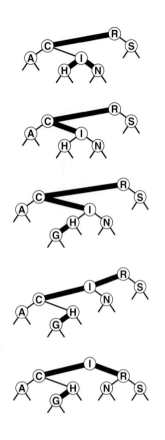

Figure 13.19
Insertion into a red–black tree, with rotations

This figure depicts the result (bottom) of inserting a record with key G into the red–black tree at the top. In this case, the insertion process consists of splitting the 4-node at I with a color flip (second from top), then adding the new node at the bottom (third from top), then (returning to each node on the search path in the code after the recursive function calls) doing a left rotation at C and a right rotation at R to finish the process of splitting the 4-node.

that is guaranteed to take a logarithmic number of steps for all searches and insertions. It is one of the few symbol-table implementations with that property, and its use is justified in a library implementation where properties of the key sequence to be processed cannot be characterized accurately.

Property 13.8 *A search in a red–black tree with N nodes requires fewer than $2 \lg N + 2$ comparisons.*

Only splits that correspond to a 3-node connected to a 4-node in a 2-3-4 tree require a rotation in the red–black tree, so this property follows from Property 13.2. The worst case is when the path to the insertion point consists of alternating 3- and 4-nodes. ∎

Moreover, Program 13.6 incurs little overhead for balancing, and the trees that it produces are nearly optimal, so it is also attractive to consider as a fast general-purpose searching method.

Property 13.9 *A search in a red–black tree with N nodes built from random keys uses about $1.002 \lg N$ comparisons, on the average.*

The constant 1.002, which has been confirmed through partial analyses and simulations (*see reference section*), is sufficiently low that we can regard red–black trees as optimal for practical purposes, but the question of whether red–black trees are truly asymptotically optimal is still open. Is the constant equal to 1? ∎

Because the recursive implementation in Program 13.6 does some work before the recursive calls and some work after the recursive calls, it makes some modifications to the tree on the way down the search path and some modifications to the tree on the way back up. Therefore, it does not have the property that the balancing is accomplished in one top-down pass. This fact is of little consequence for most applications because the depth of the recursion is guaranteed to be low. For some applications that involve multiple independent processes with access to the same tree, we might need a nonrecursive implementation that actively operates on only a constant number of nodes at any given time (see Exercise 13.66).

For an application that carries other information in the trees, the rotation operation might be an expensive one, perhaps causing us to update information in all the nodes in the subtrees involved in the rotation. For such an application, we can ensure that each insertion involves at most one rotation by using red–black trees to implement the bottom-up 2-3-4 search trees that are described at the end of Section 13.3. An insertion in those trees involves splitting 4-nodes along the search path, which involves color changes but no rotations in the red–black representation, followed by one single or double rotation (one of the cases in Figure 13.17) when the first 2-node or a 3-node is encountered on the way up the search path (see Exercise 13.59).

If duplicate keys are to be maintained in the tree, then, as we did with splay BSTs, we must allow items with keys equal to a given node to fall on both sides of that node. Otherwise, severe imbalance could result from long strings of duplicate keys. Again, this observation tells us that finding all items with a given key requires specialized code.

As mentioned at the end of Section 13.3, red–black representations of 2-3-4 trees are among several similar strategies that have been proposed for implementing balanced binary trees (*see reference section*). As we saw, it is the rotate operations that balance the trees: We have been looking at a particular view of the trees that makes it easy to decide when to rotate. Other views of the trees lead to other algorithms, a few of which we shall mention briefly here.

The oldest and most well-known data structure for balanced trees is the *height-balanced*, or *AVL, tree*, discovered in 1962 by Adel'son-Vel'skii and Landis. These trees have the property that the heights of the two subtrees of each node differ by at most 1. If an insertion causes one of the subtrees of some node to grow in height by 1, then the balance condition might be violated. However, one single or double rotation will bring the node back into balance in every case. The algorithm that is based on this observation is similar to the method of balancing 2-3-4 trees from the bottom up: Do a recursive search for the node, then, *after* the recursive call, check for imbalance and do a single or double rotation to correct it if necessary (see Exercise 13.61). The decision about which rotations (if any) to perform requires that we know whether each node has a height that is 1 less than, the same as, or 1 greater than the height of its sibling. Two bits per node are needed to encode this information in a straightforward way, although it is possible to get by without using any extra storage, using the red–black abstraction (see Exercises 13.62 and 13.65).

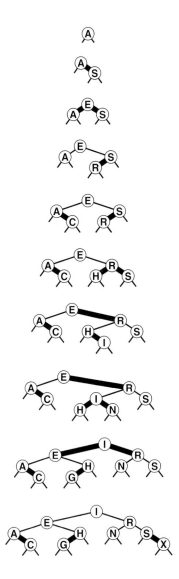

**Figure 13.20
Construction of a red–black tree**

This sequence depicts the result of inserting records with keys A S E R C H I N G X into an initially empty red–black tree.

Figure 13.21
A large red–black BST

This red–black BST is the result of inserting 200 randomly ordered keys into an initially empty tree. All search misses in the tree use between 6 and 12 comparisons.

Because 4-nodes play no special role in the bottom-up 2-3-4 algorithm, it is possible to build balanced trees in essentially the same way, but using only 2-nodes and 3-nodes. Trees built in this way are called *2-3 trees* and were discovered by Hopcroft in 1970. There is not enough flexibility in 2-3 trees to give a convenient top-down insertion algorithm. Again, the red–black framework can simplify the implementation, but bottom-up 2-3 trees offer no particular advantage over bottom-up 2-3-4 trees, because single and double rotations are still needed to maintain balance. Bottom-up 2-3-4 trees have slightly better balance and have the advantage of using at most one rotation per insertion.

In Chapter 16, we shall study another important type of balanced tree, an extension of 2-3-4 trees called *B-trees*. B-trees allow up to M keys per node for large M and are widely used for search applications that involve huge files.

We have defined red–black trees by correspondence to 2-3-4 trees. It is also amusing to formulate direct structural definitions.

Definition 13.3 *A* **red–black BST** *is a binary search tree in which each node is marked to be either* **red** *or* **black***, with the additional restriction that no two red nodes appear consecutively on any path from an external link to the root.*

Definition 13.4 *A* **balanced red–black BST** *is a red–black BST in which all paths from external links to the root have the same number of black nodes.*

Now, an alternative approach to developing a balanced tree algorithm is to ignore the 2-3-4 tree abstraction entirely and formulate an insertion algorithm that preserves the defining property of balanced red–black BSTs through rotations. For example, using the bottom-up algorithm corresponds to attaching the new node at the bottom of the search path with a red link, then proceeding up the search path, doing rotations or color changes, as per the cases in Figure 13.17, to break up any pair of consecutive red links encountered on the path. The fundamental operations that we perform are the same as in Program 13.6 and its bottom-up counterpart, but subtle differences arise, because 3-nodes can orient either way, operations can be performed in different orders, and various different rotation decisions can be used successfully.

Let us summarize: Using red–black trees to implement balanced 2-3-4 trees, we can develop a symbol table where a *search* operation for a key in a file of, say, 1 million items can be completed by comparing that key with about 20 other keys. In the worst case, no more than 40 comparisons are needed. Furthermore, little overhead is associated with each comparison, so a fast *search* is ensured, even in a huge file.

Exercises

▷ **13.48** Draw the red–black BST that results when you insert items with the keys E A S Y Q U T I O N in that order into an initially empty tree, using the top-down insertion method.

▷ **13.49** Draw the red–black BST that results when you insert items with the keys E A S Y Q U T I O N in that order into an initially empty tree, using the bottom-up insertion method.

○ **13.50** Draw the red–black tree that results when you insert letters A through K in order into an initially empty tree, then describe what happens in general when trees are built by insertion of keys in ascending order.

13.51 Give a sequence of insertions that will construct the red–black tree shown in Figure 13.16.

13.52 Generate two random 32-node red–black trees. Draw them (either by hand or with a program). Compare them with the (unbalanced) BSTs built with the same keys.

13.53 How many different red–black trees correspond to a 2-3-4 tree that has t 3-nodes?

○ **13.54** Draw all the structurally different red–black search trees with N keys for $2 \leq N \leq 12$.

● **13.55** Find the probabilities that each of the trees in Exercise 13.43 is the result of inserting N random distinct elements into an initially empty tree.

13.56 Make a table showing the number of trees for each N from Exercise 13.54 that are isomorphic, in the sense that they can be transformed to one another by exchanges of subtrees in nodes.

●● **13.57** Show that, in the worst case, almost all the paths from the root to an external node in a red–black tree of N nodes are of length $2 \lg N$.

13.58 How many rotations are required for an insertion into a red–black tree of N nodes, in the worst case?

○ **13.59** Implement *construct*, *search*, and *insert* for symbol tables with bottom-up balanced 2-3-4 trees as the underlying data structure, using the red–black representation and the same recursive approach as Program 13.6. *Hint*: Your code can be similar to Program 13.6 but should perform the operations in a different order.

13.60 Implement *construct*, *search*, and *insert* for symbol tables with bottom-up balanced 2-3 trees as the underlying data structure, using the red–black representation and the same recursive approach as Program 13.6.

13.61 Implement *construct*, *search*, and *insert* for symbol tables with height-balanced (AVL) trees as the underlying data structure, using the same recursive approach as Program 13.6.

• **13.62** Modify your implementation from Exercise 13.61 to use red–black trees (1 bit per node) to encode the balance information.

• **13.63** Implement balanced 2-3-4 trees using a red–black tree representation in which 3-nodes always lean to the right. *Note*: This change allows you to remove one of the bit tests from the inner loop for *insert*.

• **13.64** Program 13.6 does rotations to keep 4-nodes balanced. Develop an implementation for balanced 2-3-4 trees using a red–black tree representation where 4-nodes can be represented as any three nodes connected by two red links (perfectly balanced or not).

○ **13.65** Implement *construct*, *search*, and *insert* for red–black trees without using any extra storage for the color bit, based on the following trick. To color a node red, swap its two links. Then, to test whether a node is red, test whether its left child is larger than its right child. You have to modify the comparisons to accommodate the possible link swap, and this trick replaces bit comparisons with key comparisons that are presumably more expensive, but it shows that the bit in the nodes can be eliminated, if necessary.

• **13.66** Implement a nonrecursive red–black BST *insert* method (see Program 13.6) that corresponds to balanced 2-3-4 tree insertion with one top-down pass. *Hint*: Maintain links gg, g, and p that point, respectively, to the current node's great-grandparent, grandparent, and parent in the tree. All these links might be needed for double rotation.

13.67 Write a program that computes the percentage of black nodes in a given red–black BST. Test your program by inserting N random keys into an initially empty tree, for $N = 10^3$, 10^4, 10^5, and 10^6.

13.68 Write a program that computes the percentage of items that are in 3-nodes and 4-nodes in a given 2-3-4 search tree. Test your program by inserting N random keys into an initially empty tree, for $N = 10^3$, 10^4, 10^5, and 10^6.

Figure 13.22
A two-level linked list

Every third node in this list has a second link, so we can skip through the list at nearly three times the speed that we could go by following the first links. For example, we can get to the twelfth node in the list, the P, from the beginning by following just five links: second links to C, G, L, N, and then through N's first link, P.

▷ **13.69** With 1 bit per node for color, we can represent 2-, 3-, and 4-nodes. How many bits per node would we need to represent 5-, 6-, 7-, and 8-nodes with a binary tree?

13.70 Run empirical studies to compute the average and standard deviation of the number of comparisons used for search hits and for search misses in a red–black tree built by insertion of N random keys into an initially empty tree, for $N = 10^3$, 10^4, 10^5, and 10^6.

13.71 Instrument your program for Exercise 13.70 to compute the number of rotations and node splits that are used to build the trees. Discuss the results.

13.72 Use your driver program from Exercise 12.33 to compare the self-organizing–search aspect of splay BSTs with the worst-case guarantees of red–black BSTs and with standard BSTs for the search query distributions defined in Exercises 12.34 and 12.35 (see Exercise 13.29).

• **13.73** Implement a *search* method for red–black trees that performs rotations and changes node colors on the way down the tree to ensure that the node at the bottom of the search path is not a 2-node.

• **13.74** Use your solution to Exercise 13.73 to implement a *remove* method for red–black trees. Find the node to be deleted, continue the search to a 3-node or 4-node at the bottom of the path, and move the successor from the bottom to replace the deleted node.

13.5 Skip Lists

In this section, we consider an approach to developing fast implementations of symbol-table operations which seems at first to be completely different from the tree-based methods that we have been considering; but it actually is closely related to them. The approach is based on a randomized data structure and is almost certain to provide near-optimal performance for all the basic operations for the symbol-table ADT that we have been considering. The underlying data structure, which was developed by Pugh in 1990 (*see reference section*), is called a *skip list*. It uses extra links in the nodes of a linked list to skip through large portions of a list at a time during a search.

Figure 13.22 gives a simple example, where every third node in an ordered linked list contains an extra link that allows us to skip three

Figure 13.23
Search and insertion in a skip list

By adding more levels to the structure in Figure 13.22 and allowing links to skip variable numbers of nodes, we get an example of a general skip list. To search for a key in the list, we start at the highest level, moving down each time that we encounter a key that is not smaller than the search key. Here (top), we find L by starting at level 3, moving across the first link, then down at G (treating the null link as a link to a sentinel), then across to I, then down to level 2 because S is greater than L, then down to level 1 because M is greater than L. To insert a node L with three links, we link it into the three lists at precisely the places where we found links to greater keys during the search.

nodes in the list. We can use the extra links to speed up *search*: We scan through the top list until we find the key or a node with a smaller key with a link to a node with a larger key, then use the links at the bottom to check the two intervening nodes. This method speeds up *search* by a factor of 3, because we examine only about $k/3$ nodes in a successful search for the kth node on the list.

We can iterate this construction and provide a second extra link to be able to scan faster through the nodes with extra links, and so forth. Also, we can generalize the construction by skipping a variable number of nodes with each link.

Definition 13.5 *A* **skip list** *is an ordered linked list where each node contains a variable number of links, with the ith links in the nodes implementing singly linked lists that skip the nodes with fewer than i links.*

Figure 13.23 depicts a sample skip list and shows an example of searching and inserting a new node. To search, we scan through the top list until we find the search key or a node with a smaller key that has a link to a node with a larger key; then, we move to the second-from-top list and iterate the procedure, continuing until the search key is found or a search miss happens on the bottom level. To insert, we search, linking in the new node when moving from level k to level $k - 1$ if the new node has at least k extra links.

The internal representation of the nodes is straightforward. We replace the single link in a singly linked list by an array of links, and an integer that contains the number of links in the node. Memory management is perhaps the most complicated aspect of skip lists—

Program 13.7 Searching in skip lists

For k equal to 0, this code is equivalent to Program 12.6, for searching in singly linked lists. For general k, we move to the next node in the list on level k if its key is smaller than the search key, and down to level k-1 if its key is not smaller.

```
private ITEM searchR(Node t, KEY v, int k)
  {
    if (t == null) return null;
    if (t != head)
      if (equals(t.item.key(), v)) return t.item;
    if (k >= t.sz) k = t.sz-1;
    if (t.next[k] != null)
      if (!less(v, t.next[k].item.key()))
        return searchR(t.next[k], v, k);
    return (k == 0) ? null : searchR(t, v, k-1);
  }
ITEM search(KEY v)
  { return searchR(head, v, lgN - 1); }
```

we will examine the type declarations and the code for allocating new nodes shortly, when we consider insertion. For the moment, it suffices to note that we can access the node that follows node t on the $(k + 1)$st level in the skip list by accessing t.next[k]. The recursive implementation in Program 13.7 shows that searching in skip lists not only is a straightforward generalization of searching in singly linked lists, but also is similar to binary search or searching in BSTs. We test whether the current node has the search key; if it does not, we compare the key in the current node with the search key. We do one recursive call if it is larger and a different recursive call if it is smaller.

The first task that we face when we want to insert a new node into a skip list is to determine how many links we want that node to have. All the nodes have at least one link; following the intuition depicted in Figure 13.22, we can skip t nodes at a time on the second level if one out of every t nodes has at least two links; iterating, we come to the conclusion that we want one out of every t^j nodes to have at least $j + 1$ links.

Figure 13.24
Skip-list construction

This sequence depicts the result of inserting items with keys A S E R C H I N G into an initially empty skip list. Nodes have $(j+1)$ links with probability $1/2^j$.

Program 13.8 Skip-list data structures and constructor

Nodes in skip lists have an array of links, so the constructor for `node` needs to allocate the array and to set all the links to `null`. The constant L is the maximum number of levels that we will allow in the list: it might be set to the logarithm of the expected number of items on the list. The variable N keeps the number of items in the list, as usual, and lgN is the number of levels. An empty list is a head node with L links, all set to 0, with N and lgN also set to 0.

```
private class Node
  { ITEM item; Node[] next; int sz;
    Node(ITEM x, int k)
       { item = x; sz = k; next = new Node[sz]; }
  }
private static final int L = 50;
private Node head;
private int N, lgN;
ST(int maxN)
  { N = 0; lgN = 0; head = new Node(null, L); }
```

To make nodes with this property, we randomize, using a method that returns $j+1$ with probability $1/t^j$. Given j, we create a new node with j links and insert it into the skip list using the same recursive schema as we did for *search*, as illustrated in Figure 13.23. After we have reached level j, we link in the new node each time that we move down to the next level. At that point, we have established that the item in the current node is less than the search key and links (on level j) to a node that is not less than the search key.

To initialize a skip list, we build a head node with the maximum number of levels that we will allow in the list, with null links at all levels. Programs 13.8 and 13.9 implement initialization and insertion for skip lists.

Figure 13.24 shows the construction of a skip list for a sample set of keys when inserted in random order; Figure 13.25 shows the construction of a skip list for the same set of keys as in Figure 13.24, but inserted in increasing order; and Figure 13.26 shows a larger example. Like those of randomized BSTs, the stochastic properties of skip lists do not depend on the order in which keys are inserted.

> **Program 13.9 Insertion in skip lists**
>
> We generate a new j-link node with probability $1/2^j$, then follow the search path precisely as in Program 13.7, but link in the new node when we move down to each of the bottom j levels.
>
> ```
> private int randX()
>   { int i, j; double t = Math.random();
>     for (i = 1, j = 2; i < L; i++, j += j)
>       if (t*j > 1.0) break;
>     if (i > lgN) lgN = i;
>     return i;
>   }
> private void insertR(Node t, Node x, int k)
>   { KEY v = x.item.key();
>     Node tk = t.next[k];
>     if ((tk == null) || less(v, tk.item.key()))
>       {
>         if (k < x.sz)
>           { x.next[k] = tk; t.next[k] = x; }
>         if (k == 0) return;
>         insertR(t, x, k-1); return;
>       }
>     insertR(tk, x, k);
>   }
> void insert(ITEM v)
>   { insertR(head, new Node(v, randX()), lgN); N++; }
> ```

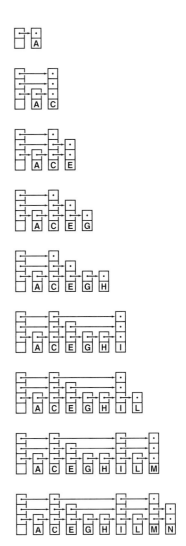

Figure 13.25
Skip-list construction with keys in order

This sequence depicts the result of inserting items with keys A C E G H I N R S *into an initially empty skip list. Stochastic properties of the list do not depend on the key insertion order.*

Property 13.10 *Search and insertion in a randomized skip list with parameter t require about $(t \log_t N)/2 = (t/(2 \lg t)) \lg N$ comparisons, on the average.*

We expect the skip list to have about $\log_t N$ levels, because $\log_t N$ is greater than the smallest j for which $t^j = N$. On each level, we expect that about t nodes were skipped on the previous level and that we should have to go through about half of them, on the average, before dropping to the next level. The number of levels is small, as is clear from the example in Figure 13.26, but the precise analysis that establishes this is not elementary (*see reference section*). ■

Figure 13.26
A large skip list

This skip list is the result of inserting 50 randomly ordered keys into an initially empty list. We can access any node by following 8 or fewer links.

Property 13.11 *Skip lists have $(t/(t-1))N$ links on the average.*

There are N links on the bottom, N/t links on the first level, about N/t^2 links on the second level, and so forth, for a total of about

$$N(1 + 1/t + 1/t^2 + 1/t^3 \ldots) = N/(1 - 1/t)$$

links in the whole list. ∎

Picking an appropriate value of t leads us immediately to a time–space tradeoff. When $t = 2$, skip lists need about $\lg N$ comparisons and $2N$ links, on the average—performance comparable with the best that we have seen with BSTs. For larger t, the time for search and insert is longer, but the extra space for links is smaller. Differentiating the expression in Property 13.10, we find that the choice $t = e$ minimizes the expected number of comparisons for searching in a skip list. The following table gives the value of the coefficient of $N \lg N$ in the number of comparisons needed to construct a table of N items:

t	2	e	3	4	8	16
$\lg t$	1.00	1.44	1.58	2.00	3.00	4.00
$t/\lg t$	2.00	1.88	1.89	2.00	2.67	4.00

If doing comparisons, following links, and moving down recursively have costs that differ substantially, we can do a more refined calculation along these lines (see Exercise 13.83).

Because the search time is logarithmic, we can reduce the space overhead to not much more than that for singly linked lists (if space is tight) by increasing t. Precise estimates of running time depend on assessment of the relative costs of following links across the lists and the recursive calls to move down to the next level. We shall revisit this kind of time–space tradeoff again in Chapter 16, when we look at the problem of indexing huge files.

Other symbol-table methods are straightforward to implement with skip lists. For example, Program 13.10 gives an implementation of the *remove* operation, using the same recursive scheme that we used for *insert* in Program 13.9. To delete, we unlink the node from the lists at each level (where we linked it in for *insert*), and we free the

Program 13.10 Removal in skip lists

To remove a node with a given key from a skip list, we unlink it at each level that we find a link to it, then delete it when we reach the bottom level.

```
private void removeR(Node t, KEY v, int k)
  { Node x = t.next[k];
    if (!less(x.item.key(), v))
      {
  if (equals(v, x.item.key()))
        { t.next[k] = x.next[k]; }
        if (k == 0) return;
        removeR(t, v, k-1); return;
      }
    removeR(t.next[k], v, k);
  }
void remove(ITEM x)
  { removeR(head, x.key(), lgN); N--; }
```

node after unlinking it from the bottom list (as opposed to creating it before traversing the list for insert). To implement *join*, we merge the lists (see Exercise 13.78); to implement *select*, we add a field to each node that gives the number of nodes skipped by the highest-level link to it (see Exercise 13.77).

Although skip lists are easy to conceptualize as a systematic way to move quickly through a linked list, it is also important to understand that the underlying data structure is nothing more than an alternative representation of a balanced tree. For example, Figure 13.27 shows the skip-list representation of the balanced 2-3-4 tree in Figure 13.10. We can implement the balanced 2-3-4 tree algorithms of Section 13.3 using the skip-list abstraction, rather than the red–black tree abstraction of Section 13.4. The resulting code is somewhat more complicated than the implementations that we have considered (see Exercise 13.80). We shall revisit this relationship between skip lists and balanced trees in Chapter 16.

The ideal skip list illustrated in Figure 13.22 is a rigid structure that is as difficult to maintain, when we insert a new node, as is the ordered array for binary search, because the insertion involves

Figure 13.27
Skip-list representation of a 2-3-4 tree

This skip list is a representation of the 2-3-4 tree in Figure 13.10. In general, skip lists correspond to balanced multiway trees with one or more links per node (1-nodes, with no keys and 1 link, are allowed). To build the skip list corresponding to a tree, we give each node a number of links equal to its height in the tree, and then link the nodes horizontally. To build the tree corresponding to a skip list, we group skipped nodes and recursively link them to nodes at the next level.

changing all the links in all the nodes after the node inserted. One way to loosen the structure is to build lists where each link skips either one, two, or three links on the level below: this arrangement corresponds to 2-3-4 trees, as illustrated in Figure 13.27. The randomized algorithm discussed in this section is another effective way to loosen the structure; we shall consider other alternatives in Chapter 16.

Exercises

13.75 Draw the skip list that results when you insert items with the keys E A S Y Q U T I O N in that order into an initially empty list, assuming that `randX` returns the sequence of values 1, 3, 1, 1, 2, 2, 1, 4, 1, and 1.

▷ **13.76** Draw the skip list that results when you insert items with the keys A E I N O Q S T U Y in that order into an initially empty list, assuming the same `randX` return values as for Exercise 13.75.

13.77 Implement the *select* operation for a skip-list–based symbol table.

• **13.78** Implement the *join* operation for a skip-list–based symbol table.

▷ **13.79** Modify the implementations of *search* and *insert* given in Program 13.7 and Program 13.9 to end lists with a sentinel node, instead of `null`.

○ **13.80** Use skip lists to implement *construct*, *search*, and *insert* for symbol tables with the balanced 2-3-4 tree abstraction.

○ **13.81** How many random numbers are needed, on the average, to build a skip list with parameter t, using the `randX` method in Program 13.9?

○ **13.82** For $t = 2$, modify Program 13.9 to eliminate the `for` loop in `randX`. *Hint*: The final j bits in the binary representation of a number t assume any particular j-bit value with probability $1/2^j$.

13.83 Choose the value of t that minimizes the search cost for the case that following a link costs α times as much as doing a comparison and that moving down one level of recursion costs β times as much as doing a comparison.

○ **13.84** Develop a skip-list implementation that has the references themselves in the nodes instead of the reference to an array of references that we used in Programs 13.7 through 13.10.

13.6 Performance Characteristics

How do we choose among randomized BSTs, splay BSTs, red–black BSTs, and skip lists for a particular application? We have concentrated on the differing nature of these algorithms' performance guarantees. Time and space are always primary considerations, but we must also consider a number of other factors. In this section, we shall briefly discuss implementation issues, empirical studies, estimates of running time, and space requirements.

All the tree-based algorithms depend on rotations; implementation of rotations along the search path is an essential ingredient of most balanced tree algorithms. We have used recursive implementations that implicitly save references to nodes on the search path in local variables on the recursion stack, but each of the algorithms can be implemented in a nonrecursive fashion, operating on a constant number of nodes and performing a constant number of link operations per node in one top-down pass through the tree.

Randomized BSTs are the simplest to implement of the three tree-based algorithms. The prime requirements are to have confidence in the random-number generator and to avoid spending too much time generating the random bits. Splay BSTs are slightly more complicated but are a straightforward extension to the standard root-insertion algorithm. Red–black BSTs involve slightly more code stillf in order to check and manipulate the color bits. One advantage of red–black trees over the other two is that the color bits can be used for both a consistency check for debugging and for a guarantee of a quick search at any time during the lifetime of the tree. There is no way to know from examining a splay BST whether or not the code that produced it made all the proper transformations; a bug might lead (only!) to performance problems. Similarly, a bug in the random-number generator for randomized BSTs or skip lists could lead to otherwise unnoticed performance problems.

Skip lists are easy to implement and are particularly attractive if a full range of symbol-table operations is to be supported, because *search*, *insert*, *remove*, *join*, *select*, and *sort* all have natural implementations that are easy to formulate. The inner loop for searching in skip lists is longer than that for trees (it involves an additional index into the link array or an additional recursive call to move down a level), so the time for search and insert is longer. Skip lists also put the programmer at the mercy of the random-number generator—debugging a program whose behavior is random is a challenge, and some programmers find it particularly unsettling to work with nodes having a random number of links.

Table 13.1 gives empirical data on both the performance of the four methods that we have discussed in this chapter and on the elementary BST implementations from Chapter 12, for keys that are random 32-bit integers. The information in this table confirms what we expect from the analytic results in Sections 13.2, 13.4, and 13.5. Red–black BSTs are much faster than the others for random keys. Paths in red–black BSTs are 35 percent shorter than in randomized or splay BSTs, and there is less work to do in the inner loop. Randomized trees and skip lists require that we generate at least one new random number for every insertion, and splay BSTs involve a rotation at every node for every insertion and every search. By contrast, the overhead for red–black BSTs is that we check the value of 2 bits at every node during insertion and occasionally need to do a rotation. For nonuniform access, splay BSTs may involve shorter paths, but this savings is likely to be offset by the fact that both search and insertion involve rotations at every node in the inner loop, except possibly in extreme cases.

Splay BSTs require no extra space for balance information, red–black BSTs require 1 extra bit, and randomized BSTs require a count field. For many applications, the count field is maintained for other reasons, so it may not represent an extra cost for randomized BSTs. Indeed, we might need to *add* this field if we use splay BSTs, red–black BSTs, or skip lists. If necessary, we can make red–black BSTs as space-efficient as splay BSTs by eliminating the color bit (see Exercise 13.65). In modern applications, space is less critical than it once was, but the careful programmer still needs to be vigilant against waste. For example, we need to be aware that some systems might use a whole 32-bit word for a small count field or a 1-bit color field in a node, and that some other systems might pack the fields in memory such that unpacking them requires a significant amount of extra time. If space is tight, skip lists with large t can reduce by nearly one-half the space for links, at the cost of a slower—but still logarithmic—search. With some programming, the tree-based methods can also be implemented with one link per node (see Exercise 12.68).

Table 13.1 Empirical study of balanced tree implementations

These relative timings for building and searching BSTs from random sequences of N 32-bit integers, for various values of N, indicate that all the methods have good performance, even for huge tables, but that red–black trees are significantly faster than are the other methods. All the methods use standard BST search, except splay BSTs, where we splay on search to bring frequently accessed keys near the top, and skip lists, which use essentially the same algorithm with a different underlying data structure.

N	construction						search misses					
	B	T	T*	S	R	L	B	T	T*	S	R	L
1250	20	28	28	10	14	15	11	10	10	10	10	16
2500	10	36	40	24	25	21	15	12	11	12	11	19
5000	22	33	65	145	42	35	26	26	26	27	19	46
12500	90	128	197	267	92	145	75	74	86	80	60	145
25000	167	569	492	215	181	385	175	180	212	195	158	355
50000	381	648	1105	1125	430	892	420	415	505	433	359	878
100000	1004	2593	2656	1148	1190	3257	1047	1041	1357	1113	861	2094
200000	2628	6121	6341	2784	2936	7493	2553	2573	2893	2649	2114	5109

Key:
- B Standard BST(Program 12.15)
- T BST built by root insertion (Program 12.19)
- T* Randomized BST (Program 13.2)
- S Splay BST(Exercise 13.33 and Program 13.5)
- R Red–black BST (Program 13.6)
- L Skip list (Programs 13.7 and 13.9)

In summary, all the methods that we have discussed in this chapter will provide good performance for typical applications, and each has its virtues for people interested in developing a high-performance symbol-table implementation. Splay BSTs will provide good performance as a self-organizing search method, particularly when frequent access to a small set of keys is a typical pattern; randomized BSTs are likely to be faster and easier to implement for a fully functional symbol table BST; skip lists are easy to understand and can provide logarithmic search with less space than the other methods, and red–black BSTs are attractive for symbol-table library implementations, because they provide guaranteed performance bounds in the worst case and the fastest search and insertion algorithms for random data.

Beyond specific uses in applications, this panoply of solutions to the problem of developing efficient implementations of the symbol-table ADT is important because it illustrates fundamental approaches to algorithm design that are available to us when we consider solutions to other problems. In our constant quest for simple, optimal algorithms, we often encounter useful near-optimal algorithms, such as the ones discussed here. Moreover, as we saw with sorting, comparison-based algorithms such as these are only the beginning of the story—by moving to a lower-level abstraction, where we can process pieces of keys, we can develop implementations that are even faster than the ones discussed in this chapter, as we shall see in Chapters 14 and 15.

Exercises

13.85 Develop a symbol-table implementation using randomized BSTs that includes a `clone` implementation and supports the *construct*, *count*, *search*, *insert*, *remove*, and *join* operations for a symbol-table ADT, with support for client handles (see Exercises 12.6 and 12.7).

13.86 Develop a symbol-table implementation using skip lists that includes a `clone` implementation and supports the *construct*, *count*, *search*, *insert*, *remove*, and *join* operations for a symbol-table ADT, with support for client handles (see Exercises 12.6 and 12.7).

CHAPTER FOURTEEN

Hashing

T HE SEARCH ALGORITHMS that we have been considering are
based on an abstract comparison operation. A significant exception to this assertion is the key-indexed search method in Section 12.2,
where we store the item with key i in table position i, ready for immediate access. Key-indexed search uses key values as array indices rather
than comparing them and depends on the keys being distinct integers
falling in the same range as the table indices. In this chapter, we consider *hashing*, an extension of key-indexed search which handles more
typical search applications where we do not happen to have keys with
such fortuitous properties. The end result is a completely different
approach to search from the comparison-based methods—rather than
navigating through dictionary data structures by comparing search
keys with keys in items, we try to reference items in a table directly by
doing arithmetic operations to transform keys into table addresses.

Search algorithms that use hashing consist of two separate parts.
The first step is to compute a *hash function* that transforms the search
key into a table address. Ideally, different keys would map to different addresses, but often two or more different keys may hash to
the same table address. Thus, the second part of a hashing search is
a *collision-resolution* process that deals with such keys. One of the
collision-resolution methods that we shall study uses linked lists and
is thus immediately useful in dynamic situations where the number of
search keys is difficult to predict in advance. The other two collision-
resolution methods that we shall examine achieve fast search times on
items stored within a fixed array. We shall also examine a way to

.513870656	51
.175725579	17
.308633685	30
.534531713	53
.947630227	94
.171727657	17
.702230930	70
.226416826	22
.494766086	49
.124698631	12
.083895385	8
.389629811	38
.277230144	27
.368053228	36
.983458996	98
.535386205	53
.765678883	76
.646473587	64
.767143786	76
.780236185	78
.822962105	82
.151921138	15
.625476837	62
.314676344	31
.346903890	34

Figure 14.1
Multiplicative hash function for floating-point keys

To transform floating-point numbers between 0 and 1 into table indices for a table of size 97, we multiply by 97. In this example, there are three collisions: at 17, 53, and 76. The most significant bits of the keys determine the hash values; the least significant bits of the keys play no role. One goal of hash-function design is to avoid such imbalance by having each bit of data play a role in the computation.

improve these methods to handle the case where we cannot predict the table size in advance.

Hashing is a good example of a *time–space tradeoff*. If there were no memory limitation, then we could do any search with only one memory access by simply using the key as a memory address, as in key-indexed search. This ideal often cannot be achieved, however, because the amount of memory required is prohibitive when the keys are long. On the other hand, if there were no time limitation, then we could get by with only a minimum amount of memory by using a sequential search method. Hashing provides a way to use a reasonable amount of both memory and time to strike a balance between these two extremes. In particular, we can strike any balance we choose, merely by adjusting hash table size, not by rewriting code or choosing different algorithms.

Hashing is a classical computer-science problem: The various algorithms have been studied in depth and are widely used. We shall see that, under generous assumptions, it is not unreasonable to expect to support the *search* and *insert* symbol-table operations in *constant* time, independent of the size of the table.

This expectation is the theoretical optimum performance for any symbol-table implementation, but hashing is not a panacea, for two primary reasons. First, the running time does depend on the length of the key, which can be a liability in practical applications with long keys. Second, hashing does not provide efficient implementations for other symbol-table operations, such as *select* or *sort*. We shall examine these and other matters in detail in this chapter.

14.1 Hash Functions

The first problem that we must address is the computation of the hash function, which transforms keys into table addresses. This arithmetic computation is normally simple to implement, but we must proceed with caution to avoid various subtle pitfalls. If we have a table that can hold M items, then we need a function that transforms keys into integers in the range $[0, M - 1]$. An ideal hash function is easy to compute and approximates a random function: For each input, every output should be in some sense equally likely.

The hash function depends on the key type. Strictly speaking, we need a different hash function for each kind of key that might be used. For efficiency, we generally want to avoid explicit type conversion, striving instead for a throwback to the idea of considering the binary representation of keys in a machine word as an integer that we can use for arithmetic computations. Hashing predates high-level languages—on early computers, it was common practice to view a value as a string key at one moment and an integer the next. Some high-level languages make it difficult to write programs that depend on how keys are represented on a particular computer, because such programs, by their very nature, are machine dependent and therefore are difficult to transfer to a new or different computer. Hash functions generally are dependent on the process of transforming keys to integers, so machine independence and efficiency are sometimes difficult to achieve simultaneously in hashing implementations. We can typically hash simple integer or floating-point keys with just a single machine operation, but string keys and other types of compound keys require more care and more attention to efficiency.

The proper place to implement a hash function in the symbol-table ADT interface that we have been using is as a method in the Key class. If desired, we could also include it in the KEY interface, which would require all implementations of Key to have a hash function implementation. (Java goes one step further and requires all Objects to have a hashCode method.) For clarity, simplicity, and flexibility, we treat the hashing primitive the same way that we have treated the less comparison primitive: we assume that all Key implementations have a hash method, but in our symbol-table implementations we use a static hash method that takes a KEY parameter. For example, this allows us to change KEY to be a primitive type without otherwise changing our code. For the rest of this section, we consider hash-method implementations for various types of keys.

Perhaps the simplest situation is when the keys are floating-point numbers known to be in a fixed range. For example, if the keys are numbers that are greater than 0 and less than 1, we can just multiply by M and round off to the nearest integer to get an address between 0 and $M - 1$; an example is given in Figure 14.1. If the keys are greater than s and less than t for any fixed s and t, we can rescale by subtracting s

16838	57	38	6
5758	35	58	58
10113	25	13	50
17515	55	15	24
31051	11	51	90
5627	1	27	77
23010	21	10	20
7419	47	19	85
16212	13	12	19
4086	12	86	25
2749	33	49	98
12767	60	67	90
9084	63	84	14
12060	32	60	53
32225	21	25	16
17543	83	43	42
25089	63	89	5
21183	37	83	91
25137	14	37	35
25566	55	66	0
26966	0	66	65
4978	31	78	76
20495	28	95	66
10311	29	11	72
11367	18	67	25

Figure 14.2
Modular hash functions for integer keys

The three rightmost columns show the result of hashing the 16-bit keys on the left with these functions:

v % 97 (left)

v % 100 (center) and

*(int) (a * v) % 100 (right) where a = .618033. The table sizes for these functions are 97, 100, and 100, respectively. The values appear random (because the keys are random). The center function (v % 100) uses just the rightmost two digits of the keys and is therefore susceptible to bad performance for nonrandom keys.*

now	6733767	1816567	55	29
for	6333762	1685490	50	20
tip	7232360	1914096	48	1
ilk	6473153	1734251	43	18
dim	6232355	1651949	45	21
tag	7230347	1913063	39	22
jot	6533764	1751028	52	24
sob	7173742	1898466	34	26
nob	6733742	1816546	34	8
sky	7172771	1897977	57	2
hut	6435364	1719028	52	16
ace	6070745	1602021	37	3
bet	6131364	1618676	52	11
men	6671356	1798894	46	26
egg	6271747	1668071	39	23
few	6331367	1684215	55	16
jay	6530371	1749241	57	4
owl	6775754	1833964	44	4
joy	6533771	1751033	57	29
rap	7130360	1880304	48	30
gig	6372347	1701095	39	1
wee	7371345	1962725	37	22
was	7370363	1962227	51	20
cab	6170342	1634530	34	24
wad	7370344	1962212	36	5

Figure 14.3
Modular hash functions for encoded characters

Each line in this table shows a 3-character word, that word's ASCII encoding as a 21-bit number in octal and decimal, and standard modular hash functions for table sizes 64 and 31, respectively (rightmost two columns). The table size 64 leads to undesirable results, because only the rightmost bits of the keys contribute to the hash value, and characters in natural-language words are not evenly distributed. For example, all words ending in y *hash to the value 57. By contrast, the prime value 31 leads to fewer collisions in a table less than one-half the size.*

and dividing by $t - s$, which puts them between 0 and 1, then multiply by M to get a table address.

If the keys are w-bit integers, we can convert them to floating-point numbers and divide by 2^w to get floating-point numbers between 0 and 1, then multiply by M as in the previous paragraph. If floating-point operations are expensive and the numbers are not so large as to cause overflow, we can accomplish the same result with integer arithmetic operations: Multiply the key by M, then shift right w bits to divide by 2^w (or, if the multiply would overflow, shift then multiply). Such methods are not useful for hashing unless the keys are evenly distributed in the range, because the hash value is determined only by the leading digits of the keys.

A simpler and more efficient method for w-bit integers—one that is perhaps the most commonly used method for hashing—is to choose the table size M to be prime, and, for any integer key k, to compute the remainder when dividing k by M, or $h(k) = k \bmod M$. Such a function is called a *modular* hash function. It is very easy to compute (k % M, in Java), and is effective in dispersing the key values evenly among the values less than M. Figure 14.2 gives a small example.

We can also use modular hashing for floating-point keys. If the keys are in a small range, we can scale to convert them to numbers between 0 and 1, multiply by 2^w to get a w-bit integer result, then use a modular hash function. Another alternative is just to use the binary representation of the key (if available) as the operand for the modular hash function.

Modular hashing applies whenever we have access to the bits that our keys comprise, whether they are integers represented in a machine word, a sequence of characters packed into a machine word, or any of a myriad of other possibilities. A sequence of random characters packed into a machine word is not quite the same as a random integer key, because some of the bits are used for encoding purposes, but we can make both (and any other type of key that is encoded so as to fit in a machine word) *appear* to be random indices into a small table.

Figure 14.3 illustrates the primary reason that we choose the hash table size M to be prime for modular hashing. In this example, for character data with 7-bit encoding, we treat the key as a base-128 number—one digit for each character in the key. The word now corresponds to the number 1816567, which also can be written as

$$110 \cdot 128^2 + 111 \cdot 128^1 + 119 \cdot 128^0$$

since the ASCII encodings of n, o, and w are $156_8 = 110$, $157_8 = 111$, and $167_8 = 119$, respectively. Now, the choice of table size $M = 64$ is unfortunate for this type of key, because the value of $x \bmod 64$ is unaffected by the addition of multiples of 64 (or 128) to x—the hash function of any key is the value of that key's last 6 bits. Surely a good hash function should take into account all the bits of a key, particularly for keys made up of characters. Similar effects can arise whenever M has a factor that is a power of 2. The simplest way to avoid such effects is to make M prime.

Modular hashing is completely trivial to implement except for the requirement that we make the table size prime. For some applications, we can be content with a small known prime, or we can look up a prime number close to the table size that we want in a list of known primes. For example, numbers of the form $2^t - 1$ are prime for $t = 2$, 3, 5, 7, 13, 17, 19, and 31 (and no other $t < 31$): these are the famous *Mersenne primes*. To allocate a table of a certain size dynamically, we would need to compute a prime number close to a certain value. This calculation is not a trivial one (although there is a clever algorithm for the task, which we shall examine in Part 8); so, in practice, a common solution is to use a precomputed table (see Figure 14.4). Use of modular hashing is not the only reason to make a table size prime; we shall consider another reason in Section 14.4.

Another alternative for integer keys is to combine the multiplicative and modular methods: Multiply the key by a constant between 0 and 1, then reduce it modulo M. That is, use the function $h(k) = \lfloor k\alpha \rfloor \bmod M$. There is interplay among the values of α, M, and the effective radix of the key that could possibly result in anomalous behavior, but if we use an arbitrary value of α, we are not likely to encounter trouble in a practical application. A popular choice for α is $\phi = 0.618033\ldots$ (the *golden ratio*). Many other variations on this theme have been studied, particularly hash functions that can be implemented with efficient machine instructions such as shifting and masking (*see reference section*).

In many applications where symbol tables are used, the keys are not numbers and are not necessarily short but rather are alphanumeric

n	δ_n	$2^n - \delta_n$
8	5	251
9	3	509
10	3	1021
11	9	2039
12	3	4093
13	1	8191
14	3	16381
15	19	32749
16	15	65521
17	1	131071
18	5	262139
19	1	524287
20	3	1048573
21	9	2097143
22	3	4194301
23	15	8388593
24	3	16777213
25	39	33554393
26	5	67108859
27	39	134217689
28	57	268435399
29	3	536870909
30	35	1073741789
31	1	2147483647

Figure 14.4
Prime numbers for hash tables

This table of the largest prime less than 2^n for $8 \le n \le 32$ can be used to dynamically allocate a hash table when it is required that the table size be prime. For any given positive value in the range covered, we can use this table to get a prime number within a factor of 2 of that value.

> ## Program 14.1 Hash function for string keys
>
> This implementation of a hash function for string keys involves one multiplication and one addition per character in the key. If we were to replace the constant 127 by 128, the program would simply compute the remainder when the number corresponding to the 7-bit ASCII representation of the key was divided by the table size, using Horner's method. The prime base 127 helps us to avoid anomalies if the table size is a power of 2 or a multiple of 2.
>
> ```
> static int hash(String s, int M)
>   {
>     int h = 0, a = 127;
>     for (int i = 0; i < s.length(); i++)
>       h = (a*h + s.charAt(i)) % M;
>     return h;
>   }
> ```

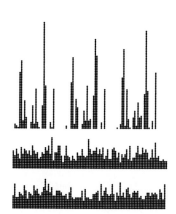

Figure 14.5
Hash functions for character strings

These diagrams show the dispersion for a set of English words (the first 1000 distinct words of Melville's Moby Dick) using Program 14.1 with

M = 96 and a = 128 (top)
M = 97 and a = 128 (center)and
M = 96 and a = 127 (bottom)

Poor dispersion in the first instance results from the combination of uneven usage of the letters and the common factor 32 in the table size and multiplier, which preserves the unevenness. The other two instances appear random because the table size and the multiplier are relatively prime.

strings and possibly are long. How do we compute the hash function for a word such as

averylongkey?

In 7-bit ASCII, this word corresponds to the 84-bit number

$$97 \cdot 128^{11} + 118 \cdot 128^{10} + 101 \cdot 128^9 + 114 \cdot 128^8 + 121 \cdot 128^7$$
$$+ 108 \cdot 128^6 + 111 \cdot 128^5 + 110 \cdot 128^4 + 103 \cdot 128^3$$
$$+ 107 \cdot 128^2 + 101 \cdot 128^1 + 121 \cdot 128^0,$$

which is too large to be represented for normal arithmetic operations in most computers. Moreover, we should be able to handle keys that are much longer.

To compute a modular hash function for long keys, we transform the keys piece by piece. We can take advantage of arithmetic properties of the mod function and use Horner's algorithm (see Section 4.10). This method is based on yet another way of writing the number corresponding to keys. For our example, we write the following expression:

$$(((((((((97 \cdot 128 + 118) \cdot 128 + 101) \cdot 128 + 114) \cdot 128 + 121) \cdot 128$$
$$+ 108) \cdot 128 + 111) \cdot 128 + 110) \cdot 128 + 103) \cdot 128$$
$$+ 107) \cdot 128 + 101) \cdot 128 + 121.$$

That is, we can compute the decimal number corresponding to the character encoding of a string by proceeding left to right, multiplying the accumulated value by 128, then adding the encoded value of the next character. This computation would eventually produce a number larger than we can represent in our machine for a long string, but we are not interested in computing the number; we want just its remainder when divided by M, which is small. We can get our result without ever carrying a large accumulated value, because we can cast out multiples of M at any point during this computation—we need to keep only the remainder modulo M each time that we do a multiply and add—and we get the same result as we would if we had the capability to compute the long number, then to do the division (see Exercise 14.10). This observation leads to a direct arithmetic way to compute modular hash functions for long strings; see Program 14.1. The program uses one final twist: It uses the prime 127 instead of the base 128. The reason for this change is discussed in the next paragraph.

There are many ways to compute hash functions at approximately the same cost as doing modular hashing using Horner's method (one or two arithmetic operations for each character in the key). For random keys, the methods hardly differ, but real keys are hardly random. The opportunity to economically make real keys appear to be random leads us to consider *randomized* algorithms for hashing—we want hash functions that produce random table indices, no matter what the keys are. Randomization is not difficult to arrange, because there is no requirement that we stick to the letter of the definition of modular hashing—we merely want to involve all the bits of the key in a computation that produces an integer less than M. Program 14.1 shows one way to do that: Use a prime base, instead of the power of 2 called for in the definition of the integer corresponding to the ASCII representation of the string. Figure 14.5 illustrates how this change avoids poor dispersion for typical string keys. The hash values produced by Program 14.1 could theoretically be bad for table sizes that are a multiple of 127 (although these effects are likely to be minimal in practice); we could choose the multiplier value at random to produce a randomized algorithm. An even more effective approach is to use *random* values for the coefficients in the computation, and a *different* random value for each digit in the key. This approach gives a randomized algorithm called *universal hashing*.

A theoretically ideal universal hash function is one for which the chance of a collision between two distinct keys in a table of size M is precisely $1/M$. It is possible to prove that using a sequence of different random values, instead of a fixed arbitrary value, for the coefficient a in Program 14.1 turns modular hashing into a universal hash function. Rather than maintaining an array with a different random number for each character in the key, we approximate universal hashing in the practical compromise shown in Program 14.2: We vary the coefficients by generating a simple pseudo-random sequence.

In summary, to use hashing for an abstract symbol-table implementation, the first step is to extend the abstract type interface to include a hash operation that maps keys into nonnegative integers less than M, the table size. The direct implementation

```
static int hash(double v, int M)
  { return (int) M*(v-s)/(t-s); }
```

does the job for floating-point keys between the values s and t; for integer keys, we can simply return v % M. If M is not prime, the hash function might return

```
(int) (.616161 * (double) v) % M
```

or the result of a similar integer computation such as

```
(16161 * v) % M .
```

All of these functions, including Program 14.1 for string keys, are venerable ones that usually spread out the keys and have served programmers well for years. The universal method of Program 14.2 is a distinct improvement for string keys that provides random hash values at little extra cost, and we can craft similar randomized methods for integer keys (see Exercise 14.1).

Universal hashing could prove to be much slower than simpler methods in a given application, because doing two arithmetic operations for each character of the key could be overly time-consuming for long keys. To respond to this objection, we can process the key in bigger pieces. Indeed, we may as well use the largest pieces that can fit into a machine word, as in elementary modular hashing. As we discussed in detail previously, an operation of this kind can be difficult or require special loopholes in some strongly typed high-level languages; but it can be inexpensive or require absolutely no work in Java if we use casting among appropriate data-representation formats. These factors

---

Program 14.2 Universal hash function (for string keys)

This program does the same computations as Program 14.1, but using pseudorandom coefficient values instead of a fixed radix, to approximate the ideal of having a collision between two given nonequal keys occur with probability $1/M$. We use a crude random-number generator to avoid spending excessive time on computing the hash function.

```
static int hashU(String s, int M)
  {
    int h = 0, a = 31415, b = 27183;
    for (int i = 0; i < s.length(); i++)
      {
        h = (a*h + s.charAt(i)) % M;
        a = a*b % (M-1);
      }
    return h;
  }
```

---

are important to consider in many situations because the computation of the hash function might be in the inner loop; by speeding up the hash function, we might speed up the whole computation.

Despite the evidence in favor of these methods, care is required in implementing them, for two reasons. First, we have to be vigilant in avoiding bugs when converting among types and using arithmetic functions on various different machine representations of keys. Such operations are notorious sources of error, particularly when a program is converted from an old machine to a new one with a different number of bits per word or with other precision differences. Second, the hash-function computation is likely to fall in the inner loop in many applications, and its running time may well dominate the total running time. In such cases, it is important to be sure that it reduces to efficient machine code.

Excessive use of type conversion and arithmetic operations are notorious sources of inefficiency—for example, the difference in running time between the simple modular method for integers and the version where we convert an integer Key to first be multiplied by 0.61616 can be startling in the absence of simple low-level optimizations.

The fastest method of all, for many machines, is to make M a power of 2, and to use the hash function

```
static int hash(int v, int M)
  { return v & (M-1); }
```

This method simply accesses the $\lg M - 1$ least-significant bits of the keys. The bitwise *and* operation may be sufficiently faster and simpler than competing calculations to offset any ill effects from poor key dispersion.

A bug that typically arises in hashing implementations is for the hash method always to return the same value, perhaps because an intended type conversion did not take place properly. Such a bug is called a *performance* bug because a program using such a hash method is likely to run correctly but be extremely slow (because it was designed to be efficient only when the hash values are well dispersed). The one-line implementations of these methods are so easy to test that we are well advised to check how well they perform for the types of keys that are to be encountered for any particular symbol-table implementation.

We can use a χ^2 statistic to test the hypothesis that a hash method produces random values (see Exercise 14.5), but this requirement is perhaps too stringent. Indeed, we might be happy if the hash method produced each value the same number of times, which corresponds to a χ^2 statistic that is equal to 0 and is decidedly not random. Still, we should be suspicious of huge χ^2 statistics. In practice, it probably suffices to test that the values are sufficiently well dispersed that no value dominates (see Exercise 14.15). In the same spirit, a well-engineered implementation of a symbol-table implementation based on universal hashing might occasionally check that hash values are not poorly dispersed. The client might be informed that *either* a low-probability event has happened *or* there is a bug in the hash method. This kind of check would be a wise addition to any practical randomized algorithm.

Exercises

▷ **14.1** Using the `digit` abstraction from Chapter 10 to treat a machine word as a sequence of bytes, implement a randomized hash method for keys represented as bits in machine words.

14.2 Check whether there is any execution-time overhead in converting from a 4-byte key to a 32-bit integer in your programming environment.

○ **14.3** Develop a hash method for string keys based on the idea of loading 4 bytes at a time, then performing arithmetic operations on 32 bits at a time.

Compare the time required for this method with the times for Program 14.1 for 4-, 8-, 16-, and 32-byte keys.

14.4 Write a program to find values of a and M, with M as small as possible, such that the hash function a*x % M produces distinct values (no collisions) for the keys in Figure 14.2. The result is an example of a *perfect hash function*.

○ **14.5** Write a program to compute the χ^2 statistic for the hash values of N keys with table size M. This number is defined by the equation

$$\chi^2 = \frac{M}{N} \sum_{0 \leq i < M} \left(f_i - \frac{N}{M}\right)^2,$$

where f_i is the number of keys with hash value i. If the hash values are random, this statistic, for $N > cM$, should be $M \pm \sqrt{M}$ with probability $1 - 1/c$.

14.6 Use your program from Exercise 14.5 to evaluate the hash function 618033*x % 10000 for keys that are random positive integers less than 10^6.

14.7 Use your program from Exercise 14.5 to evaluate the hash function in Program 14.1 for distinct string keys taken from some large file on your system, such as a dictionary.

● **14.8** Suppose that keys are t-bit integers. For a modular hash function with prime M, prove that each key bit has the property that there exist two keys differing only in that bit with different hash values.

14.9 Consider the idea of implementing modular hashing for integer keys with the code (a*x) % M, where a is an arbitrary fixed prime. Does this change mix up the bits sufficiently well that you can use nonprime M?

14.10 Prove that $(((ax) \bmod M) + b) \bmod M = (ax + b) \bmod M$, assuming that a, b, x, and M are all nonnegative integers.

▷ **14.11** If you use the words from a text file, such as a book, in Exercise 14.7, you are unlikely to get a good χ^2 statistic. Explain why this assertion is true.

14.12 Use your program from Exercise 14.5 to evaluate the hash function 97*x % M, for all table sizes between 100 and 200, using 10^3 random positive integers less than 10^6 as keys.

14.13 Use your program from Exercise 14.5 to evaluate the hash function 97*x % M, for all table sizes between 100 and 200, using the integers between 10^2 and 10^3 as keys.

14.14 Use your program from Exercise 14.5 to evaluate the hash function 100*x % M, for all table sizes between 100 and 200, using 10^3 random positive integers less than 10^6 as keys.

14.15 Do Exercises 14.12 and 14.14, but use the simpler criterion of rejecting hash functions that produce any value more than $3N/M$ times.

14.2 Separate Chaining

The hash methods discussed in Section 14.1 convert keys into table addresses; the second component of a hashing algorithm is to decide how to handle the case when two keys hash to the same address. The most straightforward method is to build, for each table address, a linked list of the items whose keys hash to that address. This approach leads directly to the generalization of elementary list search (see Chapter 12) that is given in Program 14.3. Rather than maintaining a single list, we maintain M lists.

This method is traditionally called *separate chaining*, because items that collide are chained together in separate linked lists. An example is depicted in Figure 14.6. As with elementary sequential search, we can choose to keep the lists in sorted order, or we can leave them unordered. The same basic tradeoffs as those discussed in Section 12.3 apply, but, for separate chaining, the time savings are less significant (because the lists are short) and the space usage is more significant (because there are so many lists).

We might be using a header node to streamline the code for insertion into an ordered list, but we might not want to use M header nodes for individual lists in separate chaining. Indeed, for items that are primitive types, we could even eliminate the M links to the lists by having the first nodes in the lists comprise the table (see Exercise 14.20).

For a search miss, we can assume that the hash method scrambles the key values sufficiently well that each of the M lists is equally likely to be searched. Then the performance characteristics that we studied in Section 12.3 apply, for each list.

Property 14.1 *Separate chaining reduces the number of comparisons for sequential search by a factor of M (on the average), using extra space for M links.*

The average length of the lists is N/M. As described in Chapter 12, successful searches are expected to go about halfway down some list. Unsuccessful searches go to the end of a list if the lists are unordered, halfway down a list if the lists are kept in order. ∎

Most often, we use unordered lists for separate chaining, because that approach is both easy to implement and efficient: *insert* takes constant time and *search* takes time proportional to N/M. If huge numbers of

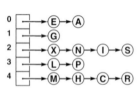

Figure 14.6
Hashing with separate chaining

This diagram shows the result of inserting the keys A S E R C H I N G X M P L into an initially empty hash table with separate chaining (unordered lists), using the hash values given at the top. The A goes into list 0, then the S goes into list 2, then the E goes into list 0 (at the front, to keep the insertion time constant), then the R goes into list 4, and so forth.

Program 14.3 Hashing with separate chaining

This symbol-table implementation is based on replacing the ST constructor, search, and insert methods in the linked-list–based symbol table
of Program 12.9 with the methods given here, and then replacing the
link head with an array of links heads. We use the same recursive list
search and deletion methods as in Program 12.9, but we maintain M
lists, with head links in heads, using a hash function to choose among
the lists. The constructor sets M such that we expect the lists to have
about five items each; therefore the other operations require just a few
probes.

```
private Node[] heads;
private int N, M;
ST(int maxN)
   { N = 0; M = maxN/5; heads = new Node[M]; }
ITEM search(KEY key)
   { return searchR(heads[hash(key, M)], key); }
void insert(ITEM x)
   { int i = hash(x.key(), M);
     heads[i] = new Node(x, heads[i]); N++; }
```

---

search misses are expected, we can speed up the misses by a factor of
2 by keeping the lists ordered, at the cost of a slower *insert*.

As stated, Property 14.1 is a trivial result, because the average
length of the lists is N/M, no matter how the items are distributed
among the lists. For example, suppose that all the items fall onto the
first list. Then, the average length of the lists is $(N+0+0+\ldots+0)/M =
N/M$. The real reason that hashing is useful in practice is that *each*
list is extremely likely to have about N/M items.

Property 14.2 *In a separate-chaining hash table with M lists and N
keys, the probability that the number of keys in each list is within a
small constant factor of N/M is extremely close to 1.*

We briefly consider this classical analysis, for readers who are familiar
with basic probabilistic analysis. The probability that a given list will
have k items on it is

$$\binom{N}{k}\left(\frac{1}{M}\right)^{k}\left(1-\frac{1}{M}\right)^{N-k}$$

by an elementary argument. We choose k out of the N items: Those k items hash to the given list with probability $1/M$, and the other $N - k$ items do not hash to the given list with probability $1 - (1/M)$. In terms of $\alpha = N/M$, we can rewrite this expression as

$$\binom{N}{k} \left(\frac{\alpha}{N}\right)^k \left(1 - \frac{\alpha}{N}\right)^{N-k},$$

which, by the classical Poisson approximation, is less than

$$\frac{\alpha^k e^{-\alpha}}{k!}.$$

From this result, it follows that the probability that a list has more than $t\alpha$ items on it is less than

$$\left(\frac{\alpha e}{t}\right)^t e^{-\alpha}.$$

This probability is extremely small for practical ranges of the parameters. For example, if the average length of the lists is 20, the probability that we will hash to some list with more than 40 items on it is less than $(40e/2)^2 e^{-20} \approx 0.0000016$. ∎

The foregoing analysis is an example of a classical *occupancy problem*, where we consider N balls thrown randomly into one of M urns and analyze how the balls are distributed among the urns. Classical mathematical analysis of these problems tells us many other interesting facts that are relevant to the study of hashing algorithms. For example, the Poisson approximation tells us that the number of empty lists is about $e^{-\alpha}$. A more interesting result tells us that the average number of items inserted before the first collision occurs is about $\sqrt{\pi M/2} \approx 1.25\sqrt{M}$. This result is the solution to the classical *birthday problem*. For example, the same analysis tells us, for $M = 365$, that the average number of people we need to check before finding two with the same birthday is about 24. A second classical result tells us that the average number of items inserted before each list has at least one item is about $M H_M$. This result is the solution to the classical *coupon collector* problem. For example, the same analysis tells us, for $M = 1280$, that we would expect to collect 9898 baseball cards (coupons) before getting one for each of 40 players on each of 32 teams in a series. These results are indicative of the properties of hashing that have been analyzed. In practice, they tell us that we can use separate chaining with great confidence, if the hash method produces values that approximate random ones (*see reference section*).

In a separate-chaining implementation, we typically choose M to be small enough that we are not wasting a huge area of contiguous memory with empty links but large enough that sequential search is the most efficient method for the lists. Hybrid methods (such as using binary trees instead of linked lists) are probably not worth the trouble. As a rule of thumb, we might choose M to be about one-fifth or one-tenth the number of keys expected be be in the table so that the lists are expected to contain about five or 10 keys each. One of the virtues of separate chaining is that this decision is not critical: if more keys arrive than expected, then searches will take a little longer than if we had chosen a bigger table size ahead of time; if fewer keys are in the table, then we have extra-fast *search* with perhaps a small amount of wasted space. When space is not a critical resource, M can be chosen sufficiently large that search time is constant; when space *is* a critical resource, we still can get a factor of M improvement in performance by choosing M to be as large as we can afford.

The comments in the previous paragraph apply to search time. In practice, unordered lists are normally used for separate chaining, for two primary reasons. First, as we have mentioned, *insert* is extremely fast: We compute the hash function, allocate memory for the node, and link in the node at the beginning of the appropriate list. In many applications, the memory-allocation step is not needed (because the items inserted into the symbol table may be existing records with available link fields), and we are left with perhaps three or four machine instructions for *insert*. The second important advantage of using the unordered-list implementation in Program 14.3 is that the lists all function as stacks, so we can easily remove the most recently inserted items, which are at the front of the lists (see Exercise 14.21). This operation is an important one when we are implementing a symbol table with nested scopes (for example in a compiler).

As in several previous implementations, we implicitly give the client a choice for handling duplicate keys. A client like Program 12.12 might *search* to check for duplicates before any *insert*, thus ensuring that the table does not contain any duplicate keys. Another client might avoid the cost of this *search* by leaving duplicates in the table, thus achieving fast *insert* operations.

Generally, hashing is not appropriate for use in applications where implementations for the *sort* and *select* ADT operations are required. However, hashing is often used for the typical situation where we need to use a symbol table with potentially a large number of *search*, *insert*, and *remove* operations, then to print out the items in order of their keys once, at the end. One example of such an application is a symbol table in a compiler; another is a program to remove duplicates, such as Program 12.12. To handle this situation in an unordered-list implementation of separate chaining, we would have to use one of the sorting methods described in Chapters 6 through 10; in an ordered-list implementation, we could accomplish the sort in time proportional to $N \lg M$ with list mergesort (see Exercise 14.23).

Exercises

▷ **14.16** How long could it take in the worst case to insert N keys into an initially empty table, using separate chaining with (*i*) unordered lists and (*ii*) ordered lists?

▷ **14.17** Give the contents of the hash table that results when you insert items with the keys E A S Y Q U T I O N in that order into an initially empty table of $M = 5$ lists, using separate chaining with unordered lists. Use the hash function $11k \bmod M$ to transform the kth letter of the alphabet into a table index.

▷ **14.18** Answer Exercise 14.17, but use ordered lists. Does your answer depend on the order in which you insert the items?

○ **14.19** Write a program that inserts N random integers into a table of size $N/100$ using separate chaining, then finds the length of the shortest and longest lists, for $N = 10^3$, 10^4, 10^5, and 10^6.

14.20 Suppose that items are `double` keys (no associated information). Modify Program 14.3 to eliminate the head links by representing the symbol table as an array of `nodes` (each table entry is the first node in its list).

14.21 Modify Program 14.3 to include an integer field for each item that is set to the number of items in the table at the time the item is inserted. Then implement a method that deletes all items for which the field is greater than a given integer N.

14.22 Modify the implementation of `search` in Program 14.3 to show all the items with keys equal to a given key, in the same manner as `show`.

14.23 Develop a symbol-table implementation using separate chaining with ordered lists that includes a `clone` implementation and supports the *construct*, *count*, *search*, *insert*, *remove*, *join*, *select*, and *sort* operations, with support for client handles (see Exercises 12.6 and 12.7).

14.3 Linear Probing

If we can estimate in advance the number of elements to be put into the hash table and have enough contiguous memory available to hold all the keys with some room to spare, then it is probably not worthwhile to use any links at all in the hash table. Several methods have been devised that store N items in a table of size $M > N$, relying on empty places in the table to help with collision resolution. Such methods are called *open-addressing* hashing methods.

The simplest open-addressing method is called *linear probing*: when there is a collision (when we hash to a place in the table that is already occupied with an item whose key is not the same as the search key), then we just check the next position in the table. It is customary to refer to such a check (determining whether or not a given table position holds an item with key equal to the search key) as a *probe*. Linear probing is characterized by identifying three possible outcomes of a probe: if the table position contains an item whose key matches the search key, then we have a search hit; if the table position is empty, then we have a search miss; otherwise (if the table position contains an item whose key does not match the search key) we just probe the table position with the next higher index, continuing (wrapping back to the beginning of the table if we reach the end) until either the search key or an empty table position is found. If an item containing the search key is to be inserted following an unsuccessful search, then we put it into the empty table space that terminated the search. Program 14.4 is an implementation of the symbol-table ADT using this method. The process of constructing a hash table for a sample set of keys using linear probing is shown in Figure 14.7.

As with separate chaining, the performance of open-addressing methods is dependent on the ratio $\alpha = N/M$, but we interpret it differently. For separate chaining, α is the average number of items per list and is generally larger than 1. For open addressing, α is the percentage of those table positions that are occupied; it must be less than 1. We sometimes refer to α as the *load factor* of the hash table.

For a sparse table (small α), we expect most searches to find an empty position with just a few probes. For a nearly full table (α close to 1), a search could require a huge number of probes and even fall into an infinite loop when the table is completely full. Typically, to avoid

Figure 14.7
Hashing with linear probing

This diagram shows the process of inserting the keys A S E R C H I N G X M P into an initially empty hash table of size 13 with open addressing, using the hash values given at the top and resolving collisions with linear probing. First, the A goes into position 7, then the S goes into position 3, then the E goes into position 9, then the R goes into position 10 after a collision at position 9, and so forth. Probe sequences that run off the right end of the table continue on the left end: for example, the final key inserted, the P, hashes to position 8, then ends up in position 5 after collisions at positions 8 through 12, then 0 through 5. All table positions not probed are shaded.

Program 14.4 Linear probing

This symbol-table implementation keeps references to items in a table twice the size of the maximum number of items expected.

    To insert a new item, we hash to a table position and scan to the right to find an unoccupied position, using null entries as sentinels in unoccupied positions in precisely the same manner as in we did in key-indexed search (Program 12.7). To search for an item with a given key, we go to the key hash position and scan to look for a match, stopping when we hit an unoccupied position.

    The constructor sets M such that we may expect the table to be less than half full, so the other operations will require just a few probes, if the hash function produces values that are similar to random ones.

```
private ITEM[] st;
private int N, M;
ST(int maxN)
  { N = 0; M = 2*maxN; st = new ITEM[M]; }
void insert(ITEM x)
  { int i = hash(x.key(), M);
    while (st[i] != null) i = (i+1) % M;
    st[i] = x; N++;
  }
ITEM search(KEY key)
  { int i = hash(key, M);
    while (st[i] != null)
      if (equals(key, st[i].key())) return st[i];
      else i = (i+1) % M;
    return null;
  }
```

---

long search times, we insist that the table *not* be allowed to become nearly full when using linear probing. That is, rather than using extra memory for links, we use it for extra space in the hash table that shortens probe sequences. The table size for linear probing is greater than for separate chaining, since we must have $M > N$, but the total amount of memory space used may be less, since no links are used. We will discuss space-usage comparisons in detail in Section 14.5; for the moment, we consider the analysis of the running time of linear probing as a function of α.

The average cost of linear probing depends on the way in which the items cluster together into contiguous groups of occupied table cells, called *clusters*, when they are inserted. Consider the following two extremes in a linear probing table that is half full ($M = 2N$): In the best case, table positions with even indices could be empty, and table positions with odd indices could be occupied. In the worst case, the first half of the table positions could be empty, and the second half occupied. The average length of the clusters in both cases is $N/(2N) = 1/2$, but the average number of probes for an unsuccessful search is 1 (all searches take at least 1 probe) plus

$$(0 + 1 + 0 + 1 + \ldots)/(2N) = 1/2$$

in the best case, and is 1 plus

$$(N + (N - 1) + (N - 2) + \ldots)/(2N) \approx N/4$$

in the worst case.

Generalizing this argument, we find that the average number of probes for an unsuccessful search is proportional to the *squares* of the lengths of the clusters. We compute the average by computing the cost of a search miss starting at each position in the table, then dividing the total by M. All search misses take at least 1 probe, so we count the number of probes after the first. If a cluster is of length t, then the expression

$$(t + (t - 1) + \ldots + 2 + 1)/M = t(t + 1)/(2M)$$

counts the contribution of that cluster to the grand total. The sum of the cluster lengths is N, so, adding this cost for all cells in the table, we find that the total average cost for a search miss is $1 + N/(2M)$ plus the sum of the squares of the lengths of the clusters, divided by $2M$. Given a table, we can quickly compute the average cost of unsuccessful search in that table (see Exercise 14.28), but the clusters are formed by a complicated dynamic process (the linear-probing algorithm) that is difficult to characterize analytically.

Despite the relatively simple form of the results, precise analysis of linear probing is a challenging task. Knuth's derviation of the following formulas in 1962 was a landmark in the analysis of algorithms (*see reference section*):

M S H P
0 3 4 8

G Ⓧ M S H P   A C E R I N
G   M S H P   A C E R I N

G   S H P   A C E R I N
G Ⓜ   S H P   A C E R I N

G M   H P   A C E R I N
G M   Ⓢ H P   A C E R I N

G M   S   P   A C E R I N
G M   S Ⓗ P   A C E R I N

G M   S H   A C E R I N
G M Ⓟ S H   A C E R I N

0 1 2 3 4 5 6 7 8 9 10 11 12

Figure 14.8
Removal in a linear-probing hash table

This diagram shows the process of removing the X from the table in Figure 14.7. The second line shows the result of just taking the X out of the table and is an unacceptable final result because the M and the P are cut off from their hash positions by the empty table position left by the X. Thus, we reinsert the M, S, H, and P (the keys to the right of the X in the same cluster) in that order, using the hash values given at the top and resolving collisions with linear probing. The M fills the hole left by the X, then the S and the H hash into the table without collisions, then the P winds up in position 2.

Property 14.3 *When collisions are resolved with linear probing, the average number of probes required to search in a hash table of size M that contains $N = \alpha M$ keys is about*

$$\frac{1}{2}\left(1 + \frac{1}{1-\alpha}\right) \qquad and \qquad \frac{1}{2}\left(1 + \frac{1}{(1-\alpha)^2}\right)$$

for hits and misses, respectively.

These estimates lose accuracy as α approaches 1, but we do not need them for that case, because we should not be using linear probing in a nearly full table in any event. For smaller α, the equations are sufficiently accurate. The following table summarizes the expected number of probes for search hits and misses with linear probing:

load factor (α)	1/2	2/3	3/4	9/10
search hit	1.5	2.0	3.0	5.5
search miss	2.5	5.0	8.5	55.5

Search misses are always more expensive than hits, and we expect that both require only a few probes in a table that is less than half full. ∎

As we did with separate chaining, we leave to the client the choice of whether or not to keep items with duplicate keys in the table. Such items do not necessarily appear in contiguous positions in a linear probing table—other items with the same hash value can appear among items with duplicate keys.

By the very nature of the way the table is constructed, the keys in a table built with linear probing are in random order. The *sort* and *select* ADT operations require starting from scratch with one of the methods described in Chapters 6 through 10, so linear probing is not appropriate for applications where these operations are frequent.

How do we delete a key from a table built with linear probing? We cannot just remove it, because items that were inserted later might have skipped over that item, so searches for those items would terminate prematurely at the hole left by the deleted item. One solution to this problem is to rehash all the items for which this problem could arise—those between the deleted one and the next unoccupied position to the right. Figure 14.8 shows an example illustrating this process; Program 14.5 is an implementation. In a sparse table, this repair process will require only a few rehash operations, at most. Another way to implement deletion is to replace the deleted key with a sentinel key

---

Program 14.5 Removal from a linear-probing hash table

To remove an item with a given key, we search for such an item and replace it with `null`. Then, we need to correct for the possibility that some item that lies to the right of the now-unoccupied position originally hashed to that position or to its left, because the vacancy would terminate a search for such an item. Therefore, we reinsert all the items in the same cluster as the removed item and to that item's right. Since the table is less than half full, the number of items that are reinserted will be small, on the average.

```
public void remove(ITEM x)
  { int i = hash(x.key(), M);
    while (st[i] != null)
      if (equals(x.key(), st[i].key())) break;
      else i = (i+1) % M;
    if (st[i] == null) return;
    st[i] = null; N--;
    for (int j = i+1; st[j] != null; j = (j+1) % M)
      { x = st[j]; st[j] = null; insert(x); N--; }
  }
```

---

that can serve as a placeholder for searches but can be identified and reused for insertions (see Exercise 14.33).

Exercises

▷ **14.24** How long could it take, in the worst case, to insert N keys into an initially empty table, using linear probing?

▷ **14.25** Give the contents of the hash table that results when you insert items with the keys E A S Y Q U T I O N in that order into an initially empty table of size $M = 16$ using linear probing. Use the hash function $11k \bmod M$ to transform the kth letter of the alphabet into a table index.

14.26 Do Exercise 14.25 for $M = 10$.

○ **14.27** Write a program that inserts 10^5 random nonnegative integers less than 10^6 into a table of size 10^5 using linear probing, and that plots the total number of probes used for each 10^3 consecutive insertions.

14.28 Write a program that inserts $N/2$ random integers into a table of size N using linear probing, then computes the average cost of a search miss in the resulting table from the cluster lengths, for $N = 10^3$, 10^4, 10^5, and 10^6.

14.29 Write a program that inserts $N/2$ random integers into a table of size N using linear probing, then computes the average cost of a search hit in the resulting table, for $N = 10^3$, 10^4, 10^5, and 10^6. Do *not* search for all the keys at the end (keep track of the cost of constructing the table).

• **14.30** Run experiments to determine whether the average cost of search hits or search misses changes as a long sequence of alternating random insertions and deletions using Programs 14.4 and 14.5 is made in a hash table of size $2N$ with N keys, for $N = 10$, 100, and 1000, and for up to N^2 insertion–deletion pairs for each N.

14.4 Double Hashing

The operative principle of linear probing (and indeed of any hashing method) is a guarantee that, when we are searching for a particular key, we look at every key that hashes to the same table address (in particular, the key itself, if it is in the table). In an open addressing scheme, however, other keys are typically also examined, particularly when the table begins to fill up. In the example depicted in Figure 14.7, a search for N involves looking at C, E, R, and I, none of which had the same hash value. What is worse, insertion of a key with one hash value can drastically increase the search times for keys with other hash values: in Figure 14.7, the insertion of M caused increased search times for positions 7–12 and 0–1. This phenomenon is called *clustering* because it has to do with the process of cluster formation. It can make linear probing run slowly for nearly full tables.

Fortunately, there is an easy way to virtually eliminate the clustering problem: *double hashing*. The basic strategy is the same as for linear probing; the only difference is that, instead of examining each successive table position following a collision, we use a second hash method to get a fixed increment to use for the probe sequence. An implementation is given in Program 14.6.

The second hash function must be chosen with some care, since otherwise the program may not work at all. First, we must exclude the case where the second hash function evaluates to 0, since that would lead to an infinite loop on the very first collision. Second, it is important that the value of the second hash function be relatively prime to the table size, since otherwise some of the probe sequences could be very short (for example, consider the case where the table size is twice the value of the second hash function). One way to enforce this policy is to make M prime and to choose a second hash function

Program 14.6 Double hashing

Double hashing is the same as linear probing except that we use a second hash function to determine the search increment to use after each collision. The search increment must be nonzero, and the table size and the search increment should be relatively prime. The `remove` method for linear probing (see Program 14.5) does *not* work with double hashing, because any key might be in many different probe sequences.

```
void insert(ITEM x)
  { KEY key = x.key();
    int i = hash(key, M); int k = hashtwo(key);
    while (st[i] != null) i = (i+k) % M;
    st[i] = x; N++;
  }
ITEM search(KEY key)
  { int i = hash(key, M); int k = hashtwo(key);
    while (st[i] != null)
      if (equals(key, st[i].key())) return st[i];
      else i = (i+k) % M;
    return null;
  }
```

that returns values that are less than M. In practice, a simple second hash function such as

```
static int hashtwo(int v) { return (v % 97) + 1; }
```

will suffice in many situations, when the table size is not small. Also in practice, any loss in efficiency stemming from the reduced dispersion that is due to this simplification is not likely to be noticeable, much less to be significant. If the table is huge and sparse, the table size itself does not need to be prime because just a few probes will be used for every search (although we might want to test for and abort long searches to guard against an infinite loop, if we cut this corner—see Exercise 14.38).

Figure 14.9 shows the process of building a small table with double hashing; Figure 14.10 shows that double hashing results in many fewer clusters (which are therefore much shorter) than the clusters left by linear probing.

A	S	E	R	C	H	I	N	G	X	M	P	L
7	3	9	9	8	4	11	7	10	12	0	8	6
1	3	1	5	5	5	3	3	2	3	5	4	2

Figure 14.9
Double hashing

This diagram shows the process of inserting the keys A S E R C H I N G X M P L into an initially empty hash table with open addressing, using the hash values given at the top and resolving collisions with double hashing. The first and second hash values for each key appear in the two rows below that key. As in Figure 14.7, table positions that are probed are unshaded. The A goes into position 7, then the S goes into position 3, then the E goes into position 9, as in Figure 14.7, but the R goes into position 1 after the collision at position 9, using its second hash value of 5 for the probe increment after collision. Similarly, P goes into position 6 on the final insertion after collisions at positions 8, 12, 3, 7, 11, and 2, using its second hash value 4 as the probe increment.

Property 14.4 *When collisions are resolved with double hashing, the average number of probes required to search in a hash table of size M that contains $N = \alpha M$ keys is*

$$\frac{1}{\alpha} \ln\left(\frac{1}{1-\alpha}\right) \qquad and \qquad \frac{1}{1-\alpha}$$

for hits and misses, respectively.

These formulas are the result of a deep mathematical analysis done by Guibas and Szemeredi (*see reference section*). The proof is based on showing that double hashing is nearly equivalent to a more complicated *random hashing* algorithm where we use a key-dependent sequence of probe positions with each probe equally likely to hit each table position. This algorithm is only an approximation to double hashing for many reasons: for example, we take pains in double hashing to ensure that we try every table position once, but random hashing could examine the same table position more than once. Still, for sparse tables, the probabilities of collisions for the two methods are similar. We are interested in both: Double hashing is easy to implement, whereas random hashing is easy to analyze.

The average cost of a search miss for random hashing is given by the equation

$$1 + \frac{N}{M} + \left(\frac{N}{M}\right)^2 + \left(\frac{N}{M}\right)^3 + \ldots = \frac{1}{1-(N/M)} = \frac{1}{1-\alpha}.$$

The expression on the left is the sum of the probability that a search miss uses more than k probes, for $k = 0, 1, 2, \ldots$ (and is equal to the average from elementary probability theory). A search always uses one probe, then needs a second probe with probability N/M, a third probe with probability $(N/M)^2$, and so forth. We can also use this formula to compute the following approximation to the average cost of a search hit in a table with N keys:

$$\frac{1}{N}\left(1 + \frac{1}{1-(1/M)} + \frac{1}{1-(2/M)} + \ldots + \frac{1}{1-((N-1)/M)}\right).$$

Each key in the table is equally likely to be hit; the cost of finding a key is the same as the cost of inserting it; and the cost of inserting the jth key in the table is the cost of a search miss in a table of $j - 1$ keys, so this formula is the average of those costs. Now, we can simplify

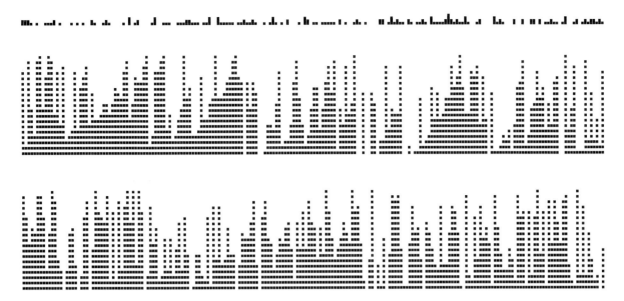

and evaluate this sum by multiplying the top and bottom of all the fractions by M:

$$\frac{1}{N}\left(1 + \frac{M}{M-1} + \frac{M}{M-2} + \cdots + \frac{M}{M-N+1}\right)$$

and further simplify to get the result

$$\frac{M}{N}(H_M - H_{M-N}) \approx \frac{1}{\alpha}\ln\left(\frac{1}{1-\alpha}\right),$$

since $H_M \approx \ln M$. ∎

The precise nature of the relationship between the performance of double hashing and the random-hashing ideal that was proven by Guibas and Szemeredi is an asymptotic result that need not be relevant for practical table sizes; moreover, the results rest on the assumption that the hash methods return random values. Still, the asymptotic formulas in Property 14.5 are accurate predictors of the performance of double hashing in practice, even when we use an easy-to-compute second hash function such as (v % 97)+1. As do the corresponding formulas for linear probing, these formulas approach infinity as α approaches 1, but they do so much more slowly.

The contrast between linear probing and double hashing is illustrated clearly in Figure 14.11. Double hashing and linear probing have

Figure 14.10
Clustering

These diagrams show the placement of records as we insert them into a hash table using linear probing (center) and double hashing (bottom), with the key value distribution shown at the top. Each line shows the result of inserting 10 records. As the table fills, the records cluster together into sequences separated by empty table positions. Long clusters are undesirable because the average cost of searching for one of the keys in the cluster is proportional to the cluster length. With linear probing, the longer clusters are, the more likely they are to increase in length, so a few long clusters dominate as the table fills up. With double hashing, this effect is much less pronounced, and the clusters remain relatively short.

similar performance for sparse tables, but we can allow the table to become more nearly full with double hashing than we can with linear probing before performance degrades. The following table summarizes the expected number of probes for search hits and misses with double hashing:

load factor (α)	1/2	2/3	3/4	9/10
search hit	1.4	1.6	1.8	2.6
search miss	1.5	2.0	3.0	5.5

Search misses are always more expensive than hits, and both require only a few probes, on the average, even in a table that is nine-tenths full.

Looking at the same results in another way, double hashing allows us to use a smaller table than we would need with linear probing to get the same average search times.

Property 14.5 *We can ensure that the average cost of all searches is less than t probes by keeping the load factor less than $1 - 1/\sqrt{t}$ for linear probing and less than $1 - 1/t$ for double hashing.*

Set the equations for search misses in Property 14.4 and Property 14.5 equal to t, and solve for α. ∎

For example, to ensure that the average number of probes for a search is less than 10, we need to keep the table at least 32 percent empty for linear probing, but only 10 percent empty for double hashing. If we have 10^5 items to process, we need space for just another 10^4 items to be able to do unsuccessful searches with fewer than 10 probes. By contrast, separate chaining would require more than 10^5 links, and BSTs would require twice that many.

The method of Program 14.5 for implementing the *remove* operation (rehash the keys that might have a search path containing the item to be deleted) breaks down for double hashing, because the deleted item might be in many different probe sequences, involving keys throughout the table. Thus, we have to resort to the other method that we considered at the end of Section 12.3: We replace the deleted item with a sentinel that marks the table position as occupied but does not match any key (see Exercise 14.33).

Figure 14.11
Costs of open-addressing search

These plots show the costs of building a hash table of size 1000 by inserting keys into an initially empty table using linear probing (top) *and double hashing* (bottom). *Each bar represents the cost of 20 keys. The gray curves show the costs predicted by theoretical analysis (see Properties 14.4 and 14.5).*

Like linear probing, double hashing is not an appropriate basis for implementing a full-function symbol table ADT where we need to support the *sort* or *select* operations.

Exercises

▷ **14.31** Give the contents of the hash table that results when you insert items with the keys E A S Y Q U T I O N in that order into an initially empty table of size $M = 16$ using double hashing. Use the hash function $11k \bmod M$ for the initial probe and the second hash function $(k \bmod 3) + 1$ for the search increment (when the key is the kth letter of the alphabet).

▷ **14.32** Answer Exercise 14.31 for $M = 10$

14.33 Implement deletion for double hashing, using a sentinel item.

14.34 Modify your solution to Exercise 14.27 to use double hashing.

14.35 Modify your solution to Exercise 14.28 to use double hashing.

14.36 Modify your solution to Exercise 14.29 to use double hashing.

○ **14.37** Implement an algorithm that approximates random hashing by providing the key as a seed to an in-line random number generator (as in Program 14.2).

14.38 Suppose that a table of size 10^6 is half full, with occupied positions chosen at random. Estimate the probability that all positions with indices divisible by 100 are occupied.

▷ **14.39** Suppose that you have a bug in your double-hashing code such that one or both of the hash methods always return the same value (not 0). Describe what happens in each of these situations: (*i*) when the first one is wrong, (*ii*) when the second one is wrong, and (*iii*) when both are wrong.

14.5 Dynamic Hash Tables

As the number of keys in a hash table increases, search performance degrades. With separate chaining, the search time increases gradually—when the number of keys in the table doubles, the search time doubles. The same is true of open-addressing methods such as linear probing and double hashing for sparse tables, but the cost increases dramatically as the table fills up, and, worse, we reach a point where no more keys can be inserted at all. This situation is in contrast to search trees, which accommodate growth naturally. For example, in a red–black tree, the search cost increases only slightly (by one comparison) whenever the number of nodes in the tree doubles.

Program 14.7 Dynamic hash insertion (for linear probing)

This implementation of insert for linear probing (see Program 14.4) handles an arbitrary number of keys by doubling the size of the table each time that the table becomes half full (this same approach can be used for double hashing or separate chaining). Doubling requires that we allocate memory for the new table and rehash all the keys into the new table.

```
private ITEM[] st;
private int N, M;
ST(int maxN)
  { N = 0; M = 4; st = new ITEM[M]; }
private void expand()
  {
    ITEM[] t = st;
    N = 0; M = M+M; st = new ITEM[M];
    for (int i = 0; i < M/2; i++)
      if (t[i] != null) insert(t[i]);
  }
void insert(ITEM x)
  { int i = hash(x.key(), M);
    while (st[i] != null) i = (i+1) % M;
    st[i] = x;
    if (N++ >= M/2) expand();
  }
```

One way to accomplish growth in a hash table is to double the table's size when it begins to fill up. Doubling the table is an expensive operation because everything in the table has to be reinserted, but it is an operation that is performed infrequently. Program 14.7 is an implementation of growth by doubling for linear probing. An example is depicted in Figure 14.12. The same solution also works for double hashing, and the basic idea applies to separate chaining as well (see Exercise 14.46). Each time that the table gets more than half full, we expand the table by doubling it in size. After the first expansion, the table is always between one-quarter and one-half full, so the search cost is less than three probes, on the average. Furthermore, although the operation of rebuilding the table is expensive, it happens

A S E R C H I N G X M P L
1 3
5 7 1 2
13 7 1 10 7 8 5 6
13 23 1 10 7 8 21 22 27 24 9 16 28

```
Ⓐ
A  Ⓢ
Ⓔ       A  S
E Ⓡ      A  S
E           S Ⓒ  R      A
E           S C Ⓗ R      A
E       Ⓘ   S C H R      A
E       I Ⓝ S C H R      A
E           C H   R      A           I N S           Ⓖ
E           C H   R      A           I N S Ⓧ         G
E           C H Ⓜ R      A           I N S X         G
E           C H M R      A    Ⓟ      I N S X         G
E           C H M R      A    P      I N S X         G Ⓛ
```

0 1 2 3 4 5 6 7 8 9 10 11 12 13 14 15 16 17 18 19 20 21 22 23 24 25 26 27 28 29 30 31

Figure 14.12
Dynamic hash-table expansion

This diagram shows the process of inserting the keys A S E R C H I N G X M P L into a dynamic hash table that expands by doubling, using the hash values given at the top and resolving collisions with linear probing. The four rows beneath the keys give the hash values when the table size is 4, 8, 16, and 32. The table size starts at 4, doubles to 8 for the E, to 16 for the C and to 32 for the G. All keys are rehashed and reinserted when the table size doubles. All insertions are into sparse tables (less than one-quarter full for reinsertion, between one-quarter and one-half full otherwise), so there are few collisions.

so infrequently that its cost represents only a constant fraction of the total cost of building the table.

Another way to express this concept is to say that the average cost *per insertion* is less than four probes. This assertion is not the same as saying that each insertion requires less than four probes on the average; indeed, we know that those insertions that cause the table to double will require a large number of probes. This argument is a simple example of *amortized analysis*: We cannot guarantee that each and every operation will be fast for this algorithm, but we can guarantee that the average cost per operation will be low.

Although the total cost is low, the performance profile for insertions is erratic: Most operations are extremely fast, but certain rare operations require about as much time as the whole previous cost of building the table. As a table grows from 1 thousand to 1 million keys, this slowdown will happen about 10 times. This kind of behavior is acceptable in many applications, but it might not be appropriate when absolute performance guarantees are desirable or required. For example, while a bank or an airline might be willing to suffer the consequences of keeping a customer waiting for so long on 10 out of every 1 million transactions, long waits might be catastrophic in other applications, such as an online system implementing a large financial transaction-processing system or in an air-traffic control system.

**Figure 14.13
Dynamic hashing**

This diagram shows the number of keys in the table (bottom) and the table size (top) when we insert keys into and remove them from a dynamic hash table using an algorithm that doubles the table when an insert makes it half full and halves the table when a removal makes it one-eighth full. The table size is initialized at 4 and is always a power of 2 (dotted lines in the figure are at powers of 2). The table size changes when the curve tracing the number of keys in the table crosses a dotted line for the first time after having crossed a different dotted line. The table is always between one-eighth and one-half full.

If we support the *remove* ADT operation, then it may be worthwhile to contract the table by halving it as it shrinks (see Exercise 14.44), with one proviso: The thresholds for shrinking have to be separated from those for growing, because otherwise a small number of *insert* and *remove* operations could cause a sequence of doubling and halving operations even for huge tables.

Property 14.6 *A sequence of t search, insert, and delete symbol-table operations can be executed in time proportional to t and with memory usage always within a constant factor of the number of keys in the table.*

We use linear probing with growth by doubling whenever an *insert* causes the number of keys in the table to be half the table size, and we use shrinkage by halving whenever a *remove* causes the number of keys in the table to be one-eighth the table size. In both cases, after the table is rebuilt to size N, it has $N/4$ keys. Then, $N/4$ *insert* operations must be executed before the table doubles again (by reinsertion of $N/2$ keys into a table of size $2N$), and $N/8$ *remove* operations must be executed before the table halves again (by reinsertion of $N/8$ keys into a table of size $N/2$). In both cases, the number of keys reinserted is within a factor of 2 of the number of operations that we performed to bring the table to the point of being rebuilt, so the total cost is linear. Furthermore, the table is always between one-eighth and one-fourth full (see Figure 14.13), so the average number of probes for each operation is less than 3, by Property 14.4. ∎

This method is appropriate for use in a symbol-table implementation for a general library where usage patterns are unpredictable, because it can handle tables of all sizes in a reasonable way. The primary drawback is the cost of rehashing and allocating memory when the table expands and shrinks; in the typical case, when searches predominate, the guarantee that the table is sparse leads to excellent performance. In Chapter 16, we shall consider another approach that avoids rehashing and is suitable for huge external search tables.

Exercises

▷ 14.40 Give the contents of the hash table that results when you insert items with the keys E A S Y Q U T I O N in that order into an initially empty table of initial size $M = 4$ that is expanded with doubling whenever half full, with collisions resolved using linear probing. Use the hash function $11k \bmod M$ to transform the kth letter of the alphabet into a table index.

14.41 Would it be more economical to expand a hash table by tripling (rather than doubling) the table in size when the table is half full?

14.42 Would it be more economical to expand a hash table by tripling the table in size when the table is one-third full (rather than doubling the table in size when the table is half full)?

14.43 Would it be more economical to expand a hash table by doubling the table in size when the table is three-quarters (rather than half) full?

14.44 Add to Program 14.7 a *remove* method that deletes an item as in Program 14.4 but then contracts the table by halving it if the deletion leaves it seven-eighths empty.

○ 14.45 Implement a version of Program 14.7 for separate chaining that increases the table size by a factor of 10 each time the average list length is equal to 10.

14.46 Modify Program 14.7 and your implementation from Exercise 14.44 to use double hashing with lazy deletion (see Exercise 14.33). Make sure that your program takes into account the number of dummy items, as well as the number of empty positions, in making the decisions whether to expand or contract the table.

14.47 Develop a symbol-table implementation using linear probing with dynamic tables that includes a `clone` implementation and supports the *construct*, *count*, *search*, *insert*, *remove*, and *join* symbol-table ADT operations, with support for client handles (see Exercises 12.6 and 12.7).

14.6 Perspective

The choice of the hashing method that is best suited for a particular application depends on many different factors, as we have discussed when examining the methods. All the methods can reduce the symbol-table *search* and *insert* operations to constant-time operations, and all are useful for a broad variety of applications. Roughly, we can characterize the three major methods (linear probing, double hashing, and separate chaining) as follows: Linear probing is the fastest of the three (if sufficient memory is available to ensure that the table is sparse), double hashing makes the most efficient use of memory (but requires extra time, to compute the second hash function), and separate chaining is the easiest to implement and deploy (provided that a good storage allocator is available). Table 14.1 gives empirical data and commentary on the performance of the algorithms.

The choice between linear probing and double hashing depends primarily on the cost of computing the hash function and on the load factor of the table. For sparse tables (small α), both methods use only a few probes, but double hashing could take more time because it has to compute two hash functions for long keys. As α approaches 1, double hashing far outperforms linear probing, as we saw in Figure 14.11.

Comparing linear probing and double hashing against separate chaining is more complicated, because we have to account precisely for memory usage. Separate chaining uses extra memory for links; the open-addressing methods use extra memory implicitly within the table to terminate probe sequences. The following concrete example illustrates the situation: Suppose that we have a table of M lists built with separate chaining, that the average length of the lists is 4, and that items and links each occupy a single machine word. The assumption that items and links take the same amount of space is justified in many situations because we would replace huge items with links to the items. With these assumptions, the table uses $9M$ words of memory ($4M$ for items and $5M$ for links), and delivers an average search time of 2 probes. But linear probing for $4M$ items in a table of size $9M$ requires just $(1 + 1/(1 - 4/9))/2 = 1.4$ probes for a search hit, a value that is 30 percent faster than separate chaining for the same amount of space; and linear probing for $4M$ items in a table of size $6M$ requires 2 probes for a search hit (on the average), and thus uses 33 percent less space than separate chaining for the same amount of time. Furthermore, we can use a dynamic method such as Program 14.7 to ensure that the table can grow while staying sparsely populated.

The argument in the previous paragraph indicates that it is not normally justifiable to choose separate chaining over open addressing on the basis of performance. However, separate chaining with a fixed

M is often chosen in practice for a host of other reasons: it is easy to implement (particularly *remove*); it requires little extra memory for items that have preallocated link fields for use by symbol-table and other ADTs that may need them; and, although its performance degrades as the number of items in the table grows, the degradation is graceful and takes place in a manner that is unlikely to harm the application because it still is a factor of M faster than sequential search.

Many other hashing methods have been developed that have application in special situations. Although we cannot go into details, we consider three examples briefly to illustrate the nature of specially adapted hashing methods.

One class of methods moves items around during insertion in double hashing to make successful search more efficient. In fact, Brent developed a method for which the average time for a successful search can be bounded by a constant, even in a full table (*see reference section*). Such a method might be useful in applications where search hits are the predominant operation.

Another method, called *ordered hashing*, exploits ordering to reduce the cost for unsuccessful search in linear probing to be close to the cost for successful search. In standard linear probing, we stop the search when we find an empty table position or an item with a key equal to the search key; in ordered hashing, we stop the search when we find an item with a key greater than or equal to the search key (the table must be constructed cleverly if this procedure is to work) (*see reference section*). This improvement by introducing ordering in the table is on the same order as what we achieved by ordering the lists in separate chaining. This method is designed for applications where search misses predominate.

A symbol table that has a fast search miss and somewhat slower search hit can be used to implement an *exception dictionary*. For example, a text-processing system might have an algorithm for hyphenating words that works well for most words, but does not work for bizarre cases (such as "bizarre"). Only a few words in a huge document are likely to be in the exception dictionary, so nearly all the searches are likely to be misses.

These examples are only a few of a large number of algorithmic improvements that have been suggested for hashing. Many of these improvements are interesting and have important applications.

Table 14.1 Empirical study of hash-table implementations

These relative timings for building and searching symbol tables from random sequences of 32-bit integers confirm that hashing is significantly faster than tree search for keys that are easily hashed. Among the hashing methods, double hashing is slower than separate chaining and linear probing for sparse tables (because of the cost of computing the second hash function) but is much faster than linear probing as the table fills, and is the only one of the methods that can provide fast search using only a small amount of extra memory. Dynamic hash tables built with linear probing and expansion by doubling are more costly to construct than are other hash tables because of memory allocation and rehashing, but they certainly lead to the fastest search times and represent the method of choice when search predominates and when the number of keys cannot be predicted accurately in advance.

	construction					search misses				
N	R	H	P	D	P*	R	H	P	D	P*
1250	7	13	19	11	2	3	2	1	1	1
2500	13	16	18	16	3	8	2	1	2	1
5000	22	16	25	10	5	19	7	3	3	3
12500	100	29	35	16	14	58	10	8	8	7
25000	201	41	31	29	45	145	25	18	19	17
50000	836	82	69	53	90	365	81	39	42	41
100000	1137	183	64	76	195	811	261	100	107	91
150000		303	110	166	385		591	248	216	135
160000		316	123	180	393		651	320	252	145
170000		325	143	190	386		773	455	298	157
180000		329	210	164	403		857	652	375	171
190000		429	259	187	424		948	1337	492	183
200000	2614	457			442	2058	997			196

Key:
R   Red–black BST (Programs 12.15 and 13.6)
H   Separate chaining (Program 14.3 with table size 20,000)
P   Linear probing (Program 14.4 with table size 200,000)
D   Double hashing (Program 14.6 with table size 200,000)
P* Linear probing with expansion by doubling (Program 14.7)

Our usual cautions must be raised against premature use of advanced methods except when the requirements are serious and the performance/complexity tradeoffs are carefully considered, because separate chaining, linear probing and double hashing are simple, efficient, and acceptable for most applications.

The problem of implementing an exception dictionary is an example of an application where we can recast our algorithm slightly to optimize performance for the most frequently performed operation—in this case, *search miss*. For example, suppose that we have a 1000-item exception dictionary, have 1 million items to look up in the dictionary, and expect virtually all the searches to end as misses. This situation might arise if the items were bizarre English-language words or random 32-bit integers. One way to proceed is to hash all the words to, say, 15-bit hash values (table size about 2^{16}). The 1000 exceptions occupy $\frac{1}{64}$ of the table, and most of the 1 million searches end immediately with search misses, finding the empty table position on the first probe. But if the table contains 32-bit words, we can do much better by converting it into a bit-exception table and using 20-bit hash values. If we have a search miss (as we do most of the time), we finish the search with one bit test; a search hit requires a secondary test in a smaller table. The exceptions occupy $\frac{1}{1000}$ of the table; search misses are by far the most likely operation; and we accomplish the task with 1 million directly indexed bit tests. This solution exploits the basic idea that a hash function produces a short *certificate* that represents a key—an essential concept that is useful in applications other than symbol-table implementations.

Hashing is preferred to the binary-tree structures of Chapters 12 and 13 as the symbol-table implementation for many applications, because it is somewhat simpler and can provide optimal (constant) search times, if the keys are of a standard type or are sufficiently simple that we can be confident of developing a good hash function for them. The advantages of binary-tree structures over hashing are that the trees are based on a simpler abstract interface (no hash function need be designed); the trees are dynamic (no advance information on the number of insertions is needed); the trees can provide guaranteed worst-case performance (everything could hash to the same place even in the best hashing method); and the trees support a wider range of operations (most important, *sort* and *select*). When these factors are not important, hashing is certainly the search method of choice, with one more important proviso: When keys are long strings, we can build them into data structures that can provide for search methods that are even faster than hashing. Such structures are the subject of Chapter 15.

Exercises

▷ **14.48** For 1 million integer keys, compute the hash-table size that makes each of the three hashing methods (separate chaining, linear probing, and double hashing) use the same number of key comparisons as BSTs for a search miss, on the average, counting the hash-function computation as a comparison.

▷ **14.49** For 1 million integer keys, compute the number of comparisons for each of the three hashing methods (separate chaining, linear probing, and double hashing) for a search miss, on the average, when they can use a total of 3 million words of memory (as BSTs would).

14.50 Implement a symbol-table ADT with fast *search miss* as described in the text, using separate chaining for secondary testing.

14.51 Do an empirical study to produce a table like Table 14.1 that compares linear probing with expansion by doubling with the Java `Hashtable` class.

CHAPTER FIFTEEN

Radix Search

S EVERAL SEARCH METHODS proceed by examining the search
keys one small piece at a time, rather than using full comparisons between keys at each step. These methods, called *radix-search
methods*, operate in a manner entirely analogous to the radix-sorting
methods that we discussed in Chapter 10. They are useful when the
pieces of the search keys are easily accessible, and they can provide
efficient solutions to a variety of practical search tasks.

We use the same abstract model that we used in Chapter 10: Depending on the context, a *key* may be a *word* (a fixed-length sequence
of bytes) or a *string* (a variable-length sequence of bytes). We treat keys
that are words as numbers represented in a base-R number system, for
various values of R (the *radix*), and work with individual digits of the
numbers. We view strings as variable-length numbers terminated by
a special symbol so that, for both fixed- and variable-length keys, we
can base all our algorithms on the abstract operation "extract the ith
digit from a key," including a convention to handle the case that the
key has fewer than i digits. Accordingly, all of our implementations
are based on the two-parameter static method digit from Chapter 10
that implements this operation. For clarity, we use the name bit when
R is 2.

This convention gives us the flexibility to accommodate complicated keys and items by defining an appripriate class or to accommodate simple keys by defining appropriate digit or bit methods for

635

Program 15.1 Binary key type

This code extends a key class such as Program 12.2, which defines
integer-valued keys, to provide radix methods with access to the key
bits. It provides a bit method that returns the indicated bit from the
key (an integer that is 0 or 1), the constants bitsword and R, and a
toString method that returns a representation of the key as a string of
bits.

```
class bitsKey extends myKey
  {
    public final static int bitsword = 31;
    public final static int R = 2;
    public int bit(int B)
      { return (val >> (bitsword-B-1)) & 1; }
    public String toString()
      { String s = "";
        for (int i = 0; i < bitsword; i++)
          s = s + bit(i);
        return s;
      }
  }
```

primitive types. For example, for integer keys, we could replace KEY
by int in our code and add to each class the following code:

```
private final static int bitsword = 31;
private final static int R = 2;
private int bit(int val, int B)
  { return (val >> (bitsword-B-1)) & 1; }
```

Program 15.1 illustrates how to achieve the same effect for class key
types by extending a key class to define the bit method (along with
B, bitsword, and toString). In this case, we would add to each class
the code

```
private final static int R = bitsKey.R;
private int bit(KEY v, int B)
  { return ((bitsKey) v).bit(B); }
```

The same approaches apply to implementing digit, using the techniques for various types of keys that are described in Section 10.1.
Program 15.9 in Section 15.4 is an example of such a class.

The principal advantages of radix-search methods are that the methods provide reasonable worst-case performance without the complication of balanced trees; they provide an easy way to handle variable-length keys; some of them allow space savings by storing part of the key implicitly within the search structure; and they can provide fast access to data, competitive with both binary search trees and hashing. The disadvantages are that some of the methods can make inefficient use of space and that, as with radix sorting, performance can suffer if efficient access to the bytes of the keys is not available.

First, we examine several search methods that proceed by examining the search keys 1 bit at a time, using them to travel through binary tree structures. We examine a series of methods, each one correcting a problem inherent in the previous one, culminating in an ingenious method that is useful for a variety of search applications.

Next, we examine generalizations to R-way trees. Again, we examine a series of methods, culminating in a flexible and efficient method that can support a basic symbol-table implementation and numerous extensions.

In radix search, we usually examine the most significant digits of the keys first. Many of the methods directly correspond to MSD radix-sorting methods, in the same way that BST-based search corresponds to quicksort. In particular, we shall see the analog to the linear-time sorts of Chapter 10—constant-time search methods based on the same principle.

We also consider the specific application of using radix-search structures for string processing, including building indexes for large text strings. The methods that we consider provide natural solutions for this application and help to set the stage for us to consider more advanced string-processing tasks in Part 6.

15.1 Digital Search Trees

The simplest radix-search method is based on the use of *digital search trees* (DSTs). The *search* and *insert* algorithms are identical to binary tree search and insertion except for one difference: We branch in the tree not according to the result of the comparison between the full keys but rather according to selected bits of the key. At the first level, the leading bit is used; at the second level, the second leading bit is

```
A 00001
S 10011
E 00101
R 10010
C 00011
H 01000
I 01001
N 01110
G 00111
X 11000
M 01101
P 10000
L 01100
```

**Figure 15.1
Binary representation of single-character keys**

As in Chapter 10, we use the 5-bit binary representation of i to represent the ith letter in the alphabet, as shown here for several sample keys, for the small examples in the figures in this chapter. We consider the bits as numbered from 0 to 4, from left to right.

Figure 15.2
Digital search tree and insertion

In an unsuccessful search for M = 01101 *in this sample digital search tree* (top), *we move left at the root (since the first bit in the binary representation of the key is* 0*), then right (since the second bit is* 1*), then right, then left, to finish at the null left link below* N*. To insert* M (bottom), *we replace the null link where the search ended with a link to the new node, just as we do with BST insertion.*

> **Program 15.2 Binary digital search tree**
>
> To develop a symbol-table implementation using DSTs, we modify the implementations of *search* and *insert* in the standard BST implementation (see Program 12.15) as shown in this implementation of *search*. Rather than doing a full key comparison, we decide whether to move left or right on the basis of testing a single bit (the leading bit) of the key. The recursive method invocations have a third parameter so that we can move the bit position to be tested to the right as we move down the tree. We use a private static bit method to test bits (*see text*). These same changes apply to the implementation of *insert*; otherwise, we use all the code from Program 12.15.
>
> ```
> private ITEM searchR(Node h, KEY v, int i)
>   {
>     if (h == null) return null;
>     if (equals(v, h.item.key())) return h.item;
>     if (bit(v, i) == 0)
>          return searchR(h.l, v, i+1);
>     else return searchR(h.r, v, i+1);
>   }
> ITEM search(KEY key)
>   { return searchR(head, key, 0); }
> ```

used; and so on, until an external node is encountered. Program 15.2 is an implementation of *search*; the implementation of *insert* is similar. Rather than using less to compare keys, we assume that a bit method is available to access individual bits in keys. This code is virtually the same as the code for binary tree search (see Program 12.15) but has substantially different performance characteristics, as we shall see.

We saw in Chapter 10 that we need to pay particular attention to equal keys in radix sorting; the same is true in radix search. Generally, we assume in this chapter that all the key values to appear in the symbol table are distinct. We can do so without loss of generality because we can use one of the methods discussed in Section 12.1 to support applications that have records with duplicate keys. It is important to focus on distinct key values in radix search, because key values are intrinsic components of several of the data structures that we shall consider.

Figure 15.1 gives binary representations for the one-letter keys used in other figures in the chapter. Figure 15.2 gives an example of insertion into a DST; Figure 15.3 shows the process of inserting keys into an initially empty tree.

The bits of the keys control search and insertion, but note that DSTs do not have the ordering property that characterizes BSTs. That is, it is *not* necessarily the case that nodes to the left of a given node have smaller keys or that nodes to the right have larger keys, as would be the case in a BST with distinct keys. It is true that keys on the left of a given node are smaller than keys on the right—if the node is at level k, they all agree in the first k bits, but the next bit is 0 for the keys on the left and is 1 for the keys on the right—but the node's key could itself could be the smallest, largest, or any value in between of all the keys in that node's subtree.

DSTs are characterized by the property that each key is *somewhere* along the path specified by the bits of the key (in order from left to right). This property is sufficient for the *search* and *insert* implementations in Program 15.2 to operate properly.

Suppose that the keys are words of a fixed length, all consisting of w bits. Our requirement that keys are distinct implies that $N \leq 2^w$, and we normally assume that N is significantly smaller than 2^w; otherwise, key-indexed search (see Section 12.2) would be the appropriate algorithm to use. Many practical problems fall within this range. For example, DSTs are appropriate for a symbol table containing up to 10^5 records with 32-bit keys (but perhaps not as many as 10^6 records) or for any number of 64-bit keys. Digital tree search also works for variable-length keys.

The worst case for trees built with digital search is much better than that for binary search trees, if the number of keys is large and the key lengths are small relative to the number of keys. The length of the longest path in a digital search tree is likely to be relatively small for many applications (for example, if the keys comprise random bits). In particular, the longest path is certainly limited by the length of the longest key; moreover, if the keys are of a fixed length, then the search time is limited by the length. Figure 15.4 illustrates this fact.

Property 15.1 *A search or insertion in a digital search tree requires about* $\lg N$ *comparisons on the average and about* $2 \lg N$ *comparisons*

Figure 15.3
Digital search tree construction

This sequence depicts the result of inserting the keys A S E R C H I N G into an initially empty digital search tree.

in the worst case, in a tree built from N random keys. The number of comparisons is never more than the number of bits in the search key.

We can establish the stated average-case and worst-case results for random keys with an argument similar to one given for a more natural problem in the next section, so we leave this proof for an exercise there (see Exercise 15.31). It is based on the simple intuitive notion that the unseen portion of a random key should be equally likely to begin with a 0 bit as a 1 bit, so half should fall on either side of any node. Each time that we move down the tree, we use up a key bit, so no search in a digital search tree can require more comparisons than there are bits in the search key. For the typical condition where we have w-bit words and the number of keys N is far smaller than the total possible number of keys 2^w, the path lengths are close to $\lg N$, so the number of comparisons is far smaller than the number of bits in the keys for random keys. ∎

Figure 15.5 shows a large digital search tree made from random 7-bit keys. This tree is nearly perfectly balanced. DSTs are attractive in many practical applications because they provide near-optimal performance even for huge problems, with little implementation effort. For example, a digital search tree built from 32-bit keys (or four 8-bit characters) is guaranteed to require fewer than 32 comparisons, and a digital search tree built from 64-bit keys (or eight 8-bit characters) is guaranteed to require fewer than 64 comparisons, even if there are billions of keys. For large N, these guarantees are comparable to the guarantee provided by red–black trees, but are achieved with about the same implementation effort as is required for standard BSTs (which can promise only guaranteed performance proportional to N^2). This feature makes the use of digital search trees an attractive alternative to use of balanced trees in practice for implementing the *search* and *insert* symbol-table operations, *provided* that efficient access to key bits is available.

Figure 15.4
Digital search tree, worst case

This sequence depicts the result of inserting the keys P = 10000, H = 01000, D = 00100, B = 00010, and A = 00001 into an initially empty digital search tree. The sequence of trees appears degenerate, but the path length is limited by the length of the binary representation of the keys. Except for 00000, no other 5-bit key will increase the height of the tree any further.

Exercises

▷ **15.1** Draw the DST that results when you insert items with the keys E A S Y Q U T I O N in that order into an initially empty tree, using the binary encoding given in Figure 15.1.

15.2 Give an insertion sequence for the keys A B C D E F G that results in a perfectly balanced DST that is also a valid BST.

Figure 15.5
Digital search tree example

This digital search tree, built by insertion of about 200 random keys, is as well balanced as its counterparts in Chapter 15.

15.3 Give an insertion sequence for the keys A B C D E F G that results in a perfectly balanced DST with the property that every node has a key smaller than those of all the nodes in its subtree.

▷ **15.4** Draw the DST that results when you insert items with the keys 0101-0011 00000111 00100001 01010001 11101100 00100001 10010101 01001010 in that order into an initially empty tree.

15.5 Can we keep records with duplicate keys in DSTs, in the same way that we can in BSTs? Explain your answer.

15.6 Run empirical studies to compare the height and internal path length of a DST built by insertion of N random 32-bit keys into an initially empty tree with the same measures of a standard binary search tree and a red–black tree (Chapter 13) built from the same keys, for $N = 10^3$, 10^4, 10^5, and 10^6.

○ **15.7** Give a full characterization of the worst-case internal path length of a DST with N distinct w-bit keys.

● **15.8** Implement the *remove* operation for a DST-based symbol table.

● **15.9** Implement the *select* operation for a DST-based symbol table.

○ **15.10** Describe how you could compute the height of a DST made from a given set of keys, in linear time, without building the DST.

15.2 Tries

In this section, we consider a search tree that allows us to use the bits of the keys to guide the search, in the same way that DSTs do, but that keeps the keys in the tree in order so that we can support recursive implementations of *sort* and other symbol-table operations, as we did for BSTs. The idea is to store keys only at the bottom of the tree, in leaf nodes. The resulting data structure has a number of useful properties and serves as the basis for several effective search algorithms. It was first discovered by de la Briandais in 1959, and, because it is useful for re*trie*val, it was given the name *trie* by Fredkin in 1960. Ironically, in conversation, we usually pronounce this word "try-ee" or just "try," so as to distinguish it from "tree." For consistency with the nomenclature that we have been using, we perhaps should use the name "binary search trie," but the term *trie* is universally used and understood. We consider the basic binary version in this section, an important variation in Section 15.3, and the basic multiway version and variations in Sections 15.4 and 15.5.

We can use tries for keys that are either a fixed number of bits or are variable-length bitstrings. To simplify the discussion, we start by assuming that no search key is the prefix of another. For example, this condition is satisfied when the keys are of fixed length and are distinct.

In a trie, we keep the keys in the *leaves* of a binary tree. Recall from Section 5.4 that a leaf in a tree is a node with no children, as distinguished from an external node, which we interpret as a null child. In a binary tree, a leaf is an internal node whose left and right links are both null. Keeping keys in leaves instead of internal nodes allows us to use the bits of the keys to guide the search, as we did with DSTs in Section 15.1, while still maintaining the basic invariant at each node that all keys whose current bit is 0 fall in the left subtree and all keys whose current bit is 1 fall in the right subtree.

Definition 15.1   *A* **trie** *is a binary tree that has keys associated with each of its leaves, defined recursively as follows: The trie for an empty set of keys is a null link; the trie for a single key is a leaf containing that key; and the trie for a set of keys of cardinality greater than one is an internal node with left link referring to the trie for the keys whose initial bit is 0 and right link referring to the trie for the keys whose initial bit is 1, with the leading bit considered to be removed for the purpose of constructing the subtrees.*

Each key in the trie is stored in a leaf, on the path described by the leading bit pattern of the key. Conversely, each leaf contains the only key in the trie that begins with the bits defined by the path from the root to that leaf. Null links in nodes that are not leaves correspond to leading-bit patterns that do not appear in any key in the trie. Therefore, to search for a key in a trie, we just branch according to its bits, as we did with DSTs, but we do not do comparisons at internal nodes. We start at the left of the key and the top of the trie and take the left link if the current bit is 0 and the right link if the current bit is 1, moving

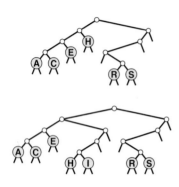

Figure 15.6
Trie search and insertion

Keys in a trie are stored in leaves (nodes with both links null); null links in nodes that are not leaves correspond to bit patterns not found in any keys in the trie.

In a successful search for the key H = 01000 in this sample trie (top), we move left at the root (since the first bit in the binary representation of the key is 0), then right (since the second bit is 1), where we find H, which is the only key in the tree that begins with 01. None of the keys in the trie begin with 101 or 11; these bit patterns lead to the two null links in the trie that are in non-leaf nodes.

To insert I (bottom), we need to add three non-leaf nodes: one corresponding to 01, with a null link corresponding to 011; one corresponding to 010, with a null link corresponding to 0101; and one corresponding to 0100 with H = 01000 in a leaf on its left and I = 01001 in a leaf on its right.

Program 15.3 Trie search

This method uses the bits of the key to control the branching on the way down the trie, in the same way as in Program 15.2 for DSTs. There are three possible outcomes: if the search reaches a leaf (with both links null), then that is the unique node in the trie that could contain the record with key v, so we test whether that node indeed contains v (search hit) or some key whose leading bits match v (search miss). If the search reaches a null link, then the parent's other link must not be null, so there is some other key in the trie that differs from the search key in the corresponding bit, and we have a search miss. This code assumes that the keys are distinct and (if the keys may be of different lengths) that no key is a prefix of another. The item member is not used in non-leaf nodes.

```
private ITEM searchR(Node h, KEY v, int d)
  {
    if (h == null) return null;
    if (h.l == null && h.r == null)
      { if (equals(v, h.item.key()))
          return h.item; else return null; }
    if (bit(v, d) == 0)
        return searchR(h.l, v, d+1);
    else return searchR(h.r, v, d+1);
  }
ITEM search(KEY key)
  { return searchR(head, key, 0); }
```

one bit position to the right in the key. A search that ends on a null link is a miss; a search that ends on a leaf can be completed with one key comparison, since that node contains the only key in the trie that could be equal to the search key. Program 15.3 is an implementation of this process.

To insert a key into a trie, we first perform a search, as usual. If the search ends on a null link, we replace that link with a link to a new leaf containing the key, as usual. But if the search ends on a leaf, we need to continue down the trie, adding an internal node for every bit where the search key and the key that was found agree, ending with both keys in leaves as children of the internal node corresponding to the first bit position where they differ. Figure 15.6 gives an example of

Program 15.4 Trie insertion

To insert a new node into a trie, we search as usual, then distinguish the two cases that can occur for a search miss.

    If the miss was not on a leaf, then we replace the null link that caused us to detect the miss with a link to a new node, as usual.

    If the miss was on a leaf, then we use a method split to make one new internal node for each bit position where the search key and the key found agree, finishing with one internal node for the leftmost bit position where the keys differ. The switch statement in split converts the two bits that it is testing into a number to handle the four possible cases. If the bits are the same (case $00_2 = 0$ or $11_2 = 3$), then we continue splitting; if the bits are different (case $01_2 = 1$ or $10_2 = 2$), then we stop splitting.

```
Node split(Node p, Node q, int d)
  { Node t = new Node(null);
    KEY v = p.item.key(), w = q.item.key();
    switch(bit(v, d)*2 + bit(w, d))
      { case 0: t.l = split(p, q, d+1); break;
        case 1: t.l = p; t.r = q; break;
        case 2: t.r = p; t.l = q; break;
        case 3: t.r = split(p, q, d+1); break;
      }
    return t;
  }
private Node insertR(Node h, ITEM x, int d)
  {
    if (h == null)
      return new Node(x);
    if (h.l == null && h.r == null)
      return split(new Node(x), h, d);
    if (bit(x.key(), d) == 0)
        h.l = insertR(h.l, x, d+1);
    else h.r = insertR(h.r, x, d+1);
    return h;
  }
void insert(ITEM x)
  { head = insertR(head, x, 0); }
```

trie search and insertion; Figure 15.7 shows the process of constructing a trie by inserting keys into an initially empty trie. Program 15.4 is a full implementation of the insertion algorithm.

We do not access null links in leaves, and we do not store items in non-leaf nodes, so we could save space by using a pair of derived classes to define nodes as being one of these two types (see Exercise 15.22). For the moment, we will take the simpler route of using the single node type that we have been using for BSTs, DSTs, and other binary tree structures, with internal nodes characterized by null keys and leaves characterized by null links, knowing that we could reclaim the space wasted because of this simplification, if desired. In Section 15.3, we will see an algorithmic improvement that avoids the need for multiple node types.

We now shall consider a number of basic properties of tries, which are evident from the definition and these examples.

Property 15.2 *The structure of a trie is independent of the key insertion order: There is a unique trie for any given set of distinct keys.*

This fundamental fact, which follows immediately by induction on the subtrees, is a distinctive feature of tries: for all of the other search tree structures that we have considered so far, the tree that we construct depends *both* on the set of keys *and* on the order in which we insert those keys. ∎

The left subtree of a trie has all the keys that have 0 for the leading bit; the right subtree has all the keys that have 1 for the leading bit. This property of tries leads to an immediate correspondence with radix sorting: binary trie search partitions the file in exactly the same way as does binary quicksort (see Section 10.3). This correspondence is evident when we compare the trie in Figure 15.6 with Figure 10.4, the partitioning diagram for binary quicksort (after noting that the keys are slightly different); it is analogous to the correspondence between binary tree search and quicksort that we noted in Chapter 12.

In particular, unlike DSTs, tries *do* have the property that keys appear in order, so we can implement the *sort* and *select* symbol-table operations in a straightforward manner (see Exercises 15.19 and 15.20). Moreover, tries are as well balanced as DSTs.

Property 15.3 *Insertion or search for a random key in a trie built from N random (distinct) bitstrings requires about $\lg N$ bit compar-*

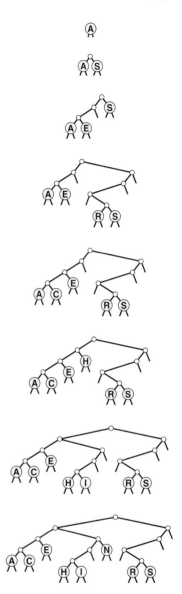

Figure 15.7
Trie construction

This sequence depicts the result of inserting the keys A S E R C H I N into an initially empty trie.

isons on the average. The worst-case number of bit comparisons is bounded only by the number of bits in the search key.

We need to exercise care in analyzing tries because of our insistence that the keys be distinct, or, more generally, that no key be a prefix of another. One simple model that accommodates this assumption requires the keys to be a random (infinite) sequence of bits—we take the bits that we need to build the trie.

The average-case result then comes from the following probabilistic argument: The probability that each of the N keys in a random trie differ from a random search key in at least one of the leading t bits is

$$\left(1 - \frac{1}{2^t}\right)^N.$$

Subtracting this quantity from 1 gives the probability that one of the keys in the trie matches the search key in all of the leading t bits. In other words,

$$1 - \left(1 - \frac{1}{2^t}\right)^N$$

is the probability that the search requires more than t bit comparisons. From elementary probabilistic analysis, the sum for $t \geq 0$ of the probabilities that a random variable is $> t$ is the average value of that random variable, so the average search cost is given by

$$\sum_{t \geq 0}\left(1 - \left(1 - \frac{1}{2^t}\right)^N\right).$$

Using the elementary approximation $(1 - 1/x)^x \sim e^{-1}$, we find the search cost to be approximately

$$\sum_{t \geq 0}\left(1 - e^{-N/2^t}\right).$$

The summand is extremely close to 1 for approximately $\lg N$ terms with 2^t substantially smaller than N; it is extremely close to 0 for all the terms with 2^t substantially greater than N; and it is somewhere between 0 and 1 for the few terms with $2^t \approx N$. So the grand total is about $\lg N$. Computing a more precise estimate of this quantity requires using extremely sophisticated mathematics (*see reference section*). This analysis assumes that w is sufficiently large that we never run out of bits during a search, but takes into account that the true value of w will only reduce the cost.

In the worst case, we could get two keys that have a huge number of equal bits, but this event happens with vanishingly small probability. The probability that the worst-case result quoted in Property 15.3 will not hold is exponentially small (see Exercise 15.30). ∎

Another approach to analyzing tries is to generalize the approach that we used to analyze BSTs (see Property 12.6). The probability that k keys start with a 0 bit and $N - k$ keys start with a 1 bit is $\binom{N}{k}/2^N$, so the external path length is described by the recurrence

$$C_N = N + \frac{1}{2^N} \sum_k \left(\binom{N}{k} (C_k + C_{N-k}) \right).$$

This recurrence is similar to the quicksort recurrence that we solved in Section 7.2, but it is much more difficult to solve. Remarkably, the solution is precisely N times the expression for the average search cost that we derived for Property 15.3 (see Exercise 15.27). Studying the recurrence itself gives insight into why tries have better balance than do BSTs: The probability is much higher that the split will be near the middle than that it will be anywhere else, so the recurrence is more like the mergesort recurrence (approximate solution $N \lg N$) than like the quicksort recurrence (approximate solution $2N \ln N$).

An annoying feature of tries, and another one that distinguishes them from the other types of search trees that we have seen, is the one-way branching required when keys have bits in common. For example, keys that differ in only the final bit always require a path whose length is equal to the key length, no matter how many keys there are in the tree, as illustrated in Figure 15.8. The number of internal nodes can be somewhat larger than the number of keys.

Property 15.4 *A trie built from N random w-bit keys has about $N/\ln 2 \approx 1.44N$ nodes on the average.*

By modifying the argument for Property 15.3, we can write the expression

$$\sum_{t \geq 0} \left(2^t \left(1 - \left(1 - \frac{1}{2^t} \right)^N \right) - N \left(1 - \frac{1}{2^t} \right)^{N-1} \right)$$

for the average number of nodes in an N-key trie (see Exercise 15.28). The mathematical analysis that yields the stated approximate value for this sum is much more difficult than the argument that we gave for

Figure 15.8
Binary trie worst case

This sequence depicts the result of inserting the keys H = 01000 *and* I = 01001 *into an initially empty binary trie. As it is in DSTs (see Figure 15.4), the path length is limited by the length of the binary representation of the keys; as illustrated by this example, however, paths could be that long even with only two keys in the trie.*

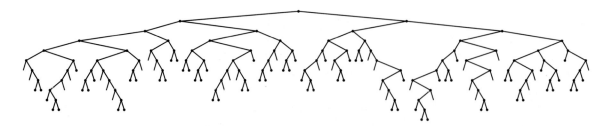

**Figure 15.9
Trie example**

This trie, built by inserting about 200 random keys, is well-balanced, but has 44 percent more nodes than might otherwise be necessary, because of one-way branching. (Null links on leaves are not shown.)

Property 15.3, because many terms contribute values that are not 0 or 1 to the value of the sum (*see reference section*). ■

We can verify these results empirically. For example, Figure 15.9 shows a big trie, which has 44 percent more nodes than does the BST or the DST built with the same set of keys; nevertheless, it is well balanced, with a near-optimal search cost. Our first thought might be that the extra nodes would raise the average search cost substantially, but this suspicion is not valid—for example, we would increase the average search cost by only 1 even if we were to double the number of nodes in a balanced trie.

For convenience in the implementations in Programs 15.3 and 15.4, we assumed that the keys are of fixed length and are distinct so that we could be certain that the keys would eventually distinguish themselves and that the programs could process 1 bit at a time and never run out of key bits. For convenience in the analyses in Properties 15.2 and 15.3, we implicitly assumed that the keys have an arbitrary number of bits so that they eventually distinguish themselves except with tiny (exponentially decaying) probability. A direct offshoot of these assumptions is that both the programs and the analyses apply when the keys are variable-length bitstrings, with a few caveats.

To use the programs as they stand for variable-length keys, we need to extend our restriction that the keys be distinct to say that no key be a prefix of another. This restriction is met automatically in some applications, as we shall see in Section 15.5. Alternatively, we could handle such keys by keeping information in internal nodes, because each prefix that might need to be handled corresponds to some internal node in the trie (see Exercise 15.32).

For sufficiently long keys comprising random bits, the average-case results of Properties 15.2 and 15.3 still hold. In the worst case, the height of a trie is still limited by the number of bits in the longest keys. This cost could be excessive if the keys are huge and perhaps have some uniformity, as might arise in encoded character data. In the next two sections, we consider methods of reducing trie costs for long keys. One way to shorten paths in tries is to collapse one-way branches into single links—we discuss an elegant and efficient way to accomplish this task in Section 15.3. Another way to shorten paths in tries is to allow more than two links per node—this approach is the subject of Section 15.4.

Exercises

▷ **15.11** Draw the trie that results when you insert items with the keys E A S Y Q U T I O N in that order into an initially empty trie.

15.12 What happens when you use Program 15.4 to insert a record whose key is equal to some key already in the trie?

15.13 Draw the trie that results when you insert items with the keys 0101-0011 00000111 00100001 01010001 11101100 00100001 10010101 01001010 into an initially empty trie.

15.14 Run empirical studies to compare the height, number of nodes, and internal path length of a trie built by insertion of N random 32-bit keys into an initially empty trie with the same measures of a standard binary search tree and a red–black tree (Chapter 13) built from the same keys, for $N = 10^3$, 10^4, 10^5, and 10^6 (see Exercise 15.6).

15.15 Give a full characterization of the worst-case internal path length of a trie with N distinct w-bit keys.

15.16 Implement a lazy *count* operation for the trie-based symbol-table implementation of Programs 15.3 and 15.4.

15.17 Add an integer field N to Node and modify the trie code in Programs 15.3 and 15.4 to implement an eager *count* operation that takes constant time.

• **15.18** Implement the *remove* operation for the trie-based symbol-table implementation of Programs 15.3 and 15.4.

○ **15.19** Implement the *select* operation for the trie-based symbol-table implementation of Programs 15.3 and 15.4.

15.20 Implement the *sort* operation for the trie-based symbol-table implementation of Programs 15.3 and 15.4.

▷ **15.21** Write a program that prints out all keys in a trie that have the same initial t bits as a given search key.

○ **15.22** Use a pair of derived classes to develop implementations of *search* and *insert* using tries with non-leaf nodes that contain links but no items and with leaves that contain items but no links.

15.23 Modify Programs 15.4 and 15.3 to keep the search key in a machine register and to shift one bit position to access the next bit when moving down a level in the trie.

15.24 Modify Programs 15.4 and 15.3 to maintain a table of 2^r tries, for a fixed constant r, and to use the first r bits of the key to index into the table and the standard algorithms with the remainder of the key on the trie accessed. This change saves about r steps unless the table has a significant number of null entries.

15.25 What value should we choose for r in Exercise 15.24, if we have N random keys (which are sufficiently long that we can assume them to be distinct)?

15.26 Write a program to compute the number of nodes in the trie corresponding to a given set of distinct fixed-length keys by sorting them and comparing adjacent keys in the sorted list.

• **15.27** Prove by induction that $N \sum_{t \geq 0} \left(1 - (1 - 2^{-t})^N\right)$ is the solution to the quicksort-like recurrence that is given after Property 15.3 for the external path length in a random trie.

• **15.28** Derive the expression given in Property 15.4 for the average number of nodes in a random trie.

• **15.29** Write a program to compute the average number of nodes in a random trie of N nodes and print the exact value, accurate to 10^{-3}, for $N = 10^3$, 10^4, 10^5, and 10^6.

•• **15.30** Prove that the height of a trie built from N random bitstrings is about $2 \lg N$. *Hint*: Consider the birthday problem (see Property 14.2).

• **15.31** Prove that the average cost of a search in a DST built from random keys is asymptotically $\lg N$ (see Properties 15.1 and 15.2).

15.32 Modify Programs 15.3 and 15.4 to handle variable-length bitstrings under the sole restriction that records with duplicate keys are not kept in the data structure. In particular, decide upon a convention for the return value of `bit(v, d)` for the case that d is greater than the length of v.

15.33 Develop a trie-based class that implements an existence table ADT for *w*-bit integers. Your class should include a constructor and support *insert* and *search* operations that take integer parameters, where *search* returns `false` for search miss and `true` for search hit (see Program 15.10).

15.3 Patricia Tries

Trie-based search as described in Section 15.2 has two inconvenient flaws. First, the one-way branching leads to the creation of extra nodes in the trie, which seem unnecessary. Second, there are two

---

Program 15.5 Patricia trie symbol-table implementation

Nodes in patricia tries contain a field that indicates which bit position distinguishes keys on the right from keys on the left. We use a dummy node head at the top of the trie that is always the result of a search for the null (all 0s) key. The root of the trie is at head.l (the link head.r is unused).

```
class ST
  {
    private class Node
      { ITEM item; Node l, r; int bit;
        Node(ITEM x, int i) { item = x; bit = i; }
      }
    private Node head;
    ST(int maxN)
      { head = new Node(null, -1); head.l = head; }
    ITEM search(KEY key)
      // See Program 15.6
    void insert(ITEM x)
      // See Program 15.7
    public String toString()
      // See Program 15.8
  }
```

---

different types of nodes in the trie, which leads to complications (see Exercise 15.22). In 1968, Morrison discovered a way to avoid both of these problems, in a method that he named *patricia* ("practical algorithm to retrieve information coded in alphanumeric"). Morrison developed his algorithm in the context of string-indexing applications of the type that we shall consider in Section 15.5, but it is equally effective as a symbol-table implementation. Like DSTs, patricia tries allow search for N keys in a tree with just N nodes; like tries, they require only about $\lg N$ bit comparisons and one full key comparison per search, and they support other ADT operations. Moreover, these performance characteristics are independent of key length, and the data structure is suitable for variable-length keys.

Starting with the standard trie data structure, we avoid one-way branching via a simple device: we put into each node the index of

Program 15.6 Patricia-trie search

The recursive method `searchR` returns the unique node that could contain the record with key v. It travels down the trie, using the bits of the tree to control the search, but tests only 1 bit per node encountered—the one indicated in the bit field. It terminates the search when it encounters an external link, one which points up the tree. The search method `search` calls `searchR`, then tests the key in that node to determine whether the search is a hit or a miss.

```
private ITEM searchR(Node h, KEY v, int i)
  {
    if (h.bit <= i) return h.item;
    if (bit(v, h.bit) == 0)
        return searchR(h.l, v, h.bit);
    else return searchR(h.r, v, h.bit);
  }
ITEM search(KEY key)
  { ITEM t = searchR(head.l, key, -1);
    if (t == null) return null;
    if (equals(t.key(), key)) return t;
    return null;
  }
```

Figure 15.10
Patricia search

In a successful search for R = 10010 *in this sample patricia trie (top), we move right (since bit 0 is 1), then left (since bit 4 is 0), which brings us to* R *(the only key in the tree that begins with* 1***0*). On the way down the tree, we check only the key bits indicated in the numbers over the nodes (and ignore the keys in the nodes). When we first reach a link that points up the tree, we compare the search key against the key in the node pointed to by the up link, since that is the only key in the tree that could be equal to the search key.*

In an unsuccessful search for I = 01001, *we move left at the root (since bit 0 of the key is 0), then take the right (up) link (since bit 1 is 1) and find that* H *(the only key in the trie that begins with* 01*) is not equal to* I.

the bit to be tested to decide which path to take out of that node. Thus, we jump directly to the bit where a significant decision is to be made, bypassing the bit comparisons at nodes where all the keys in the subtree have the same bit value. Moreover, we avoid external nodes via another simple device: we store data in internal nodes and replace links to external nodes with links that point back upwards to the correct internal node in the trie. These two changes allow us to represent tries with binary trees comprising nodes with a key and two links (and an additional field for the index), which we call *patricia tries*. With patricia tries, we store keys in nodes as with DSTs, and we traverse the tree according to the bits of the search key; but we do not use the keys in the nodes on the way down the tree to control the search; we merely store them there for possible later reference, when the bottom of the tree is reached.

As hinted in the previous paragraph, it is easier to follow the mechanics of the algorithm if we first take note that we can regard standard tries and patricia tries as different representations of the same abstract trie structure. For example, the tries in Figure 15.10 and at the top in Figure 15.11, which illustrate search and insertion for patricia tries, represent the same abstract structure as do the tries in Figure 15.6. The search and insertion algorithms for patricia tries use, build, and maintain a concrete representation of the abstract trie data structure different from the search and insertion algorithms discussed in Section 15.2, but the underlying trie abstraction is the same.

Program 15.6 is an implementation of the patricia-trie search algorithm. The method differs from trie search in three ways: there are no explicit null links, we test the indicated bit in the key instead of the next bit, and we end with a search key comparison at the point where we follow a link up the tree. It is easy to test whether a link points up, because the bit indices in the nodes (by definition) increase as we travel down the tree. To search, we start at the root and proceed down the tree, using the bit index in each node to tell us which bit to examine in the search key—we go right if that bit is 1, left if it is 0. The keys in the nodes are not examined at all on the way down the tree. Eventually, an upward link is encountered: each upward link points to the unique key in the tree that has the bits that would cause a search to take that link. Thus, if the key at the node pointed to by the first upward link encountered is equal to the search key, then the search is successful; otherwise, it is unsuccessful.

Figure 15.10 illustrates search in a patricia trie. For a miss due to the search taking a null link in a trie, the corresponding patricia trie search will take a course somewhat different from that of standard trie search, because the bits that correspond to one-way branching are not tested at all on the way down the trie. For a search ending at a leaf in a trie, the patricia-trie search ends up comparing against the same key as the trie search but without examining the bits corresponding to one-way branching in the trie.

The implementation of insertion for patricia tries mirrors the two cases that arise in insertion for tries, as illustrated in Figure 15.11. As usual, we gain information on where a new key belongs from a search miss. For tries, the miss can occur either because of a null link or because of a key mismatch at a leaf. For patricia tries, we need to

**Figure 15.11
Patricia-trie insertion**

To insert I into the sample patricia trie in Figure 15.10, we add a new node to check bit 4, since H = 01000 and I = 01001 differ in only that bit (top). On a subsequent search in the trie that comes to the new node, we want to check H (left link) if bit 4 of the search key is 0; if the bit is 1 (right link), the key to check is I.

To insert N = 01110 (bottom), we add a new node in between H and I to check bit 2, since that bit distinguishes N from H and I.

do more work to decide which type of insertion is needed, because we skipped the bits corresponding to one-way branching during the search. A patricia-trie search always ends with a key comparison, and this key carries the information that we need. We find the leftmost bit position where the search key and the key that terminated the search differ, then search through the trie again, comparing that bit position against the bit positions in the nodes on the search path. If we come to a node that specifies a bit position higher than the bit position that distinguishes the key sought and the key found, then we know that we skipped a bit in the patricia-trie search that would have led to a null link in the corresponding trie search, so we add a new node for testing that bit. If we never come to a node that specifies a bit position higher than the one that distinguishes the key sought and the key found, then the patricia-trie search corresponds to a trie search ending in a leaf, and we add a new node that distinguishes the search key from the key that terminated the search. We always add just one node, which references the leftmost bit that distinguishes the keys, where standard trie insertion might add multiple nodes with one-way branching before reaching that bit. That new node, besides providing the bit-discrimination that we need, will also be the node that we use to store the new item.

We use the convention that the leftmost link (the one corresponding to a key that is all 0 bits) does not point to any internal node. We need such a convention because the number of external links exceeds the number of internal nodes by precisely 1 in every binary tree. To make sure that no search ever follows that link, we further adopt the convention for class types that only the null key has all 0 bits. This convention is easy to enforce by implementing bit so as to always return 0 for the null key and to return 1 after exhausting the bits of any non-null key (see Exercise 15.34). Figure 15.12 shows the initial stages of the construction of a sample trie, which illustrate these conventions.

Program 15.7 is an implementation of the patricia-trie–insertion algorithm. The code follows directly from the description in the previous paragraph, with the additional observation that we view links to nodes with bit indices that are not larger than the current bit index as links to external nodes. The insertion code merely tests this property of the links, but it does not have to move keys or links around at all. The upward links in patricia tries seem mysterious at first, but

Figure 15.12
Patricia-trie construction

This sequence depicts the result of inserting the keys A S E R C H into an initially empty patricia trie. Figure 15.11 depicts the result of inserting I and then N into the tree at the bottom.

Program 15.7 Patricia-trie insertion

To insert a key into a patricia trie, we begin with a search. The method
searchR from Program 15.6 gets us to a unique key in the tree that
must be distinguished from the key to be inserted. We determine the
leftmost bit position at which this key and the search key differ, then
use the recursive method insertR to travel down the tree and to insert
a new node containing v at that point.

In insertR, there are two cases, corresponding to the two cases
illustrated in Figure 15.11. The new node could replace an internal link
(if the search key differs from the key found in a bit position that was
skipped) or an external link (if the bit that distinguishes the search key
from the found key was not needed to distinguish the found key from
all the other keys in the trie).

This code assumes that KEY is a class type and depends upon bit
being implemented so that null is the only key that is all 0s (see text).

```
private Node insertR(Node h, ITEM x, int i, Node p)
  { KEY v = x.key();
    if ((h.bit >= i) || (h.bit <= p.bit))
      {
        Node t = new Node(x, i);
        t.l = bit(v, t.bit) == 0 ? t : h;
        t.r = bit(v, t.bit) == 0 ? h : t;
        return t;
      }
    if (bit(v, h.bit) == 0)
        h.l = insertR(h.l, x, i, h);
    else h.r = insertR(h.r, x, i, h);
    return h;
  }
void insert(ITEM x)
  { int i = 0;
    KEY v = x.key();
    ITEM t = searchR(head.l, v, -1);
    KEY w = (t == null) ? null : t.key();
    if (v == w) return;
    while (bit(v, i) == bit(w, i)) i++;
    head.l = insertR(head.l, x, i, head);
  }
```

Program 15.8 Patricia-trie sort

This recursive procedure shows the records in a patricia trie in order of their keys. We imagine the items to be in (virtual) external nodes, which we can identify by testing when the bit index on the current node is not larger than the bit index on its parent. Otherwise, this program is a standard inorder traversal.

```
private String toStringR(Node h, int i)
   {
     if (h == head) return "";
     if (h.bit <= i) return h.item + "\n";
     return toStringR(h.l, h.bit) +
             toStringR(h.r, h.bit);
   }
public String toString()
   { return toStringR(head.l, -1); }
```

---

the decisions about which links to use when each node is inserted are surprisingly straightforward. The end result is that using one node type rather than two simplifies the code substantially.

By construction, all external nodes below a node with bit index k begin with the same k bits (otherwise, we would have created a node with bit index less than k to distinguish two of them). Therefore, we can convert a patricia trie to a standard trie by creating the appropriate internal nodes between nodes where bits are skipped and by replacing links that point up the tree with links to external nodes (see Exercise 15.52). However, Property 15.2 does not quite hold for patricia tries, because the assignment of keys to internal nodes does depend on the order in which the keys are inserted. The structure of the internal nodes is independent of the key-insertion order, but external links and the placement of the key values are not.

An important consequence of the fact that a patricia trie represents an underlying standard trie structure is that we can use a recursive inorder traversal to visit the nodes in order, as demonstrated in the implementation given in Program 15.8. We visit just the external nodes, which we identify by testing for nonincreasing bit indices.

Patricia is the quintessential radix search method: it manages to identify the bits that distinguish the search keys and to build them into

Figure 15.13
Patricia-trie example

This patricia trie, built by insertion of about 200 random keys, is equivalent to the trie of Figure 15.9, with one-way branching removed. The resulting tree is nearly perfectly balanced.

a data structure (with no surplus nodes) that quickly leads from any search key to the only key in the data structure that could be equal to the search key. Figure 15.13 shows the patricia trie for the same keys used to build the trie of Figure 15.9—the patricia trie not only has 44 percent fewer nodes than the standard trie but also is nearly perfectly balanced.

Property 15.5 *Insertion or search for a random key in a patricia trie built from N random bitstrings requires about $\lg N$ bit comparisons on the average, and about $2 \lg N$ bit comparisons in the worst case. The number of bit comparisons is never more than the length of the key.*

This fact is an immediate consequence of Property 15.3, since paths in patricia tries are no longer than paths in the corresponding trie. The precise average-case analysis of patricia is difficult; it turns out that patricia involves one fewer comparison, on the average, than does a standard trie (*see reference section*). ∎

Table 15.1 gives empirical data supporting the conclusion that DSTs, standard binary tries, and patricia tries have comparable performance (and that they provide search times comparable to or shorter than the balanced-tree methods of Chapter 13) when keys are integers, and certainly should be considered for symbol-table implementations even with keys that can be represented as short bitstrings, taking into account the various straightforward tradeoffs that we have noted.

Note that the search cost given in Property 15.5 does *not* grow with the key length. By contrast, the search cost in a standard trie typically does depend on the length of the keys—the first bit position that differs in two given keys could be arbitrarily far into the key. All the comparison-based search methods that we have considered also depend on the key length—if two keys differ in only their rightmost bit, then comparing them requires time proportional to their length.

Table 15.1 Empirical study of trie implementations

These relative timings for construction and search in symbol tables with random sequences of 32-bit integers confirm that digital methods are competitive with balanced-tree methods, even for keys that are random bits. Performance differences are more remarkable when keys are long and are not necessarily random (see Table 15.2), or when careful attention is paid to making the key-bit–access code efficient (see Exercise 15.23).

N	construction				search hits			
	R	D	T	P	R	D	T	P
1250	25	14	14	16	5	3	4	3
2500	43	23	29	29	9	7	6	5
5000	70	43	43	60	19	15	12	11
12500	116	96	100	102	59	47	36	32
25000	298	204	251	305	147	115	87	80
50000	1120	464	476	604	356	290	198	180
100000	2476	1189	1172	1411	853	665	456	429
200000	3591	4487	2505	3240	1884	1579	1012	945

Key:
- R   Red–black BST (Programs 12.15 and 13.6)
- D   DST (Program 15.2)
- T   Trie (Programs 15.3 and 15.4)
- P   Patricia trie (Programs 15.6 and 15.7)

Furthermore, hashing methods *always* require time proportional to the key length for a search in order to compute the hash function. But patricia immediately takes us to the bits that matter and typically involves testing less than $\lg N$ of them. This effect makes patricia (or trie search with one-way branching removed) the search method of choice when the search keys are long.

For example, suppose that we have a computer that can efficiently access 8-bit bytes of data, and we have to search among millions of 1000-bit keys. In this case, patricia would require accessing only about 20 bytes of the search key for the search, plus one 125-byte equality comparison; in contrast, hashing would require accessing all 125 bytes of the search key to compute the hash function (plus a few equality comparisons), and comparison-based methods would require 20 to 30 full key comparisons. It is true that key comparisons, particularly in the early stages of a search, require only a few byte comparisons, but later stages typically involve many more bytes. We shall consider comparative performance of various methods for searching with lengthy keys again in Section 15.5.

Indeed, there needs to be no limit at all on the length of search keys for patricia. Patricia is particularly effective in applications with variable-length keys that are potentially huge, such as the one discussed in Section 15.5. With patricia, we generally can expect that the number of bit inspections required for a search among N records, even with huge keys, will be roughly proportional to $\lg N$.

Exercises

15.34 Modify the implementation of the two-parameter `bit` method in the text after Program 15.1 to return 1 if its second parameter is not less than `bitsword` and to always return 0 if its first parameter is `null`.

15.35 What happens when you use Program 15.7 to insert a record whose key is equal to some key already in the trie?

▷ **15.36** Draw the patricia trie that results when you insert the keys E A S Y Q U T I O N in that order into an initially empty trie.

▷ **15.37** Draw the patricia trie that results when you insert the keys 01010011 00000111 00100001 01010001 11101100 00100001 10010101 01001010 in that order into an initially empty trie.

○ **15.38** Draw the patricia trie that results when you insert the keys 01001010 10010101 00100001 11101100 01010001 00100001 00000111 01010011 in that order into an initially empty trie.

15.39 Run empirical studies to compare the height and internal path length of a patricia trie built by insertion of N random 32-bit keys into an initially empty trie with the same measures of a standard binary search tree and a red–black tree (Chapter 13) built from the same keys, for $N = 10^3$, 10^4, 10^5, and 10^6 (see Exercises 15.6 and 15.14).

15.40 Give a full characterization of the worst-case internal path length of a patricia trie with N distinct w-bit keys.

15.41 Implement a lazy *count* operation for the patricia-based symbol table implementation of Programs 15.5 through 15.7.

15.42 Add an integer field N to `Node` and modify the patricia code in Programs 15.5 through 15.7 to implement an eager *count* operation that takes constant time.

15.43 Implement the *select* operation for a patricia-based symbol table.

• 15.44 Implement the *remove* operation for a patricia-based symbol table.

• 15.45 Implement the *join* operation for patricia-based symbol tables.

○ 15.46 Write a program that prints out all keys in a patricia trie that have the same initial t bits as a given search key.

15.47 Modify standard trie search and insertion (Programs 15.3 and 15.4) to eliminate one-way branching in the same manner as for patricia tries. If you have done Exercise 15.22, start with that program instead.

15.48 Modify patricia search and insertion (Programs 15.6 and 15.7) to maintain a table of 2^r tries, as described in Exercise 15.24.

15.49 Show that each key in a patricia trie is on its own search path and is therefore encountered on the way down the tree during a *search* operation as well as at the end.

15.50 Modify patricia search (Program 15.6) to compare keys on the way down the tree to improve search-hit performance. Run empirical studies to evaluate the effectiveness of this change (see Exercise 15.49).

15.51 Use a patricia trie to build a data structure that can support an existence table ADT for w-bit integers (see Exercise 15.33).

• 15.52 Write programs that convert a patricia trie to a standard trie on the same keys, and vice versa.

15.4 Multiway Tries and TSTs

For radix sorting, we found that we could get a significant improvement in speed by considering more than 1 bit at a time. The same is true for radix search: By examining r bits at a time, we can speed up the search by a factor of r. However, there is a catch that makes it necessary for us to be more careful in applying this idea than we had to be for radix sorting. The problem is that considering r bits at a time corresponds to using tree nodes with $R = 2^r$ links, and that can lead to a considerable amount of wasted space for unused links.

Program 15.9 Radix key type example

This code is an example of extending a key class such as Program 12.2, which defines integer-valued keys, in order to provide radix methods with access to the key digits. It provides a `digit` method that returns the indicated digit from the decimal representation of the key (an integer that is 0 through 9) and the constants R and END. Numbers of type int have only ten decimal digits; our convention is to return END if a client asks for a digit beyond the end of the number.

```
class radixKey extends myKey
  {
    public final static int R = 10;
    public final static int END = -1;
    private int[] p =
      {1000000000, 100000000, 10000000,
        1000000, 100000, 10000, 1000, 100, 10, 1 };
    public int digit(int B)
      { int v = val;
        if (B > 9) return END;
        return (v/p[B]) % 10;
      }
  }
```

Program 15.9 is an example of a key type implementation that provides access to key digits. As with `bit`, if we were to use this type of key, we would add to each class the code

```
private final static int R = radixKey.R;
private int digit(KEY v, int i)
  { return ((radixKey) v).digit(i); }
```

to give us the flexibility to substitute a direct implementation for keys that are primitive types (see Exercise 15.53).

In the (binary) tries of Section 15.2, the nodes corresponding to key bits have two links: one for the case when the key bit is 0, and the other for the case when the key bit is 1. The appropriate generalization is to R-ary tries, where we have nodes with R links corresponding to key digits, one for each possible digit value. Keys are stored in leaves (nodes with all links null). To search in an R-way trie, we start at the root and at the leftmost key digit and use the key digits to guide

Figure 15.14
R-way trie for base-10 numbers

This figure depicts the trie that distinguishes the set of numbers

.396465048
.353336658
.318693642
.015583409
.159369371
.691004885
.899854354
.159072306
.604144269
.269971047
.538069659

(see Figure 12.1). Each node has 10 links (one for each possible digit). At the root, link 0 points to the trie for keys with first digit 0 (there is only one); link 1 points to the trie for keys with first digit 1 (there are two), and so forth. None of these numbers has first digit 4, 7, 8, or 9, so those links are null. There is only one number for each of the first digits 0, 2, and 5, so there is a leaf containing the appropriate number for each of those digits. The rest of the structure is built recursively, moving one digit to the right.

us down the tree. We go down the ith link (and move to the next digit) if the digit value is i. If we reach a leaf, it contains the only key in the trie with leading digits corresponding to the path that we have traversed, so we can compare that key with the search key to determine whether we have a search hit or a search miss. If we reach a null link, we know that we have a search miss, because that link corresponds to a leading-digit pattern not found in any keys in the trie. Figure 15.14 shows a 10-way trie that represents a sample set of decimal numbers. As we discussed in Chapter 10, numbers typically seen in practice are distinguished with relatively few trie nodes. This same effect for more general types of keys is the basis for a number of efficient search algorithms.

Before doing a full symbol-table implementation with multiple node types and so forth, we begin our study of multiway tries by concentrating on the *existence-table* problem, where we have only keys (no records or associated information) and want to develop algorithms to *insert* a key into a data structure and to *search* the data structure to tell us whether or not a given key has been inserted. Program 15.10 defines an ADT for existence tables. The existence-table implementation that we consider next clearly exposes the structure of multiway tries, is useful in its own right, and paves the way for using tries in a standard symbol-table ADT implementation.

Definition 15.2 *The **existence trie** corresponding to a set of keys is defined recursively as follows: The trie for an empty set of keys is a null link; and the trie for a nonempty set of keys is an internal node with links referring to the trie for each possible key digit, with the leading digit considered to be removed for the purpose of constructing the subtrees.*

For simplicity, we assume in this definition that no key is the prefix of another. Typically, we enforce this restriction by ensuring that the keys are distinct and either are of fixed length or have a termination

> **Program 15.10 Existence-table ADT**
>
> This interface defines the simplest kind of symbol table, where we have keys but no associated information. Clients can insert a key and search to determine whether or not a given key has been inserted.
>
> ```
> class ET // ADT interface
>   { // implementations and private members hidden
>     ET()
>     boolean search(KEY)
>     void insert(KEY)
>   }
> ```

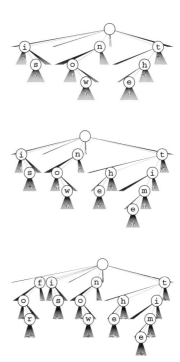

digit with value END, a sentinel that is used for no other purpose. The point of this definition is that we can use existence tries to implement existence tables, without storing *any* information within the trie; the information is all implicitly defined within the trie *structure*. Each node has $R + 1$ links (one for each possible character value plus one for END) and no other information. To search, we use the digits in the key to guide us down the trie. If we reach the link to END at the same time that we run out of key digits, we have a search hit; otherwise we have a search miss. To insert a new key, we search until we reach a null link, then add nodes for each of the remaining characters in the key. Figure 15.15 is an example of a 27-way trie; Program 15.11 is an implementation of the basic (multiway) existence-trie search and insert procedures.

If the keys are of fixed length and are distinct, we can dispense with the link to the terminal character and can terminate searches when we reach the key length (see Exercise 15.60). We have already seen an example of this type of trie when we used tries to describe MSD sorting for fixed-length keys (Figure 10.10).

In one sense, this pure abstract representation of the trie structure is optimal, because it can support the *search* operation in time proportional to the length of a key and in space proportional to the total number of characters in the key in the worst case. But the total amount of space used could be as high as nearly R links for each character, so we seek improved implementations. As we saw with binary tries, it is worthwhile to consider the pure trie structure as a particular representation of an underlying abstract structure that is

Figure 15.15
R-way existence trie search and insertion

The 26-way trie for the words now, is, *and* the *(top) has nine nodes: the root plus one for each letter. The nodes are labeled in these diagrams, but we do not use explicit node labels in the data structure, because each node label can be inferred from the position of the link to it in its parents' link array.*

To insert the key time, *we branch off the existing node for* t *and add new nodes for* i, m, *and* e *(center); to insert the key* for, *we branch off the root and add new nodes for* f, o, *and* r.

Program 15.11 Existence-trie search and insertion

This implementation of the *search* and *insert* existence-table ADT operations for multiway tries stores the keys implicitly within the structure of the trie. Each node contains R linkss to the next level down the trie. We follow the ith link at level l when the tth digit of the key is i.

```
private boolean searchR(Node h, KEY v, int d)
  { int i = digit(v, d);
    if (h == null) return false;
    if (i < 0) return true;
    return searchR(h.next[i], v, d+1);
  }
boolean search(KEY key)
  { return searchR(head, key, 0); }
private Node insertR(Node h, KEY v, int d)
  { int i = digit(v, d);
    if (h == null) h = new Node();
    if (i < 0) return h;
    h.next[i] = insertR(h.next[i], v, d+1);
    return h;
  }
void insert(KEY v)
  { head = insertR(head, v, 0); }
```

---

a well-defined representation of our set of keys and then to consider other representations of the same abstract structure that might lead to better performance.

Definition 15.3 *A* **multiway trie** *is a multiway tree that has keys associated with each of its leaves, defined recursively as follows: The trie for an empty set of keys is a null link; the trie for a single key is a leaf containing that key; and the trie for a set of keys of cardinality greater than one is an internal node with links referring to tries for keys with each possible digit value, with the leading digit considered to be removed for the purpose of constructing the subtrees.*

We assume that keys in the data structure are distinct and that no key is the prefix of another. To search in a standard multiway trie, we use the digits of the key to guide the search down the trie, with three possible outcomes. If we reach a null link, we have a search miss; if we reach a leaf containing the search key, we have a search hit; and if we reach a leaf containing a different key, we have a search miss. All leaves have R null links, and when we are implementing a symbol table we can put the items in the leaves (as we did for binary tries) so that different representations for leaf nodes and non-leaf nodes are appropriate, as in Section 15.2. We consider such an implementation in Chapter 16, and we shall consider another approach to an implementation in this chapter. In either case, the analytic results from Section 15.3 generalize to tell us about the performance characteristics of standard multiway tries.

Property 15.6 *Search or insertion in a standard R-ary trie requires about $\log_R N$ byte comparisons on the average in a tree built from N random bytestrings. The number of links in an R-ary trie built from N random keys is about $RN/\ln R$. The number of byte comparisons for search or insertion is no more than the number of bytes in the search key.*

These results generalize those in Properties 15.3 and 15.4. We can establish them by substituting R for 2 in the proofs of those properties. As we mentioned, however, extremely sophisticated mathematics is involved in the precise analysis of these quantities. ∎

The performance characteristics listed in Property 15.6 represent an extreme example of a time–space tradeoff. On the one hand, there are a large number of unused null links—only a few nodes near the top use more than a few of their links. On the other hand, the height of a tree is small. For example, suppose that we take the typical value $R = 256$ and that we have N random 64-bit keys. Property 15.6 tells us that a search will take $(\lg N)/8$ character comparisons (8 at most) and that we will use fewer than $47N$ links. If plenty of space is available, this method provides an extremely efficient alternative. We could cut the search cost to 4 character comparisons for this example by taking $R = 65536$, but that would require over $5900N$ links.

In practical applications, the space cost is likely to be even higher, because real sets of keys tend to have long stretches where parts of subsets of keys are equal. The trie for such a set of keys will have many nodes with $R - 1$ null links.

In particular, this analysis shows that it is unwise to use tries for standard Java Unicode strings, because the amount of space they consume when $R = 65536$ is excessive. One way to ameliorate this difficulty is to implement digit so as to break characters into multiple pieces, perhaps restricting attention to ASCII so that we only need half of each character (see Exercise 15.63). Next, we consider an algorithmic approach that is even more effective.

In the remainder of this section, we shall consider an alternative representation of multiway tries: the *ternary search trie (TST)*, which help us avoid the excessive space cost normally associated with multiway tries. In a TST, each node has a character and *three* links, corresponding to keys whose current digits are less than, equal to, or greater than the node's character. Using this arrangement is equivalent to implementing trie nodes as binary search trees that use as keys the characters corresponding to non-null links. In the standard existence tries of Program 15.11, trie nodes are represented by $R + 1$ links, and we infer the character represented by each non-null link by its index. In the corresponding existence TST, all the characters corresponding to non-null links appear explicitly in nodes—we find characters corresponding to keys only when we are traversing the middle links. A sample TST is illustrated in Figure 15.16.

The search algorithm for implementing the existence table ADT with TSTs is so straightforward as nearly to write itself; the insertion algorithm is slightly more complicated, but mirrors directly insertion in existence tries. To search, we compare the first character in the key with the character at the root. If it is less, we take the left link; if it is greater, we take the right link; and if it is equal, we take the middle link and move to the next key character. In each case, we apply the algorithm recursively. We terminate with a search miss if we encounter a null link or if we encounter the end of the search key before encountering END in the tree, and we terminate with a search hit if we traverse the middle link in a node whose character is END. To insert a new key, we search, then add new nodes for the characters in the tail of the key, just as we did for tries.

Program 15.12 gives the details of the implementation of these algorithms, and Figure 15.17 has TSTs that correspond to the tries in Figure 15.15. Since one of the most important and natural applications of multiway tries is to process strings, Program 15.12 is coded as an

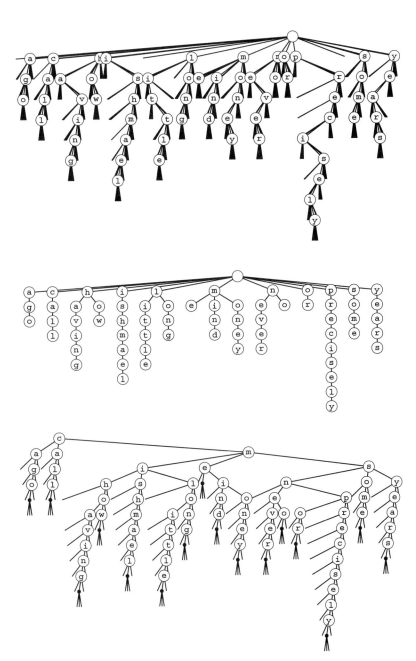

Figure 15.16
Existence-trie structures

These figures show three different representations of the existence trie for the 16 words call me ishmael some years ago never mind how long precisely having little or no money: *The 26-way existence trie (top); the abstract trie with null links removed (center); and the TST representation (bottom). The 26-way trie has too many links, but the TST is an efficient representation of the abstract trie.*

The top two tries assume that no key is the prefix of another. For example, adding the key not *would result in the key* no *being lost. We can add a null character to the end of each key to correct this problem, as illustrated in the TST at the bottom.*

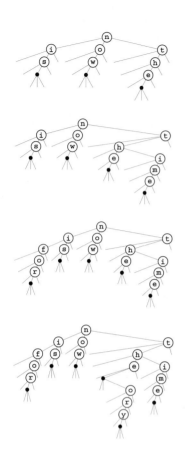

Figure 15.17
Existence TSTs

An existence TST has one node for each letter, but only 3 children per node, rather than 26. The top three trees in this figure are the RSTs corresponding to the insertion example in Figure 15.15, with the additional change that an end-of-key character is appended to each key. We can then remove the restriction that no key may be a prefix of another, so, for example, we can insert the key theory *(bottom).*

implementation of the existence table ADT interface of Program 15.10 for String keys; it is a straightforward matter to change it to use digit and therefore implement the interface for the general KEY type that we have been using (see Exercise 15.62).

Continuing the correspondence that we have been following between search trees and sorting algorithms, we see that TSTs correspond to three-way radix sorting in the same way that BSTs correspond to quicksort, tries correspond to binary quicksort, and M-way tries correspond to M-way radix sorting. Figure 10.12, which describes the recursive call structure for three-way radix sort, is a TST for that set of keys. The null-links problem for tries corresponds to the empty-bins problem for radix sorting; three-way branching provides an effective solution to both problems.

We can make TSTs more efficient in their use of space by putting keys in leaves at the point where they are distinguished and by eliminating one-way branching between internal nodes as we did for patricia. At the end of this section, we examine an implementation based on the former change.

Property 15.7 *A search or insertion in a full TST requires time proportional to the key length. The number of links in a TST is at most three times the number of characters in all the keys.*

In the worst case, each key character corresponds to a full R-ary node that is unbalanced, stretched out like a singly linked list. This worst case is extremely unlikely to occur in a random tree. More typically, we might expect to do $\ln R$ or fewer byte comparisons at the first level (since the root node behaves like a BST on the R different byte values) and perhaps at a few other levels (if there are keys with a common prefix and up to R different byte values on the character following the prefix), and to do only a few byte comparisons for most characters (since most trie nodes are sparsely populated with non-null links). Search misses are likely to involve only a few byte comparisons, ending at a null link high in the trie, and search hits involve only about one byte comparison per search key character, since most of them are in nodes with one-way branching at the bottom of the trie.

Actual space usage is generally less than the upper bound of three links per character, because keys share nodes at high levels in the tree. We refrain from a precise average-case analysis because TSTs are most

Program 15.12 Existence-TST search and insertion

This code implements the existence table ADT for string keys. Each
node contains just one digit and three links: one each for keys whose
next digit is less than, equal to, or greater than the corresponding digit
in the search key, respectively.

The character value END is used as an end-of-string marker in the
TST (this code uses 0, as in C-style strings) but strings need not end with
END.

```
class StringET
  {
    private final static int END = 0;
    private class Node
      { char c; Node l, m, r; }
    private Node head;
    StringET()
      { head = null; }
    private Node insertR(Node h, char[] s, int i)
      { char ch = (i < s.length) ? s[i] : END;
        if (h == null) { h = new Node(); h.c = ch; }
        if (ch == END && h.c == END) return h;
        if (s[i] < h.c) h.l = insertR(h.l, s, i);
        if (s[i] == h.c) h.m = insertR(h.m, s, i+1);
        if (s[i] > h.c) h.r = insertR(h.r, s, i);
        return h;
      }
    void insert(String s)
      { head = insertR(head, s.toCharArray(), 0); }
    private boolean searchR(Node h, char[] s, int i)
      {
        if (h == null) return false;
        if (i == s.length) return h.c == END;
        if (s[i] < h.c) return searchR(h.l, s, i);
        if (s[i] > h.c) return searchR(h.r, s, i);
        return searchR(h.m, s, i+1); // s[i] == h.c
      }
    boolean search(String s)
      { return searchR(head, s.toCharArray(), 0); }
  }
```

useful in practical situations where keys neither are random nor are derived from bizarre worst-case constructions. ∎

The prime virtue of using TSTs is that they adapt gracefully to irregularities in search keys that are likely to appear in practical applications. There are two main effects. First, keys in practical applications come from large character sets, and usage of particular characters in the character sets is far from uniform—for example, a particular set of strings is likely to use only a small fraction of the possible characters. With TSTs, we can use a 256-character ASCII encoding or a 65536-character Unicode encoding without having to worry about the excessive costs of nodes with 256- or 65536-way branching, and without having to determine which sets of characters are relevant. Unicode strings in non-Roman alphabets can have thousands of characters—TSTs are especially appropriate for standard Java String keys that consist of such characters. Second, keys in practical applications often have a structured format, differing from application to application, perhaps using only letters in one part of the key, only digits in another part of the key, and special characters as delimiters (see Exercise 15.79). For example, Figure 15.18 gives a list of library call numbers from an online library database. For such keys, some of the trie nodes might be represented as unary nodes in the TST (for places where all keys have delimiters); some might be represented as 10-node BSTs (for places where all keys have digits); and still others might be represented as 26-node BSTs (for places where all keys have letters). This structure develops automatically, without any need for special analysis of the keys.

A second practical advantage of TST-based search over many other algorithms is that search misses are likely to be extremely efficient, even when the keys are long. Often, the algorithm uses just a few byte comparisons (and chases a few references) to complete a search miss. As we discussed in Section 15.3, a search miss in a hash table with N keys requires time proportional to the key length (to compute the hash function), and at least $\lg N$ key comparisons in a search tree. Even patricia requires $\lg N$ bit comparisons for a random search miss.

Table 15.2 gives empirical data in support of the observations in the previous two paragraphs.

A third reason that TSTs are attractive is that they support operations more general than the symbol-table operations that we have

```
LDS___361_H_4
LDS___485_N_4_H_317
LDS___625_D_73_1986
LJN___679_N_48_1985
LQP___425_M_56_1991
LTK__6015_P_63_1988
LVM___455_M_67_1974
WAFR_____5054____33
WKG_____6875
WLSOC_____2542____30
WPHIL_____4060____2__55
WPHYS_____39____1__30
WROM_____5350____65___5
WUS_____10706_____7__10
WUS_____12692_____4__27
```

Figure 15.18
Sample string keys (library call numbers)

These keys from an online library database illustrate the variability of the structure found in string keys in applications. Some of the characters may appropriately be modeled as random letters, some may be modeled as random digits, and still others have fixed value or structure.

Table 15.2 Empirical study of search with string keys

These relative timings for construction and search in symbol tables with string keys such as the library call numbers in Figure 15.18 confirm that TSTs, although more expensive to construct, provide the fastest search for search misses with string keys, primarily because the search does not require examination of all the characters in the key.

N	construction				search misses			
	B	H	T	T*	B	H	T	T*
1250	6	5	15	7	6	5	4	4
2500	11	9	23	12	13	11	8	7
5000	29	18	48	39	31	22	17	13
12500	78	64	264	145	99	66	51	45
25000	223	93	509	251	253	151	119	101
50000	558	189	1234	495	608	322	275	249
100000	1328	516	2917	1008	1507	690	640	563

Key:
- B   Standard BST (Program 12.15)
- H   Hashing with separate chaining ($M = N/5$) (Program 14.3)
- T   TST (Program 15.12)
- T*   TST with R^2-way branch at root (Programs 15.15 and 15.16)

been considering. For example, Program 15.13 gives a program that allows particular characters in the search key to be unspecified and prints all keys in the data structure that match the specified digits of the search key. An example is depicted in Figure 15.19. Obviously, with a slight modification, we can adapt this program to visit all the matching keys in the way that we do for *sort*, rather than just to print them (see Exercise 15.65).

Several other similar tasks are easy to handle with TSTs. For example, we can visit all keys in the data structure that differ from the search key in at most one digit position (see Exercise 15.66). Operations of this type are expensive or impossible with other symbol-table implementations. We shall consider in Part 6 these and many other algorithms for finding approximate matches in a string search.

Program 15.13 Partial-match searching in TSTs

With judicious use of multiple recursive calls, we can find close matches in the TST structure of Program 15.12, as shown in this program for printing all strings in the data structure that match a search string with some characters unspecified (indicated by asterisks).

```java
private char[] w;
private void matchR(Node h, char[] s, int i)
  {
    if (h == null) return;
    if (i == s.length && h.c == END)
      Out.println(w + "");
    if (i == s.length) return;
    if ((s[i] == '*') || (s[i] == h.c))
      { w[i] = h.c; matchR(h.m, s, i+1); }
    if ((s[i] == '*') || (s[i] < h.c))
      matchR(h.l, s, i);
    if ((s[i] == '*') || (s[i] > h.c))
      matchR(h.r, s, i);
  }
void match(String s)
  { w = new char[s.length()];
    matchR(head, s.toCharArray(), 0); }
```

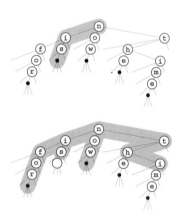

Figure 15.19
TST-based partial-match search

To find all keys in a TST matching the pattern i* (top), we search for i in the BST for the first character. In this example, we find is (the only word that matches the pattern) after two one-way branches. For a less restrictive pattern such as *o* (bottom), we visit all nodes in the BST for the first character, but only those corresponding to o for the second character, eventually finding for and now.

Patricia offers several of the same advantages; the main practical advantage of TSTs over patricia tries is that the former access key bytes or characters rather than key bits. One reason that this difference represents an advantage is that machine operations for this purpose are found in many machines, and Java provides direct access to bytes and characters through arrays or charAt in strings. Another reason is that, in some applications, working with bytes or characters in the data structure naturally reflects the orientation of the data itself—for example, in the partial-match search problem discussed in the previous paragraph (although, as we shall see in Part 6, we can also speed up partial-match search with judicious use of bit access).

To eliminate one-way branching in TSTs, we note that most of the one-way branching occurs at the tail ends of keys, which is not a factor if we evolve to a symbol-table implementation where we keep

---

Program 15.14 Hybrid TST symbol-table implementation

This TST-based implementation of our standard symbol-table ADT uses
R-way branching at the root node: the root is an array `heads` of R links,
indexed by the first key digit. Each link points to a TST built from all
the keys that begin with the corresponding digit. This hybrid combines
the benefits of tries (fast search through indexing, at the root) and TSTs
(efficient use of space with one node per character, except at the root).

```
class ST
  {
    private class Node
      { int d; ITEM item; Node l, m, r;
        Node(ITEM x) { item = x; d = END; }
        Node(int k) { d = k; }
        Node(Node h, int k) { d = k; m = h; }
        boolean internal()
          { return l!=null || m!=null || r!=null; }
      }
    private Node[] heads;
    ST(int maxN)
      { heads = new Node[R]; }
    void insert(ITEM x)
      // See Program 15.15
    ITEM search(KEY v)
      // See Program 15.16
```

---

records in leaves that are placed in the highest level of the tree that
distinguishes the keys. We also could maintain a byte index in the
same manner as in patricia tries (see Exercise 15.72) but will omit this
change, for simplicity. The combination of multiway branching and
the TST representation by themselves is quite effective in many applications, but patricia-style collapse of one-way branching will further
enhance performance when the keys are such that they are likely to
match for long stretches (see Exercise 15.79).

Another easy improvement to TST-based search is to use a large
explicit multiway node at the root. The simplest way to proceed is to
keep a table of R TSTs: one for each possible value of the first letter
in the keys. If R is not large, we might use the first two letters of

---

Program 15.15 Hybrid TST insertion for symbol-table ADT

This implementation of *insert* for Program 15.15 uses a TST with items in leaves (generalizing Program 15.4) for all words beginning with each character. If the search ends at a null link, we create a leaf to hold the item. If the search ends at a leaf, we create the internal nodes needed to distinguish the key found from the search key.

```
private Node split(Node p, Node q, int d)
  { int pd = digit(p.item.key(), d),
       qd = digit(q.item.key(), d);
    Node t = new Node(qd);
    if (pd < qd) { t.m = q; t.l = new Node(p, pd); }
    if (pd == qd) { t.m = split(p, q, d+1); }
    if (pd > qd) { t.m = q; t.r = new Node(p, pd); }
    return t;
  }
private Node insertR(Node h, ITEM x, int d)
  { int i = digit(x.key(), d);
    if (h == null)
      return new Node(new Node(x), i);
    if ((h.d == END) && (i == END)) return h;
    if (!h.internal())
      return split(new Node(x), h, d);
    if (i < h.d) h.l = insertR(h.l, x, d);
    if (i == h.d) h.m = insertR(h.m, x, d+1);
    if (i > h.d) h.r = insertR(h.r, x, d);
    return h;
  }
void insert(ITEM x)
  { int i = digit(x.key(), 0);
    heads[i] = insertR(heads[i], x, 1); }
```

---

the keys (and a table of size R^2). For this method to be effective, the leading digits of the keys must be well distributed. The resulting hybrid search algorithm corresponds to the way that a human might search for names in a telephone book. The first step is a multiway decision ("Let's see, it starts with 'A' "), followed perhaps by some two-way decisions ("It's before 'Andrews,' but after 'Aitken' "), followed by sequential

---

Program 15.16 Hybrid TST search for symbol-table ADT

This *search* implementation for TSTs (built with Program 15.15) is like
multiway-trie search, but we use only three, rather than R, links per
node (except at the root). We use the digits of the key to travel down
the tree, ending either at a null link (search miss) or at a leaf that has a
key that either is (search hit) or is not (search miss) equal to the search
key.

```
private ITEM searchR(Node h, KEY v, int d)
  {
    if (h == null) return null;
    if (h.internal())
      { int i = digit(v, d);
        if (i < h.d) return searchR(h.l, v, d);
        if (i == h.d) return searchR(h.m, v, d+1);
        if (i > h.d) return searchR(h.r, v, d);
      }
    if (equals(v, h.item.key())) return h.item;
    return null;
  }
ITEM search(KEY v)
  { return searchR(heads[digit(v, 0)], v, 1); }
```

---

character matching (" 'Algonquin,' ... No, 'Algorithms' isn't listed,
because nothing starts with 'Algor'!").

   Programs 15.14 through 15.16 comprise a TST-based implementation of the symbol-table *search* and *insert* operations which uses R-
way branching at the root and keeps items in leaves (so there is no
one-way branching once the keys are distinguished). These programs
are likely to be among the fastest available for searching with string or
long radix keys. The underlying TST structure can also support a host
of other operations.

   In a symbol table that grows to be huge, we may want to adapt
the branching factor to the table size. In Chapter 16, we shall see a
systematic way to grow a multiway trie so that we can take advantage
of multiway radix search for arbitrary file sizes.

Property 15.8 *A search or insertion in a TST with items in leaves
(no one-way branching at the bottom) and R^t-way branching at the*

root requires roughly $\ln N - t \ln R$ byte accesses for N keys that are random bytestrings. The number of links required is R^t (for the root node) plus a small constant times N.

These rough estimates follow immediately from Property 15.6. For the time cost, we assume that all but a constant number of the nodes on the search path (a few at the top) act as random BSTs on R character values, so we simply multiply the time cost by $\ln R$. For the space cost, we assume that the nodes on the first few levels are filled with R character values and that the nodes on the bottom levels have only a constant number of character values. ∎

For example, if we have 1 billion random bytestring keys with $R = 256$, and we use a table of size $R^2 = 65536$ at the top, then a typical search will require about $\ln 10^9 - 2 \ln 256 \approx 20.7 - 11.1 = 9.6$ byte comparisons. Using the table at the top cuts the search cost by a factor of 2. If we have truly random keys, we can achieve this performance with more direct algorithms that use the leading bytes in the key and an existence table, in the manner discussed in Section 14.6. With TSTs, we can get the same kind of performance when keys have a less random structure.

It is instructive to compare TSTs without multiway branching at the root with standard BSTs, for random keys. Property 15.8 says that TST search will require about $\ln N$ *byte* comparisons, whereas standard BSTs require about $\ln N$ *key* comparisons. At the top of the BST, the key comparisons can be accomplished with just one byte comparison, but at the bottom of the tree multiple byte comparisons may be needed to accomplish a key comparison. This performance difference is not dramatic. The reasons that TSTs are preferable to standard BSTs for string keys are that they provide a fast search miss; they adapt directly to multiway branching at the root; and (most important) they adapt well to bytestring keys that are *not* random, so no search takes longer than the length of a key in a TST.

Some applications may not benefit from the R-way branching at the root—for example, the keys in the library-call-number example of Figure 15.18 all begin with either L or W. Other applications may call for a higher branching factor at the root—for example, as just noted, if the keys were random integers, we would use as large a table as we could afford. We can use application-specific dependencies of this sort to tune the algorithm to peak performance, but we should not lose sight of the fact that one of the most attractive features of TSTs is that they free us from having to worry about such application-specific dependencies, providing good performance without any tuning.

Perhaps the most important property of tries or TSTs with records in leaves is that their performance characteristics are *independent* of the key length. Thus, we can use them for arbitrarily long keys. In Section 15.5, we examine a particularly effective application of this kind.

Exercises

▷ **15.53** Write a `digit` method that corresponds to Program 15.9 for keys that are of type `int`.

▷ **15.54** Draw the existence trie that results when you insert the words `now is the time for all good people to come the aid of their party` into an initially empty trie. Use 27-way branching.

▷ **15.55** Draw the existence TST that results when you insert the words `now is the time for all good people to come the aid of their party` into an initially empty TST.

▷ **15.56** Draw the 4-way trie that results when you insert items with the keys 01010011 00000111 00100001 01010001 11101100 00100001 10010101 0100-1010 into an initially empty trie, using 2-bit bytes.

▷ **15.57** Draw the TST that results when you insert items with the keys 0101-0011 00000111 00100001 01010001 11101100 00100001 10010101 01001010 into an initially empty TST, using 2-bit bytes.

▷ **15.58** Draw the TST that results when you insert items with the keys 0101-0011 00000111 00100001 01010001 11101100 00100001 10010101 01001010 into an initially empty TST, using 4-bit bytes.

○ **15.59** Draw the TST that results when you insert items with the library-call-number keys in Figure 15.18 into an initially empty TST.

○ **15.60** Modify our multiway-trie search and insertion implementation (Program 15.11) to work under the assumption that keys are (fixed-length) w-byte words (so no end-of-key indication is necessary).

○ **15.61** Modify our TST search and insertion implementation (Program 15.12) to work under the assumption that keys are (fixed-length) w-byte words (so no end-of-key indication is necessary).

15.62 Develop a TST-based implementation of Program 15.10, by modifying Program 15.12 to use parameters of type KEY for `search` and `insert` and using `digit` instead of array indexing to access characters.

15.63 Modify Program 15.11 to implement an existence table for `String` keys (like Program 15.12) by using parameters of type `String` for `search` and `insert` and using array indexing instead of `digit` to access characters. Assume that the strings are ASCII so that you can use byte arrays instead of character arrays.

15.64 Run empirical studies to compare the time and space requirements of an 8-way trie built with random integers using 3-bit bytes, a 4-way trie built with random integers using 2-bit bytes, and a binary trie built from the same keys, for $N = 10^3$, 10^4, 10^5, and 10^6 (see Exercise 15.14).

15.65 Modify Program 15.13 such that it invokes a method in an object passed as a parameter with each matching string as a parameter (instead of just printing it).

○ **15.66** Write a method that prints all the keys in a TST that differ from the search key in at most `k` positions, for a given integer `k`.

• **15.67** Give a full characterization of the worst-case internal path length of an R-way trie with N distinct w-bit keys.

• **15.68** Develop a symbol-table implementation using multiway tries that includes a `clone` implementation and supports the *construct*, *count*, *search*, *insert*, *remove*, and *join* operations for a symbol-table ADT, with support for client handles (see Exercises 12.6 and 12.7).

• **15.69** Develop a symbol-table implementation using TSTs that includes a `clone` implementation and supports the *construct*, *count*, *search*, *insert*, *remove*, and *join* operations for a symbol-table ADT, with support for client handles (see Exercises 12.6 and 12.7).

▷ **15.70** Write a program that prints out all keys in an R-way trie that have the same initial `t` bytes as a given search key.

• **15.71** Modify our multiway-trie search and insertion implementation (Program 15.11) to eliminate one-way branching in the way that we did for patricia tries.

• **15.72** Modify our TST search and insertion implementation (Program 15.12) to eliminate one-way branching in the way that we did for patricia tries.

15.73 Write a program to balance the BSTs that represent the internal nodes of a TST (rearrange them such that all their external nodes are on one of two levels).

15.74 Write a version of *insert* for TSTs that maintains a balanced-tree representation of all the internal nodes (see Exercise 15.73).

• **15.75** Give a full characterization of the worst-case internal path length of a TST with N distinct w-bit keys.

15.76 Write an implementation of `radixKey` for 80-byte ASCII string keys (see Exercise 10.23). Then write a client that uses Program 15.11 to build a 256-way trie with N random keys, for $N = 10^3$, 10^4, 10^5, and 10^6, using *search*, then *insert* on search miss. Instrument your code to print out the total number of nodes in each trie, the total amount of space used by each trie, and the total amount of time taken to build each trie. Compare these statistics with the corresponding statistics for a client that uses `String` keys (see Exercise 15.63).

15.77 Answer Exercise 15.76 for TSTs. Compare your performance results with those for tries (see Program 15.12 and Exercise 15.62).

15.78 Write an implementation of `radixKey` that generates random keys by shuffling a random 80-byte sequence of ASCII characters (see Exercise 10.25). Use this key generator to build a 256-way trie with N random keys, for $N = 10^3$, 10^4, 10^5, and 10^6, using *search*, then *insert* on search miss. Compare your performance results with those for the random case (see Exercise 15.76).

○ **15.79** Write an implementation of `radixKey` that generates 30-byte random strings made up of three fields: a 4-byte field with one of a set of 10 given ASCII strings; a 10-byte field with one of a set of 50 given ASCII strings; a 1-byte field with one of two given values; and a 15-byte field with random left-justified ASCII strings of letters equally likely to be 4 through 15 characters long (see Exercise 10.27). Use this key generator to build a 256-way trie with N random keys, for $N = 10^3$, 10^4, 10^5, and 10^6, using *search*, then *insert* on search miss. Instrument your program to print out the total number of nodes in each trie and the total amount of time taken to build each trie. Compare your performance results with those for the random case (see Exercise 15.76).

15.80 Answer Exercise 15.79 for TSTs. Compare your performance results with those for tries.

15.81 Develop an implementation of *search* and *insert* for bytestring keys using multiway *digital* search trees.

▷ **15.82** Draw the 27-way DST (see Exercise 15.81) that results when you insert items with the keys `now is the time for all good people to come the aid of their party` into an initially empty DST.

● **15.83** Develop an implementation of multiway-trie search and insertion using linked lists to represent the trie nodes (as opposed to the BST representation that we use for TSTs). Run empirical studies to determine whether it is more efficient to use ordered or unordered lists, and to compare your implementation with a TST-based implementation.

15.5 Text-String–Index Algorithms

In Section 12.5, we considered the process of building a *string index*, and we used binary search in a table of indexes into a text string to provide the capability to determine whether or not a given key string

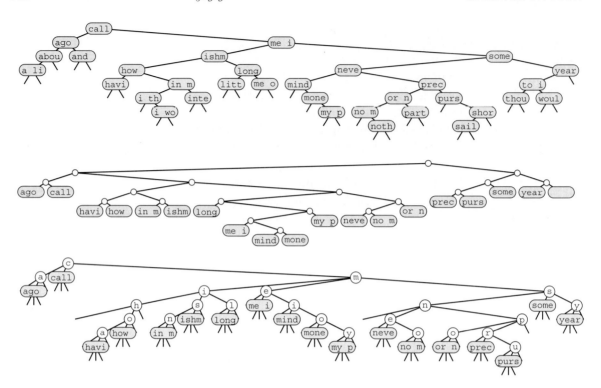

Figure 15.20
Text-string index examples

These diagrams show text-string indexes built from the text call me ishmael some years ago never mind how long precisely ... *using a BST (top), a patricia trie (center), and a TST (bottom). Nodes with string pointers are depicted with the first four characters at the point referenced by the pointer.*

appears in the text. In this section, we look at more sophisticated implementations of this ADT using multiway tries.

As in Section 12.5, we consider each position in the text to be the beginning of a string key that runs all the way to the end of the text and build a symbol table with these keys, using indexes into the text. The keys are all different (for example, they are of different lengths), and most of them are extremely long. The purpose of a search is to determine whether or not a given search key is a prefix of one of the keys in the index, which is equivalent to discovering whether the search key appears somewhere in the text string.

A search tree that is built from keys defined by indexes into a text string is called a *suffix tree*. We could use any algorithm that can admit variable-length keys. Trie-based methods are particularly suitable, because (except for the trie methods that do one-way branching at the tails of keys) their running time does not depend on the key length but rather depends only on the number of digits required to distinguish among the keys. This characteristic lies in direct contrast to, for example, hashing algorithms, which do not apply immediately to this problem because their running time is proportional to the key length.

Figure 15.20 gives examples of string indexes built with BSTs, patricia, and TSTs (with leaves). These indexes use just the keys starting at word boundaries; an index starting at character boundaries would provide a more complete index, but would use significantly more space.

Strictly speaking, even a random string text does not give rise to a random set of keys in the corresponding index (because the keys are not independent). However, we rarely work with random texts in practical indexing applications, and this analytic discrepancy will not stop us from taking advantage of the fast indexing implementations that are possible with radix methods. We refrain from discussing the detailed performance characteristics when we use each of the algorithms to build a string index, because many of the same tradeoffs that we have discussed for general symbol tables with string keys also hold for the string-index problem.

For a typical text, standard BSTs would be the first implementation that we might choose, because they are simple to implement (see Exercise 12.82). For typical applications, this solution is likely to provide good performance. One byproduct of the interdependence of the keys—particularly when we are building a string index for each character position—is that the worst case for BSTs is not a particular concern for huge texts, since unbalanced BSTs occur with only bizarre constructions.

Patricia was originally designed for the string-index application. To use Programs 15.7 and 15.6, we need only provide an implementation of bit that, given a string pointer and an integer i, returns the ith bit of the string (see Exercise 15.89). In practice, the height of a patricia trie that implements a text string index will be logarithmic. Moreover, a patricia trie will provide fast search implementations for misses because we do not need to examine all the bytes of the key.

TSTs afford several of the performance advantages of patricia, are simple to implement, and take advantage of built-in byte-access operations that are typically found on modern machines. They also are amenable to simple implementations, such as Program 15.13, that can solve search problems more complicated than fully matching a search key. To use TSTs to build a string index, we need to remove the code that handles ends of keys in the data structure, since we are guaranteed that no string is a prefix of another, and thus we never will be comparing strings to their ends. This modification includes changing the definition of `equals` to regard two strings as equal if one is a prefix of the other, as we did in Section 12.5, since we will be comparing a (short) search key against a (long) text string, starting at some position in the text string. A third change that is convenient is to keep a string index rather than a character in each node so that every node in the tree refers to a position in the text string (the position in the text string following the first occurrence of the character string defined by the characters on equal branches from the root to that node). Implementing these changes is an interesting and informative exercise that leads to a flexible and efficient text-string–index implementation (see Exercise 15.88).

Despite all the advantages that we have been discussing, it is important to remember that the text itself is usually fixed for typical text indexing applications, so we do not need to support the dynamic *insert* operations that we have become accustomed to supporting. That is, we typically build the index once, then use it for a huge number of searches, without ever changing it. Therefore, we may not need dynamic data structures like BSTs, patricia tries or TSTs at all: the basic binary search algorithm in Section 12.5 is sufficient. The primary advantage of using binary search over a dynamic data structure is the space savings. To index a text string at N positions using binary search, we need just N string indexes; in contrast, to index a string at N positions using a tree-based method, we need at least $2N$ references (for at least two links per node) in addition to the N indexes. Text indexes are typically huge, so binary search might be preferred because it provides guaranteed logarithmic search time but uses less than one-third the amount of memory used by tree-based methods. If sufficient memory space is available, however, TSTs or tries will lead to a faster *search* for many applications because they move through the key without retracing its steps, and binary search does not do so (though it is possible to improve binary search to examine fewer characters in string keys, as we will see in Part 6).

If we have a huge text but plan to perform only a small number of searches, then building a full index is not likely to be justified. The *string-search* problem is to determine quickly whether a given text contains a given search key (without preprocessing the text). There are numerous string-processing problems that fall between these two extremes of needing no preprocessing and requiring a full index. Part 6 is devoted to such problems.

Exercises

▷ **15.84** Draw the 26-way DST that results when you build a text-string index from the words now is the time for all good people to come the aid of their party.

▷ **15.85** Draw the 26-way trie that results when you build a text-string index from the words now is the time for all good people to come the aid of their party.

▷ **15.86** Draw the TST that results when you build a text-string index from the words now is the time for all good people to come the aid of their party, in the style of Figure 15.20.

▷ **15.87** Draw the TST that results when you build a text-string index from the words now is the time for all good people to come the aid of their party, using the implementation described in the text, where the TST contains string pointers at every node.

○ **15.88** Modify the TST search and insertion implementations in Programs 15.15 and 15.16 to provide a TST-based string index.

○ **15.89** Implement an interface that allows patricia to process String keys as though they were bitstrings.

○ **15.90** Draw the patricia trie that results when you build a text string index from the words now is the time for all good people to come the aid of their party, using a 5-bit binary coding with the ith letter in the alphabet represented by the binary representation of i.

15.91 Find a large (at least 10^6 bytes) text file on your system and compare the height and internal path length of a standard BST, patricia trie, and TST, when you use these methods to build an index from that file.

15.92 Run empirical studies to compare the height and internal path length of a standard BST, patricia trie, and TST, when you use these methods to build an index from a text string consisting of N random characters from a 32-character alphabet, for $N = 10^3$, 10^4, 10^5, and 10^6.

○ **15.93** Write an efficient program to determine the longest repeated sequence in a huge text string.

○ **15.94** Write an efficient program to determine the 10-character sequence that occurs most frequently in a huge text string.

• **15.95** Build a string index that supports an operation that returns the number of occurrences of its parameter in the indexed text and supports a *search* operation that calls a method in a client-supplied object for all the text positions that match the search key.

o **15.96** Describe a text string of N characters for which a TST-based string index will perform particularly badly. Estimate the cost of building an index for the same string with a BST.

15.97 Suppose that we want to build an index for a random N-bit string, for bit positions that are a multiple of 16. Run empirical studies to determine which of the bytesizes 1, 2, 4, 8, or 16 leads to the lowest running times to construct a TST-based index, for $N = 10^3$, 10^4, 10^5, and 10^6.

CHAPTER SIXTEEN

External Searching

$\mathbf{S}$EARCH ALGORITHMS THAT are appropriate for accessing items from huge files are of immense practical importance. Searching is the fundamental operation on huge data sets, and it certainly consumes a significant fraction of the resources used in many computing environments. With the advent of world wide networking, we have the ability to gather almost all the information that is possibly relevant to a task—our challenge is to be able to search through it efficiently. In this chapter, we discuss basic underlying mechanisms that can support efficient search in symbol tables that are as large as we can imagine.

Like those in Chapter 11, the algorithms that we consider in this chapter are relevant to numerous different types of hardware and software environments. Accordingly, we tend to think about the algorithms at a level more abstract than that of the Java programs that we have been considering. However, the algorithms that we shall consider also directly generalize familiar searching methods and are conveniently expressed as Java programs that are useful in many situations. We will proceed in a manner different from that in Chapter 11: We will develop specific implementations in detail, consider their essential performance characteristics, and then discuss ways in which the underlying algorithms might prove useful under situations that might arise in practice. Taken literally, the title of this chapter is a misnomer, since we will present the algorithms as Java programs that we could substitute interchangeably for the other symbol-table implementations that we have considered in Chapters 12 through 15. As such, they are not "external" methods at all. However, they are built in accordance with a simple abstract model, which makes them precise specifications of how to build searching methods for specific external devices.

Detailed abstract models are less useful than they were for sorting because the costs involved are so low for many important applications. We shall be concerned mainly with methods for searching in huge files stored on any external device where we have fast access to arbitrary blocks of data, such as a disk. For tapelike devices, where only sequential access is allowed (one model that we considered in Chapter 11), searching degenerates to the trivial (and slow) method of starting at the beginning and reading until completion of the search. For disklike devices, we can do much better: Remarkably, the methods that we shall study can support *search* and *insert* operations on symbol tables containing billions or trillions of items using only three or four references to blocks of data on disk. System parameters—such as block size and the ratio of the cost of accessing a new block to the cost of accessing the items within a block—affect performance, but the methods are relatively insensitive to the values of these parameters (within the ranges of values that we are likely to encounter in practice). Moreover, the most important steps that we must take to adapt the methods to particular practical situations are straightforward.

Searching is a fundamental operation for disk devices. Files are typically organized to take advantage of particular device characteristics to make access to information as efficient as possible. In short, it is safe to assume that the devices that we use to store huge amounts of information are built to support efficient and straightforward implementations of *search*. In this chapter, we consider algorithms built at a level of abstraction slightly higher than that of the basic operations provided by disk hardware, which can support *insert* and other dynamic symbol-table operations. These methods afford the same kinds of advantages over the straightforward methods that BSTs and hash tables offer over binary search and sequential search.

In many computing environments, we can address a huge *virtual memory* directly and can rely on the system to find efficient ways to handle any program's requests for data. The algorithms that we consider also can be effective solutions to the symbol-table implementation problem in such environments.

A collection of information to be processed with a computer is called a *database*. A great deal of study has gone into methods of building, maintaining, and using databases. Much of this work has been in the development of abstract models and implementations to support *search* operations with criteria more complex than the simple "match a single key" criterion that we have been considering. In a database, searches might be based on criteria for partial matches, perhaps including multiple keys, and might be expected to return a large number of items. We touch on methods of this type in Parts 6 and 7. General search requests are sufficiently complicated that it is not atypical for us to do a sequential search over the entire database, testing each item to see if it meets the criteria. Still, fast search for tiny bits of data matching specific criteria in a huge file is an essential capability in any database system, and many modern databases are built on the mechanisms that we describe in this chapter.

16.1 Rules of the Game

As we did in Chapter 11, we make the basic assumption that sequential access to data is far less expensive than nonsequential access. Our model will be to consider whatever memory facility that we use to implement the symbol table as divided up into *pages*: contiguous blocks of information that can be accessed efficiently by the disk hardware. Each page will hold many items; our task is to organize the items within the pages such that we can access any item by reading only a few pages. We assume that the I/O time required to read a page completely dominates the processing time required to access specific items or to do any other computing involving that page. This model is oversimplified in many ways, but it retains enough of the characteristics of external storage devices to allow us to consider fundamental methods.

Definition 16.1 *A* **page** *is a contiguous block of data. A* **probe** *is the first access to a page.*

We are interested in symbol-table implementations that use a small number of probes. We avoid making specific assumptions about the page size and about the ratio of the time required for a probe to the time required, subsequently, to access items within the block. We expect these values to be on the order of 100 or 1000; we do not need to be more precise because the algorithms are not highly sensitive to these values.

This model is directly relevant, for example, in a file system in which files comprise blocks with unique identifiers and in which the purpose is to support efficient access, insertion, and deletion based on that identifier. A certain number of items fit on a block, and the cost of processing items within a block is insignificant compared to the cost of reading the block.

This model is also directly relevant in a virtual-memory system, where we simply refer directly to a huge amount of memory and rely on the system to keep the information that we use most often in fast storage (such as internal memory) and the information that we use infrequently in slow storage (such as a disk). Many computer systems have sophisticated paging mechanisms, which implement virtual memory by keeping recently used pages in a *cache* that can be accessed quickly. Paging systems are based on the same abstraction that we are considering: They divide the disk into blocks and assume that the cost of accessing a block for the first time far exceeds the cost of accessing data within the block.

Our abstract notion of a page typically will correspond precisely to a block in a file system or to a page in a virtual-memory system. For simplicity, we generally assume this correspondence when considering the algorithms. For specific applications, we might have multiple pages per block or multiple blocks per page for system- or application-dependent reasons; such details do not diminish the effectiveness of the algorithms and thus underscore the utility of working at an abstract level.

We manipulate pages, references to pages, and items with keys. For a huge database, the most important problem to consider now is to maintain an *index* to the data. That is, as discussed briefly in Section 12.5, we assume that the items constituting our symbol table are stored in some static form somewhere and that our task is to build a data structure with keys and references to items that allows us to produce quickly a reference to a given item. For example, a telephone company might have customer information stored in a huge static database, with several indexes on the database, perhaps using different keys, for monthly billing, daily transaction processing, periodic solicitation, and so forth. For huge data sets, indexes are of critical importance: We generally do not make copies of the basic data, not only because we may not be able to afford the extra space, but also because we want to avoid the problems associated with maintaining the integrity of the data when we have multiple copies.

Accordingly, we generally assume that each item is a *reference* to the actual data, which may be a page address or some more complex interface to a database. For simplicity, we do not keep copies of items in our data structures, but we may keep copies of keys—an approach that is often practical. Also, for simplicity in describing the algorithms, we do not use an abstract interface for item and page references— instead, we just use references to Item objects. Thus, we can use our implementations directly in a virtual-memory environment but have to convert the references and object accesses into more complex mechanisms to make them true external sorting methods.

We shall consider algorithms that, for a broad range of values of the two main parameters (block size and relative access time), implement *search*, *insert*, and other operations in a fully dynamic symbol table using only a few probes per operation. In the typical case where we perform huge numbers of operations, careful tuning might be effective. For example, if we can reduce the typical search cost from three probes to two probes, we might improve system performance by 50 percent! However, we will not consider such tuning here; its effectiveness is strongly system- and application-dependent.

On ancient machines, external storage devices were complex contraptions that not only were big and slow but also did not hold much information. Accordingly, it was important to work to overcome their limitations, and early programming lore is filled with tales of external file access programs that were timed perfectly to grab data off a rotating disk or drum and otherwise to minimize the amount of physical movement required to access data. Early lore is also filled with tales of spectacular failures of such attempts, where slight miscalculations made the process much slower than a naive implementation would have been. By contrast, modern storage devices not only are tiny and extremely fast but also hold huge amounts of information; so we generally do not need to address such problems. Indeed, in modern programming environments, we tend to shy away from dependencies on the properties of specific physical devices—it is generally more important that our programs be effective on a variety of machines (including those to be developed in the future) than that they achieve peak performance for a particular device.

For long-lived databases, there are numerous important implementation issues surrounding the general goals of maintaining the integrity of the data and providing flexible and reliable access. We do not address such issues here. For such applications, we may view the methods that we consider both as the underlying algorithms that will ultimately ensure good performance and as a starting point in the system design.

16.2 Indexed Sequential Access

A straightforward approach to building an index is to keep an array with keys and item references, in order of the keys, then to use binary search (see Section 12.4) to implement *search*. For N items, this method would require $\lg N$ probes—even for a huge file. Our basic model leads us immediately to consider two modifications to this simple method. First, the index itself is huge and, in general, will not fit on a single page. Since we can access pages only through page references, we can instead build an explicit fully balanced binary tree with keys and page references in internal nodes, and with keys and item references in external nodes. Second, the cost of accessing M table entries is the same as the cost of accessing 2, so we can use an M-ary tree for about the same cost per node as a binary tree. This improvement reduces the number of probes to be proportional to about $\log_M N$. As we saw in Chapters 10 and 15, we can regard this quantity to be constant for practical purposes. For example, if M is 1000, then $\log_M N$ is less than 5 if N is less than 1 trillion.

Figure 16.1 gives a sample set of keys, and Figure 16.2 depicts an example of such a tree structure for those keys. We need to use relatively small values of M and N to keep our examples manageable; nevertheless, they illustrate that the trees for large M will be flat.

The tree depicted in Figure 16.2 is an abstract device-independent representation of an index that is similar to many other data structures that we have considered. Note that, in addition, it is not far removed from device-*dependent* indexes that might be found in low-level disk access software. For example, some early systems used a two-level scheme, where the bottom level corresponded to the items on the

706	111000110
176	001111110
601	110000001
153	001101011
513	101001011
773	111111011
742	111100010
373	011111011
524	101010100
766	111110110
275	010111101
737	111011111
574	101111100
434	100011100
641	110100001
207	010000111
001	000000001
277	010111111
061	000110001
736	111011110
526	101010110
562	101110010
017	000001111
107	001000111
147	001100111

Figure 16.1
Binary representation of octal keys

The keys (left) that we use in the examples in this chapter are 3-digit octal numbers, which we also interpret as 9-bit binary values (right).

pages for a particular disk device, and the second level corresponded to a master index to the individual devices. In such systems, the master index was kept in main memory, so accessing an item with such an index required two disk accesses: one to get the index, and one to get the page containing the item. As disk capacity increases, so increases the size of the index, and several pages might be required to store the index, eventually leading to a hierarchical scheme like the one depicted in Figure 16.2. We shall continue working with an abstract representation, secure in the knowledge that it can be implemented directly with typical low-level system hardware and software.

Many modern systems use a similar tree structure to organize huge files as a sequence of disk pages. Such trees contain no keys, but they can efficiently support the commonly used operations of accessing the file in sequential order, and, if each node contains a count of its tree size, of finding the page containing the kth item in the file.

Historically, because it combines a sequential key organization with indexed access, the indexing method depicted in Figure 16.2 is called *indexed sequential access*. It is the method of choice for applications in which changes to the database are rare. We sometimes refer to the index itself as a *directory*. The disadvantage of using indexed sequential access is that modifying the directory is an expensive operation. For example, adding a single key can require rebuilding virtually the whole database, with new positions for many of the keys and new values for the indexes. To combat this defect and to provide for modest growth, early systems provided for overflow pages on disks and overflow space in pages, but such techniques ultimately were not very effective in dynamic situations (see Exercise 16.3). The methods that we consider in Sections 16.3 and 16.4 provide systematic and efficient alternatives to such ad hoc schemes.

Property 16.1 *A search in an indexed sequential file requires only a constant number of probes, but an insertion can involve rebuilding the entire index.*

We use the term *constant* loosely here (and throughout this chapter) to refer to a quantity that is proportional to $\log_M N$ for large M. As we have discussed, this usage is justified for practical file sizes. Figure 16.3 gives more examples. Even if we were to have a 128-bit search key, capable of specifying the impossibly large number of 2^{128}

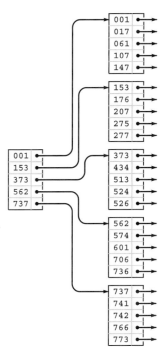

**Figure 16.2
Indexed sequential file structure**

In a sequential index, we keep the keys in sequential order in full pages (right), with an index directing us to the smallest key in each page (left). To add a key, we need to rebuild the data structure.

different items, we could find an item with a given key in 13 probes, with 1000-way branching. ∎

We will not consider implementations that search and construct indexes of this type, because they are special cases of the more general mechanisms that we consider in Section 16.3 (see Exercise 16.17 and Program 16.2).

Exercises

▷ **16.1** Tabulate the values of $\log_M N$, for $M = 10$, 100, and 1000 and $N = 10^3, 10^4, 10^5$, and 10^6.

▷ **16.2** Draw an indexed sequential file structure for the keys 516, 177, 143, 632, 572, 161, 774, 470, 411, 706, 461, 612, 761, 474, 774, 635, 343, 461, 351, 430, 664, 127, 345, 171, and 357 , for $M = 5$ and $M = 6$.

○ **16.3** Suppose that we build an indexed sequential file structure for N items in pages of capacity M, but leave k empty spaces in each page for expansion. Give a formula for the number of probes needed for a search, as a function of N, M, and k. Use the formula to determine the number of probes needed for a search when $k = M/10$, for $M = 10$, 100, and 1000 and $N = 10^3, 10^4, 10^5$, and 10^6.

○ **16.4** Suppose that the cost of a probe is about α time units, and that the average cost of finding an item in a page is about βM time units. Find the value of M that minimizes the cost for a search in an indexed sequential file structure, for $\alpha/\beta = 10$, 100, and 1000 and $N = 10^3, 10^4, 10^5$, and 10^6.

10^5	words in dictionary
10^6	words in *Moby Dick*
10^9	Social Security numbers
10^{12}	phone numbers in the world
10^{15}	people who ever lived
10^{20}	grains of sand on beach at Coney Island
10^{25}	bits of memory ever manufactured
10^{79}	electrons in universe

Figure 16.3
Examples of data set sizes

These generous upper bounds indicate that we can assume safely, for practical purposes, that we will never have a symbol table with more than 10^{30} items. Even in such an unrealistically huge database, we could find an item with a given key with less than 10 probes, if we did 1000-way branching. Even if we somehow found a way to store information on each electron in the universe, 1000-way branching would give us access to any particular item with less than 27 probes.

16.3 B Trees

To build search structures that can be effective in a dynamic situation, we build multiway trees, but we relax the restriction that every node must have *exactly* M entries. Instead, we insist that every node must have *at most* M entries so that they will fit on a page, but we allow nodes to have fewer entries. To be sure that nodes have a sufficient number of entries to provide the branching that we need to keep search paths short, we also insist that all nodes have *at least* (say) $M/2$ entries, except possibly the root, which must have a least one entry (two links). The reason for the exception at the root will become clear when we consider the construction algorithm in detail. Such trees were named *B trees* by Bayer and McCreight, who, in 1970, were the first researchers to consider the use of multiway balanced trees for external searching. Many people reserve the term *B tree* to describe the exact data structure built by the algorithm suggested by Bayer and McCreight; we use it as a generic term to refer to a family of related algorithms.

We have already seen a B-tree implementation: In Definitions 13.1 and 13.2, we see that B trees of order 4, where each node has at most four links and at least two links, are none other than the balanced 2-3-4 trees of Chapter 13. Indeed, the underlying abstraction generalizes in a straightforward manner, and we can implement B trees by generalizing the top-down 2-3-4 tree implementations in Section 13.4. However, the various differences between external and internal searching that we discussed in Section 16.1 lead us to a number of different implementation decisions. In this section, we consider an implementation that

- Generalizes 2-3-4 trees to trees with between $M/2$ and M nodes
- Represents multiway nodes with an array of items and links
- Implements an index instead of a search structure containing the items
- Splits from the bottom up
- Separates the index from the items

The final two properties in this list are not essential but are convenient in many situations and are normally found in B tree implementations.

Figure 16.4 illustrates an abstract 4-5-6-7-8 tree, which generalizes the 2-3-4 tree that we considered in Section 13.3. The generalization is straightforward: 4-nodes have three keys and four links, 5-nodes have four keys and five links, and so forth, with one link for each possible interval between keys. To search, we start at the root and move from one node to the next by finding the proper interval for the search key in the current node and then exiting through the corresponding link to get to the next node. We terminate the search with a search hit if we find the search key in any node that we touch; we terminate with a search miss if we reach the bottom of the tree without a hit. As with top-down 2-3-4 trees, we can insert a new key at the bottom of the tree after a search if, on the way down the tree, we split nodes that are full: If the root is an 8-node, we split it into

**Figure 16.4
A 4-5-6-7-8 tree**

This figure depicts a generalization of 2-3-4 trees built from nodes with 4 through 8 links (and 3 through 7 keys, respectively). As with 2-3-4 trees, we keep the height constant by splitting 8-nodes when encountering them, with either a top-down or a bottom-up insertion algorithm. For example, to insert another J into this tree, we would first split the 8-node into two 4-nodes, then insert the M into the root, converting it into a 6-node. When the root splits, we have no choice but to create a new root that is a 2-node, so the root node is excused from the constraint that nodes must have at least four links.

Figure 16.5
B tree construction, part 1

This example shows six insertions into an initially empty B tree built with pages that can hold five keys and links, using keys that are 3-digit octal numbers (9-bit binary numbers). We keep the keys in order in the pages. The sixth insertion causes a split into two external nodes with three keys each and an internal node that serves as an index: Its first entry refers to the page containing all keys greater than or equal to 000 but less than 601, and its second entry refers to the page containing all keys greater than or equal to 601.

a 2-node connected to two 4-nodes; then, any time we see a k-node attached to an 8-node, we replace it by a $(k+1)$-node attached to two 4-nodes. This policy guarantees that we have room to insert the new node when we reach the bottom.

Alternatively, as discussed for 2-3-4 trees in Section 13.3, we can split from the bottom up: We insert by searching and putting the new key in the bottom node, unless that node is a 8-node, in which case we split it into two 4-nodes and insert the middle key and the links to the two new nodes into its parent, working up the tree until encountering an ancestor that is not a 8-node.

Replacing 4 by $M/2$ and 8 by M in descriptions in the previous two paragraphs converts them into descriptions of search and insert for $M/2$-...-M trees, for any positive even integer M, even 2 (see Exercise 16.9).

Definition 16.2 *A* **B tree** *of order M is a tree that either is empty or comprises* **k-nodes**, *with $k-1$ keys and k links to trees representing each of the k intervals delimited by the keys, and has the following structural properties: k must be between 2 and M at the root and between $M/2$ and M at every other node; and all links to empty trees must be at the same distance from the root.*

B tree algorithms are built upon this basic set of abstractions. As in Chapter 13, we have a great deal of freedom in choosing concrete representations for such trees. For example, we can use an extended red-black representation (see Exercise 13.69). For external searching, we use the even more straightforward ordered-array representation, taking M to be sufficiently large that M-nodes fill a page. The branching factor is at least $M/2$, so the number of probes for any search or insert is effectively constant, as discussed following Property 16.1.

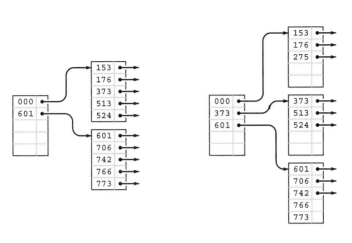

Instead of implementing the method just described, we consider a variant that generalizes the standard index that we considered in Section 16.1. We keep keys with item references in *external pages* at the bottom of the tree and copies of keys with page references in *internal pages*. We insert new items at the bottom and then use the basic $M/2$-...-M tree abstraction. When a page has M entries, we split it into two pages with $M/2$ pages each and insert a reference to the new page into its parent. When the root splits, we make a new root with two children, thus increasing the height of the tree by 1.

Figures 16.5 through 16.7 show the B tree that we build by inserting the keys in Figure 16.1 (in the order given) into an initially empty tree, with $M = 5$. Doing insertions involves simply adding an item to a page, but we can look at the final tree structure to determine the significant events that occurred during its construction. It has seven external pages, so there must have been six external node splits, and it is of height 3, so the root of the tree must have split twice. These events are described in the commentary that accompanies the figures.

Program 16.1 gives the outline of our B-tree symbol table implementation. We do not specify the structure of nodes in the detail that would be required in an actual implementation, because that should involve reference to specific disk pages. For clarity, we use one node type, each node consisting of an array of entries that each contain an

Figure 16.6
B tree construction, part 2

After we insert the four keys 742, 373, 524, and 766 into the right-most B tree in Figure 16.5, both of the external pages are full (left). Then, when we insert 275, the first page splits, sending a link to the new page (along with its smallest key 373) up to the index (center); when we then insert 737, the page at the bottom splits, again sending a link to the new page up to the index (right).

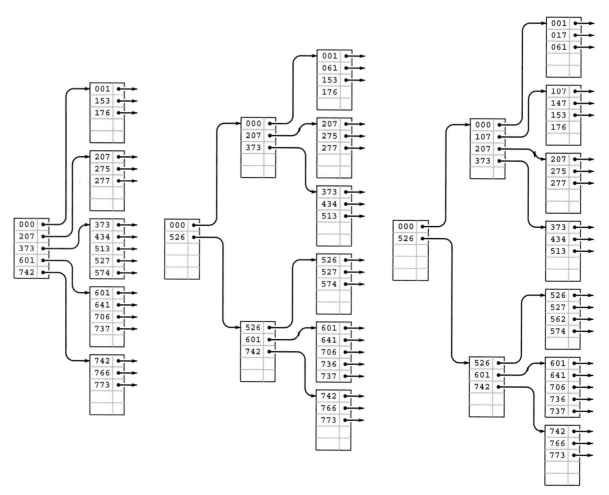

Figure 16.7
B tree construction, part 3

Continuing our example, we insert the 13 keys 574, 434, 641, 207, 001, 277, 061, 736, 526, 562, 017, 107, and 147 into the right-most B tree in Figure 16.6. Node splits occur when we insert 277 (left), 526 (center), and 107 (right). The node split caused by inserting 526 also causes the index page to split and increases the height of the tree by one.

item, a key, and a link. Each node also contains a count giving the number of active entries. We do not refer to the items in internal nodes; we do not refer to the links in external nodes; and we do not refer to the keys within the items in the tree. The precise data structure that we would choose in an application might save space by using derived classes. We could also choose to trade space for time by using links to items everywhere in the tree instead of keys. Such design decisions involve straightforward modifications to our code and depend on the precise nature of an application's keys, items, and links.

> **Program 16.1 B tree symbol-table implementation**
>
> Each node in a B tree contains an array and a count of the number of
> active entries in the array. Each array entry is a key, an item, and a
> node reference. In internal nodes, we use only the keys and references;
> in external nodes, we use only the keys and items.
>
> ```
> class ST
>   {
>     private class entry
>       { KEY key; ITEM item; Node next;
>         entry(KEY v, ITEM x) { key = v; item = x; }
>         entry(KEY v, Node u) { key = v; next = u; }
>       }
>     private class Node
>       { int m; entry[] b;
>         Node(int k) { b = new entry[M]; m = k; }
>       }
>     private Node head;
>     private int HT;
>     ST(int maxN)
>       { HT = 0; head = new Node(0); }
>     ITEM search(KEY key)
>       // See Program 16.2
>     void insert(ITEM x)
>       // See Program 16.3
>   }
> ```

With these definitions and the example trees that we just considered, the code for *search* that is given in Program 16.2 is straightforward. For external nodes, we scan through the array of nodes to look
for a key matching the search key, returning the associated item if we
succeed and null if we do not. For internal nodes, we scan through
the array of nodes to find the link to the unique subtree that could
contain the search key.

Program 16.3 is an implementation of *insert* for B trees; it too
uses the recursive approach that we have taken for numerous other
search-tree implementations in Chapters 13 and 15. It is a bottom-up
implementation because we check for node splitting *after* the recursive

Program 16.2 B-tree search

This implementation of *search* for B trees is based on a recursive method, as usual. For internal nodes (positive height), we scan to find the first key larger than the search key, and do a recursive call on the subtree referenced by the previous link. For external nodes (height 0), we scan to see whether or not there is an item with key equal to the search key.

```
private ITEM searchR(Node h, KEY v, int ht)
  {
    if (ht == 0)
      for (int j = 0; j < h.m; j++)
        { entry e = h.b[j];
          if (equals(v, e.key)) return e.item; }
    else
      for (int j = 0; j < h.m; j++)
        if ((j+1 == h.m) || less(v, h.b[j+1].key))
          return searchR(h.b[j].next, v, ht-1);
    return null;
  }
ITEM search(KEY key)
  { return searchR(head, key, HT); }
```

call, so the first node split is an external node. The split requires that we pass up a new link to the parent of the split node, which in turn might need to split and pass up a link to its parent, and so forth, perhaps all the way up to the root of the tree (when the root splits, we create a new root, with two children). By contrast, the 2-3-4–tree implementation of Program 13.6 checks for splits *before* the recursive call, so we do splitting on the way down the tree. We could also use a top-down approach for B trees (see Exercise 16.10). This distinction between top-down versus bottom-up approaches is unimportant in many B tree applications, because the trees are so flat.

The node-splitting code is given in Program 16.4. In the code, we use an even value for the variable M, and we allow only $M - 1$ items per node in the tree. This policy allows us to insert the Mth item into a node *before* splitting that node and simplifies the code considerably without having much effect on the cost (see Exercises 16.20 and 16.21). For simplicity, we use the upper bound of M items per node in the

Program 16.3 B-tree insertion

We insert an item by recursively calling insertR for the node in the entry with the largest key smaller than the item's key.

At the bottom level (when ht is 0), we move larger items to the right by one position, as in insertion sort. If the insertion overfills the node, we call split (see Program 16.4) to divide the node into two halves, and then insert the reference to the new node into the parent internal node, which could also split, possibly propagating the insertion all the way up to the root.

To split the root, we create a new head node with two entries, one for the old head and the other for the new reference created by the split. The node at the root is the only node in the tree that can have fewer than $M/2$ entries.

```
private Node insertR(Node h, ITEM x, int ht)
  { int i, j; KEY v = x.key(); Node u;
    entry t = new entry(v, x);
    if (ht == 0)
      for (j = 0; j < h.m; j++)
        { if (less(v, (h.b[j]).key)) break; }
    else
      for (j = 0; j < h.m; j++)
        if ((j+1 == h.m) || less(v, (h.b[j+1]).key))
          { u = insertR(h.b[j++].next, x, ht-1);
            if (u == null) return null;
            t.key = (u.b[0]).key; t.next = u; break;
          }
    for (i = h.m; i > j; i--) h.b[i] = h.b[i-1];
    h.b[j] = t; h.m++;
    if (h.m < M) return null; else return split(h);
  }
void insert(ITEM x)
  { Node u = insertR(head, x, HT);
    if (u == null) return;
    Node t = new Node(2);
    t.b[0] = new entry((head.b[0]).key, head);
    t.b[1] = new entry((u.b[0]).key, u);
    head = t; HT++;
  }
```

> ### Program 16.4 B-tree node split
>
> To split a node in a B tree, we create a new node and move the larger half of the keys to the new node. This code assumes that M is even and uses an extra position in each node for the item that causes the split. That is, the maximum number of keys in a node is M-1, and when a node gets M keys, we split it into two nodes with M/2 keys each.
>
> ```
> private Node split(Node h)
>   { Node t = new Node(M/2); h.m = M/2;
>     for (int j = 0; j < M/2; j++)
>       t.b[j] = h.b[M/2+j];
>     return t;
>   }
> ```

analytic results later in this section; the actual differences are minute. In a top-down implementation, we would not have to resort to this technique, because the convenience of being sure that there is always room to insert a new key in each node comes automatically.

Property 16.2 *A search or an insertion in a B tree of order M with N items requires between $\log_M N$ and $\log_{M/2} N$ probes—a constant number, for practical purposes.*

This property follows from the observation that all the nodes in the interior of the B tree (nodes that are not the root and are not external) have between $M/2$ and M links, since they are formed from a split of a full node with M keys and can only grow in size (when a lower node is split). In the best case, these nodes form a complete tree of degree M, which leads immediately to the stated bound (see Property 16.1). In the worst case, we have a root with two entries that each refer to a complete tree of degree $M/2$. ∎

When M is 1000, the height of the tree is less than three for N less than 125 million. In typical situations, we can reduce the cost to two probes by keeping the root in internal memory. For a disk-searching implementation, we might take this step explicitly before embarking on any application involving a huge number of searches; in a virtual memory with caching, the root node will be the one most likely to be in fast memory, because it is the most frequently accessed node.

We can hardly expect to have a search implementation that can guarantee a cost of fewer than two probes for *search* and *insert* in huge files, and B trees are widely used because they allow us to achieve this ideal. The price of this speed and flexibility is the empty space within the nodes, which could be a liability for huge files.

Property 16.3 *A B tree of order M constructed from N random items is expected to have about $1.44N/M$ pages.*

Yao proved this fact in 1979, using mathematical analysis that is beyond the scope of this book (*see reference section*). It is based on analyzing a simple probabilistic model that describes tree growth. After the first $M/2$ nodes have been inserted, there are, at any given time, t_i external pages with i items, for $M/2 \leq i \leq M$, with $t_{M/2} + \ldots + t_M = N$. Since each interval between nodes is equally likely to receive a random key, the probability that a node with i items is hit is t_i/N. Specifically, for $i < M$, this quantity is the probability that the number of external pages with i items decreases by 1 and the number of external pages with $(i + 1)$ items increases by 1; and for $i = 2M$, this quantity is the probability that the number of external pages with $2M$ items decreases by 1 and the number of external pages with M items increases by 2. Such a probabilistic process is called a *Markov chain*. Yao's result is based on an analysis of the asymptotic properties of this chain. ∎

We can also validate Property 16.3 by writing a program to simulate the probabilistic process (see Exercise 16.11 and Figures 16.8 and 16.9). Of course, we also could just build random B trees and measure their structural properties. The probabilistic simulation is simpler to do than either the mathematical analysis or the full implementation and is an important tool for us to use in studying and comparing variants of the algorithm (see, for example, Exercise 16.16). The implementations of other symbol-table operations are similar to those for several other tree-based representations that we have seen before and are left as exercises (see Exercises 16.22 through 16.25). In particular, *select* and *sort* implementations are straightforward, but, as usual, implementing a proper *remove* can be a challenging task. Like *insert*, most *remove* operations are a simple matter of removing an item from an external page and decrementing its counter, but what do we do when we have to remove an item from

Figure 16.8
Growth of a large B tree

In this simulation, we insert items with random keys into an initially empty B tree with pages that can hold nine keys and links. Each line displays the external nodes, with each external node depicted as a line segment of length proportional to the number of items in that node. Most insertions land in an external node that is not full, increasing that node's size by 1. When an insertion lands in a full external node, the node splits into two nodes of half the size.

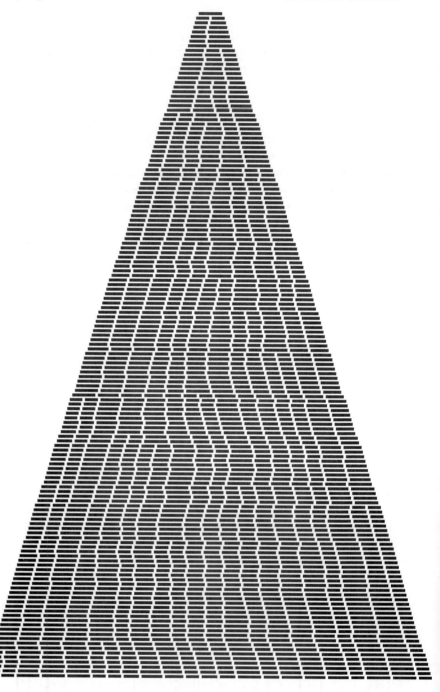

a node that has only $M/2$ items? The natural approach is to find items from sibling nodes to fill the space (perhaps reducing the number of nodes by one), but the implementation becomes complicated because we have to track down the keys associated with any items that we move among nodes. In practical situations, we can typically adopt the much simpler approach of letting external nodes become underfull, without suffering much performance degradation (see Exercise 16.25).

Many variations on the basic B-tree abstraction suggest themselves immediately. One class of variations saves time by packing as many page references as possible in internal nodes, thereby increasing the branching factor and flattening the tree. As we have discussed, the benefits of such changes are marginal in modern systems, since standard values of the parameters allow us to implement *search* and *insert* with two probes—an efficiency that we could hardly improve. Another class of variations improves storage efficiency by combining nodes with siblings before splitting. Exercises 16.13 through 16.16 are concerned with such a method, which reduces the excess storage used from 44 to 23 percent, for random keys. As usual, the proper choice among different variations depends on properties of applications. Given the broad variety of different situations where B trees are applicable, we will not consider such issues in detail. We also will not be able to consider details of implementations, because there are so many device- and system-dependent matters to take into account. As usual, delving deeply into such implementations is a risky business, and we shy away from such fragile and nonportable code in modern systems, particularly when the basic algorithm performs so well.

Exercises

▷ **16.5** Give the contents of the 3-4-5-6 tree that results when you insert the keys E A S Y Q U E S T I O N W I T H P L E N T Y O F K E Y S in that order into an initially empty tree.

○ **16.6** Draw figures corresponding to Figures 16.5 through 16.7, to illustrate the process of inserting the keys 516, 177, 143, 632, 572, 161, 774, 470, 411, 706, 461, 612, 761, 474, 774, 635, 343, 461, 351, 430, 664, 127, 345, 171, and 357 in that order into an initially empty tree, with $M = 5$.

○ **16.7** Give the height of the B trees that result when you insert the keys in Exercise 16.6 in that order into an initially empty tree, for *each* value of $M > 2$.

16.8 Draw the B tree that results when you insert 16 equal keys into an initially empty tree, with $M = 4$.

Figure 16.9
Growth of a large B tree, page occupancy exposed

This version of Figure 16.8 shows how pages fill during the B tree growth process. Again, most insertions land in a page that is not full and just increase its occupancy by 1. When an insertion does land in a full page, the page splits into two half-empty pages.

• **16.9** Draw the 1-2 tree that results when you insert the keys E A S Y Q U E S T I O N into an initially empty tree. Explain why 1-2 trees are not of practical interest as balanced trees.

• **16.10** Modify the B-tree–insertion implementation in Program 16.3 to do splitting on the way down the tree, in a manner similar to our implementation of 2-3-4–tree insertion (Program 13.6).

• **16.11** Write a program to compute the average number of external pages for a B tree of order M built from N random insertions into an initially empty tree, using the probabilistic process described after Property 16.1. Run your program for $M = 10$, 100, and 1000 and $N = 10^3$, 10^4, 10^5, and 10^6.

○ **16.12** Suppose that, in a three-level tree, we can afford to keep a links in internal memory, between b and $2b$ links in pages representing internal nodes, and between c and $2c$ items in pages representing external nodes. What is the maximum number of items that we can hold in such a tree, as a function of a, b, and c?

○ **16.13** Consider the *sibling split* (or B* *tree*) heuristic for B trees: When it comes time to split a node because it contains M entries, we combine the node with its sibling. If the sibling has k entries with $k < M - 1$, we reallocate the items giving the sibling and the full node each about $(M + k)/2$ entries. Otherwise, we create a new node and give each of the three nodes about $2M/3$ entries. Also, we allow the root to grow to hold about $4M/3$ items, splitting it and creating a new root node with two entries when it reaches that bound. State bounds on the number of probes used for a search or an insertion in a B* tree of order M with N items. Compare your bounds with the corresponding bounds for B trees (see Property 16.2), for $M = 10$, 100, and 1000 and $N = 10^3$, 10^4, 10^5, and 10^6.

•• **16.14** Develop a B* tree *insert* implementation (based on the sibling-split heuristic).

• **16.15** Create a figure like Figure 16.8 for the sibling-split heuristic.

• **16.16** Run a probabilistic simulation (see Exercise 16.11) to determine the average number of pages used when we use the sibling-split heuristic, building a B* tree of order M by inserting random nodes into an initially empty tree, for $M = 10$, 100, and 1000 and $N = 10^3$, 10^4, 10^5, and 10^6.

• **16.17** Write a program to construct a B tree index from the bottom up, starting with an array of references to pages containing between M and $2M$ items, in sorted order.

• **16.18** Could an index with all pages full, such as Figure 16.2, be constructed by the B-tree–insertion algorithm considered in the text (Program 16.3)? Explain your answer.

16.19 Suppose that many different computers have access to the same index, so several programs may be trying to insert a new node in the same B tree at about the same time. Explain why you might prefer to use top-down B trees instead of bottom-up B trees in such a situation. Assume that each program can (and does) delay the others from modifying any given node that it has read and might later modify.

● **16.20** Modify the B-tree implementation in Programs 16.1 through 16.3 to allow M items per node to exist in the tree.

▷ **16.21** Tabulate the difference between $\log_{999} N$ and $\log_{1000} N$, for $N = 10^3$, 10^4, 10^5, and 10^6.

▷ **16.22** Implement the *sort* operation for a B-tree–based symbol table.

○ **16.23** Implement the *select* operation for a B-tree–based symbol table.

●● **16.24** Implement the *remove* operation for a B-tree–based symbol table.

○ **16.25** Implement the *remove* operation for a B-tree–based symbol table, using a simple method where you delete the indicated item from its external page (perhaps allowing the number of items in the page to fall below $M/2$), but do not propagate the change up through the tree, except possibly to adjust the key values if the deleted item was the smallest in its page.

● **16.26** Modify Programs 16.2 and 16.3 to use binary search (see Program 12.10) within nodes. Determine the value of M that minimizes the time that your program takes to build a symbol table by inserting N items with random keys into an initially empty table, for $N = 10^3$, 10^4, 10^5, and 10^6, and compare the times that you get with the corresponding times for red–black trees (Program 13.6).

16.4 Extendible Hashing

An alternative to B trees that extends digital searching algorithms to apply to external searching was developed in 1978 by Fagin, Nievergelt, Pippenger, and Strong. Their method, called *extendible hashing*, leads to a *search* implementation that requires just one or two probes for typical applications. The corresponding *insert* implementation also (almost always) requires just one or two probes.

Extendible hashing combines features of hashing, multiway-trie algorithms, and sequential-access methods. Like the hashing methods of Chapter 14, extendible hashing is a randomized algorithm—the first step is to define a hash function that transforms keys into integers (see Section 14.1). For simplicity, in this section, we simply consider keys to be random fixed-length bitstrings. Like the multiway-trie algorithms of Chapter 15, extendible hashing begins a search by using the leading bits of the keys to index into a table whose size is a power of 2. Like B-tree algorithms, extendible hashing stores items on pages that

Figure 16.10
Directory page indices

With a directory of eight entries, we can store up to 40 keys by storing all records whose first 3 bits match on the same page, which we can access via a reference stored in the directory (left). Directory entry 0 contains a reference to the page that contains all keys that begin with 000; table entry 1 contains a reference to the page that contains all keys that begin with 001; table entry 2 contains a reference to the page that contains all keys that begin with 010, and so forth. If some pages are not fully populated, we can reduce the number of pages required by having multiple directory references to a page. In this example (left), 373 is on the same page as the keys that start with 2; that page is defined to be the page that contains items with keys whose first 2 bits are 01.

If we double the size of the directory and copy each reference, we get a structure that we can index with the first 4 bits of the search key (right). For example, the final page is still defined to be the page that contains items with keys whose first three bits are 111, and it will be accessed through the directory if the first 4 bits of the search key are 1110 or 1111. This larger directory can accommodate growth in the table.

are split into two pieces when they fill up. Like indexed sequential-access methods, extendible hashing maintains a directory that tells us where we can find the page containing the items that match the search key. The blending of these familiar features in one algorithm makes extendible hashing a fitting conclusion to our study of search algorithms.

Suppose that the number of disk pages that we have available is a power of 2—say 2^d. Then, we can maintain a directory of the 2^d different page references, use d bits of the keys to index into the directory, and can keep, on the same page, all keys that match in their first k bits, as illustrated in Figure 16.10. As we do with B trees, we

Program 16.5 Extendible symbol-table implementation

An extendible hash table is a directory of references to pages (like the external nodes in B trees) that contain up to $2M$ items. Each page also contains a count (m) of the number of items on the page, and an integer (k) that specifies the number of leading bits for which we know the keys of the items to be identical. As usual, N specifies the number of items in the table. The variable d specifies the number of bits that we use to index into the directory, and D is the number of directory entries, so $D = 2^d$. The table is initially set to a directory of size 1, which refers to an empty page.

```
class ST
  {
    private class Node
      { int m; ITEM[] b; int k;
        Node() { b = new ITEM[M]; m = 0; k = 0; }
      }
    private Node[] dir;
    private int d, D;
    ST(int maxN)
      {
        d = 0; D = 1;
        dir = new Node[D];
        dir[0] = new Node();
      }
    ITEM search(KEY v)
      // See Program 16.6
    void insert(ITEM x)
      // See Program 16.7
  }
```

keep the items in order on the pages and do sequential search once we reach the page corresponding to an item with a given search key.

Figure 16.10 illustrates the two basic concepts behind extendible hashing. First, we do not necessarily need to maintain 2^d pages. That is, we can arrange to have multiple directory entries refer to the same page, without changing our ability to search the structure quickly, by combining keys with differing values for their leading d bits together on the same page, while still maintaining our ability to find the page

Program 16.6 Extendible hashing search

Searching in an extendible hashing table is simply a matter of using the leading bits of the key to index into the directory, then doing a sequential search on the specified page for an item with a key equal to the search key. The only requirement is that each directory entry refer to a page that is guaranteed to contain all items in the symbol table that begin with the specified bits.

```
private ITEM search(Node h, KEY v)
  {
    for (int j = 0; j < h.m; j++)
      if (equals(v, h.b[j].key())) return h.b[j];
    return null;
  }
ITEM search(KEY v)
  { return search(dir[bits(v, 0, d)], v); }
```

containing a given key by using the leading bits of the key to index into the directory. Second, we can double the size of the directory to increase the capacity of the table.

Specifically, the data structure that we use for extendible hashing is much simpler than the one that we used for B trees. It consists of pages that contain up to M items, and a directory of 2^d references to pages (see Program 16.5). The reference in directory location x refers to the page that contains all items whose leading d bits are equal to x. The table is constructed with d sufficiently large that we are guaranteed that there are less than M items on each page. The implementation of *search* is simple: We use the leading d bits of the key to index into the directory, which gives us access to the page that contains any items with matching keys, then do sequential search for such an item on that page (see Program 16.6).

The data structure needs to become slightly more complicated to support *insert*, but one of its essential features is that this search algorithm works properly without any modification. To support *insert*, we need to address the following questions:

- What do we do when the number of items that belong on a page exceeds that page's capacity?
- What directory size should we use?

For example, we could not use $d = 2$ in the example in Figure 16.10 because some pages would overflow, and we would not use $d = 5$ because too many pages would be empty. As usual, we are most interested in supporting the *insert* operation for the symbol-table ADT so that, for example, the structure can grow gradually as we do a series of intermixed *search* and *insert* operations. Taking this point of view corresponds to refining our first question:

- What do we do when we need to *insert* an item into a full page?

For example, we could not insert an item whose key starts with a 5 or a 7 in the example in Figure 16.10 because their pages are full.

Definition 16.3 *An* **extendible hash table** *of order d is a directory of 2^d references to pages that contain up to M items with keys. The items on each page are identical in their first k bits, and the directory contains 2^{d-k} references to the page, starting at the location specified by the leading k bits in the keys on the page.*

Some d-bit patterns may not appear in any keys. We leave the corresponding directory entries unspecified in Definition 16.3, although there is a natural way to organize references to null pages; we will examine it shortly.

To maintain these characteristics as the table grows, we use two basic operations: a *page split*, where we distribute some of the keys from a full page onto another page; and a *directory split*, where we double the size of the directory and increase d by 1. Specifically, when a page fills, we split it into two pages, using the leftmost bit position for which the keys differ to decide which items go to the new page. When a page splits, we adjust the directory entries appropriately, doubling the size of the directory if necessary.

As usual, the best way to understand the algorithm is to trace through its operation as we insert a set of keys into an initially empty table. Each of the situations that the algorithm must address occurs early in the process, in a simple form, and we soon come to a realization of the algorithm's underlying principles. Figures 16.11 through 16.13 show the construction of an extendible hash table for the sample set of 25 octal keys that we have been considering in this chapter. As occurs in B trees, most of the insertions are uneventful: They simply add a key to a page. Since we start with one page and end up with eight pages, we can infer that seven of the insertions caused a page split; since we start with a directory of size 1 and end up with a directory of size 16, we can infer that four of the insertions caused a directory split.

Property 16.4 *The extendible hash table built from a set of keys depends on only the values of those keys and does not depend on the order in which the keys are inserted.*

Consider the trie corresponding to the keys (see Property 15.2), with each internal node labeled with the number of items in its subtree. An internal node corresponds to a page in the extendible hash table if and only if its label is less than M and its parent's label is not less than M. All the items below the node go on that page. If a node is at level k, it corresponds to a k-bit pattern derived from the trie path in the normal way, and all entries in the extendible hash table's directory with indices that begin with that k-bit pattern contain references to the corresponding page. The size of the directory is determined by the deepest level among all the internal nodes in the trie that correspond to pages. Thus, we can convert a trie to an extendible hash table without regard to the order in which items are inserted, and this property holds as a consequence of Property 15.2. ∎

Program 16.7 is an implementation of the *insert* operation for an extendible hash table. First, we access the page that could contain the search key, with a single reference to the directory, as we did for search. Then, we insert the new item there, as we did for external nodes in B trees (see Program 16.2). If this insertion leaves M items in the node, then we invoke a split method, again as we did for B trees, but the split method is more complicated in this case. Each page contains the

Figure 16.11
Extendible hash table construction, part 1

As in B trees, the first five insertions into an extendible hash table go into a single page (left). Then, when we insert 773, *we split into two pages (one with all the keys beginning with a 0 bit and one with all the keys beginning with a 1 bit) and double the size of the directory to hold one reference to each of the pages (center). We insert* 742 *into the bottom page (because it begins with a 1 bit) and* 373 *into the top page (because it begins with a 0 bit), but we then need to split the bottom page to accommodate* 524. *For this split, we put all the items with keys that begin with* 10 *on one page and all the items with keys that begin with* 11 *on the other, and we again double the size of the directory to accommodate references to both of these pages (right). The directory contains two references to the page containing items with keys starting with a 0 bit: one for keys that begin with* 00 *and the other for keys that begin with* 01.*

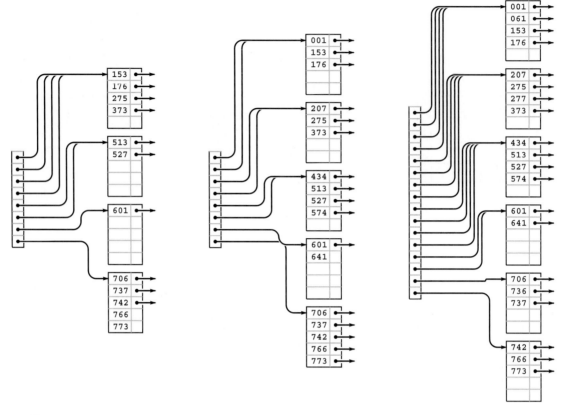

Figure 16.12
Extendible hash table construction, part 2

We insert the keys 766 and 275 into the rightmost B tree in Figure 16.11, without any node splits. Then, when we insert 737, the bottom page splits, which causes a directory split because there is only one link to the bottom page (left). Then, we insert 574, 434, 641, and 207 before 001 causes the top page to split (center). Then, we add 277, 061, and 736 (which causes the bottom page to split) (right).

number k of leading bits that we know to be the same in the keys of all the items on the page, and, because we number bits from the left starting at 0, k also specifies the index of the bit that we want to test to determine how to split the items.

Therefore, to split a page, we make a new page, then put all the items for which that bit is 0 on the old page and all the items for which that bit is 1 on the new page, then set the bit count to $k + 1$ for both pages. Now, it could be the case that all the keys have the same value for bit k, which would still leave us with a full node. If so, we simply go on to the next bit, continuing until we get a least one item in each page. The process must terminate, eventually, *unless we have M values of the same key.* We discuss that case shortly.

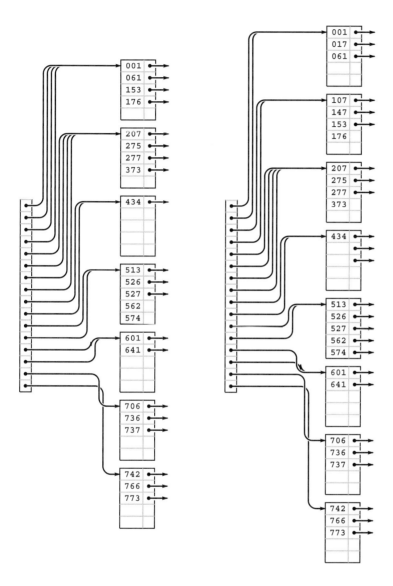

Figure 16.13
Extendible hash table con-
struction, part 3

Continuing the example in Figures 16.11 and 16.12, we insert the 5 keys 526, 562, 017, 107, *and* 147 *into the rightmost B tree in Figure 16.6. Node splits occur when we insert* 526 *(left) and* 107 *(right).*

Program 16.7 Extendible hashing insertion

To insert an item into an extendible hash table, we search; then we insert the item on the specified page; then we split the page if the insertion caused overflow. The general scheme is the same as that for B trees, but the search and split algorithms are different. The split method creates a new node, then examines the kth bit (counting from the left) of each item's key: if the bit is 0, the item stays in the old node; if it is 1, it goes in the new node. The value $k+1$ is assigned to the "leading bits known to be identical" field of both nodes after the split. If this process does not result in at least one key in each node, we split again, until the items are so separated. At the end, we insert the reference to the new node into the directory.

```
private void insertDIR(Node t, int k)
  // See Program 16.8
private void split(Node h)
  { Node t = new Node();
    while (h.m == 0 || h.m == M)
      {
        h.m = t.m = 0;
        for (int j = 0; j < M; j++)
          if (bits(h.b[j].key(), h.k, 1) == 0)
                h.b[h.m++] = h.b[j];
          else t.b[t.m++] = h.b[j];
        h.k += 1; t.k = h.k;
      }
    insertDIR(t, t.k);
  }
private void insert(Node h, ITEM x)
  { int j; KEY v = x.key();
    for (j = 0; j < h.m; j++)
      if (less(v, h.b[j].key())) break;
    for (int i = h.m; i > j; i--)
      h.b[i] = h.b[i-1];
    h.b[j] = x; h.m += 1;
    if (h.m == M) split(h);
  }
void insert(ITEM x)
  { insert(dir[bits(x.key(), 0, d)], x); }
```

As with B trees, we leave space for an extra entry in every page to allow splitting after insertion, thus simplifying the code. Again, we can ignore the effect of using this technique in the analysis.

When we create a new page, we have to insert a reference to it in the directory. The code that accomplishes this insertion is given in Program 16.8. The simplest case to consider is the one where the directory, prior to insertion, has precisely two references to the page that splits. In that case, we need simply to arrange to set the second reference to refer to the new page. If the number of bits k that we need to distinguish the keys on the new page is greater than the number of bits d that we have to access the directory, then we have to increase the size of the directory to accommodate the new entry. Finally, we update the directory entries as appropriate.

If more than M items have duplicate keys, the table overflows, and the code in Program 16.7 goes into an infinite loop, looking for a way to distinguish the keys. A related problem is that the directory may get unnecessarily huge, if the keys have an excessive number of leading bits that are equal. This situation is akin to the excessive time required for MSD radix sort, for files that have large numbers of duplicate keys or long stretches of bit positions where they are identical. We depend on the randomization provided by the hash function to stave off these problems (see Exercise 16.43). Even with hashing, extraordinary steps must be taken if large numbers of duplicate keys are present, because hash functions take equal keys to equal hash values. Duplicate keys can make the directory artificially large; and the algorithm breaks down entirely if there are more equal keys than fit in one page. Therefore, we need to add tests to guard against the occurrence of these conditions before using this code (see Exercise 16.35).

The performance parameters of interest are the number of pages used (as with B trees) and the size of the directory. Randomization for this algorithm is provided by the hash functions, so average-case performance results apply to any sequence of N distinct insertions.

Property 16.5 *With pages that can hold M items, extendible hashing requires about $1.44(N/M)$ pages for a file of N items, on the average. The expected number of entries in the directory is about $3.92(N^{1/M})(N/M)$.*

This (rather deep) result extends the analysis of tries that we discussed briefly in the previous chapter (*see reference section*). The exact con-

Program 16.8 Extendible-hashing directory insertion

This deceptively simple code is at the heart of the extendible-hashing process. We are given a link t to a node that carries items that match in the first k bits, which is to be incorporated into the directory. In the simplest case, where d and k are equal, we just put t into d[x], where x is the value of the first d bits of t.b[0] (and of all the other items on the page). If k is greater than d, we have to double the size of the directory, until reducing to the case where d and k are equal. If k is less than d, we need to set more than one directory entry—the first for loop calculates the number of entries that we need to set (2^{d-k}), and the second for loop does the job.

```
private void insertDIR(Node t, int k)
  { int i, m;
    KEY v = t.b[0].key(); int x = bits(v, 0, k);
    while (d < k)
      { Node[] old = dir;
        d += 1; D += D;
        dir = new Node[D];
        for (i = 0; i < D; i++) dir[i] = old[i/2];
        for (i = 0; i < D/2; i++) old[i] = null;
        if (d < k) dir[bits(v, 0, d)^1] = new Node();
      }
    for (m = 1; k < d; k++) m *= 2;
    for (i = 0; i < m; i++) dir[x*m+i] = t;
  }
```

stants are $\lg e = 1/\ln 2$ for the number of pages and $e \lg e = e/\ln 2$ for the directory size, though the precise values of the quantities oscillate around these average values. We should not be surprised by this phenomenon because, for example, the directory size has to be a power of 2, a fact which has to be accounted for in the result. ∎

Note that the growth rate of the directory size is faster than linear in N, particularly for small M. However, for N and M in ranges of practical interest, $N^{1/M}$ is quite close to 1, so we can expect the directory to have about $4(N/M)$ entries, in practice.

We have considered the directory to be a single array of references. We can keep the directory in memory, or, if it is too big, we can keep a root node in memory that tells where the directory pages are, using the same indexing scheme. Alternatively, we can add another level, indexing the first level on the first 10 bits (say), and the second level on the rest of the bits (see Exercise 16.36).

As we did for B trees, we leave for exercises the implementation of all of the other symbol-table operations (see Exercises 16.38 through 16.41). Also as it is with B trees, a proper *remove* implementation is a challenge, but allowing underfull pages is an easy alternative that can be effective in many practical situations.

Exercises

▷ **16.27** How many pages would be empty if we were to use a directory of size 32 in Figure 16.10?

16.28 Draw figures corresponding to Figures 16.11 through 16.13 to illustrate the process of inserting the keys 562, 221, 240, 771, 274, 233, 401, 273, and 201 in that order into an initially empty table, with $M = 5$.

○ **16.29** Draw figures corresponding to Figures 16.11 through 16.13 to illustrate the process of inserting the keys 562, 221, 240, 771, 274, 233, 401, 273, and 201 in that order into an initially empty table, with $M = 5$.

○ **16.30** Assume that you are given an array of items in sorted order. Describe how you would determine the directory size of the extendible hash table corresponding to that set of items.

● **16.31** Write a program that constructs an extendible hash table from an array of items that is in sorted order, by doing two passes through the items: one to determine the size of the directory (see Exercise 16.30) and one to allocate the items to pages and fill in the directory.

○ **16.32** Give a set of keys for which the corresponding extendible hash table has directory size 16, with eight references to a single page.

●● **16.33** Create a figure like Figure 16.8 for extendible hashing.

● **16.34** Write a program to compute the average number of external pages and the average directory size for an extendible hash table with page capacity M built from N random insertions into an initially empty table. Compute the percentage of empty space, for $M = 10$, 100, and 1000 and $N = 10^3$, 10^4, 10^5, and 10^6.

16.35 Add appropriate tests to Program 16.7 to guard against malfunction in case too many duplicate keys or keys with too many leading equal bits are inserted into the table.

● **16.36** Modify the extendible-hashing implementation in Programs 16.5 through 16.7 to use a two-level directory, with no more than M references per directory node. Pay particular attention to deciding what to do when the directory first grows from one level to two.

• **16.37** Modify the extendible-hashing implementation in Programs 16.5 through 16.7 to allow M items per page to exist in the data structure.

○ **16.38** Implement the *sort* operation for an extendible hash table.

○ **16.39** Implement the *select* operation for an extendible hash table.

•• **16.40** Implement the *remove* operation for an extendible hash table.

○ **16.41** Implement the *remove* operation for an extendible hash table, using the method indicated in Exercise 16.25.

•• **16.42** Develop a version of extendible hashing that splits pages when splitting the directory so that each directory entry refers to a unique page. Develop experiments to compare the performance of your implementation to that of the standard implementation.

○ **16.43** Run empirical studies to determine the number of random numbers that we would expect to generate before finding more than M numbers with the same d initial bits, for $M = 10$, 100, and 1000, and for $1 \leq d \leq 20$.

• **16.44** Modify hashing with separate chaining (Program 14.3) to use a hash table of size $2M$, and keep items in pages of size $2M$. That is, when a page fills, link it to a new empty page so that each hash table entry points to a linked list of pages. Empirically determine the average number of probes required for a search after building a table from N items with random keys, for $M = 10$, 100, and 1000 and $N = 10^3$, 10^4, 10^5, and 10^6.

○ **16.45** Modify double hashing (Program 14.6) to use pages of size $2M$, treating accesses to full pages as "collisions." Empirically determine the average number of probes required for a search after building a table from N items with random keys, for $M = 10$, 100, and 1000 and $N = 10^3$, 10^4, 10^5, and 10^6, using an initial table size of $3N/2M$.

16.5 Perspective

The most important application of the methods discussed in this chapter is to construct indexes for huge databases that are maintained on external memory—for example, in disk files. Although the underlying algorithms that we have discussed are powerful, developing a file-system implementation based on B trees or on extendible hashing is a complex task. First, we cannot use the Java programs in this section directly—they have to be modified to read and refer to disk files. Second, we have to be sure that the algorithm parameters (page and directory size, for example) are tuned properly to the characteristics of the particular hardware that we are using. Third, we have to pay attention to reliability, error detection, and error correction. For example, we need to be able to check that the data structure is in a consistent state and to consider how we might proceed to correct any of the scores of errors that might crop up. Systems considerations of this kind are critical—and are beyond the scope of this book.

On the other hand, if we have a programming system that supports virtual memory, we can put to direct use the Java implementations that we have considered here in a situation where we have a huge number of symbol-table operations to perform on a huge table. Roughly, each time that we access a page, such a system will put that page in a *cache*, where references to data on that page are handled efficiently. If we refer to a page that is not in the cache, the system has to read the page from external memory, so we can think of cache misses as roughly equivalent to the probe cost measure that we have been using.

For B trees, every search or insertion references the root, so the root will always be in the cache. Otherwise, for sufficiently large M, typical searches and insertions involve at most two cache misses. For a large cache, there is a good chance that the first page (the child of the root) that is accessed on a search is already in the cache, so the average cost per search is likely to be significantly less than two probes.

For extendible hashing, it is unlikely that the whole directory will be in the cache, so we expect that both the directory access and the page access might involve a cache miss (this case is the worst case). That is, two probes are required for a search in a huge table—one to access the appropriate part of the directory and one to access the appropriate page.

These algorithms form an appropriate subject on which to close our discussion of searching, because, to use them effectively, we need to understand basic properties of binary search, BSTs, balanced trees, hashing, and tries—the basic searching algorithms that we have studied in Chapters 12 through 15. As a group, these algorithms provide us with solutions to the symbol-table implementation problem in a broad variety of situations: they constitute an outstanding example of the power of algorithmic technology.

Exercises

• **16.46** Develop a symbol-table implementation using B trees that includes a `clone` implementation and supports the *construct*, *count*, *search*, *insert*, *re-*

move, and *join* operations for a symbol-table ADT, with support for client handles (see Exercises 12.6 and 12.7).

• **16.47** Develop a symbol-table implementation using extendible hashing that includes a `clone` implementation and supports the *construct*, *count*, *search*, *insert*, *remove*, and *join* operations for a symbol-table ADT, with support for client handles (see Exercises 12.6 and 12.7).

16.48 Modify the B-tree implementation in Section 16.3 (Programs 16.1 through 16.3) to use an ADT for page references.

16.49 Modify the extendible-hashing implementation in Section 16.4 (Programs 16.5 through 16.8) to use an ADT for page references.

16.50 Estimate the average number of probes per search in a B tree for S random searches, in a typical cache system, where the T most-recently-accessed pages are kept in memory (and therefore add 0 to the probe count). Assume that S is much larger than T.

16.51 Estimate the average number of probes per search in an extendible hash table, for the cache model described in Exercise 16.50.

○ **16.52** If your system supports virtual memory, design and conduct experiments to compare the performance of B trees with that of binary search, for random searches in a huge symbol table.

16.53 Implement a priority-queue ADT that supports *construct* for a huge number of items, followed by a huge number of *insert* and *remove the maximum* operations (see Chapter 9).

16.54 Develop an external symbol-table ADT based on a skip-list representation of B trees (see Exercise 13.80).

• **16.55** If your system supports virtual memory, run experiments to determine the value of M that leads to the fastest search times for a B-tree implementation supporting random *search* operations in a huge symbol table. (It may be worthwhile for you to learn basic properties of your system before conducting such experiments, which can be costly.)

•• **16.56** Modify the B-tree implementation in Section 16.3 (Programs 16.1 through 16.3) to operate in an environment where the table resides on external storage. If your system allows nonsequential file access, put the whole table on a single (huge) file and use offsets within the file in place of references in the data structure. If your system allows you to access pages on external devices directly, use page addresses in place of references in the data structure. If your system allows both, choose the approach that you determine to be most reasonable for implementing a huge symbol table.

•• **16.57** Modify the extendible-hashing implementation in Section 16.4 (Programs 16.5 through 16.8) to operate in an environment where the table resides on external storage. Explain the reasons for the approach that you choose for allocating the directory and the pages to files (see Exercise 16.56).

References for Part Four

The primary references for this section are the books by Knuth; Baeza-Yates and Gonnet; Mehlhorn; and Cormen, Leiserson, and Rivest. Many of the algorithms covered here are treated in great detail in these books, with mathematical analyses and suggestions for practical applications. Classical methods are covered thoroughly in Knuth; the more recent methods are described in the other books, with further references to the literature. These four sources, and the Sedgewick-Flajolet book, describe nearly all the "beyond the scope of this book" material referred to in this section.

The material in Chapter 13 comes from the 1996 paper by Roura and Martinez, the 1985 paper by Sleator and Tarjan, and the 1978 paper by Guibas and Sedgewick. As suggested by the dates of these papers, balanced trees are the subject of ongoing research. The books cited above have detailed proofs of properties of red–black trees and similar structures and references to more recent work.

The treatment of tries in Chapter 15 is classical (though complete implementations are rarely found in the literature). The material on TSTs comes from the 1997 paper by Bentley and Sedgewick.

The 1972 paper by Bayer and McCreight introduced B trees, and the extendible hashing algorithm presented in Chapter 16 comes from the 1979 paper by Fagin, Nievergelt, Pippenger, and Strong. Analytic results on extendible hashing were derived by Flajolet in 1983. These papers are must reading for anyone wishing further information on external searching methods. Practical applications of these methods arise within the context of database systems. An introduction to this field is given, for example, in the book by Date.

R. Baeza-Yates and G. H. Gonnet, *Handbook of Algorithms and Data Structures*, second edition, Addison-Wesley, Reading, MA, 1984.

R. Bayer and E. M. McCreight, "Organization and maintenance of large ordered indexes," *Acta Informatica* **1**, 1972.

J. L. Bentley and R. Sedgewick, "Sorting and searching strings," Eighth Symposium on Discrete Algorithms, New Orleans, January, 1997.

T. H. Cormen, C. E. Leiserson, and R. L. Rivest, *Introduction to Algorithms*, second edition, MIT Press/McGraw-Hill, Cambridge, MA, 2002.

C. J. Date, *An Introduction to Database Systems*, seventh edition, Addison-Wesley, Boston, MA, 2002.

R. Fagin, J. Nievergelt, N. Pippenger and H. R. Strong, "Extendible hashing—a fast access method for dynamic files," *ACM Transactions on Database Systems* **4**, 1979.

P. Flajolet, "On the performance analysis of extendible hashing and trie search," *Acta Informatica* **20**, 1983.

L. Guibas and R. Sedgewick, "A dichromatic framework for balanced trees," in *19th Annual Symposium on Foundations of Computer Science*, IEEE, 1978. Also in *A Decade of Progress 1970–1980*, Xerox PARC, Palo Alto, CA.

D. E. Knuth, *The Art of Computer Programming. Volume 3: Sorting and Searching*, second edition, Addison-Wesley, Reading, MA, 1997.

K. Mehlhorn, *Data Structures and Algorithms 1: Sorting and Searching*, Springer-Verlag, Berlin, 1984.

S. Roura and C. Martinez, "Randomization of search trees by subtree size," Fourth European Symposium on Algorithms, Barcelona, September, 1996.

R. Sedgewick and P. Flajolet, *An Introduction to the Analysis of Algorithms*, Addison-Wesley, Reading, MA, 1996.

D. Sleator and R. E. Tarjan, "Self-adjusting binary search trees," *Journal of the ACM* **32**, 1985.

Appendix

FOR SIMPLICITY and flexibility, we have used input and output sparingly in the programs in this book. Most of our programs are ADT implementations intended for use with diverse clients, but we also exhibit the driver programs that you need to run and test the programs on your own data. Programs 1.1, 6.1, and 12.6 are typical examples. In these drivers:

- We use the command line to get values of parameters.
- We take input data from the standard input stream.
- We print out results on the standard output stream.

The conventions for taking parameter values are standard in Java (and the mechanism is described in Section 3.7); in this Appendix, we present the classes that we use for input and output.

Rather than directly using Java library classes for input and output in our code, we use the adapter classes In and Out.

The code for Out is trivial, since the methods that we use are precisely the methods that print a string (perhaps followed by a newline character) from Java's System.out class:

```
public class Out
  {
    public static void print(String s)
      { System.out.print(s); }
    public static void println(String s)
      { System.out.println(s); }
  }
```

To use the programs in this book that use the Out class, either put this code in a file named Out.java or just replace "Out" with "System.out" in the program code. The System.out class overloads print and println to take primitive-type parameters; we do not bother to do so because our client code usually prints strings and can otherwise easily use type conversion.

724

The code for In is more complicated because we have to arrange for reading different types of data. (Type conversion for output is straightforward because of Java's convention that every type of data have a toString method that converts it to a string.) The following implementation of In uses the Java System.in class to define methods for initializing itself; reading integers, floating point numbers, and strings; and testing whether the input stream is empty:

```
import java.io.*;
public class In
  { private static int c;
    private static boolean blank()
      { return Character.isWhitespace((char) c); }
    private static void readC()
      {
        try
          { c = System.in.read(); }
        catch (IOException e)
          { c = -1; }
      }
    public static void init()
      { readC(); }
    public static boolean empty()
      { return c == -1; }
    public static String getString()
      {
        String s = "";
        while (!(empty() || blank()))
          { s += (char) c; readC(); }
        while (!empty() && blank()) readC();
        return s;
      }
    public static int getInt()
      { return Integer.parseInt(getString()); }
    public static double getDouble()
      { return Double.parseDouble(getString()); }
  }
```

To use the programs in this book that use the In class, put this code in a file named In.java.

Our driver programs are intended for our own use in running and testing algorithms on known test data. Accordingly, we normally know that a program's input data is in the format that it expects (because we construct both the program and data in such a fashion), so we do not include error checking in In. Our programs explicitly initialize the input stream by calling In.init and test whether it is empty by calling In.empty, often just using the construct

```
for( In.init(); !In.empty(); )
```

with calls to one or more of the get methods within the body of the loop. The get methods return 0 or an empty string rather than raising an exception if we attempt to read from an empty input stream, but our drivers do not make use of those return values.

Using these adapter classes gives us the flexibility to change the way that we do input and output without modifying the code in the book at all. While the implementations given here are useful in most Java programming environments, other implementations of In and Out might be called for in various special situations. If you have classes for input and output that you are accustomed to using, it will be a simple matter for you to implement appropriate In and Out adapter classes to replace the ones given here. Or, as you gain experience developing and testing the algorithms in this book, writing the more sophisticated drivers called for in many of the exercises, you may develop more sophisticated implementations of these classes for your own use.

Exercises

• **A.1** Write a version of In that prints an informative message about what is wrong with the input for each possible exception that might arise.

• **A.2** Write a class that extends Applet and provide implementations of In and Out so that you can accept input and provide output in an applet window. Your goal is to make it possible for driver code in programs such as Program 1.1 to be used with as few changes as possible.

Index

ALGORITHMS

Essential Volumes for Every Programmer's Library

Robert Sedgewick has thoroughly rewritten his long popular work to provide current and comprehensive coverage of the most important algorithms and data structures. His substantially expanded *Third Edition* now comprises three volumes, with implementations in key programming languages.

Parts 1–4. The first volume published covers basic algorithms and data structures, with implementations available in Java, C++, or C.

**Algorithms in Java,
Third Edition, Parts 1–4**
*Fundamentals, Data Structures,
Sorting, Searching*

ISBN 0-201-36120-5
© 2003
Paperback

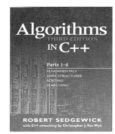

**Algorithms in C++,
Third Edition, Parts 1–4**
*Fundamentals, Data Structures,
Sorting, Searching*

ISBN 0-201-35088-2
© 1999
Paperback

**Algorithms in C,
Third Edition, Parts 1–4**
*Fundamentals, Data Structures,
Sorting, Searching*

ISBN 0-201-31452-5
© 1998
Paperback

> **Bundles**
>
> C++, Parts 1–5 and C, Parts 1–5 are now available in a single package. Instructors should contact their local Addison-Wesley representative for details.

Part 5. The second volume published focuses on graph algorithms, with implementations available in C or C++.

**Algorithms in C,
Third Edition, Part 5**
Graph Algorithms

ISBN 0-201-31663-3
© 2002
Paperback

**Algorithms in C++,
Third Edition, Part 5**
Graph Algorithms

ISBN 0-201-36118-3
© 2002
Paperback

Parts 6–8. A future third volume will cover strings, geometry, and a variety of other advanced topics.

http://www.awprofessional.com